The International

GU00734300

THE ENGLISH PRISON
AND BORSTAL SYSTEMS

Founded by KARL MANNHEIM

The International Library of Sociology

THE SOCIOLOGY OF LAW AND CRIMINOLOGY
In 15 Volumes

THE ENGLISH PRISON AND BORSTAL SYSTEMS

An account of the prison and Borstal systems in England
and Wales after the Criminal Justice Act 1948, with a
historical introduction and an examination of the
principles of imprisonment as a legal punishment

by

LIONEL W. FOX

Routledge
Taylor & Francis Group

LONDON AND NEW YORK

First published in 1952
by Routledge

Reprinted 1998, 2001
by Routledge
2 Park Square, Milton Park, Abingdon, Oxon, OX14 4RN
711 Third Avenue, New York, NY 10017

Transferred to Digital Printing 2007

Routledge is an imprint of the Taylor & Francis Group
First issued in paperback 2013

© 1952 Lionel W. Fox

All rights reserved. No part of this book may be reprinted or reproduced
or utilized in any form or by any electronic, mechanical, or other means,
now known or hereafter invented, including photocopying
and recording, or in any information storage or retrieval system, without
permission in writing from the publishers.

The publishers have made every effort to contact authors/copyright holders
of the works reprinted in *The International Library of Sociology*.
This has not been possible in every case, however, and we would
welcome correspondence from those individuals/companies
we have been unable to trace.

British Library Cataloguing in Publication Data
A CIP catalogue record for this book
is available from the British Library

The English Prison and Borstal System
978-0-415-17738-2 (hbk)
978-0-415-86386-5 (pbk)
The Sociology of Law and Criminology: 15 Volumes
978-0-415-17832-7
The International Library of Sociology: 274 Volumes
978-0-415-17838-9

Publisher's Note
The publisher has gone to great lengths to ensure the quality of this reprint
but points out that some imperfections in the original may be apparent

PREFACE

M Y first aim in preparing this book was to describe and explain our prison and Borstal systems as they face the tasks laid on them by the Criminal Justice Act, 1948. But since the purposes of this Act, and the methods followed to further them, can be understood only against their historical and philosophical background I have ventured to add, as Part I of the book, a brief history of thought and practice in the application of legal punishment and in the development of the idea of imprisonment as a form of punishment.

The systems described are those under the administration of the Prison Commissioners for England and Wales. The systems of Scotland and Northern Ireland have, however, developed along parallel lines under their separate administrations, and making due allowance for differences in scale it may be said that principles and practice are in general similar throughout the United Kingdom.

I am indebted to the Permanent Under Secretary of State for the Home Department for permission to publish this book, but it should be understood that while the facts and figures, so far as they relate to the English systems, are derived almost entirely from published official documents, the responsibility for their accurate presentation and for any inferences drawn from them rests solely with myself.

My grateful thanks are due to the many colleagues and friends who have kindly helped me with correction and advice. The text itself, particularly in Part I, speaks on nearly every page of my debt to many workers and thinkers in this wide field whose valuable publications have enabled me to extend the scope of this book much beyond my own experience. The Bibliographical Notes contain more specific acknowledgments.

May I in conclusion warn readers that while the text represents the situation as it appeared at the beginning of 1951, it is a fluid and developing situation. Information received after the completion of the text to the latest possible date will be included in Appendix K.

L. W. F.

June 1951

BIBLIOGRAPHICAL NOTES

The following notes refer only to the principal works quoted or used in the text, and are not intended to constitute a bibliography of the subject. Where the name of the author is used alone for short reference in the text, it is shown in brackets at the end of the note.

The State of the Prisons, John Howard, 1777.

An Inquiry whether Crime and Misery are Produced or Prevented by our Present System of Prison Discipline, T. Fowell Buxton, 1818.

The Prison Chaplain, Rev. W. Clay (Macmillan), 1861.
A memoir of the work of the Rev. John Clay, Chaplain of Preston Prison. A valuable source-book of information on early nineteenth-century opinion and historical development. [Clay.]

Elizabeth Fry, Janet Whitney (Guild Books, Harrap), 1937. [Whitney.]

The Punishment and Prevention of Crime, Sir E. du Cane (Macmillan), 1885.
The first Chairman of the Prison Commission here describes and explains the system for which he was responsible for over twenty years. [du Cane.]

The English Prison System, Sir E. Ruggles-Brise (Macmillan), 1921.
Sir E. du Cane's successor takes the story up to 1921. [Ruggles-Brise.]

English Prisons under Local Government, Sidney and Beatrice Webb (Longmans), 1922.
The standard history of our prison system up to 1898, of which any subsequent historical work must be to some extent a summary. A stimulating preface by George Bernard Shaw on crime, punishment, and prisons in general. [Webb.]

English Prisons Today, edited by S. Hobhouse and A. Fenner Brockway (Longmans), 1922.
The Report of the Prison System Enquiry Committee established in 1919 by the Labour Research Department.

The Modern English Prison, L. W. Fox (Routledge), 1934.
An account by the present writer, then Secretary of the Prison Commission, of the English prisons and Borstals in 1933.

The Home Office, Sir E. Troup (Putnam), 1925.
A short account of the Home Office, its functions, and the way it works with a history of the development of the office of Secretary of State. Sir E. Troup was Permanent Under-Secretary of State in the Home Office, 1908–1922. [Troup.]

English Social History, G. M. Trevelyan (Longmans, Green), 1944. [Trevelyan.]

vii

A History of English Criminal Law from 1750, Vol. I, L. Radzinowicz (Stevens), 1948.

A detailed and definitive history, by the Asst. Director of the Department of Criminal Science of Cambridge University, which sets the development of English criminal law and its administration, and of penal thought, against a wide social and political background. [Radzinowicz.]

The Dilemma of Penal Reform, H. Mannheim (Geo. Allen & Unwin), 1939

Dr. Mannheim, Lecturer in Criminology at the London School of Economics and Political Science, makes a searching study of the social and economic aspects of penal reform. [Mannheim.]

Penal Reform, M. Grünhut (Oxford University Press), 1948.

A comparative study of the history, purposes and developments of penal reform in Europe and America by the Reader in Criminology in the University of Oxford. [Grünhut.]

Crime and the Community, Sir Leo Page (Faber and Faber), 1937.

Sir Leo Page was a magistrate of long experience on the Bench and as Chairman of the Visiting Committee of one of H.M. Prisons. His book is a valuable contribution to contemporary thought on the problems of legal punishment, its principles, and its application in practice. [Page.]

Meet the Prisoner, John A. F. Watson (Cape), 1939.

Mr. Watson is a London Juvenile Court magistrate, and a former Chairman of the National Association of Prison Visitors. From his intimate knowledge of prisons and prisoners he gives a vivid account of English prisons and their problems at the time, with particular reference to education, religion, welfare, and the work of Prison Visitors. [Watson.]

Society and the Criminal, Sir Norwood East (Stationery Office), 1949.

Sir Norwood East, a former Medical Commissioner of Prisons, is Lecturer on Forensic Psychiatry at the Maudsley Hospital (London University). These collected essays deal authoritatively with the nature of criminals, criminal responsibility, psychopathic personalities, and the medico-legal aspects of crime. [East.]

Should Prisoners Work, L. N. Robinson (Winston, Philadelphia), 1931.

A study of the prison labour problem in the United States, with some discussion of principles of general application. [Robinson.]

The Clarke Hall Lectures, published annually by the Clarke Hall Fellowship, particularly:

The Ethics of Penal Action, (First Lecture) by the late Archbishop Temple. [Temple.]

Is the Criminal to Blame, or Society, (Fourth Lecture) by Lord Samuel [Samuel.]

Mental Health and the Offender, (Seventh Lecture) by Dr. J. R. Rees. [Rees.]

Criminal Justice; Problems of Punishment, (Eighth Lecture) by Lord Justice Birkett. [Birkett.]

The Institutional Treatment of Offenders, (Ninth Lecture) by Sir A. Maxwell. [Maxwell.]

The following books would have been included above had they been received before my text was complete:

Arms of the Law, Margery Fry (Gollancz), 1951.

Paterson on Prisons, ed. S. K. Ruck (F. Muller), 1951. (The collected papers of the late Sir Alexander Paterson.)

STATIONERY OFFICE PUBLICATIONS

Making Citizens (1945). A review of the aims, methods and achievements of the Approved Schools in England and Wales. Price 1s. 0d.

Prisons and Borstals (1950). Price 2s. 6d.
A short account of policy and practice in the administration of prisons and Borstal Institutions in England and Wales, issued under the authority of the Home Office. Illustrated by photographs.

Reports of the Commissioners of Prisons and Directors of Convict Prisons. Published annually. Price 4s.

Criminal Statistics, England and Wales. Published annually. Price usually 3s.

Report from the Select Committee of the House of Lords on the Present State of Discipline in Gaols and Houses of Correction, 1863.

Report from the Departmental Committee on Prisons, 1895.

Report from the Select Committee of the House of Commons on Debtors (Imprisonment), 1908.

Report from the Departmental Committee on the Treatment of Young Offenders, 1927. Price 2s. 6d.

Report from the Departmental Committee on Persistent Offenders, 1932. Price 1s. 6d.

Report from the Departmental Committee on the Employment of Prisoners. Part I. 1933. Price 1s. 6d.

Do. Part II. 1935. Price 1s. 3d.

Report from the Departmental Committee on Imprisonment by Courts of Summary Jurisdiction in Default of Payment of Fines, etc., 1934. Price 1s. 6d.

Report on the Psychological Treatment of Crime, by W. Norwood East and W. H. de B. Hubert, 1939. Price 2s. 6d.

Report of a Committee to Review Punishments in Prisons, Borstal Institutions, Approved Schools and Remand Homes. Parts I and II, Prisons and Borstal Institutions. Price 3s. 6d. (H.M. Stationery Office).

CONTENTS

V. YOUNG OFFENDERS

APPENDICES

PART ONE

WHAT IS PRISON FOR?

Carcer ad terrorem aedificatur.—Livy, i. 33.

Carcer ad continendos homines, non ad puniendos haberi debet.—Justinian, *Digest*.

Parum est coercere improbos poena nisi probos efficias disciplina.—Inscription in House of Correction of St. Michael, Rome. (cit. John Howard, *State of the Prisons*, 1777.)

May God preserve the City of London, and make this place a terror to evil doers.—Commemorative inscription on foundation stone deposit of Holloway Prison, 1849.

We do not consider that the moral reformation of the offender holds the primary place in the prison system.—House of Lords Committee of 1863.

(The primary object) is deterrence, through suffering, inflicted as a punishment for crime, and the fear of a repetition of it.—Lord Chief Justice Cockburn, in evidence to that Committee.

Prison treatment should have as its primary and concurrent objects deterrence and reformation.—Gladstone Committee of 1895.

You cannot train men for freedom in a condition of captivity. —Sir Alexander Paterson, 1932.

The purposes of training and treatment of convicted prisoners shall be to establish in them the will to lead a good and useful life on discharge, and to fit them to do so.—Prison Rules, 1949, Rule 6.

CHAPTER ONE

THE QUESTION

BETWEEN the Criminal Justice Act of 1948 and the Prisons Act of 1898, which was the last previous statute affecting the administration of our prison system, lie fifty years. Through these years the system has steadily followed a course which it will be the purpose of this book to explain and define, with a particular description of the methods by which it is being and will be pursued in the light of the Act of 1948.

But in this first part we shall be concerned less with means than with ends. What is done in a prison can make sense only in the light of some answer to the question—what is prison for? And if one can hope today to find that answer with more certainty than was possible before 1948, it still has to be found: it is nowhere given to us ready-made, authoritative, and of general acceptance.

For this one may offer explanations, the first particular to this country, the second of general validity.

The first, then, lies in the nature of English tradition and the structure of English law. 'It is characteristic of the English genius for practical affairs that we are suspicious of system . . . the English tend rather to deal with the situation confronting them and afterwards discover on what principles they have done so, and what precedent for future action they have established.' [1] Thus our law is not disposed to arrange itself in consistent, comprehensive, and logical codes: certainly neither our prison system nor the penal system of which it forms part derives from such a code. Indeed it is not until the Act of 1948 that one can hope to learn from the law—and then largely by inference—what place Parliament has assigned to the prison in its general order of battle for the attack on crime.

To the modern development of our prison system this situation has been of great advantage—has indeed permitted it to acquire such merit as it may possess. In particular, flexibility and freedom of experiment

[1] Temple, p. 1.

3

were assured by the decision, in the Prison. Act of 1898, to discard the detailed regulation of the prison régime embodied in earlier Acts, and to leave this to the subordinate legislation of Statutory Rules made by the Secretary of State. Desirable change could thus be made without the need for fresh legislation on each occasion, and legislation has harvested the fruit of administrative development. Sir Evelyn Ruggles-Brise had developed the Borstal system for some years before it received statutory recognition: the conception of 'training' prisoners was well established before the word made its statutory début in 1948: and when in one historic handful of words the Act of 1948 abolished penal servitude, hard labour and the triple division of imprisonment, and so established, almost by inadvertence, the single sentence of undifferentiated imprisonment—the 'peine unique' of classic criminological controversy—it did no more than recognise *de lege* a situation already existing *de facto* through the normal and logical development of the principles of 1898.

We may therefore be grateful on the whole that, as Dr. Grünhut points out, 'England, with her traditional system of non-codified law, has been spared the cumbersome way of total reform' [1]—even though one effect be the inevitability of cumbersome explanation. Another effect will be that when we come to view our prison system at work, and perhaps find much to call in question, it can only explain itself as Topsy did—'I never was born, I just growed.' We shall not see a machine running to blueprint specifications, but the contemporary phase of a long historical process, a vital organism claiming to be judged not only by what it now is but by what it has been and what it is becoming.

The second explanation of our uncertainties will take longer. It derives from the fact that since a prison system is part of a penal system it cannot—to put it no higher at this stage of the argument—be dissociated from the idea of punishment. And as to the ends, the means, or the values of punishment it does not appear either that philosophers or psychologists are yet agreed among themselves, or that such conclusions as some of them may have reached necessarily commend themselves to the general sense of the man in the street. With the general ethics of punishment we cannot concern ourselves here: it is not the easiest branch of metaphysics. But when it is brought into relation with the particular field of penal action by society against criminal offenders, particular difficulties arise, and these we cannot ignore even if in the end we cannot resolve them. Some conclusions on them, if only as a working hypothesis, are essential if an answer is to be given to our question: yet it would not be easy to formulate any which could with certainty be said to be of general acceptance among those concerned with these matters, be they jurists or judges, penologists

[1] Grünhut, p. 106.

or politicians,[1] prison administrators, police, or just plain members of the public—the actual or potential victims of crime. And though the views of these last may rarely become articulate, they are of central importance; for the prevention of crime, which is here our concern as a matter of abstract speculation, is for every member of the community a matter of serious actuality.

First, then, let us consider what crime is.

'It is plain that in every community professing to be civilised there must be rules and regulations which the citizens must obey, and standards of behaviour to which they must conform; and those rules and regulations, designed for the benefit of all, and made by the Parliament the citizens themselves have chosen, must be enforced.'[2] Crime, in its broadest sense, is the breach of such of these rules as the community decides to enforce through its penal system. But these may range from playing football in the street to being drunk while driving a motor-car; from hawking without a licence to publishing a false balance-sheet; from stealing an apple to embezzling millions; from a minor assault to a homicide or rape. In neither popular nor technical thought are all these offences 'criminal'; yet our concern is with all, since, as we shall see, all may in the end be the concern of the prison.

Apart from these distinctions of degree, opinion as to what kind of conduct should be deemed criminal has varied widely from time to time and from place to place: few indeed are those classes of offence of which it can be said 'quod semper, quod ubique, quod ab omnibus . . .' 'Even from the point of view of legal policy there is hardly any uniformity of opinion as to whether—to give only a few examples— attempted suicide, homosexual activities, adultery, euthanasia, and certain types of abortion should or should not be generally treated as criminal offences'[3]; and where conduct of one of these types is treated as an offence, there is often a strong body of opinion against convictions, with no disposition on the part of those who hold that opinion to consider the offenders as criminals.

While therefore we cannot forget that 'there are in the world a considerable number of extremely wicked people, disposed when opportunity offers to get what they want by force or fraud, with complete indifference to the rights of others, and in ways that are inconsistent with the existence of civilised society',[4] we must also remember that it is not with those alone, nor mainly, that the penal system and therefore the prisons are concerned. And in particular we must avoid the pitfall of treating crime and sin as synonymous terms, and confusing the criminal law with a code of ethics. It is not through its

---

[1] "It cannot be said that the theories of criminal punishment current among either our judges or our legislators have assumed . . . either a coherent or even a stable form." Kenny, *Outlines of Criminal Law*, 15th edition, 1947, p. 38.

[2] Birkett, pp. 18, 19.   [3] Mannheim, p. 23.   [4] Stephen J. cit Birkett, p. 24.

penal system that society seeks to vindicate its moral basis. That system has in view a much more limited and practical end, which we may see more clearly, so far as concerns our own system, by the inductive process of asking what in fact are the actions which in this country, at this time, are treated as criminal offences.

Of those more serious offences, known to the law as indictable offences, which are usually referred to as crime, the Criminal Statistics list 70, of which in one form or another 35 are offences of dishonesty in relation to property, and 25 of violence, including sexual offences, against the person: the remaining few include such comparatively rare offences as perjury, libel, attempted suicide, and certain offences against the State. Of the persons guilty of these crimes who come to prison, some 88 per cent will have committed offences against property and 9 per cent offences against the person. From these facts the effective purpose of our penal system in relation to serious crime might seem to be the protection of our property and persons against dishonesty and violence.

But of every 100 offenders convicted in 1947, no less than 81 had committed non-indictable offences, and ten years earlier the percentage was 90. These non-indictable offences, though for the most part they are rather of the order of 'breaches of regulations', do include certain offences, such as assaults and offences against property of a minor nature and cruelty to or neglect of children, which are more akin to crime than to such social nuisances as immoderate drunkenness, tactless begging, and parking cars in the wrong place. There has also been, since the late war, a range of offences, which unfortunately cannot be isolated statistically, deriving from economic controls and restrictions. These are, in one sense, more clearly offences against society than many which excite greater public resentment, yet the amount of odium attaching to them has tended to vary with the individual social conscience.

These considerations having suggested the need for care in making generalisations about criminals and crime, whether in relation to prevention or to treatment, we now approach what Lord Justice Birkett has described as 'the central problem . . . what is to be done when it is proved that these rules and regulations have been broken?' [1]

The prevention of crime in the widest sense calls for action in many fields outside that of the penal system. 'To expect from a penal system that it should by itself create law-abiding citizens can only be regarded as a grotesque over-estimation of its powers.' [2] Lord Samuel has isolated three causal factors of crime—heredity, environment, and individual choice.[3] Society may seek to influence all these through education and the work of the Churches, as well as by such remedial measures as the care of deprived or maladjusted children and mentally

[1] Birkett, p. 19.   [2] Mannheim, p. 19.   [3] Samuel, p. 17.

subnormal or abnormal persons, eugenics, and improved housing conditions. But the concern of penal law is with the last factor only, and its operation is twofold—directly, against those persons whose reactions to influences pre-disposing to crime produce a wrong choice of action; indirectly, against every one subject to those influences— for, as Lord Samuel puts it, 'the penal law is itself one of the elements that help to determine the choice.' In the more technical language of penology, the preventive effect of the penal system is said to be both 'individual' and 'general'. Lord Justice Birkett's 'central problem' is that of individual prevention, in that it is concerned with the treatment of the individual against whom an offence has been proved, but it is impossible to treat this question apart from the considerations arising from general prevention.

The theory of general prevention is that potential offenders will be deterred from offence by the fear of what will happen to them if they are found out. If this theory is to be effective in practice it must rest on a general assumption that offenders will, on the whole, be detected, brought to justice, and in proper cases suitably punished. 'Something must be done to assert the power of the law and to make it plain that the law must be observed; and any weakness here is the greatest possible disservice to the life of the whole community. The punishment of the offender, ordained by the law itself, must not only be a just punishment but it must be recognised to be just, and will vary with the proved facts of each particular case; but whatever is done it is important that the law itself shall be vindicated, and disobedience to it never merely condoned.' [1]

Thus the action of the courts in relation to each individual offender has a certain ambivalence: it looks to the effect on that individual, who has not been deterred from offence by general prevention but may be prevented from offending again; but it looks also to the effect on all who may be tempted to commit that sort of offence. It is this ambivalence which has led to some, though not all, of the difficulties that have arisen in relation to the punishment by society of individual offenders.

Punishment is defined by the Oxford English Dictionary as 'to cause an offender to suffer for an offence', and legal punishment is defined by Dr. Grünhut as 'a legal sanction against unlawful acts committed with a guilty mind'. Given that to cause suffering is an evil, unless it can be justified as the means to a good end, the problem posed has been the justification of the use of evil as a legal sanction.

'Punishment,' said George Bernard Shaw (speaking of legal punishment), 'is a mistake and a sin.' [2] That Mr. Justice Stephen meant to express the same view when he said 'the object of criminal law is to overcome evil with evil' should not perhaps be assumed, since he also

---

[1] Birkett, p. 19.   [2] Preface to Webb, p. lii.

said, 'The criminal law thus proceeds upon the principle that it is morally right to hate criminals, and . . . I think that the punishments inflicted on them should be so contrived as to give expression to that hate and to justify it.' [1] It may be that Dr. Grünhut had this view in mind when he wrote, 'Legal punishment is inseparably linked with the idea of justice. . . . A just punishment is more than the overcoming of evil with force. It is also a spiritual power which may make an appeal to the moral personality of man.' [2]

For two centuries or more this argument has ranged 'about it and about', but it must suffice here to give an impression of the contemporary climate of opinion, within which those concerned with the administration of the penal system must carry out their work. The different standpoints adopted at different stages of development in this country, and their effects in practice, will be noticed in the following chapters.

It is first necessary to consider the present view of those classic justifications of punishment as an end in itself, the doctrines of Expiation and Retribution. The former suggests that it is morally good and necessary that an offender should expiate his offence by a punishment which adjusts his suffering to his sin. This view finds little support today. In so far as it equates crime with sin, it invites the reply—even if it be so, why select those sins which happen to have been brought within the scope of penal law for public vindication of this moral need? And Archbishop Temple expressly deprecated, for himself, 'the intuition . . . that it is good that the wicked should suffer'.[3] Most discussions of the theory now conclude that the judgment of moral guilt is a function of religion rather than of law. Sir Leo Page and Dr. Grünhut both emphasise the difficulties of a judge in face of this confusion of law and morality. 'Be it once accepted that expiation is a necessary constituent of the punishment of an offender, then, whenever the courts of law found a defendant guilty of a legal offence, they would be bound to impose such a penalty as would cause him pain and suffering . . . (and) . . . to require a judge to determine precisely the degree of pain adequate to expiate moral guilt is patently impossible. No human judge, but God alone, can read the secrets of the heart.' [4] 'The infliction of punishment by human judges with their limited insight into character and motives is acceptable only in so far as it is necessary for the protection of the community.' [5]

The doctrine of Retribution calls for closer consideration, for it lies closer to the roots of common feeling. It has been described by Archbishop Temple and Dr. Grünhut in almost identical terms—'It is concerned that the evil-doer should get what he deserves',[6] and '(Retribution) implies the notion that the offender has deserved his punish-

1 Cit. Birkett, p. 20.   3 Temple, p. 28.   5 Grünhut, p. 3.
2 Grünhut, p. 3.   4 Page, p. 68.   6 Temple, pp. 27, 28.

ment, that it is "his due".' [1] This feeling is, as Professor Sidgwick put it, [2] 'universalised in criminal justice', and emphasis is added to this view by Lord Justice Birkett, out of his wide experience as both advocate and judge in the criminal courts, when he says 'The element of retribution is always present, I think, in the sentences imposed for the more serious offences. The advocates of retribution insist that in any well-ordered state, the citizens feel that when the laws are broken it is just and proper that punishment shall overtake the wrong-doer. And the sense of satisfaction that this arouses, it is urged, is by no means an unimportant consideration.' [3] The sting of this last statement lies in the tail, for the assumption of a certain public sentiment to be satisfied has had no small influence on the action of the penal system in all its phases. The present Lord Chief Justice, in an address to the Magistrates Association, said 'The public conscience will not be satisfied if gross, violent, savage, and sometimes bestial crimes are not punished in a way that will satisfy it . . .' [4]

This dictum of the Lord Chief Justice was however in terms of limited application, and the doctrine of Retribution in the sense of 'what the offender deserves' must be stated in wider terms for complete reconciliation with current thought and practice. What is due to the offender can be no more and no less than a sentence which is just in the terms predicated by Lord Justice Birkett (p. 7) and Dr. Grünhut (p. 8), that is to say a sentence which keeps in balance the interests of the community as a whole and those of the offender as a member of the community. If such a sentence leads to the infliction of pain and suffering as punishment, then in so far as that is calculated, no more and no less, both to demonstrate that the law cannot be broken with impunity and to prevent the offender from repeating the offence, it is justified as a means to a good end in that it will promote his moral welfare, whereby the community benefits equally with the offender.

Discussions of the doctrine of punishment do not always distinguish in this sense between Expiation and Retribution, and condemnation of Retribution as a principle may often appear on analysis to be rather a condemnation of that 'adjustment of suffering to sin' which has here been brought under the heading of Expiation—as when Lord Justice Asquith described Retribution as 'a theory . . . now so discredited that to attack it is to flog a dead horse.' [5] It is however sufficiently clear that the reaction against the most extreme statements of the doctrine of Retribution has now gone so far that some would eliminate it, or convert it into terms which at least suggest that it 'may be more accurately described as restorative than retributive, since its function is to

---

[1] Grünhut, pp. 3, 4.   [2] Cit. Kenny, p. 35.   [3] P. 23.
[4] Reported in *The Magistrate* (July 1948).
[5] *The Listener*: May 11, 1950: p. 821.

repair the damaged order of society, and since it does not necessarily carry with it the wish to inflict pain . . . The nature of the punishment (the State) imposes is determined not by the intrinsic guilt of the offence but by the need to prevent its repetition. The motive for the punishment which the State inflicts in a Christian society is not the demand for retribution, that the guilty should be made to pay, but the positive impulse to restore the broken order of society.' [1]

This position appears to find support at one point from the Law—This hope of preventing a repetition of an offence is not only a main object, but the sole permissible object, of inflicting a criminal punishment' [2]; and at another from the Church, in Archbishop Temple's reference to 'the essential element in so-called retributive punishment . . . the assertion of the good-will of the community against his (the offender's) evil will.' [3] To state the position in these terms implies further that the 'restoration of the broken order of society', or 'the assertion of the good-will of the community against the offender's evil will', or even the plain 'vindication of the law' does not necessarily require that the action taken against the offender should include punishment in the sense of pain and suffering, so that the tendency today is to speak rather of the 'treatment' than of the 'punishment' of offenders, it being always and clearly understood that treatment may include punishment, and severe punishment, in a proper case. 'We nowadays realise that the basic vindication of the law is that the offender is put within the power of the court. And the court has the choice of punishment, that is of treatment . . .' [4]

It would at least appear to be in the light of such considerations that legal punishment can today be defined as 'the action which the court sees wise to take towards a person on conviction' [5] or 'the totality of the legal consequences of a conviction for crime.' [6] Certainly there is support for them in the actual practice of the courts in recent years. In 1947, 633,459 persons were dealt with by the criminal courts in England and Wales. Of these 78·9 per cent were fined; 15 per cent were bound over; dismissed, or placed under supervision under the Probation of Offenders Act; and only 4·7 per cent were sentenced to imprisonment.

It is now necessary to consider how far this view of the principles of punishment in relation to individual prevention is affected by considerations arising from general prevention and from the need which has been expressed to satisfy a demand of the public conscience for severe

[1] *The Times Literary Supplement*: April 21, 1950: leading article on 'Retribution'.
[2] Kenny, *Outlines of Criminal Law*, 15th edition, p. 32.
[3] Temple, p. 31.
[4] *The Courts and Punishment*, Dr. F. J. O. Coddington: *The Magistrate*, May–June, 1950.
[5] Page, p. 76.
[6] B. A. Wortley, in *The Modern Approach to Criminal Law* (Macmillan), p. 50.

retributive punishment for certain offences or classes of offence. And here we are not concerned with the special and quite separate problem of the persistent offender.

The principle of general prevention is that the penal system should have the effect of deterring potential offenders by fear of what will happen to them if they are found out. Therefore the court in dealing with each individual offender should consider the effect of its sentence not only on him but on all who may be tempted to commit a like offence. In considering the practical effects of this principle, it seems necessary first to answer the question—what is it that the potential offender fears?

It was the assumption that the only answer to this question was 'severity of punishment' that be-devilled the penal systems of the eighteenth and nineteenth centuries, since it led to the complete subordination of the interests of the individual to a conception of the interests of the community which was based not on reason and experience but on ignorance and fear. It was this sentiment which was epitomised in the pronouncement of the eighteenth-century judge, 'You are to be hanged not because you have stolen a sheep but in order that others may not steel sheep.' Since severity was the only acceptable criterion of deterrence, it followed that when it failed in its effect—as it invariably did—the only remedy was to call for further severity; and any attempt to break the vicious circle in which the system thus enmeshed and stultified itself met with the state of mind exemplified in Lord Ellenborough's now classic reply to Romilly's attempt to remove the death penalty for stealing 5s. or more from a shop, 'Your Lordships will pause before you assent to a measure so pregnant with danger for the security of property. The learned judges are unanimously agreed that the expediency of justice and public security require that there should not be a remission of capital punishment in this part of the criminal law.'

What most contributed to defeat this system was that it did not satisfy the public conscience. 'It must never be forgotten that the law is enforced by ordinary people. . . . Drastic punishment arouses in many minds such a sympathy for the accused that they will have no part or lot in inflicting it.' [1] Sir Leo Page, in illustration of this point, tells us that in 1830 a petition signed by 725 bankers was presented in Parliament 'praying that Parliament would not withhold from them that protection to their property which they would derive from a more lenient law',[2] and that in fifteen years to 1833 it was said that 555 perjured verdicts were returned at the Old Bailey alone for the single offence of stealing from a dwelling-house.

Indeed, whether or no there be scientific and statistical support for the view that 'crime decreases in every country as the pain inflicted for

1 Birkett, p. 22.   2 Page, p. 54.

it is diminished',[1] the plain lesson which students of criminal science draw from the history of penal law is that a policy of uniform deterrent severity has never been effective for either individual or general prevention.

On the principle of punishment with general deterrence in view as a primary aim, Archbishop Temple had this to say: 'In the infliction of a deterrent sentence the State is treating the offender as a means to the good of others rather than as an end in himself; and if this is all that the State has in view it will be acting immorally, for it will be contravening the fundamental principle of morality as expressed in the Kantian maxim: "Treat humanity, whether in your own person or in others, always as an end withal and never only as a means" . . . the moral relationship of the State towards the offending member cannot be exhausted by what has so little of moral quality about it as mere deterrence.'[2]

Attention has also been drawn to an effect of undue emphasis on severity of punishment in aid of general prevention which is more than a mere debating point. If the principle is of general validity and logically applied, it would follow that the commonest offences should attract the greatest deterrence. Traffic offences, for example, should be more seriously treated than offences that are, comparatively, rare. Indeed Mr. Alan Paton has pointed out that in Sweden, where ordinary crime is not a serious problem but traffic offences are, 'the same community that tolerates a humane and dispassionate approach to ordinary crime asks for sterner measures against dangerous traffic offenders.'[3] The practical difficulties of pursuing this line of thought to its logical conclusion are apparent.

Contemporary opinion, therefore, while accepting that the action of the penal system should be strong enough to vindicate the law, and that this action must therefore lead to punishment, and even severe punishment, in proper cases, rejects both in principle and for the practical reason that it does not work a conception of general prevention which wholly subordinates the interests of the individual offender.

It remains still to answer the question, what then is it that the potential offender fears?[4]

An answer of general acceptance could perhaps be best expressed, by adapting Mr. Wortley's definition of legal punishment (p. 10), as 'the totality of the consequences of being found out'. First in order

[1] Margaret Wilson: *The Crime of Punishment*, (Cape) p. 25.

[2] Temple, pp. 25, 27.

[3] *Freedom as a Reformatory Instrument* (Penal Reform League of S. Africa), p. 8.

[4] On the whole question of the adequacy of the sanction of fear as a safeguard against law-breaking, see *Arms of the Law* by Margery Fry, Part II, 'A Digression on Fear.'

comes the fear of being found out in itself. As Lord Samuel puts it, 'If every offence were certain of detection it would not be worth while for anyone to commit offences';[1] and clearly the first line of penal defence is an adequate and efficient police. The second is the swift and certain administration of justice, a point which in this country at this time does not require elaboration, though as we shall see the lesson had to be learned. Then, for the offender who has been detected and brought to justice, unless he be already an habitué, there is enough pain and suffering in the shame, hardship, and stigma which must attend his arrest, his public trial, and his conviction to carry in itself considerable deterrent force, even if the chances of any severe punishment be slight. And none can feel sure that he will not be punished, or how he will be punished: the mental agony of fearing a sentence of imprisonment may be greater than that of serving it. While therefore the expectation of punishment must remain, 'the essence of deterrence is found rather in the threat of the penalty than in the execution',[2] and the conclusion would seem to be that deterrence, for purposes of general prevention, is inherent in the whole action of the penal system and is not required to assume a primary place in the treatment of the individual.

Notable confirmation of this change in the attitude of informed opinion towards the deterrent function of the penal system is found in the House of Lords debate of 23 November 1948, on the motion of the Archbishop of York, about the serious increase in crime during 1947 and 1948. Rightly anxious as Their Lordships showed themselves in face of the grave facts before them, it is remarkable that, throughout the debate in that repository of a robust and conservative tradition in penal affairs, the sole reference to deterrence was made by the Archbishop himself—and that for repudiation. It was to the strengthening of the police, and to remedial measures outside the penal system, that every speaker directed his attention.

We are left therefore, for modification of the principle of the just sentence predicated by the argument, with one more factor—the need, in particular cases, to 'satisfy the public conscience' by retributive punishment of a severity beyond what is necessary, so far as concerns the individual offender, to vindicate the law and prevent repetition of the offence. To establish what these cases are, it is necessary to look rather to practice than to penological principle, which offers no clear guide. Recent discussion has dealt with three categories.

The first is that which Sir Leo Page would appear to have had in mind when he said 'The interests of the individual are ruthlessly and necessarily sacrificed by reason of the peculiar danger to the community of such crimes. Salus populi suprema lex.'[3] Such would be treason, or breaches of trust by policemen or public servants; and it may be also crimes against property outstanding in scale so as to bring widespread

---

[1] P. 25.   [2] Temple, p. 23.   [3] P. 245.

ruin or threaten public confidence in financial institutions, as major depredations by bank officials or the operations of such historic swindlers as Jabez Balfour and Horatio Bottomley. In such cases the argument can still proceed from the principle of 'balance', but the scale is weighted more strongly in favour of the general interest. It is a question rather of degree than of kind.

The second category was dealt with by Lord Justice Asquith as follows:

'Everyone has heard of an "exemplary" sentence: and nearly everyone agrees that at times such sentences are justified. But it is not always observed that an exemplary sentence is unjust; and unjust to the precise extent that it is exemplary. Assume a particular crime is becoming dangerously frequent. In normal times the appropriate sentence would be, say, two years. The judge awards three: he awards the third year entirely to deter others. This may be expedient; it may even be imperative. But one thing it is *not*: it is not just. The guilt of the man who commits a crime when it happens to be on the increase is no greater than that of another man who commits the same crime when it is on the wane. The truth is that in such cases the Judge is not administering strict justice but choosing the lesser of two practical evils. He decides that a moderate injustice to the criminal is a lesser evil than the consequences to the public of a further rise in the crime-wave.' [1]

The third category, which includes those cases which the Lord Chief Justice would appear to have had in mind (p. 9), comprises those crimes, usually associated with gross cruelty or violence, which are likely to excite, at any rate in the minds of many, peculiar repugnance and disgust—likely, in short, to make one 'see red'.

With this category the argument from principle is difficult. Many of us, no doubt, looking within ourselves, recognise both the repugnance and, when 'exemplary punishment' is meted out, the satisfaction—whether of conscience or of something more elemental. But no doubt also these effects are excited in different sorts of people by different sorts of offences: and experience suggests that among such offences are at least some of those on which opinion is divided as to whether they be truly criminal or no.

The path of justice therefore may here be beset with difficulty. The figure of Justice is blindfold, and may not 'see red'. And there is no index or measure of the movement of public conscience in these matters. One called to sit in judgment may well, in these circumstances, be in danger either of reading his own conscience for that of the public, or of finding it opposed to what he believes to be that of the public.

The conclusion must be that in these cases, as finally in all, justice

[1] Asquith, L. J., op. cit., p. 821.

can only confide in the knowledge, wisdom, and humanity of those who are called to the hard duty of making these decisions.

Such, then, are the considerations in the light of which an answer must be given today to the question—why punishment? The next question is—what punishment?

The kinds of punishment which are, or have been, at the disposal of English courts fall into six main categories, (1) death, (2) banishment, (3) public shame, (4) physical punishments (5) forfeiture of property, (6) deprivation of liberty. Of these the first, at the time of writing, remains, though its scope and indeed its retention at all come under more or less continuous public inquiry and debate. The second ceased with the abolition of transportation in the nineteenth century. The third, in which was included such devices as the pillory and the stocks, went rather earlier. The fourth, since the abolition of flogging in 1948, has also gone. We are left therefore, for offences not subject to capital punishment, with the last two categories only. Forfeitures are now limited to monetary penalties such as fines, damages, costs, and compensation: but the significance of 'deprivation of liberty' must be extended to include a range of greater or less limitations of self-determination such as are implied in 'binding over' and the conditions of a probation order (which may include a condition of residence in a home or hostel or mental hospital), as well as imprisonment, corrective training for incipient persistent offenders, and preventive detention for those persistent offenders who must be interned for long periods for the protection of society.[1]

Having thus placed the prison against its background, we may now knock on the gate and directly put the question—what is prison for?

Let us begin by asking what classes of person are in fact sent to prison. The statistics for 1947 [2] show that only about half the people received in prison in that year had been sentenced to imprisonment in the first instance as a punishment for an offence, and of these a bare majority were 'criminals' in the narrower sense of the word. Of the remainder, many were there because they could not or would not pay sums of money adjudged by the courts to be due, whether as fines or otherwise in connection with offences, or as civil debts. The remainder had been sent for safe-custody while on remand or awaiting trial or sentence, or under certain of the Aliens Orders. From time to time, also, there would be some awaiting execution of the death sentence, while others sentenced to corporal punishment under the law as it then stood would there be flogged.

Clearly, then, whatever prison is for it is not for one clear and single purpose. Indeed, three main purposes can be distinguished, which may

[1] For young offenders there is still another range of graduated limitations of liberty.
[2] Annual Report of the Prison Commissioners for 1948.

conveniently be defined as (1) custodial, for the unconvicted, (2) coercive, for those who can secure release by paying what they owe, and (3) correctional, for the convicted.

The duties of the prison as maid-of-all-work to the penal system will be dealt with elsewhere. Our present concern is only with the 'central problem', the treatment of convicted offenders: leaving aside the persistent offenders, these fall into two categories—those who have been sentenced to imprisonment in the first instance, and those who, having in the first instance been ordered to pay a fine or comply with conditions, have failed to do so and have in consequence been sent to prison.

From these facts, and from those given on p. 10 as to the recent practice of the courts, and from the principles of legal punishment, two preliminary statements can be made. First, that imprisonment is one of the methods at the disposal of the courts for the punishment of convicted offenders, though rarely used except for the more serious offences: it is also used as a sanction against the failure of more usual methods. Second, that the purpose of this as of other punishments is to prevent the offender from offending again. And if these statements seem to be mere glimpses of the obvious, they are nevertheless necessary because they condition the answer to the question, the root question implicit from the beginning in the words 'prison reform'—how is the prison to effect that purpose?

The answers that have been given to that question will, in effect, be the subject of this book, and at this stage we shall approach it only so far as to see what it implies, and to outline certain preliminary considerations which will later be established in their historical development.

The first of these is that the use of imprisonment as a form of punishment in itself is, in historical perspective, a comparatively recent idea, and that in England it had hardly gained acceptance before it was overtaken by the doubt whether after all it was a very good idea, so that subsequent legislation was devoted rather to abating than developing its use. It is not therefore surprising that in this matter thought should still be tentative, and practice empiric.

The second consideration concerns the nature and meaning of imprisonment. To sentence a person to imprisonment means, in itself and at Common Law, no more than to order him for the period stated to be deprived of his liberty by confinement in a lawful prison. Whether the prisoner, while so confined, should be treated in this way or in that, and why, depends solely on such directions as may from time to time be given to the keepers of the prison by statute or by statutory rule. In so far as the court may be deemed to be acting in knowledge of those directions, the treatment the prisoner will receive may be said to be implicit in the sentence, but all that is explicit is deprivation of liberty in the manner stated. By way of illustration, consider the condition of a convicted prisoner, serving a sentence, as recently observed by the present writer in a continental prison. In an adequately furnished room, over what looked like an adequate meal, he was reading a newspaper at ease in his own shirtsleeves. If he cared to do some work in the garden, it was welcome, but not expected. His sole obligations were to stay there and obey the rules. That is simple imprisonment in essence —though perhaps the provision of food and bedding might be regarded as a special modification: they have not always been held to be of the essence.

In the light of these considerations, our question now appears in this form—in what ways should this deprivation of liberty be modified so that as a punishment it may best serve its purpose of preventing the offender from offending again?

We shall find that, in the long-drawn thread of this still lively argument, three strands recur by way of answer, constant and inter-woven.

The first is the simplest, and perfect if carried to its logical conclusion —prolong the deprivation of liberty *sine die*, since for so long as the offender is 'taken out of circulation' he clearly cannot offend again. This principle, which may be called Prevention, is seen in its fullest action in the 'indeterminate sentence', or the sentence for 99 years or the like, known to American law; to a lesser degree in the 'preventive detention' for up to 14 years of persistent offenders under English law; and indeed in any sentence of any length for so long as it lasts. However, expressed in this way it is for our present purpose a mere abstraction: in the first place it does not, in principle, require any modification of the custodial function: in the second place, in the present state of penal law and public conscience in this country, sentences are not in practice —excepting always the special case of the persistent offender—based on this conception. The treatment of the offender in prison, save in exceptional cases, must therefore be based on the assumption that he will in a few months, or years, be returned to the community.

The second answer, which has been called Deterrence, suggests that the treatment in prison should be such that on his return to the community the offender will refrain from further offence through fear of having to repeat such an experience.

The third, which has been called Reform, suggests that the protection of society will be not less effectively secured if the offender returns to it with his mind set against further offence not from fear, which may or may not be an abiding restraint, but from an inner conviction which will remain with him. The treatment should therefore be designed to this end.

A more recent variation on these themes suggests that, whether the offender on discharge has been deterred or whether he has been reformed, in any event the protection of society will not be served unless he returns to it not only willing but able to take a normal and useful place: it therefore emphasises the need of Training.

Such then are the three classic principles—Prevention, Deterrence, and Reform. Under which of these, or under what combination of them, could or should we seek to regulate the treatment of persons punished by deprivation of liberty in a prison? Or is it possible, by an extension of the conception of Training, to effect a viable synthesis?

That is the question as it faces us today.

CHAPTER TWO

THE QUESTION IS POSED

(1) BEFORE JOHN HOWARD. THE QUESTION DID NOT ARISE

IMPRISONMENT as a punishment of first instance has developed, as a complete conception, almost within the time of men now living, but legal punishment, in the sense of formal action by society against the law-breaker, goes to the primitive roots of social history. Banishment and vengeance were the earliest reactions to offence, and they have never wholly ceased to work in penal systems. The first goes back very far: an offender against tribal tabu became a danger to the safety of the tribe, which could be assured only by his complete expulsion. This thread will run through the story as far at least as Devil's Island and Botany Bay. The second has undergone many mutations: social utility enforced some limitation of the right of private vengeance —'an eye for an eye, a tooth for a tooth'; then substituted compensation for physical vengeance; and finally required society to take into its own hands the responsibility of securing justice for private wrongs. So came in England the conception of 'the King's Peace', under which any offences against private persons likely to lead to reprisals, and therefore disorder, were deemed to be 'against the Peace of our Sovereign Lord the King'. It is a matter of continuing significance that legal punishment for a crime against a private person is in origin a substitute for that private vengeance which society forbids the victim.

The first principle of justice enforced by the community was compensation, the *lex talionis*. Even banishment came to be redeemable by the forfeiture of property instead of life. The later medieval system of corporal and defamatory penalties was largely of economic origin 'because almost the only worldly goods that had been left to the great masses were their bodies and, perhaps, their citizenship'.[1] Where there were prisons, their part was only to hold offenders till the proper punishments could be inflicted, and imprisonment was not a proper punishment. Indeed, for a thousand years after Justinian had enunciated

[1] Mannheim, p. 40.

19

this principle (p. 2), the penal law of Europe was dominated by the idea of the illegality of imprisonment as a punishment.

The English, however, must have their heresy, and in 1275 the Statute of Westminster provided two years imprisonment as a legal punishment for rape—also their illogicality, for Bracton had little earlier 'referred to prisons as places where men waited to be liberated or sentenced by judicial decision' [1] and stated that 'fetters and all such things are forbidden by law, because a prison is a place of detention and not of punishment'.[2] Certainly when the judges of the King's High Court went on circuit their commission was one of 'gaol delivery'; they went to clear the gaols, not to fill them. It is interesting, however, to note that at a very early stage the prison assumed the coercive as well as the custodial function. When forfeitures came to be made to the Crown, prisons were found helpful in persuading the offender or his family to pay. 'The word fine is still reminiscent of this form of "finishing" a prison term.' [3]

In English legal theory the gaols, as well as the Peace, were the King's, and though private prisons were kept by corporations, nobles, or bishops under franchise, it was only in the common or county gaol that the Sheriff as King's officer for the county had his authority. And today it is still the Sheriff who is charged with the execution in prisons of sentence of death. In 1403 we find what is perhaps the first statutory regulation of imprisonment, providing that Justices should commit only to the Common Gaol.[4]

These gaols were not specially provided buildings. Dr. Grünhut, speaking of prisons in Europe generally, says, 'Towers, gate-houses, dungeons, cellars of town-halls and market-houses were used as prisons.' [5] In England the position was no better, and could hardly have been worse. Anything might serve, from the cellar of an inn to the gate-house of an abbey, and neither the Sheriff nor the local Justices were effectively responsible either for the upkeep of the buildings or for the treatment of the prisoners—or even indeed for their maintenance, saving a small allowance of bread for convicted felons. The public or private authorities or persons owning the gaols farmed them out to private keepers on a purely profit-making basis.

Since this mediæval system continued, with little significant change, right through the eighteenth century and into the nineteenth, it will be convenient to give an impression of these establishments now, and finish with them. We will look at them as Howard found them—the gaols of Dr. Johnson's England—the England of Adam Smith and Blackstone, of Fielding and Smollett, of Hogarth and 'The Beggars' Opera', of the Gordon Riots and cheap gin.

To the common gaol, be it first remembered, all were committed

[1] Grünhut, p. 12.   [2] Buxton, p. 10.   [3] Grünhut, p. 12.
[4] 5 H. IV, cap. 10.   [5] p. 13.

alike—felons and misdemeanants, convicted or unconvicted; civil debtors (except where there were separate Debtors Prisons); men, women, and children. In the smaller gaols there was no provision whatever for separation of different classes of prisoners, and usually little or none for segregation of the sexes—nor, where that existed, would the keeper require or expect it to be observed. A night room and a day room or yard would serve for everybody. Larger gaols built for the purpose were not essentially better, they only held more; and possibly by providing two or more yards and wards enabled some rudimentary separation. All were usually unheated, unfurnished except for straw, and unprovided with any but the most primitive sanitary arrangements.

The only duty of the gaoler to the prisoners was to hold them, his only interest to make what he could from his duty. The economic basis of the business was the fee—legal or illegal. A fee was charged for admission, and happy the gaoler who received a prisoner on several commitments, for he could charge a separate fee on each: another was payable before the prisoner could obtain his discharge. Irons were a fruitful source of fees. Their use was illegal in theory, but they were much cheaper than secure buildings: useless then for Lord Chief Justice King to 'reply to those who urged that irons were necessary for safe-custody that they might build their walls higher'.[1] So fees were charged both for the hammering on and knocking off of irons, and fastidious gentlemen like Captain MacHeath could select lighter or better fitting irons for a higher fee.

On this basis it was good business to make everything as pleasant as possible for those who would pay, and equally unpleasant for those who would not. So, at a price, special rooms might be hired, and special meals provided, and of such amenities the tap and the brothel were not the least lucrative.

Such were the gaols of which it was written 'that disease, cold, famine, nakedness, a contagious and polluted air, are not lawful punishments in the hands of a civil magistrate, nor has he a right to poison or starve his fellow creature'.[2] Poison indeed, for they were forcing houses not only of lechery, debauchery and moral corruption, but of a contagious pestilence. The gaol-fever had been known at least since 1414: at Oxford, in the Black Assizes of 1577, 'within five weeks 500 persons died, among them the Lord Chief Baron and many jurymen and witnesses. . . . In 1750 a Lord Mayor of London, an Alderman, and two Judges were among the victims.'[3] At this time it was computed that every year one quarter of the prisoners were thus destroyed, and none who has read contemporary accounts of the conditions need doubt it.

[1] Buxton, p. 12.
[2] *State of Jails* by W. Smith, 1776, cit. Buxton.   [3] Grünhut, p. 28.

The age which fostered these conditions was one, as Dr. Trevelyan tells us, 'of the growth of humanitarian and philanthropic feeling and endeavour . . . a keener sensitiveness to the needs and sufferings of others (which) melted the hard prudence of statesmen'; an age which saw 'the foundation first of Charity Schools, then of Hospitals . . . and of Sunday Schools'.[1] Yet it is not unfair to say that before Howard began his work in 1773, no effective protest against this national disgrace was heard in public life beyond the parliamentary inquiry of 1729 under General Oglethorpe, which was forced by public scandal when several debtors died in the Fleet and Marshalsea prisons of sheer brutality and negligence: Dr. Grünhut records no more than a report of 1702 by the S.P.C.K. into the conditions of certain London prisons, some sharp observations in the works of Henry Fielding, and a sermon of 1740 by Bishop Butler. It is a suggestive field for the student of social history.

Fortunately the history of the common gaol is not all that the period under review has to offer us; but before we turn to a more hopeful field let us look first at the contemporary system of criminal justice. This, until at least 1823, was so chaotic as to be almost beyond description or understanding. By the time of the Tudors the mediaeval system of penalties was giving way, for felonies, to the domination of the penalty of death. For misdemeanours there were fines and various corporal and defamatory punishments. This tendency continued through the seventeenth century, and by 1688 some fifty offences were punishable by death. Then, in the eighteenth century, came such a pouring panic of capital statutes that by the end of the century they were literally beyond number: Dr. Radzinowicz concludes that they probably exceeded two hundred, and quotes Romilly as saying, in 1810, that 'there is probably no other country in the world in which so many and so great a variety of human actions are punishable with loss of life as in England.' [2]

This was the ferocity of fear. As any new offence gained prominence, it was countered by a new capital statute: and when there was no diminution of offence it must in the nature of that sentiment, since death was not a sufficient deterrent, be required to aggravate death by torture and degradation. For some offences the victim was dragged to the scaffold at a horse's tail, strangled, mutilated, and disembowelled; women for others might be burned alive. Even more ingenious measures were publicly propounded for diminishing the rise in crime by prolonging the agony of death. Nor was the horror mitigated for children of tender years. On the other hand, Blackstone was able to illustrate the increased humanity of his time by pointing to the provision that the victim might be drawn to the scaffold on a hurdle and not along the ground.

[1] G. M. Trevelyan, *English Social History*, pp. 336, 347.   [2] Radzinowicz, p. 3.

The social psychology of these conditions is of great interest, but less relevant for our purpose than those causes of them which derived from the preventive deficiencies of the penal system. These, as summed up by Dr. Trevelyan, strikingly illustrate the point made in the previous chapter that the first lines of defence in a penal system must be an adequate and efficient police and the swift and certain administration of justice: 'The effect of increased legal severity in an age that was becoming more humane, was that juries often refused to convict men for minor offences that would lead them to the scaffold. Moreover it was easy for a criminal, by the help of a clever lawyer, to escape on purely technical grounds from the meshes of an antiquated and over elaborate procedure. Out of six thieves brought to trial, five might in one way or another get off, while the unlucky one was hanged. It would have been more deterrent if they had all six been sure of a term of imprisonment. To make matters worse, the chances of arrest were small, for there was no effective police in the island, except the 'runners' of the office which the Fielding brothers, about the middle of the century, set up in their house in Bow Street.' [1] A second factor was the absence of any adequate alternative to the system, for the gaols were incapable of development into an effective penal instrument as they were then conceived.

Fortunately not all of those convicted on capital charges were executed. Dr. Radzinowicz, examining the figures for London and Middlesex for the last half of the eighteenth century, finds that out of 3680 capitally convicted 1696 were executed: he also points out that in one of those years, out of 97 executions, only one was for murder and 96 were for offences against property. The curious complications of 'benefit of clergy', with its division of felonies into the clergyable and the non-clergyable, saved those who could read the 'neck verse', at the cost of a branding, and the Prerogative of Mercy was available for others. This is not the place to discuss either Clergy or Prerogative: the former stayed till 1827, when the death penalty was limited to treason and the felonies which had been non-clergyable: the relevance of the Prerogative is its use as the instrument for bringing banishment back to the penal system. Following the acquisition of territory in America, the practice developed during the seventeenth century of granting Crown Pardons to condemned felons on condition of their agreeing to be 'transported beyond the seas', where they provided valuable labour in the plantations. The practice was placed on a statutory basis in 1679,[2] and in 1717 [3] was more precisely regulated, 7 years in the American plantations being prescribed for clergyable felonies and 14 years for non-clergyable. In 1767 [4] the Judges were

---

[1] Trevelyan, pp. 348, 349.

[2] 31 Car. 2, cap. 2.

[3] 4 Geo. 1, cap. 11.

[4] 8 Geo. 3, cap. 15.

empowered to order transportation as a sentence, such order having the effect of a conditional pardon.

So we leave our gaols, for a time, in the condition in which they were described by a contemporary wit—'An ante-room, to the New World—or the next.' It was through another channel, outside the penal system, that the function of correction was to be introduced into the prisons.

The social and economic conditions of the Tudor age, with its increase of unemployed and unemployable, vagrants and 'sturdy beggars', led to the institution of 'a proper system of Poor Relief, based upon compulsory rates and discriminating between the various classes of the indigent'.[1] Moreover, the strong central government of the Tudor monarchy saw to it that this was effectively enforced through the local Justices of the Peace, who were given increasing powers not only of justice but of local government administration. The system aimed to provide not only relief for the poor but work for the unemployed, and for the latter purpose Working Houses or Houses of Correction were set up for those classes who required a measure of compulsion to get them to work—especially such as vagabonds, beggars, prostitutes, idle apprentices and others who required 'to be corrected in their habits by laborious discipline'. This situation has a parallel today in the law of some Swiss cantons, where both idleness and prostitution rate high enough as social disorders to bring commital to a penal establishment. The first of these Houses was founded in the former royal palace of Bridewell, given by Edward VI in 1553, and thence came the popular name of these institutions which lingers here and there to this day. In 1576 [2] the Justices were required to provide a House of Correction in every county.

The idea of reform was implicit in these institutions, and at first it seems to have been effective. 'Coke stated, that unlike those suffering from the bad and even deteriorating effects of the common gaol, people commited to the Working House come out better.' [3] Certainly they tried to live up to their name, and the essence of the discipline was hard and useful industrial work, from the proceeds of which the inmates were paid wages for their maintenance. But the idea of deterrence was also implicit, and quickly rose to parity and then predominance. Bridewells soon came to be more an arm of the penal than of the poor law, and the practice grew of committing to them all sorts of minor offenders. Industry as a training gave way to hard work as a deterrent, and in 1609 Justices were authorised by statute [4] to institute 'hard labour' in the Bridewells as a purely penal measure.

The similarity of the continental trend is of interest. The first House of Correction was the Rasp Huis at Amsterdam of 1595, and the idea

[1] Trevelyan, p. 113.   [3] Grünhut, p. 16.
[2] 18 Eliz., cap. 3.   [4] 7 J. i, cap. 4.

spread across Europe. It was, as in England, an idea at first of reform by hard work, with wages, education, and religious instruction. 'The whole tendency of the new foundation was fundamentally opposed to contemporary criminal law. It did not involve an exclusion from society by death, mutilation, and branding with permanent degradation. The ultimate aim was to lead the prisoner back into society. As to the results, contemporary writers are full of praise.' [1] But in Europe too committal to the Rasp House became a purely penal measure, and during the eighteenth century developed all the characteristics not only of deterrence but of defamation. Some eighteenth-century prints [2] of the Amsterdam Rasphuis show groups of half-naked prisoners rasping huge logs with desperate energy; close by, bound to an elegant Ionic column, is one who undergoes violent chastisement. Groups of ladies and gentlemen watch with a detached air.[3]

Yet fresh ideas developed which had a continuing life. In the House of Correction at Ghent, before the end of the eighteenth century, were to be found the elements of a modern prison system. And in 1703, in the House of Correction of St. Michael in Rome, there was founded the first separate reformatory for young delinquents and for what today we should call 'beyond control' or 'care and protection' cases. It was here that Howard found the famous inscription 'Parum est coercere improbos poena nisi probos efficias disciplina.'

In England the remaining history of the Bridewell is unhappy and short. Early in the seventeenth century it became the practice to establish them alongside the gaols: in 1719 the practice of committing to them minor offenders was given statutory sanction: [4] during the eighteenth century the two classes of institution became almost completely assimilated, being commonly under the same roof and the same keeper, and in 1823 [5] this position was recognised by law, and the Justices were given a definite responsibility for the whole of the 'united or contiguous buildings': in 1865 the distinction between gaol and Bridewell, long lost in practice, was finally abolished in law.[6]

(2) HOWARD AND AFTER. THE MOVEMENT FOR REFORM

Although it was the peculiar merit of John Howard to focus attention on the scandal of the prisons, his work was but one aspect—though for our purpose the most important—of a European movement for the reform of penal systems which was characteristic of the Age of Enlightenment. A few philosophers isolated principles of enduring value; a few more men of good will, under their inspiration, fought for

---

[1] Grünhut, p. 18.
[2] Formerly in the office of the Penal and Penitentiary Commission at Bern.
[3] See Appendix K.   [5] 4 G. iv, cap. 64.
[4] 6 G. i, cap. 19.   [6] See Appendix K.

improvement; but effective action was blanketed by administrative inadequacy and legal and political reaction.

In France the movement of thought had started with Voltaire and Montesquieu, but it was the publication in Italy in 1764 of Beccaria's essay 'On Crimes and Punishments' which stirred the penal systems of Europe and laid the foundations of criminal science. This potent work stated most of the principles that have come to be accepted as the basis of thought on legal punishment—that the sole justifiable purpose of such punishment was the protection of society by the prevention of crime; that for this purpose the principle of uniform maximum severity, particularly by capital punishment, was not only wrong but ineffective; and that milder punishments proportioned to the offences; but inflicted with promptness and certainty, would be more effective in preventing crime than haphazard severity.

In England, under the influence of Beccaria and the leadership of Eden, Romilly, and Blackstone, the attack was pressed incessantly but fruitlessly for half a century. But the main battleground was the legal system itself, and the main issue the rationalisation of the use of capital punishment. Howard, in association with this group, fought mainly on what seemed then the secondary issue of the state of the prisons, though we may now see that neglect of the question of 'secondary punishments' was a strong reason for failure in the main field.

John Howard was a very English character. A nonconformist land-owner of humane and progressive views, with a developed social conscience, he was led into his life work simply by doing his public duty as he saw it with conscience and a single mind. When in 1773 he became High Sheriff of Bedfordshire 'he did what none of his predecessors had tried before; he inspected the prisons of his county'.[1] What he saw struck him so forcibly that he thought it well to see some other prisons, and before his sense of duty was satisfied he had visited most English prisons and many in Europe. In 1777 he published his conclusions in 'The State of the Prisons in England and Wales with some Preliminary Observations, and an Account of some foreign Prisons'. A second volume followed in 1789, and in 1790 he died of the plague in the Ukraine while investigating hospital conditions in the Middle East. As Bentham said later, 'he died a martyr after living an apostle'.

Howard's work and abiding influence were not limited to the ascertainment and exposure of evil: he proposed remedies, and influenced others to work for them. He was concerned not only with the elementary material decencies and necessities, but with spiritual values: he wished to bring back the forgotten notion that Houses of Correction should correct—'parum est coercere improbos poena nisi probos efficias disciplina'. Prisons should be sanitary and secure; the sexes should be effectively separated; the keeper should be a paid and responsible servant

1 Grünhut, p. 32.

of the Justices; and the Justices themselves should exercise effective supervision. But above all physical and moral corruption should be prevented by the provision of separate cells for sleeping; moral improvement should be sought through the influence of religion by the appointment of Chaplains; and last, but by no means least, prisoners should be provided with useful work by day in proper workshops. Between 1774 and 1791, largely through the efforts of Eden and Blackstone and the personal prestige of Howard with Parliament, a well-intentioned group of Acts was passed in which most of these ideas were embodied.

But though informed opinion had moved, the machinery of administration was powerless to enforce it against the inertia of general opinion. The Acts were permissive, not mandatory, and their enforcement rested with the local Justices: the central government had no means even of knowing whether recommendations of Parliament were being followed or not. Some of the better Magistrates, personally influenced by Howard, were able to get some improvement in their counties, but local authorities were not generally disposed to increase the rates for the benefit of prisoners: in the year of Waterloo the Aldermen of the City of London, in whose prisons a debtor had recently died of starvation, and two women prisoners were shortly to be found with only a rug to hide their joint nakedness, declared that 'their prisoners had all they ought to have, unless gentlemen thought they should be indulged with Turkey carpets' [1]—perhaps the first public protest of common sense against the ' pampering of prisoners '. And so, although the increasing menace of the gaol-fever forced some improvement of sanitation, the prisons in general, twenty years after Howard's death, were very much as he found them when he first began his tour in 1773.

Let us see how they looked to another inquiring missionary, Thomas Fowell Buxton, in the years after Waterloo—the age of an England, after the victories of Nelson and Wellington, at her brilliant best—the England of Wordsworth, Shelley, and Keats, of Cobbett, Jane Austen, and Sir Walter Scott, of the flower of English architecture and English art. In Appendix A are given extracts from Buxton's *An Inquiry whether Crime and Misery are produced or prevented by our present System of Prison Discipline, illustrated by Descriptions of (ten prisons at home and abroad) and the Proceedings of the Ladies Committee at Newgate.* It is dreadful reading. Its effect cannot be better summarised than by Buxton himself in his Preliminary Observations (p. 19): 'In short, by the greatest possible degree of misery, you produce the greatest possible degree of wickedness; . . . receiving (the prisoner) because he is too bad for society, you return him to the world impaired in health, debased in intellect, and corrupted in principles.'

[1] Clay, p. 91.

Yet we should remember that, after the long years of the Napoleonic Wars, England had no more than in our own day 'saved herself by her exertions' without paying the price. It was moreover an age of serious economic disorder and rapid social change. Increasing population and growing industrialisation brought with them slum-towns, unemployment, and serious distress. The growing demands of the new proletariat were at odds with the natural anti-Jacobin sentiment of the time. Crime was increasing and the prisons were overfull. The age of the Luddites and Peterloo was not propitious for reform of the penal system. Twice in our own time we have seen that prisons after a war have low priority as a charge on public purse and conscience; their consequent condition lays them open to attack, and their reaction may carry them a long bound forward. So, in degree, it fell out after Waterloo.

Those who now took up the work of Howard were a remarkable group. Centred on the great Quaker banking families—Gurneys, Barclays, Frys, and Hoares—they had the urge of their religion to do practical good, the wealth to furnish it, and the social standing to make themselves felt in high places. Among these Elizabeth Fry, née Gurney, was not only pre-eminent in her time but still keeps her place, comparable with that of Florence Nightingale, among the greatest Englishwomen.

Mrs. Fry's first visits to the women's side of Newgate—then a new prison, and so providing a separate side for women—were made at the suggestion of her brothers-in-law, Samuel Hoare and Thomas Fowell Buxton, the founders, in 1816, of the Society for the Reformation of Prison Discipline.[1] She found it, says Buxton, 'in a situation which no language can describe' [2]; she visited the sick, and helped the mothers with their children, but it was not till 1816 that she was moved to grapple in earnest with the problems of a place of which a contemporary wrote that 'of all the seats of woe on this side Hell, few, I suppose, exceed or equal Newgate'.[3] Now that she saw that something must be done, she did not, being a woman and Elizabeth Fry, write a book about it, but went into the prison and did it. Sheriffs, Governor, and prisoners alike were brought under the spell of her simple goodness and practical single-minded determination, and with the help of a Ladies Committee of her Quaker friends she had, within a few months, brought into this bedlam of harridans the calm and industrious order of a cloister. As the fame of her miracle spread, she visited other prisons to set up Ladies Committees, and in 1818 was

[1] It is remarkable that the Howard League, virtually the lineal descendant of this Society, still numbers among its officers a Fry, a Fowell Buxton, and a Samuel Hoare (Lord Templewood).

[2] For the language in which he nevertheless attempted to describe it, see extracts in Appendix A.

[3] Whitney, p. 142.

called as an expert witness before a Committee of Parliament, 'the first woman other than a queen to be called into the councils of the government in an official manner to advise on matters of public concern'.[1] Her fame preceded her visits to the prisons of Europe, and before her death in 1845 she was a regular correspondent of kings and princes in matters of prison reform.

What was her secret? It is worth while to know it, for Mrs. Fry was more than an historical episode—she was the prophet, a hundred years before her time, of our present system. All that she asked of Parliament for her women in 1818 was granted by Parliament—in 1948. It may be found in the Statutory Rules made under the Criminal Justice Act. She started from the principle that 'punishment is not for revenge, but to lessen crime and reform the criminal'. For accommodation she required a separate building for women, under the care of women, providing separate cells by night with proper workshops and common rooms by day. For training, plenty of useful work, careful religious instruction, a library, and attention to education. So far, perhaps, as principles, nothing very striking or fresh: but her special contribution was to show conclusively that they worked, and this carried conviction even in her own time. In 1818 the Grand Jury of the City of London said 'that if the principles which govern her regulations were adopted towards the males, as well as the females, it would be the means of converting a prison into a school of reform: and instead of sending criminals back into the world hardened in vice and depravity, they would be restored to it repentant, and probably become useful members of society'.[2] But the question remained, what made her principles work? Here the report of the Parliamentary committee went to the root of the matter. 'The benevolent exertions of Mrs. Fry and her friends have indeed etc., etc. But much must be ascribed to unremitting personal attention and influence.'[3]

Unremitting personal attention and influence—there lay her secret. This was a method not easily transmitted in her time and the years to come, and it was not until, more than a hundred years after, it was again both preached and practised that her work took root in our prison system. How did she exercise that influence? Her simple rules may be seen in Appendix A. First, she believed that 'prisoners should be treated as human beings with human feelings'; second, that their willing co-operation should be sought; and third, that they should learn responsibility through a measure of self-government. And the result? 'I have never,' she told the Committee, 'punished a woman during the whole time, or even proposed a punishment to them; and yet I think it is impossible, in a well-regulated house, to have rules more strictly attended to.'[4] Each element of this method also finds

---

[1] Whitney, p. 164.
[2] Whitney, p. 160.
[3] Whitney, p. 168.
[4] Whitney, p. 166.

its place in the new Statutory Rules, and the Governor of a women's prison, in her Annual Report for 1948, repeated in similar words the exact sense of Mrs. Fry's statement of the result. *Eppur si muove.*

But these 'benevolent exertions' were concerned with the lot of people in prison, not with the function of the prison in the penal system,' though this question was already being canvassed in other connections which we shall consider in the   next section. Mrs. Fry's Newgate was still 'no more than an ante-room', and her women for all her care would pass to the transports or the scaffold. Indeed much of the Ladies' time was spent in calming and comforting unhappy girls about to be hanged for stealing a floor-cloth or a few shillings, and in dealing with the 'transports'. With these they first took charge of the removal from the prison to the docks. This had been a horrible business; first a hysterical struggle as the turnkeys fought to iron the crazed and half-drunken women, then a popular procession in closely guarded open wagons. Now it took place quietly, in closed hackney coaches, with Quaker ladies instead of chains for control. Then they organised the ships, and brought to them also the order, decency, and industry of Newgate. And in time Mrs. Fry's influence reached out to New South Wales itself—but that is another story.[1]

(3) SECONDARY PUNISHMENTS. DEATH OR . . .?

During the period covered by the preceding section, the parliamentary battle for reform of the whole penal system had been joined. The great increase in crimes of violence, and the ineffectiveness of the system in face of it, forced the House of Commons to appoint Committees in 1750 and 1770: on each occasion a rationalisation and reduction of the capital statutes was recommended by the Commons but defeated by the Lords. The Committee of 1750 went further, and made a series of far-sighted suggestions covering the improvement of social conditions predisposing to crime, a more efficient police system, a better administration of criminal justice, and the removal of defects in the Houses of Correction. But nothing could be done, and there the matter rested until, under the leadership of Sir Samuel Romilly, the ten year battle was joined which ended, soon after his death, with the appointment of another Committee in 1819. The leadership had now passed to Fowell Buxton and James Mackintosh, and although they were again checked by the Lords, they did succeed in changing the climate of opinion and preparing the way for the radical changes effected by Peel when he became Home Secretary in 1821.

Simultaneously, the problem of 'secondary punishments' was being forced on the reluctant attention of Parliament through the 'divers

---

[1] For the story of Sarah Martin, a humble follower of the methods of Mrs. Fry at Yarmouth, see Appendix B.

difficulties and inconveniences' to which the system of transportation had become subject during the War of Independence in America. Bills were passed to meet the situation in 1775 and 1779, but general opinion still inclined to the simple view that the best thing to do with convicted felons was to get rid of them, one way or another, and forget about them. It was therefore with relief that the Government was able, in 1787, to resume transportation to the new continent conveniently discovered by Captain Cook. But though the Acts of 1775 and 1779 had little or no immediate effect, they gave a fresh turn to thought and practice on the function of correction, as distinct from custody, in prisons, and deserve to be noticed in some detail.

The first Act provided for convicted felons not transported to be set to hard labour for various terms, in dredging the river Thames or 'other such laborious services'. They might be confined in the hulks—transports, as it were, in suspense [1]—or in 'any proper place of confinement', and Justices were required to prepare their Houses of Correction for the setting of convicts to hard labour. These were temporary arrangements, and the permanent scheme appeared in the Act of 1779.[2] This 'Hard Labour Bill' provided for the building of two Penitentiaries in which convicts were to be imprisoned and set to hard labour, viz. 'Labour of the hardest and most servile kind, in which drudgery is chiefly required . . . such as treading in a wheel or drawing in a capstern for turning a mill or other machine, sawing stone, etc., etc., or any other hard and laborious service', with 'other less laborious employment' according to age and sex for those unfitted for the heavier work. The penitentiary buildings were to provide for the separation of the sexes, separate cells, an infirmary and a Chapel: but in fact, Captain Cook intervening, they were never built.

Meanwhile there had been another influential intervention. Jeremy Bentham, under the influence of Beccaria, had led the Utilitarians into the battle for penal reform, and was now moved by the Hard Labour Bill to devote to the question of prisons the gifts of his brilliant mind. On themes of the school of Howard he elaborated endless variations, many extremely sensible, many less so: but above all he fought for the principle of useful work as against sterile hard labour. It was unfortunate that his fertility in over-ingenious notions and curious mechanical contrivances led him to canalise his efforts towards his novel plan for a penitentiary, which he called a panopticon. He developed this to a point at which Parliament actually agreed, in 1794, to take it up under his direction, and a site for it was bought on Millbank. But again time passed; nothing was done; Parliament thought again—perhaps wisely; and when in 1812 another Act was passed for the building of a penitentiary it was not to be Bentham's. The new building was started in 1816 on the site bought for the panopticon, and

[1] See Appendix K. [2] 19 Geo. III cap. 74.

by two curious exchanges on Thames side between the fine arts and crime, Scotland Yard now rises from the foundations of an opera house, while the Tate Gallery replaces our first penitentiary. Some structural remains of Millbank penitentiary may still be seen, and the gravestone of one of its governors is still legible in St. John's churchyard nearby.

Bentham's brilliant irruption into the field of secondary punishments left little of practical effect behind. Indeed the whole period is one of false starts and fumbling uncertainty. But there were three new ideas in the field—punitive hard labour, the hulks, and (in posse) the penitentiary, of which the important feature was that it was a Government and not a local affair. The idea of hard labour made little impact on the local prisons. An Act of 1791 required Justices to make Rules for Hard Labour on the lines of the Hard Labour Act of 1779, but their prisons were quite unfit for the prolonged detention of large numbers of convicts, and they were not prepared to go to the trouble and expense of making them so. Since the Government could not shelve on to the local authorities its responsibility for convicts, these until they could be transported were kept in the hulks down the Thames or wherever else they could be employed in dredging or public works.

The time, in short, was not yet ripe in England for serious consideration of imprisonment as a method of legal punishment, and it was not until 1823, as one part of Peel's reforms, that an effective start was made. It was in that year also that Parliament learned of the New World having been brought in to redress the balance of the Old, and since the effects of this beneficent process were nowhere more marked than in our prison system, it is across the Atlantic that we must look for the opening of the next act.

(4) THE QUESTION IS POSED. THE BATTLE OF THE SYSTEMS

Long before the Declaration of Independence the Quaker state of Pennsylvania, anticipating the course of penal reform by over 100 years, had abolished both whipping and (except for murder) hanging, and had substituted as the punishment for felony as well as misdemeanour imprisonment on the model of the best Houses of Correction. But this experiment did not survive the death of William Penn in 1718, and it was not till after 1776 that the Quakers, under the influence of Howard, again took up the cause of penal reform. Once again murder alone was made capital, and the prison was made the prime instrument of legal punishment.

This time, however, the system was different. Taking perhaps too much account of the value Howard placed on the separate cell, and too little of the rest of his doctrine, it was based on solitary confinement in its most absolute form. 'This practice was intended to promote "that calm contemplation which brings repentance", and reminded the visitors of fasting and abstinence among certain religious sects. Apparently this group were not allowed either to work or to receive visitors. Prisoners convicted of minor offences, and felons after the expiration of the solitary stage of their confinement, worked in association . . . . Disciplinary punishment consisted in transferring the prisoner to solitary confinement.' [1] A variation of this Solitary System, under which prisoners might be removed from their cells, provided they were kept strictly separate, was known as the Separate System: this in its perfection provided rows of enclosures like large pig-sties, but with high walls, in which each prisoner took separate exercise, turned the Chapel into a honeycomb of separate cubicles from which only the chaplain and the altar were visible, and even provided the prisoners with masks.

But the fertility of thought and experiment which has in different periods distinguished the penal systems of the United States was already active. The beneficent effects of the Pennsylvania System were not everywhere taken for granted, and Boston was soon in the field with a school of thought different from that of Philadelphia, and closer to the views of Bentham and Howard. This was based on the Separate System for sleeping, but provided workshops for useful employment by day, and starting from New England and New York spread considerably. Many prisons were built on this model, including the historic Sing-Sing and Auburn (1819), and from the strict rule of silence enforced at the latter this system was known sometimes as the Silent System and sometimes as the Auburn System.

This rapid building of great new prisons gave the United States a lead in prison construction which they have never lost, and in the early years of the nineteenth century, as today, there was a regular flow of European visitors to inspect and report on new systems and new model prisons—among which, to the comfort and encouragement of Bentham, there was even a version of his Panopticon.[2] The impact on European thought and practice was considerable, and may still be traced: within recent years the writer has visited continental prisons which still retain the apparatus of the Separate System, (including the 'préaux' or separate exercise pens and the chapel cubicles), and others which were introduced as representing 'le système Auburn'. The monthly Bulletin of the Belgian prison service for February 1949 reported that, during 1948, 'furent ordonnées progressivement la suppression des stalles individuelles dans les chapelles et la démolition des préaux cellulaires, autres vestiges des temps où la discipline rigide des Quakers était en honneur'.

In England, effective progress in penal reform began with the

[1] Grünhut, p. 46.
[2] Another version of the Panopticon still exists at Breda, Holland.

historic tenure (1821–27) of the office of Secretary of State for the
Home Department by Sir Robert Peel, 'who of all Home Secretaries has
left the deepest impress on the laws and institutions of the country'.[1]
Peel was neither a missionary nor an innovator, but an able and
energetic administrator with a strong sense of the politically practicable.
Having taken stock of those ideas concerning penal reform which
seemed to him right and practicable, from the Committee of 1750
through Howard and Bentham to Romilly and Mackintosh, he proceeded systematically to put them into effect, with all the authority of
the government, in a series of statutes which cleared broad avenues
through the mediaeval chaos of the penal system. The capital statutes
were consolidated and reduced in number; benefit of clergy was
abolished (1827) and transportation or imprisonment up to two
years prescribed as penalties for the felonies which, broadly,
had been clergyable; the scale of punishments for many minor
offences was reduced; the administration of justice was overhauled
to make for greater certainty and speed; and in 1829 the Metropolitan Police was established on substantially its present basis,
to become a model shortly followed by all the county and borough
forces.

It was a necessary part of this comprehensive plan that the prisons
should be put in a state to become an effective instrument of secondary
punishment, and the Gaol Act of 1823,[2] 'the first measure of general
prison reform to be framed and enacted on the responsibility of the
national executive'[3] made a well-concerted attack on most of the
major evils of the system as Peel found it. It consolidated the twenty-
three pre-existing statutes on the subject of gaols and houses of correction, took the first step towards assimilating these institutions, and
'for the first time it made it peremptorily the duty of Justices to organise
their prisons on a prescribed plan, and to furnish quarterly reports to
the Home Secretary upon every department of their prison administration. They were expressly required to adopt, as the basis, Howard's
four principles of the adoption of sufficient secure and sanitary accommodation for all prisoners, the transformation of the gaoler or master
from an independent profit-maker into the salaried servant of the local
authority, the subjection of all criminals to a reformatory regimen, and
the systematic inspection of every part of the prison by visiting
justices.'[4] The nature of the reformatory regimen, however, was something of a compromise between the religious and the utilitarian schools,
for while provision was made both for religious and for educational
instruction, the principle of separate confinement was specifically
rejected and its place was taken by the Benthamite idea of classified
association in five groups, viz. debtors (or, in the bridewells, vagrants),

[1] Troup, p. 22. [3] Troup, p. 115.
[2] 4 Geo. IV, cap. 64. [4] Webb, p. 74.

unconvicted felons, unconvicted misdemeanants, convicted felons, and convicted misdemeanants. Each group was to be associated in productive employment, from the profits of which the prisoners were to be maintained. All the worst abuses of the old system were now swept away, including irons and chains, fees, taps, unauthorised punishments, and the supervision of women by men, and the Act prescribed a Code of Rules of which many survive, in whole or in part, to this day.

It was no fault of this admirable statute or its sponsors that the constitution lacked the machinery to secure its enforcement: indeed, the major problem throughout this period was not so much to decide what should be done as to bring the various Benches and Corporations to do what was decided, or, indeed, to do anything at all. Nevertheless, although in a large number of counties and most of the small-town and franchise gaols the Act was only enforced partially, or not at all, it did act as a tremendous stimulus to the more progressive, and a considerable number of the more important prisons were rebuilt under its influence.

But though the Gaol Act laid the foundations of the elementary physical and moral decencies for which Howard had fought, as a solution of the question of how the prisons were to carry out their new functions it was a dead end. Three years later Peel himself felt deep anxiety about the state of secondary punishments. In a remarkable letter of March 24, 1826, to Sydney Smith of the *Edinburgh Review*, he wrote:

'I admit the inefficiency of transportation to Botany Bay, but the whole subject of what is called secondary punishment is full of difficulty; . . . I can hardly devise anything as secondary punishment in addition to what we have at present. We have the convict ships. . . . There is a limit to this, for without regular employment found for the convicts, it is worse even than transportation. . . . Solitary imprisonment sounds well in theory, but it has in a peculiar degree the evil that is common to all punishment, it varies in its severity according to the disposition of the culprit. . . . To some intellects its consequences are indifferent, to others they are fatal. . . . Public exposure by labour on the highways, with badges of disgrace, and chains, and all the necessary precautions against escape, would revolt, and very naturally, I think, public opinion in this country. . . . As for long terms of imprisonment without hard labour, we have them at present, for we have the Penitentiary with room for 800 penitents. When they lived well, their lot in the winter season was thought by people outside to be rather an enviable one. . . . We reduced their food . . . there arose a malignant and contagious disorder which at the time emptied the prison, either through the death or removal of its inmates. The present occupants are therefore again living too comfortably, I fear, for penance. . . . I despair of any remedy but that which I wish I could hope for—a great reduction in the amount of crime.' [1]

Well might Peel cry for a decrease in crime, for in the period of his Home Secretaryship 'commitments in England and Wales (excluding London and Middlesex) showed an increase of 86 per cent over the period 1811–1817.' [2] So it happened that, as news of Pennsylvania and Auburn began to cross the Atlantic and the Battle of the Systems was joined, the issues were to some extent obscured by a growing reaction against the mitigations of the penal system, and the question about prisons—the 'reformed prisons', as they were called, was more often whether they were sufficiently deterrent than whether they were sufficiently reformative.

The condition of the county prisons in the 'Thirties was confused. A few had been rebuilt, from the time of Howard, on the separate cell system, following the lead set in 1792 by Sir George Onesiphorous Paul at Gloucester, which 'appears to have been the fountain-head of information on silence and solitude'.[3] But to most Justices this seemed an expensive concession to cranky reformist ideas, and the Benthamite idea of 'reform by industry' had proved more attractive. The prisons in these counties had become busy workshops, profitable not only to the county but to the prisoners, who were often able to repay the cost of their maintenance and have something over for themselves. But many prisons were still in the old state of idle and corrupt disorder. Into this confusion had infiltrated first the idea of punitive hard labour by treadwheel or crank, and later that of the Silent System: this gained some popularity, since it suited the construction of prisons rebuilt on the classification system of 1823 and permitted the continuance of industry. Even the treadwheel, since it could be made to 'turn a mill or other engine', might be adapted to profitable use by letting out the man-power to the local miller for grinding corn, while at the same time the prisoners could be kept in separate compartments as they toiled at their dreary task.

Meanwhile those who saw that the basic evils of the prisons could only be removed by the separate cell system continued to press their view, while those who called for greater deterrence in the face of the crime wave pressed for the enforcement of strict hard labour, meaning the use of the treadwheel or crank not only in silence and separation, but for no useful purpose, since in this view labour, to be fully deterrent, should be not only monotonous and severe but quite useless, this being more likely to 'plague the prisoner'. Employment in useful and interesting work, on the other hand, seemed to be positively encouraging crime.

[1] Radzinowicz, p. 572. [2] Radzinowicz, p. 588.
[3] Report of the Inspector for the S.W. District, 1836 (see p. 37).

The only hope of clearing this confusion of both principles and practice was a strong lead from the central government backed by adequate powers to enforce its views on the local authorities; and the Home Office as Peel had left it was gradually putting itself into a position to give that lead and secure those powers. The Act of 1823, in addition to prescribing Rules, had required Justices to make quarterly reports to the Home Secretary on their enforcement, though he had no power to do anything but receive them. In the general agitation of the 'Thirties about the state of the penal system this aspect of the problem received special attention, and as the matter fell to be dealt with by the Reformed Parliament, and a Whig ministry 'dominated by two leading assumptions . . . namely . . . uniformity of administration . . . and the impossibility of attaining that uniformity without a large increase in the activity of the central government',[1] it was dealt with at once by a method that was to have immediate and continuing effect. The Home Secretary was, by an Act of 1835, empowered to appoint persons to inspect prisons on his behalf and to report to him, and by the same Act Justices were required to make Rules for the government of their prisons and to submit them to the Home Secretary. By a later Act of 1844 the Home Secretary was also empowered to appoint a Surveyor-General of prisons, to advise the Home Office and the local authorities on all matters concerning the construction of prisons.

The inspectors appointed under the Act included some able, active, and zealous men, whose reports[2] were not only factual accounts of what they saw, but reasoned analyses of the problems presented with suggestions for their solution. They acted and thought independently, each reporting to the Secretary of State on his own District, but the most influential seem to have been the Rev. Whitworth Russell and William Crawford, the Inspectors of the Home District. These two, with the later collaboration of Col. Jebb, R.E., the first Surveyor-General of prisons, were convinced by their study and experience of the Separate System both in the United States and in England that it must be wholly and quickly adopted if the prisons were to be effective for any purpose at all, and by their recognised expertise and the publication of their reports they played a considerable part in influencing official and parliamentary opinion.

Meanwhile the Home Office had been forced by circumstances to become constructively active. It was in fact developing a prison system of its own, in which the Separate System was positively demonstrated. The Home Secretary was already responsible for the General Penitentiary at Millbank, which had been completed in 1821, and was used for convicts who were awaiting transportation or were not to be transported, though most of these were still in the hulks. This building was based on the separate cell system, with a curious plan, akin to that

---

[1] Webb, p. 110.   [2] Extracts in Appendix B.

of the admired Maison de Force at Ghent, of six pentagonal blocks radiating from a central space. Further development of central prisons followed a general attack on the whole of the government's arrangements for dealing with convicts, not only because they were alleged to fail in deterrent effect, but because of revelations of the revolting conditions which prevailed in the hulks, and of alarming reports from the penal settlements. The general dissatisfaction was strongly expressed in the report of the Parliamentary Committee of 1837, which condemned the whole system. The government made a considerable effort to put it on a proper basis: the period spent abroad was divided into the Probation Period, during which the convicts were employed in gangs on public works; the Probation Pass Period, during which they might be assigned to private employment; then the Ticket-of-Leave. For selected convicts believed to be susceptible to reform a preliminary period was added, not exceeding 18 months, of separate confinement in a penitentiary, according to their conduct in which was decided the stage into which they would pass in Australia. Millbank being inadequate, the government, in 1842, built a large prison at Pentonville, not only to serve as a penitentiary for convicts, but to provide local authorities with a 'model prison' in which they could see how the Separate System ought to work in proper conditions.[1] It served this latter purpose so well that 'in six years after Pentonville was built 54 new prisons were built after its model, affording 11,000 separate cells'.[2] The architect of Pentonville was Major J. Jebb, R.E.,[3] whose achievement in practice as in precept was so enduring that of him if of any it may still be said 'si monumentum requiris, circumspice': Pentonville, after being closed for some years and badly damaged by bombs in the late war, was reopened shortly after its centenary and is again one of the principal prisons of London, while its immediate successors are still, with few exceptions, the only walled prisons available to fulfil the purposes of the Act of 1948.

The success of the Pentonville experiment enabled the Government, when (in 1846) it became necessary for the time being to suspend transportation, to formulate a definite system for the treatment of convicts without transportation to penal settlements. The first 15–18 months of the sentence were to be spent in separate confinement, with hard labour, in Millbank or Pentonville, or in cells rented by the Government in the county gaols: then followed a period of employment in association on public works, for which the convict was removed to a 'Public Works Prison' at such harbours as Portland or Chatham, or (in the earlier stages) Gibraltar or Bermuda: some of these prisons were, in fact, the old hulks,[4] but large prisons of the cellular type were

---

[1] See Appendix K.   [2] Du Cane, p. 56.
[3] Later, as Colonel Jebb, C.B., Surveyor-General of Prisons.
[4] The last hulk in this country was destroyed in 1857.

built at Portland (1848), Dartmoor (1850), and Chatham (1856), while in 1853 Brixton Prison was taken over for the reception of the female convicts.

As one consequence of this central activity the 'beginning of the end' of the Battle of the Systems on the local prison front was signalled by the Act of 1839,[1] which repealed so much of the Act of 1823 as related to classification, and substituted permission for the Justices to adopt the Separate System. But for some years to come the adoption of separate confinement and the purely penal conception of hard labour was neither complete nor undisputed. Different authorities continued to take their own line, and the dispute boiled up again in the late 'Forties with a violent press campaign against the separate system and 'reformatory discipline' generally: this resulted in 1850 in another Parliamentary Committee, which, while supporting the separate system, gave general satisfaction by coming out strongly in favour of hard labour in individual separation, with crank or treadwheel, instead of 'useful industry'. The day of the Silent System was now nearly over: a return made to Parliament in 1856 showed that 'in about one-third of the prisons in England the (separate) system was fully carried out; in another third partially; while the rest were either on the Silent System or in the old disorderly state'.[2]

So by mid-century the outlines of the situation to be faced were sufficiently clear. Governments could no longer rely on the gallows and the transports to remove its responsibility for convicted felons. Imprisonment had ceased to be a 'secondary punishment': it was the one potentially effective instrument at the disposal of the penal system. The adhesions of the moribund transportation system must be cut away, and in the prisons under central control there must be created an actually effective system of imprisonment based on self-supporting principles: within such a system must be incorporated the local prisons, and administrative machinery devised adequate to pursue and sustain these purposes. The new system would be based on the prison with separate cells—that was already clear. What was not yet clear was what answer should be given to the question—what is the prison for? Deterrence? Reform? Both? And whatever its expressed ends, by what means should it seek them?

[1] 2 and 3 Vic., cap. 56.   [2] Clay. p. 264.

CHAPTER THREE

THE NINETEENTH CENTURY ANSWERS

(1) THE FIRST ANSWER (1865)

THE first stage of the new dispensation was the Act of 1850,[1] which enabled the Secretary of State to appoint Directors of Convict Prisons in whom would vest the powers and duties of the Superintendent of the Hulks, and of the various bodies which had been created to manage Millbank, Pentonville, and Parkhurst [2] prisons. So, with the now well-established Inspectors, there was at the Home Office a permanent body of administrators who directly controlled a vital part of the prison system and indirectly exercised a considerable influence over the rest. Their first Chairman was the Surveyor-General, soon to be Sir Joshua Jebb. The establishments for which they assumed responsibility were: [3]

Prisons for separate confinement—Millbank and Pentonville.
Cells for separate confinement rented in eight local prisons.
Prisons for public works—Portland and Dartmoor.[4]
Prison for Juveniles—Parkhurst.
Hulks—two at Woolwich, two at Portsmouth.
Invalid Depots—one hulk and Shornclif Barracks.

The system in force consisted of 'three probationary periods of discipline, viz.:

1st. Twelve months separate confinement.
2nd. Labour in association on public works.
3rd. A ticket-of-leave in one of the colonies.'

[1] 13 and 14 Vic. cap. 39.
[2] Established 1839 as a prison for juvenile convicts: see Chapter 19.
[3] Report on the Discipline and Management of the Convict Prisons, 1850, p. 2.
[4] The 'old war prisons on Dartmoor' were appointed to be a prison for male offenders under sentence of transportation by the Secretary of State's warrant of 24 Oct. 1850, and their conversion by convict labour from Millbank was started at once.

Colonel Jebb set about his work with the practical spirit and constructive energy to be expected of an engineer. 'It has been well remarked,' he said, 'that whatever is found to be practically right is not theoretically wrong.' The first thing was to get rid of the hulks: among other good reasons, he evidently disliked hearing from brother officers of his convicts 'dragging their chains about the ordnance depots and dockyards seeing how little they could do'. His report for 1850 advises new prisons to replace the hulks at Portsmouth and Woolwich: in 1851 he reported that the new convict prison at Portsmouth was nearly completed, and urged a start at Woolwich. One is lost, in these lean years, in admiration and envy of the formidable energy and resources which could thus produce great new prisons at the rate of one every year or so. Portland was first envisaged in the summer of 1847, and by 1849 accommodated 840 prisoners and the necessary staff. The conversion of Dartmoor, started in October 1850, had provided for 1017 prisoners by November 1851. And in this uprush there was no instability: indeed these prisons show all too well the qualities of 'rocky solidity and indeterminate duration' observed by Dr. Johnson in Durham Cathedral, and the persistence of the latter quality in such buildings as Dartmoor gives rise to mixed feelings in those who have to use them today.

In building a system of treatment for their prisoners the Directors were less assured. They had to take over the stock of ideas current at the time, and do their best with them within the limits imposed by close political control and persisting confusion of public opinion on basic principles. From the practice of imprisonment at home they inherited only the sterile ideas of separate confinement and punitive hard labour. From the transportation system however, scandalous and ineffective as it had proved itself, they were able to take certain seminal ideas which were to have a potent influence on the future. These were, the release before the expiration of sentence of well-conducted convicts on ticket-of-leave; the valuable use of prison labour on public works; and the system of 'progressive stages', which gave to prisoners the stimulus of hope and interest by allowing them, through good conduct and industry, to make quicker progress towards the goal of ticket-of-leave.

Though these ideas had been much developed at home in the course of adapting the transportation system to domestic use, they owed much also to pioneers in the penal settlements abroad, and particularly to Captain Alexander Maconochie, who in 1840 became Superintendent of the punitive settlement on Norfolk Island. This remarkable man not only developed the 'marks system' of registering progress in conduct and industry, but showed in his general attitude to a painful and difficult task much of the spirit of Elizabeth Fry. 'I sought generally,' he said, 'by every means to recover the men's self-respect, to gain his own goodwill towards his reform, to visit moral offences severely, but to reduce the number of those that were purely contraventional, to mitigate the penalties attached to these, and then gradually to awaken better and more enlightened feelings among both officers and men.' [1]

It is a little saddening to follow the early attempts of the Directors to come to terms with these quite different sets of ideas. In spite of grave doubts as to whether it was theoretically deterrent, they could feel no doubt that their public works system was practically right. Their enthusiasm for useful employment on valuable work, and for progressive 'classes' with good-conduct badges and increasing monetary gratuities, shines through their early reports. Portland represents 'a new era in the moral and industrial training of convicts', and watching the cheerful energy of the gangs hauling blocks of Portland stone to build the great new harbour, they 'have seldom seen a greater amount of willingness and industry displayed by men whose livelihood depended on their exertions'—sentiments which in the years since the late war have been repeated by many employers of prison labour in most of the counties of England.

Their views on the selection and conduct of staff were also singularly just, and were expressed [2] in words which could hardly be bettered today and may still be found in use both at home and overseas.[3] 'In a system of discipline in which the reformation of the offender is a leading principle, it would on all accounts be desirable to employ an officer who was under the influence of religious principle, and of strictly moral character.' 'It is the duty of all officers to treat the prisoners with kindness and humanity, and to listen patiently to, and report, their complaints or grievances, being firm, at the same time, in maintaining order and discipline, and enforcing complete observance of the rules and regulations of the establishment. The great object of reclaiming the criminal should always be kept in view by every officer in the prison, and they should strive to acquire a moral influence over the prisoners, by performing their duties conscientiously, but without harshness. They should especially try to raise the prisoners' mind to a proper feeling of moral obligation by the example of their own uniform regard to truth and integrity even in the smallest matters. Such conduct will, in most cases, excite the respect and confidence of prisoners, and will make the duties of the officers more satisfactory to themselves, and more useful to the Public.'

It will be noted that in these expressions, it may be in an unguarded

[1] Maconochie, *Norfolk Island*, p. 6, cit. Grünhut, p. 79.
[2] In their Report dated 16/3/50, pp. 27 and 49.
[3] Cf. New Zealand Prison Regulation 25, which reads:
'The great object of reclaiming the criminal should always be kept in view by all officers, and they should strive to acquire a moral influence over the prisoners. . . . They should especially try to raise the prisoners' minds to a proper feeling of moral obligation.'

moment, Col. Jebb and his colleagues left no doubt as to what in their minds was the 'great object' and 'leading principle' of the system they were required to administer.

It is therefore right to assume that they were sincere in their belief that the 'high moral tone and good discipline' among the prisoners on public works would have been unattainable without the preliminary period of separate confinement and hard labour in the penitentiaries or county gaols, and one must simply accept the fact that Col. Jebb could return from Portland harbour to devote himself to calculating the number of revolutions per hour that a prisoner might reasonably be expected to perform on a crank, to the practical perfection of that machine, and to expressing the view that 'my own impression is that the generality of prisoners would have a greater distaste for the labour if it were not applied to any useful purpose'.[1]

The system of separate confinement they accepted without question in principle, but they were earnestly concerned with its application in practice. In the light of medical evidence as to the increasing incidence of insanity and tuberculosis, they advised that the normal maximum of 18 months was too long, and that it should be suitably varied to individual needs so as to give an average of not more than 12 months. They also applied a practical mitigation: the separate exercise pens or 'airing yards' at Pentonville were cleared away, and to allow of 'brisk exercise' there were laid down in their place a series of concentric circular paths, such as may still be seen as a principal feature of the grounds of all our prisons. The use of caps with visors to 'prevent recognition' was still thought desirable, and the view of the Chaplain of Pentonville was accepted that the use of separate cubicles in Chapel was 'not oppressive to the mind to any perceptible degree', though the prevalence of punishments for defacing or knocking holes in these might have seemed to raise a question.

During their Pentonville stage the education of the convicts was treated very seriously: perhaps too seriously, for while the Chaplain felt that 'to confer the advantages of a superior education on convicts was wrong in principle', he was convinced that every convict should be taught to read so that they might acquaint themselves with the truths of religion. Yet if that were done, it would certainly be necessary, he felt, to do something 'to meet the most pernicious efforts continually being put forth by authors and publishers . . . to the detestable purpose of mere money gain, neutralising the benefits of education to the lower classes, and poisoning the sources of their temporal as well as their eternal happiness'. These doubts, as appears from the Addenda to his Report,[2] were particularly occasioned by 'professed works of fiction . . . of the "Jack Sheppard" school . . . issued from the London press to be continued in weekly numbers at a penny and three-halfpence

[1] Report for 1850, p. 59. [2] For the year 1852, p. 30.

each'. The 'evil tendency of those writings' is strikingly illustrated by the case of J. A., aged 18, who 'first began to read these bad books; and from them to the beer-shop; from these to the concert-room; and from these to the dancing school, which finally brought me within these walls'.

While the new Directors were acquiring this valuable experience, the government was fighting a stubborn rear-guard action in defence of the moribund transportation system. In Australia the 'Eastern Colonies' after 1846 refused absolutely to receive any more convicts in any shape or form; a project for a penal settlement in North Australia broke down, and the Cape of Good Hope forcibly resisted an attempt to plant convicts on its shores; there remained therefore only the small settlement in Western Australia, a struggling colony which welcomed labour of any sort. In these difficulties it became necessary to devise a system under which not only would the whole of the sentence be served in England, but the convicts would be released in England. This was the origin of the sentence of Penal Servitude, which by the Act of 1853 [1] was substituted for sentences of transportation of less than 14 years. The sentences legalised were related to, but shorter than, those of transportation, with a minimum of three years and no remission; but this caused considerable resentment among the convicts, and in 1857 a second Penal Servitude Act [2] restored the correspondence with the lengths of transportation sentences together with remission on a 'ticket', though this was now called a 'licence to be at large'. By this Act also penal servitude was legalised for any crime punishable by transportation. It is interesting to note that until the end of the system in 1948 the lengths of penal servitude sentences passed by the Courts were still conditioned by the transportation tradition, tending to be of 3, 5, 7, 10, or 14 years. Interesting, too, that no sooner was the system well established than the then Chairman of Directors pointed out that it was unnecessary to distinguish between penal servitude and imprisonment 'now that they are both carried out in the United Kingdom, and it is misleading, for both classes of prisoner are undergoing "imprisonment", and are equally in a condition of "penal servitude".' [3]

The system as it stood after the Act of 1857 consisted of three distinct parts: (1) separate confinement for 9 months in Pentonville or one of the local prisons; (2) associated labour in a Public Works prison: this part of the sentence was divided into three equal 'progressive stages', carrying increasing privileges and gratuities, so that the convict might have a definite stimulus to work hard and behave well; (3) release on 'licence' to be at large for the remainder of the sentence, the period of licence varying with the length of the sentence. For some

---

[1] 16 and 17 Vic. cap. 99.   [2] 20 and 21 Vic. cap. 3.

[3] *An Account of Penal Servitude*; Sir E. du Cane; printed at H.M. Convict Prison Millbank, 1882.

years small numbers of convicts continued to be removed overseas after their period of separate confinement, either to Bermuda or Gibraltar or the still receptive colony of W. Australia. But eventually, 'in deference mainly to the repeated and urgent wishes of the eastern colonies', this last line of defence was abandoned and transportation finally ceased in 1867.

It is of more than historical interest to note here the concurrent development of penal servitude in Ireland, under the influence of Sir Walter Crofton, Chairman of the Irish Directors of Convict Prisons, who appears to have applied the lessons to be drawn from the transportation system not only with greater completeness but with greater faith and imagination than his English contemporaries. In the Irish system there was equally an initial 9 months of separate confinement, followed by a period on public works with progressive stages. The interesting feature was the interpolation, between 'public works' and 'licence', of an 'intermediate stage' corresponding to some extent with the Probation Pass stage of a transportation sentence. This is described by Dr. Grünhut (p. 84) as follows—'This "filter between prison and the community" was the main characteristic of the Irish system. The idea was that employment of convicts "under circumstances of exposure to the ordinary temptations and trials of the world where the reality and sincerity of their reformation may be fairly and publicly tested, will present the most favourable chances for their gradual absorption into the body of the community". Therefore prisoners worked without supervision or went to work unattended. There were no disciplinary measures, but the possibility of recommitment to a former stage. The work was similar to what the prisoner would probably do at large; agricultural work, carpentry, etc. There was a special technical education.' Special attention was also paid to the supervision and after-care of convicts on release, and the whole system was evidently based on a belief that imprisonment not only could be 'reformatory' but should be so.[1] Dr. Grünhut traces the considerable influence of 'the Irish system' on the continent,[2] but our more immediate interest is to note the resemblances, particularly in the 'intermediate stage', between this system and the new system of Preventive Detention for persistent offenders introduced in England by the Rules made under the Criminal Justice Act, 1948 (see Chapter 18).

Having progressed so far with its central system for convicts, the

---

[1] But it must also be noted that even Sir W. Crofton attached great importance to the preliminary period of 'stringent punishment' for the sake of simple deterrence, irrespective of what he agreed were its 'degrading effects': cf. his evidence before the Committee of 1863 quoted in Appendix C. See also Appendix K.

[2] Ruggles-Brise however rightly points out (p. 29) that 'the idea of progressive reformatory discipline' in itself was of English origin, and was introduced into Ireland by Jebb himself.

government still had to face the problem of the uncoordinated local prisons, and, being no longer able to rid itself of responsibility for its prisoners by getting rid of them, to settle some principles on which imprisonment as a system should operate. This function fell to a Committee of the House of Lords of 1863, which met, as Sir E. du Cane recalls (p. 155) under the influence of 'an increase of crime, marked by an outbreak of a practice of garrotting', which was attributed by public opinion *inter alia* to the release of 'a flood of criminals' in this country under the new penal servitude system. Thus this historic Committee, whose views are summarised in Appendix C as a landmark in the movement of opinion on penal questions, took within its scope both the penal servitude system and the condition of the ordinary prisons. The answers it gave to the questions it asked itself were clear, and their effects were conclusive for a generation.

In the view of the Committee the object of imprisonment was deterrence—'hard labour, hard fare, and a hard bed' were the proper elements of a prison régime, and the foundations of such a system must be separate confinement and the crank. In this view they had the undoubted support of a considerable body of public opinion, including, it would seem, the Church, since Archbishop Whately had pronounced that 'we cannot admit that the reformation of the convict is an essential part of the punishment; it may be joined incidentally, but cannot necessarily belong to a penal system'; and including certainly the Bench, which in 1847 had definitely declared 'reform and imprisonment to be a contradiction in terms and utterly irreconcilable. They expressed a doubt as to the possibility of such a system of imprisonment as would reform the offender, and yet leave the dread of imprisonment unimpaired.' [1] Similar views on behalf of the Judges were again placed before the Committee through the redoubtable Lord Chief Justice Cockburn, and are printed in Appendix C. Under such influences as these, and in the face of public alarm over the increase of violent crime, it would have required a committee of very different constitution to reach any other conclusions.

They also handled the penal servitude system rather roughly, calling for an increase in the minimum sentence from 3 to 5 years, a severe supervision of convicts released on licence, and a tightening up of the disciplinary system. To this end they advocated a considerable remission of the sentence to be earned by industry, with the introduction of Captain Maconochie's 'marks system' for its measurement, a reduction in the rate of gratuities, and arrangements for greater speed and certainty in the infliction of flogging for serious offences. Effect was given to these proposals by the Act of 1864,[2] and by subsequent administrative arrangements.

To the principles advocated by the Committee for the conduct of the

[1] Ruggles-Brise, p. 89.   [2] 27 and 28 Vic. cap. 47.

ordinary prisons Parliament gave approval by the important Prison Act of 1865,[1] which revised and consolidated previous Acts, amalgamated the Gaols and Houses of Correction into what were henceforth to be known as 'Local Prisons' as distinct from 'Convict Prisons', and took the first definite and peremptory steps to secure uniform compliance by all the Justices. The provisions of this Act were not permissive but mandatory, and effect was given to them by a detailed code of regulations which were enacted as a schedule to the Act and given the force of law. Every prison was henceforth to provide separate cells for the confinement of all its prisoners, and for the first time precise definition was given to the term 'imprisonment with hard labour'. For at least 3 months of his sentence the offender serving a sentence 'with hard labour' was to be kept to First-Class Hard Labour, which included the heavier forms of exercise (treadwheel, crank, shot drill, etc.) duly set out in detail; but thereafter he might, at the discretion of the Justices, be employed on Second-Class Hard Labour, which was defined as 'such other description of bodily labour as might be appointed by the Justices'. It is interesting to note that the liability of the County to maintain all criminal prisoners having been established, prisoners not sentenced to hard labour were now required to work without pay,[2] but there was still so much delicacy about forcing them to work, that they might not be punished for neglect of work save by alteration of diet.

The foundations of a coherent and uniform system of imprisonment had now been laid. Principles and practice had been firmly settled and prescribed in detail: what still lacked was the means of enforcing them in the local prisons. The Act of 1865 had stripped the local authorities of almost the last vestige of discretion in the management of their prisons, and gave the Secretary of State power to enforce compliance by withholding the Grant in Aid from recalcitrant prison authorities. But even this was not enough. Although it had one desirable result in securing the closing of a large number of the smaller prisons, there were still too many local prisons: they were already expensive, and to put them all into a state to comply with the law and satisfy the Inspectors was not only in many cases a waste of money, but would have imposed an intolerable burden on the county rates. Further, there was still a lamentable lack of uniformity in the methods of enforcing the statutory code.

It was at this stage that 'the General Election of 1874 brought into power a government pledged not to increase but actually to relieve the burden of rates upon the rural districts'; [3] the opportunity seemed a

---

[1] 28 and 29 Vic. cap. 126.
[2] The Act of 1782 had provided that they should on discharge receive half the profits of their labour.
[3] Webb, p. 198.

fitting one to revive a proposal already made by the Committee of
1850, but never seriously entertained, to transfer the whole administration of local prisons to a central Board; and in 1877 Parliament took
the plunge.

By the Prison Act of that year [1] the ownership and control of all
local prisons, with all the powers and duties of the Justices relative
thereto, were vested in the Secretary of State, and the cost of their
maintenance was transferred to public funds. Their general superintendence, subject to the control of the Home Secretary, was vested
in a board of Prison Commissioners, assisted by Inspectors appointed
by the Home Secretary, and a departmental staff. The rule-making
power of Justices having passed to the Secretary of State, a new code
of rules was issued in 1878, and as from the 1st April of that year all
the local prisons came for the first time under one central control and
a single code of rules. The first Chairman of the Commissioners was
Sir Edmund du Cane, R.E., who had succeeded Sir Joshua Jebb as
Surveyor-General and Chairman of Directors of Convict Prisons: in
effect therefore the whole of the prisons, convict and local, were now
brought under one administration.

So by 1878 ,when the new Prison Act came into force, the nineteenth
century had given its first answer to our question: it was the answer of
Lord Chief Justice Cockburn—the primary object is deterrence, both
general and individual, to be realised through 'suffering, inflicted as a
punishment for crime, and the fear of a repetition of it'. If as a by-
product of this process the reformation of the offender is achieved, so
much the better; if not, no matter—it is hardly to be expected. The
government had its directive, its detailed operation orders, and, for
the first time, full power and resources. And for nearly twenty years
the new machine was allowed to run without further parliamentary
interference.

(2) THE SECOND ANSWER (1895)

Colonel Sir Edmund F. du Cane, K.C.B., R.E., Chairman of the
Prison Commissioners, Chairman of the Directors of Convict Prisons,
Surveyor-General of Prisons, and Inspector-General of Military
Prisons, was without doubt, in 1878, the right man in the right place.
As a soldier, he would wish his orders to be clear, and he found them
so: 'The objects which the Prisons Act 1877, was intended to secure
were two, viz. the application to all prisoners, wherever confined, of a
uniform system of punishment, devised to effect in the best method
that which is the great object of punishment, viz. the repression of crime;
and economy in the expenses of prisons.' [2] He would wish them to be
firm, and they were. Under the Act of 1877 the Secretary of State

---

[1] 40 and 41 Vic. cap. 21.   [2] Du Cane, p. 99.

could make rules for the governance of prisons in detail, but the essentials were immutably fixed by the Statutory Code of the Act of 1865. He would prefer to find himself in agreement with them, and he did so. In the first chapter of 'The Punishment and Prevention of Crime' he fully argues the view that while penal methods 'must be founded on a combination of penal and reformatory elements in their due proportions', the penal element (except with younger criminals) 'should have the *first* place—both on account of its effect on themselves and its influence in deterring others', and that while sight should never be lost of the desirability of 'reformatory elements' these could only be introduced so far as they were compatible with the needs of deterrence. And the penal element must, as the Lord Chief Justice had said, be one of evident severity: 'if you are going to punish, you must find something that does punish, and is disagreeable'.[1]

In this strong position, he was able with an undivided mind to devote his great abilities as an administrator and an engineer to what he rightly saw as the first necessity of his task—the production of order out of chaos. Ruling both his Boards, as Sir Edward Troup tells us, 'with a rod of iron', he set himself to secure strict economy, sound administration, and rigid uniformity, and his success here was a rock on which his successors could confidently build as they would. Of 113 local prisons taken over, 38 were closed forthwith, and by 1894 only 56 were still open.

In the system of treatment of prisoners in local prisons which the Commissioners proceeded to develop, they relied for deterrent effect mainly on 'the punishment of hard, dull, useless, uninteresting, monotonous labour'[2] with rigid enforcement of separate confinement and the rule of silence—these latter being still regarded as the necessary basis of the 'reformatory influences'. The theory was that the more deterrent part of the sentence should come first, and accordingly prisoners sentenced to Hard Labour were placed on 'penal labour' (standardised as so many revolutions per diem on the treadwheel) for at least the first[3] month of the sentence. Thereafter a prisoner by good conduct might, as a reward, earn the 'privilege' of being placed on 'useful' labour, which the Commissioners regarded as 'one of the principal reformatory influences in the prison system'.[4] This 'useful labour' (the Second-Class Hard Labour of the Act of 1865) was, however, limited to such processes as could be carried out in cellular confinement, and it would seem that, except for prisoners in the later stages of long sentences who might be brought out to work in the

---

[1] Evidence before Departmental Committee on Prisons, 1895, Q. 10832.
[2] Du Cane, p. 175.
[3] The minimum period of three months on First-Class Hard Labour had been reduced to one month by the Act of 1877.
[4] Evidence before Departmental Committee on Prisons, 1895, p. 617.

domestic services about the prison, separate confinement (except at exercise and chapel) was rigidly enforced throughout the sentence. Prisoners not sentenced to hard labour were placed on 'useful labour' from the beginning.

This advancement from 'penal labour' to 'useful labour' formed the initial stage of the contribution of this period to the development of the Progressive Stage System of 'managing the prisoners by appealing to their better qualities' instead of 'governing by mere fear of punishment', which had for some time been in use in the convict prisons. This is described by Sir E. du Cane as follows:

'The principle on which this system is founded is that of setting before prisoners the advantages of good conduct and industry by enabling them to gain certain privileges or modifications of the penal character of the sentence by the exertion of these qualities. Commencing with severe penal labour—hard fare and a hard bed—he can gradually advance to more interesting employment, somewhat more material comfort, full use of library books, privilege of communication by letter and word with his friends, finally the advantage of a moderate sum of money to start again on his discharge, so that he may not have the temptation or the excuse that want of means might afford for falling again into crime. His daily progress towards these objects is recorded by the award of marks, and any failure in industry or conduct is in the same way visited on him by forfeiture of marks and consequent postponement or diminution of the prescribed privileges.'

It is, however, sufficiently clear that this progress was achieved by emphasising rather the rigours of the earlier stages than the comfort of the later stages. In the first stage no mattress was allowed, and no books of any sort; in the second and third stages school books were allowed and a mattress on certain nights; it was not till the fourth and last stage that the full 'material comfort' of a mattress every night was achieved, with the 'full use of library books and privilege of communication with friends'. In retrospect, the value of this system as a 'reformatory influence', replacing the 'mere fear of punishment', seems open to question.

Apart from separation and such habits of industry as a prisoner with a long enough sentence might form from employment on useful labour, the only other reformatory influences to which any importance was attached were 'religious instruction'—the value of which Sir Godfrey Lushington [1] put down as 'very little indeed'—and 'literary education', which Sir E. du Cane confessed had 'not the reformatory influence on prisoners which was once expected of it'.[2] Nevertheless it

---

[1] Permanent Under Secretary of State of the Home Office; in his evidence before the Departmental Committee on Prisons, 1895, Q. 11480.

[2] Du Cane, p. 79.

is clear that devoted work was done by many Chaplains, and there was a useful educational organisation: if its efforts were limited to element- ary instruction in the 'three R's' it must be remembered that such instruction, at a time when public elementary education was in its infancy, was the only form of education possible for the large majority of the prison population—and it was perhaps too much to expect any 'reformatory influence' from even Standard III of the National Society's Reading Book.

And so, in the English prison system, the lights that had been lit in Newgate by Elizabeth Fry, on Norfolk Island by Captain Maconochie, and at Portland by Colonel Jebb, went out: for twenty years our prisons presented the pattern of deterrence by severity of punishment, uni- formly, rigidly, and efficiently applied. For death itself the system had substituted a living death. It became legendary, as Sir Evelyn Ruggles- Brise tells us, even in Russia. When, in the course of time, this view prevailed, criticism centred on the Chairman of the Prison Commission. This was unjust. Sir E. du Cane was a public servant, and with less freedom of action than his successors. Parliament, the Judges, and the public had called for such a system, and he provided it: he was even required, so hard was it so satisfy the more convinced exponents of deterrence, to defend it against the charge of 'exaggerated senti- mentality'. That he was able to do his duty as he saw it without com- punction might merit the question of posterity, but not of his own time.

Fortunately the lights had not gone out all over Europe. The ideas of 'reformatory discipline' and 'progressive stages', developed in England and transmitted through Ireland, had aroused great interest and fertile experiment in several continental systems, and were now to form the basis of a fresh impulse in the United States, then in the flush of social reconstruction after the Civil War. The two great names in this American movement were E. C. Wines and Z. R. Brockway. To Dr. Wines is due not only much of the strong impulse in his own country, but the foundation of the international movement repre- sented by the International Penal and Penitentiary Commission at Berne.[1] Sir E. Ruggles-Brise, for many years President of the Com- mission, describes how 'in 1870, a joint resolution of both Houses of Congress, that a conference on prison questions might usefully be held, and that London would be the most suitable place for holding it, led the President of the United States to appoint a special committee to organise the proceedings. Dr. Wines was selected for the duty.'[2] The first International Prison Congress was accordingly held in London in 1872, as a result of which a permanent organisation was established

[1] Appendix K.
[2] *Prison Reform At Home and Abroad*, Sir E. Ruggles-Brise; Macmillan, 1924; p. 18.

at Geneva, and a system of Quinquennial Congresses inaugurated, to be held in the capitals of the different states-members, which with interruptions by two World Wars has continued ever since.[1]

The difference between the spirit of the London Congress of 1872 and that of the system of their English hosts is shown by 'what they described as the leading principles which should lie at the root of a sound prison system:

1. That though fundamentally the protection of society is the object for which penal codes exist, such protection is not only consistent with, but absolutely demands that the moral regeneration of the prisoner should be the primary aim of prison discipline, and that for this purpose Hope must always be a more powerful agent than Fear.

2. That in the treatment of criminals, anything that inflicts unnecessary pain or humiliation should be abolished; that the true principle is to make a prisoner depend on his own exertions, and to gain the will of the convict by showing that he will profit by such exertion.

3. That unsuitable indulgence is as pernicious as undue severity.

4. That religion, education, labour, must be the basis of any good system, to the working of which a capable, highly trained, and well-paid staff is essential.

5. Lastly, that it is in preventive work, ragged schools, and all the institutions for saving young life, that the battle against crime is to be won, and that the influence of women devoted to such work is of the highest importance.' [2]

In this spirit may be traced the influence of the first American National Prison Congress held at Cincinnati in 1870, from which emerged the celebrated 'Declaration of Principles' which still holds a reverend place in the literature of penal reform, together with the novel idea of the Reformatory. This type of institution was to provide, on the basis of the 'indeterminate sentence', for the purely reformatory treatment of young persons between the ages of 16 and 30, and its first example was the famous New York State Reformatory at Elmira opened under the charge of Z. R. Brockway in 1877. 'The spirit of Cincinnati', Dr. Grünhut tells us, 'died with the first generation of humanitarian reformers.' But not altogether; as the torch had passed to America from England, so it was to pass from Elmira back again, for it was here that Sir E. Ruggles-Brise learned much that encouraged him to found his Borstal system in England.

But the published evidence does not suggest that the coming upheaval of the English system resulted from any wide uprising of reformers inspired by liberal ideas from abroad: it is rather more suggestive of a 'palace revolution.' In 1892 Sir E. du Cane, old and in failing health, had come after over twenty years of undisputed sway

---

[1] The last Congress was held at The Hague, in August 1950.
[2] *Prison Reform At Home and Abroad*; Sir E. Ruggles-Brise; p. 32.

to be 'regarded as the embodiment of bureaucratic despotism and arrogance . . . absorbing all matters great and small into his own hands. His word was law.' [1] In that year the Home Secretary, Mr. Matthews, 'wished on to him' as a Prison Commissioner Mr. (later Sir Evelyn) Ruggles-Brise, a civil servant who had for the past ten years been the valued and influential Private Secretary to a succession of Home Secretaries. Sir Evelyn made it clear in his autobiography [2] that his new position was difficult: he was required to take a nominal responsibility for a system of which he did not approve under a chief who, the first time he tried to assert himself, 'as far as I remember never spoke to me again'. In this position Sir E. du Cane, doing what he must do, brought down his whole system. A certain Dr. Morrison, after ten years' experience as a prison Chaplain, was no longer able to contain himself: he wrote an article in the press criticising the prison system, and Sir Edmund at once dismissed him. Dr. Morrison then opened a press campaign which elicited so much latent dislike of the system and its administration that a point was reached when 'in magazines and in the newspapers, a sweeping indictment had been laid against the whole of the prison administration. In brief, not only were the principles of prison treatment as prescribed by the Prison Acts criticised, but the prison authority itself, and the constitution of that authority, were held to be responsible for many grave evils which were alleged to exist.' [3] In 1894 the Home Secretary, Mr. Asquith, for this or other reasons, set up a Departmental Committee with limited terms of reference under the chairmanship of his Under Secretary of State, Mr. H. J. Gladstone (later Lord Gladstone), and in 1895 this Committee presented the Report which remains the foundation stone of the contemporary prison system.

The Gladstone Committee was both courageous and radical: its terms of reference had been carefully drawn so as to exclude from its consideration both the principles of 1865 and the methods of administration of the Commissioners. 'This limitation,' they said, 'we found it impossible to make.' Certainly they acquitted the administration of many of the charges brought against it; they emphasised the success with which it had achieved the objects for which it was set up; and pointed out—a truth of permanent validity—that while 'it is easy to find fault, to form ideal views, and to enunciate lofty speculations as if they were principles arrived at by experience', yet 'nothing is more common than to find persons whose attention has been attracted only to some disadvantage in the system finally decided on discussing it without being aware that any alternative would produce still greater

[1] Private autobiography of Sir E. Ruggles-Brise quoted in *Sir Evelyn Ruggles-Brise*, Shane Leslie (John Murray 1938), pp. 85 and 86.
[2] Quoted in *Sir Evelyn Ruggles-Brise*, op. cit.
[3] Report of the Gladstone Committee, para. 5.

evils'; but on the central questions their findings amounted to an indictment of the whole ideology of the du Cane régime.

Their fundamental conclusion was that 'the prisoners have been treated too much as a hopeless or worthless element of the community, and the moral as well as the legal responsibility of the prison authorities has been held to cease when they pass outside the prison gates'. In the Committee's view it was the duty of the administration to emphasise all those elements of prison life which might make for the reclamation of the prisoner, and mitigate whatever elements made for degradation and deterioration.

They condemned the one unquestionable achievement of the administration—so far as it had concerned itself with prisoners and not with prisons—uniformity of treatment. 'To Sir Edmund du Cane a prisoner was a prisoner, and practically nothing else'; [1] but 'we think,' said the Committee, 'that the system should be made more elastic, more capable of being adapted to the special cases of individual prisoners; that prison discipline and treatment should be more effectually designed to maintain, stimulate, or awaken the higher susceptibilities of prisoners, to develop their moral instincts, to train them in orderly and industrial habits, and, whenever possible, to turn them out of prison better men and women physically and morally than when they came in.''

This emphasis on reclamation, they believed, was not incompatible with the maintenance of the deterrent aspect of imprisonment, and they were at pains to shatter the belief that the pursuit of deterrence as an end in itself had even achieved its own ends. 'The diminution in the average prison population which had been so triumphantly adduced as a proof of the success of the du Cane régime was shown to be almost entirely accounted for by a reduction in the average length of sentence awarded. . . . The recidivism [2] was as great as ever.' [3]

It is a feature of this Report that many of its most pregnant observations are scattered *obiter*, e.g.:

'Since 1865 the main principles of prison treatment have not been altered, except in detail and in so far as they may have been affected by the radical change in the administration effected by the Act of 1877. Indeed, it may be said generally that neither those principles, nor the administrative system laid down by the Acts of 1865 and 1877, have been brought into question until the present inquiry was instituted.'

'We do not consider that it is right to lay the burden of all the shortcomings of the prison system on the central prison authorities who have carried into effect under successive Secretaries of State the Acts approved by Parliament; who have loyally and substantially carried

---

1 Webb, p. 204.
2 *The habit of relapsing into crime* (O.E.D.).   3 Webb, p. 222.

out the various recommendations made from time to time by Commissions and Committees; and who, as administrators, have achieved in point of organization, discipline, order, and economy, a striking administrative success.'

'The difficulty of laying down principles of treatment is greatly enhanced by the fact that while sentences may roughly speaking be the measure of particular offences, they are not the measure of the characters of the offenders; and it is this fact which makes a system of prison classification, which shall be at once just, convenient, and workable, so difficult to arrive at.'

'While scientific and more particularly medical observation and experience are of the most essential value in guiding opinion on the whole subject, it would be a loss of time to search for a perfect system in learned but conflicting theories, when so much can be done by the recognition of the plain fact that the great majority of prisoners are ordinary men and women amenable, more or less, to all those influences which affect persons outside.'

'But under this orderly equality there exist the most striking inequalities. The hardened criminal bears the discipline without much trouble. Others are brutalised by it. Others suffer acutely and perhaps are permanently weakened by it in mind and body. What is a temporary inconvenience to the grown criminal, may be to lads and younger men a bitter disgrace from which they never recover to their dying day. It is impossible to administer to each man a relatively exact amount of punishment. But yet it is these very inequalities which often must produce that bitterness and recklessness which lead on to habitual crime.'

'It is certain that the ages when the majority of habitual criminals are made lies between 16 and 21. It appears to us that the most determined effort should be made to lay hold of these incipient criminals and to prevent them by strong restraint and rational treatment from recruiting the habitual class. It is remarkable that previous inquiries have almost altogether overlooked this all important matter. The habitual criminals can only be effectually put down in one way, and that is by cutting off the supply.'

And last, but by no means least, 'we start from the principle that prison treatment should have as its primary and concurrent objects deterrence and reformation'.

To these ends they condemned unproductive penal labour absolutely, and recommended the employment of all prisoners on useful industrial work. They even laid hands on the separate system, 'swept aside the old-fashioned idea that separate confinement was desirable on the ground that it enables a prisoner to meditate on his misdeeds' and 'held that association for industrial labour under proper conditions could be productive of no harm, and this view was supported by the fact that association for work on a large scale had always been the practice at Convict Prisons'.[1] In short, they held that separate confinement (except, of course, by night) was simply a deterrent instrument which they clearly viewed with grave mistrust, in the light of the known facts as to its effect on the physical and mental condition of prisoners; but.they did not feel able to condemn it absolutely, contenting themselves with the hope that it would prove possible to reduce the periods. The 'Rule of Silence' received equal condemnation.

In one sense, this second answer of the Nineteenth Century to our question can be thought of as final. Within the classical line of thought running from Beccaria through Howard, Bentham, and Elizabeth Fry it leaves little more to be said as to principles and ends. For fifty years it has held its place, comparable with that of the Cincinatti Principles in America, as the scriptural sanction of the English prison system. Like other scriptures, it is a mine where each may find what he will: but though its principles may call for reinterpretation, its methods for re-adaptation, the basis of its gospel has not been put to question. Much that has been done in the last twenty-five years, novel as it seemed at the time, is no more than a late working out of suggestions in this Report. Indeed, to the task of making 'better men and women' there can be no finality, and the story of the next fifty years will be one of means rather than ends. Even the entirely new thought and method latterly introduced by the development of psychiatric medicine can but be another means to the same end, unless by a full turn of the Erewhonian wheel it removes this problem altogether from the purview of the penal system.

[1] Ruggles-Brise, p. 137.

CHAPTER FOUR

THE TWENTIETH CENTURY ANSWERS

(1) THE PRISON ACT 1898 AND ITS ADMINISTRATION TO 1921

SHORTLY after the publication of the Gladstone Report Sir Edmund du Cane, having reached the age of superannuation, retired, and for twenty-seven years Sir Evelyn Ruggles-Brise ruled in his place. In this long course of time the new Chairman, an Amurath to Amurath succeeding, established a personal position which makes it as natural to speak of the 'Ruggles-Brise régime' as of the 'du Cane régime' which preceded it. His mandate from Mr. Asquith was 'that the views of the Committee should, as far as practicable, be carried into execution', [1] and that mandate has descended, implicitly or explicitly, through successive Home Secretaries to successive Chairmen to this day. The words deserve a moment's study: the Home Secretary spoke not of the 'recommendations' of the Committee but of its 'views', and these, as we have seen, were diverse and radical; and in 'as far as practicable' is implicit the whole slow process of development over fifty years. The action possible to each generation is conditioned by the climate of opinion of its time and by the physical and financial resources at its disposal, as well as by the courage and faith of those called to 'carry into execution' views that could lead us still further than we have yet thought to go.

Meanwhile the new administration, still cumbered about with 'the stage-properties of the Victorian melodrama',[2] set to work with the instruments to its hands. These were the Prison Act 1898 [3] and the Statutory Rules of 1899, which, with the unrepealed portions of the acts of 1865 and 1877, formed the substantial legal basis of the administration (other than for young offenders and habitual criminals) until the Criminal Justice Act 1948.

Not the least important provisions of the Act of 1898 were those which repealed the statutory regulations of 1865, and left the whole of

---

[1] Ruggles-Brise, p. 77.
[2] Sir Samuel Hoare, in the debate on the Criminal Justice Bill, 1938.
[3] 61 and 62 Vic. cap. 41.

the detailed regulation of the system to the Secretary of State, who was given power to make all rules necessary for the government of both local and convict prisons. The code of rules made in 1899, with such amendments as from time to time proved necessary, remained in force until 1933, when a consolidated and simplified code was substituted with certain revisions of detail to bring it into line with more recent developments. This code, with occasional amendments, remained in force until 1949.[1] The value of this more elastic procedure, which made it possible for changes to be effected without fresh legislation on each occasion, is indicated by the fact that under it the natural development of fifty years was able to proceed without further intervention by Parliament.

This removal of detailed control from the parliamentary sphere was also facilitated by the adoption as a normal instrument of the Departmental Committee appointed by the Home Secretary, following the model of the Gladstone Committee, in place of the Parliamentary Committees which had so often sat during the eighteenth and nineteenth centuries. These Committees have been appointed as occasion required to examine and report on specific problems (as the treatment of young offenders or persistent offenders, the employment of prisoners, and punishments in prisons and Borstals), and may have the advantage of including experts in the matters under consideration, with M.Ps., officials, and members of the general public. Subsequent legislation, or changes in administrative practice, have commonly been based on the Reports of these Committees, which form a valuable part of the literature of our penal system.

The more important changes of principle introduced by the Act into the prison system, and their subsequent history, were as follows:

Classification—The Gladstone Committee had pointed out that 'no adequate attempt had yet been made to secure a sound system of classification in local prisons', and the Commissioners had responded by introducing into the Local Prisons the Star Class system started in the Convict Prisons in 1879, thus providing for 'the complete separation of first offenders from habitual criminals'.[2] Later, they placed young prisoners between 16 and 21 in a separate Juvenile Adult Class. For the purposes of classification alone, therefore, the provision by the Act of 1898 of the Triple Division of Offenders, under which the Court might order a sentence of imprisonment *without hard labour* to be served in the First, Second, or Third Division, was scarcely necessary. As the Commissioners said, 'The principle here given expression to is very far-reaching, and, as far as we are aware, is in advance of the

---

[1] Rules for the government of prisons are now made under the Act of 1948, the Rules now in force dating from 1949. Rules must lie in draft on the Table of the House of Commons for forty days before they are made.

[2] Annual Report 1899–1900, paras. 3 and 34.

penal systems in force on the Continent of Europe. By it is destroyed, in emphatic language, the theory that had prevailed largely hitherto, and had found expression in divers reports, viz., that the duty of classification is a matter for prison officials, and not for the Court of Law having the individual offender and all the circumstances of his case fully detailed before it. It is obvious what an enormous responsibility is thus thrown upon Courts of Law, and, as we stated in our last year's report, the degree of success which this new departure may attain must depend on the extent and manner in which Courts of Law realise and act upon this responsibility.' [1]

It appears from the Commissioners' Reports that this system was doomed to failure from the outset, largely because the Courts found it difficult to refrain from passing sentences 'with hard labour' even when in later years this form of sentence had ceased to have any significance. In 1910 the Commissioners reported that 'the exercise of this power is becoming rarer still, until we are almost forced to realise that the classification aimed at by the prison reformer will not be attained by relying on the discretionary power of the Courts of Law'.[2] This position remained virtually unchanged, and by the Act of 1948 the Triple Division was abolished. All measures for classification and for the individualisation of punishment are thus left to the prison administration.

Hard Labour—First-Class Hard Labour was abolished, and all prisoners were from the beginning of their sentences to be employed on 'useful industrial labour'. The unfortunate hedging of the Gladstone Committee on this question was, however, reflected in the curious provision of the Rules that a prisoner sentenced to hard labour 'shall for 28 days be employed in strict separation on hard bodily or hard manual labour . . . after that period he shall, provided his conduct and industry are good, be employed on labour of a less hard description, in association if practicable'.

This clinging to the shadow of 'hard labour' and 'separate confinement' long after the substance had escaped them led the Commissioners into a somewhat illogical position, later set out by their successors as follows:

'The practical difficulties raised by the requirements (1) that work shall be productive, (2) that for the first month the work shall be "hard bodily or hard manual labour", and (3) that subsequently it shall be labour of "a less hard description" are obvious. To find various useful employments suitable for various types of prisoners is a standing difficulty of prison administration, and it was a baffling problem to find for every prisoner sentenced to hard labour two kinds of work—one harder than the other but nevertheless of such a character that it could be carried on for a month by a prisoner confined to a cell.

[1] Annual Report 1899–1900, para. 4. [2] Annual Report 1909–1910, para. 42.

'Moreover, the conception that a prisoner who behaves and works well shall be rewarded by being allowed to work less hard is irreconcilable with the conception that the period of imprisonment is to be utilised as a period of training. If training is effective, a prisoner should in the second month of his sentence be working harder, i.e. with more aptitude and more concentration, than in the first month.

'Oakum picking was originally the task for the first month of a man's hard labour sentence, but when this work was given up, little could be done to render effective the distinction in the Rule between "hard bodily or hard manual labour," and "labour of a less hard description," and the distinctive character of a hard labour sentence lay—not in the nature of the prisoner's work—but in the fact that for the preliminary part of his sentence he was liable to be kept in separate confinement, i.e. to be employed in his cell and not in an associated working party.' [1]

In fact, what this provision did was to ensure that for 28 days a hard-labour prisoner worked less hard than an ordinary prisoner, and the restriction to prisoners so sentenced of the vestige of separate confinement that was retained was presumably intended simply to preserve in another way the aspect of greater deterrence implied in sentences to hard labour.

Except for these hard labour prisoners during the first 28 days of their sentences, all work during the day was henceforth done in association in workshops or outdoor parties. The Separate System from now onwards meant only separate cells for sleeping and meals, all other activities being in associated parties under strict supervision and the Rule of Silence: in effect, the Silent System had again come into favour, though with the modification that absolute silence was less rigidly required, and 'the privilege of talking' recommended by the Gladstone Committee might be earned by long-sentence prisoners in their later stages.

The construction of sufficient and suitable workshops for this new obligation was a long task, which after the First World War had scarcely been brought to completion for the much smaller numbers of prisoners for whom work had then to be found. Today, when the numbers are again comparable with those of the Ruggles-Brise régime, the shortage is again noticeable and many additional shops have been and are being erected.

To complete the story of hard labour, separate confinement was abolished when, in the course of the First World War, it became necessary in the public interest for hard labour prisoners to work as hard as others; in 1945 the last vestige of special treatment—deprivation of mattress for the first fourteen days—was removed by an amendment

[1] Annual Report 1930, p. 23.

of the Rules; and by the Act of 1948 this form of sentence was finally abolished.

Remission of Sentence—A further important change authorised by the Act was that provision might be made by the Rules for enabling a local prisoner to earn by special industry and good conduct a remission of a portion of his imprisonment, and that on his discharge his sentence should be deemed to have expired. The Rules fixed the maximum period of remission to be earned at one-sixth of the sentence, and the system of awarding daily marks for industry, already operating in connection with the Progressive Stage System, was applied also to the earning of remission. The Commissioners were immediately impressed by the beneficial effects on conduct and industry of this measure, which remains to the present time one of the basic sanctions of prison discipline.

Corporal Punishment—The use of corporal punishment for offences against prison discipline was limited to the offences of mutiny, incitement to mutiny, and gross personal violence to an officer of the prison. Its award was subject to confirmation by the Secretary of State. This is substantially the position today (see Chapter 10).

The legislative way was now wide open to the realisation of a prison system in which deterrence and reform should be primary and concurrent objects. Yet when in 1921 Sir E. Ruggles-Brise retired, having reached the age of superannuation, there was a discouraging repetition of the story of 1895: the end of his long rule, like that of Sir E. du Cane, was marked by the publication of a Report which condemned it unsparingly, and on strikingly similar grounds. The administration was criticised as autocratic and irresponsible, rigid, and remote; the treatment of prisoners as founded on 'retributory and deterrent factors, to the exclusion of truly preventive and educational principles'. [1]

On this occasion, however, the enquiry was neither parliamentary nor official, but a reversion to the tradition of Howard and Fowell Buxton. A general dissatisfaction with the conditions of the prisons among those interested in their reform, among whom the Howard Association [2] had been prominent, was intensified by the first-hand experience of imprisonment gained during the First World War by some hundreds of conscientious objectors and others drawn from social groups outside the normal catchment area of the prisons. In these circumstances, since 'there had been no systematic enquiry since the Departmental Committee of 1894–5, and . . . there seemed to be at the time no prospect of any Government enquiry', [3] in January 1919 the Labour Research Department set up a Prison System Enquiry

[1] *English Prisons Today*, chapters III and IV.
[2] Shortly, by marriage with the Penal Reform League, to become the Howard League.
[3] *English Prisons Today*, Foreword.

Committee. Naturally the Committee received no official support, but making all reservations that must be made in respect of an enquiry conducted in these circumstances, with no direct official evidence or information and no direct access to the prisons, their Report is an important document in our knowledge of the system with which it deals.

The broad conclusions of this Committee were that, making every allowance for the slow and cautious development by the Commissioners of certain of the recommendations of the Gladstone Committee, the principles and effects of their régime were scarcely distinguishable from those of the du Cane régime. In its detailed practice the treatment of the prisoners was held to be 'humiliating and dehumanising', and 'the effects of imprisonment are of the nature of a progressive weakening of the mental powers and of a deterioration of character in a way which renders the prisoner less fit for useful social life, more predisposed to crime, and in consequence more liable to reconviction' (p. 561). This, so far as it may have been justified, was lamentably far from 'stimulating the higher susceptibilities of the prisoners' and sending them out of prison 'better men and women, physically and morally, than when they came in'.

It is evidently important, if this sweeping indictment of 25 years' untrammelled implementation of the Gladstone Report was justified, to establish why this was so. And that there was substantial justification for the broad conclusions reached may be deduced not only from the Commissioners' own Reports but from the actions of their immediate successors. We have already noted that the system in the local prisons was still dominated by nineteenth-century conceptions of the value of 'separate confinement' and the 'rule of silence', and much else remained unchanged, including the personal humiliation of cropped heads and drab and shapeless dress besprinkled with broad arrows. It is difficult to find evidence of any positive elements making for reform or rehabilitation. Much stress is laid on the work of the Chaplains and the influences of religion, but those influences had long been active in our prisons. The methods of education appear to have been very little in advance of those of the du Cane régime, and the privileges to be earned under the stage system were still little more than a slow increase in the number of letters and visits permitted and in the quality and quantity of library books. Nor was there any notable change of principle or practice in the convict prisons.

Yet Sir Evelyn Ruggles-Brise was a humane and high-minded administrator, well versed in the literature of penology, and as President of the International Penal and Penitentiary Commission for many years he well knew what could be done and what was done in the penal systems of the world. He brought to life many of the major recommendations of the Gladstone Report: in particular, his foundation of the Borstal system [1] of treating young offenders on the lines suggested by the Committee has passed into honourable history. He also, after the Prevention of Crime Act 1908, started the novel system of preventive detention for habitual criminals; [2] and he was active in forwarding many of the measures for keeping offenders out of prison altogether which are discussed in the following section. Why, then, did such a man so far fail to realise the spirit of the principles handed to him as terms of reference on his appointment?

The answer is sufficiently clear from his own pronouncements, which suggest that he never really accepted the possibility of a system of treatment in which reform would hold a primary and concurrent place with deterrence. Indeed at the International Congress of Washington in 1910 he was reported to have 'shelled and shattered' the American delegates for having 'swung too violently away from the classical traditions of punishment', and to have pronounced that 'In Europe we place the constituent elements of punishment in the following order: Retributory, deterrent, and reformatory. Possibly in the United States this last named method is placed first in importance.' [3] Nor was this thunder-bolt discharged only for the occasion. He repeats it with equal emphasis in his Annual Reports, and indeed in one statement of the theme goes back almost to the position of 1865: 'Our constant effort is to hold the balance between what is necessary as punishment ... from a penal and deterrent point of view, and what can be conceded, consistently with this, in the way of humanising and reforming influences.' [4]

And this is to say no more than that Sir Evelyn was not in advance of the norm of penological thought on these questions in his time, at least in Europe. It would have been more than difficult for him, at any rate prior to 1910, to follow the heretic Americans so far from the 'classical tradition' as to put reformation first, though his own order does appear to depart a little in emphasis from his terms of reference. In the England of his time the doctrine of general deterrence was still too deeply engrained in the texture of penal thought and prison tradition for it to be possible to envisage a treatment of prisoners not definitely directed to deterrence by fear, and the Gladstone Committee itself was constrained here and there to rather obvious hedging in the need to accommodate its wish to 'turn out better men and women' with the necessities of deterrence. All official authority, Parliament, Church, and Bench, had denied the compatibility of deterrence with reform, and none in more memorable and disturbing words than Sir Godfrey Lushington, who said in his evidence before the Committee 'I regard as unfavourable to reformation the status of a prisoner throughout his whole career; the crushing of self-respect, the starving of all moral

[1] See Chapter 21.
[2] See Chapter 18.
[3] Shane-Leslie, op. cit., p. 163.
[4] Annual Report 1911–12, p. 27.

instinct he may possess, the absence of all opportunity to do and receive a kindness, the continual association with none but criminals, and that only as a separate item among other items also separate; the forced labour and the denial of liberty. I believe the true mode of reforming a man or restoring him to society is exactly in the opposite direction of all these. But of course this is a mere idea; it is quite impracticable in a prison. In fact the unfavourable features I have mentioned are inseparable from prison life.'

On any view of the functions of a prison which it would have been possible for Sir E. Ruggles-Brise at that time to carry into effect, we may now see that Sir Godfrey's 'mere idea' *was* quite impracticable. In order to justify the innate confidence of the Committee that the reconciliation of deterrence and reform in the treatment of prisoners was possible, a re-interpretation of the deterrent function of a prison was necessary which the Committee itself was not ready to make. And Sir Godfrey's uncomfortable words have remained and must remain in the minds of all concerned with prison administration. Nearly thirty years later Sidney and Beatrice Webb said, 'We suspect that it passes the wit of man to contrive a prison which shall not be gravely injurious to the minds of the vast majority of the prisoners, if not also to their bodies. So far as can be seen at present the most practical and the most hopeful of prison reforms is to keep people out of prison altogether.' [1] And in our own time the problem has been well stated by James V. Bennett, Director of the Federal Prisons of the U.S.A. —'Our basic problem is how to use imprisonment, which is inherently a symbol of punishment, to achieve a purpose almost completely antithetical to punishment—rehabilitation.' [2]

Yet we may wonder whether the prison administration, at any rate after 1910, might not have been encouraged to go further and faster along the road if a young and ardent Home Secretary had been less transient in that office. In the year in which Sir Evelyn was shattering the surprised penologists of Washington, Mr. Winston Churchill said in the House of Commons, 'The mood and temper of the public with regard to the treatment of crime and criminals is one of the most unfailing tests of the civilisation of any country. A calm, dispassionate recognition of the rights of the accused, and even of the convicted, criminal against the State—a constant heart-searching by all charged with the duty of punishment—a desire and eagerness to rehabilitate in the world of industry those who have paid their due in the hard coinage of punishment: tireless efforts towards the discovery of curative and regenerative processes: unfailing faith that there is a treasure, if you can only find it, in the heart of every man. These are the symbols, which, in the treatment of crime and criminal, mark and measure the stored-up strength of a nation, and are sign and proof of the living

[1] Webb, p. 248.   [2] Federal Prisons Report 1947, p. 4.

virtue in it.' [1] That 'constant heart-searching', that 'unfailing faith', were to come into our prison administration, but it required the upheaval of the First World War to release the fresh climate of opinion in which they could do their work.

(2) THE ABATEMENT OF IMPRISONMENT

It may be that in the early years of this century a pessimistic view of the social value of imprisonment, derived from long experience of the du Cane régime, tended to act as a brake on progress in prison treatment; but it certainly brought a long way towards realisation the Webbs' 'most practical of all prison reforms, to keep people out of prison altogether'. Nor has the passage of time changed that view. In 1947 Sir Alexander Maxwell, recently retired from the office of Permanent Under Secretary of State in the Home Office, said, 'The first of the Home Office functions in relation to prisons is to keep as many people as possible out of them', [2] and in 1948 Mr. Claud Mullins, recently retired after fifteen years' service as a Metropolitan Magistrate, said, 'A tradition is growing up that nobody should receive a sentence to prison unless all other sentences are impracticable." [3]

The legislative course followed before the First World War to make that tradition possible may seem, in retrospect, to have been the most significant contribution of those years to practical penology. They were marked by a remarkable series of statutes seeking to keep out of prison large classes of offenders for whom imprisonment is neither suitable nor necessary, and to provide better ways of dealing with them. First came the Probation of Offenders Act 1907, followed in 1908 by the Children Act and the Prevention of Crime Act. Of these two the first established juvenile courts for offenders under 16 (later 17) and provided better methods both for dealing with child offenders and for preventing them from becoming offenders: the second sought to remove from the normal prison system on the one hand young people under 21 who ought not to be subject to it, and on the other habitual criminals who were neither reformed nor deterred by it. The Mental Deficiency Act 1913 kept out of, or removed from, the prisons a large number of unfortunates for whom imprisonment was indefensible. And finally, a provision of the Criminal Justice Act 1914 required magistrates to allow time for the payment of fines unless there were good reasons for not doing so. 'As a consequence partly of this change in the law and partly of a decrease in drunkenness, the number of persons sent to prison in default of payment of fines fell from 85,000 in

---

[1] Cit. Ruggles-Brise, p. 4.
[2] Second Annual Lecture in Criminal Science delivered to the Department of Criminal Science, Cambridge University, Stevens, p. 17.
[3] *Fifteen Years Hard Labour*, Claud Mullins (Gollancz), p. 100.

E.P.B.S.—5

1910 to 15,000 in 1921.' [1] The numbers of committals in default of payments of fines were further reduced by the Money Payments Act 1935, which required magistrates to make enquiries as to means before committing to prison an offender who had not paid his fine. In the five years 1937–41 the average number of committals in default was 6054, and in 1947 it had fallen to 2952.

The effect of all these measures, and of the resulting 'tradition', has been shown on p. 10. The Criminal Justice Act 1948 is, in its broad effect, a summing up of all these tendencies: in so far as it could be described at all as a 'prison reform Act', it would be in the sense in which the Webbs would have had us use those words. It supplements and improves the existing powers and methods of dealing with convicted offenders by fine or by one of the procedures under the Probation Acts; it makes further provision for dealing with offenders of unsound mind other than by imprisonment; it still further restricts the imprisonment of young people under 21 and provides alternative methods of dealing with them outside the prison system; and it facilitates the use of Borstal training for young people. Except in its provisions for the treatment of persistent offenders, it is above all an Act for keeping people out of prison.

(3) THE CONCEPTION OF TRAINING

The history of English prison administration from the inception of the Prison Commission in 1878 seems to fall almost too neatly into three periods of similar length divided by years of war, each, under the influence of one dominating personality, offering its answer to our question through the reinterpretation of one dominating principle. Historical analogies may be as misleading as historical periods, but it is tempting to see the growth of our English way of treating prisoners as we see that of our English style of Gothic architecture: Leyhill prison is as little like Dartmoor as Lincoln cathedral is like Durham, but each later building derives from the continuous organic development of a principle already latent in the earlier, and through similar periods of 'style'. First, the old style, the powerful and perdurable Norman of du Cane, ending with the South African War; second the Transitional style of Ruggles-Brise, with the structural features modifying though the feeling of the older style tends to persist; and the third, after the First World War, the 'Early English' of Alexander Paterson, releasing the true spirit of the structure in a 'first fine careless rapture' of seminal ideas which his successors may not hope to recapture, but can strive to bring to full fruition, working out all their implications in a manner which may come, in the course of history, to be regarded as a 'Second English' style in its own right. Nor will the visitor informed with the spirit of this analogy be surprised, in looking at a building

[1] Sir A. Maxwell, op. cit., p. 8.

which the guide-book tells him is Second English, to find here and there a feature of earlier style, or even what he suspects to be an original Norman wall. He may reflect, too, on the similarity of the problem which each system, penal and architectural, was engaged in working out—a problem essentially of balance, of reconciling in one harmonious structure two principles apparently opposed—deterrence and reform, stability and light.

And now to return to historical fact. Sir E. Ruggles-Brise retired in 1921, though at the special request of the Secretary of State he remained as British delegate to the International Penal and Penitentiary Commission, of which body he had become President in 1910, so that he might preside over the forthcoming London Congress of 1925. His successor was Mr. M. L. Waller, afterwards Sir Maurice Waller, C.B. Here again history repeated itself, since Mr. Waller, like his predecessor, had been Private Secretary to the Home Secretary before becoming a Prison Commissioner in 1910. At about the same time, Mr. Alexander Paterson, M.C. (later Sir Alexander Paterson) was appointed to be a Prison Commissioner. This appointment was remarkable in that it was the first from outside the Prison Service or the Home Office, and it was destined to have remarkable results—results such as might have followed, had there been Prison Commissioners in her time, the appointment of Elizabeth Fry. To say that for the next twenty-five years Paterson was the mainspring and inspiration of the changes that revitalised our prison and Borstal systems, and breathed life into the honoured formulae of the Gladstone Report, is in no way to derogate from the contributions of the distinguished Chairmen under whom he served between the two wars, particularly that of Sir Maurice Waller, under whose leadership till his untimely retirement in 1928 most of the major steps had been taken or projected. Paterson himself neither became nor sought to become Chairman: in his own words, he was 'a missionary, not an administrator'.

The first Annual Report over the signatures of Waller and Paterson, for the year 1921, showed that they had not wasted time. Gusts of fresh air begin to blow through the pages. The convict crop and the broad arrows had gone; a substantial breach had been made in the Rule of Silence; new cell furniture and new clothing were being planned; arrangements were being made for suitable prisoners to receive visits from their friends at tables in a room; and 'prison visitors' were being introduced for men, as had long been done for women, to visit them regularly in their cells in the evenings. The activities of voluntary workers from the outside world, long valued for their help in providing lectures and concerts, were also being extended in other directions, particularly in the teaching of handicrafts and gymnastics.

And already the Commissioners were finding it necessary to reply to the criticism that the prisoners were being 'pampered'. 'Pampering' they said 'is not the object, nor is it the result. It is our duty, as custodians of those who are for a time forcibly separated from life in the civic community, to restore them to it at least as fit as when we received them. To this end we should feed and exercise their minds as well as their bodies; else we shall return them to the stern competition outside torpid in mind and nerve, and quite unfit to take their part. It is therefore reasonable that we should make it our aim to balance the hour of physical exercise each day with an hour of mental exercise each evening; to provide brain food in the form of books and social intercourse as regularly as we issue wholesome food for the body.'

In the 1922 Report further important changes were recorded. 'Last summer we received authority from the Secretary of State to suspend, as an experiment, the period of separate confinement which had hitherto been in force at the beginning of every convict's sentence. This separate confinement used to be carried out partly in the local prison at the place of conviction before transfer, and partly in the convict prison after transfer. The old idea with regard to separate confinement was (a) to prevent contamination, and (b) to give the man a quiet period in which to review his past life and his present position, and make better resolutions for the future. Our opinion was, on the contrary, that a man brooding alone in his cell became morose and vindictive. Abolition was, therefore, tried, the Governors of local prisons being merely authorised to keep a man working in his cell for the first day or two, if he should be received in so violent a frame of mind as to make it necessary in the interests of discipline. The reports which were received after six months' trial were satisfactory. Governors reported that they were in favour of this step, and that discipline was equally maintained; while Medical Officers gave definite opinions that the men were better in physical and mental health. The Secretary of State has authorised us to continue this plan pending the necessary revision of the statutory rules. At the same time, the Boards of Visitors at Convict Prisons were requested not to impose separate confinement as part of a punishment. Separate confinement is now being regarded as in the nature of a restraint, only to be used when necessary for the maintenance of discipline.'

'We are aiming at a minimum of eight hours' associated work for all prisoners. This has so far been attained only at some of the local prisons, but at the others the period is, at any rate, seven to seven and a half hours per day. Compared with the very short periods which were being worked by the associated parties only a year or two ago, this does represent a satisfactory advance.'

In that year also, in co-operation with the Adult Education Committee of the Board of Education, a start was made with organising an adult education system throughout the local prisons. This scheme was based on voluntary teachers, and at each prison there was appointed an Educational Adviser to the Governor to help both in procuring the teachers and framing the schemes: the Adviser himself was also a volunteer, the list for 1922 including Professors from the Universities, Headmasters, and Directors of Education. Under these arrangements it became possible at last to view the education of prisoners in a more liberal spirit than that of the Chaplain of Pentonville (see p. 43), and we read in the 1922 Report that 'while more simple elementary teaching was still required, the need for education on a broader basis, suitable for backward adults, was even more urgent. The teaching in simple subjects which is given to normal children is not wholly suitable for adults, whatever their degree of ignorance. They find it difficult to concentrate their attention upon it, and, while it remains necessary that their reading, writing, and arithmetic should be brought up to a certain minimum standard, even these ends can be better attained through the medium of subjects of general interest.' And again in 1924 that 'the great point is to arouse mental activity, and to give some kind of healthy mental outlook; and to this end the personality of the teacher is more important than the choice of subject. Subjects requiring real mental effort are to be preferred to those which merely impart information.' This enlightened scheme soon spread to all prisons, regular annual meetings of Educational Advisers and teachers were held at the Prison Commission, and it remained a vital part of the system until the late war. A little later the Prison Visitors also organised a National Association of Prison Visitors, which held annual meetings in the same way.

Other significant changes recorded in 1922 were the introduction of regular shaving; arrangements for Star Class and Second Division prisoners to dine together in association; 'honour parties' of prisoners trusted to work together without continuous supervision; and, in the Chapels, the removal of the officers from raised seats facing the congregation to the back and sides where 'they take part in the service as ordinary members of the congregation'.

In the following years was initiated the idea of 'classification of prisons' as a necessary step in the use of classification to secure the positive results of better training rather than the mere negative of mitigating 'contamination'. The first steps in establishing what has become known as the Wakefield System were recorded in 1923, and were followed by the setting apart of Wormwood Scrubs as a prison for Star Class prisoners only.

The two further developments of major significance between the wars were the establishment of 'open' institutions, first for Borstal boys at Lowdham Grange in 1930, then for selected prisoners from Wakefield at New Hall Camp in 1936; and the institution from 1929 of 'earnings schemes' of small cash payments related to effort in order to stimulate industry among the prisoners.

These details are here briefly recorded simply to show the scope and speed of the attack: their practical significance will be considered as we come to consider the structure and working of the system as it stands today, since the elements of that system are all implicit in the work of these few years. Our present purpose is rather to assess their total effect in relation to the question, 'What is prison for?'

The Commissioners for their part saw quite clearly what they meant to do and why, and in their Reports for 1924 and 1925 set it out equally clearly in these words:

'*The Object in View*—We are dealing with persons who have to return to the life of a free community after a period which is seldom very long, and, in most cases, is only a few weeks ahead. Our object, therefore, must be to restore them to ordinary standards of citizenship, so far as this can be achieved in the time at our disposal. If this is not done, society will only have been protected during the brief period of their sojourn in prison, and on leaving its doors they will again become nuisances, and some of them dangers. The means to be employed are reasonably long hours of hard and steady work, which, in the case of the longer sentences, should if possible give some useful industrial training; and, after the day's work is over, education of a kind suitable for backward adults. Self-respect has to be promoted; the influence, both spiritual and secular, of people of strong character and personality, prison officials and voluntary workers, must be brought to bear; and also, so far as prison conditions admit, such measures of trust as will arouse a sense of personal responsibility. The prisoner's daily round should make as much demand as possible on the activities of both mind and body; the whole being a coherent scheme of training. Every development of prison methods forms part of this scheme, and is directed to this end.'

'It is the policy of the administration to carry out its duty of protecting society by training offenders, as far as possible, for citizenship; and every change in the prison system is directed to that end. Prisons exist to protect society, and they can only give efficient protection in one of two ways, either (a) by removing the anti-social person from the community altogether or for a very long period; or (b) by bringing about some change in him. Any general application of the first method would not be supported by public opinion. The prison administration must therefore do its utmost to apply the second; that is to say, to restore the man who has been imprisoned to ordinary standards of citizenship, so far as this can be done within the limits of his sentence. Unless some use can be made of the period of imprisonment to change the anti-social outlook of the offender and to bring him into a more healthy frame of mind towards his fellow citizens, he will, on leaving the prison gates after a few weeks or months, again become a danger, or at any rate a nuisance. He may, indeed, be worse than before, if the only result has been to add a vindictive desire for revenge on society to the selfish carelessness of the rights of others which he brought into prison with him. The change can be, and is, effected in a good many cases by vigorous industrial, mental, and moral training, pursued on considered lines by officers, teachers, and prison visitors of character and personality. The effect of such training, properly conducted, is to induce self-respect, to lessen self-conceit (characteristic of many prisoners on first reception) and to arouse some sense of personal responsibility. Failures there are, and always will be, but the records of successes justify the system and the efforts of those who work to carry it out.'

Perhaps the most notable feature of these statements, in the light of what had gone before, was not so much what was said as what was not said. For the first time, we find no anxious balancing of how much, without undue derogation from deterrence, can safely be conceded to reform: in fact we find no mention whatever of either. What we do find is that 'every development of prison methods' is directed towards 'a coherent scheme of training'.

It is not to be assumed from these statements that, in the minds of those who formed them, neither deterrence nor reform was henceforth an object of prison treatment, but rather that a more realistic approach to the problem of reconciling them within a system intended to 'turn out better men and women' would suggest that, if less attention were paid to words and more to facts, more might in practice be achieved. This approach calls for a somewhat radical revaluation, in the light of practical experience, of these two well-worn coins of penological currency.

To take deterrence first, we have already seen [1] that for general deterrence, viz. the preventive effect of the penal system on the potential offender at large, contemporary thought relies not on the punitive treatment of the individual offender but on 'the totality of the consequences of being found out'—general prevention is inherent in the whole action of the penal system. Equally, individual deterrence is not to be sought by devising deliberately punitive measures as part of the treatment of the individual in prison, and that for two reasons. It is unlikely that men or women will become better, either physically, mentally, or morally, if the régime to which they are subjected is seeking simultaneously to punish, humiliate, and hurt them. And even for those prisoners who are in any event unlikely to become better, there is sufficient evidence that such methods are most likely to make them worse. The deterrent effect of imprisonment on the individual is therefore held to rest not on any specific features of his treatment in prison but on the fact of being in prison, and all that is inevitably inherent in that condition—the subjection of the prisoner to forced labour and disciplinary control, separation from home and the normal human

[1] Chapter 1, pp. 10–13.

associations of life, deprivation of most of its amenities and comforts, and absolute loss of personal liberty. In short, the offender comes to prison 'as a punishment, not for punishment.' [1]

The concept of 'reform' is less easy to evaluate. If reform can be defined as the substitution of a will to do right for a will to do wrong, we have to face the fact that for many prisoners the problem does not arise in that form at all: there never was for them a settled will to do wrong—all too often there was no will at all, just social inadequacy in one form or another, physical or mental. Some again, who could not be classed as socially inadequate, may well have reached at least that necessary condition precedent to reform, the humility of repentance, before ever their sentence begins. Others, and today they are many, have no personal standards by which they can measure right and wrong.

It is in fact no more practical to seek a prison system which will 'reform' all those subjected to it than one which will 'deter' them. Reform is not some specific which can be prescribed either from the prayer-book or the pharmacopoeia. It must come from something inside the man. All the prison can do is to provide the sort of conditions in which that something can be reached by the right personal influences, for this is of all things one for a rather delicate and practised personal approach. Some will be reached by the message of the Gospel, others by a friendly hint, a sympathetic touch. For one it may be necessary to prick a bladder of self-conceit, for another carefully and patiently to build or rebuild his self-respect. For some the mere withdrawal for a time from the circumstances leading to the offence will serve, for others complete re-education is required. There are many whose rehabilitation can be effected by the removal of some mental disability by psychiatric treatment, or of some physical defect by surgery. Indeed the subtlety of variety may almost equal the number of individuals concerned.

The conception of 'training' therefore seeks to provide a background of conditions favourable to reform, and where necessary and possible to foster this delicate and very personal growth by personal influences rather than by specific features of treatment labelled 'reformative'. Then, leaving deterrence to speak for itself, it concentrates on the social rehabilitation of the prisoner, so as to remove as many obstacles as possible to the maintenance, after discharge from prison, of such will to do right as may have become established or incipient therein. Whether a prisoner has been reformed or whether he has been deterred by his experience, or even if the effect has been quite negative, the protection of society is not well served if he comes back to it unfitted rather than fitted to lead a normal life and earn an honest living, or as an embittered man with a score against society that he means to pay off.

It has been said, and well said, that it is easy to imprison a man—

[1] Alexander Paterson.

the difficulty is to release him; and again, that the true test of a prison system is what happens to the prisoner when he comes out; and yet again, that it is on release that the prisoner faces the hardest part of his punishment. All this means that whatever is done in prison may be wasted unless the hard transition to normal life is eased and guided by a humane and efficient system of after-care: this subject will be dealt with in a separate chapter, but it must be said here that it forms an essential part of the whole system.

Such then are the principles underlying the contemporary system of prison treatment, as they were conceived by Sir Maurice Waller and Sir Alexander Paterson, and as they have a quarter of a century later been recognised and established by Parliament in the Criminal Justice Act 1948, which provides that rules shall be made for 'the training of prisoners', and sets in the forefront of those rules the statement that 'The purposes of training and treatment of convicted prisoners shall be to establish in them the will to lead a good and useful life on discharge, and to fit them to do so'.

It is fitting that, before passing to examination of the present system, something should be said of Alexander Paterson, to whom especially it owes what merit it may have. After his death in 1947 Sir Alexander Maxwell wrote:

'Alexander Paterson will be affectionately remembered in the Home Office and the Prison Service as an honoured leader who won loyalty and devotion not only by his intellectual gifts, his zest and driving energy, his humanity and sympathetic understanding of men and women of all types, his wisdom, wit and humour, but by his ever-present sense of life's high ends. The many activities of his crowded official career were lifted above the common level by the intensity of his faith and vision. A practical idealist, whose grasp of reality was as firm as his aspirations were lofty, he was as fertile of constructive ideas as he was powerful to kindle enthusiasm. To his imagination and inventive force we owe almost all the schemes of penal reform which have been developed in this country in the last twenty-five years.'

Nor was his influence confined to England—

'His labours in the international field were untiring. He had known and made himself known in the penal systems of most of the countries of Europe and North America, and carried out many missions of inspection and advice in the prisons of Africa and Asia on behalf of our Colonial Office. During the late war, he also visited and advised on internment camps for aliens in Great Britain and in Canada. One may well ask whether any one man has had a knowledge at once so deep and so wide of the condition of man in captivity. As British delegate to the International Penal and Penitentiary Commission for over twenty years, he was always in the van of the fight for humane values in our penal systems, whether in the preparation of the Standard Minimum Rules for the League of Nations, in the fight against Nazi ideology at the Congress of Berlin in 1935, or in the last resolution which he placed before us in 1946, condemning the outrage of the concentration camps.' [1]

Out of all his rich contribution to the revolution in the spirit of our prison and Borstal systems, perhaps that part which above all bore the stamp of Paterson's personality was his insistence that it is through men and not through buildings or regulations that this work must be done; his flair for finding the right men to do it; and his ability to inspire them with his own faith.

[1] Obituary notice in the Bulletin of the I.P.P.C.

PART TWO

ADMINISTRATION AND ACCOMMODATION

CHAPTER FIVE

CENTRAL ADMINISTRATION

(1) THE HOME SECRETARY

IN other countries it is usual to find the 'penitentiary administration' in the Ministry of Justice. Since England has no such Minister, it is natural that our administration should come under the Home Secretary, who 'takes a part in the administration of criminal justice, so great that for some of its purposes he might be described as the Minister of Justice'.[1] If that were not enough, he is also the King's adviser on the exercise of the Prerogative of Mercy, and is especially responsible for the keeping of the King's Peace, which brings into the Home Office all matters concerning police and public order; and finally, 'he is charged with all the home affairs of England and Wales except those . . . which are assigned to other and newer departments'.[2] It would therefore have been difficult, one way and another, for the administration of prisons and kindred institutions to have fallen anywhere but the Home Office, where it keeps company with the departments responsible for the probation service and for the approved schools for children and young persons who come before the Courts.

But while the Home Secretary is the Minister responsible to Parliament for the prevention of crime and the treatment of offenders in general, his powers and duties in relation to prisons and any other institutions to which by statute the Prisons Acts or parts of them apply (e.g. Borstals, Remand Centres, and Detention Centres) do not depend on the Prerogative or inherent powers of his office. They are statutory powers and duties under the Prisons Acts 1865–98 or the Criminal Justice Act 1948. All such institutions are vested in the Secretary of State, and he makes the Statutory Rules for their governance, appoints their Boards of Visitors,[3] and appoints all those officers of prisons and Borstals who are described by statute as 'superior officers', viz. Governors, Chaplains, and Medical Officers: the dismissal or reduction in

[1] Troup, p. 73.   [2] Troup, p. 1.
[3] Where applicable: see p. 85.

rank of a prison officer on disciplinary grounds also requires his approval.

In carrying out these statutory duties the Home Secretary receives the advice of the Prison Commissioners, in whom is vested, subject to his general control, the superintendence, control, and inspection of institutions to which the Prisons Acts apply. The nature, composition, and organisation of the Prison Commission are described in the following section of this chapter. It is sufficient to say here that, subject to submission to the Secretary of State of questions of policy of major interest, or of particular cases which have aroused or may arouse public or political interest, or of such matters as by statute are reserved to the Secretary of State (e.g. those aforementioned, or the confirmation of awards of corporal punishment on prisoners) the work of the Prison Commission is self-contained, and they are primarily responsible for both the formulation and the application of policy. Their work is however necessarily carried out in close co-operation with other departments of the Home Office concerned with the prevention of crime and the treatment of offenders, and with the Principal Establishment Officer, the Legal Adviser, the Statistical Adviser, and the Public Relations Officer.

Since 1944, the Home Secretary has had the assistance of an Advisory Council on the Treatment of Offenders. The membership includes magistrates and others with special knowledge or experience in the work of the Courts, the police, and the treatment of offenders, together with men and women of various experience outside the specialised field. The Chairman since its inception has been Mr. Justice Birkett,[1] and the Vice-Chairman the Permanent Under Secretary of State for the Home Department. The Council meets several times a year, and considers and reports on questions referred to it by the Home Secretary or raised by its own members, a considerable amount of work being done by sub-committees between the meetings of the Council. The Council also acts as the National Working Group in this field for the Economic and Social Council of the United Nations, and as the National Committee of the International Penal and Penitentiary Commission: [2] for these purposes it may appoint sub-committees on such questions as are referred to it, with power to co-opt members from outside the Council, e.g. appropriate members of the Home Office or Prison Commission staff, academic experts, or representatives of the Magistrates Association. The meetings of the Council are held in private, and its proceedings are normally not published.

---

[1] Mr. Justice Birkett retired in December 1950, on becoming a Lord Justice of Appeal, and was succeeded by Sir Granville Ram, Chairman of the Hertfordshire Quarter Sessions.

[2] See Appendix K.

(2) THE PRISON COMMISSION

The constitution of the Prison Commission is, in the Civil Service of today, something of a curiosity, and its organisation and relations with the Home Office may more easily be appreciated by experience than by explanation. Prior to the Prisons Act 1877, local prisons were a local service administered on much the same principles as today still govern the administration of other such public services, e.g. the Police, the convict prisons being in a special relation to the Home Office akin to that of the Metropolitan Police. When Parliament decided to adopt for this service the principle of centralised ownership and control, there was no Civil Service such as we know today to take over its management, and the establishment of statutory Commissioners employing their own staff was still the normal expedient of the time as it had been when the Metropolitan Police was set up in 1829.

The Prisons Board as thus established is a body corporate, with a common seal and power to hold land, and with the consent of the Secretary of State it may under the Criminal Justice Act 1948 exercise powers of compulsory purchase. The Commissioners, whose numbers may not exceed five, are appointed by the Crown under the Sign Manual and are full-time pensionable civil servants.

The Chairman of the Board is appointed by the Home Secretary. Since the time of Sir E. Ruggles-Brise, Chairmen have been drawn from experienced administrators of the Home Office staff: Maurice Waller and his successor Alexander Maxwell had both been Private Secretaries to the Home Secretary, and Harold Scott and C. D. Carew Robinson, who followed, had each been in charge of the Criminal Division of the Home Office, which dealt *inter alia* with prisoners and prisons. The present Chairman was transferred from an administrative post in that Division to be Secretary of the Prison Commission (1925-34), and served at New Scotland Yard before receiving his present appointment in 1942. The composition of the Board has varied through the years in both numbers and qualifications, including at different times administrators of the Home Office staff, men with experience as Governors of prisons or Borstals, medical men from the Prison Medical Service and in the one case of Sir A. Paterson a man whose experience lay in social and educational work outside the service.

Following the passage of the Criminal Justice Act, there was a considerable change in the responsibilities, status and composition of the Board. In the preparation of the Bill, it had been contemplated that the arrangements of 1877 should be revised, and that the Prison Commission should be abolished so as to allow of a reorganisation on different lines of all the departments of the Home Office concerned with the treatment of offenders. Parliament however preferred to retain the Prison Commission, and the Secretary of State decided to place under their control the new types of establishment, known as Remand Centres and Detention Centres, to be set up under the Act for the treatment of young offenders.

In consequence of this enlargement of the responsibilities of the Commissioners, it was further decided that their organisation should be strengthened on the administrative side and that they should in future be responsible direct to the Secretary of State through the Permanent Under Secretary of State, and not as hitherto through the Criminal Division of the Home Office. One of the steps taken to this end was the enlargement of the Board to include the Establishment Officer and the Woman Director in addition to the five Commissioners, who are at present the Chairman, the Deputy Chairman, the Secretary, and two Commissioners who respectively direct the Prisons and the Borstals (including Remand and Detention Centres). The collective responsibility of the Prisons Board to the Secretary of State is, under this arrangement, shared by its seven *de facto* members and not only by the five Commissioners who constitute the Board *de lege*.

The Board is assisted by four specialist Directors, with the necessary professional or technical qualifications, for Education and Welfare,[1] Medical Services,[2] Industries, and Works; and the Directors of Prisons and Borstals are assisted by five Assistant Commissioners who are also Inspectors under the Prisons Acts and as such appointed by the Home Secretary, on the recommendation of the Commissioners, from among the best qualified Governors.

Each of the three Assistant Commissioners on the prisons side is responsible for the general control and regular inspection of the group of prisons allotted to him: it is his duty to interpret the policy and views of the Commissioners to the Governors, to see that they are carried out, and to keep the Commissioners in touch with the views and difficulties of the Governors and their staffs. After each visit to a prison an Assistant Commissioner makes a written report which is seen by all the Commissioners and any other officers of the Department concerned. The duties on the Borstal side are similar, but also include the planning and development of Remand and Detention Centres.

The women's prisons and girls' Borstals are inspected and controlled by the woman Director.

The Head Office staff also includes the Chaplain Inspector, who assists and advises the Commissioners in all matters relating to the Chaplains and their spiritual work, the chapels and their equipment, and questions concerning religion in general. He spends much of his time visiting the Chaplains to help and advise them.

The two Commissioners known as the Director of Prisons Administration and the Director of Borstals Administration visit all their

---

1 Appendix K.
2 There are also an Assistant Director of Medical Services and a Chief Psychologist.

prisons or Borstals at least once a year and more frequently where necessary, while the Chairman and other members of the Board visit as often as their closer concern with office administration permits. Thus the Board as a whole is in reasonably close and constant touch, directly or indirectly, with the actual work in the field, and great importance is attached to the maintenance of this personal contact between the centre and the periphery. These contacts by visit are most valuably supplemented by annual conferences, at which prison Governors and their Assistant Governors, Borstal Governors and their Assistant Governors, Chaplains, and Medical Officers meet (in their respective groups at separate times) to discuss questions of general professional interest among themselves and with the Commissioners, who also keep in touch with the work of the Visiting Committees and Boards of Visitors, and of the National Association of Prison Visitors, by attending the annual meetings organised in London by these bodies.[1] Consultation with the subordinate staff is maintained through the Whitley Council (see p. 95), and occasionally *ad hoc* meetings are arranged for the discussion of particular topics at which all grades may be represented. Other methods used to bring the staff at the prisons and Borstals into consultation in the formulation of policy are the 'working party' to prepare proposals on particular subjects, or the method of consultation through representative panels. This interesting device, which is capable of further development, has been used as follows: the questions on which the views of the staff are desired are put to the Governor of each establishment, who is asked to arrange meetings of all grades at his establishment to discuss them and submit their views. Panels of five representatives of each of the grades of Governor, Chaplain, Medical Officer, and Chief Officer then meet and receive the reports of their grades, synthesise them, and submit a report to the Commissioners: for the staff below the rank of Chief Officer the report is prepared by the Executive Committee of the Prison Officers' Association (see p. 95).

Within the Prison Commission there is a regular Monthly Conference of the Board with all the Directors and Assistant Commissioners and such other senior officers as may be required for particular topics.

While therefore it is unlikely that the charges of 'remoteness' and 'autocracy' levelled against earlier administrations would again be raised, the system of uniform and centralised administration initiated by Sir E. du Cane still remains the basis of management today. Structurally, so to speak, the system is the same in all establishments, and is based on a volume of Standing Orders of formidable size and remarkable scope. But different types of establishment develop their own variations, and especially in the Borstals and Training Prisons Governors

---

[1] The former meetings are now organised by the Prisons and Borstals Committee of the Magistrates Association.

have a good deal of latitude, except in matters of business management, to develop their establishments along their own lines. Even in the local prisons, though in general these are, save for size, 'much of a muchness', there is scope for initiative and experiment within the general framework of the Statutory Rules and the policy laid down by the Commissioners.

To return to the Commissioners' office, this is organised as a separate and self-sufficient Department; its funds are provided by a separate Parliamentary Vote for which the Chairman accounts to the Public Accounts Committee of Parliament, and it deals direct with the Treasury on matters of finance, establishments, and supply. Formerly located in the main Home Office building in Whitehall, it is now, after some years of peregrination, settled [1] within a stone's-throw of the vestiges of Millbank Penitentiary. Apart from the higher direction already described, it employs at its Head Office some 270 persons of the administrative, professional, executive, clerical, technical, and minor grades. These are organised as follows.

The Secretary of the Department (an Assistant Secretary of the Administrative Class) is responsible for presenting material for the consideration of the Board, for carrying into effect its decisions and for what may be called its external relations—legal, public and parliamentary. He is directly assisted by a group of administrative and executive officers known as the Secretariat.

The Establishment Officer (also an Assistant Secretary of the Administrative Class) controls the Establishment Branch, which is responsible for the organisation and staffing of the Head Office and the prisons and Borstals: the departmental Registry is also under his control.

The Finance Officer controls the Finance Branch, whose functions are implied in its name.

The Director of Industries is assisted by a small staff of technical officers at the Head Office, and controls the work in the prisons and Borstals through travelling area Supervisors and resident Industrial Managers. In close relation with him is the Controller of Stores and Manufactures, whose branch is responsible for the placing of contracts for supply of raw materials, etc., and generally for all stores, clothing, furnishing and victualling. Specialists included in this organisation include a Supervisor of Farms and Gardens, Vocational Training Officers and a full-time Catering Adviser who deals with dietary questions, meal service, kitchen equipment and the training of cooks.

The Director of Works, with his Deputy Director, controls all the architectural, engineering, estate management and other technical and specialist staffs required for the management and maintenance of the

---

[1] At Horseferry House, Dean Ryle St., Westminster, S.W.1.

considerable lands and buildings vested in the Commissioners, and for the design and erection of new buildings.[1]

Such is the organisation charged not only with the safe-custody of over 20,000 men and women of all ages and from every level of society, but with their housing, feeding, clothing and doctoring; their industrial employment; their education and religious and moral training; their social welfare during and after their sentences; the legal questions arising from their various states as prisoners; and the grievances and complaints, reasonable or unreasonable, which may be expected to arise from men and women in their condition and from their relatives, friends, and legal advisers. To this is to be added the responsibility for recruiting, training, managing, clothing and housing the staff required to these ends in the prisons and Borstals, which number some 6,000 men and women in about 100 different grades. And since it is by the quality of its staff that the system stands, this last task is not the least.

The scope of this work is a world in little, and the motto of the Prison Commissioners must be 'humani nihil a me alienum', for there are few aspects of life and conduct on which they may not be required to form a view in the course of a day's work. Nor is their view bounded by the establishments in England and Wales for which they are legally responsible. They act in close co-operation with the Scottish administration in Edinburgh, and their woman Director and Director of Industries respectively visit, once a year, the women's establishments and industrial arrangements in Scotland and report to the Scottish Home Department. They are represented on the Treatment of Offenders Sub-Committee of the Colonial Office, and in this way, and by furnishing officers of various grades to the Colonial Prison Service and providing courses of instruction in the Home Service for Colonial officers, they help to create and maintain standards in prisons and Borstals throughout the Empire. In the wider international field they provide the first delegate of H.M. Government to the International Penal and Penitentiary Commission and assist in collaboration with the Social Defence Section of the United Nations Secretariat.[2]

A word, in conclusion, on publicity. Whether or not there was justification for the Webbs, in 1922, to have described the prisons of this country as 'a silent world, shrouded, so far as the public is concerned, in almost complete darkness',[3] or for the Labour Research Department Enquiry to have levelled against the administration of the day the charge of 'undue secrecy', it must be said flatly that when such assertions are made today they are made without reference to the facts.

[1] Major new building schemes are undertaken by the Ministry of Works from preliminary plans prepared by the Director.
[2] Appendix K.   [3] Webb, p. 235.

As publicity in this sense official publications can be said to have a limited value, but for those who wish to read them there are two: the Commissioners are required by statute to present an annual report [1] to the Secretary of State which is laid before Parliament, and this provides in addition to complete statistics of the prison and Borstal populations and their characteristics a reasonably full account of the major activities of the administration in the preceding year: in addition the Stationery Office publishes, for public sale, an illustrated pamphlet issued on the authority of the Home Secretary giving a short account for the general reader of what is being done in the prisons and Borstals, and why. [2]

What is said or not said in official publications is open to check not only by the hundreds of voluntary workers who co-operate in the work of the staff, by the Boards of Visitors and Visiting Committees and the magistrates who visit the prisons privately, but by a great number of non-official visitors from at home and abroad—research workers, social science and other students, [3] penologists, indeed anyone with a serious and responsible interest in the work or in related fields.

As regards newspaper publicity, it may be doubted whether an editor of a responsible newspaper or journal could be found to say that access to prisons or Borstals for this purpose had been unreasonably refused to his representative on proper application to the Press Officer at the Home Office: the number of newspaper articles, including illustrated articles, which have been published in the last few years as a result of facilities granted in this way is certainly considerable. Moreover, Governors have standing instructions to report at once to the Press Officer any incident likely to be of public interest, so that a notice may be sent to the Press Association, and when the terms of the notice are settled, Governors are authorised to communicate it to the local Press.

Nor have other methods been neglected: film companies have been allowed to acquire correct local colour for commercial films, and an official film of prison life ('Four Men in Prison') has been prepared by the Central Office of Information for private showing to audiences of magistrates and others concerned with the administration of criminal justice. From time to time members of the staff have spoken of their work in radio programmes, and the B.B.C. have made in one of the prisons a feature for broadcasting.

[1] Published by H.M. Stationery Office, Kingsway, W.C.2, from whom, or through any bookseller, it may be obtained at a charge of (at present) 4s.

[2] *Prisons and Borstals* (1950). Price 2s. 6d.

[3] Research workers and selected students have not only visited establishments but lived and worked in them.

CHAPTER SIX

LOCAL ADMINISTRATION

(1) VISITING COMMITTEES AND BOARDS OF VISITORS

BEFORE the local prisons were transferred to the Secretary of State by the Act of 1877, they were administered by the Justices in Quarter Sessions, acting through the Visiting Justices whom they appointed, and the Act reserved certain of the powers of these Visiting Justices to new bodies called Visiting Committees. The Committees were to be appointed annually by the Benches committing to the prisons, their composition, method of appointment, powers and duties being prescribed by the Secretary of State in the Statutory Rules. For convict prisons, and later for Borstal institutions, which were under central control and to which the courts did not commit direct, similar bodies were appointed by the Secretary of State from among suitable local people, including a proportion of magistrates.

However this experiment in dual control may have appealed in 1877 to Sir E. du Cane, it has come to be accepted as a necessary and advantageous part of the administrative system of today, and was re-enacted by the Act of 1948 and the Rules of 1949 with very little change. The bodies appointed for local prisons to which the courts commit direct are still called Visiting Committees, while those appointed by the Secretary of State for other prisons, and for Borstals, are called Boards of Visitors. For simplicity, 'Visiting Committee' will hereafter be used to refer to both bodies, except where the context otherwise indicates.

The powers and duties prescribed by the Rules for Visiting Committees fall into three main groups. First, they are an independent and non-official body with a right to enter the prison or Borstal at any time and to see any prisoner or inmate. Any prisoner or inmate may apply to see them, or any of their number who may be visiting, to make a complaint or application. This is a valuable safeguard for the prisoner against harshness or oppression by authority.

The Rules require that 'A Committee shall meet at the prison once a month to discharge its functions under these Rules or, if the Committee resolves that, for reasons specified in the resolution, less frequent meetings are sufficient, not less than eight times in twelve months', and that 'Members of a Visiting Committee and of a Board of Visitors shall pay frequent visits to the prisons for which they are appointed, and (a) at least one member of a Visiting Committee shall visit the prison once in each week; (b) at least one member of a Board of Visitors shall visit the prison once between each meeting of the Board and the next meeting'.

Second, the Visiting Committee is the superior authority for the maintenance of discipline in the establishment. The Governor can deal only with minor offences against the rules: more serious offences must come before the Visiting Committee. In particular, any offence in a prison for which corporal punishment may be imposed must be dealt with by the Visiting Committee.

Third, they are charged with a general oversight of the management of the prisons and Borstals, and report to the Secretary of State on the way in which the statutes and Statutory Rules are applied by the Governors and their staffs. This is done by means of a formal Annual Report, though this does not preclude interim representations on particular matters where necessary.

In Borstal Institutions and for Preventive Detention prisoners the Boards of Visitors have the further function of advising the Commissioners as to the date of release of the inmates or prisoners.

The Magistrates Association has established a Prisons and Borstals Committee composed of members of Visiting Committees. This Committee arranges an annual conference in London of all members of Visiting Committees who are able to attend. The conference is usually opened by the Secretary of State and attended by representatives of the Prison Commissioners, who are invited to take part in discussion of the resolutions placed before the Conference.

In their Annual Report for 1947, p. 11, the Commissioners said of this system:

'It makes for public confidence in the administration of discipline; it creates local sympathy and interest in the work going on inside the walls; it spreads necessary knowledge among magistrates of what is the actual result of the sentences they pass in court; and it places at the disposal of the Home Secretary and the Prison Commissioners knowledge and ideas about the working of the system from experienced public men and women who see it with a fresher eye than those who are immersed in its daily work. These ideas may be conveyed either in informal talks at the prisons, where the Commissioners are always happy to meet Visiting Magistrates, or through the discussions at the Annual Conferences, or in their Annual Reports.'

(2) GOVERNORS, CHAPLAINS AND MEDICAL OFFICERS

These three grades are, by a provision of the Act of 1877, known as 'superior officers', the remainder of the staff as 'subordinate officers'. Apart from hierarchical and functional differences, the statutory significance of this not very happy nomenclature is that the former are appointed by the Secretary of State, the latter by the Prison Commissioners. With the growth of years in variety of work in the prisons and Borstals, this distinction has come at times to be rather blurred at the edges, though the appointment of these three superior grades by the Secretary of State remains clear-cut.

If the English prison and Borstal systems of today have any merits, they derive above all from the belief that what counts for most in them is not buildings or systems, but men. 'A school is a teacher with a building round him, not a building with a teacher inside.' So for some thirty years past the first care of the administration has been the selection and training of staff, and though with the increasing complica-, tion of the work much remains to be done for training, this care has provided a staff with a tone and tradition, and a professional competence, that are constantly remarked with admiration by experienced administrators from abroad.

Governors

In any type of penal establishment the Governor is the keystone of the arch. Within his own prison, he is in much the same position as the captain of a ship—supreme in an isolated community, responsible for the efficiency and welfare of his crew as well as for the safe arrival of his passengers at their journey's end. The time is long past when the post of prison Governor was a suitable niche for the retired officer with the reputation of 'a good disciplinarian'. The command of a large prison today calls not only for a vocation for such work but for special personal qualities and adequate educational and administrative qualifications. Quite apart from the control and training of his prisoners, and the leadership of his staff, the Governor is responsible for extensive and various buildings and machinery; for large industrial and, maybe, agricultural activities; for close co-operation with the courts and the police and the machinery of justice in general; for enlisting voluntary workers in different fields and seeing that they work harmoniously with his administration and with each other; for keeping on good terms with the local authorities who run the prison library and evening education; and often enough—too often for those who do not enjoy hearing themselves talk—for 'selling' his job in private to the more important visitors to the prison and in public at a variety of local meetings and functions.

The duties of the Governor, as the responsible head of each

establishment, are defined by the Rules, and supplemented by more detailed instructions in Standing Orders. Governors are divided into three classes, according to the size and responsibility of their establishments, and are assisted in all Borstals and the larger prisons by Assistant Governors, who are deemed to be Governors for the purposes of the Prisons Act 1877 and are appointed by the Secretary of State. Assistant Governors are divided into two classes: those in Class I act as Deputy Governors or in junior posts of special responsibility, such as the charge of an outlying camp: those in Class II act as Housemasters in Borstals, or in similar posts in Training Prisons, or as assistants to the Principal of the staff Training School, and generally as required. The grades and titles for women follow exactly those for men.

Appointments are no longer made to governorships direct: all candidates start as Assistant Governors II, except that Chief Officers who are promoted may pass direct to the grade of Assistant Governor I. Thus all governors will have learned the elements of the work in the junior grades before succeeding to the command of prisons or Borstals.

Since the late war the Commissioners, with the approval of the Secretary of State, have followed the principle that vacancies in the ranks of Assistant Governors should be filled by promotion from within the service to the extent that suitably qualified candidates are forthcoming. There are two channels for this purpose, the first being the promotion of selected Chief Officers already mentioned. The second is through a special machinery devised to bring forward young officers with the necessary personal qualifications early in their careers. Each year the Civil Service Commissioners hold a qualifying examination, which is a simple test of literacy and intelligence, for which any established officer with over two years service may apply. A given number of those who qualify are then seen by a selection board of representatives of the Civil Service and Prison Commissions, which has before it the reports of a 'week-end test' [1] as well as reports from Governors and Assistant Commissioners who know the candidates. The board selects up to twelve candidates for a six-month Staff Course at the Imperial Training School at Wakefield, which in conjunction with Leeds University provides a general educational course with a slant towards the future work of a potential governor—its purpose however is not so much to give a professional training as to test the capacity of minds and personalities to develop and respond to such a training. It is rewarding to find how men whose social and educational opportunities may have been narrow will broaden and burgeon under these influences. At the end of the course the selection board again sees the candidates, with the reports of the Wakefield staff before it, and marks them as either qualified or not qualified for the rank of Assistant Governor. The 'Qs' receive promotion as vacancies occur; for the

1 Held at the Imperial Training School, Wakefield.

'NQs' it is 'as you were', so far at least as concerns immediate promotion.

The results of the four Staff Courses held since the war have been, for reasons which it may be hoped are transitory, disappointing, only 14 men and 2 women having been selected through this channel. It is no part of the intention that the high standards required for a Governor should be relaxed. But it remains true that any young man who enters the service as a prison officer, if he can reach those standards, can become a Governor.

Thus in recent years the majority of vacancies for Assistant Governor have been filled by direct entry through open competition, which is equally open to any member of the service.[1] Since Governors, like all established members of the prison service, are permanent pensionable civil servants, the competition is held by the Civil Service Commissioners. After public advertisement a selection board of representatives of the Civil Service and Prison Commissions sees the 'short list' and the selected candidates are recommended to the Secretary of State for appointment. No special qualifications are required as a *sine qua non*, but an adequate educational background, some vocation for the work, a knowledge of the lives and background of those sections of the community from which delinquents mainly derive, a promise of some administrative capacity—all these will help, if the candidate is the right sort of person in himself, a person of sincerity, integrity, humanity and goodwill, with at any rate one foot firmly on the ground.

Assistant Governors are appointed on probation for two years, the first few months being spent in a prison or Borstal on a syllabus of training before joining for duty: at some time during his first year he also attends a short 'background' course at the Imperial Training School. Owing to the higher proportion of Borstal housemaster posts, the chances are that an Assistant Governor will start in this way, as did the majority of the Assistant Commissioners now serving and one of the Commissioners. There is a complete fluidity of promotion between prisons and Borstals, though those who show a decided vocation for one side rather than the other will usually stay where they are best fitted.

Chaplains

The Chaplain must by statute be a priest of the Established Church, but by the Prison Ministers Act 1863, provision is made for spiritual ministration to prisoners who are not members of that Church by Prison Ministers, who are appointed by the Prison Commissioners on the recommendation of the Bishop of the Diocese in the case of the Roman Catholic Church, or of the governing body in the case of one of the Protestant Free Churches. There are at every establishment a

[1] Some prison officers have in fact become Assistant Governors in this way

Roman Catholic Priest and a Nonconformist Minister, and Ministers of other denominations are appointed or specially called in as occasion arises. Prison Ministers are appointed on a part-time basis and may be remunerated either by fixed salaries or by fees fixed on a capitation basis, according to the numbers of their congregations.

The duties of the Chaplain in the majority of establishments are performed by local clergymen appointed on a part-time basis at a remuneration appropriate to the size of the prison. At the larger establishments where a full-time post is necessary the Chaplains are appointed for seven years in the first instance, and are not usually retained for longer, this being the period at the end of which they become entitled to a small superannuation gratuity. The reason for this is that the Commissioners attach great importance to the work of Chaplains: they believe therefore that a Chaplain should always be at his best, and that a man who spends too many years in the highly specialised, difficult, and often discouraging work of a penal establishment tends to lose that spiritual zest, that freshness of touch, which is essential in what must always be uphill work, however rewarding. They have therefore reached an agreement with the Bishops, through the good offices and with the cordial approval of the Archbishop of Canterbury, under which the Bishop of a candidate's diocese is consulted as to and approves his appointment to prison work, and agrees to take him back into the diocese in due course. The arrangement also provides for the Chaplains to keep in touch with their Deanery and Diocese.

In the appointment of Chaplains selections are made by a Board on which the Prison Commissioners are assisted by a Bishop.

Medical Officers

Although the Prisons Medical Service is a separate service, under the control of the Director of Medical Services in the Prison Commission, its full-time Medical Officers form part of the general class of Government Medical Officers, their conditions of service being the same and their recruitment being through the competitions for this class held by the Civil Service Commissioners. When there are vacancies for Prison Medical Officers, the Director of Medical Services attends the selection board. Experienced practitioners are required, preferably with knowledge of and experience in psychological medicine. A proportion of these officers have the rank of Principal Medical Officer: they are employed at the prisons with the heaviest medical responsibilities, and have certain advisory and supervisory functions over the medical work of other prisons and Borstals in their 'group'. Establishments where the numbers are not high enough to justify a full-time officer are served by local practitioners on a part-time basis. At the largest prisons there may be two or even three full-time doctors, though unfortunately the shortage of doctors since the late war has been such that many of these posts have remained unfilled.

The duties of the medical officers, and the arrangements for consultative and specialist services, and co-operation with the National Health Service and civil hospitals and clinics, are dealt with in Chapter 14.

(3) OTHER STAFF

The 'subordinate' officers engaged in the control and supervision of prisoners, and to a considerable extent in their instruction, have for over thirty years been officially styled Prison Officers, though the Press and the public are still disposed to call them Warders or Wardresses. The change of name in 1919 coincided with and symbolised a change of spirit—warder suggests the turnkey and the guard, officer the leader. However, to the prisoner he remains the 'screw'.

They are divided, men and women, into three grades, Chief Officer, Principal Officer, and Officer. The Chief Officer is the head of the subordinate staff, and where there is no Assistant Governor he takes charge in the absence of the Governor: taking account of annual leave, sick leave and absence at Assizes and Sessions, this may be for a substantial portion of the year. These officers are therefore carefully selected men of high responsibilities and corresponding qualities. At the larger establishments they are Class I, with second Chief Officers of Class II in the largest; at the smaller establishments they are Class II. The position of women Chief Officers corresponds with that of men in the two large separate establishments for women, but in the small women's wings of mixed prisons it is rather different: there the woman in charge is a Chief Officer under the male Governor of the whole establishment, and her rank derives rather from her special responsibility under the Rules than from the size of her charge, which is often quite small. In the largest of these women's wings, at Manchester, the woman in charge is a Deputy Governor with a Chief Officer under her.

Principal Officers in prisons are in charge of wings of the prison, or in specially responsible posts. They also take charge of the dock and arrangements for the custody of prisoners at Assizes and Sessions. In many prisons too a senior Principal Officer is required to act as Chief Officer while the Chief is away or acting for the Governor. Many of the more responsible specialist posts, such as Instructors or Cooks, are also graded as Principals. In Borstals these supervisory functions are not required to the same extent, and the role of the Principal Officer is rather to act as assistant to the Housemaster in the general running of the House.

The basic grade of Prison Officer covers a wide variety of work. In an ordinary local prison much of this is of necessity of a routine nature; prisoners must be unlocked in their cells and locked up again at the regular times; meals served; workshops, exercises and associations supervised; applications collected; numbers checked; cells and kits examined—all this forms the framework of the daily round. But there is also a variety of specialised work, such as librarian, gymnastic instructor, cooking, instructing in trades, and hospital work—all of which carry additional pay—for which officers who acquire the necessary qualifications are eligible. There are also 'staff' jobs such as charge of the gate or stores, or Chief Officer's clerk, which are coveted for a change of work, and escorts to courts or to other prisons give a change of air, as does the charge of parties working away from the prison on farms or elsewhere.

In the regional training prisons, as will be seen when we come to describe them, the work of the officer tends to be less of a routine and purely supervisory kind, in the open prisons still less, and in the Borstals scarcely at all. In the central prisons for 'long-timers' it has a special character of its own. There is also all the difference in the world between life in a big London prison and life in a small country prison. One way and another, therefore, in the course of ten years service, a prison officer may see more change than the nature of the job might suggest.

The established prison officials do not do night duty, except that one of them remains on duty as Orderly Officer till the prison is finally locked up, and then sleeps in the prison so as to be available in case of emergency, while another 'sleeps in' at the gate. The night-patrols are specially recruited for their duty. Stoking and other such industrial work is done by regular workmen under normal Trade Union rates and conditions for the job.

The Works Staff, who are responsible under the Director of Works and his staff for all constructional, engineering and maintenance work in the prisons, the officers' quarters, farm buildings and other adjuncts, form a separate branch of the subordinate staff. They are recruited on the basis of their trade experience as 'Trade Assistants', and after the normal training of a prison officer—since they must take charge of prisoners—pass straight to their work. They may later pass by examination into the ranks of the Engineers II, and by a further examination to Engineer I or Foreman of Works. This is a highly skilled and qualified technical service, which must be prepared to face a wider variety of constructional, mechanical, electrical and civil engineering problems than falls to the lot of most who call themselves in any sense engineers. They carry out practically all their work with prison or Borstal labour which they must train themselves, though for special jobs skilled local workmen may also be engaged as necessary.

In addition to these main bodies, there are other specialist officers in control of prisoners, mainly on the industrial side. For a number of trades however Civilian Instructors skilled in that trade are recruited, as also for the Vocational Training Classes: for these posts Prison Officers with the necessary qualifications may apply. The farms and gardens are under the control of Farm Bailiffs and Farm Instructors, with a sufficient number of skilled agricultural workers to supplement and instruct the prison or Borstal labour.

On a somewhat separate basis is the 'business' staff of the establishment, under the Steward, who is responsible to the Governor for the cash and accounts, the stores and manufactures, victualling and the general office work of the establishment. These responsible posts are filled by members of the Executive Class of the Civil Service —Senior Executive Officers in the largest, Higher Executive Officers in the majority, and Executive Officers with an allowance in the remainder. The Stewards are assisted by Executive and Clerical Officers of appropriate ranks and numbers. These two classes are interchangeable with their colleagues at the Head Office, the whole service being treated as one for promotion purposes.

Since the basic grade of prison officer forms the foundation of the service, great care has for long been taken with their selection and training. At the time of writing, however, conditions are very different from those of the days before the war. Then it was necessary only to replace the normal wastage of something more than 100 a year, and there was usually a long waiting list of applicants of whom a high proportion were ex-N.C.Os. of the Regular Forces. After preliminary sifting formalities the final selection was made by a Commissioner or Assistant Commissioner by personal interview, and the chosen went to the Imperial Training School at Wakefield for an 8 weeks' course: this served two purposes, a general grounding in the work, and a testing of suitability for the service, concluding with a final examination by a Commissioner. The successful were posted to prisons as probationers for 2 months' further training in practical routine, and if still found satisfactory after 12 months' probation were then posted for duty.

After six years suspension of recruiting during the war, the prison service was faced in 1946 with a formidable staff deficit at a time when recruiting was limited by Government direction of man-power: indeed in 1945 and 1946 the pressure of an increasing prison population on the seriously diminished and over-taxed staff had strained the machine almost to breaking point. The steps taken to meet this situation were described by the Commissioners in their Annual Report for 1946 as follows:

'It was provisionally estimated that, in order to bring the numbers of staff up to the level necessary to put all establishments on to a shift-system covering the full day, as before the war, it would be necessary, in relation to the increased population and larger number of establishments, to recruit some 1700 additional men officers and 170 additional women officers. This was a formidable undertaking, which required as a first step the building up of an adequate staff in the Establishment Branch to deal with the volume of work entailed. It was further complicated by the housing situation, which made it virtually impossible to post the majority of recruits to any station except one close to any home they might have.

'It was clear that, if anything like these numbers were to be recruited and trained in any reasonable time, the pre-war system of posting selected candidates direct to the Imperial Training School at Wakefield for two months' training would have to be suspended.

'In place of this system it was decided to continue to enlist recruits in the first instance as Auxiliary Officers at the establishment nearest their homes, and to give them three months' practical training at the place of joining. This training was to follow a prescribed syllabus at the end of which a recommendation would be made by a board of senior officers of the establishment as to whether the candidate was suitable for permanent employment as a Prison or Borstal Officer. Candidates so recommended and approved by the Commissioners were then to be sent for a two weeks' course of special training and testing at the Imperial Training School at Wakefield, at the end of which successful candidates would be posted to their prisons as established officers on 12 months' probation.

'The function of the Training School in this scheme was to provide a short period more of testing than of training, and a study was therefore made of the novel methods introduced during the war by the War Office Selection Boards and subsequently adopted in the 'country-house test' by the Civil Service Commissioners. Some of these methods were applied, and in addition, the candidates were given instruction in the background and principles of their work. For the first time also women were included with men at Wakefield, an innovation which has been entirely successful and much appreciated by the women's staff.

'It is interesting to record here that with the opening of this system the present buildings of the Imperial Training School, which were not completed till the end of 1939, were used for the first time for the purpose for which they were built. Accordingly, on 5th April 1946, a formal opening ceremony was held, at which a large and representative gathering was addressed by the Home Secretary, the Rt. Hon. J. Chuter Ede, M.P. The buildings were erected by prison labour to the plans and under the direction of the present Director of Works.'

This system still continues, though the Wakefield period was later extended to 3 weeks and may shortly be increased to 5 weeks.

Although recruiting proceeded at a gratifying rate, the numbers in the basic grade for men increasing from 1610 on 1st January 1947 to 2784 on 31st December 1950, the prison and Borstal populations increased ever more steeply, and it became necessary to open many more establishments. At the time of writing, therefore, the staff is still no more than adequate to man the prisons properly on a single-shift system, and the possibility constantly recedes of returning generally to a two-shift system, which would make possible a full working day for the prisoners and a full scale of evening activities. If recruiting remains satisfactory during 1951, however, it will be possible to effect improvements at some of the special training prisons.

This long-standing condition of staff shortage has also restricted the possibilities of improving the professional training of officers: as soon as circumstances permit, the Commissioners would wish both to lengthen the preliminary training and to introduce courses of more advanced training for senior officers of the basic grade.

The Executive and Clerical Classes receive the training provided under the normal Civil Service training programmes, which are controlled by a Training Officer at the Head Office.

(4) WHITLEY COUNCILS AND CONDITIONS OF SERVICE

Members of the staffs of all grades partake, through the appropriate representative staff Associations, in the Whitley Council [1] machinery which was set up for the Civil Service in 1919.

For the subordinate staff there is a separate Departmental Whitley Council for the Prison Service, on which all grades are represented through the Prison Officers' Association. The constitution follows the model constitution prescribed by the National Whitley Council, and meetings are held once or twice a year.

The Prison Officers' Association is a registered Trade Union with a full time General Secretary and Assistant General Secretary, who are not members of the service. It also has the services as Advisers of Mr. W. J. Brown and Mr. L. C. White, the former and present General Secretaries of the Civil Service Clerical Association. These gentlemen, by an extra-constitutional arrangement personal to themselves, attend meetings of the Council, where their expert knowledge of Civil Service affairs has often been advantageous to its working. The Prison Officers' Association has a branch in each local establishment, with a Chairman, Secretary and Committee, with whom Governors are empowered to consult on questions affecting the local conditions of service of the staff, and who may submit to the Governor resolutions concerning those conditions. These local matters ought to be and usually are settled locally, but failing agreement may be referred to the Commissioners,

[1] The Whitley Council is an adaptation to the needs of the Civil Service of Joint Industrial Councils, with Official Side and Staff Side representing employers and employees. It is named after Mr. Speaker J. H. Whitley, from whose proposals it originated.

and if the staff are still not satisfied they may ask their central Executive Committee to pursue the matter. The Association owns and publishes an organ called 'The Prison Officers' Magazine.''

The Whitley Council has in general worked to the advantage of the service as a harmonious and effective instrument of negotiation, both centrally and locally. On occasion Joint Sub-committees have dealt with special subjects, such as housing and uniform, and produced agreed recommendations. A great deal of business is also carried out by correspondence or discussion between the Establishment Officer and the General Secretary.

Failing agreement on the Whitley Council, all the representative associations have access to the Civil Service Arbitration Tribunal on such matters and for such grades as come within the Civil Service Arbitration Agreement. The Prison Officers' Association have frequently succeeded in improving their pay or conditions of service through this medium.

These conditions of service are designed to compensate for some of the disadvantages of prison life. To those who may find confinement in the somewhat unnatural atmosphere of a prison, with its need for constant alertness, a mental or physical strain, the reasonable working hours (84 in the fortnight) and long leave (18 working days rising after 10 years to 21, plus 9 days for public holidays) [1] will be of advantage, as will the special superannuation arrangements which allow retirement on pension at 55 instead of 60, with full pension after 30 years' service instead of after 40 years.

The cash value of the emoluments must be taken as a whole to obtain its real comparative value with other employments: it includes free unfurnished quarters or an allowance in lieu, and free uniform and boots or an allowance in lieu: both these emoluments are pensionable. Taking the value of these emoluments together with the weekly pay, the minimum earnings of a man in the basic grade are approximately 147s. per week at entry, 178s. 6d. after 7 years, 183s. after 15 years, and 187s. 6d. after 20 years; of a woman 133s. 5d., 159s. 8d., 163s. 5d., and 167s. 2d.

To be added to this minimum, apart from overtime earnings which are substantial in total, is a number of special allowances of various incidence: apart from special duty allowances (trade instructors, cooks, hospital, etc.) these include an allowance of 4s. 6d. a week for all officers employed in Borstals, and allowances payable at certain remote establishments for 'inconvenience of locality' which range from 2s. 6d. to 15s.

Promotion tends to be slow: in 1950 the average length of service of officers promoted to Principal Officers was 17 years and 8 months, and of Principal Officers to Chief, 8 years.

[1] For women 21 days, rising after 10 years to 24.

All grades of the subordinate staff in the prisons from Chief Officer downwards wear uniform, excepting women Chief Officers and the Foremen of Works. All Borstal staffs wear plain clothes, and receive an allowance of £24 a year in lieu of uniform. The uniform is of navy blue, not unlike the police except that the buttons are gilt and a gilt HMP is worn on the shoulder straps: and like the police, it is in process of changing over from a high closed collar to an open-necked jacket with collar and tie. Men wear a flat peaked cap with a gilt metal badge. Principal Officers wear a black cord epaulette, and Chief Officers a gilt one. Women wear a navy blue jacket and skirt with shoulder-badges, and a blue felt hat and badge.

Prison Officers are civil servants, and as such their recruitment is under Civil Service Commission control and subject to the issue by the Civil Service Commissioners of a Certificate of Qualification, which requires preliminary medical and educational tests. Their conditions of service also follow Civil Service practice. But in some respects they are more closely comparable with two other services outside the Civil Service which come under Home Office control—the Police and Fire Services: not only do they wear uniform but they are subject to a statutory Code of Discipline. The Prison Rules require the Prison Commissioners to formulate such a code with the approval of the Secretary of State. The present code, which was drafted by the Commissioners in consultation with the Staff Side of the Whitley Council, is analogous to those in force for the Police and Fire Services, and sets out clearly not only what acts constitute an offence against discipline, and what awards may be made in respect of them and by what authority, but also the procedure for dealing with such offences and the rights and safeguards of an accused officer. The dismissal of an Officer or his reduction in rank requires the approval of the Secretary of State.

Details of the grades, numbers and pay of all ranks of the service are given in Appendix D.

CHAPTER SEVEN

ACCOMMODATION

(1) NATURE AND DISTRIBUTION OF PRISON BUILDINGS

AT least it may be said for the subject-matter of this chapter that it is more fluid, novel and various than it could ever have been before or will, in all probability, ever be again. There have been in the history of the Prison Commission two periods of contraction, the first after 1877 when du Cane reduced from 113 to 56 the local prisons handed over to him under the Act; the second after the First World War, when 29 more were closed as local prisons, though 3 of these were turned by the Commissioners to other uses. Of the remainder, 18 were discontinued and disposed of, the others were kept in reserve.

So there was never, before the present time, any shortage of cellular accommodation: never therefore any necessity for new building such as, before the First World War, might have been occasioned by new ideas of prison treatment, or after it might have prevailed against the recurrent drives for economy in public expenditure. Between the wars, the economic shadow of the first war hung over all such possibilities; when this began to lift, and at long last a 'new Holloway' was actually on the drawing-board, it was lost in the deepening shadow of the second. So it comes that in England there is only one prison building of the twentieth century, the former preventive detention prison built at Camp Hill in the Isle of Wight after the Act of 1908. Equally there is only one Borstal which was built as such—Lowdham Grange: and this was made possible only because it was built over a long period of years almost entirely by Borstal labour—in fact the last house was opened in 1949, and there are more buildings to come. To see a modern prison in Great Britain, one must cross the Border to Edinburgh.

The years immediately following the Second World War provided for the first time a period of expansion, and again in conditions which, though they called for immediate action on a wide scale, ruled out all possibility of new building for some years ahead.

In the autumn of 1945, after the close of hostilities, the Commissioners, with all their spare prisons in other hands and several cell-blocks destroyed by bombing, found that to meet their immediate requirements they needed 'at least six more Borstals and five more prisons more or less simultaneously'.[1] In the course of 1946 they acquired in new premises one Reception Centre and four Borstals for boys, one Borstal for girls, one prison for men, and one for women: the closed prisons at Pentonville, Northallerton, Reading, and Canterbury were also recovered and taken into use, and the two remaining prisons at Portsmouth and Preston followed later—this exhausted the cellular accommodation available in the country.[2] In 1947 and 1948 two 'satellite camps' and an additional prison were opened. In 1949, as the population continued to grow, another satellite camp and two more prisons were opened, and the small portion of Hull prison which had not been damaged was taken into use for a working party of prisoners. In 1950 the population was still higher, and two new Borstals were opened to release cellular buildings for prison purposes: at the end of the year one more open prison was taken into use.

So in the space of five years the number of prisons and Borstals in use had grown from 39 to 59 (plus four satellite camps), and one more is in course of adaptation. Of this swift accretion only seven were in prison buildings: the 'modern English prison'—or Borstal—may be found in an American army hospital, an Elizabethan house, a Land Army hostel, a nobleman's country seat, a R.A.F. airfield, a Victorian fort or—across the Border—in a mediaeval castle.

As 1951 opens, history repeats itself. Notwithstanding the economic conditions, the Commissioners had in 1950 secured agreement in principle to initiate a substantial new building programme, to include three prisons for men, two boys' Borstals, and two small Borstals for girls to replace Aylesbury. Sites were being sought, and with eager anticipation preliminary plans had been prepared, at last, for a prison to meet the needs of the contemporary prison system. The present international situation, with the diversion of the nation's resources once more to re-armament, is scarcely favourable to any early fruition of such plans.

So it is that the structural basis of our system is still the local prison of the post-Pentonville era and the convict prison of Sir Joshua Jebb. The brutally limited space within the twenty-foot walls of these ancient buildings, except where occasionally a little land could be bought outside, must still confine and cramp the multifarious activities of today. For one thing however thanks are due to our predecessors and to the conditions in which our prison system grew: we are not cumbered with the very large prison. In only three prisons does the accommodation approach or exceed 1,000, and it is only in the London prisons,

[1] Annual Report for 1945, p. 5.
[2] Excepting one very small prison in use as a military prison, and the war-damaged ruins at Hull.

and at times of exceptional pressure, that a population of 1,000 or more is likely to be reached. Even in the peak population pressure of 1949, when additional huts were in use for sleeping and in most prisons some prisoners were sleeping three in a cell, only twelve prisons exceeded a population of 500.

Such is the general situation as to buildings in use. To turn now to their numbers and distribution, it should first be noted that the concentration of local prisons after the First World War put an end to the traditional idea of the 'county gaol', to which were committed all prisoners from the Assizes and Quarter Sessions for the county and from its Petty Sessional Courts. A prisoner sentenced to imprisonment, or committed to prison on remand or to await trial, may be lawfully confined in any prison to which the Prisons Acts apply, and must be committed by the Courts to such prisons as the Secretary of State may from time to time direct. So all prisoners, convicted or unconvicted, are received in the first instance into the nearest of twenty-five local prisons: there is nothing in the English system corresponding with the wide distribution of small 'gaols' of American practice or 'district prisons' of continental European practice. While this might seem to have disadvantages for visitors to untried prisoners, little or nothing is heard of these in practice, and the prisoner certainly has the advantage of the better conditions of the larger prisons under central control: on the other hand, with such large 'committal areas' the cost of escorting prisoners and the drain on man-power are unduly high. This is particularly marked in the case of women, since the very small numbers call for only six local women's prisons: one of these is no more than a small depot for untried women, while Holloway prison in London, on the other hand, collects from all the south-eastern counties of England from the Solent to the Wash.

In addition to the twenty-five local prisons which receive direct committals there are five others used for special purposes, mainly for the segregation of local prisoners of the Star Class [1] and civil prisoners.

In the next tier above the local prisons come the regional prisons: their functions and characteristics will be described in Chapter 9, but it may be said here that they include four regional training prisons for men at Wakefield (part), Maidstone, Sudbury, and the Verne (Portland); one for women, at Askham Grange (Yorks) in the north and one in preparation at Hill Hall (Essex) in the south; a separate prison for young prisoners at Lewes; and an allocation centre at Reading for corrective training.

The central prisons for long-term prisoners (over 3 years) are as follows: for men of the Ordinary Class,[1] Parkhurst and Dartmoor,[2] of the Star Class, Wakefield (part) and Leyhill: for women of the Ordinary Class, Holloway, of the Star Class, Aylesbury. Long-term young

---

[1] These classifications are explained on p. 116.   [2] See Appendix K.

prisoners are in a separate block at Wakefield. Of these establishments Parkhurst and Dartmoor are former convict prisons: the first, situated in the Isle of Wight, originated as a convict prison for young 'transports' in 1838, while the second needs no further introduction. Both have considerable areas of land outside the walls, affording healthy out-door work in agriculture, forestry or land reclamation. Wakefield has long had a famous name in prison history, first as the House of Correction for the West Riding, then for many advanced experiments in the early part of the nineteenth century, and a hundred years later, reopened after a long rest, as the starting place of the new methods of Waller and Paterson in prison training. It is also known to every officer in the English service and to many in prisons and Borstals overseas as the home of the Imperial Training School for prison officers. It is a large walled prison, with plenty of intra-mural space, containing what are really three establishments in one—a central prison in two wings for long-term Stars, a regional training prison in two other wings, and the long-term young prisoners in a separate block.

Some miles out of Wakefield, on a high space cleared from the woods, stands a curious little cabin: it is built of the discarded doors of prison cells. This, the first building of New Hall Camp, symbolises the start of the open prison system in England. The camp still takes up to 100 men from the 'training side' of Wakefield. Its direct descendant at Leyhill, in Gloucestershire, was opened some ten years later in an ex-American Army hospital in the grounds of Tortworth Court. The adjoining mansion has been adapted for use as a regional training prison.

The handful of long-term Star women are in a wing of the walled prison at Aylesbury, which gives them space in a pleasantly rural air with gardens. The Ordinaries are less well placed at Holloway, a large London prison of the classic nineteenth-century castellated style, said to be inspired by Warwick Castle, which has of unhappy necessity become an 'omnium gatherum' of women prisoners of any and every kind: the dissolution of this anachronism has for too long been regarded as a first priority.

The prisons for corrective training are, for men, Chelmsford, Camp Hill, Nottingham, two wings of Liverpool, a wing of Durham, and two wings of Wormwood Scrubs: for women, inevitably, a wing of Holloway. For preventive detention, a part of Parkhurst for men, and for women a part of Holloway.

Such is the outline of the pattern: details of planning and equipment will be filled in in the following section; of function in the appropriate chapters. A detailed list of all establishments is given in Appendix E.

(2) PLANNING AND ACCOMMODATION

Excepting the former convict prisons, all English cellular prisons, including those now serving other than local purposes, are the county gaols of mid-nineteenth century built under the influence of Pentonville. They follow, with minor variations, some form of the radial plan by which two or more wings, according to size, radiate from a centre like spokes from the hub of a wheel: in some there is a separate block which was formerly the 'female prison', in others this was—or is—one of the spokes. This plan had the advantages of economy of supervision, since all could be controlled from the centre, and elasticity, since spokes could be added or lengthened: on the other hand the space in the angles cannot be well used, and for modern requirements in classification the inevitable mixing at the centre prevents complete segregation. The convict prisons were built in separate blocks, with or without a connecting corridor.

The cell blocks or halls are from two to five storeys high according to the size and general planning of the prison. On the ground floor the cell-doors give on to a central corridor usually 16 ft. in width, which reaches to and is lighted from the roof. On the upper floors, or landings, the cells open on to railed galleries about 3 ft. wide, supported on wall brackets. The well between the galleries is bridged at intervals, and the bridges serve also as landings for open stair-flights from floor to floor. At the gallery-level above the ground floor wire netting is stretched across the well, to check the fall of anyone who by accident or design drops over the gallery railings. The interior walls are lime-washed to within four feet of ground level, where a line of green paint borders a cream-painted dado, giving a clean and light interior effect.

To this nucleus of cell-blocks the administrative and auxiliary buildings are attached in various ways. The offices and stores commonly form a 'spoke' through which lies the entrance to the prison proper. For convenience of service and administration the kitchen and bakery and the chapel will be close to the centre: the laundry will usually be attached to the hall that is (or was) set aside for women. The hospital arrangements are described in Chapter Fourteen. In a separate building towards the Gate is the 'Reception', where prisoners on arrival are received, examined, bathed, fitted out with prison clothing and detained till they have been passed medically fit for admission to the main prison. The stores for prison clothing and for prisoners' private clothing will usually be connected with this block. The general bath-house may be here or elsewhere.

Although it would seem that the local prisons were usually built outside the county towns, the towns have long since caught up with most of them and have closed around the prison walls. In the exceptions, it has been possible to buy some adjoining land which serves as a lung, with market gardens and perhaps a football pitch. Otherwise, the activities of the prison of today must all be worked somehow into the limited space within the walls, much of which since 1898 has increasingly been taken up by the provision of workshops, which had not been required for prisons built to enforce the separate system. Since the late war alone, to provide for the higher prison population and new industries requiring more space, 38 industrial workshops have been provided, and a number of shops for vocational training. More space too is required today for exercise; grounds must be provided where possible for physical training, as well as for the concentric exercise rings, which since the war have been increased in width to allow prisoners to walk two or three abreast instead of in silent single file. In some prisons there is still sufficient space for small vegetable gardens, and everywhere any cultivable patch is brightened with flowers.

It is evident that these buildings, meant to serve a system of punitive repression, strict separation, silence and the discipline of the treadmill, will be ill adapted to the different purposes of today. Mr. Herbert Morrison, when he was Home Secretary, emulated the elder Cato's 'delenda est Carthago' in his constantly expressed wish that all English prisons could be blown up. And there were times during his term of office when it seemed that his wish might be gratified. In the light of the post-war economic situation it now seems well that it was not: for a long time to come Pentonville and its whole grim brood will still have to serve.

But one need not therefore despair. If the prison population fell so as to give a little elbow room, and funds could be made available not indeed to replace but to remodel these buildings, something worth while might yet be done. Experiment has already shown that it is possible to convert a standard cell into a not displeasing little room, and the provision of up-to-date sanitary annexes of adequate size on each remodelled landing would remove one of the most distressing features of the cell-blocks as they are. Priority should then be given to the building of new blocks for visiting rooms, with pleasant waiting rooms for the visitors, for these arrangements rank only after the sanitation among the major eyesores of a prison.

The next need would be to gut a cell-block to provide on one floor dining and common rooms, and on the floor above a large assembly room and some class-rooms. It would not then be necessary for eating and every associated activity to take place on the narrow floors of the cell-blocks, as also classes except where two or three cells can be knocked together to make one small room, nor would a screen need to be drawn across the altar while the Chapel served for a concert or a film-show.

Of the standard local prison there are of course many variations, both of planning and of atmosphere—from Armley Gaol in Leeds, where all an imprisoned Yorkshireman can see below the sky is the surrounding wall black with a century's soot, to Lewes in Sussex, where the young prisoners at exercise can lose sight of the wall and see for miles the sweep of the South Downs. There are many interesting structural links with early prison history: Gloucester keeps its connection with Sir Onesiphorus Paul, while Oxford, on the site of the ancient castle, has in good preservation not only a row of eighteenth-century dungeons but a Norman crypt and the tower from which Queen Matilda in her mantle of white escaped across the snow.

As to the prisons of recent acquisition, there can be no generalisation. Such premises were taken as were quickly available and could easily be made serviceable. The central prison at Leyhill and the regional prison at Sudbury are in the well-built brick structures of American Army hospital camps; the regional prison at The Verne, Portland, is within the high earthwork and moat of the island fortress; one is in the one-time country seat of a noble family, another on a war-time airfield. For women the northern training prison is in a country house in a park some miles from York, while that for the south is being prepared in the historic beauty of Hill Hall, Essex. It is a curious comment on the times that it should be the Prison Commissioners who, in these great houses of the past, find themselves the custodians not only of their precious heritage of art and natural beauty but of their long tradition of service to the local community.

(3) CELLS AND THEIR EQUIPMENT

The abandonment of the Separate System in England implied no weakening of belief in the separate cell for sleeping. In principle, strict separation by night remains fundamental to the system. In practice, in more recent years, circumstances have forced more than one breach in the principle. The first followed the introduction of 'minimum security' establishments: these had to be hutted camps or nothing, and camps imply dormitories. It remains an open question, whether, if funds were available to build an 'open prison', it should be based on dormitories or on separate rooms: the argument is well balanced. The second breach is due simply to overcrowding: before the late war there had always been cells enough for all comers, but post-war pressure on the available accommodation has led first, to the creation inside the prisons of small dormitories in whatever rooms could be made available, and next to the regrettable necessity, in the majority of local prisons, of sleeping a proportion of the prisoners three in a cell—three being the maximum allowed by Rule, while for other reasons two men are not allowed to sleep in a cell. Where this must be done, three-tier bunks are used. Although the practice has many undesirable consequences, it is certainly not unpopular among the prisoners, provided that reasonable care is taken in the selection of cell-mates and suitable adjustments are made when necessary. And the Medical Officers have found no evidence of adverse effects on health.

Normally however the prisoner, for all his sleeping time and—in present conditions at least—for far too many of his waking hours as well, is in his cell, locked in, and alone. What this cell, and what is in it, may come in the course of months or long years to seem to him, only a prisoner can tell. This account must be objective and impersonal.

There is no prescribed specification of a standard cell, but the Rules provide that every cell in which a prisoner sleeps must be certified by the Prison Commissioners as reaching a proper standard of size, construction, heating, lighting, ventilation and equipment.

The majority of cells in local prisons are 13 ft. × 7 ft. × 9 ft. high, giving 819 cubic feet of air space: this was the size adopted, after careful inquiry, at Pentonville, which as we have seen was the model for most of the prisons built after 1842. It was intended to provide an adequate size for strictly separate confinement with cellular labour. The size of cell subsequently adopted by the Directors for Convict Prisons was 10 ft. × 7 ft. × 9 ft. high, giving only 630 cubic feet of air space, since the convicts worked outside and not in their cells.

The stone or brick wall surfaces and the ceiling are lime-washed, with a dado painted like that in the halls: the outer-wall surface only is plastered, and this is done for security so that any attempt to tamper with the brickwork would show up. The floors vary, concrete, stone flags, tiles, slate and wood planks or blocks all being found.

Cell doors are of solid construction, both doors and frames often being lined with sheet-iron to prevent tampering by ingenious prisoners. A small glass peep-hole, covered by a movable shutter, gives observation of the cell to the patrolling officer. The lock is strong and heavy, and inaccessible from the inside of the cell.

There are many patterns of cell-window: the majority are of the old Pentonville type, with 14 small panes in two rows; a later pattern was of 21 panes in three rows; during the present century the pattern used has been of 35 panes in five rows, each pane being $4\frac{7}{8}$ in. × $6\frac{7}{8}$ in. The panes are glazed with clear glass, and two sliding panes give direct access to the outer air. With older types of window the sash was of cast iron, and this necessitated strong guard-bars outside the window: the later type has a manganese-steel sash, which renders guard-bars unnecessary. With the old 14-pane window the sill was approximately 6 ft. 9 in. above floor-level, but with the later type the height from floor to sill is about 5 ft. Today it would not be thought necessary to construct windows on these principles: those of the new Edinburgh prison are of more normal pattern, and in English prisons experiments have been made on similar lines against the day when reconstruction can be started. Security must be retained, but it is no longer thought wrong that a prisoner should be able to look out of his window.

For artificial lighting electricity has now replaced gas in all establishments, and since the late war a start has been made on increasing the wattage of cell lights from 20 to 40.

The old system of heating and ventilation provided for fresh air, warmed in winter by low pressure hot-water pipes, to be passed into the cell by an intake flue near the ceiling and out by an extraction flue in the opposite corner near the floor. This system, originated at Penton-ville, is with little modification still used with satisfactory results in many prisons. In systems of more modern installation heating is by direct radiation from low pressure hot-water pipes carried through the cells themselves, and ventilation is not by ventilating flues but by circulation from the outer air secured by the sliding panes in the win-dows and ventilators. A daily record is kept of the temperatures of different parts of the prison, which must be maintained in conformity with a prescribed standard.

Prisoners are required to open the ventilators on leaving their cells, and it is the landing officer's duty to see that at least once a day doors and sliding sashes are open for long enough to give the cells a thorough airing. The general intention is that all temperatures should be kept at about 60° F. in winter, and that both in summer and winter there should be a regular current of fresh air through the cells. Equal care is devoted to the heating and ventilation of halls, workshops and other parts of the building.

The above relates to ordinary cells, but there are many special types of cell: the hospital cell is larger and lighter, and its plastered walls are painted ivory white: the observation cell, for certain medical and mental cases, has an iron gate as well as a door, the latter being left open to allow full observation into the cell at all times: cells for tubercular cases are similar to hospital cells, with a larger portion of the window made to open, rounded angles, and impervious floors: there are matted cells for epileptics, with observation gates, coir floor mats, and coir matting round the walls to a height of 5 feet, and padded cells for insane prisoners who may endanger their lives without this protection: the 'special' cells are fitted with a minimum amount of immovable equip-ment that cannot be 'smashed up', and windows and lights high out of reach for the same reason—a certain number of such cells are specially isolated and fitted with double doors, for the discouragement of those who disturb the prison by outbursts of shouting and offensive noise.

In accordance with the Rules every cell is fitted with a bell and out-side indicator so that the duty officer may be summoned in case of need. At the times when prisoners are locked up there is a minimum staff on duty, and after 10 p.m. only one with a cell-key: it may be inferred that, particularly in large prisons where several flights of steps may have to be climbed and considerable lengths of stone landing traversed to reach a distant cell, the prisoners come to understand that the unnecessary ringing of bells is unwelcome.

These considerations, to anyone familiar with prison life, at once carry the mind's eye in the cell to the chamber-pot (enamel, with lid) which symbolises one of the major difficulties of that life—one which at the same time leads to more criticism than almost any other while still resisting any immediately practicable solution. It has been the practice in some countries to instal a water-closet in every cell. Whether or not that be the best solution, and modern practice abroad appears to move away from it, it has at least in England been found to have serious practical disadvantages: Pentonville was thus equipped when built, but experience showed that the combined malice, ignorance and carelessness of prisoners resulted in such constant stoppage of the drains that the system had to be taken out. And experience suggests that a hundred years later the result would be the same: the stoppage of W.C. drains in prisons is a constant nuisance. It is therefore not proposed, in the new prison plans in preparation, to provide water-closets in the cells. So the chamber-pot remains, though consideration of the whole range of its disadvantages will be better reserved for a later discussion of sanitation.

It may be that ideally a new prison should have wash-basins with running water, possibly even 'h. and c.', in the cells, though this would add enormously to the cost: the present plans provide for adequate lavatory and sanitary annexes on each landing. At present, there is an enamel wash basin and water jug on a wooden stand, and a set of toilet requisites to go with it—nail-brush, soap and towel; toothbrush and tooth-powder; hair-brush and comb; a small looking-glass; and for men a safety-razor holder and shaving-brush.

For furniture there is first the bed—still commonly a movable plank bed, though these are gradually being replaced by iron hospital-type beds, which have already been issued to all women's prisons. The bedding consists of a mattress, two blankets, and a bed-rug to go on top, with an extra blanket in winter, sheets, pillow and pillow-case. By day the bed stands on one side against the wall, with the bedding neatly folded to hang over the top; this allows of airing and a clean floor, and disallows lying on the bed until 'beds-down' in the evening.

Next in importance after the bed comes the table and chair: the table is of wood, fixed between the door and the side-wall, this being the position of the old 'gas-box' when the cells were gas-lit: the chair is an ordinary straight-backed wooden piece. On the table will be eating utensils—enamel plate and mug, salt-cellar, and knife, fork and spoon, though the 'knife' is a prison speciality of soft metal without a cutting edge—window bars have been cut through with an ordinary table-knife to which a prisoner had given a saw-edge.

On the wall opposite the bed is a batten with hooks from which hang the cell-cards of information and guidance provided under the Rules, and maybe a calendar or some Christmas or other cards, or photographs. Prisoners are allowed to have a reasonable number of such things in their cells, so long as they do not paste or pin them on the walls.

The last fixed object is a corner shelf on the window side, on which will be found the prisoner's devotional and library books, and when one looks behind the books usually a jackdaw cache of miscellaneous objects for which there is no other obvious place. On the floor is a strip of coconut matting, and the brushes and cloths supplied for cleaning; also, if the prisoner has a 'cell-task', which is invariably the sewing or patching of mail-bags, a heap of canvas and the necessary implements.

All these articles must, before the occupant of the cell goes out to work in the morning, be laid out for inspection according to the regulation pattern of the prison, the cell having first been cleaned out. From dinner-time onwards, there is a rather more homely appearance. And while 'homely' may not seem to be the *mot juste* for a prison cell, it is remarkable how this impersonal collection of unattractive barrack utilities can reflect the personality of its incumbent. Of the short-sentence ins-and-outs of local prisons one does not expect more than a cell tidy enough to escape notice; they have neither the time nor the interest. But there will usually be the cell of some favourite 'old lag' which the Chief Officer will point out with amused admiration—a dazzle of 'spit and polish' set out with mathematical precision. At the other extreme one recognises the student, his books double-banked on the shelf and note-books and technical journals piled on the table. Indeed there are few cells, used for any length of time by the same person, man or woman, which will not to a few moments' observation give back some human reflections—in one the shelf is made a little shrine of photographs of husband or wife and children, in another no photographs at all, but a collection of old Christmas cards set out with careful art; in this cell are some reproductions of good pictures cut from magazines and ingeniously backed and framed, in that a riot of 'pin-up girls'.

The complicated and colourful miracles wrought by long-term women in their cells we shall see when we reach them, and arrangements have recently been completed for extending the use of personal possessions in cells to all long-term prisoners at a certain stage of their sentence.

Outside the cell door a small wooden frame of cards contains information for the staff about the occupant. On one appears the name and register number, sentence and classification: this card varies in colour according to religious denomination, so that Chaplains and Ministers may pick out members of their flock at a glance. Here, too, are kept notes of the party the prisoner is allotted to for work, the tools he should have in his cell, any special diet he is allowed, and other such matters.

PART THREE

THE TRAINING AND TREATMENT
OF ADULTS

CHAPTER EIGHT

THE PRISON POPULATION

(1) COMPOSITION

WHILE it is well to start this chapter by remembering, from Chapter 1, that the majority of those who come to prison are not criminals and the majority of criminals do not come to prison, it is also necessary to qualify this statement by adding that in recent years the first part of it has very nearly ceased to be true. At p. 195 of *The Modern English Prison* it is stated, in respect of 1931, that 'only about one-quarter of the persons received into prison are convicted of crime in the ordinary sense, i.e. of indictable offences': in 1949 those persons numbered almost one-half.

It is also desirable to explain at the outset that in considering numbers reference will be made both to 'receptions' and to 'daily average population'. But x receptions in a year does not mean that x separate individuals have been received: many persons are 'received' more than once in a year, and a special record kept in 1927 showed that in that year 35,964 individuals accounted for 43,674 receptions. There is no fixed ratio between the number of receptions and the daily average population,[1] which reflects not only the volume of receptions but the average length of sentences: thus x receptions for an average of three months would give a d.a.p. only half as large as x receptions for an average of six months.

Analysis of the receptions—The receptions for the year 1949, as shown in the Annual Report for 1950, are analysed in Table A at the end of this chapter.

In this table, omitting those sentenced by Courts-Martial and those sent to Borstal, it is only those persons in categories 4 (ii), 5 and 6 who had been convicted of crimes, except that of those committed in default of fines 1·7 of the men and 1·1 of the women had been fined for indictable offences. Thus some 45 per cent of the men and some 35 per cent of the women were convicted of indictable offences, a striking

[1] Hereafter referred to as 'd.a.p.'

111

increase since 1938, when the comparable figures were 28·8 per cent and 21·5 per cent.

A second point of general interest is that 20·3 per cent of the men and 13·3 per cent of the women had been committed for non-payment of sums of money, whether debts or fines. This represents the present extent of what has been called the coercive function of the prison, in that its purpose is to persuade these people to pay, and if they pay they can go. There has been a remarkable contraction of this function since the years before the late war: for 1931 the comparable figures were 41·3 for men and 41·7 for women, and for 1938 they were 32·0 and 34·8. This drop has been equally marked for both debts and fines, but the debtors—or civil prisoners as they are now called—form a trifling proportion of the prison population and their problems will be considered in a later chapter. For our present purpose interest centres on the important question of committal for non-payment of fines, which through the present century has had considerable effect on the numbers of persons coming to prison.

Imprisonment in default of fines—Reference has already been made (p. 81) to the effects of the Criminal Justice Act 1914 and the Money Payments Act 1935 on the abatement of imprisonment in default: this is shown in detail in the following table from the Annual Report for 1950.

Imprisonments in Default of Payment of Fines

Quinquennial Averages or Calendar Years

	Total Imprisonments in default
1909–13 [1]	83,187
1926–30	13,433
1931–35	11,214
1936 [2]	7,022
1937–41	6,054
1942–46	3,488
1947	2,952
1948	4,059
1949	4,329

[1] The Criminal Justice Administration Act, 1914 required time to be given for the payment of fines.

[2] The Money Payments (Justices Procedure) Act, 1935, came into force in 1936.

It may be that this process has now been taken almost as far as it can go, for in the absence of an effective alternative sanction imprisonment must remain. In 1938 the numbers committed in default were 7,936, only 1·25 per cent of the total number of fines imposed, as compared with 75,152 or 14·9 per cent in 1913. But in spite of this great reduction only 2,469 or 31 per cent of the persons actually committed in default in 1938 had been allowed time to pay, and in 1949 the percentage was still lower, being only 29·9 per cent of the 4,329 committals.

Length of sentences—The statistics of length of sentences shown in Table B affect not only the size of the prison population but its distribution and the nature of the training which can be given to it. The d.a.p. of the prisons may be more affected by the average length of sentence of the prisoners received than by their numbers. Thus in their Annual Report for 1948 the Commissioners said:

'From the following table it will be observed that notwithstanding the increase in 1940 of the amount of remission to be earned, an increase in receptions between 1938 and 1947 of only 8 per cent produced an increase in the daily average population of over 54 per cent.

Convicted Men

	1938	1945	1946	1947
Receptions .	28,815	28,887	28,331	31,116
Daily Average population .	9,330	11,899	13,221	14,448

But an increase in the average length of sentence may be due either to a disposition on the part of the Courts to pass longer sentences in certain conditions, or to an increase in the proportion of more serious offences: thus, in commenting on the foregoing figures, the Commissioners said:

'Broadly, this position was due to the proportion of receptions on conviction for indictable offences, carrying longer sentences, being much higher in the post-war years than in 1938.

In 1938 the percentages were:
Non-indictable 51·3 per cent. Indictable 48·7 per cent.

In 1947 they were:
Non-indictable 23·4 per cent. Indictable 76·6 per cent.'

The distribution of the population is affected since long-term prisoners (over 3 years) are detained in central prisons, and increases in the numbers of long sentences will increase the pressure on the limited number of prisons suitable for this purpose: thus in 1948 prisoners of this category, owing to the increase in their numbers, had to wait over a year in local prisons before there was room for them in central prisons.[1]

Training is affected from two angles. Regional training prisons take only prisoners with sentences of 12 months or over, and their populations will therefore depend on the numbers of prisoners otherwise suitable for training who are received with such sentences. In local prisons the training that can be given will affect only those who are

[1] Annual Report 1948, p. 24.

there long enough to profit by it. Of the many misuses and abuses of imprisonment as a system, none has been more unsparingly condemned, at home and abroad, by penologists, prison administrators and informed opinion in general, than the short sentence—which for this purpose may be taken to mean one of under 6 months. It may be that for certain first offenders who stand in no need of constructive training but for whom the courts find no alternative to imprisonment a sentence of less than 6 months may serve some positive purpose; it is certain that for those already inured to prison the effect is purely negative. Unfortunately, as will be seen from Table B, the position in this respect in this country, though better than it once was, is still far from satisfactory. In 1949, 9·9 per cent of the receptions of men and 18·6 per cent of women sentenced to imprisonment were for periods of not more than 14 days; 51·3 per cent of men and 69·3 per cent of women were for not more than 3 months; and 70·2 per cent of men and 86·8 of women were for not more than 6 months. These men and women for the most part represent a dreary stage army of 'ins-and-outs' to whom these periodic visits to prison are no more than an accepted if unwelcome risk of the trade: they clog the efficiency of the prison system, add greatly to its cost, and distract it most wastefully from its proper function, which is the protection of society against crime: in the 14 day and under cases, they reduce the prison to the status of a cleansing centre.

At the other end of the scale it is notable that the English courts do not favour the very long sentence. In 1949 sentences of 5 years and upwards for men numbered only 286 or 1·0 per cent of the total receptions, a trifling increase over 1913 in spite of the grave increase in serious crime which might well have led to a period of very heavy sentences. This disposition is welcome to the prison administration, since one of their major problems is to counteract the mental and physical deterioration which for most men and women may be the result of many years in prison.

To conclude this section, it is to be noted that the large numbers received for short periods, although each of them causes as much work on reception and discharge as if he were in for life, do not, because of their rapid turn-over, bulk large in the d.a.p.: figures given in the Annual Report for 1950 show that the d.a.p. for 1949, if divided according to length of sentences, fell into the following groups:

	Men	Women
Under 1 month	318	36
1 month and less than 3 months .	650	81
3 months and less than 6 months .	1,087	96
6 months and less than 12 months .	2,094	124
12 months and less than 18 months .	2,261	109
18 months and less than 3 years .	2,977	122
3 years and over	4,001	113
	13,388	681

(2) CHARACTERISTICS

The following section, which could be the most interesting part of this book, may well prove to be the least. To describe what manner of men and women prisoners are, why they have been led to do whatever has brought them to prison, how they behave in prison and what effect imprisonment has on their behaviour, would be the work not of one section of a book but of many books from many hands—criminologists, social research workers, psychologists, those who have lived with prisoners whether as officers of a prison or as prisoners themselves, and others with experience and qualifications which the present writer cannot claim.

Sir Norwood East, whose published work throws on these questions as much light as the life-work of a medical psychiatrist among prisoners can hope to throw, quotes [1] Sir A. Maxwell, in an address to the Cambridge University Medical Society, as follows:

'That persons found guilty of criminal offences are, for the most part, ordinary folk, seldom showing abnormal characteristics, is one of the first things noted by everyone who is brought into contact with a considerable number of offenders. In a prison one prisoner differs from another as one clerk or one labourer differs from another, but between a hundred prisoners and a hundred persons chosen at random from the street outside the resemblances are more noticeable than the differences. In each group there will be found a similar mixture of good and bad qualities, strains of kindness and streaks of selfishness, companionable fellows and self-centred people, masterful personalities and weaker characters, a few who are specially intelligent and a few who are noticeably dull. In each group there will be some accustomed to comfortable circumstances and many who are poor. Perhaps among the prisoners the proportion of noticeably egotistic and noticeably shiftless characters will be higher than in the other group, but otherwise the ordinary observer will find it hard to discover differences between the two groups.''

As a broad statement of the human truth about prisoners this must stand. Nevertheless the writer must add the strong personal impression that when he enters a workshop in one of the large London prisons with its thousand or more hardened recidivists, and feels the furtive glances flicking above rows of canvas-draped knees, he has a quick and painful impression that here are 'the right men in the right place'. Looking at a shop in a 'star' prison or one of the training prisons, the question that starts to his mind is 'why are these men here?' Is it that the recidivist prison stamps its own character on its prisoners, or is it . . .? But these are speculations which could fill another book: here

---

[1] *Society and the Criminal*, pp. 167, 168.

we must be content with such thin and uncertain light as may come from the published statistics.

Nature of Offences—Table C gives in respect of 1913, 1938 and 1949 a summary of the principal types of offence for which convicted prisoners were received into prison. It is interesting as showing again in statistical form that protection against crime means in practice protection against dishonesty and personal violence, and also how the various types of offence have fluctuated through the years: in relation to the treatment of offenders in prison its interest is limited—what matters there is not the nature of the offence but the nature of the offender, what he is and what he is capable of becoming. In the individual study of a prisoner the facts of the offence may or may not be of interest: in the arrangements for the classification and training of prisoners in general they are of no account, except in relation to selection for open establishments: even the special consideration given to homosexuals is not necessarily connected with their offences, since they may well have been convicted of some other offence.

Classes of prisoner—In accordance with the provisions of Statutory Rule 9, 'in order so far as possible to prevent contamination and facilitate training', prisoners are divided into three classes, as follows:

Prisoners under 21 years of age shall be placed in the Young Prisoners' Class.

Prisoners of 21 years of age and over who have not previously been in prison on conviction shall be placed in the Star Class unless the reception board considers that, in view of their record or character, they are likely to have a bad influence on others. The reception board may also place in the Star Class a prisoner of 21 years of age and over who has previously been in prison on conviction if they are satisfied, having regard to the nature of the previous offence, or to the length of time since it was committed, or to the prisoner's general record and character, that he is not likely to have a bad influence on others.

Other prisoners shall be placed in the Ordinary Class.

The d.a.p. of persons sentenced to imprisonment was in 1949 divided among these statutory classes as follows: [1]

	Men	Women
Young Prisoners	486	25
Star Class, serving less than 3 years . .	3,483	188
Ordinary Class, serving less than 3 years .	5,418	355
All classes serving 3 years or over . .	4,001	113
	13,388	681

[1] The figures are given in this form in the Annual Report for 1950 because they had not in previous years included sentences of penal servitude (3 years and over), and the change could not be made in respect of 1949.

The arrangements for classification will be discussed in the following chapter, together with the relation between classification and training: here we are concerned only with the make-up of the classes. The first thing to be said about the foregoing table is that compared with the years between the wars the proportion in the Star class is very much higher: exact figures cannot be quoted, first because the system of classification before the war was rather different, second because a Star cannot be mathematically defined and practice as to the making of Stars may vary with the views of individual Governors as well as on long term tendencies. Arising out of that is a further point, that these figures do not indicate how many of those classed as Stars were in prison for the first time, or of those who were in for the first time, how many had previous proved offences. These considerations raise interesting questions concerning the movement of crime and the effect of imprisonment on crime, which will be studied in a later chapter: here we are only concerned to establish that the prison population of today contains a very much higher proportion of the Star class than has been the case previously, with the effect that positive training takes a much greater part and the need for accommodation in training prisons becomes more pressing.

Sex and age—Table D shows the grouping by sex and age of each main class of the convicted prisoners received in 1949, with a percentage comparison with 1913 and 1938. The striking factors are the growing predominance of the 21–30 age-group among the men, and the uprush of both the younger age-groups of women in 1949. The annual reports of prison governors in the post-war years constantly reflected their almost despairing amazement at the character of the young men between 21 and 30 who were coming to prison in such great numbers, convicted usually of serious offences—insolent, a-moral, unco-operative, and unashamed. The salvage of this war-corroded generation from lives of habitual crime is a terrible responsibility for the prison system of our day. The even more discouraging problems of young people under 21 are reflected less in the prisons than elsewhere, and will be discussed as a whole in Part V.

Occupations—Table E summarises the occupations of convicted prisoners, according to their own statements, as given in the Annual Report for 1946, since when it has not been published. Its main interest is perhaps in comparison with pre-war years, e.g. in 1938 'Vagrants, etc.' numbered 2,843 as compared with 113 in 1945, 'Labourers, etc.' had fallen from nearly 15,000 to nearly 11,000. 'Skilled work-people, had gone up by some 1,500, and 'Armed Forces' had gone up from 487 to 4,546, though of course this last figure is meaningless since like is not compared with like—the Forces of 1913 were not those of 1945. If any deduction could be ventured from these figures, it might be that they tend to support the view of experienced prison officials that too much and too easy money is as likely to lead to crime as too little.

(3) SIZE AND DISTRIBUTION

Size—In the years following the Second World War the English prison system was dominated by the problem of over-crowding. In the immediate pre-war years the d.a.p. had been of the order of 10–11,000, and the war did not bring a fall as did the First World War, when a 'record low' of about 9,000 was reached. Instead, it mounted steadily to 12,915 in 1944, then rapidly to 17,067 in 1947, and in 1948 reached 19,765, at or about which level it remained in 1949. During 1950 it moved up again to 20,462. In October 1951 the number was 22,500.[1] A population of this order, doubling the pre-war average, had not been known since the bad first decade of the century.

To see this position in its proper perspective, it should be placed against its historical background, and to this end Graph A (p. 127) shows, from the early years of the Prison Commission to the present time, the fluctuations in the numbers of both receptions and d.a.p.

Since the subject of this book is not crime but the treatment of prisoners, no attempt will be made to draw such inferences from this graph as to the movement of crime or the practice of the courts as it might appear to reflect. Two general observations may however be made which appear to be both relevant and safe.

First, the reason for the very striking divergence of the curves in the post-Second War years is the great increase during those years of serious crime, resulting in a high proportion of long sentences, as has been explained on p. 113. Second, as the converse of this, the enormous reduction of committals for minor offences which followed the First World War has progressively continued: the receptions on conviction of 'other non-indictable offences', which in 1913 numbered over 70,000 men and nearly 28,000 women, had by 1938 fallen to 10,819 men and 2,009 women, and in 1949 to 5,088 men and 854 women. The broad effect of these movements is to concentrate the prison increasingly on its central task of training criminal prisoners.

Distribution—The following table shows how the d.a.p. for 1949 was distributed among the different categories of prisoners:

Category	Men	Women
Untried Prisoners . . .	1,153	94
Civil Prisoners . . .	467	1
Imprisonment . . .	13,388	681
Corrective Training . .	390	18
Preventive Detention . .	123	7
Borstal Training . . .	3,088	275
Other Convicted Prisoners .	174	20
Total d.a.p.	18,783	1,096

[1] This was the highest figure recorded since the records began in 1878.

It is unfortunate that the latest available annual statistics should be those for a year for only a part of which was the Criminal Justice Act in force, since after April 1949 the categories of prisoners were altered following the abolition of penal servitude and the introduction of corrective training and preventive detention in its new form. The situation at the end of 1950 is however shown, on a slightly different basis, by the following summary of the weekly population return for the week ended December 26th:

Categories	Men	Women
Local prisoners . . .	11,600	730
Imprisonment over 3 years .	2,391	49
Corrective training . .	2,077	88
Preventive detention . .	497	17
Borstal training . . .	2,895	235

Attention may be drawn to certain aspects of these figures. Firstly the very small proportion of women, which makes many difficulties in providing the most suitable' arrangements for their classification, accommodation and training: during 1949, for example, the number of girls under 21 in custody averaged only about 25 over the whole country! Second, the significant change in the numbers serving sentences of preventive detention, after less than two years' experience of the provisions of 1948: out of some 500 [1] cases, only about 30 were serving sentences passed under the Act of 1908.

It is of interest, in conclusion, to note that in 1949 the d.a.p. of men and women in our prisons and Borstals represented 117 for each 100,000 of the male population of England and Wales, and 6·2 for each 100,000 of the female population (the populations in both cases being of persons of 16 years of age or over).

[1] In October 1951 this number was approaching 700.

TABLE A

Analysis of receptions in the year 1949

	Men		Women	
	Numbers	Percentage	Numbers	Percentage
1. Committals on remand or for trial, not followed by return to prison on conviction	8,510	19·4	1,668	36·3
2. Committals by civil process	5,176	11·8	32	0·7
3. Committals in default of paying fines . . .	3,749	8·5	580	12·6
4. Imprisonment:				
(i) For non-indictable offences . . .	5,183	11·8	590	12·8
(ii) For indictable offences	17,509	40·0	1,485	32·3
(iii) By Courts-Martial .	371	0·8	—	—
5. Sentences of corrective training. . . .	1,106	2·5	54	1·2
6. Sentences of preventive detention . . .	268	0·6	11	0·2
7. Sentences of Borstal training	1,812	4·1	115	2·5
8. Other convicted prisoners*	208	0·5	66	1·4
Total Receptions	43,892	100·0	4,601	100·0

* E.g. Capital and H.M. Pleasure cases, committals under the Mental Deficiency Act, 1913 to 1927, committals to Approved Schools, etc.

TABLE B

Lengths of Sentences of Receptions in 1949

	1913		1938		1949	
	Receptions on conviction with sentences of Imprisonment or Penal Servitude	Percentage of total receptions on conviction with sentences of Imprisonment or Penal Servitude	Receptions on conviction with sentences of Imprisonment or Penal Servitude	Percentage of total receptions on conviction with sentences of Imprisonment or Penal Servitude	Receptions on conviction with sentences of Imprisonment or Penal Servitude	Percentage of total receptions on conviction with sentences of Imprisonment or Penal Servitude
MEN						
Not exceeding 1 month .	81,986	78·2	13,865	51·0	6,868	26·0
Over 1 month and not more than 3 months .	13,932	13·3	6,518	23·9	6,686	25·3
Over 3 months and not more than 6 months .	4,204	4·0	3,634	13·4	4,981	18·9
Over 6 months and not more than 12 months.	2,651	2·5	1,770	6·5	3,881	14·7
Over 12 months and not more than 18 months.	993	0·9	659	2·4	1,719	6·5
Over 18 months and not more than 2 years .	304	0·3	284	1·0	1,038	3·9
Over 2 years and less than 3 years . .	2	—	—	—	25	0·1
3 years . . .	492	0·5	288	1·1	718	2·7
Over 3 years and not more than 4 years .	76	0·1	72	0·3	237	0·9
Over 4 years and not more than 5 years .	155	0·2	88	0·3	214[1]	0·8
Over 5 years and not more than 7 years .	32	—	17	0·1	63	0·2
Over 7 years and not more than 10 years .	10	—	8	—	8	—
Over 10 years and not more than 14 years .	5	—	5	—	3	—
Over 14 years . .	4	—	—	—	—	—
Life sentences . .	8	—	—	—	—	—
Death sentences[2] commuted to penal servitude-imprisonment for life	8	—	11	—	11	—

[1] Includes 212 sentences of 5 years
[2] Disregarded in calculating the percentages in this table.

TABLE B—*continued*

Lengths of Sentences of Receptions in 1949

	1913		1938		1949	
	Receptions on conviction with sentences of Imprisonment or Penal Servitude	Percentage of total receptions on conviction with sentences of Imprisonment or Penal Servitude	Receptions on conviction with sentences of Imprisonment or Penal Servitude	Percentage of total receptions on conviction with sentences of Imprisonment or Penal Servitude	Receptions on conviction with sentences of Imprisonment or Penal Servitude	Percentage of total receptions on conviction with sentences of Imprisonment or Penal Servitude
WOMEN						
Not exceeding 1 month .	29,334	87·7	2,430	70·7	1,107	41·7
Over 1 month and not more than 3 months .	2,930	8·8	525	15·3	732	27·6
Over 3 months and not more than 6 months .	866	2·6	313	9·1	466	17·5
Over 6 months and not more than 12 months.	222	0·7	111	3·2	196	7·4
Over 12 months and not more than 18 months.	40	0·1	35	1·0	78	3·0
Over 18 months and not more than 2 years .	4	—	9	0·3	31	1·2
Over 2 years and less than 3 years . .	—	—	—	—	—	—
3 years . . .	30	0·1	11	0·3	32	1·2
Over 3 years and not more than 4 years .	2	—	3	0·1	3	0·1
Over 4 years and not more than 5 years .	7	—	1	0·0	7[1]	0·3
Over 5 years and not more than 7 years .	2	—	—	—	3	—
Over 7 years and not more than 10 years .	—	—	—	—	—	—
Over 10 years and not more than 14 years .	—	—	—	—	—	—
Over 14 years . .	—	—	—	—	—	—
Life Sentences . .	4	—	—	—	—	—
Death sentences [2] commuted to penal servitude-imprisonment for life	4	—	3	—	3	—

[1] All sentences of 5 years.
[2] Disregarded in calculating the percentages in this table.

TABLE C

Analysis of the offences of receptions in the year 1949

	1913	1938	1949
MEN			
Indictable Offences.			
Violence against the person . . .	514	529	923
Sexual offences (including bigamy) . .	1,064	839	1,361
Burglary, housebreaking, etc. . .	1,956	2,498	5,610
Other offences against property . .	16,806	9,649	12,863
Forgery and coining	115	152	241
Other offences	543	330	631
Totals	20,998	13,997	21,629
Non-Indictable Offences.			
(i) Offences akin to indictable offences:			
Assaults	7,486	1,691	1,058
Frequenting, etc.	1,770	701	695
Malicious damage	1,650	536	455
Indecent exposure	866	449	347
Cruelty to children	1,028	181	172
Other offences	1,558	329	391
Totals	14,358	3,887	3,118
(ii) Other Offences:			
Drunkenness	37,033	5,078	2,167
Offences against the Poor Law . .	4,343	1,004	—
Begging and Sleeping-out . . .	14,822	1,300	510
Breach of Police Regulations . . .	5,897	391	131
Offences in relation to Railways . .	866	194	162
Other offences	7,193	2,852	2,118
Totals	70,154	10,819	5,088
Grand Totals	105,510	28,703	29,835

TABLE C—*continued*

Analysis of the offences of receptions in the year 1949

	1913	1938	1949
WOMEN			
Indictable Offences.			
Violence against the person . . .	114	82	59
Offences against property . . .	2,593	921	1,648
Bigamy	10	22	13
Other offences	154	123	43
Totals	2,871	1,148	1,763
Non-Indictable Offences.			
(1) Offences akin to indictable offences:			
Assaults	1,136	71	26
Cruelty to children	731	120	168
Indecent exposure	242	81	26
Malicious damage	392	43	21
Brothel-keeping, etc.	419	32	39
Other offences	134	18	4
Totals	3,054	365	284
(ii) Other Offences:			
Drunkenness	15,116	1,543	407
Disorderly behaviour of prostitutes. .	8,063	172	92
Breach of Police Regulations . . .	2,730	92	32
Begging and Sleeping-out . . .	1,049	41	33
Other offences	850	161	290
Totals	27,808	2,009	854
Grand Totals	33,733	3,522	2,901

TABLE D

Grouping by sex and age of receptions on conviction in the year 1949

Offences	1 Totals of convicted prisoners			2 Under 21		3 21 and under 30		4 30 and under 40		5 40 and under 50		6 50 and under 60		7 60 and above	
	Totals	M	W	M	W	M	W	M	W	M	W	M	W	M	W
Indictable . . .	23,392	21,629	1,763	2,661	177	9,125	579	5,138	462	3,004	304	1,201	166	500	75
Non-indictable: (i) akin to Indictable .	3,402	3,118	284	126	14	1,404	116	766	91	490	43	220	14	112	6
(ii) other offences .	5,942	5,088	854	244	48	1,441	244	1,187	189	1,096	130	720	92	400	151
Total	32,736	29,835	2,901	3,031	239	11,970	939	7,091	742	4,590	477	2,141	272	1,012	232
Percentages 1949 .	—	—	—	10·2	8·2	40·1	32·4	23·7	25·6	15·4	16·5	7·2	9·3	3·4	8·0
,, 1931 . .	—	—	—	8·5	3·3	30·6	16·1	26·0	27·0	18·0	29·0	9·6	15·8	7·3	8·8
,, 1913 . .	—	—	—	6·1	2·6	24·8	18·4	29·0	34·2	21·3	29·1	10·0	11·3	8·8	4·4

TABLE E

Occupations of receptions on conviction in the year 1945

(1)	(2)	Offences		
Occupations	Total Number of Convicted Prisoners	(3) Indictable Offences	(4) Non-Indictable Offences (akin to Indictable Offences)	(5) Other Non-Indictable Offences
Vagrants and prostitutes and others of known bad character	113	56	13	44
Labourers, charwomen, and other unskilled workpeople .	10,955	7,166	1,278	2,511
Domestic servants . . .	870	465	157	248
Miners, farm hands, factory operatives, merchant seamen, and other skilled workpeople.	10,963	7,555	959	2,449
Members of the Army, Navy or Air Force	4,546	3,879	380	287
Shop assistants, clerks, waiters, etc.	1,169	867	85	217
Shopkeepers, tradesmen, farmers, etc.	323	263	19	41
Professional employments, merchants, and persons of independent means, etc. . .	176	117	19	40
Unclassified	2,775	1,377	543	855
Total	31,890	21,745	3,453	6,692

Graph A—Fluctuations in receptions and daily average.
Population 1880–1950

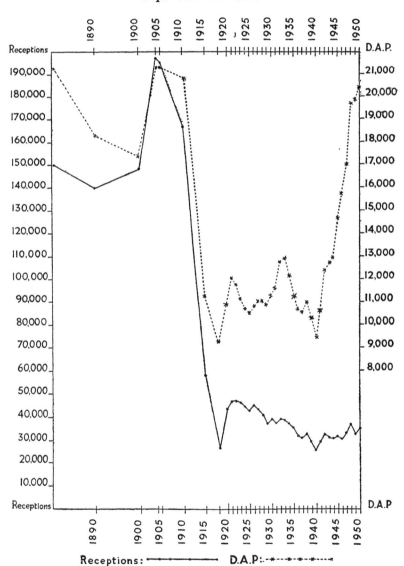

Receptions: ————— D.A.P.: -*-*-*-*-*-*-*

CHAPTER NINE

CLASSIFICATION AND TRAINING

(1) PRINCIPLES AND THEIR APPLICATION

'THE purposes of training and treatment of convicted prisoners shall be to establish in them the will to lead a good and useful life on discharge, and to fit them to do so.'

Having dealt with the historical and penological considerations which have led to the establishment of the central purpose of the prison system in the terms of the foregoing Rule, with the organisation created to effect that purpose, the buildings within which it must be effected, and the numbers and types of offender with whom it is concerned, we now turn to the practical working of the system as it is organised under the Criminal Justice Act and the Prison Rules 1949. In this chapter we shall consider the broader outlines and general framework of the system, and in this section the principles on which it is based and the difficulties, inherent or contingent, which condition the translation of those principles into practice.

The prison system of 1950 is in principle and in method the natural growth of the seminal ideas of the years between the wars, as set out in the third section of Chapter Four. Its basic ideas have been summarised as follows:

'First, that for all suitable prisoners with sentences of suitable length, the prison régime should be one of constructive training, moral, mental and vocational; second, that such training can be fully carried out only in homogeneous establishments set aside for the purpose, though the principle should apply, so far as practicable in the limitations of an ordinary prison, to all prisoners in all prisons; third, that the special training prisons need not, for all prisoners, provide the security of normal prison buildings, since men can only acquire a sense of responsibility by exercising it, and experience has shown that a high proportion of prisoners can be trusted to exercise it in open conditions; fourth, that the outside community should be brought into the training at every practicable point, so as to break down the tradition that the prisoner is cut off from society; and fifth, that this continuing responsibility of society should be maintained after his discharge by effective aid towards social rehabilitation.' [1]

Before developing the application of these ideas, let us consider the difficulties which condition that application.

The first we have already discussed: it lies in the inherent contradiction between punishment and rehabilitation, and the inherent doubt whether the prison can become an effective instrument for reconciling these two purposes. The duty of the administration is to do its best, but it does not operate *in vacuo*: it must deal with the human material it receives, and the selection of that material is itself conditioned by these doubts and contradictions. The people who come to prison must be somehow fitted into the general pattern, whether from the point of view of fitting in they be well selected or ill, either as persons or in the length of time they are to be kept there.

And here one inevitable feature of prison life must be mentioned: writing in 1931 of the general standards of a prison system the present writer said:

'And these standards, at whatever level fixed, must be applied rigidly and impartially to all alike. Inflexibility and impartiality are of the essence of a prison system: a prison cannot make the punishment fit either the crime or the criminal. The sentence is meted out by the Court according to an established scale of time-lengths, which may be some measure of the offence but can be no measure of the effect upon the offender. Once in prison each has for his appointed term to tread the same road, at the same step, and in the same standard shoe—some it may pinch in one place, some in another; some it may fit pretty well, others it may painfully crush; many are already hardened to it, but of the others few will escape without bruises and callosities.

'Yet the contrast between the standardisation of the punishment and the variety of the offender grows progressively greater. In the last hundred years the increasing complexity of society has brought with it a proportionately complex increase in the number of offences against society, and in the kinds of people who are convicted of such offences. The prison population today shows a vertical section through society from peer to vagrant: and to all these people their punishment must mean something quite different according to the differences in temperament, mental and moral calibre, education and previous social circumstances and training.' [2]

Neither the changes of time nor maturity of reflection have led him to wish to modify this as a broad generalisation, though he might now

---

[1] *Prisons and Borstals*, p. 11.   [2] *The Modern English Prison*, p. 33.

qualify it by adding that there are two or three standard shoes made on different lasts, and 'American fittings' may be available.

Again, though the English administration is fortunate in its comparative freedom to experiment and develop, it must still do its work within the climate of opinion of its time, with a constant regard to the effect on the value of that work of public and parliamentary criticism; and that opinion again reflects the contradictions inherent in the question. That it is greatly changed from the times of Sir Evelyn Ruggles-Brise is sufficiently shown by the fact that the publication of the Rule which heads this chapter should have passed without comment: undoubtedly there is today a much wider circle of opinion which is well informed on the realities of penal administration. This may be due to several causes. One of these is the belated development in certain of our Universities of an interest in penology and criminology as valuable spheres of knowledge: it is a curious fact, that in spite of the great English contribution to international thought on these matters in the eighteenth and early nineteenth centuries—witness only Blackstone, Howard, Bentham and Maconochie—there has been until recently almost no modern English penology. Even the valuable work now being done here is for the most part that of eminent penologists from abroad who have honoured us by preferring to work in our Universities. But to balance our deficiency in the professional academic field we have lately had, as one fruit of the policy of enlisting the community in the service of the prison system, the published work of such practical amateurs as Mrs. le Mesurier, Sir Leo Page and Mr. John Watson, who have learned about prisons and prisoners by working in and with them. Fuller access for the Press to prisons and Borstals, with freedom of comment within the limits of accurate presentation, has also paid occasional dividends in the form of a more balanced and understanding treatment of matters of news interest as they arise, and of a willingness to give space to informed accounts of what is being done and why. It remains necessary, nevertheless, to distinguish between informed and uninformed Press comment on what happens in prisons.

But when all is said and done, responsible publications on penal matters affect the minds of a minimal number of the public. One cannot be unaware that what Mr. G. M. Young has called the 'body of assumptions underlying the common talk of common people, and directing their praise and blame' [1] are not, in these matters, the assumptions on which contemporary prison administration is based. As to whatever he may understand by the phrase 'prison reform', the man-in-the-street is at best apathetic, commonly cynical, and at worst frankly hostile. And while it must be for an administration to lead, it cannot afford to get out of touch with the common sense of the community as a whole. Its position in relation to public criticism tends therefore to

[1] In *The Sunday Times*, October 16th 1949.

resemble that of the Romans who happened to be in the middle of the bridge when 'those behind cried forward, and those in front cried back'. In such a position, they may do well to remember the words of a former Home Secretary:

'The harm done by crime is caused by a few members of the community; but for the harm done by wrong methods of punishment the whole community is answerable. The responsibility for our penal laws and for the operations of our criminal courts rests on us all, and if society continues to tolerate unenlightened methods of dealing with offenders when better methods are known and are practicable, all members of society are guilty of sinning against the light.' [1]

Where the administration thinks it knows the better way it has no option but to follow it if it may: but this duty makes it all the more necessary to examine and answer all objections which may be felt by the majority of the community in whose name it acts and to whom it is finally responsible. It is therefore important to consider what are the main 'assumptions underlying the common talk of common people' in these matters: to dogmatise on this would be unwise, but the opinion may be ventured that there are perhaps three. The first has already been adumbrated in Chapter 2, p. 19, in the reference to legal punishment being in origin a substitute for private vengeance: the second was put by Professor Bruno Salmiala when he spoke [2] of its being 'an almost intuitive conception, sprung from a people's age-old experience' that justice requires suffering as an element of punishment: the third, though related to the second, is really distinct. It is that repugnance to what is believed to be a policy of 'pampering prisoners' which has been very fully explored by Dr. Mannheim as a translation into this sphere of the 'principle of less eligibility' of the old Poor Law.

The place of the first two of these popular assumptions in the theory of punishment on which the contemporary prison system is based has been discussed in principle in Part I: it may however be well at this point to elaborate a little the facts behind the official assumption that a prisoner is 'sent to prison as a punishment, not for punishment'—that is, that so far as suffering is a necessary element of punishment it is inherent in the fact of imprisonment, and that it is no part of the duty of the prison authorities to devise a régime intended to add to it.

The essence of imprisonment is deprivation of personal liberty: when Dame Ethyl Smyth, after imprisonment in Holloway as a suffragette, was asked what for her was the worst part of the experience, she replied shortly but sufficiently, 'Couldn't get out.' Nor is it only freedom to

[1] Mr. Herbert Morrison, speaking in Birmingham on 28th March 1944.
[2] Annual Meeting of 1948 of the Northern Association of Criminalists, in the discussion of The Purpose of Punishment, *Yearbook of the Northern Association of Criminalists*, 1947–48.

come and go that is cut off, it is freedom to do as you like at almost every point of personal life. 'The whole existence of great masses of the population receives its vital stimulus mainly from that small margin of personal freedom that still remains to them after their daily work is done'; [1] but the person sentenced to forfeiture of freedom by imprisonment is 'placed under the control of custodians whose powers of supervision and coercion are such that if (he is) recalcitrant (he) can be forced to comply with the rules. . . . They control his time, his food, his clothing and all the details of his life. He lives within a framework of supervision and control, whether he is in a prison cell or working on an outlying farm. The control is not dependent on walls or bolts and bars: it is constituted by the legal powers of his custodians. Those powers are unaffected by such changes as the institution of 'open prisons' or arrangements for the offender to work at a distance from the prison or Borstal establishment. The essence of his punishment is that he is in subjection to his custodians and can do only what they allow or direct. The right of citizens to freedom from restraint is a precious right, and the loss of that right is a severe deprivation. If anyone is illegally held in captivity by some other person or persons, he suffers a grave injury, for which the courts will award him heavy damages, however considerately he may have been treated by his captors. When an offender is held in legal custody, he suffers a grave punishment, however free from punitive conditions his treatment may be.' [2]

There are other conditions of confinement which may cause more or less suffering according to the circumstances and temperament of the individual. Save for infrequent letters, and even less frequent visits in what for most are distressing circumstances, the prisoner is wholly cut off from his family, friends and all familiar life, with perhaps the added suffering of knowing that his crime has left them in want and trouble. The troubles of complete separation from the other sex in what Paterson has described as 'a monastery of men unwilling to be monks'—and these are not absent in the nunnery—must be common to imprisonment in any form. For many prisoners for many months, at any rate in present conditions, nearly every evening must be spent in silence in a locked cell. If to all this be added the nature of the company for those who do not like it—and few prisoners of any type enjoy each other's company—and the fact that this life is to be lived in physical surroundings which for many are a punishment in themselves, it may be understood that the idea that imprisonment is a punishment *per se* is not without substance.

It is of course implicit in the nature of imprisonment that as a punish-

[1] Mannheim, p. 70.
[2] 'The Institutional Treatment of Offenders', Ninth Clarke Hall Lecture, by Sir Alexander Maxwell, pp. 39, 40.

ment it does not fall equally on all subjected to it: what punishment does? It is one purpose of classification to secure so far as may be, in the broad, the 'individualisation of the punishment', which implies a certain levelling out of inherent inequalities as well as fitting the training to the needs of the individual. Not all of these conditions therefore fall equally today, for the whole of their sentences, on all classes of prisoner in every type of prison: there is more than one 'standard shoe'. But broadly they are and must be the common lot, the punishment inherent in the sentence.

Now as to the third assumption, the recurrent question of 'pampering', Dr. Mannheim has treated one aspect of it as follows. The Poor Law principle of 'less eligibility' was defined by Sidney and Beatrice Webb [1] as follows—'that the condition of the pauper should be *less eligible* than that of the lowest grade of independent labourer'. This had been re-stated by Bentham,[2] in relation to the penal system, thus— 'saving the regard due to life, health and bodily ease, the ordinary condition of a convict doomed to punishment, which few or none but individuals of the poorest class are apt to incur, ought not to be made *more eligible* than that of the poorest class of subjects in a state of innocence and liberty'. The justness of one or other of these principles is deeply ingrained in common thought about the treatment of convicted prisoners, and the second at least has not been specifically rejected by any English prison administration. But the application of the principle is beset with many problems, both theoretical and practical. Dr. Mannheim, basing his argument on the view that, in law, imprisonment is fundamentally no more than deprivation of liberty, takes account of the additions to this fundament which occur in fact, and suggests that 'it becomes the duty of the state to compensate the prisoner for this excess of evil that the execution of the penalty has inflicted upon him'; and he adds to this that 'modern treatment . . . while often implying greater leniency, may . . . lead to the imposition of long-term penalties for comparatively petty offences which would previously have been visited with much smaller sentences'.[3] He concludes that these principles (less eligibility or non-superiority) are 'incompatible with the idea of reformation . . . and equally . . . with the idea of individual treatment,' pointing out in particular that 'for all members of the better situated classes a rigid adherence to the principle of less eligibility makes their punishment much more severe than that of others'.[4]

This last point deserves a moment's elaboration. We have moved far from the situation in which Bentham could write of imprisonment as something which 'none but individuals of the poorest class are apt to incur'. Table E (p. 126) shows that the great majority of those who come to prison today are of or above the standing of 'skilled work-people',

---

[1] Cit. Mannheim, p. 56.   [3] P. 98.
[2] Cit. Mannheim, p. 57.   [4] Pp. 100, 101.

who in modern social conditions are by no means 'individuals of the poorest class'. And considering the application of this principle on the plane of purely physical standards—food, clothing, furniture and accommodation, and so on—it must be emphasised that these standards at least, at whatever level fixed, apply with complete impartiality to every prisoner alike—no methods of classification or individualisation significantly affect this.

There are also practical difficulties. Any public institution charged with the residential care of persons committed to its charge is bound for reasons of health and good order alone to require a certain level in its physical standards, and where that institution charges itself with preserving at least and enhancing if possible the self-respect of its charges, and with training them if it can in good citizenship, that level must in some respects be higher still. In the matter, for instance, of personal appearance, it might be adequate on a minimum basis to clothe its prisoners in drab, shapeless, and shaming dress, crop their heads close, and balance this with a week's stubble on the chin. This was done within the present century. But if today men and women are given clothes of normal type, wear their hair—in reason—as they like, shave every day if they are men and use their cosmetics if they are women, that is not to 'pamper' them but to avoid the evil of making their personal appearance a source of constant humiliation: not that, with the best will of all concerned, prison dress ever seems to contrive an air much above its station. As to food, again, health might be preserved by a reasonably varied diet of adequate nutritional value, but it is not with the intention to pamper that attention is also paid to the conditions in which it is served: to require that men or women eating together should have a clean table, properly set with the minimum requirements of civilised eating, and should use it properly, is the merest necessity of a system which allows of common meals, even if some visitors remark with almost shocked surprise that the effect is little different from a good works canteen.

In fact all these physical standards remain, and often by the inevitable conditions of their surroundings are bound to remain, at a level which most prisoners used to a modicum of material comfort or refinement find at the least austere; and harder words have been used by those accustomed to more than that modicum who have not appreciated the principle of less eligibility. Certainly they do not offer much of what for *l'homme moyen sensuel* might seem the smallest comforts of life. There is no beer for the thirsty, for the weary no armchair: and the troubles of a smoker suddenly reduced to one cigarette or less a day which he cannot even smoke when he likes are not small.

But even so these standards, at their minimum, will remain above those which many prisoners are able, or willing, to provide for themselves outside. Hence the traditional stories of people who so much prefer prison to the workhouse (cidevant), or regularly winter in their favourite prison. There may well be such people, though Table E (p. 126) shows that the class from which they are likely to be drawn is nowadays minimal in the prison population, and the Report of the Casual Poor Committee 1930 [1] found little factual foundation for these stories. The answer given by Edwin Chadwick, one of the Poor Law Commissioners in the days when Bentham's principle was young and strong, is valid in its degree today:

'The prisons (he wrote) were formerly distinguished for their filth and bad ventilation; but the descriptions given by Howard of the worst prisons he visited in England (which he states were among the worst he had seen in Europe) were exceeded in every wynd in Edinburgh and Glasgow inspected by Dr. Arnott and myself. More filth, worse physical suffering and moral disorder than Howard describes are to be found amongst the cellar populations of the working people of Liverpool, Manchester or Leeds and in large portions of the Metropolis.' [2]

The conclusion is well stated by Dr. Mannheim: 'The old materialistic idea that prison conditions can be considered one by one, and that each calorie of food, each cubic foot of air, enjoyed by the prisoner should be compared and contrasted with conditions outside . . . has proved fundamentally wrong. No comparison is possible between social conditions that have no common factor.' [3]

But in spite of some adverse comment in Parliament and the Press when in recent years, at a time of potato shortage, prisoners were thought to be receiving more potatoes than those 'in a state of innocence and liberty', and it became necessary to publish a calorific balance sheet, it is less to these purely physical conditions than to methods of treatment and control that the flavour of pampering seems nowadays to attach. This can be ascribed only to a failure to appreciate either the nature or the purpose or the methods of imprisonment.

In the light of the foregoing description of the nature of imprisonment, we may appreciate the truth of Sir Alexander Maxwell's conclusion 'that when an offender is confined in an institution the constriction of his life and his isolation from society have harmful effects on his mind and character, that to mitigate these harmful effects should be the aim of institutional treatment, and that methods of treatment adopted for punitive purposes aggravate the harmful effect and should be avoided. . . . How far it is practicable to make men and women better by methods of prison treatment may be arguable. That it is possible to make them worse is incontestable; and the primary object of prison reform is to mitigate the deformative effects of detention.' [4] To prevent actual deterioration, moral, mental or physical,

[1] Cit. Mannheim, p. 85. [3] P. 70.
[2] Cit. Trevelyan, p. 529. [4] Ninth Clarke Hall Lecture, pp. 25, 38.

must clearly be a primary, if negative, duty of the administration, especially for those serving long sentences, and to this end alone such small progress as has been made towards normalising the abnormal and deforming conditions of prison life would have been essential. But the positive duty enjoined in Rule 6 calls not only for this but for more than this. The traditional 'punitive' discipline and treatment was entirely negative; it was humiliating, repressive, dead and dull. It allowed the prisoner who could 'take it' to shuffle through his sentence with the minimum of mental and physical effort so long as he knew enough to appear to be keeping within the rules. It was symbolised by the 'face to the wall' order whenever a person of sufficient importance entered or passed by—a practice by which the writer has himself been humiliated while visiting a war-time military prison in this country, but not, fortunately, of it. If for 'discipline' of this type there has been substituted a method of control which is positive and constructive, this does not mean that discipline in its proper sense has been in any way relaxed: it does mean that, in the words of the relevant Rule, 'Discipline and order shall be maintained with firmness, but with no more restriction than is required for safe custody and well ordered community life', and that 'At all times the treatment of prisoners shall be such as to encourage their self-respect and a sense of personal responsibility.' Self-respect and a sense of personal responsibility are qualities that can only be acquired by exercising them: they will not come from the 'fugitive and cloistered virtue' of men and women walking in silence from cell to workshop and back again, seeking no more than to keep out of trouble. This is not to pamper: it is to substitute for what was merely repressive something more strenuous and more exacting.

Similar considerations apply to every technique which the system devises to get prisoners out of their cells for as long as possible, so as to quicken rather than deaden their moral, mental and physical responses to so much of life as a prison can offer them. The final development and test of these principles, the practical application of Paterson's dictum that 'you cannot train men for freedom in a condition of captivity', is the open prison. Although men and women placed in these conditions are still, in all the implications of the word, in captivity, at least it is a form of captivity less subject to deformative effects, more likely to turn out better men and women, than any that has yet been tried. And it is for that reason and that alone that open prisons are used. They are in no sense 'holiday camps'; save for the different buildings and the open view, the standards of material life are the same as in a closed prison; work is just as hard, probably harder, the standard of discipline just as high, probably higher.

Here the man-in-the-street, may well raise his hand and put a point that for some time has been pressing from the back of his mind.

'This,' he may say, 'may be all very well. But what about your really bad men—your recidivists, old lags, habitual criminals, or whatever you call them. Those who keep coming back for more. Is there nothing more to be done about them? This system doesn't seem either to reform them or deter them.' This is a valid point and must be answered. First, the system recognises this type, and classification sorts them out: if there is no apparent hope that training can help them, they will get very little in the fuller sense of the word—perhaps indeed too little: many men could serve many sentences in our prisons today without benefit of much that is described in these pages as training—but the system cannot do everything for the best for everybody, or not yet.

Second, it remains as true for the recidivists as for the first offenders that if you cannot make them better at least you must not make them worse: and it is a basic assumption that deliberately punitive measures will make them worse. That conclusion of the Gladstone Committee was confirmed by one who suffered the deterrent system at its sharpest in Reading Gaol in 1898. Wilde wrote in *De Profundis* that:

'prison life with its endless privations and restrictions makes one rebellious. The most terrible thing about it is not that it breaks one's heart—hearts are made to be broken—but that it turns one's heart to stone. One sometimes feels that it is only with a front of brass and a lip of scorn that one can get through the day at all. And he who is in a state of rebellion cannot receive grace . . .'

Third, a question—what is it suggested that, in actual practice, such measures should be? Work harder? But all are made to work as hard as they can. More confinement in cells? That will only deaden or embitter. Lower the physical standards of treatment? But where is this to stop, short of a bread and water diet in dungeons? The prisons cannot include an entirely different kind of system directed *in terrorem* against 'the criminal class'. Among other reasons, the 'criminal class' is too diverse: it includes many who are dangers to society in prison and out, brutal, cunning and vicious, but many also who are not so much anti-social as a-social misfits who through mental or physical deficiencies slip into crime because they cannot keep out of it. Each offender presents an individual human problem, and the administration cannot assume the responsibility of adjusting the physical severity of the punishment in accordance with some criterion of moral guilt prescribed by—whom? Not by the courts, who must be assumed to have expressed their sense of the gravity of offences in the *lengths* of the punishments they award. No, the problem is not to be solved on these lines: that way leads straight back to the opinion Sir Godfrey Lushington gave to the Gladstone Committee that 'a mediaeval thief who had his right hand chopped off was much more likely to turn over a new leaf than a convict who has had penal servitude'. The contemporary solution is that provided by the Criminal Justice Act: follow the better way so long as it is open—when it is clear that the offender will not take it, then for the protection of society shut him up out of harm's way for a very long time.

Such are the answers to be returned to those who, believing that 'prison reform' goes too far or too fast, would seek to curb it. To those who, thinking it goes neither far nor fast enough, would serve it in the office of a spur, there are others. Pressure from this direction is however less urgent since the fuller developments of the training system, and is directed for the most part against conditions in the local prisons.

So far as this criticism is directed against physical conditions in and arising from the buildings, it is at the same time pushing at an open door and beating its head against a stone wall. No' one charged with responsibility in these matters for many years past has not at some time publicly raised his voice in bitterness on this question; equally no one so charged today does not realise that the economic conditions of the time will prevent any substantial changes for some years to come. Nevertheless, by the use of huts and other improvisations, steady improvement goes on in the teeth of steady reduction of available funds.

Within this rigid and unsuitable framework, the staff of a local prison cannot, as in a training prison, concentrate on its central function. There is a constant ebb and flow of receptions and discharges, surges of family visitors, a great and growing amount of work in escorting prisoners to and from courts and other prisons and a special drain on the staff at every sitting of the many Assizes and Sessions which a local prison serves: often on these occasions there are hardly enough officers left in the prison to man the essential posts. Again, as we have seen in Chapter Eight, a considerable proportion of the prisoners are not criminals but either civil prisoners or untried prisoners who cannot yet be deemed criminal, and each of these categories has to be treated separately under special rules. Of the convicted prisoners, many are merely on their way to some other kind of prison; many are there for so short a time that there is nothing to be done with or for them except provide board, lodging and work; and those who stay longer are only those who are unsuitable to go anywhere else. It is a valid criticism of the system of specialised prisons that it tends to concentrate the more interesting and constructive work in a few prisons and leave to the majority little that is encouraging and much that is mere routine. But these distracting features, in their degree, are inseparable from a local prison, and the balance of advantage seems to lie in doing the best for those prisoners who are most likely to profit by removing them to prisons where the conditions are more settled and favourable, and the staff is able to concentrate on its fundamental job.

There is another aspect of prison treatment which, though it affects every kind of prison, especially governs the working of local prisons. The essence of the punishment being deprivation of liberty, it must be of the essence of prison life that the prisoners be kept in safe-custody. The methods of securing this will vary from one type of prison to another, but in the conditions of a local prison only rigid attendance to the needs of security at every point will suffice. What this entails in detail is fully described in Chapter Ten.

Without doubt many of these difficulties could with time and thought be removed or mitigated, and without doubt, in time, they will be. But the bright prospect opened out by the Criminal Justice Act is clouded by unfavourable conditions which may be transient, but are a serious check on progress while they last. The overcrowding of the prisons caused by the increase of population (p. 118) clogs the administration of the local prisons and tends to an atmosphere of rush and pressure making for frayed tempers among both prisoners and staff, of which the substantial increase of offences of violence by prisoners in 1949 was perhaps one unhappy effect, though the unduly high proportion of inexperienced staff may also have contributed. In 1947 the Commissioners reported as follows:

'One result of the overcrowding was that in almost every prison from time to time, and in many all the time, it became necessary to sleep three men in a cell. The effects were not so bad as might have been expected. Some prisoners, of course, disliked it, but the more general reaction seems to have been to find the advantage of company outweighing the drawbacks of 'crowding in'. The hygienic effects must be disagreeable, but have not so far affected the general state of health. The staff and the general tempo and standards of administration have perhaps suffered most. When there are three times the normal number of prisoners on a landing to be locked up and unlocked, 'slopped out', searched, and served with meals, speed must tend to take the place of care. It is a situation in which an officer can rarely feel satisfaction in his work, and particularly bad for the training of so many young officers.

'There are other bad effects of over-crowding. The results in the industrial sphere have been mentioned. In the largest prisons the administration is simply clogged by the unwieldy masses of men who have to be moved from place to place, so that workshop hours as well as tempers become shorter. There is a perpetual general post of prisoners and officers, the prisoners being moved from the more overcrowded prisons to the less, the officers detached on temporary duty from the more fortunate prisons to the less. In most prisons every room that could be used for education or recreation has been pressed into use as a dormitory. And when every cell has to be used, classification by wings and landings is preserved more in principle than in effective practice.' [1]

Throughout 1950 these conditions had not improved and a daily average of some 2,000 men were still sleeping three in a cell, though their lot had been improved by the introduction of tiered bunks and suitable furniture. These conditions were not allowed to affect the regional training prisons and the central prisons, though here there were balancing disadvantages: a large number of men qualified for training prisons could not go to them, and the average period of waiting for removal to a central prison was, for men of the Ordinary Class, about 15 months.

These difficulties were capable of relief by expansion of accommodation, or mitigation by expansion of staff. But by 1947 every available cell in the country had been taken into use; expansion thereafter could only be into open conditions; and there are limits to the numbers of prisoners who can properly be placed in those conditions. The opening of new prisons is also a heavy drain on staff, and the fall in recruiting in 1949 strictly limited the possibilities of further expansion. The effects of this serious staff shortage on the administration of prisons and the training of prisoners have already been touched on: in March 1951 the numbers of established officers in post were still below the number reckoned to be necessary to maintain even a one-shift system with full efficiency. Women prisoners, it may be added, are not overcrowded, but the women's prisons are equally understaffed.

In these circumstances it is a tribute to the tradition and morale of the service that health, discipline and good order were kept at a satisfactory level and that substantial progress was made in improving the methods of training even in the local prisons. But 1949 was a bad year in which to face the substantial reorganisation of the whole system required by the provisions, so long and so hopefully awaited, of the Act of 1948.

Before we finally leave principle for practice, it is of interest to note the international diffusion of the 'climate of opinion' in which the contemporary English prison system has developed. This may be seen in the spirit which characterises the Resolutions of the Twelfth International Penal and Penitentiary Congress at The Hague (1950) (Appendix F), and in the selection in Appendix G of recently published reports and studies which show a striking correspondence of thought, whether as to the principles of penal punishment or its application, across the five continents of the world.

(2) CLASSIFICATION

Classification is a word which has come, like democracy, to mean very much what the user wants it to mean. It first gained currency in

[1] A.R. for 1947, p. 34.

England to describe a system intended to break down the contamination of the common wards and yards of the eighteenth century gaols: as established by Peel's Gaol Act of 1823 it was based on Bentham's division of the prisoners into five groups—debtors (or, in the bridewells, vagrants), unconvicted felons, unconvicted misdemeanants, convicted felons and convicted misdemeanants. Although this method was shortly abandoned for the separate system, it did establish two principles that have governed all subsequent methods of classification, viz. the necessity for the prevention of contamination, and the complete separation of debtors and unconvicted prisoners from convicted prisoners. The latter principle has for over fifty years been as much a matter of course as the separation of the sexes, though it does present its own anomalies: any collection of untried prisoners is likely to include every degree of criminality, while among civil prisoners there may well be criminal records—and the ethical distinction between some forms of debt and some forms of crime is rather fine. It is equally a matter of course that young prisoners under 21 will be separated from all other categories. The questions to be considered here will therefore relate solely to adult convicted prisoners, the treatment of the three special categories above-mentioned being dealt with in later chapters.

The ground must be further cleared by eliminating those who are dealt with under section 21 of the Act of 1948 as persistent offenders. This is in fact a major act of classification, since it separates out two significant classes of offender for appropriate treatment of different forms: but since it places them under a separate statutory system, they will also be dealt with in a separate chapter.

But having reduced the present subject-matter to adult convicted offenders sentenced to imprisonment, we have by no means reduced the terms of the problem to simplicity. Dr. Grünhut, for instance, devotes 17 pages [1] to a study of classification without approximating to a statement corresponding with current English practice. We may however take as a point of departure his opening statement that 'classification means a method of assigning certain types of prisoner to different forms of custody and treatment', together with his further statement (p. 182) that 'classification is a means to an end'. But when the inquiry is pursued along the lines of 'what types, to what forms of (a) custody (b) treatment, to what ends, and why?' we shall find considerable confusion of both theory and practice in respect of each separate part of this question.

At the London Congress of the International Penal and Penitentiary Commission in 1925 the following statement emerged from a full discussion by higly qualified and experienced experts of many countries:

'The prevention of the contamination of the less criminal prisoner

[1] *Penal Reform*, pp. 179 seqq.

by those more experienced in crime is one of the first essentials in prison treatment.

'After the necessary divisions according to age and sex have been made and the mental status of the prisoner has been taken into account, classification should be according to character and ability to be reformed of each prisoner.

'The shorter term prisoners should be treated apart from those with longer sentences in order that a régime or course of training, appropriate to the latter but not possible with the former, may be applied.

'The various classifications of prisoners should be located separately and where possible in different buildings on the same ground under one administrative head.

'It is difficult to apply the necessary individual treatment of prisoners where the number in any one establishment exceeds five hundred.' [1]

This statement implies two ends to which classification is a means—first, prevention of contamination; second, individualisation of treatment, taking account of 'mental status, character and ability to be reformed'. It also implies, in addition to these vertical divisions, a horizontal division according to the length of sentences, and suggests the classification of prisons as well as of prisoners.

Dr. Grünhut also deals with classification under the headings of 'horizontal' and 'vertical', though along different lines. He includes under the former the division of prisoners 'into a number of treatment groups', and under the latter the 'differentiation of the prison term into a number of consecutive stages': in English practice the stage system is not regarded as an aspect of classification, being itself adapted to the special needs of each 'treatment group'. In his discussion of the assignment of types of prisoner to appropriate treatment groups, Dr. Grünhut distinguishes two leading principles; the first is based on 'a distinction between offenders committing crimes from strong motives or the lack of counter-motives, and those whose offences seem an almost inevitable expression of deep-rooted anti-social tendencies'; the second on 'the consideration whether every prisoner needs the same amount of safe-custody in order to prevent assaults and escapes'. He also gives as the basis of a classification proposed in the *Handbook of Case Work and Classification Methods* of the American Prison Association, 'a differentiation into first offenders, recidivists, mentally abnormal, and physically defective prisoners'. More recently and nearer home, the Report on the Scottish Prison System by the Scottish Advisory Council on the Treatment and Rehabilitation of Offenders (1949) recommends that 'convicted prisoners whose sentences are over 6 months should be classified in the first instance according to their mental ability irrespec-

---

[1] For a later statement by The Hague Congress 1950, see I (3), Appendix F.

tive of their age, criminal record or character, and divided into two groups—those of low intelligence and the mentally agile' (para. 105).

In considering what is meant by classification in current English practice, we shall find that in outline it corresponds almost exactly with the specifications of the Congresses of London and The Hague, but that in its detailed application to types and individuals not more than one or two of the systems and considerations mentioned by Dr. Grünhut, the *American Prison Association Handbook*, or the Scottish Report are even indirectly relevant.

The main structure is based on one vertical division by type and two horizontal divisions by length of sentence. The vertical division is into two classes, Star and Ordinary, in accordance with the provisions of Rule 9, which (omitting certain paras. relevant only to young prisoners) reads as follows:

9. (1) 'In order so far as possible to prevent contamination and to facilitate training the arrangements set out in the following paragraphs of this Rule shall be made in classifying prisoners.

(3) 'Prisoners of 21 years of age and over who have not previously been in prison on conviction shall be placed in the Star Class unless the reception board considers that, in view of their record or character, they are likely to have a bad influence on others. The reception board may also place in the Star Class a prisoner of 21 years of age and over who has previously been in prison on conviction if they are satisfied, having regard to the nature of the previous offence, or to the length of time since it was committed, or to the prisoner's general record and character, that he is not likely to have a bad influence on others.

(4) 'Other prisoners shall be placed in the Ordinary Class.

(5) (*b*) 'The Governor may in his discretion at any time remove from the Star Class to the Ordinary Class a prisoner whose character has shown him to be unfit to associate with other prisoners of the Star Class.

(6) 'Arrangements shall be made in all local prisons to provide so far as practicable for the effective separation at all times of the three classes of convicted prisoners.

(7) 'Prisoners of the Star Class transferred to a central prison shall normally be placed in a prison set aside for prisoners of that class and, where they are in the same prison as prisoners of the Ordinary Class, the two classes shall so far as practicable be effectively separated.

(8) 'The Commissioners may set up such other classes, or may authorise in particular cases or at particular prisons such departures from the provisions of this Rule, as may in their opinion be desirable for the purposes of paragraph (1) of this Rule."

It will be observed that this Rule, like the statement of the Congress of London, lays down two objects of classification—prevention of contamination and facilitation of training: but as to the methods of achieving these objects, it goes no further in terms than the division into two classes, and provision for their effective separation. This division serves primarily the prevention of contamination, though the training of the two classes is facilitated by separation, since different methods of treatment are appropriate. In the break-down of these two statutory classes into appropriate treatment groups the Commissioners are left a fairly free hand under para. (8) of the Rule.

Of the horizontal divisions, the first is based on the view that prisoners who have to serve really long terms of imprisonment require different treatment from those serving shorter terms, and in separate establishments; accordingly the Rules provide that the Commissioners may set aside particular prisons, or parts of prisons, for such prisoners or classes of prisoner serving sentences of 3 years and upwards as they may determine. These are known as central prisons, and at present the prisoners removed to them are normally those serving sentences of over 4 years,[1] though this may be varied from time to time or for particular prisoners. The vertical division of this long-term group is preserved by setting aside separate prisons for those of the Star class and those of the Ordinary class, whether men or women. One of the two prisons for the Star class men is an open prison (Leyhill).

For the prisoners below this horizontal line there is another line drawn below 12 months, this being the minimum sentence required before transfer to a regional training prison is considered. The regional training prison represents one aspect of the principle recommended by the Congress of London of setting aside particular prisons for particular classes of prisoner: the second aspect (again leaving aside the provision for young prisoners) is met by providing so far as possible separate prisons for the Star class. These latter arrangements are at the time of writing in process of reorganisation, but in principle there are two prisons, one in the north and one in the south, for Stars with sentences of over 6 months, and two more for those with sentences of up to 6 months.[2] The two last mentioned prisons are of medium or minimum security: they were opened primarily to relieve overcrowding, though having become available they are used in a manner to assist the process of classification in accordance with the principle of 'custodial differentiation' mentioned by Dr. Grünhut, the convicted prisoners sent to them being of types which by length of sentence are not eligible for training prisons, but which both by length of sentence and by character are suitable for treatment in conditions of minimum security, since

[1] For Stars, 3 years. See also Appendix K.
[2] Civil prisoners are also sent to these prisons. See also Appendix K.

they are unlikely either to think it worth while to escape or to require conditions of close control.

While for short-sentence Stars the principle of custodial differentiation is applied to the class as a whole, individuals being held back on special grounds only (e.g. medical unfitness or some doubtful factor in the offence or record), in other categories it is based on rigorous personal selection after careful observation. For the long-term (over 3 year) Stars the practice is to send them first to that half of Wakefield which serves as a central prison, where their characters and accommodation to prison conditions are periodically considered by a board: when it is thought that they are suitable and ready to go to the open central prison at Leyhill, a recommendation is made to the Commissioners, who again give the case most careful consideration before either approving or postponing transfer. No type of case is automatically excluded, but the greatest care is taken with men who have committed offences of violence, particularly sexual offences, homosexuals and younger men with any suggestion of mental instability. The Commissioners feel that they have a considerable responsibility to the public among whom they place some hundreds of men serving sentences of from 4 years to life for serious offences, including murder, with no physical restrictions against escape. They are, moreover, acutely conscious that too many escapes, or even a very few serious offences committed against members of the public by prisoners, might seriously shake public and parliamentary confidence in the system. Most prisoners, therefore, serve some months, and many much longer, before the Commissioners can feel satisfied that they are able and ready to settle down and co-operate in a system which requires a high standard of self-discipline: moreover any who show that they cannot maintain that standard are at once returned to a closed prison.

The same methods are applied, in relation to short-term prisoners eligible for training prisons, in considering whether they are suitable for an open training prison, except that they do not pass through Wakefield. In any case of doubt it is thought right to place the interests of the system before those of the individual, and on this basis the English experience since the first open prison was established in 1933 has been fortunate, in that the number of escapes has been insignificant and only two prisoners have been charged with offences against local inhabitants.

From this divagation into 'custodial differentiation' we return to consider how the two divisions of short-term (up to 3 years) prisoners are further subdivided into appropriate 'treatment groups'.

Let us first take those above the horizontal line which qualifies for a training prison, i.e. 12 months to 3 years. These may be either Stars or Ordinaries. For a Star, the assumption is that he will go to a training prison unless some exceptional reason appears against it: the main

E.P.B.S.—10

question for decision is whether the prison shall be open or closed. The disposal of Ordinaries is more complicated, and calls for another divagation from the main theme.

In their origin training prisons were for the Star class only, since it was thought that only with prisoners of that type could the atmosphere of trust and self-responsibility required for such prisons be maintained. But in more recent years the Commissioners came to the conclusion that to devote this intensive system of training solely to a class of offender of whom it was statistically certain that some 80 per cent would not in any event return to prison was in some sense a waste. In the fight against recidivism the hard core of the problem was the 20 per cent who did return to prison: these were the people who above all needed the best training that could be given. But to attempt to create the atmosphere of a training prison with prisoners drawn only from this group was out of the question. The somewhat revolutionary solution decided on was to break down, under the powers of Rule 9 (8), the vertical division into Stars and Ordinaries and substitute a division into 'trainable' and 'non-trainable'. This implied a revaluation of 'contamination': the possibilities of contamination are, perhaps, no easier to evaluate than the possibilities of reform without a much more subtle and precise method of probing the depths of the human mind than is yet available to prison staffs—there may be many who must be classed as Stars who are more likely to corrupt the minds of their fellows than many who must be classed as recidivists. Nor is a burglar or a pickpocket likely to teach his trade to a defaulting solicitor or a public servant who has committed a breach of his trust. However that may be, it was decided to look the bogy of contamination firmly in the face and to act on the optimistic view that, provided the recidivists were selected with sufficient care, and remained a minority, it was more reasonable to suppose that they would be influenced for the good by a majority of better men than the other way about. Accordingly machinery was devised for selecting prisoners of the Ordinary Class whose records suggested that they were not yet beyond hope of rehabilitation, and whose characters appeared to be such that they would co-operate in and profit by the special régime of a training prison. These 'trainable ordinaries' were slowly infiltrated into the training prisons until they reached a proportion of 40 to 60 per cent of Stars, though within the training prisons there is no classification—all are treated alike. Governors of closed training prisons, like those of open prisons, are free to send back to their local prisons any who cannot or will not co-operate, after they have done their best with them—and they do not like to admit failure too easily. After three years' trial, there has been no reason to regret this experiment, either in the administration of the training prisons or in the results after discharge of either class of prisoner.[1]

[1] Appendix K.

Finally, for those who, being disqualified either by character or shortness of sentence from transfer to a training prison, serve their sentences in their local prisons, there remains nothing but the division into the two normal classes, with appropriate treatment for each class so far as the conditions of such prisons permit of differentiation, and such physical separation as is practicable of the Stars who will not be, or have not yet been, transferred to a separate prison.

It will be noticed that this system translates into practice with some precision the recommendations of the Congress of London, except that it appears to take no account of 'mental status', whether this term be taken to mean, as in the criterion favoured by the Scottish Report, 'mental ability', or as in that of the American Prison Association, 'mental abnormality'. Nor has account been taken of certain other features mentioned in Dr. Grünhut's study, e.g. the nature and motive of the offence and physical defect. Nevertheless, although none of these criteria is used as the basis of a separate treatment *group*, any one of them may be relevant to the question whether an *individual* should be selected either for a training prison or an open prison. The nature of the offence and even its motives, so far as they could be discovered, might well decide whether or not a man was sent to a particular type of prison, as would a medical diagnosis of psychopathy or psycho-neurotic disturbance: but neither subnormal intelligence nor physical defect would affect a prisoner's selection for a particular form of training unless it were such that he would evidently be unable to co-operate in and profit by the training. This does not mean that serious consideration has not been given to the separation for appropriate treatment of the group described by Sir Norwood East as the 'non-sane non-insane': this has long been accepted in principle, but this whole important question may be more properly considered as a medical one, and is dealt with as such in Chapter Fourteen. Another related question which has occasioned much doubt in the English as in other prison systems is whether homosexual offenders should, as such, be separated from other groups: the view so far taken in this country, not without consideration of other methods and their effects, is against such separation. But so far, rightly or wrongly, consideration has not been given to the practice followed in some systems of setting up separate establishments for e.g. the tuberculous, or those requiring continuous treatment in hospital.

A word in conclusion about women. Although the foregoing discussion has been throughout in the masculine gender, the whole of it applies equally to women, except in so far as modifications are necessary owing to the much smaller numbers to be dealt with—it is, for example, impossible to provide training centres for girls under 21 when the total number eligible [1] at any one time, all over the country, rarely reaches

---

[1] I.e. with sentences of 3 months or over.

twenty. Apart from Holloway, the characteristics of which have already been described, there are only four local prisons which have wings for women, plus one which keeps a small block of cells for untried women only, and in only one of these is the population likely to exceed 100. These small and ill-provided premises offer little facility either for complete separation of classes or for active training. However, subject to these limitations of the local prisons, the general principles above described are applied except that there is no separate prison for short-term Stars—the long-term (over 3 year) Stars go to a separate prison at Aylesbury, the long-term Ordinaries to a separate wing of Holloway. There is one regional training prison for women at Askham Grange in Yorkshire, and a second in preparation at Hill Hall in Essex, both being open prisons. In the 'Five Year Plan' presented by the Commissioners to the Secretary of State at the end of the war [1] the building of modern prisons for women was given a high priority, but of these hopeful plans, five years later, only the sense of urgency remains.

(3) TRAINING

Having divided the prisoners into appropriate treatment groups, we pass to consideration of how, in the broad, the principles of training and treatment already described are applied to the different groups, working our way up from the local prisons, through the regional training prisons, to the central prisons. In the local prisons we are concerned with those members of the Star class whose sentences are too short for training prisons, or who are awaiting their turn to go to one, but principally with the common run of 'in-and-out' Ordinaries— mostly with short sentences, but a fair proportion also with sentences up to 4 years whose character and record offer little hope that they will profit by any sort of training. The operation of section 21 of the Criminal Justice Act is now diverting a number of these last, with what result remains to be seen, into the channel of corrective training.

Methods of treatment concerned with security and control, material conditions of life and so forth make no differentiation between the two classes; and in smaller prisons where only one or two industries are available there will be little if any differentiation in work, though in general the Stars would be put to the better class work where practicable. But in practice this would not always work out, as the more skilled industries call for men with longer sentences, and these will *ex hypothesi* be Ordinaries. On the other hand, Stars will generally be found in positions of trust, as in the library, or in small 'honour parties' working without the direct supervision of an officer, or working on the prison gardens or in outside agricultural parties: and in the separate Star prisons the industries are of the better class. Trust and responsi-

[2] Annual Report for 1945, Appendix 2A.

bility are not, in the hurly-burly of local prison life, to be attributed with any freedom to the general run of the Ordinary class: those who are given the 'red-band' of the prisoner who is allowed to pass to and fro, or do his special job, without continuous supervision, are as likely to be reliable old customers who know the ropes as men selected for the inculcation of a sense of responsibility.

The main differentiation lies in the application to the two classes of the Stage System. This has, in recent years, undergone such changes of both principle and practice as may almost have excluded it from any of the classical definitions or descriptions. We have seen how, at least from the time of Maconochie on Norfolk Island, the conception of Progressive Stages, coupled with Maconochie's marks system, became almost the dominating idea in prison reform in both Europe and America. In its earliest form, it amounted to little more than permission to pass from a stage of desperate hopelessness, through one of mere existence, to the ultimate goal of hope that some remission might be earned. Its second form, corresponding in England roughly with the du Cane régime, added to this some progressive mitigation of the severer physical deprivations, though convicts with their longer sentences received a little more encouragement. Under the Ruggles-Brise régime the main features were a slow increase in the numbers of letters and visits allowed, and in the quality and quantity of library books—one 'good' book in the First Stage, one good book and one less good but more interesting in the Second, two good ones and one interesting one in the Third, and so on. Indeed this sort of thing remained the substantial basis of the system until recent years, with some provision for periodicals to be sent in, attendance at concerts and lectures, and the privilege of association at certain meals for Stars: with the introduction of earnings at work the right to earn also became a stage privilege, while convicts had continued to receive their traditional 'stage gratuities' of a few pence increasing year by year.

Under the modifications gradually introduced since the war, and standardised in the revised stage system introduced in 1949, almost the whole of this machinery has been discarded. The marks system had gone some years earlier, having long become a piece of labour-wasting routine which served no perceptible purpose: in practice every prisoner was automatically credited with the necessary marks for both remission and stage unless he had forfeited them by idleness or misconduct—it was therefore much simpler all round to assume that he had earned these privileges unless they had been taken away, which could more conveniently be done in terms of days than of marks.

It appeared to the Commissioners that a system of this traditional pattern was open to two objections in principle. In so far as the 'privileges' had a value as elements of training, the sooner a prisoner was able to profit by them the better: and in so far as they were useful as aids to discipline, a prisoner might be more affected by the loss of something he was actually enjoying than by deferment of the hope of enjoying it. Accordingly it was decided that since good reading, the stimulation of industry by earning, and the maintenance of family relations by letters and visits were all valuable for training, they should be divorced from the stage system and made available as fully as possible to all prisoners from the beginning of their sentences. Further, that except for long-term Ordinaries the system should no longer be progressive through a number of stages, but that the prisoners should be either 'in stage' or 'out of stage', this being already the practice in the training prisons before the war. For the long-term Ordinaries it seemed desirable, for a variety of reasons, to keep a progressive system. The feeling of progress through a term of years is helpful to men to whom it is neither practicable nor desirable to give at an early stage the privileges which the modern system affords to Stars; and the old lag is a conservative person who values his place in a well-defined class system, with its cachet of distinctive dress and separate 'club room' in the higher ranks, and he will usually try to live up to it. Long-term Stars however get all available privileges as soon as they come into stage. Another feature of the new system is that any one privilege, whether it be a stage privilege or not, may be forfeited independently, but Governors are advised that certain privileges, e.g. letters, library books and educational facilities should normally be forfeited only if they are abused. A list of all the features of treatment which are defined as privileges which may be forfeited is given in Appendix H, together with a detailed account of the operation of the Stage System. Certain features of this call for special comment.

The differentiation in the application of the short-term system to the two classes is two-fold. The Star gets into stage after a month, this being in some sense a period of quarantine to make sure that he is a Star, and suitable to be trusted in the fairly full association allowed to his class: the Ordinary is out of stage for 4 months, which means that he has to have a sentence of over 6 months (allowing one-third off for remission) to get into stage. This decision was deliberately taken to exclude the mass of short-sentence recidivists for whom their imprisonment could have no training value, who could not be trusted in association, and for whom there would be no room if they could be trusted: it should nevertheless be noted that while out of stage they now receive every privilege which they could have earned in the second stage of the previous progressive system. The second difference relates to the amount of association allowed in stage: to allow prisoners to mix freely together for meals and recreation is a means of allowing the staff to form some judgment of a prisoner's real character—it is also a privilege so highly valued by the majority that they will try to conform to the required standards of behaviour rather than lose it, and for many there is a positive gain in having succeeded in living up to a standard for some months, however reluctantly and for whatever motives. Nor is it compulsory—those who prefer their own company or wish to read or study quietly can stay in their cells. But this privilege can be awarded much more sparingly to Ordinaries than to Stars, not only because of their nature but because in a local prison, which normally has only the floors of the halls available for association, there simply is not room for them: so the Governor is given complete discretion as to allowing them to associate either at meals or for evening recreation, and it is only after 12 months in stage that they come out in the evenings.

The long-term system gives to all prisoners from the beginning everything that was formerly a second-stage privilege, and for the rest is based mainly on the gradual extension of the periods of association— an arrangement that is conditioned as much by the limited accommodation of the central prisons as by any principle of treatment or training, though over a period of years too much purposeless association does tend to diminish its value.

The shorter periods of the progressive stages for women are due primarily to the fact that the women's prisons are better able to provide the necessary facilities for association.

There are two important aspects of training which are not dependent on stage or class—education in all its forms, and what may broadly be termed social welfare. Both these subjects will be fully discussed elsewhere, and it is only necessary to say of them here that in a local prison all prisoners of both classes may benefit from all the facilities available to the extent of their capacity and will.

In a training prison nothing turns on either stage or class—all, whether in their local prisons they were Stars or Ordinaries, are on the same footing, and all are in stage from the start. And there are two other features which are not found in local prisons—stability and homogeneity: all the prisoners are there for at least six months and often much longer. The staff get to know them because they are not being constantly taken off their regular work by extraneous jobs, and the whole establishment and every one in it is working to one and the same end. The principles are not different from those in a local prison, but they can be more fully and intensively practised. All the industries are of good quality, with three or four vocational training classes in skilled trades, and the staff is sufficient to allow a working week of reasonable length. The evening educational and recreational programmes are full and varied, so that little or no time need be spent in cells—indeed these stand open all day and are used for little else but sleeping. And the teaching of self-discipline and self-responsibility is taken much further in many ways besides the daily freedom of association from getting up to going to bed: although security cannot be neglected it is not obtruded, and prisoners move freely about the place without the direct supervision of officers. This is one result of the 'leader' system. A leader is something quite different from the 'red-band' of a local prison, though he has none of the attributes of the 'trustie' of some American practice or of the N.C.O. prisoner of some colonial practice—at Wakefield they are traditionally called 'strokes', because their job is not to command the crew but to set the pace: each mess of some ten men has its stroke, and in this prison each mess has its own small room where it eats and lives, and the stroke sees to it that the standards of the prison and the mess are maintained—but he has no disciplinary authority and no special privileges or remuneration. At Maidstone there are no separate mess-rooms so the system is rather different: here leaders are responsible, for example, for the cleanliness and turn-out of their halls, for arranging evening activities and taking parties to and fro, and generally they play a fairly responsible part in the life of the prison. The writer was in a block of this prison one evening while a number of educational classes were going on, for the most part under prison teachers; while he was in one such class, the lights fused and the building was in darkness; although there was no uniformed officer in the block, there was no disorder—prisoners from a technical class quickly located the fault and restored the light, and all went quietly on. Such can be the effect of self-discipline through trust.

An essential part of the training in regional prisons is personal knowledge by the staff of every prisoner and attention to the problems he presents as an individual, whether in relation to his past or his future, his training inside the prison or his family and social relations outside. The subordinate staff, as we have seen, are in a much better position to help here than in a local prison; there is a resident Welfare Officer appointed by the National Association of Discharged Prisoners' Aid Societies [1]; the Medical Officers are skilled in psychological medicine and play a full and essential part in the training; the Chaplain is in a much better position than in a local prison to get to know his flock as individual souls, and to find the way to reach them; and finally, though this cannot be carried so far as in a Borstal, appropriate blocks or divisions of the prisons are placed under Assistant Governors who bring to the men in their charge much the sort of care that a Borstal housemaster brings to his house.

The culminating feature of the training for many men is the transfer to camp. Both Wakefield and Maidstone have camps, which normally take up to 100 men, some miles away in the country. These are entirely without security, the men sleeping in wooden huts and the bounds designated, if at all, by whitewash marks on the trees. An Assistant Governor is in charge, with a Principal Officer and a staff of three or four officers who lead a bachelor life on the premises. Work is entirely agricultural; at Wakefield, in clearing the woodland for cultivation and

[1] See Chapter 16.

then cultivating it, with minor stock-raising (pigs, hens, rabbits); at Maidstone, by supplying parties of workers to surrounding farms or for public works [1] (catchment, land drainage, etc.). Selection for camp will usually be considered in the latter part of a man's sentence, as forming a valuable half-way house to freedom, an opportunity for conditioning to the feel of normal life after the distortions of life behind a wall. It is not, however, either valuable or possible, or not equally so, for everyone; some men from their records, the nature of their offences (especially if it is a sexual offence or one of violence), their observed characters in the prison, are bad risks; others may be completing a trade training course and prefer to stick to their lasts; others are just not tempted by a rather hard physical life out of doors with dormitory life and modest amenities. But wise selection can bring to many men an influence which is of determining value for their future: there have been many cases of men with dubious records, on whom other forms of treatment had little apparent effect, who lost in camp their 'old-lag' mentality and did well after discharge. With this careful selection, and the rigorous return to the prison of any who cannot stand up to the strain of self-discipline, experience has shown that the public is not asked to undergo any special risk in the interests of this form of training: from New Hall Camp at Wakefield, since 1936, only seven prisoners have escaped, and only one has been charged with an offence against a local inhabitant, while from Aldington Camp at Maidstone, since it was opened in 1947, there has been one escape and no known offences.

This experience led the Commissioners, in 1948, to establish at Sudbury, Derbyshire, in the premises of a former American army hospital, an independent training prison for up to 300 men in entirely open conditions. This establishment was built up slowly with an initial population of selected Stars, and now takes up to 40 per cent of trainable Ordinaries or corrective trainees [2] like the closed training prisons —to the extent, that is, to which a sufficient number of these categories suitable for open conditions can be found. Its traditions are now well-established, and are based on the fullest responsibility and initiative in a communal life which is less cramped and distorted than that of a walled prison. There is first-class workshop accommodation, ample space for indoor and outdoor recreation (including a good theatre), and a valuable educational programme provided by the County Education Authority.

The fourth of the present training prisons for men might technically be described as a 'medium security' prison—not because the system recognises a place for medium security in principle, but because the premises became available and happened to be built that way. This

---

[1] For the conditions of extra-mural employment of prisoners in all prisons, see Chapter 11. [2] See Appendix K, note on p. 146.

institution is situated within the formidable earthwork and moat of the Verne Citadel on the Island of Portland. The security of the perimeter is thus impressive, but the conditions within are quite open, the prisoners using the former accommodation of the garrison. The premises lend themselves admirably to their new purpose, the dining-room and kitchen, common-rooms and workshops being exceptionally good. The prison was opened early in 1949 by a pioneer party of Stars, and the population was slowly built up towards the optimum of 300, of whom up to 40 per cent will be trainable Ordinaries or corrective trainees as elsewhere. A football field has been levelled and prepared within the 'wall', and the Dorset County Education Authority provide a programme of evening education.[1]

The first training prison for women, at Askham Grange near York, is also on the 60-40 basis, but there is rather more elasticity about the types of women sent there. The prison was established early in 1947 in a large country house, not because premises of this type were thought to be the most appropriate for the purpose, but because, in the circumstances of the time, if anything was to be done for women it had to be done in a house of this sort or not at all. Many visitors have raised the question, both here and in the similar but more beautiful house for Borstal girls at East Sutton Park, whether it is wise to accustom women and girls to this standard of amenity when most of them must shortly go back to something so depressingly different. It is a valid question— but would it have been better or worse, on the whole, to have left them behind the walls of Holloway or Strangeways? And again, may there not be some continuing value in having given them, perhaps for the first time, the feeling of a way of life with standards and values outside the possibility of their own experience? Apart from this doubt, it may also be thought that mature women would be better placed in single rooms than in the small dormitories that the structure of Askham Grange requires. But given these conditions as inevitable, one can only put them to the test of experience and remark that after two years' experience the Governor was able to report that no woman had escaped, none had been punished and none had been reconvicted.[2]

The principles at Askham are the same as for men, but the methods are modified to meet the needs of women, and of a small unit of women, for the house will take only 60. It has not yet been possible to find an industry in which vocational training could be given to women on the lines of that given to men, and the day's work is based on a thorough training in the various aspects of home-making, including cookery, housewifery, needlework, gardening and laundry-work. It is worth while to emphasise that this is *training*, and that the conditions of the house make it possible, in a way that is not possible in an ordinary

---

[1] Another open training prison was opened in 1951 at Falfield, Glos.
[2] Annual Report for 1948, p. 27. In 1949 two reconvictions were reported.

prison, to relate the training to the needs of ordinary life: the women become really competent cooks and needlewomen, learn how to do home washing, and finally go through a course of Cookery and Home Management prescribed by the County Council, who examine them at the end. The painting and decorating has also been done by the women themselves, and done very well. There is plenty of outdoor work, not only in gardening and poultry-keeping in the grounds but (in supervised parties) for local farmers. The evening educational activities have a useful bias, including teaching in embroidery, dress-making, toymaking and leatherwork, and lectures in Child Welfare, Home Nursing, First Aid and Personal Hygiene. There are also classes in English and other subjects. All this is of real value to women who will for the most part return to their homes or be called on to make homes. After a time the women are allowed to go for local walks in small groups without supervision, and in a spirit of good-neighbourliness 'the Grange', in spite of its new use, remains within proper limits the local centre for both recreation and social welfare.

On the effects of this homely community life on character the Governor reported as follows:

'A code of honour takes the place of what is generally known as discipline; this is rarely abused even in a small way. The improvement in manners, appearance, industry and co-operation of the women has been well maintained, there is always an atmosphere of friendliness, and freedom from fear and anxiety makes a noticeable difference in their behaviour in a short time. Their readiness to shoulder responsibility is praiseworthy. Friendship with the local inhabitants is now firmly established, they are invited to all our social activities, and always come in full force.' [1]

We pass now to the central prisons, taking first those for the Ordinary Class at Parkhurst and Dartmoor. Dartmoor, in spite of its reputation, climate and buildings, does provide good facilities for training: there is a variety of good class industry, and almost unlimited work outside the walls on the extensive farm-lands, quarries and land maintenance and reclamation. Notwithstanding the isolation of the prison the Devon County Council provides a good programme of evening education, and the use of the library and of correspondence courses shows a high level of serious interest. The two great draw-backs to this prison, apart from archaic buildings, are its isolation, which minimises the amenities of life for the staff and the application of outside resources to the training of the prisoners, and the sensational reputation which has been attached to it. It has been doomed to discontinuance for so long that it will now be a long and costly business to bring its buildings and staff accommodation up to the standards which might make of it the

[1] Annual Report for 1948, p. 28.

healthy and active training establishment which, given a fair chance, it is capable of becoming. Nevertheless, with the growing need for prisons of this type to provide for the large number of long-term prisoners flowing from the 'persistent offenders' provisions of the Criminal Justice Act, it became necessary in 1949 to grant this ancient prison a reprieve from its long-impending doom, and to set to work on its reorganisation and modernisation.

Dartmoor is built of hard granite on the high moors. Parkhurst, brick-built in the softer climate of the Isle of Wight, is a different affair. Steeped in the 'old-lag mentality', it harboured until 1950 [1] the 'old-age party', the pre-1948 preventive detention men, a considerable hospital which has long been the convict medical centre, and generally favoured the feeling of doing one's time quietly. There are few elements of hope in the Parkhurst population. Nevertheless, as is desirable for men serving long sentences, there are good industries, out-door work on the farm and in the forest, and a football-field in an adjoining compound, where the week-end games offer an outlet alike for the physical energies of the more robust and the gambling instincts of all. The whole prison turns out for the game, and the break from routine is good for discipline and morale. There is little to be said of any constructive evening activities.

Long-term men of the Star Class, for so long as they remain at Wakefield (see p. 175), are treated under a régime similar to that of the 'training' side of the prison which has already been described. It remains to consider those who in due course are passed on to the open prison at Leyhill. Although this prison represents the most advanced experiment in training prisoners so far attempted in this country, not in the fact of its being in open conditions but in the resolution to trust in those conditions men serving very long sentences for serious offences, there is little fresh to be said of principles: all the methods that have been described as applicable in training prisons are applied here. First, plenty of high-class industrial work, with outside work on surrounding farms, to which some men go out individually on bicycles. Then, the provision of ample and various opportunities for the valuable use of leisure—a good educational programme organised by the Local Education Authorities in conjunction with Bristol University, and a variety of recreational and sporting activities organised by the men themselves—the Leyhill Amateur Dramatic Society puts on two or three shows a year in its own theatre from its own resources; the cricket and football clubs stand high in the sporting esteem of neighbouring leagues, though they play only 'home' matches; regular concerts are

[1] In the summer of 1950 the first of the 'new-style' preventive detention men under the Act of 1948 began to arrive—see Chapter 18. It seems probable that by the end of 1951 Parkhurst, except for medical cases, will be full of preventive detention men. Dartmoor will then be the only prison for long-term Ordinaries.

supported by the prison orchestra; there is a monthly periodical edited and produced by the men . . . in short nothing in reason is omitted which may keep the bodies and minds of the prisoners healthy, active and interested, and prepare them for normal life; during their long years of confinement. Here, as in other open prisons, there is a noticeable absence of the tensions of ordinary prison life, and a high standard of discipline is required and maintained with little need to resort to punishment—for which indeed there are few facilities: the real sanction against failure to keep up is to be sent back to a closed prison. And last but not least, knowledge of each man by the staff—Governor and Assistant Governors, Chaplain, Medical Officer and every one else, so that their problems both inside and outside the prison may be understood and so far as possible resolved—for even in an open prison any mole-hill may quickly become a mountain in the mind of a prisoner.

The picture for women fills neither so broad nor so various a canvas. Long-term women are few: some 30 Stars at Aylesbury and about the same number of Ordinaries in a separate wing at Holloway. Aylesbury is an ordinary cellular prison within a wall, though there is space for gardens. The women have in the past been for the most part elderly abortionists, with others who have committed serious offences which may often be classed as 'accidental', though since the war the proportion of younger women has increased. For this type of women it has been found that a rather homely and informal atmosphere, allowing closer personal contacts with the staff, is more successful than a regimented though possibly more constructive régime to which few would be likely to respond. Those for whom something more positive may be needed, especially the younger women, may be transferred to Askham Grange after a time. Certainly the régime appears to serve its primary purpose, since a reconviction is almost unknown. Nevertheless, it would be refreshing to see the women housed in some more pleasant and appropriate buildings which would encourage a more tonic and normal life. Even more would one wish this for the Ordinaries, who behind the grim walls of Holloway lead a life very much that of the local prison, save for their privileges of association and the efforts made by the staff, under an Assistant Governor who has them in her special charge, to understand and help them, keep the peace, and make their evenings as interesting and constructive as possible. Again, certain carefully selected women may be sent to Askham Grange to be 'finished'.[1]

[1] See also Appendix K.

CHAPTER TEN

SECURITY AND CONTROL

(1) GENERAL

THE régime of a prison is founded, and must be firmly founded, on the twin rocks of security and good order: if these are not sound the superstructure, whatever its purpose, must sooner or later crack: this holds true in its degree for prisons of every type, though methods of securing the foundations will vary. Classification brings together in separate prisons those who can be trusted to exercise self-discipline, and there control by the staff, though not less effective, should be less obtrusive. The serious problems are presented in the local prisons and in those for long-term Ordinaries and persistent offenders: it is essential here that the staff should not only have complete and unquestioned control but that they should manifestly and openly be seen to have it. Many of these prisoners are malicious, cunning and often violent men whose ónly interests, throughout their sentences, are to score points in their incessant poker-game against authority and to bend to their purposes such weaker prisoners as they can dominate: and once this section feels itself to be on top, there is no more peace in that prison. Firm control is therefore necessary in the interests not only of the administration but of the majority of prisoners who want to do their time quietly, and they recognise and welcome it.

Above all therefore a prison officer must know his men—on the one hand those who can be allowed some latitude, or checked with a quiet word, on the other those who are out to make trouble, and especially those who, while skilfully keeping out of trouble themselves, know how to make others fire their bullets for them: he must be able to keep order fairly and firmly without too much fuss—he should not often need to place a prisoner 'on report', but he should never hesitate if it is necessary for that man at that time. Long periods of superficial calm must not be allowed to dull alertness—in the abnormal associations of a prison any trifling incident, fumbled in its handling, may lead for no apparent reason to disorder, assault or mutinous riot.

158

It is against this background that we should consider the first of the Statutory Rules under this heading, which reads:

'The Rules in this section shall be applied, due allowance being made for the differences of character and response to discipline of different types of prisoner, in accordance with the following principles:

(i) Discipline and order shall be maintained with firmness, but with no more restriction than is required for safe custody and well ordered community life;

(ii) In the control of prisoners officers shall seek to influence them through their own example and leadership, and to enlist their willing co-operation;

(iii) At all times the treatment of prisoners shall be such as to encourage their self-respect and a sense of personal responsibility.'

In Star prisons and training prisons, and in dealing with Stars in local prisons, the régime and the conduct of the staff can be and are confidently based on those principles. For the rest they are valid, as the Rule implies, as far as they can be taken, and the farther that is the better will be the tone of that prison: but it needs a well selected, trained and experienced staff to do it. There is more than one system of controlling prisoners: in America the tendency is to strengthen the prison wall with watch-towers, searchlights, armed sentries and every mechanical aid, and within this impregnable circuit to allow relaxed control— the prisoners suffer little immediate restriction of their doings, but they know that tear-gas and fire-arms are not far in the background. The English prison officers carry staves (concealed in a special pocket) for use only when essential and in self-defence, but no fire-arms or tear-gas or the like are held in prisons,[1] and the staff is on a minimum functional basis without reserves against violent contingencies. It may here be mentioned that a Statutory Rule to which the greatest importance is attached is that 'No officer when dealing with prisoners shall use force unnecessarily, and when . . . force is necessary, no more force than is necessary shall be used.' Nothing is more likely to result in dismissal than a breach of this Rule, and though it cannot be confidently stated that illicit 'beatings-up' never happen, they are very rare and are never condoned. To avoid violence, officers are instructed in certain Judo holds for the control of refractory prisoners.

This system of control does call for a somewhat regimented routine with close and constant supervision by the staff: it also requires high qualities from the staff and a high standard of discipline from the prisoners: but if discipline is regarded as a willing response to authority,

---

[1] Except at Dartmoor, where armed patrols cover the large parties working outside the wall.

and the staff is able on the whole to secure that response by fairness and humanity, there is something of value gained. And it may be doubted whether the American system, whatever its advantages, would travel so well as other ideas which have been successfully transplanted across the Atlantic. However that may be, order is maintained under this system with little recourse to punishment: for ten years before the late war the average number of prisoners punished in local prisons was about 4·5 per cent—since the war, overcrowding and shortage of experienced staff have resulted in an increase to over 8 per cent, but even so, in a recent year in a large and difficult local prison less than 2 men a day were reported for offences out of over 800. Serious or concerted disorder is very rare, and only three times since the First World War have there been serious outbreaks of mutinous violence.

Of all restrictions on the conduct of prisoners, the most notorious has been the Rule of Silence. It is, therefore, well to emphasise that in English prisons today there is no such rule. Broadly, talking is restricted, though not forbidden, on certain occasions, and entirely unrestricted on others. During working hours, gossip and unnecessary chatter will be discouraged, as also when parties of prisoners are moving about under supervision, or waiting to see the Governor or Medical Officer when there may be prisoners of different classes in the same party: on all these 'parade' occasions a prisoner who does not stop talking when he is warned is likely to be reported. 'Off parade', during meals, recreation, exercise and on educational occasions, talking is quite unrestricted. There is a story that, shortly after talking at exercise was first allowed, an officer of the old school reported a prisoner for 'not conversing on conversational exercise'—apocryphal perhaps, but it does hint at the danger of a certain traditionalism, tending to rigidity, which is still latent in our system.

The qualities this system seeks in its officers are not those of an amateur psychologist, or even of a strong vocation for social service, but humanity, fairness, self-responsibility, self-control and complete integrity—and it must be said that it is this last which is likely to be most sorely assailed among the type of prisoner we are primarily considering—and even among the Star class there are not a few who are dangerous here. Every prison officer in regular contact with prisoners is constantly open to corruption, and the root of this evil is tobacco. There has always been a certain amount of illegal traffic in tobacco, even when its presence in a prison was most strictly forbidden. But then it was fairly easy to detect illicit tobacco. When, with the introduction of the earnings scheme, the purchase of tobacco by prisoners was allowed, detection became less easy; and since the level of earnings can only provide enough tobacco to stimulate the craving for more, the effects have been bad—so bad as to raise the question whether the disadvantages of this step have not outweighed the advantages. Tobacco, or the lack of it, leads to more corruption, secret and overt violence and general bad feeling and evil conduct than almost any other aspect of prison life. The 'tobacco-baron' who, with the help of his jackals, gets a hold on the weak and hard-up who have been led into borrowing, is a menacing feature of the unsavoury underlife of all too many prisons.

An even greater menace may be the corrupt officer, rare though he fortunately is: to bring illicit tobacco, letters and other specified articles into a prison, or to 'plant' them outside for the purpose, is an offence punishable by imprisonment and (for a member of the staff) automatic forfeiture of office, but the profits are so great that the risks may still be taken. The danger to the officer is insidious—if he gives way, however little, he cannot withdraw; once a prisoner has moved him from the strict path of duty it is the prisoners who control him, not he the prisoners—*facilis descensus* . . .

This is a situation of real difficulty for prison administrators, who cannot but know that in this sort of atmosphere moral training is unlikely to do well: it is one of the strongest reasons for the separate training prison. The present combination of high prices for tobacco with restrictions on the cost of the earnings scheme required by public economy is unfavourable to a simple economic solution; to allow prisoners a reasonable ration of tobacco below cost, when so many 'in a state of innocence and liberty' cannot now afford to smoke at all, might prove to be too flagrant a breach of the principle of less eligibility; the radical solution of abolishing smoking in prisons is probably impracticable. Recently some improvement has been effected by a modest increase of earnings, by allowing all to earn and to smoke from the beginning, and by experiments in substituting book-credits for cash payments. But this may well remain as a troublesome problem in any prison of mixed or recidivist population, or to a lesser degree in other prisons should an officer become corrupted and escape detection. Fortunately the determination of the staff as a whole to resist and expose this evil of 'trafficking' keeps it within very small dimensions.

(2) SECURITY

The essence of commitment to prison for any purpose being that the prisoner is deprived of his liberty, the basic charge on the keepers of the prison is, today as yesterday, safe-custody. If today other 'primary and concurrent' charges are laid on the prison which cannot be fully discharged if safe-custody is treated as an over-riding consideration, that raises questions of method and emphasis rather than of principle. Where the value of a particular system of training for the prevention of crime is such that, in order to preserve it, reasonable risks must be taken as to safe-custody, such risks may properly be taken for so long as the balance of results justifies them—for so long, that is, as escapes do not cause trouble to the police and the public, and disturbance in the administration of the prison, which are disproportionate to the additional value of the system over one of greater security.

But in prisons which rely on physical restraints—walls, locks and bars—there can be no half-measures. To many prisoners this type of safe-custody offers a challenge which they are always ready to accept, and they show great skill, perseverance and daring in their attempts to defeat it. For the defenders therefore a certain professional pride also becomes involved, if no more. In the local prisons, then, and those for long-term prisoners and persistent offenders, the requirements of security have a dominating influence on the life and routine of the prison.

The structural features of the security system condition the whole plan and atmosphere of the prison. The sheer 20-foot wall encloses all, with its massive gate-house of which the outer and inner gates must never be open at the same time. Every entrance to the main prison blocks has an iron-barred gate on a double lock opened with a special key of limited issue, and the day's routine is regularly punctuated by the unlocking and locking up of the prisoners in their cells. The prison officer of today is a good deal more than a turnkey, but turning keys, checking them, and accounting for them remain a prominent and permanent feature of his daily life.

This locking and unlocking of gates and cell doors, with the 'proving' and checking required to ensure that they are always properly secured, requires a specialised technique, as do the various ceremonies of the keys—a stray key may give sleepless nights to the whole staff till it is found. The checking of numbers is the next essential of security. This requires the careful supervision of every party of prisoners at all times, and a sort of running audit and balancing up of numbers at each unlocking and locking-up comparable with the operations of a bank. The first thing reported to a visiting superior is the number on the roll, whether of the whole prison or a particular shop or party, and the standard greeting of every prison officer, as he salutes the visitor, is 'Fourteen men, sir, all correct.' When prisoners are locked up at dinner-time, and again at supper-time, every officer has to report his roll, and the senior officer balances up. The staff cannot dismiss till the balance is correct, and many a careless officer has appeared before the Governor charged with 'giving an incorrect roll, thereby delaying the staff for 20 minutes'. When account is taken of all the comings and goings of prisoners, the odd men who are sick, or on report, or waiting to see the Governor, or taken away from their parties for a bath or a visit, the complication of this technique, and the constant care required to keep the record straight, become almost distressingly clear. But it is not difficult for an experienced prisoner to 'escape notice disappearing' in the to-and-fro of a busy prison day, and without this somewhat rigid and exacting routine his absence might not be noticed for hours, and then it might take a very long time to find out who it was that was missing, where he was last seen, whether he was not perhaps somewhere where he might legitimately be, and so on. It is easier to fade away during the day and lie-up somewhere till night-fall than to break out of a cell, and much more disturbing to the administration.

But breaking out of a cell is a possible and, with a limited number of skilled operators, a popular project. It has been done in many different ways—by making keys, by filing window-bars, by making a hole in the wall, or even by cutting a hole in the floor and going out through a ventilating shaft. But it requires time, care and tools of sorts, and the counter-move to this gambit is searching. About once a fortnight, at irregular intervals to secure a surprise effect, every cell and its occupant should have a 'special search' designed to lay bare any filing or picking or scratching, or any illicit objects that could serve as tools. Many 'unauthorised articles' are revealed on these occasions, perhaps the most striking of recent years being a little wireless receiver made out of bits and pieces of broken-down telephone equipment smuggled in from a workshop—though, as it was put by the officer displaying this ingenious bit of work, 'the poor chap was wasting his time because after all it seemed he could only get the Third Programme!' Every party is, in principle, searched on coming in from work, but this is no more than a superficial rub-down supposed to ensure that nothing is concealed in the clothing. It is not surprising that, in the general rush, this should have developed into little more than a formal gesture by the officer carrying it out, though it may still have some deterrent effect. The 'shadow-boards' for tools in the workshops are part of the same set of precautions, to ensure that the officers responsible for checking tools at the end of each period can see at a glance whether one is missing. A break out from a cell is usually made at night, though it has been done by day (and once by a girl of about 16), and must include the operation of 'selling the dummy' to the night-patrol, that is of placing in the bed objects giving the appearance of a sleeping occupant: since the night-patrols have no cell-key (lest they should be overpowered by someone at large who could then unlock the whole prison) this is not difficult—indeed the night-patrols are not effective as a security measure, and escapers can always gauge their operations so as to evade inspection.

Having broken out of the cell, it is necessary to get over the wall, and this seems to present surprisingly little difficulty to the enterprising. Security measures against this move include the careful locking up of ladders, timber, ropes and other articles that would help, but somehow the escaper is usually able to construct and conceal somewhere a rope and hook, or get hold of a long piece of timber. The expense of manpower in yard-patrols by night has not seemed justifiable.

On top of all this precaution is the blanket-measure of the Escape List, on which the Governor is required to place all prisoners who are known to have escaped or tried to escape before. These men are located together in cells placed where they can most easily be supervised, and have to put all their clothing outside the door at night, while a dim light is kept on in their cells. During the day every officer who takes such a man over signs for him and duly hands him over on receipt to his successor, and to make sure that they are not overlooked they wear coloured patches of an unobtrusive sort on their jackets and trousers. The Governor has complete discretion to take a man off the Escape List at any time he thinks it right to do so.

The dispassionate observer, considering the enormous effort put into this complicated system of security, and its effect in adding to the repression and artificiality of prison life, may well wonder if there may not be more sorrow over one offender who escapes safe-custody than over ninety-and-nine who escape reform. What, he may ask, are its effects? After all this trouble, how many prisoners do escape from conditions of security? The answer, as given by the Commissioners in their Annual Report for 1947 (p. 35) is that prior to 1939 the average number of escapes from secure conditions was about 5 a year; the conditions during and after the war, already described, had led to an increase, wholly disproportionate to the increase of population, to between 40 and 50 a year. A great improvement was however recorded in 1950, when escapes fell to 20 for a much larger population.

(3) MECHANICAL RESTRAINTS AND REMOVAL

Here it may be said first that the chaining of prisoners who have tried to escape is no longer permitted in English prisons. Indeed the use of any form of mechanical restraint inside the prison is strictly forbidden by the Statutory Rules except on medical grounds by direction of the Medical Officer, or when it appears to the Governor that it is necessary in order to prevent a prisoner injuring himself or others, or damaging property, or creating a disturbance. If the Governor does so order, he must at once inform the Visiting Committee and the Medical Officer in writing, and if the Medical Officer does not concur the Governor must act on his recommendations. No prisoner must be kept under restraint longer than is necessary for the purpose for which it was ordered, nor for a longer period than 24 hours without the written authority of the Visiting Committee or the Commissioners.

Outside the prison, when convicted men (but not women or, except by special direction of the Governor, young prisoners) are being removed to another prison, or to or from court, they may be and usually are handcuffed, or attached to a chain when being moved in parties. On these occasions the Rules prescribe that 'they shall be exposed to public view as little as possible, and proper safeguards shall be adopted to protect them from insult and curiosity': this of course applies whether the prisoners are handcuffed or not, and to all classes of prisoner. Effect is given to the rule by using road transport direct from place to place as much as possible, and where rail is used by securing reserved compartments and making special arrangements with the railway authorities to ensure the inconspicuous entraining and detraining of the prisoners and their escort. These arrangements do not always work to perfection, and on occasion the sensitive may still be shocked by the sight of chained prisoners at a railway station: but at least such a sight is accidental, unforeseen and undesired by those responsible. We have moved far in such matters from the days, not much more than a hundred years ago, when a party of unconvicted women were taken down the public street to York Assizes not only handcuffed, but chained by their necks; or from those, some fifty years ago, when Oscar Wilde, handcuffed and in prison garb, was kept for twenty minutes on the crowded platform of Clapham Junction waiting for the train to Reading.

(4) REMISSION

From the days of transportation and the early penal servitude system, eligibility to earn a remission of part of the sentence by good conduct and industry has been the first and most valuable privilege accorded to prisoners, as the power to forfeit remission has been and remains one' of the strongest sanctions against bad conduct. Under the penal servitude system a convict did not, strictly, earn a remission of his sentence, but became eligible for earlier release on a conditional licence: the sentence remained in force and on breach of licence he might be required to serve the unexpired portion, again with the power to earn earlier release on a fresh licence. But when by the Prison Act 1898 this privilege was extended from penal servitude to imprisonment, the person sentenced to imprisonment could earn an absolute remission: when he was discharged the sentence was deemed to have expired. On the abolition of penal servitude by the Criminal Justice Act 1948, this system of absolute remission was continued for all sentences of imprisonment of whatever length, save for young prisoners (see Chapter 20). For persons sentenced to corrective training or preventive detention the conditional licence system is retained (see Chapter 18).

The amount of remission which may be earned is prescribed not by the Act but by the Statutory Rules. After 1898 the amount to be earned on a sentence of penal servitude was one-quarter of the sentence for men and one-third for women, and on one of imprisonment one-sixth. During the Second World War, primarily as a measure to reduce the prison population, a flat-rate of one-third for all sentences was introduced, and this rate was continued in the Statutory Rules 1949. Remission applies only to sentences above one month, and cannot serve to reduce a sentence to less than 31 days. A prisoner is discharged in the early morning of the day following that on which he earns full remission.

It is not easy to define any principle on which the amount of remission to be earned has been or should be based. On the one hand, the amount must be enough to enable its forfeiture to be effective as a disciplinary sanction: if a badly behaved prisoner loses all his remission in the early days of his sentence, he is left with nothing to hope or work for, while if he continues to behave badly the Governor has no resource but continued physical punishments such as close confinement or reduced diet. On the other hand, if the amount went beyond a certain point, the Courts might feel constrained to pass longer sentences than they would otherwise consider appropriate. Although the present rate was fixed on grounds of expediency rather than of principle, it appears to strike a reasonable balance.

Since the abolition of the marks system, it is perhaps hardly correct to speak of a prisoner 'earning' his remission. It is, like his privileges under the new stage system, credited to him at the beginning and he keeps it unless it is forfeited by his own fault.

(5) OFFENCES AND PUNISHMENTS

A prisoner may be punished only for one of the 'offences against discipline' set out as such in the Statutory Rules, and by one of the punishments prescribed in the Rules. Punishments may be awarded only by the Governor or the officer authorised to act for him, or, for more serious offences, by the Visiting Committee or a Commissioner or Assistant Commissioner.[1]

The Rules prescribe that 'A prisoner shall, before a report against him is dealt with, be informed of the offence for which he has been reported and shall be given a proper opportunity of hearing the facts alleged against him and of presenting his case.' This Rule follows an enactment of the Criminal Justice Act 1948, in the course of debate on which concern was shown by the Committee of the House of Commons as to whether, in the special circumstances of a prison, prisoners charged with offences are enabled to make an effective defence: in particular, the view was expressed that an accused prisoner should be assisted or represented by a 'friend', who might even in certain circumstances be a legal adviser. In deference to the feeling of the House, the Secretary of State appointed a Departmental Committee to examine the whole question of offences and punishments in prisons and Borstals, and it

[1] This power is in practice rarely used by Commissioners or Assistant Commissioners, except where a recaptured escaper has to be dealt with in another prison.

may be that the Report of this Committee will suggest reconsideration of some of the present Rules, or of the practice in applying them.[1]

Pending any such changes, the present procedure is that when an officer finds it necessary to report a prisoner, he completes a form, which is handed to the prisoner, setting out the precise paragraph of the Rule under which the charge is made (the prisoner has a copy of this in his cell) and the time and place: there is a space on the form on which the prisoner can make a written reply if he wishes. Pending adjudication the prisoner is kept in his cell: this will not be for long, except at the week-end, for the Governor is required to adjudicate on reports every morning except on Sundays and public holidays.

When the prisoner's turn comes he is brought before the Governor under escort, and is first ordered to 'give your full name and number to the Governor': this is done whenever a prisoner is brought before the Governor for any purpose, and is not, as might appear, meaningless routine—it could happen, and has happened, that by some accident the man present is not the man named in the records before the Governor. The Governor then reads out the charge, and hears the evidence of the reporting officer, which is of course also heard by the prisoner: the prisoner is then invited to say whatever he has to say in his defence, and here the written statement of defence may be helpful to those who are too over-awed or incoherent to express themselves to advantage. Usually in these cases there is no question of difficulty about the facts, or of an alibi, or the like, and the Governor has little difficulty in making up his mind as to guilt, though there may be a certain amount of question and answer between the prisoner and the officer, and it may even be necessary to call other evidence. But in cases within his own competence the Governor can usually despatch the matter then and there, perhaps after sending the prisoner out while he consults with the Chief Officer, in the light of the prisoner's record, on the best way to deal with him. The proceedings may be brusque, but one thing about which there is, on the whole, virtually no complaint by prisoners is the standard of fairness and justice in Governors' adjudications. The Governor makes a full note of the proceedings, and these are sent to the Prison Commission weekly for information. Each Assistant Commissioner scrutinises these reports from his prisons.

Frequently an admonition to a prisoner is sufficient, but when punishment is necessary the Governor may choose from the following:

(a) forfeiture of remission of sentence for a period not exceeding fourteen days;

(b) forfeiture or postponement of privileges for a period not exceeding twenty-eight days;

[1] For a summary of the recommendations of this Committee, which were published in May 1951, see Appendix I.

(c) exclusion from associated work for a period not exceeding fourteen days;

(d) cellular confinement for a period not exceeding three days;

(e) restricted diet No. 1 for a period not exceeding three days;

(f) restricted diet No. 2 for a period not exceeding fifteen days;

(g) stoppage of earnings for a period not exceeding fourteen days.

Where the misconduct is so serious or repeated that the Governor considers the punishments within his power inadequate, he may report the prisoner to the Visiting Committee, and he must do so if the offence charged is one of the following:

(a) escaping or attempting to escape from prison or from legal custody;

(b) gross personal violence to a fellow prisoner;

(c) mutiny or incitement to mutiny;

(d) gross personal violence to an officer.

Pending adjudication by the Visiting Committee the prisoner will again, unless the Governor orders otherwise, be kept in his cell, except for Chapel and exercise, but again not for more than a few days in the ordinary course, since except for mutiny and gross personal violence to an officer the powers of the Visiting Committee may be exercised by any one of them, and a member visits by rota every week.

The investigation by the Visiting Committee is more formal, especially when it is taken by the full Committee, though in normal practice this means a panel of from three to five of the members presided over by the Chairman. The investigation may be on oath if the Committee so decides. It is within the discretion of the Committee to decide what additional evidence should be called, and in the peculiar circumstances of a prison this may give rise to difficulty, and even to an appearance of injustice if the standards of the Courts are applied. In a conflict between the word of an officer and that of a prisoner, without corroboration, the prisoner may well feel that the odds are on the officer, though this position is not peculiar to a prison—the private soldier in the Orderly Room, or the citizen in the Magistrates' Court, may equally gain the impression that his word carries less weight than that of a sergeant-major or a police constable. If the officer calls corroborative evidence, the prisoner may suppose that the 'screws' will naturally support each other, and if the prisoner wishes to call other prisoners to support his version he may be faced with difficulties: the natural disposition of most prisoners is to 'keep out of trouble', and unless they have some personal axe to grind they will not usually be anxious either to give the lie to an officer on oath or to give away a fellow prisoner. The Committee may also be unconvinced of the relevance of the evidence which a prisoner claims to call, and where they hear evidence which remains in clear conflict with that of the officer or officers on the other side, they are still faced with their original dilemma—on the one side the voice of authority, which should be supported unless it is clearly being abused, on the other that of a man or men of, in all probability, known bad character and dubious motives. Yet an officer is not to be believed because he is an officer, nor a prisoner disbelieved because he is a prisoner. In spite of these difficulties, no ground has been given for supposing that, on the whole, the magistrates who undertake these difficult duties do not succeed in doing substantial justice, and the Chairman usually regards it as his duty to assist the accused in making the best of his defence and in questioning the evidence against him.

The punishments which a Visiting Committee may award are as follows:

(a) forfeiture of remission of sentence;

(b) forfeiture or postponement of privileges;

(c) exclusion from associated work for a period not exceeding twenty-eight days;

(d) restricted diet No. 1 for a period not exceeding fifteen days;

(e) restricted diet No. 2 for a period not exceeding forty-two days;

(f) cellular confinement for a period not exceeding fourteen days or, where the prisoner is found guilty of mutiny or incitement to mutiny, or of gross personal violence to an officer, not exceeding twenty-eight days;

(g) stoppage of earnings for a period not exceeding twenty-eight days.

For the two offences of mutiny or incitement to mutiny, and gross personal violence to an officer, there are special provisions in view of their gravity and of the fact that they may, by the provisions of the Criminal Justice Act 1948, be punished by corporal punishment. This is now the sole relic of flogging as a legal punishment in England, and since its retention in support of prison discipline has so recently been approved by Parliament, discussion of merits in a matter of so much controversy would here be out of place. The grounds on which it has been defended have been clearly and fairly stated by a prominent opponent of corporal punishment as follows: 'The case for the retention of flogging for breaches of prison discipline rests upon the need of defending prison officers against violence in the particular circumstances in which they are placed. An outstanding feature of the English Prison Service is the absence of brutality, or of the manhandling of prisoners by warders. The rule against brutality is rigidly enforced even in cases of violent attack. It is held that as individual retaliation is forbidden to the officer he must be specially protected, not so much for his own safety as in the interests of good discipline in the service.' [1]

[1] *Corporal Punishment—An Indictment*, George Benson and Edward Glover (Howard League for Penal Reform. Price 6d.), p. 12.

The procedure of the Visiting Committee on these charges is the same, except that a special meeting must be summoned at which not more than five nor less than three members, two at least being magistrates, must be present, and the proceedings must be on oath.

If corporal punishment is awarded, the number of strokes is by statute restricted to 18 with the cat o' nine tails or birch rod [1], the former being inflicted on the back, the latter on the buttocks; and cellular confinement or restricted diet may not be awarded in addition. Only male prisoners serving sentences of imprisonment, corrective training or preventive detention are eligible for corporal punishment.

All awards of corporal punishment must be confirmed by the Secretary of State, who sees all such cases personally. When they are not confirmed, an alternative punishment is substituted by the Visiting Committee.

Corporal punishment may not be awarded unless the Medical Officer has examined the prisoner and certified that he is medically and physically fit for it, and he must again examine him immediately before the punishment is inflicted and be present during its infliction: if on medical grounds the Medical Officer advises that it should stop, the Governor, who must also be present, must remit the remainder.

A note in conclusion of this section on the nature of the various punishments permitted.

Forfeitures of remission and privileges have been discussed elsewhere, though it may be added that privileges need not be forfeited en bloc—any one may be forfeited if it has been abused or if that seems the most appropriate punishment, and Governors are advised that such privileges as letters and visits, use of the library, and education facilities should be forfeited in the ordinary course only if they are abused.

Exclusion from associated work is usually awarded in the prisoner's own interests to keep him out of trouble: he then works in his cell.

Cellular confinement does not connote a dark cell or a dungeon: there is nothing of this sort in English practice. The prisoner works in his cell and is deprived of all forms of association: in some prisons, for convenience, a separate block of cells or part of a landing is set aside for prisoners undergoing punishment, but these do not differ in construction or equipment from ordinary cells. There are advantages in keeping these prisoners away from the normal life of the prison.

Although not relevant to the heading of punishment, it is convenient to mention here that as distinct from the foregoing 'separate' cells there are also 'special' cells, which again are not dark though they are silent, or as near so as may be, with double-doors and a minimum of fixed unbreakable furniture with the window well out of reach. These are for the temporary confinement of violent, noisy or

2 For a person under 21, twelve strokes with the birch rod.

hysterical prisoners who would otherwise smash up their cells, possibly injure themselves or others, keep the prison awake with their noise, or otherwise violently disturb the peace. The Statutory Rules provide that 'no prisoner shall be confined in such a cell as a punishment or after he has ceased to be refractory or violent'. Restricted Diet No. 1 is one pound of bread per diem with water. If given for more than 3 days, the first 3 days bread and water are followed by 3 days ordinary diet, then 3 more days bread and water, and so on, so that the maximum period of 15 days means 9 days bread and water and 6 days ordinary diet. A prisoner on this diet is not required to work, but may work in his cell if he so wishes. Restricted diet No. 2 consists of 8 oz. of bread with water for breakfast and supper, and 1 pint of oatmeal porridge, 8 oz. of potatoes, and 8 oz. of bread with water for dinner. If given for more than 21 days, it must be interrupted after 21 days by 7 days ordinary diet. This prolonged excess of carbo-hydrates is now regarded as unsatisfactory, and alternatives are under consideration.

No prisoner may be awarded cellular confinement or dietary punishment unless he has been certified fit for such punishment by the Medical Officer, and the Governor, Chaplain and Medical Officer are required to pay a daily visit to every prisoner undergoing cellular confinement or No. 1 diet.

(6) INFORMATION AND COMPLAINTS

The Statutory Rules are explicit as to the necessity of informing prisoners fully about the Rules governing their treatment and generally as to their rights and obligations, and ensuring that this information has been read and understood. This is done by a series of cell-cards. The prisoner meets the first of these in the reception-cell, its purpose being to assure him that he is not going to serve his sentence in this bleak cubicle, and to instruct him as to the processes through which he will pass in the reception block. On the wall of his cell, when he reaches the main prison, he will find a collection of cards dealing with all contingencies. For the untried and recently convicted there will be a batch dealing with Bail, Legal Aid and Appeals: for more sustained reading there are four cards, one giving 'Notes for Guidance' on most aspects of prison life not covered by the other three, which deal with Discipline, Privileges and Stage; Diet; and Aid on Discharge. These large and closely-printed cards make neither for convenient reading nor, after a time, for amenity as a wall-decoration, and their combination in some form of booklet or folder is under consideration: the variety of cards required for different categories and classifications will, however, make it difficult to secure a system at once effective and economical.

1 See Appendix I.

One matter to which a prisoner's attention is fully and precisely directed in his 'Notes for Guidance' is his right to make complaints and the channels through which he may make them, which are both numerous and, in time and trouble expended from the landing officer up to the Home Secretary himself, costly. The English prison system is especially sensitive to any possibility of abuse of authority without redress.

The care taken here can perhaps be best shown by quoting the information actually given to the prisoner, which reads as follows:

'2. (a) If you want to make a request or complaint, you can have an interview with any of the following:

Governor, Chaplain or Medical Officer.
Member of the Visiting Committee or Board of Visitors at his next visit.
Commissioner or Assistant Commissioner at his next visit.

'If you want to see any of the first three you should ask your landing officer when your cell is opened in the morning: to see the others you should apply to the Governor.

'(b) If you are taken suddenly ill, you may ask for the Medical Officer at any time.

'(c) You may if you wish submit a petition to the Secretary of State, but before doing so you should enquire of the Governor whether the matter about which you desire to petition is one which which the Governor or the Visiting Committee or the Board of Visitors are authorised to deal. If it is such a matter you should take steps to bring it to the notice of the Governor or the Visiting Committee or the Board of Visitors and should await their decision before submitting a petition.

'3. If you wish to write to a Member of Parliament to complain about your conviction or sentence or your treatment in prison, you may do so on the following conditions:

'(a) If your complaint is about your treatment in prison you must first make it through the usual channels set out in Note 2 above. You will not be allowed to write to a member of Parliament about a complaint of this sort on which you have written a petition till you have had a reply to the petition.

'(b) You must use one of your ordinary letters unless you have been 2 months in prison, when you may on application be allowed one special letter.

'(c) You must not put in the letter any enclosures for the M.P. to send to the Home Office, or any matter intended for insertion in the Press.

'(*d*) You must not ask the M.P. to approach on your behalf any Judge, Foreign Minister or Consul, or other public department or authority at home or abroad.

'(*e*) Your letter must comply with the regulations as to outgoing letters: in particular, you must not use any threatening or improper language.'

As further evidence, one may note the care with which the Secretary of State thought it necessary to justify to the House of Commons certain restrictions on the right of prisoners to communicate with Members of Parliament: in reply to a Question on 29 July 1949, Mr. Chuter Ede said:

'In July of last year, after consultation with my right hon. Friend the Secretary of State for Scotland, I decided, as I announced to the House at the time, to issue instructions that prisoners might be permitted to use letters from their ordinary allowance to write to a Member of Parliament of their choice, and that such letters might be permitted in certain circumstances.

'I am anxious to maintain this concession, which I think is right in principle, and in accordance with the wishes of the House, but experience of its working has shown that certain limitations are necessary in the interests of the maintenance of discipline and the proper management of prisons. Under the Prison Standing Orders a prisoner is not permitted to make complaints in his letters to friends and relatives about his treatment in prison, because there are appointed channels by which grievances of this kind can be considered and redressed. A prisoner can ask to see the Governor, and if dissatisfied with the Governor's decision, can ask to see the Visiting Committee or Board of Visitors, and he has the further remedy of petitioning the Secretary of State. He can also request an interview with one of the Prison Commissioners or Assistant Commissioners or in Scotland with an officer of the Secretary of State at his next visit to the prison. Moreover, if a prisoner makes, either to the visiting magistrates or in a petition, allegations against a prison officer, which are established to be false and malicious, he is liable to be punished.

'Hon. Members will appreciate that if a prisoner is to be allowed to use a letter to a Member of Parliament for the purpose of making complaints about his treatment, which he would not be allowed to make in an ordinary letter, and which he has never made to the prison authorities, the result would be that a prisoner could by-pass the appointed channels for the investigation of such complaints, and could make with impunity the most malicious and unfounded allegations against particular officers. This seems to be most undesirable and likely eventually to undermine the authority of the Visiting Committee or

Board of Visitors who are the independent check on prison administration for which Parliament has made provision. My right hon. Friend the Secretary of State for Scotland and I therefore propose to issue instructions that a prisoner shall not be allowed to make complaints about his prison treatment in a letter to a Member unless he has already exhausted his right of making the complaint through the proper channels in one or other of the ways I have mentioned.

'Under the Prison Standing Orders there are certain matters which may not be included in letters written by prisoners. These are:

'(1) Discussion of methods of committing crime, instigation of criminal offences, attempts to defeat the ends of justice by suborning witnesses or tampering with evidence, or attempts to facilitate escapes.

'(2) Complaints about the courts and the police which are deliberately calculated to hold the authorities up to contempt.

'(3) Threats of violence.

'(4) Matter intended for insertion in the Press.

'(5) Grossly improper language.

'(6) Attempts to stimulate public agitation about matters other than the prisoner's own conviction and sentence.

'There can be no grounds upon which it would be justifiable to allow a prisoner to include in a letter to a Member of Parliament any of these matters, which are objectionable in themselves, irrespective of the person to whom the letter is addressed, and my right hon. Friend and I propose, therefore, to issue instructions that the rule prohibiting the inclusion of such matters in prisoners' letters shall be applied to letters addressed to Members of Parliament.' [1]

This statement by the Secretary of State gives a sufficient explanation of the principles and practice in this matter, but a few foot-notes may be of interest.

If a prisoner puts himself down to see the Governor, Chaplain, Medical Officer, Visiting Magistrate or Commissioner, he does not have to explain why—he sees the members of the staff that day or (on a late application) the next, and the visitors on their next visit, without question.

If he asks for a petition form he is given one, unless he already has an unanswered petition outstanding, and he can petition about anything he likes so long as he does not use improper language. If the matter is one with which the Visiting Committee is competent to deal the petition is first laid before them, and if the prisoner is then satisfied he may

---

[1] Hansard, Vol. 467, No. 160, Cols. 181–183.

withdraw it: otherwise it is posted at once with all relevant information and reports, and dealt with by the administrative staff of the Prison Commission or of the Criminal Division of the Home Office, according to its subject-matter, in consultation as necessary with the appropriate Directorate of the Commission. If necessary, a petition may well be considered by the Permanent Under Secretary of State or by Ministers. It is desirable to state this in view of a commonly expressed belief by prisoners that their petitions are answered by the Governor's clerk!

The Home Secretary's statement referred to one question which from time to time causes particular difficulty—the making of complaints against officers by prisoners. It is important to protect prisoners against abuse of authority, but it is equally important to protect the staff, in the proper discharge of their difficult duties, against accusations which are malicious and unfounded and likely to damage their reputation or even their livelihood. Prisoners are, therefore, advised on their cell-cards that they should always consult the Governor before committing themselves to any serious accusation against a member of the staff. A Governor so consulted will advise the prisoner that he should consider carefully, before he makes his charge, whether he will be able to prove it, because it will be carefully investigated and, if it is found to be false and made with malice knowing it to be false, he is liable to punishment. If he wishes to go on, the prisoner is then told to put it in writing, and a copy is sent to the officer concerned. The subsequent proceedings depend on the facts and circumstances, but a full-dress inquiry by the Visiting Committee, and if necessary by the Commissioners, may well follow. It is an inevitable feature of imprisonment that men and women, especially the more unbalanced, brood excessively over trifles and make mountains out of every molehill. The last thing wanted is the appearance of frightening them out of what may be mere 'blowing off steam' or the making of legitimate complaints. To steer a fair and sympathetic course between this evil and the equal evil of leaving the staff a prey to the malice of some of the cunning and wicked people in their charge is not easy.

CHAPTER ELEVEN

WORK

(1) PRINCIPLES AND PROBLEMS

SHOULD prisoners work? The fact that, as recently as 1931, an authoritative work [1] should have been published under this title implies all the still unresolved questions surrounding this central problem of prison administration. Should prisoners be required to work? If so, for what purpose? What sort of work should they do? On what economic basis should the work be found and organised? What incentives, if any, should be offered to induce them to work well? Any or all of these questions may still be asked today in the penal systems of the world without finding answers of general acceptance in principle or applicability in practice. [2] The integration of social, economic and penal theory required for a clear and consistent set of principles on which such answers could be based is far from complete, in England or elsewhere.

As before, consideration starts from the basic fact that imprisonment at common law is deprivation of liberty in a lawful prison and no more. While the function of the prison was no more than custodial, therefore, there was no doubt as to the answer to the first question—prisoners could not be required to work: nor is the position different today in respect of the custodial function. By the Statutory Rules of 1949 neither untried prisoners nor those 'convicted of sedition etc.' may be required to work in the service or industries of the prison without their consent, and if they do so work they must be paid for it. The same held good until recent years in respect of the coercive function in its application to debtors. It appears, therefore, that the right to exact work is to be considered as inherent, if at all, in the corrective function of the prison and not in imprisonment as such: if the State does not claim the right to exact from all whom it commits to its penal institutions that they should work, whether for their keep or on other

[1] *Should Prisoners Work*, L. N. Robinson. Philadelphia, 1931.
[2] See however Resolution II (3), Appendix F.

176

grounds, the principles on which work-is to be exacted from those who are subject to the corrective function are still to seek.

During the eighteenth and early nineteenth centuries, when the local prison authorities were under no liability to maintain their prisoners, they might be allowed to work to keep themselves from starvation, and at a later stage the authorities might be glad to ease the burden of prisons on the rates by providing industries in the prisons and even paying the prisoners well for working in them; but these practices derived from economic considerations, not from penal theory. Setting aside the early practice of Houses of Correction, which again did not derive from penal theory, the first clear principle of work generally applied in English prisons was that of 1865—hard labour as a form of punishment over and above the punishment by deprivation of liberty: the derivation here was entirely from penal theory divorced from social or economic principles, since its essence was that the labour should be unproductive—it aimed at punishment of the body and spirit by monotony and fatigue and nothing more. This principle, though in historical perspective it now seems no more than a temporary deviation from the true line of development, did have the effect of importing into the prison system the idea of 'work as a part of the punishment' which has never since been wholly exorcised from consideration of the question. This conception was limited in its application to persons sentenced to penal servitude or to imprisonment with hard labour: for those not so sentenced, productive work was still provided, but after 1865, the liability of the county to maintain all criminal prisoners having been established, it was forbidden to pay the prisoners for their work. It is interesting to note here that there seems still to have lingered a doubt as to whether such prisoners should be forced to work, since for neglect of work the Rules specifically limited punishment to alteration of diet: the implication seems to be that the governing principle here, expressed or not, was the social-economic 'he who does not work, neither shall he eat'.

But as to any principle governing productive work in penal theory, serious consideration is lacking until 1895; the thought of Howard, Bentham and Mrs. Fry in relation to prisoners' work, valuable and constructive as it was, was not concerned with the prison as a primary instrument of legal punishment: the prisoners with whom they were concerned, saving the untried, debtors and minor offenders, were to be *punished* not by imprisonment but by transportation or death. It is, therefore, a matter for continuing regret that, when it had become not only possible but essential to define the function of work in the régime of the prison, the examination of the question by the Gladstone Committee was neither exhaustive nor convincing.

The Committee opened its observations under the heading of Prison Labour by pointing out that notwithstanding its 'great intrinsic importance . . . in previous inquiries it has been passed over with but little notice': but although their own consideration started from the principle, revolutionary in its time, 'that prison treatment should have as its primary and concurrent objects deterrence and reformation', their conclusions were still conditioned by the conception of 'work as part of the punishment'. 'It follows, therefore,' they continued, 'that it is desirable to provide labour which in conjunction with the general prison discipline does not impair the one, and which does include the other.' From this somewhat Delphic utterance of principle one clear recommendation only resulted, that 'the mechanical labour should be discontinued wherever practicable' and replaced by—what? Here was the crux, the test of the Committee's faith in the principle from which they started. But here they faltered: the authority of the idea of deterrence was still too great for them to separate it altogether from the function of work, and instead of a courageous statement of the place of work in a régime intended to be reformative, the conclusion is that 'we recommend that every effort should be made to find work for prisoners which would be a fitting equivalent to hard labour of the 1st class as now defined'.

In England, therefore, the first phase of the twentieth-century system opened without benefit of real examination of the place of work in a prison régime which included reformation in its objects, and so with no clear view of a purpose behind the requirement that its prisoners should be set to productive work. The provision of useful work was regarded as in itself a 'reformative element', and indeed that provision was and is basic, on many grounds. The first was put by Elizabeth Fry when, in answer to the question 'Do you think any reformation possible without employment?' she said 'I should believe it impossible. We may instruct as we will, but if we allow them . . . nothing to do they must return to their evil practices.' [1] To the mere avoidance of Satan's mischief the Gladstone Committee had added the value of 'training in orderly and industrial habits', and a third and most cogent point was well put by Mr. E. R. Cass [2] when he said 'idleness in a prison is subversive of discipline and hurtful to the moral, intellectual and physical well-being of the inmates. No greater cruelty can possibly be inflicted on prisoners than enforced idleness.' No prison treatment can hope to reform a person on whom it inflicts this cruelty as an addition to the punishment of deprivation of liberty. But at this stage perception of the reformative value of useful work was still balanced by the feeling that, deterrence being a 'primary and concurrent object', work must also be regarded as part of the punishment, 'the fitting equivalent of 1st class Hard Labour'.

The true line of development, from the original principle of the

[1] Whitney, p. 167.

[2] General Secretary of the American Prison Association, cit. L. N. Robinson, p. 2.

Houses of Correction that work should be the instrument of restoration of offenders to good citizenship, was not resumed till that integration of deterrence and reform in the conception of training which marked the second phase of the twentieth-century system. This principle, expressed by the Commissioners in those passages which have been quoted from their Annual Reports in Chapter 4, was fully endorsed by a Departmental Committee appointed in 1933 to report on the whole question of employment of prisoners. 'We cannot,' said the Committee, 'stress too strongly . . . that suitable employment is the most important factor in the physical and moral regeneration of the prisoner.'[1] While one might linger over possible qualifications of this robust declaration, the Commissioners themselves had already made it clear at least that a full working-day of useful and interesting work was central to the scheme of training, and the Statutory Rules of 1949 provide that 'Every prisoner shall be required to engage in useful work for not more than ten hours a day, of which so far as practicable at least eight hours shall be spent in associated or other work outside the cells.'

From this Rule, read in conjunction with that which lays down that the purpose of the training and treatment of prisoners is 'to establish in them the will to lead a good and useful life on discharge *and to fit them to do so*', may be derived the second clear statement of the purpose of prison work in English penal theory, well put by Dr. Grünhut (p. 209) as follows, 'the object of prison labour in a rehabilitative programme is twofold: training for work and training by work'.

It does not appear to derogate from this principle to suggest that, in so far as a prisoner has, by his offence, caused loss or damage to the community, it is right that he should make some restitution by his labour; for an appreciation of this as a moral obligation would also mark some advance in moral training. Nor is it inconsistent to advance the economic argument that the burden on the community of maintaining prisons should be eased so far as possible by the product of prison labour, so long as the argument is not pressed to the prejudice of the true purpose of the prison, which is to prevent crime: elsewhere, though not hitherto in this country, the demand that prisons should at all costs be self-supporting has led to distortion of their function and gross exploitation of prison labour.

In the English system of today, therefore, the answers to the first two questions posed at the beginning of this chapter are, in principle, clear and settled: they are the fruits of long practical experience, fully endorsed by the report of a Departmental Committee, and finally translated into statutory form by an act of the legislature. But when we come to consider the further questions, which concern the translation

[1] Report of the Departmental Committee on Employment of Prisoners, 1933, Part I, p. 64.

of the principle into practice, we shall unfortunately find that this is no more than 'the end of the beginning'. Before practice becomes wholly consistent with principle there are many and major difficulties still to be overcome. Some of these are internal, in that they are (or at present seem to be) inherent in the conditions of work in prisons; some are external, in that they concern the integration of that work into the economic framework of society—prisons do not produce in an economic vacuum.

Of the internal difficulties, the first is that the prison management has absolutely no control over its labour force in respect of either quantity or quality. As to quantity, it must accept and employ whatever numbers are received from the Courts: it may be that it has been organised for some years to provide industrial work for 5,000, and then finds its numbers have grown, for reasons it could not foresee or provide against, to 10,000: should it undertake capital expansion of workshops and machinery to meet this situation, it may find the numbers sink again to 7,000 or 4,000. As to quality, the situation has not substantially changed since the Gladstone Committee said, 'The capacities of prisoners range from a high standard to the lowest to be found anywhere in an almost endless variety. . . . (The population) is of a low order of physical and mental development, it is constantly changing, and in short presents no favourable feature whatever for the development of industrial work' (p. 22): or, as Dr. Grünhut puts it (p. 223), 'Prisoners, though not different from people at large, are a negative selection with regard to ability and inclination for regular work.' The Departmental Committee of 1933, in illustration of the same point, quoted Sir Norwood (then Dr.) East, the Medical Commissioner, as saying 'Many prisoners purposely avoid hard work and have lost permanently the capacity for sustained effort, others are untrained or cannot be trusted to work with machines or tools. Thirty-seven per cent of the male admissions in 1930 were 40 years of age or over. Some are of poor physique, indifferent mental capacity or temperamentally unstable. In short the human material in prison differs considerably from that in the general labour market. It is seldom efficient, it is often indifferent and is sometimes useless. No doubt many of the first offenders—30 per cent of the admissions in 1930—would be retained by a private employer working for profit. Only few recidivists would escape dismissal if staffs were being reduced, (p. 14).

This situation is further complicated by the special care which the prison authorities must exercise to see that no prisoner suffers injury to his health through being put to work unsuitable to his physical condition. This is one of the oldest and strongest traditions of the English prisons, deriving in part from the days of Hard Labour, in part from a real care for the rights and welfare of those so completely subject to authority. The Statutory Rules provide that 'The Medical

Officer may excuse a prisoner from work on medical grounds, and no prisoner shall be set to any work unless he has been certified as fit for that type of work by the Medical Officer.' So all prison work is roughly classified, for medical purposes, into No. 1, No. 2 and Light, and the Departmental Committee found that, in 1932–33, the percentage of admission to each of these categories was 74 to No. 1, 17 to No. 2, 6 to Light and 3 unfit for any work.

The next factor is that a high proportion of the prisoners received have sentences so short that there is no question of teaching them in the time available more than the simplest operations, even when they are both able and willing to learn. The proportions of this problem have been dealt with in Chapter 8.

The effect of these various factors is that one of the gravest and most persistent problems of prison work is not strictly concerned with work as training at all: it is the problem of finding sufficient work suitable for this large number of unskilled short-sentence prisoners. It must be work that can be easily taught in a short time, does not require valuable material or delicate machines that can be spoiled through ignorance, carelessness or malice and does not require much skilled supervision. Further, on the economic side, it must be work for the product of which a regular demand can be foreseen and a steady flow of orders relied on. So it happens that in most prison systems there is a traditional occupation, of a low industrial grade, which comes to bear particularly the stigma of prison: on the Continent, it is sticking paper-bags, in England it is making or repairing mailbags. This is one of the sore spots of our prison administration. Nobody likes it, inside or outside the prisons. It fits a man for no form of work he is likely to do outside, and few are likely to feel anything but dislike for doing it inside. And you do not even train men in 'orderly and industrial habits' by setting them to work in which they do not take and can scarcely be expected to take any intelligent interest. But not even the Departmental Committee was able to make a concrete suggestion for a better alternative, and continuous criticism since 1933 has equally produced no constructive suggestion which meets all the conditions.

There could be a brighter side even to this picture. Given a sufficient flow of orders in relation to the labour potential, the making of new bags could be carried out entirely on machines, with which the prisons are well equipped, and this is reasonably skilled and interesting work. But all too often, for long periods, expensive batteries of power machines stand idle while the work is done by hand to make the order last out till the next one is received. The prisons cannot stand men off when orders fall off, and 'redeployment' is no easier inside than outside. The worst features of this situation can only be mitigated by offering incentives for work of good quality and quantity: this question will be discussed separately, but it may be said here that on the one hand the present piece-work earnings scheme does ensure that even when employed on no more arduous and interesting work than sewing or patching canvas by hand the prisoners on the whole work fast and well, and that is not without training value; but on the other hand if work is really short the application of this incentive is obviously difficult.

There are certain other internal difficulties which are not inherent but are the result of conditions which are, it may be hoped, transitory.

The first of these is shortage of work shops. The prisons were not built with the intention of employing prisoners in association, and workshop construction in local prisons, with some exceptions, began in the early years of the century. The Departmental Committee found that in 1933 there were 94 shops employing 42·9 per cent of the total prison population out of some 60·5 per cent employed in manufacturing work (as distinct from farm and building work and domestic services). Additional workshops were built after that date, and the position before the Second World War was reasonably satisfactory and would have become entirely so, had it not been for the post-war increase of population: in 1947-8 the Commissioners reported 8,992 prisoners engaged in manufacturing work as compared with 5,925 ten years earlier. Several workshops had been lost by enemy action in the war, and a major effort was therefore necessary to keep pace with the situation, within the limits of new construction permitted by the economic situation. In their Report for 1948 the Commissioners reported that 8 industrial workshops and 23 vocational training shops [1] had been completed during the year, and others were in progress. Nevertheless it was still no uncommon sight in 1949 to see the narrow space of a long prison wing filled with men, elbow to elbow on their stools, sewing their dreary canvas. [2]

After shortage of shops shortage of staff ranks next as an obstacle to the full development of work. The effect of being able to employ only one shift of staff is to make it impossible (except in training prisons and a few special shops) to preserve the 8-hour workshop day predicated by the Rules and always sought by the administration. The Committee of 1933 said on this question, after quoting the Statutory Rule then in force (which was of similar effect to the Rule of 1949), 'This Rule gave effect to what had become at that time the general practice in all prisons, viz. the employment of all prisoners in association for as nearly as practicable 8 hours a day. In practice it was not found possible to secure that prisoners were actually employed in association for eight hours since this period included the time spent in getting men to and from their cells, a time which varied according to the size and construction of the prison, and it was further liable to be interrupted

[1] Some of these would be in Borstals.
[2] This situation had notably improved in 1951.

by intervals for attendance at chapel, exercise, bathing, visits, etc. On an average the period of actual employment might be fairly stated as 6½ hours daily. The rule giving statutory authority for the enforcement of an eight-hour associated working day had only been made three months when the financial crisis forced upon the Commissioners in July, 1931, a reduction of the staff of the prisons in England and Wales. This reduction made it impossible to continue to employ all prisoners for a nominal eight-hour day of associated labour (6½ hours actual work) and in most prisons the actual period of associated labour was reduced to under 5 hours daily. A longer period continues to be worked in the Borstal Institutions, in certain specialised prisons such as Wakefield and by certain parties of prisoners in other prisons. In consequence of the reduction in the hours of associated labour a corresponding increase was made in the hours of cell labour when work was available.'

By 1939 the position had been almost restored, and with a full shift-system the approximate 8-hour day was general. Then, substituting 'war' for 'financial crisis', history repeated itself almost precisely, and with minor variations the foregoing will serve for a description of the position today: one variation would be to underline 'when work was available' at the end of the quotation, for in recent years, in order to keep the shops working, the cell-task has become almost a matter of history.

Other writers on this subject have dealt with the classification system as an internal obstacle to the best organisation of work, but this and similar considerations are relevant only to the economic aspects of prison industry. If a prison were a factory and nothing else much might be more efficiently and economically done. But a prison is a prison first, and the proper treatment and training of the prisoners in accordance with the Statutory Rules, and the maintenance of good order and safe-custody, cannot be subordinated to considerations of good business.

We now pass to those external considerations which affect the quality and quantity of the work that can be provided for prisoners; and on this one may begin by saying that he who wills the end may be supposed to will the means, and that if society, expressing its will through the elected legislature in statutory form, has decided that prisoners should be employed for 8 hours a day in useful productive work, which should so far as possible be such as to assist both in the character-formation of the prisoner inside and in fitting him to earn an honest living outside, then society should be prepared to modify its economic and social practices, so far as may be reasonable and necessary, to assist in securing these ends. Prison managements in general have not found, and do not find today, that that position has been reached: as Dr. Mannheim puts it, 'Nowhere else has the inconsistency between

penological progress and real or imagined demands of national economy become so glaringly unmasked. This is true not only of the fundamental problem whether prisoners should be given work at all, but
also of the further question of *how* they should be employed.' [1] Here
again the principle of less eligibility is found operating in many direc-
ions; prisoners should work, no doubt, but only in such a way that
the product of their work does not compete with that of free workers;
indeed, as Dr. Grünhut points out,[2] in social-economic conditions
where work has come to be regarded not as a 'damned duty' but as a
fundamental right, the question may even be raised of a prisoner's
right to work if that right cannot be enjoyed by honest men at liberty;
and where it has been proposed to give prisoners vocational training
in a skilled trade, objection has been raised both in England [3] and
abroad on the grounds that such training may not be available to
honest citizens who might profit by it. It is still necessary in England to
face fairly and openly all the implications of 'less eligibility', and of
complaints of unfair competition by prison industries, if the intentions
of Parliament in regard to 'the training of prisoners by work and for
work' are to be properly fulfilled.

One problem has been recurrently posed and left unsolved ever since
serious attention was first given to it. In 1895 the Gladstone Committee
said, 'Difficulty of a greater or less extent is experienced almost in every
prison in getting a sufficiency of suitable work for the male prisoners'
(p. 21); in 1933 the Departmental Committee said, 'The root of all
evil in the employment of prisoners is the definite shortage of work';
in 1948 Dr. Grünhut, writing not only of England, said, 'It is the overwhelming problem of prison management to provide penal institutions
constantly with useful work.' The nature of these difficulties still, in
1951, conditions the answers to questions as to what sort of work
prisoners in English prisons should do, and how it should be found
and organised.

The story is not a new one: indeed, Mrs. Fry, as so often, said most
of what needs saying about it—'The benefit which society derives
from the employment of criminals greatly outweighs the inconvenience
which can possibly arise to the mass of our labouring population
from the small proportion of work done in our prisons.' [4] 'My idea
with regard to the employment of women is that it should be a regular
thing, undertaken by Government; considering that there are so many
to provide for; there is the Army and the Navy and so many things
required for them; why should not Government make use of the
prisoners?' [5] The Gladstone Committee, on the same subject, said,

---

[1] Mannheim, p. 75.   [2] Grünhut, p. 197.
[3] Report of the Departmental Committee on Employment of Prisoners, 1933,
Part I, pp. 82–84.
[4] Whitney, p. 161.   [5] Whitney, p. 167.

'This difficulty (shortage of work) has been largely added to by outside agitation against competition of prisoners with free labour. In consequence of the agitation, and of proceedings in the House of Commons, some suitable industries and in particular mat-making have been to a large extent given up' [1]: yet they accepted evidence that the conversion, of all prisoners from non-productive to productive labour 'would only increase the interference of prison with outside labour in the proportion of 1 to 2,500'. Dr. Grünhut, surveying the international position in 1948, says '. . . almost throughout its whole history prison labour has been denounced by trade and free labour as unfair competition'. Yet in America, he points out,[2] 'in 1923 prison-made goods reached the volume of 0·12 per cent of all goods manufactured in establishments doing business of 5,000 dollars or more.' And he adds, 'The economic loss through crime is considerable, and far surpasses the alleged detrimental effects of prison labour on private enterprise. What is indispensable for social readjustment must be accepted. But apart from rational weighing-up, men and women in prison are members of a wider community. Neither crime nor punishment would justify forfeiture of the right to work.'

The Departmental Committee of 1933 started from the propositions that 'Continuous and useful employment must be regarded not as a punishment but as an instrument of discipline and reformation. In order that this idea may be achieved, the first requirement is that useful and suitable work should be provided *and that there should be plenty of it*' (para. 128). 'But the most serious problem which the Prison Authorities have to face is the shortage of simple work suitable for unskilled and short-term prisoners' (para. 122).

As remedies for this difficulty they proposed that (1) 'The maximum amount of suitable Government work should be allocated to the prisons.' They did not recommend 'a compulsory system of state use as in certain American States' but that 'where it is known that goods required by Government Departments can be made satisfactorily by prison labour, the Prison Department should be given the opportunity in all cases of undertaking the work at a price based on that ruling in the outside market', and that in order that prison work could be planned ahead such orders should be given on a regular annual programme, with manufactures for stock of goods in regular use (133–136).

(2) That the requirements of local authorities should be met in the same way as those of Government Departments (140).

(3) 'Work for prison purposes and for Government Departments provides practically the entire occupation of the English prisoners today, and the Commissioners have hitherto been deterred by the fear of objection from outside manufacturers or workpeople from undertaking any considerable volume of outside work.

[1] Pp. 21 and 22.　　　　[2] P. 53, quoting L. N. Robinson, op. cit.

'In principle the competition of prison labour with free labour is the same whether the articles made are for Government Departments or for sale in the outside market, though the effects of prison competition in the outside market are more obvious. We think it desirable that so far as possible prisoners should be employed on Government work, but in so far as such work may be found insufficient to keep prisoners fully employed we see no objection to outside work being undertaken subject to the conditions laid down in the Report of the Gladstone Committee of 1895, viz. that prison goods are not sold below the market price, and that every consideration is shown to the special circumstances of particular industries outside so as to avoid undue interference with wages or the employment of free labour.

'The number of prisoners likely to be employed on such work at any time is so small in comparison with the outside labour market that the effect of their competition will be negligible provided there is a careful avoidance of concentration on a particular industry in a particular district' (141).

(4) 'Wherever it is possible to obtain suitable land in the vicinity of a prison on reasonable terms we are strongly of opinion that it should be acquired and brought under cultivation with a view both to the provision of employment and to making the prisons, so far as possible, self-supporting in the matter of vegetables' (143).

(5) As regards works of public utility such as drainage work, land reclamation, afforestation, etc., 'we are impressed by the importance in the existing state of unemployment of avoiding any step which might give to prisoners work which might otherwise be allocated to the unemployed. We are satisfied, however, that there is a considerable volume of useful work of this kind available and it seems probable that in many cases it will not be put in hand even as a scheme for alleviating unemployment. We recommend that such work should be considered available for prison labour in suitable cases' (144).

The effect of these recommendations, so far as they were applied, and especially of the new system of industrial management instituted on the Committee's recommendation, was such that Dr. Grünhut, surveying the international position as it was in 1938, was able to say 'the percentage of prisoners productively employed varies between 74·2 in England and Wales and 43·5 in the United States, where one-fifth of the prisoners have no work at all. . . . England with a pre-war ratio of less than 10 per cent of prisoners without work,[1] comes very

---

[1] In 1950, in U.S.A., 'probably less than thirty per cent of the prisoners in State prisons and reformatories are gainfully employed' (Report of the Federal Bureau of Prisons, 1950, p. 3). The position in the English prisons in 1949, as stated on p. 233, shows that all prisoners available for work were employed. The 10 per cent quoted by Dr. Grünhut refers to 'ineffectives', not to unemployment among prisoners available for work.

near to the optimum of full employment. . . . The good record of English prisons not only testifies to successful labour management, but is also one of the beneficial results of the centralisation of administration, the reduction of local gaols, and the small number of remand prisoners.' (P. 200.)

The war, naturally, solved all problems of under-employment in prisons as elsewhere. Prison industries played their full part in the industrial war effort, and responded magnificently to the various and urgent calls made on them, including—in preparation for 'D Day'— 'the work of anti-rust treating, wrapping and cartoning of military spare parts for the Royal Army Ordnance Corps (approx. 2,000,000 cartons).'[1] But in the post-war contraction of demand by Government Departments this record was of little avail. Before long the principle of less eligibility was ironically illustrated when English prisoners were refused permission to prepare a site for housing prison staff, on prison land, in favour of German war-prisoners; and in their Annual Report for 1949 (p. 41) the Commissioners reported that, 'In the latter part of 1949 there was a marked decline in the orders from Government Departments. This affected particularly the simpler types of work required for short-sentence prisoners, and caused a curtailment of the cellular work. The mat-making industry, which had been greatly expanded since the war, has also suffered a serious set-back through the competition of cheap imported mats, and much useful work has been lost here. There is also a shortage of more skilled work suitable for the training of long-term prisoners, which is particularly unfortunate at a time when the introduction of Corrective Training requires an increase in that class of work. There is a prospect of serious under-employment in the prisons in 1950, and the position is under review, with the Departments concerned, with a view to preventing such a situation and to securing the position for the future.'

As a result of this review, a more satisfactory appreciation of the principles of 1933 was reached, and methods were devised for their practical application—so far as concerned government contracting departments—which marked a distinct advance. There was under-employment in 1950, but it never became so serious as had been anticipated. Nevertheless, if this is the position in a period of full employment nationally, when the great majority of prisoners are working no more than 25 hours a week instead of 44, it is sufficiently clear that the provision of useful work is still, as ever, 'the overwhelming problem of prison management'.[2]

(2) PROVISION AND ORGANISATION OF WORK

Many different systems of employing prisoners have been and are in use in the penal systems of the world: Dr. L. N. Robinson in 1931

[1] *Annual Report*, 1945, p. 33.   [2] See Appendix K.

listed five as being in use in the U.S.A., and most of these, or combinations or modifications of them, may still be found in the systems of Europe. They are as follows.[1]

Lease System.—The State contracts with a lessee to feed, clothe, house and guard the prisoners, subject to inspection, the lessee paying an agreed amount for the prisoners' labour.

Contract System.—The State keeps the prisoners but lets their labour to a contractor, who manages the business side and superintends the work.

Piece-price System.—This is a variation of the contract system under which the contractor pays for output by the piece or article. 'The supervision of the work is generally performed by a prison official, although sometimes by the contractors. The officials of the prison not only maintain discipline, but also dictate the daily quantity of work required.'

State-account System.—'The State enters the field of manufacturing on its own account . . . has the entire care and control of the convicts and with them conducts an ordinary factory.'

State-use System.—As in the State-account system, but manufacture is for use of State institutions only. 'The principle . . . is that the State shall produce . . . for its own consumption alone and shall not compete directly with the business of manufacturers employing free labour.'

The first of these systems may be disregarded; Dr. Robinson indicated that it had virtually fallen into disuse, or had been pronounced illegal, in most of the States of America. The second, though it would be regarded as incompatible with the requirements of the English system, was legal in some States of America and has been used in Europe since the late war.

The English system may be said to be primarily 'State-use' as above defined, though it should be noted that this term is sometimes applied also to a system whereby States are required by law to purchase certain manufactures of prison industries—this is 'compulsory State-use' as considered and rejected by the Departmental Committee of 1933 (p. 185 above), and there is no such provision in English law or practice. But in so far as, in a few industries and on a small scale, English prisons make goods for sale on the outside market, they may be said to operate also the State-account System. During the late war they also made substantial use of the Piece-price System—the prisons acted as sub-contractors to Government contractors, who supplied the tools, materials and technical supervision, paying for the output on pricing systems agreed, usually, through the Ministry of Supply: this system may still, in principle, be used, and a certain number of workshops today are employed on doing work for outside contractors though entirely under prison supervision. During the war much highly skilled

---

[1] See *Should Prisoners Work*, pp. 79, 80.

work, such as assembly of radio-sets, electrical equipment for tanks and the like was carried out on this system.

Somewhere between 'Piece-price' and 'Contract' falls the system, originated during the war and still continued, of extra-mural employment of prisoners by farmers, public bodies and private firms in suitable industries. Here we have a somewhat paradoxical position. No system of employing prisoners is more open to abuse and has been more roundly condemned than the Contract System. Yet no step by the English administration in recent years has given more cause for satisfaction, both to the administration and to the interested public, than its moves towards a system of this type. The explanation may lie in the strictness of the safeguards to ensure on the one hand that no interest of normal labour is prejudiced, and on the other that no employer is at any financial advantage through the employment of prison labour. No such labour may be employed without the prior consent of the local office of the Ministry of Labour, who ensure that no local labour is available for the job and that there is no Trade Union objection; and every employer must pay over to the prison the full local rate for the job for every man-hour worked.

But so far as concerns industrial work, the prisons must rely for the great bulk of their work on making what they need for themselves—clothing, underclothing and shoes; beds and bedding; furniture and equipment of all kinds—and on orders from other Government Departments for such articles as the prisons can make. The methods of allocating such orders, and of extending their volume and variety to meet the growing shortage of work in prisons, have recently been much improved in consultation with all the departments concerned.

The responsibility for finding the orders and organising production in workshops and farms falls to the Director of Industries in the Prison Commission. He is assisted by a staff of Industrial Supervisors and a Supervisor of Farms and Gardens, with other technical staff, at the Head Office, and by Industrial Managers at the larger prisons and groups of smaller prisons.

In their Annual Report for 1949, the Commissioners reported that of a daily average population of 20,043 [1] there were 16,932 available for employment and 3,111 non-effectives, i.e. untried who did not choose to work, sick, under punishment, in transit, etc. The labour available was utilised as follows:

(1) Domestic Services .	3,618
(2) Farms and gardens.	538
(3) Building Services .	1,622
(4) Manufactures .	10,158
(5) Outside work. .	996

[1] This and the subsequent figures include Borstal inmates; the figures for prisons are not published separately.

A survey of these categories one by one will give a complete picture of the work now done in prisons.

Domestic services include much more than the unskilled work of cleaning the prison and working in the grounds. There are parties doing fairly skilled and interesting work in the kitchens and laundries: the latter over a period of years have been gradually centralised and modernised, and are conducted either by a civilian or a prison officer who has been through a course of training in laundry methods. Where there is a women's section they usually do the laundry work. Some of the larger power laundries take in work from other Government establishments.

There is also in this category a number of individual jobs as orderlies, stokers and the like which are usually assigned to 'red-band men' who are allowed to move about the prison and do their work without constant supervision.

The amount of work provided by the gardens varies from prison to prison. All have flower-beds or vegetable gardens in any cultivable space within the walls, and a few have market-gardens outside the main wall. At Dartmoor and Parkhurst there are substantial mixed farms, but farming is not carried out at the local or regional prisons except on the land reclaimed at New Hall Camp, Wakefield. It is often suggested that it would be beneficial to extend the employment of prisoners on farms, but there are certain practical objections: local prisons are in towns, and it would be necessary to buy land at some distance for cultivation; it is to be assumed that most cultivable land is already under cultivation by farmers who would not necessarily be willing to be dispossessed, while the Ministry of Agriculture would require to be convinced that the interests of food production would be served by such a change; and it would require some hundreds of acres, with substantial capital expenditure in buildings and machinery, to employ more than a handful of men except for seasonal periods.

The employment provided at all prisons by the Works Department is various, interesting and often skilled. Except for an occasional specialised job the maintenance of the buildings and equipment of the prisons, and the erection of all new buildings and installations (including electrical installations) within the walls is carried out entirely by prisoners working under the engineers and tradesmen of the Works Department. Considerable works have also been undertaken outside the walls, including the erection of staff quarters [1] and such substantial buildings as the Imperial Training School at Wakefield and the Borstal Institution at Lowdham Grange. The provision of doors, window-frames and other wooden and metal fittings for the Works Department

[1] At the end of 1949 over 800 additional quarters had been completed or were under construction since the war, but the greater part of this large programme was completed by contractors.

provides skilled work for the carpenters, joiners and metal shops on the industrial side. At several prisons where there are large new building programmes the Works Department maintain training classes in brick-laying and painting from which men pass out to practical work on the job. During and since the war women have also been extensively employed on painting and decorations: the whole of the redecoration of Askham Grange, including a good deal of such complicated detail as may be expected in an Edwardian mansion, was recently completed by the women with equal satisfaction and skill.

The list of manufactures in Appendix 6 to the Annual Report of the Prison Commissioners for 1949 includes 36 different trades, and of over 11,150 persons engaged in them rather less than half are making or repairing mailbags: the implications of this have already been dis-cussed. Other trades in this unskilled category, such as bed-making, sack-making and rope-making, employ some 250; but the largest group, of over 650, under the heading Pickers & Sorters, is engaged for the most part in the transitory post-war work of stripping and sorting into its component parts surplus government stores of many kinds from telephone equipment to bandages—useful work and not uninteresting, though of little constructive or vocational value. This is the pathetic obverse of the high and strenuous days of 1944, when prisoners worked long hours packing such stores for the invasion of Europe.

First of the semi-skilled trades is the making of coir mats—door mats, gymnasium mats, floor-matting, small coloured mats. These are made either on frames or looms; the methods are not those of an outside factory, but the work is harder, more skilful, and more interest-ing than sewing canvas. After the late war this industry was rapidly expanded to meet both the increased prison population and the in-creased demand, and in 1949 employed nearly 1,000. Today, much of this market has been lost to foreign competition, and many mat-shops are dwindling to stagnation. Basket-making and brush-making are two valuable trades employing over 230, while knitting, shoe-making and shoe-repairing absorb over 370. Needleworkers and dressmakers (some 420), mostly women, include all grades of work from unskilled to skilled, as do over 420 tailors: between them they make and repair all the cloth-ing, both under and outer, for the use of men and women prisoners, and in some shops do high-grade work in making clothing for other Government departments.

Of the more skilled trades the largest are the carpenters (245); the metal-workers—moulders, smiths, fitters and tinsmiths (118); and weavers (126), who make all the cloth, calico, sheeting, blankets, etc. required for prison dress and bedding. There is a printing shop at Maidstone where most of the forms and internal publications of the department are printed. Over 100 prisoners are also engaged in book-binding; this is at present confined to the needs of prison libraries, but arrangements have recently been made for prisoners to undertake the binding of Government papers for the official libraries, which will provide a skilled and interesting occupation for a number of long-term men.

The last group of workers to be considered is those who work outside the walls, not on the prison lands and buildings but on work of public value through or for public authorities. This development was first described by the Commissioners in their Annual Report for 1942-44 as follows:

'The work done for private farmers by boys from the Usk Borstal Institution was described in the previous report. Since that time the original idea has developed in a remarkable manner. In co-operation with the Ministry of Agriculture and Fisheries and the local County War Agricultural Executive Committees in 26 counties, men and women, boys and girls, from nearly every prison and Borstal Institution in the country have been regularly working on farms far from the prisons and have made a valuable contribution to the country's food production. The quality and quantity of their work has received high praise from their employers, and though only token supervision was provided by the prisons, escapes and unfortunate incidents were rare in proportion to the numbers employed. Wage Board rates are paid to the Commissioners in all cases, the workers receiving the normal payments under the prison or Borstal earnings schemes. The approximate revenue was £67,500 for 1943 and £92,000 for 1944.

'Further work by outside parties was arranged with the Timber Control Section of the Ministry of Supply. These operated in timber yards and colliery pit prop sites, and even unloaded barges in London Docks. A small number of selected men were allowed to work in power saw mills. As in the case of land workers they had the minimum of supervision. The arrangements for pay were the same as for land workers. The approximate revenue was £30,000 in 1943 and £28,000 in 1944.'

In 1945 the daily average numbers employed in this way were 985, and this sort of level was maintained in the next three years. In 1948 the Commissioners reported that work was being done in this way in agriculture (through the County Committees); river drainage; laying of gas and water mains and drains for housing; and at store-depots, etc., for the Service Departments: £120,560 was credited to the Commissioners for wages, and 407,500 hours were worked free of charge for other Government Departments.

Two things were perhaps surprising about these developments: first, the high reputation earned by prison labour, which was always in strong demand and usually described by farmers as the best labour they had

had from any source; second, the very small number of abscondings or misbehaviour in relation to the number of man-hours worked—and a high proportion of these workers have been prisoners of the Ordinary Class. A typical report from one Governor, quoted by the Commissioners in their Annual Report for 1948 (p. 73) was as follows:

'During most of the year 30 prisoners were employed, in three parties, on agricultural work, land drainage etc.· for the Local Agricultural Executive Committees. During November a further party of 14 prisoners was started on potato picking. I have received several letters from farmers, for whom these parties were working, speaking very highly of their work, conduct and industry. One such letter is reproduced below for information:

'Sir,
    'A party of prisoners working for the A.E.C. have just completed the picking of 12 acres of potatoes on the farm and my father and I felt that we could not let the way they did the job pass unnoticed.
    'They tackled the job wholeheartedly, quickly and thoroughly, and it was a great pleasure to see the cheerful spirit in which they set about their work and were always willing to lend a helping hand, besides being so well mannered and well behaved.

Yours faithfully.

'This type of work is appreciated by the men and the privilege of working outside the prison is seldom abused. During the year under review there have been no absconders from any of these parties.'

What was not surprising was the remarkable benefit not only to the physical and mental health of the men so employed, and to their morale, but to the general morale of the prison: competition to get into an outside party was keen, and only to be earned by proof of trustworthiness —there was no better culmination to a system of training in self-responsibility, for it must be emphasised that the supervision by one officer of a dozen or twenty men spread over a tract of farmland could only be nominal. Many stories to illustrate this are recorded: a party whose lorry broke down, and remained for some hours in the dark while the officer went to see about repairs—another caught by fog and benighted as the guests of a golf-club—another party (recidivists) lost four of its members and reported them as absconders; shortly the Governor received a 'transferred trunk-call' from one of them asking to be fetched—they had strayed to pick chestnuts and missed the bus!

There have been variations of the normal procedure of work in parties of 10–20 going out daily from the prison with an officer. At Leyhill, following a Borstal precedent, selected men go out singly on bicycles to work for local farmers, and when this valuable form of

E.P.B.S.—13

training was temporarily discontinued when local labour was found to be available, the farmers publicly voiced their disappointment.

Another variation was the location of a party on the site, in camp conditions, to carry out a specific job. This is a method of which much valuable use may yet be made in suitable conditions, as may be seen from the following description by the Commissioners of their first essay in this mode of operation.

'A development at Stafford Prison during the year provides a classic example of the use of prison labour to the maximum advantage of the public, both direct, in that it gets necessary work done which would in all probability not get done otherwise, and indirect, in that it provides precisely that form of training most likely to lead to the social re-adaptation of the prisoner and therefore to the protection of the public which is the purpose of imprisonment. This might also have been said of the employment of women in hospitals, and of all other schemes for employing prisoners outside the prison on work of public importance where normal labour interests are not prejudiced.

'The Governor, in his Annual Report, describes this scheme as follows:

'*Hanbury and the Camp.*

'In November 1944 an explosion took place in the R.A.F. Bomb Store at Fauld, near Burton-on-Trent, which resulted in the loss of some 100 lives and the devastation of some 350 acres of the best grazing land in the County.

'In February 1945 I was asked to provide a small party to do some drainage work there and on March 14th the first party of men started work in a setting of appalling desolation.

'I do not think the full significance of what their work really meant came to them until I took the party to a memorial service to the 18 who were still missing from the explosion, when they realised that this was more than a job of just clearing up a mess and that it had deeper possibilities for each man on the job. Much has been done since then, and by the end of the year some 100 acres had been restored and were under cultivation, some miles of fencing and ditching had been completed, and a start had been made on a large afforestation scheme.

'With the progress of the work the Air Ministry were good enough to provide and the Commissioners to sanction a Camp, and on July 23rd the first party of men moved into a series of huts some two miles from the job. At the end of the year 36 men were living in the Camp and 80 others were coming out from Stafford daily to the working site.

'Here in the Camp are all the needs of civilian training met under rational conditions, from the huts to the attendance at the village Church at Hanbury each Sunday evening as part of an ordinary congregation. Freed from the prison machine men behave naturally and the good can be sifted from the bad. I hope to see the whole of my working-out parties living under similar conditions.

'Those 100 acres of green pasture and fertile ploughland, set against the 200 acres of remaining devastation reminiscent of the Ypres salient in 1918, were indeed to the Commissioners, as to the Governor and his staff, a source both of pride and of inspiration.' [1]

In 1948 the Commissioners reported that 'There is a tendency for this employment to decline owing to the use of European Voluntary Workers, Government efforts to encourage youths to take up land work as a career and also the slight rise in unemployment in some districts. The Commissioners are taking such steps as are open to them to maintain the volume of this valuable form of employment.' [2] Unhappily this tendency continued during 1949, when the number fell to 826.

On occasion by arrangement with the Ministry of Labour extramural parties have been employed on suitable work for private employers, e.g. quarrying: this differs in principle from other such work only in that it is not work for a public authority.[3]

(3) VOCATIONAL TRAINING

In recent years the training value of work has been increased by the installation at certain prisons of vocational training classes in skilled trades. These had for some time been active in the regional prisons at Wakefield and Maidstone, which during the war discharged hundreds of men direct to skilled work in the engineering trades for which they had been trained in the prisons. Later an engineering course was started at Wormwood Scrubs, and since the war courses in moulding, weaving, bricklaying and .painting and decoration have been started at Wakefield and Maidstone. Similar courses have been or will be opened at all regional or corrective training prisons, including among other trades taught carpentry, black-smithing, shoe-making and tin-smithing. All these courses are based on the Ministry of Labour syllabus for civilian training courses, last for 26 weeks, and include both theoretical and practical training under skilled civilian instructors recruited from the trades. There are also courses in bricklaying and painting and decorating at certain local and central prisons where the men after training can be employed in these trades by the Works

---

[1] *Annual Report* for 1945, para. 78. This work is now virtually complete.
[2] *Annual Report* for 1948, p. 37.   [3] See Appendix K.

Department. In 1949 the Commissioners reported that there were 24 classes in operation for adult prisoners engaging 320 men.

At the end of 1950 it was decided to make a fresh approach to this question of industrial training. Instead of having the training courses quite separate from the production shops of the same trade, they will now be amalgamated, and instead of a separate six months course each man selected for a trade will get 'on-the-job' training over a longer period. He will begin with 10 weeks' training before he starts on production, so that he knows the use of tools and materials: the rest of the present 26-week syllabus will not be lost, but will be given at intervals by withdrawing a certain number of men from the production end of the shop for a short period of special training, practical or theoretical.

It is unfortunate that, despite careful enquiry, it has not so far proved possible to find trades in which it would be both useful and practicable to train women in prison: at Askham Grange, however, the work is so arranged as to give the women a complete course of training in the domestic arts, each woman doing a period of training in the kitchen, the laundry, the sewing-room, the gardens and the care of the house, with periodical examinations by the Local Education Authority in cookery and housewifery. In the evenings there are classes in fine dressmaking, toy-making, leather-work and other handicrafts, and many women are known to have established flourishing little businesses on the basis of a craft learned in the prison.

From time to time the question is raised whether men who have been trained in a trade can be placed in that trade on discharge, and if not whether the training is really worth while. There can be no general answer to the first part of the question: a prison course is not recognised by the Trade Unions as qualifying a man for entry to the trade as a skilled worker, nor as counting towards the apprenticeship of a younger man, and on occasion hostility has been shown by particular Unions both to the principle of giving such training in prisons and to the employment of such men in their trades after discharge: nevertheless, many men trained in prison have found work in their trades, especially where the local Employment Exchange manager understands the difficulties and co-operates in removing them. Even if they do not, the training is still worth while; it wholly enlists a man's interest; to acquire a new skill is a valuable piece of character formation, making for increased self-control and self-respect; and at least it gives the man a skill which he may be able to turn to advantage after discharge.

(4) INCENTIVES TO WORK

Once work is treated as part of the training and not as part of the punishment, it follows that prisoners should work fast and work well.

True, a certain level of industry can be maintained by the discipline of fear, but there is a wide gap between the quality and quantity of work a man will do to escape punishment, and what he will do when doing his best: and to get the best out of a man requires the discipline not of fear but of interest—in prison this will not always come from the nature of the work itself, but it may well come from normal economic self-interest if suitable incentives can be offered.

This question has been approached from many angles. In some countries hunger has been used as the spur: the basic ration is bare and unappetising, but may be supplemented by a variety of additional food to be bought with earnings. At the other extreme lies the conception of an 'economic wage', out of which a prisoner will keep both himself and his family, maintain his insurances, compensate those he has wronged, and do as he will with the balance—if any. This has advantages in principle, as making both for self-respect and self-responsibility, as well as for interest and industry at work. But imagination and reason alike recoil from the prospect of trying to realise this conception. It is difficult to visualise a system of this sort which would not in practice be wholly artificial and unrelated to actual economic conditions, honey-combed with anomaly and inequity, almost impossible to administer, and unduly costly to the taxpayer: nor, in the opinion at least of the present writer, would it be likely to produce in practice the advantages attributed to it in theory. This view would appear to have been shared by the Departmental Committee of 1933, which briefly considered the idea and rejected it, adding that their enquiries showed that in certain countries where 'in theory wages are paid on the basis of outside scales, in practice the prisoner receives only a much smaller sum arbitrarily fixed by the prison authority' (para. 166).[1]

In England, at least after the Act of 1865, the only incentive to industry was the marks system, under which both 'stage' and 're-mission' were earned on the basis of a daily allocation of marks which in theory were proportioned to the amount of industry shown. But in the course of years the award of marks became a time-wasting formal-ity, and during the late war it was abolished as a measure of economy. The prisoner was then credited with full remission from the beginning, and if he had to be reported for idleness or other misconduct some of it might be forfeited—the discipline of fear. But before the war other methods had been tried: the Departmental Committee expressed itself (para. 167) as 'greatly impressed by the good results of the experimental systems of payment in force at Wakefield and Lowdham, and we think that the extension of a system of payment to other establishments on

---

[1] See however para. 6. of Resolution II (3) of The Hague Congress (Appendix F). In view of the recommendation of the Congress, and of a similar recommendation by the Scottish Advisory Council on the Treatment of Offences in 1949, this question is further considered in Appendix K.

similar lines should be made.' Before the war this system had been extended to all establishments, and the present scheme has developed out of it with little change of principle.

Although the earnings scheme has in fact acted, and still acts, as a considerable incentive to industry, it may be said at once both that it has other purposes and justifications, and that it is open to many valid criticisms, the nature of which reflects the difficulties that would be met in attempting to apply a system based on economic wage rates in outside industry. Try as one may to 'normalise' prison life, the fact remains that a prison is a wholly artificial community, in which the economic conditions of outside life can no more easily be reproduced than its social conditions. Rightly or wrongly, it is a basic principle of the English system that, subject to such variations and privileges as may be accorded to defined groups in accordance with stated principles known to all prisoners, every prisoner should be treated alike in respect of the material conditions of life and the grant of specific concessions or privileges: absolute fairness as between man and man is the essence of successful management of a community where small things count for so much. Again, a prisoner is not free to choose his work, or to change it when he wishes: the management, on the other hand, is bound to employ him for so long as he is there, however stupid, malicious or incompetent he may be—and a considerable number are virtually unemployable. Yet another peculiar feature of prison life is that skill in normal prison trades, which may result in high output, will usually result from experience born of long years in prison—the novice for all his effort will never make so much: and as for specialist trades, a serious offender may have a trade at his finger-tips that he happens to be able to follow in prison, while a minor offender has another trade which he cannot follow in prison. These are random examples of the many conditions peculiar to a prison which inevitably create anomalies in any system of payment for work. Two other considerations may be mentioned. First, wages may be expressed in terms of cash, but the true currency is the tobacco into which the great majority at once convert the cash: the real value of earnings varies exactly with the price of tobacco. Second, when the value of a prisoner's work is not enough to pay the cost of keeping him in prison, any sum paid to him is by way of an unconvenanted benefit, the cost of which to the taxpayer should not become unduly high.

The system at present in force is as follows. Work is divided into what can be measured and therefore paid at piece-rates, and what cannot be measured and must therefore be paid at flat-rates. The majority of prisoners, including many skilled tradesmen, are employed in flat-rate parties; the scheme must therefore seek to preserve an approximation to equality as between the two rates of earning.

All prisoners for the first eight weeks of their sentences are paid the 'beginners' rate' of 10*d*. a week. Thereafter, piece-workers go on to a basic rate of 1*s*. 8*d*. a week for a minimum output of approved quality: sums in excess of 1*s*. 8*d*. may be earned by increased output according to the rates fixed in the different trades, but though there is no ceiling for piece-rate earnings the rates are fixed in the expectation that they will produce an overall average of about 3*s*. a week—an exceptional worker may earn 4*s*., but more would be rare. Flat-rate workers after the initial eight weeks go into grade C at 1*s*. 8*d*. a week, and from this semi-skilled and particularly useful men may be promoted to grade B in which they can earn supplements up to 1*s*. 3*d*. a week on the basis of the party officer's assessment of their skill and effort. Fully skilled tradesmen placed in grade A may earn from 3*s*. to 4*s*. on the same basis. Prisoners who through no fault of their own are unable to work are paid 10*d*. a week.

While it is the expressed intention of the scheme that workers should be paid according to their merits, and that payments should be related rather to genuine endeavour than to dexterity, it is difficult to realise these intentions in practice: flat-rates may tend to become automatic, and piece-rates to be proportioned to quantity rather than to quality or effort. Certainly piece-rates have had a remarkable effect on output, but it is a minority who—beyond the original eight weeks—are so employed: the flat-rates, if flexibly and intelligently administered, should have the effect of keeping the workers 'on their toes', but cannot of course influence output in the same way as piece-rates.

It may well be that over all the true value of earnings lies rather in their contribution to the training scheme as a whole than in their direct stimulus to industry. It makes for self-responsibility and self-respect that a man should have some reward for his effort, that he should have something to spend in his pocket and have to think about how he should spend it. There is a humanising influence too: many a father and mother in prison regularly save their earnings to buy chocolates for their children. Certainly it was the general opinion of Governors that the revision of the scheme in 1949, with its increased rate of earnings and closer assimilation of flat-rates to piece-rates, had a beneficial effect not only on output but on morale. Finally, it is not to be denied that another of the, so to speak, uncovenanted benefits of an earnings scheme is to place a potent disciplinary sanction in the hands of authority, for there is nothing that touches the recalcitrant more than stoppage of earnings, which means stoppage of tobacco.

The criticism may well be made that the level of earnings under this scheme is too low—even that it is derisory. But to assess the validity of this argument, it is necessary to establish some criterion by which the suitability of any level can be judged. There is no contract of service and no legal entitlement. No ordinary economic considerations apply. The prisoner, and as may be necessary his family also, are maintained at the public expense, and it is unlikely that the product of the prisoner's work approaches that expense in value. Any payment at all is by way of an act of grace, and its purpose must be considered in the more general light indicated above rather than in relation to economic considerations. The conclusion would seem to be that the least amount necessary to effect that purpose is the most that the taxpayer should be asked to pay.

However that may be, since in fact the average prisoner has only a shilling or two to dispose of each week, his normal disposition will be to spend it, and arrangements are made to ensure that he or she shall have a reasonable range of choice in the weekly shopping. Every prison has a canteen, in which are displayed for sale tobacco, sweets, jams and pickles, hair-cream, cosmetics and such other articles as may be in demand.

Before leaving the question of industrial conditions in prisons, it may be mentioned that all workshops are inspected to secure compliance with the Factory Acts as to health and safety, and that prisoners are fully compensated for industrial injury (see p. 221).

CHAPTER TWELVE

THE CHAPLAIN'S DEPARTMENT

THROUGHOUT history the better part of what has been done for prisoners beyond the maintenance of a marginal existence and the provision of work originated in pastoral work. Education and welfare work in prison—even more than in the world at large—are a secularisation of tasks undertaken originally by the Church and her ministers. The prison chaplain's original importance was that he was the one neutral force in an otherwise impersonal and repressive régime.' [1] This statement is true both of the historical development of education and welfare in English prisons and of their present practice: all the matters dealt with in this chapter fall, in principle, within 'the Chaplain's Department', though developments in spheres other than that of religion tend increasingly and necessarily to their 'secularisation'. As more importance is given to education and libraries, it becomes increasingly difficult in the larger or more specialised prisons for the Chaplain to manage them without detraction from his first duty—the spiritual welfare of the prisoners.

Nor is the Chaplain today the only 'neutral force' in a prison régime. The normal agencies of society are active in all the prisons, so that education becomes the business of the Local Education Authority, and the library that of the County or City Public Library, while the Prison Visitors represent the generalised good-will of the community.

This dichotomy is now carried into the Head Office organisation. The Assistant Commissioner (Education and Welfare) is responsible to the Board for all secular aspects of the work of 'the Chaplain's Department' in prisons and Borstals. In matters of religion and of the organisation and work of Ministers of religion the Board receives the advice and reports of the Chaplain Inspector.

(1) RELIGION

It is not enough that Statutory Rules should require that all the formal necessities of the practice of religion be at a prisoner's disposal

[1] Grünhut, p. 253.

—a Minister of his denomination, a chapel, a regular service, books of devotion and instruction in his cell, pastoral visits and even the right —on good grounds—to change his religious denomination. All this is ensured, and whether the offender wishes it or not at least he will find his feet more firmly set on this road in prison than in any other situation in which he is likely to find himself. But whether he will follow it, and in what spirit, and to what end, will depend on more than this. If a Minister is to preach Christ in prison, the whole ethos of the prison should sustain and justify his work. Nor are the purposes of English prisons dissonant from an aspiration to this condition, however far they may, at times and places, fall short in practice. Let us now consider how they are applied to the particular questions of religious practice and instruction.

The care taken in the selection of full-time Chaplains, particularly in order to preserve their freshness and zeal, has already been described (Chapter 6), and the more numerous body of part-time Chaplains and Ministers of other denominations than the Established Church bring to the work no less devotion and interest. In the larger prisons the Chaplains are assisted by Church Army Evangelists, on a full-time basis, selected by the Church Army and changed from time to time: their work is invaluable on every side of the Chaplain's department.

Prison chapels vary in the possibilities they offer of providing an inspiring centre for the spiritual life of the prison. Many are perhaps as beautiful as the average Victorian parish church, others are neutral, some an affront to beauty and piety alike. A real effort is being made to bring the decorations, furniture and fittings up to the level of their purpose—sometimes with outstanding success—but this programme will take some years to complete. The officers are no longer placed on high seats facing the prisoners, and though they are definitely there on duty and not as voluntary members of the congregation, this marks at least an advance from the chapel of Walnut Street Prison, Philadelphia, where the first preacher in 1790 is said to have been protected by a guard with a lighted torch beside a loaded cannon! [1]

In most prisons there is a separate Roman Catholic chapel, and in a few a Jewish synagogue. It can only be deplored that the absence of any other suitable hall makes it necessary in most prisons to use the chapel for such secular entertainment as is provided.

The Rules require the Chaplain to conduct Divine Service for the prisoners of the Church of England at least once on every Sunday, on Christmas Day and Good Friday, and 'such celebrations of Holy Communion and such services on weekdays as may be arranged'. Prison Ministers conduct Divine Service for prisoners of their denominations at convenient times. There is, therefore, no question that every prisoner has the opportunity of attending a service once a week: what

[1] Grünhut, p. 257.

is still to some extent in question is how far he should be compelled to take advantage of it. The arguments against compulsory worship are strong, and have prevailed more completely elsewhere than in our prisons: here opinion has been divided, the balance falling hitherto in favour of a compromise under which all must attend the Sunday morning services unless they have formally 'opted out' with the Governor's consent. Thus no-one is compelled to attend against his conscience, but it is not open to a man who has not opted out to decide on any Sunday that he would rather do something else.

There is usually a voluntary service on Sunday afternoons and another during the week: sometimes the Sunday afternoon service is replaced by a suitable concert or band performance. The mid-week service is held after work in the evening, except in a few prisons where at present staff shortages preclude this, and it has to be held in the morning. These are usually well attended.

The Chaplains regularly celebrate Holy Communion, and the majority prepare candidates for confirmation and arrange for Confirmation Services in the prison chapels. Some Chaplains however take the view that it is better, after preparing a candidate, to recommend him to his parish priest on discharge: they believe this to be a better test of a man's sincerity, and a safeguard against a sort of opportunist formalism known as 'prison religion'. This manifestation may be more emotional than spiritual, but at least it does no harm: what is more dangerous is the hypocritical approach which looks for some material advantage from playing up to the Chaplain—not always perhaps so naïve as that of the candidate for confirmation who, on being told that he would be given a course of preparation, replied 'Why, Chaplain, I don't need no preparation! I've been confirmed three times already—Borstal, Dartmoor, and Wormwood Scrubs!'

There is no prescribed form of Service: each Chaplain, on the basis of the liturgy of the Church of England, seeks in his own way to bring beauty, variety and conviction into the different forms: it is common to seek freshness by inviting an outside clergyman to take the Service now and then. There are also occasional Mission Services, and the Film Mission conducted by the Rev. W. Upright of the Methodist Church has often been welcomed. Since the war it has become a general practice, either in place of or as well as one of the voluntary services, to have a 'Chaplain's Hour' when questions are answered and points of doctrine and ritual explained and discussed. And some Chaplains, realising that the minds of most of their congregation are virtually a blank on any question of Christian practice or belief, start patiently at the beginning with classes of elementary instruction. In the end the Chaplain's Annual Report usually states that his congregation is encouragingly reverent, attentive and—especially in the North— harmonious, and it may well be right to believe that whatever a man's motives his presence once a week in this place and this atmosphere may give him something of lasting value.

In several Borstals and open prisons, where there is no chapel, the inmates go to the parish church as ordinary members of the congregation. All the Chaplains concerned find much good in this. The prisoners feel that they are taking part in a normal activity of the community in which they share like anyone else, and many realise perhaps for the first time that corporate worship *is* a normal activity, in which they can go on sharing after their release, and not a peculiar feature of prison life. They will not be shy of entering a church. And it is pleasant to learn how they are welcomed and made to feel at home by the congregations.

Music in chapel presents less difficulty than might be supposed with a congregation of this sort, thanks to the devotion of organists, choirmasters and Chaplains. An organ, or at worst a harmonium, is provided, and the central and regional prisons at least seem to be fortunate in finding a succession of competent organists and choirmasters among their prisoners, though usually this work is done by a local gentleman for a small—a surprisingly small—fee. The prison choir often forms the basis of a musical society in the prison.

Apart from prayer-books and hymn-books for use in chapel, the Rules require that, so far as practicable, every prisoner shall have available for his personal use 'such of the Scriptures and books of religious observance and instruction recognised for his denomination as are accepted by the Commissioners for use in prisons'. For Protestants, the present application of this Rule is conditioned to some extent by war experience. Under the Rules then in force, a Bible was provided in every cell as a normal piece of cell equipment, and was so regarded and treated by most of the prisoners—indeed it seemed that many, in the general shortage of paper, used it principally as a source of cigarette and toilet paper. When this situation was taken in hand, all the mutilated Bibles were withdrawn, and a new system was instituted. Chaplains were asked to give each prisoner personally a New Testament at his reception interview, and to tell him that if later he wished for a complete Bible he might come and ask for one: if a prisoner does not wish to have the Testament it is not pressed on him, and his refusal is noted. In addition to the Scriptures, the Chaplain gives to Church of England prisoners who will profit by them suitable books from 'the Chaplain's Library', and for prisoners of other denominations devotional and instructional books are allowed from lists agreed between the Commissioners and the church authorities. The general effect of the present practice is that Scriptures and other devotional books are treated with respect: it is no longer a matter for pleased surprise to find a complete Bible in a cell, for it is there because the prisoner wants to have it there—to read.

Many Chaplains feel that much of their most valuable and rewarding work is done not in the chapel but in the cells, or wherever they may find opportunity for quiet private talks with those who can be helped. This work is naturally selective—the Chaplain sees every prisoner on reception, but there is no regulation visit to all and sundry thereafter. Indeed in the active evening life of many prisons it becomes increasingly difficult to make opportunities for these talks, though the Chaplain may make his influence felt and valued by being about and accessible during periods of associated activity.

(2) PRISON VISITORS

Prison Visitors started with Elizabeth Fry and her Quaker Ladies, and though after her time they did not last long, the idea was not dead. Sir E. du Cane must have allowed some limited revival, for the Gladstone Committee reported (para. 33) that 'the governor of the female Convict Prison was of the decided opinion that lady visitors to female prisoners did good': and they evidently contemplated an extension of the system, and not only for women, for in discussing the necessity for 'adequate individual attention' and for 'power to give or obtain for an individual prisoner that guidance, advice or help which at such a crisis in his life may make a priceless change in his intentions or disposition', they thought that 'under proper rules and regulations outside helpers could be brought in to supplement the work of the prison staff . . . There are many men and women . . . who by training and temperament are amply competent to render valuable assistance' (para. 27)'

Although it was not until 1922 that the Commissioners began to develop the full implications of this idea, from the beginning of the century there was a great extension of Visitors to women. In 1901 the Lady Visitors Association (later the National Association of Visitors to Women Prisoners) was constituted under the presidency of Adeline, Duchess of Bedford, and first under her guidance and later under that of Lady Ampthill, the lady members did valuable work at all prisons for women. Visitors to men prisoners started in 1922, and in 1924 followed the example of their women colleagues by forming the National Association of Prison Visitors. The two Associations worked side by side for some twenty years in happy collaboration, but in 1944 a marriage was arranged and the N.A.P.V. (as we shall hereafter call it), with a Women's Committee, now manages the affairs of all the Prison Visitors. The Association has a branch in each prison, with a local Secretary, and manages its affairs centrally through the good will of those members who, by election to office, voluntarily shoulder an administrative burden on top of their work in the prisons: it keeps its members in touch by a monthly News-letter, and by an annual general meeting which is devoted in part to the business of the Association and in part to discussion of matters of interest with the Commissioners, who attach real value to views based not on theory but on knowledge of the problems of the individual prisoner and the ways in which imprisonment affects him. The Commissioners reported that in 1949 there were some 720 men and women Visitors engaged in this valuable social service, organised in 39 Branches.

Perhaps at this point we should stop to consider why this service is valuable, and how it fits into the general scheme of training. We should remember first that, except in the regional training prisons and—to a certain extent—in the later stages of a long sentence, the normal fate of an Ordinary Class prisoner is to be locked in his cell by 5 p.m., and unless it is his night for a class he may not see anybody to speak to again till he is unlocked next morning. Even those out in association will usually be locked up by 7 p.m. This is a bleak and lonely period for many, since not all are capable of concentrated reading, and the cell task is monotonous and easily disposed of by the experienced prisoner. It is at this time that a visit from someone from the outside world, quite unconnected with the prison staff—someone to talk and listen [1] about ordinary matters of everyday interest, to take an interest in his family, perhaps to help him to understand how he has gone wrong and to discuss the future—may not only prevent the prisoner from solitary brooding over real or fancied grievances, but may actively direct his thoughts in profitable directions, give him fresh hopes and interests, and assist to restore his self-respect by letting him see that someone thinks it worth while to come and talk to him and take an interest in his affairs.

There is a considerable value in this last aspect, which is well assessed by Mr. John Watson when he says, 'The visitor's position is that of one man paying a friendly call on another and he is anxious to show himself in that light from the beginning. Prison visitors are sometimes called the 'unofficial visitors' and there is more meaning in the adjective than a mere distinction between the voluntary workers and the official panel of visiting justices. The deeper significance of the word 'unofficial' makes its most obvious appeal to the prisoner himself. He knows that the visitor has no official status, is unpaid and comes to the prison because he wants to and for no other reason.' [2] In short, the visitor provides that element of social conversation which is necessary to the ordinary life of most of us; he restores and confirms the prisoner's sense of community with what is good and valuable; he refreshes his mind with topics outside the stagnant and often unhealthy flow of

---

[1] 'Mathilde Wrede, the Finnish pioneer of prison welfare, when asked what she told the prisoners, replied, "So many people talk to them; what they want is someone who listens to what they are saying." Grünhut, p. 249.

[2] *Meet the Prisoner*, John A. F. Watson. Jonathan Cape, 1939.

normal prison talk, and perhaps gets him to see his prison problems in better balance and perspective; he may, by showing interest and sympathy in a prisoner's private affairs, improve his attitude towards his present situation; he may help and advise him in his studies and his reading; and he may direct his mind to the future. In this last connection, the closest co-operation is encouraged between visitors and Aid Societies or After-Care agencies, and at every local prison the visitors are represented on the committee of the Aid Society. Work of this sort is not for everybody. It needs particular qualities, and to learn what these are we cannot do better than consult Mr. John Watson, one of the pioneers of prison visiting to men, Hon. Secretary of the N.A.P.V. from 1928 to 1938 and its Chairman for some years thereafter. 'The allocation of prisoners to a visitor demands much care, for the visitors vary between one and another as greatly as do the prisoners themselves, and both need grouping according to their individual qualities. Socially, visitors are drawn from every class. But whether the prison visitor graduated in the Board School or at Balliol, there are certain qualities he *must* possess—breadth of outlook, sympathy and, above all, a sense of humour. He should not be too young; most certainly he must not be too old. He must have a hard head—which is quite unrelated to a hard heart—and be devoid of all false sentiment or morbidity . . . he will (not) sentimentalise with the prisoner on his present situation and seek his confidence by seeming to side with him in his antagonism to society. Equally he will refrain, particularly in the early stages, from delivering any kind of moral homily; for no one likes to be preached at. . . . Obviously the visitor will not embroil himself in political argument—indeed he should bear no political label—and in any case he will find that the average prisoner is much more interested in the fortunes of the 'Arsenal' than in the Government's foreign policy. The visitor should look upon it as part of his job to know enough about the principal forms of sport to be able to discuss any of them with reasonable intelligence. . . . It is objected that the prison visitor is not there to make light-hearted conversation on frivolous topics. I venture to disagree. Conversation on any topic is justified if it helps to lift the prisoner out of himself and enables his visitor to get to know him. I have little faith in the prison visitor with the long face and the pocket full of tracts. Prisons are gloomy enough without long-faced prison visitors, and I believe that Christianity needs to be something more live and vital than can be proffered second-hand in a pamphlet. Only cheerful people should be prison visitors, for there is dire need for brightness and laughter—especially laughter. In prison life there is little to laugh at.' [1] The official advice to visitors underlines two of Mr. Watson's points. Visitors should not discuss with prisoners their grievances about their convictions and sentences—

[1] *Meet the Prisoner*, pp. 101–109.

there are other channels for these, and the visitor's purpose is to shake the prisoner out of the mood of morbid brooding over real or imaginary grievances, not to encourage it: and they should not discuss religion —that approach is for the Chaplains and Ministers. This is not work for those who are 'interested in crime' or whose primary motive is the saving of souls.

It follows that great care must be taken in selecting men and women for the work, and that if they turn out to be unsuitable they should not go on with it. Recommendations are made to the Commissioners by Governors with the advice of their Chaplains, and if they approve the Commissioners invite the visitor to serve for a year. There is an annual review, after which each visitor receives a letter which either invites him to serve for another year or thanks him for his services, but does not renew the invitation. The Commissioners, in agreement with the N.A.P.V., make it a rule never to tell visitors why they are not again invited to serve: it is difficult to explain their shortcomings to voluntary workers without giving offence, and the Commissioners feel that their discretion must not be limited by the necessity of embarrassing explanations. The case is of course different when a visitor's services are discontinued because of some grave indiscretion or breach of the rules [1] laid down, by agreement with the N.A.P.V., for the proper conduct of their work.

Two points in conclusion. Every prisoner does not have a visitor— 720 visitors with some 10 prisoners each on their lists would cover less than half of the eligible prisoners. They are not necessary for most short-sentence prisoners, and would be wasted on many recidivists— though cases have been known of most intractable prisoners, whose hostile attitude no efforts of the staff could affect, having been completely changed by the insight and patience of a visitor. It is one of the functions of the Reception Board to allocate visitors to prisoners. And finally, though we have spoken of women visitors to women and men to men, there are also women visitors to young men: it has been found that well-chosen women may have a most helpful influence on young prisoners, and though the experiment was at first thought rash, their presence is now as welcome to the Governors as to the boys.

(3) EDUCATION AND RECREATION

The linking of education and recreation suggests both the virtues and the defects of education in prison. The purpose of prison training is not primarily to inculcate particular skills, but to train the whole man. So education is not to be treated as a thing apart, but must be related to the whole scheme. In its relation to work, therefore, the general

---

[1] Breaches of this sort are fortunately rare, and may generally be ascribed to the heart being stronger than the head.

purpose will be to produce in the prisoner an attitude of mind, a desire to work well for the sake of good work rather than a vocational skill, though for persons who want them vocational courses [1] will be arranged. Nor does formal education in academic subjects take a primary place, though it may be there for those who need it, particularly the illiterate and backward on the one hand and serious students of superior education on the other.

Many prisoners, too, cannot easily profit by normal educational processes, but can find satisfaction and often obtain mental relief by acquiring a manual skill or learnng to express themselves through some sort of creative work, such as drawing or singing—the writer has heard of more than one case of intractable and inaccessible prisoners whose attitude to life was completely changed by a box of paints, though they had never handled a brush before. So hobby and handicraft classes, and the encouragement of any form of creative expression, must hold an important place.

Again, since it is often through failure in some sort of social adaptation that delinquency has occurred, prison education should have a social content, and that aimed not only at normal life outside but at the abnormal life inside: if prisoners' relations with each other are to be tolerable, and if their conversation is to be of anything but the usual dark and dirty topics of prison life, they must be given some healthy food for their starved minds. A prison syllabus, therefore, is likely to show as many hours devoted to discussion groups, debates, play-readings and musical appreciation classes as to arithmetic, shorthand and French.

There will, too, be regular lectures, concerts and cinematograph shows: there will be the wireless, the library and the newspaper. Who is to say where, in all this, education and recreation divide? To read a good book, to take part in producing a play, to hear a symphony, to see an interesting documentary film, to listen to an expert lecture—is it education, or is it recreation?

The origins of the Adult Education Scheme in our prisons in 1922, and its development up to the late war, have already been described (pp. 68, 69). 'From the operation of this scheme much was learned. It was found that the prisoner generally responded well. He was willing and anxious to learn, and it was remarkable that in the thousands of classes taken by outside teachers scarcely a single case of indiscipline had been reported, although no prison officers were present. The prisoner was generally ill-nourished mentally, however, with no reserves for meditation, his taste untrained and with little equipment mentally for learning and temperamentally for self-discipline and concentration. It was found too that the voluntary teacher had great value, coming as

[1] The reference here is to evening education courses, not to Vocational Training as part of the day's work, though the two may naturally be related.

E.P.B.S.—14

he did to the prisoner as one who approached him simply as a member of the community wishing to make the prisoner feel that the community still interested itself in him and wished to help him. The voluntary teacher was also in the happy position, owing to his individual approach, of acting in some sense as a personal tutor rather than a class teacher, and the prisoner above all needed and responded to this form of approach. On the other hand the system had its limitations. The curriculum at any prison was apt to depend on what the available teachers had to offer at any given time, and it therefore lacked cohesion and continuity. So the intellectually undernourished prisoner was offered not a diet prescribed by experts for his condition, but an assortment of dishes that happened to be on the menu at the moment.' [1]

This scheme was virtually killed by the war, and in 1946 the Commissioners had to consider what to put in its place. They began by obtaining authority for the appointment in their office of a Director of Education and Welfare, and by seeking the advice of a small informal committee of educational experts whose first Report was discussed in the Annual Report of the Commissioners for 1948.

The Committee had before it information about various expedients adopted during and since the war in order to fill the educational gap. Much use had been made of correspondence courses for individual prisoners provided by various organisations; these were in some ways more valuable than classes and lectures, since prisoners could choose the subjects nearest to their needs; and to work at them in their cells suggested a serious wish to learn, whereas it may be that many prisoners go to classes mainly to get out of their cells for an hour in the evening. These courses had the additional value that a prisoner on transfer or discharge could take his course with him. This method has continued to develop since the war. In their 1948 Report the Commissioners said that some 2,000 prisoners had entered for courses. Many had gained diplomas, and some have been enabled to get work through the knowledge thus acquired.

A by-product of correspondence courses was the tutorial system, under which a teacher, instead of taking a class, coaches a small group of prisoners engaged in private study either as a group or individually in their cells.

The use of suitably qualified prisoners as teachers had also extended and has continued since the war: in their Report for 1948 the Commissioners remarked that of 63 classes a week held in one prison 14 were taken by prison teachers.

But the most notable and pregnant development was initiated at Durham Prison in 1945. Informal conversations between the Director of Education for the County and the Governor led to the suggestion that the County Education Authority should take over responsibility

[1] Extract from the Report of the Prisoners' Education Advisory Committee.

for the provision of evening education in the prison. The Commissioners and the Ministry of Education cordially welcomed the idea. There was little equipment and no class-rooms, but plenty of enthusiasm, and soon, on any evening, the dim lengths of the prison halls were punctuated at regular intervals by groups of prisoners seated round a teacher and a blackboard. The success of this scheme was such that in their Report for 1946 the Commissioners said 'it was agreed in principle between the Ministry of Education and the Commissioners that it was a proper function of an Education Authority to provide Further Education for the citizen in prison as for the citizen outside, and plans were prepared for future development on these lines.' The Advisory Committee encouraged these plans, which are now in force at all prisons and Borstals.[1] At the end of 1949 over 700 regular classes were in progress.

The normal arrangement is for the Education Authority to establish in the prison an Evening Institute with a Supervising Teacher, the classes being staffed by qualified teachers supplied by the Authority. In the larger prisons blocks of class-rooms in huts are gradually being supplied where possible: otherwise the teachers make the best of what rooms there are, or the floors of the prison halls. The work is regularly inspected by divisional inspectors of the Ministry of Education, at whose headquarters a controlling inspector keeps in close touch with the Assistant Commissioner charged with education in the Prison Commission.

The extent to which prison education may be taken in favourable conditions is shown by the reference in the Annual Report for 1949 to Wormwood Scrubs Prison, which then housed over 1,000 prisoners of the Star and Young Prisoner classes. There were 62 classes each week of 15–20 men each. These were taken by 37 professional teachers provided by the London County Council, 4 voluntary teachers, 8 members of the staff and 13 prisoners. In addition 45 men were taking correspondence courses and 11 diplomas in such courses were gained in the year.

There are two features of this scheme that should be emphasised. Education in prison, as for workers in ordinary life, takes place in the workers' own time when the working day is over, and it is entirely voluntary. In training prisons especially a certain amount of encouragement, even pressure, may be used, since the prisoners are there to be trained and this is an important part of the training: but no teacher would welcome a conscript class. Usually, there are waiting lists for vacancies.

These arrangements are elastic enough to cover special tuition for the illiterate and backward at one end of the scale,[2] and for the more

---

[1] Similar arrangements had been provided before the war at two Borstals by the L.E.As. concerned.

[2] This may be during working hours, and may be compulsory.

advanced at the other: for the latter, the University of London has kindly allowed long-sentence prisoners to enter for its Matriculation, Intermediate and Degree courses.

The Commissioners communicated to all Governors the Report of the Advisory Committee, 'and expressed the desire that its recommendations should be brought into effect as soon as practicable'. (Annual Report 1948.) Broadly, this has now been done, and it is fitting to leave this aspect of education with a quotation from the Report:

'The social education of a prisoner, in its widest sense, should be taken to cover everything that is concerned with living as a member of society including the proper use of leisure.

'We agreed that the basis for all prisoners should be training in the use of English, both written and spoken; citizenship, in its widest sense; and creative work of some sort whether in crafts, art or music.

'Training in English should include both basic training and play-readings, discussions, etc.

'We attach particular importance to the treatment of the illiterate, by whom we mean those who can not, or can only with difficulty, read, write or interpret drawings. In our view every effort should be made to bring the illiterate up to the best possible standard in the time available, and we suggest that where necessary and practicable time should be taken from the working day for this purpose: where this is done the evening period might be devoted to handicrafts.

'For more advanced training, both in English and in what we have called citizenship, we consider that the most fruitful methods will be not so much formal classes as discussion groups, lectures followed by discussion, Brains Trusts, the following of B.B.C. discussion series and the like.'

And now we approach the boundary line between education and recreation, around which may be found both the cinema and the wireless. As to the former, every prison has a projector, which is used to provide a show as often as the limited funds available for film-hire permit: since 'documentary' and 'educational' films come cheaper than more popular features, it may be that to the audience the educational rather than the entertainment value of many film shows seems to predominate. Film-strips are also a recognised visual-aid adjunct of education.

Each prison also has a wireless equipment, but on the use of this the Commissioners in their Annual Report for 1944 gave a rather pessimistic view. 'In 1943 the Commissioners decided to collect information about the use of wireless in prisons, and subsequently issued the following circular:

'On consideration of the information recently obtained from Governors on the use of wireless sets in prisons, the Commissioners think it desirable to give some guidance as to the policy they wish to be followed.

'The introduction of wireless into prisons is not intended to provide entertainment for the general body of prisoners, but to keep them in touch with the outside world, and to serve as a supplement to the educational and recreational programme of the prison. For the prison as a whole, therefore, it should only be used for broadcasting the news bulletins (not more than once a day) and any important speeches or events of national importance.

'Where its separate use is allowed by prisoners who have the privilege of association, it may be used as those prisoners wish during the hours of association, subject to such control as Governors may think necessary.

'In hospitals it may be used at the discretion of the Medical Officer.

'No doubt it will also be found valuable in connection with educational classes (e.g. for discussion groups) and on occasion it may well be used, when a suitable programme is available, to give a concert under the conditions of S.O. 426.'

In 1944, in the hope of reaching more definite conclusions as to how wireless could best be made to fit into the scheme of training, they made further inquiries, but found the subject so beset with difficulties that no clear opinions could easily be formed. There are considerable technical difficulties, which even the latest sets have not entirely overcome, in obtaining effective broadcasting in the special acoustic conditions of a prison, and it does not yet appear practicable, even if it were desirable, to provide a broadcast to penetrate a closed cell. Effective use is therefore limited to times when prisoners are out of their cells, which means that generally speaking the only 'all prisoners' broadcast is the news. At a number of establishments the wireless is used during the association hours of stage prisoners; but save in a few special establishments, this tends to be no more than 'background noise', and may be the cause of more discord than harmony. There are, it seems, still those who prefer their books, chess, or conversation without a musical background; mutual agreement in a mixed company on a programme to be listened to rather than heard would be difficult to achieve; and any attempt to require attention to officially selected programmes would probably, and properly, meet with small success. Loudspeakers in the hospitals present obvious difficulties, and headphones would seem to be the only practicable method here. There remains the use for educational purposes, including in this not only discussion groups but selected talks, plays and musical programmes. 'This seems to be the most hopeful approach to a really constructive use of wireless in prisons, and along these lines the Commissioners propose to explore the subject further, so soon as staffing and other conditions make it possible to resume a full programme of evening activities.' Nor, it is to be feared, has the position substantially changed since then.

The newspaper also occupies a marginal place. Daily papers to meet most tastes and opinions are supplied to the association messes. The primary purpose is to keep the prisoners informed of what goes on in the outside world, but authority does not concern itself with the relative attention paid by readers to the parliamentary and sporting reports. Before the late war a small prison-service news-sheet was printed and distributed to all prisoners. When this had to be discontinued, the Chaplains used to read a news-bulletin after the Sunday service. With the general introduction after the war of wireless and newspapers this unhappy expedient came to an end: it was less than seemly that Divine Service should be looked forward to as the time for checking one's football pools. In general, with the present arrangements, all prisoners are sufficiently in touch with the news of the day. Prisoners may also have sent in to them by their friends the weekly editions of local and national newspapers, and such periodicals as may help to keep them in touch with current thought and events or with any hobbies or specialised interests.

From the Press we pass to the Library. Since the War, everything has been done to encourage a full and intelligent use of the prison library. The divorce of reading matter from the Stage System has already been noted: the present wish is to encourage reading, not to restrict it. With few exceptions the County or Borough Libraries now run the prison library as a branch of their own, and the prisoners are given direct access to the books on the shelves except where the physical conditions forbid. The libraries are on the whole well stocked with an adequate selection of all categories of books, new and old, in normal demand, and will usually take considerable trouble to meet special demands. There is at Wakefield Prison a central library of technical and foreign books. Although in a few prisons with specially unfavourable conditions traces of the older system may still persist, these are gradually being eliminated, and it ought to be, and in no long time will be, possible to say that (saving the often unsuitable premises) any prisoner may get as good a library service inside a prison as out. And in addition they may have books sent to them from outside on condition that they become the property of the prison library when done with. There is, therefore, every facility for both educational and recreational reading, and much is done to encourage and help those who need it. Many a man who had never read anything but a certain type of Sunday paper has left prison with a taste for good reading. An encouraging lesson from this development of prison libraries has been that it has practically killed the nasty and endemic prison disease of mutilating and scribbling in library-books, perhaps because these outlets for repressed resentments are no longer needed, perhaps because prisoners will live up to a good standard as easily as down to a bad one. Prison libraries are under the control of a selected prison officer who, after a short course at the local library, is paid an allowance for this specialised work. The best of these take great trouble to see that the prisoners get what they want, or where, as often, they do not know what they want, to help and advise them. But it is an interesting question whether at the largest prisons a professional librarian might not be employed with advantage. Prisoners are also employed in the libraries, and this work is usually reserved for the better type of Star.[1]

Still in the borderland we find the regular concerts and lectures, varied sometimes by an amateur dramatic performance, that have at least since the days of Sir Evelyn Ruggles-Brise been a regular feature of prison life. These in general are held about once a month, and in the local prisons are open to every prisoner 'in stage', and to those 'out of stage' too if there is room for them. One cannot generalise about the scope and nature of these. Governors and Chaplains, according to their initiative, imagination and connections, get the best they can find—and many a well-known concert artiste, actor or actress, or music-hall star, as well as kind-hearted 'local talent', have come into the prisons and given their best. The variety of lectures too is surprisingly rich, and first-class authorities may be heard on most aspects of life and thought: here the Commissioners have acknowledged special debts of gratitude to Mrs. J. W. Field, who has for long organised regular fortnightly lectures in the London Prisons, and to the Central Office of Information, who have given constant help in the supply both of lectures and of film shows.

But even more important than hearing plays or music is that prisoners should be encouraged to make their own plays and music. Mr. John Watson has given a vivid account of the first play-readings at Wormwood Scrubs in 1922, and the help the volunteer teachers were given by well-known actors and actresses, leading to 'an excellent production of Julius Caesar with Leslie Banks as Cassius against Claude Rains' Brutus'.[2] Today at many regional and central prisons there are flourishing Dramatic Societies staging one or two performances a year. In such prisons too, and in not a few local prisons, music-making and appreciation of music are fostered through choirs, bands, gramophone clubs, musical appreciation classes and the like.

It is desirable for completeness to mention one small matter, which has nevertheless occasioned no small controversial heat. Prisoners had long been allowed note-books to use in connection with any educational

[1] See Appendix K.   [2] *Meet the Prisoner*, J. F. Watson, Jonathan Cape, p. 137.

class or study in which they might be engaged, and these (if properly used) they could take out on discharge: in 1947, however, there was a development described by the Commissioners on pp. 37 and 38 of their Annual Report for that year as follows:

'The Standing Orders required the use of the notebooks to be strictly limited to the technical or educational purpose for which they were issued, and specially prohibited verse or prose compositions, drawings, etc. "for the purpose of subsequent publication or sale". On condition that the regulations were complied with, the notebooks might be taken out on discharge. Nevertheless, "educational purpose" was liberally interpreted, and marginal questions of whether the contents of a given notebook were notes on English literature or a prose composition were likely to arise. A conflict—haunted by the ghosts of Bunyan and of Wilde—also became evident between the principle that a prisoner must not be allowed to use his leisure to work for personal gain, and the fear that some great work of literature might be untimely strangled by red-tape. In an attempt to resolve these difficulties, the Commissioners decided to divide notebooks into two classes, educational and general. The former may be issued to any prisoner at any time after reception to enable him to profit by an approved course of study, whether it be followed as a member of a class or individually: the interpretation of "approved course" is still liberal—anything tending to improve general education, or vocational fitness, or wise use of leisure is encouraged, but "compositions for publication" are prohibited. These "educational" notebooks, if properly used, may be taken out on discharge. The "general" notebooks may be issued to 2nd Stage prisoners on application, and there is no restriction, within the bounds of propriety and discipline, on the use to which they may be put, but they may not in any circumstances be taken out. Thus their use may extend from idle jottings, which may still be more beneficial to a man alone in his cell than mental stagnation, to the work of some future Bunyan. We certainly see no reason why a man with an urge to express himself creatively should be prevented from doing so because he is a prisoner, though he may not be allowed to profit financially by the use of his manuscript.'

This statement attracted further attention to the problem, which was eventually referred by the Home Secretary to the Advisory Council on the Treatment of Offenders for their advice on the general question of whether prisoners should be allowed to take out of prison work they had done in their spare time, and the particular question of whether matter in notebooks which might have a sales value should be excepted from any general prohibition, so that the prisoners might be able to take their 'general' notebooks out with them. The Council advised in favour of maintaining the principle that prisoners should not work for profit in their spare time, but felt that it was so desirable that prisoners should be allowed to take their notebooks out with them that the very slight risk of some saleable matter going out might well be taken, provided that control was exercised to prevent objectionable or sensational matter being taken out. The Secretary of State having accepted this advice, matters have been arranged accordingly. The prisoner can now write what he likes in his book, provided it is not indecent or subversive of discipline, and he can take it out provided it contains nothing against the security or good order of the prison, and no autobiographical writing or other 'crime stuff' or descriptions of prison life. These notebooks are not issued for the preparation of sensational stories for such newspapers as might be disposed to publish them; on the contrary they are intended, as part of the process of training, to divert the prisoner's mind from his criminal activities and his real or alleged grievances to more constructive attitudes.

In future, therefore, there need be no fear that any work of art conceived in a prison cell will never see the light. If it be retorted that under these restrictions 'De Profundis' would have remained buried, there are several answers. First, that 'De Profundis' did in fact emerge. Second, that Oscar Wildes do not come into prison with any frequency: since 'De Profundis' only one man of letters is known to have written anything of note in a prison—oddly enough, Lord Alfred Douglas. Third, it has long been the rule that if any prisoner claimed that his notebook contained matter worthy of preservation it should be kept for ten years. What was to happen at the end of the ten years was not, at the time, decided; and it may be fortunate that under present practice the question is unlikely to arise. The Advisory Council examined all the notebooks retained in the prisons over a long period of years, and found in them nothing of the slightest literary or artistic value.

It would be wrong to close this section without special reference to the value of handicrafts in the educational training scheme. A substantial proportion of the evening classes are devoted to hand-work of many kinds. Some are taken by the Local Education Authority or voluntary teachers, many by members of the prison staff, who obtain strikingly attractive results. In different prisons may be found carpentry, rug-making, leather work, plastics, toy-making, embroidery, knitting, dress-making and many other useful and enjoyable crafts. The results range from the commonplace to the spectacular, as when the wireless class at one prison made themselves a television set which worked. Apart from classes, prisoners in stage may have the privilege of carrying on permitted 'arts or crafts' in their cells, while those taking part in classes may also carry on in their cells where the work is suitable, e.g. rug-making.

The economics of these classes should be explained. There is no question of the prisoners making anything out of it financially. There is a 'handicraft fund' at each prison from which tools and raw materials are supplied, and this must be kept self-supporting by the sale of the product. The prices are fixed by a committee at an approximation to market value, and sales are made to staff and the public, any surplus going usually to the Discharged Prisoners' Aid Society. Prisoners are allowed to buy articles they have made at the prices so fixed to send out as presents to their family, and many a doll's house or teddy-bear or baby's frock has been sent home at Christmas or for birthdays.

At one women's prison the D.P.A.S. will set up a released prisoner with tools and materials to carry on a craft she has learned, and more than one woman has in this way managed to establish a useful little spare-time business.

Altogether, the humanising, vocational and educational value of these classes is great, and it is a pity that it is not practicable to extend the practice of handicrafts to any prisoners who wish to pass the evenings usefully in their cells.

(4) SOCIAL RELATIONS AND WELFARE

In this section we shall consider what may be called the external relations of a prisoner—the preserving or fostering of all those interests [1] outside the prison wall which may serve either his better adaptation to his present situation or his re-adaptation in due course to normal life. The forcible severance of an offender from family and community life raises many problems, both for himself and others, which cannot be neglected by a system which claims to seek his social rehabilitation. 'An even more important question concerns those needs which have been revealed or caused by the punishment itself. From a legal point of view imprisonment is deprivation of liberty in an enclosed institution, minutely regulated and strictly limited to years, months, weeks, or days. Any additional hardship for the prisoner's family or his future career is without legal foundation and ought to be prevented or removed. From a social point of view imprisonment is not a forfeiture of a man's position in life, but an opportunity for adapting him to the community of law-abiding citizens. This cannot be achieved by individual persuasion alone. Much has to be done to disentangle difficult family and other personal relationships, to protect legitimate economic interests, and to prepare the ground for a fresh start. All this is the responsibility of the social services in penal institutions.' [2]

The phrase 'forfeiture of a man's position in life' raises in the first place the question of 'forfeiture of civil rights' as a consequence of imprisonment. Dr. Mannheim says of this: 'Whilst the different legal

[1] Except those relating to after-care and aid-on-discharge, which are dealt with separately in Chapter 16.
[2] Grünhut, p. 245.

systems show wide variations in detail, certain fundamental characteristics are common to most of them. The offender who is convicted of a
serious crime may have to suffer, for instance, loss of his offices, professional or honorary, and of eligibility for future office, of his pension,
of the right to wear decorations and to bear titles and academic degrees,
of the right to elect and to be elected in parliamentary and municipal
elections, to act as guardian, trustee or witness, and so on. Sometimes
these deprivations follow as automatic consequences attached to every
severe sentence; sometimes, however, it is left to the discretion of the
judge to make a specific order to that effect.' [1] He also emphasises
that while many such provisions may be defended as being for the
protection of society their actual effect is social defamation.

To define English practice in these matters is difficult. What, in
England, are our 'civil rights'? It does not appear to be possible either
to give them the legal definition which they receive in some legal systems
or to say, with any authoritative precision, what is the effect on whatever
one may deem them to be of a sentence of imprisonment. So far as
statute law takes us, certain of the consequences set out by Dr. Mannheim may result from a conviction of felony, but not from imprisonment *per se*. These derive from the Forfeiture Act 1870, as amended
by the Criminal Justice Act 1948. Prior to the Act of 1870 a convicted
felon, among other disabilities, forfeited his property to the Crown:
the Act was intended as a measure of relief, substituting for forfeiture
certain disabilities on dealing with his property during the currency of
the sentences: these disabilities in turn were removed by the Criminal
Justice Act 1948. The effect of the remaining disabilities may be summarised as follows. A person convicted of treason or felony, who is
sentenced to death, preventive detention, corrective training, or any
term of imprisonment over 12 months, must vacate certain public
offices and forfeit any pension connected with them. He also becomes
incapable of holding such offices, or of being elected or sitting or
voting as a member of either House of Parliament, or of exercising any
right of parliamentary or municipal franchise, until he has completed
his punishment or received a free pardon.

A further statutory provision (section 59 (1) Local Government Act
1933) disqualifies a person from being elected or being a member of a
local authority if he has 'within five years before the day of election
or since his election been convicted in the United Kingdom, the Channel
Islands or the Isle of Man of any offence and ordered to be imprisoned
for a period of not less than three months without the option of a fine'.

Further disabilities and disqualifications may result from the action
of professional associations (e.g. the striking off the rolls in certain
circumstances of a convicted doctor or solicitor), or from administrative action (e.g. forfeiture of honours or decorations).[2]

---

[1] Mannheim, pp. 109, 110.   [2] See Appendix K.

Where a prisoner is not subject to a statutory disability, the position would appear to be as follows: a sentence of imprisonment does not of itself impose on an offender any 'loss of civil rights', but his position as a prisoner may disable him from exercising them, and any relief of this disability rests in the discretion of the Secretary of State. As an example of the exercise of this discretion, in 1948 a convicted prisoner petitioned to be allowed to offer himself as a parliamentary candidate at a bye-election, and the petition was granted, though he was not nominated. Subsequently, he was further allowed to petition against the election result and the Courts accepted his petition: he was not allowed to proceed because he had not lodged his security.[1] Again, when in 1948 postal voting became permissible for voters absent from their constituencies in certain conditions, it appeared that prisoners confined in prisons outside their constituencies (if not disqualified under the Forfeiture Act from voting) would be accepted by Returning Officers as eligible to vote by post. It was, therefore, decided that they should be allowed to post their votes in the subsequent General Election, notwithstanding the anomaly that other prisoners in the same prison who normally resided in the constituency in which the prison was situated were not in a position to go to the polling-booths! [2]

From these examples it is clear that, so far at any rate as concerns parliamentary franchise and elections, the Home Office has not been disposed to interfere arbitrarily with the exercise of a prisoner's 'civil rights', in so far as they can be exercised from within the prison walls. But whether a prisoner would have any remedy if the Secretary of State declined to exercise a discretion in his favour it does not seem possible to say until a case in point has been decided by the Courts.

Within the category of what may be called for this purpose civil rights, the position of a prisoner in regard to marriage is of interest. Requests are frequently made for the temporary release of prisoners so that they may marry, sometimes on grounds of considerable force in relation to the welfare either of the prisoner or of the other party. Hitherto, however, the practice has been to refuse such requests.[3]

Again, any citizen has a right to seek a remedy at law for any wrong that he may conceive himself to have suffered, or at least to seek advice to that end. This right, however, is not conceded to persons under sentence of imprisonment, the Commissioners holding themselves free to decide on the merits of each case whether a prisoner should be allowed to initiate legal proceedings, or to seek legal advice to that end. Their discretion is, however, exercised fairly widely in favour of the prisoners. Broadly speaking, prisoners have not been prevented from initiating proceedings against the Crown where they claimed to have suffered

[1] *Daily Herald*, 9 April 1948.
[2] Weekly Hansard, Vol. 163, cols. 379, 380, 383, 384, 676. See also Appendix K.
[3] See Appendix K.

damage arising out of their detention, and permission has been given in other categories of actions where it appeared that the prisoner's interests would be prejudiced if he had to wait until his release, or where the action was already under consideration before committal to prison. In such cases the legal advisers of a prisoner are, by Statutory Rule, allowed reasonable facilities for visits out of the hearing of a prison officer.

The next category of interests comprises what may be called the social insurance group, including health and industrial insurance. Every care has been taken to ensure that, so far as is legally and administratively practicable, the punitive effects of imprisonment do not extend to the prejudice of this important aspect of contemporary social life.

In the benefits of the National Health Service, as will appear in a subsequent chapter, every prisoner may fully participate—including dental, ophthalmological and other subsidiary services.

Although prisoners are formally outside the scope of the Industrial Injuries Acts, not being persons employed under a contract of service, it has been decided that, where a prisoner is injured in the course of his prison employment, any incapacity which persists beyond the expiration of his sentence will attract an *ex gratia* grant calculated by reference to those Acts. To ensure the proper assessment of such injuries, prisoners are examined by the Medical Boards of the Ministry of National Insurance. Nor is a prisoner debarred from taking action against the Commissioners at common law if he suffers injury through their alleged negligence, though where such cases arise they are usually settled by negotiation between the Treasury Solicitor and solicitors acting for the injured party. The position of the prisoner in both these respects is equally safeguarded if he is working for another public department or for a private employer.

The position of prisoners under the National Insurance Act, which covers *inter alia* sickness and unemployment benefits and old age pensions, is less completely safeguarded. Title to benefits under this Act is conditional on payment of a minimum number of contributions and on the maintenance of an annual credit of at least fifty contributions: further, benefits and contribution rates vary according to whether the contributor is classed as an employed, self-employed, or non-employed person. For the purpose of the Act persons in legal custody are deemed to be non-employed persons, but they are excused from the statutory liability to pay the contributions appropriate to that category, known as Class 3 contributions.

This statutory position, if unmitigated, would have two potentially adverse effects on a prisoner's insurance position after discharge. In the first place, for certain persons in certain circumstances there could be a loss or reduction of unemployment or sickness benefits to which they might otherwise become entitled after release, while the amount of the old age pension might also be affected. In the second place, the state of the prisoner's insurance card could be such as to disclose the fact that he has been in prison. Adequate steps have been taken, in collaboration with the Ministry of National Insurance, to avert the second contingency. The first cannot be wholly averted: it is not legally practicable for prisoners to pay Class 2 contributions while in custody, and no sufficient grounds have been shown for the State to assume the heavy financial responsibility of paying their contributions from public funds, whether direct or behind the façade of increasing prisoners' earnings to enable them to pay. While the arguments advanced in favour of such a course have a certain validity, they do not take account of two factors: first, that this would be to put prisoners in a privileged position as compared with many citizens in Bentham's 'state of innocence and liberty' who are unable for various reasons to maintain their contributions: second, the considerable and complicated administrative labour of ascertaining the precise insurance position of prisoners on reception and assessing the nature and amount of the contributions due in each case. What has been done, after exhaustive consideration by all Departments concerned of all the possibilities, is to provide that any convicted or civil prisoner who wishes to maintain his insurance position to the extent of paying Class 3 contributions may do so, either from such private money as he has in his possession or through his friends. A prisoner who was self-employed immediately before being taken into custody may also opt to pay a Class 1 contribution. All prisoners are informed by a special cell-card of the machinery available for this purpose.[1]

Relations with past and potential employers being more conveniently dealt with in connection with after-care, we now pass to what for many, perhaps most, prisoners are the most necessary and valuable of the social services which the prison must seek to provide for them—those concerned with their families. And here it may be that more remains to be done than in any other part of this field of work.

If one fact can be accepted as established in the field of criminology, it is the overwhelming influence of unsatisfactory home conditions in the formation of delinquency, and that not only among juveniles. Dr. W. F. Roper, in a detailed survey of over 1,400 adult prisoners at Wakefield and Dartmoor,[2] found not only that faulty home training and bad family relations had a preponderating influence on subsequent criminality—this was to be expected: he also found that '25 per cent of the marriages represented have been broken by separation or divorce' and that 'the man from a faulty home tends to recreate faults in his own home, when he comes to found one, and this hands evil down the gen-

---

[1] See Appendix K, note on p. 219.

[2] *The British Journal of Delinquency*, July 1950—'A Comparative Survey of the Wakefield Prison Population in 1948', by W. F. Roper, Principal Medical Officer, Wakefield Prison.

erations'. These observations suggest how wide a field of work there may be, hitherto almost untouched, in seeking the rehabilitation of an offender through his family as well as through his personal training.

And family relations may be of central importance in the treatment of prisoners before as well as after their release. Their adaptation to their situation as prisoners may be materially eased by the sorting out of domestic tangles and difficulties: this is work to which Governors and their Assistants, Chaplains and Welfare Officers willingly give much time and trouble, knowing how great the reward may be in ease of mind among their charges and so in their better co-operation. Many an escape, especially from open prisons, and many an outburst of bad conduct has resulted from some molehill of domestic trouble magnified into a mountain by the helpless brooding of the prisoner.

And here perhaps we may turn aside to consider a problem which is increasingly engaging attention, though in this country hitherto merely as a matter of abstract discussion. How far is it possible, within the limits of prison treatment as those are now understood, to continue the 'normalisation' of prison life by filling its greatest gap—the absence of all those normal and necessary human influences, ties and responsibilities which centre round the life of the family, including the deprivation of all normal sexual life? The problems thus raised are so various and difficult that it is not possible here to do more than recognise them. In their wider aspects they have led so distinguished and experienced an authority as M. Paul Cornil, Secretary-General of the Ministry of Justice of Belgium and for long head of the Belgian prison administration, to ask [1] whether it may not be right so to arrange prisons that the family life of prisoners may be continued within their confines: and reports from Russia have told of certain prisons where that is in fact done. In certain prison systems in Europe and South America the narrower sex problem is recognised, whether or not it be resolved, by regular arrangements in the prisons for 'connubial visits' between husband and wife. If these questions have assumed less importance in this country, it is not from failure to recognise their existence. The problems of homosexuality in prisons are patent to all familiar with prison life, though the desirability of a hetero-sexual antidote has not hitherto been brought into discussion.[2]

In the wider sphere, no more has been done than to reduce the limitations on visits and letters, and so far as may be within these limits to encourage and promote all valuable ties between a prisoner and his family. But prison letters and visits at the best must be cold

---

[1] In an address to the XII International Penal and Penitentiary Congress at The Hague, 1950.

[2] It has however been suggested by an outside observer that the efflorescence of 'pin-up-girls' in the rooms of Borstal boys may have, in this connection, an effect as much therapeutic as decorative. (Mark Benney, 'Leader.' 3 December 1949.)

channels for the human affections. Letters must be censored, and kept within reasonable limits of length. The conditions in which visits take place at most prisons are commonly repugnant to any sensitive mind. What can be done to humanise these things is done. For example, immediate agreement was given to the suggestion that a prisoner writing to a child in the care of a school or foster-home should be allowed to use plain paper and a 'camouflage' address. Experiment to improve visiting conditions is continuous, and many different systems will be found in use in different types of prison. At one end of the scale is the traditional system of 'visiting-boxes'—a row of cubicles, in which the prisoner sits in one half and the visitor in the other, separated by glass and a wire grille, so permitting sight and sound without the possibility of physical contact: at the other end, in open prisons and some training prisons, the prisoners and their visitors may walk about the grounds and have tea and a cigarette together under the trees. Between these extremes experiments continue, seeking to devise a system of 'open visits', away from the 'boxes', without loss of essential control and supervision. A common plan is a long table, with a partition down the centre to prevent contraband being flicked across, and supervising officers at the ends: but the paradoxical situation was reached that, although this system was devised primarily for Stars and prisoners of the better sort, such prisoners began to ask for visits in the boxes 'as a privilege'—they and their friends could not stand the noise and elbow-to-elbow publicity of the public tables. It should be understood that these difficulties are not due to mere obtuseness or conservatism in the prisons, but to inherent difficulties—first, as in so many other things, inadequate space; second, that visiting times must suit the visitors, and they all tend to come at the same time, especially on Saturdays; and third, that control must be kept to prevent contraventions of the law and the prison Rules—it is a mistake to think of all visitors to prisoners as innocent and sensitive persons; many of them are them-selves members or associates of the criminal class and up to every trick of the trade, with extraordinary ingenuity in getting across a pound note or a packet of cigarettes or a hack-saw blade, and even visitors to Stars will often go to some lengths to circumvent the Rules in this way. The tax-payers' bill is sensibly relieved by the amount of contraband annually confiscated, as no doubt are many prisoners by the unknown amount which escapes detection. The latest experiment is to rely for control on searching after the visit, and to allow each party a small separate table and chairs, spaced at reasonable distances. Observation of the practice of other prison systems suggests a similar variety of approach: in the U.S.A., for example, the writer has seen 'guest-rooms' suggesting the foyer of the Waldorf-Astoria, with up-holstered couches and chairs; wooden benches and tables in a basement passage; and boxes similar to our own.

One point to which criticism has been directed illustrates the perplexities of prison life. Is it right that young children should be brought to visit their parents in prison, and in such conditions as often prevail? To many the answer may seem at once to be a shocked 'no'. But do the imprisoned parents think so? And how if the mother, or father, cannot come unless the children come too? The conclusion so far has been, rightly or wrongly, that this is a matter for the parents to decide for themselves: it is not for authority to say no.

Certainly, among the many improvements which our ancient prisons still await, the building of completely new blocks for visiting should, when the time comes, have a high priority.

Before we leave the question of family relations, there are certain other points of interest, actual and potential. In their Annual Reports for 1947 and 1948 the Commissioners described an interesting new scheme as follows:

'The Commissioners were able during the year to help in filling a gap in social assistance for women prisoners. It was brought to their notice through the Howard League that many women, on being sent —perhaps unexpectedly—to prison, are faced with immediate domestic problems which may be small but can cause acute anxiety to themselves and much inconvenience or worse to their families if they are not seen to at once and on the spot. The Commissioners felt that there was a situation here that ought to be dealt with somehow, but was beyond the scope of the existing welfare agencies in a prison. They were fortunate in being able to enlist the interest of the Women's Voluntary Services an experimental scheme was started at Holloway.

'Here W.V.S. representatives attend every evening in the reception, and see any woman who wishes to see them soon after she is brought in. The service is essentially one of "first-aid", and any but immediate difficulties are referred to the D.P.A.S. But with the urgent problems that call for action at once the W.V.S., with its wide organisation of helpful women on the spot, is excellently fitted to deal. These problems have included disposal of keys and ration books, securing luggage and rooms, making arrangements for children at home or at school, looking after the dog left behind, or stopping a woman in Durham from leaving to visit her sister who was by then in Holloway. . . .

'The W.V.S. "First-Aid" scheme for meeting the immediate domestic problems of women on reception has continued successfully at Holloway. Since the scheme started on July 28th 1947, 2,144 women have been interviewed, and help has been given to 346 of them. It is apparent therefore, that although the need may not be frequent it exists, and where it exists it is usually urgent. A similar scheme was tried at Birmingham, Durham and Manchester, but for reasons which defy speculation there was not one request for help in these prisons: the service was therefore reduced to a "shadow" organisation.

'In all these experiments the Commissioners met with the most willing co-operation from the W.V.S., who have throughout regarded this unsensational and often apparently unwanted service as amply justified by the cases in which a real need has been met and a woman saved much unnecessary distress.'

For the future, the power now available [1] to release prisoners on parole may well be used to afford to certain classes of prisoner 'home leave' on the lines long established for Borstal boys. This would enable prisoners to resume contact with their homes and families before release, and give them a better sense of the future and its responsibilities.

Given the importance of the family background as a factor in the causation of crime, it may be that valuable help could be given in many cases by boldly including the prisoner's family in the process of his rehabilitation. This would require a various, tactful and skilled approach. In one case their understanding co-operation might be all that it was necessary to secure, in another the family itself might need rehabilitation. The development of a professional social-welfare service in prisons, which has recently been advocated (see p. 264), might enable progress towards this end.

[1] Criminal Justice (Scotland) Act 1949, 11th Schedule and Prison Rules, 1951 See also Appendix K.

CHAPTER THIRTEEN

PHYSICAL WELFARE

(1) HYGIENE

THE Statutory Rules under this heading are as follows:

'94. The Medical Officer shall oversee and shall advise the Governor upon the hygiene of the prison and the prisoners, including arrangements for cleanliness, sanitation, heating, lighting and ventilation.

'95. Arrangements shall be made for every prisoner to wash at all proper times, to have a hot bath at least once a week, and for men (unless excused or prohibited on medical or other grounds) to shave or be shaved daily and to have their hair cut as required. The hair of a male prisoner may be cut as short as is necessary for good appearance but the hair of a female prisoner shall not be cut without her consent, except by the direction of the Medical officer for the eradication of vermin, dirt or disease.

'96. Every prisoner shall be provided on admission with such toilet articles as are necessary for health and cleanliness, and arrangements shall be made for the replacement of these articles when necessary.'

These general statements of principle call for little elaboration. The washing arrangements and toilet equipment in cellular prisons have already been described (p. 131). Men are required to shave every morning on getting up, blades being issued and collected on each occasion: each man has his own blade, and they may buy blade-sharpeners, or have them sent in. Certain additional toilet articles may be bought in the canteen.

Bathing takes place once a week in the central bath-house, and is usually the occasion for change of underclothing.

Haircutting is not very satisfactory. This is one of the activities which, when prisons are staffed for an evening shift, should certainly take place after working hours. As things are, one may find in any workshop a prisoner in process of having his hair cut by another. The result is that the phrase 'as short as is necessary for good appearance' gets a strikingly elastic interpretation, and the younger men rival the women in the elaborate complication of their 'hair-dos', generally with less taste. It may be that this can be justified as being the one expression of personality left to a man in prison uniform. But it may also be that the reaction against the 'convict crop' has gone too far, and that the pendulum could with aesthetic advantage begin to swing the other way. The proper solution is undoubtedly a barber's shop, with trained men doing the work under skilled supervision.

This problem does not arise for women, who may do what they will with their hair, though they do not have the advantage of 'beauty-parlours' as do many of their American cousins in distress. They are however free to act as their own beauticians with such lip-stick and powder as they may bring in with them, or purchase at the canteen. Much detrition of crimson book-bindings is thereby saved.

The last words of Rule 95 are 'the eradication of vermin, dirt or disease', and it must be emphasised that this is one of the first and nastiest duties of the reception staff, particularly in women's prisons. A considerable number of prisoners, notably among the short-sentence class, are received in a filthy condition, and the greatest care has to be taken to detect and isolate cases of vermin and contagious skin disease. There is special apparatus for dealing with women's hair, and special baths and cells are set aside for 'dirt diseases'. Every prisoner of course has to take a hot bath before leaving the reception block, and personal cleanliness is enforced thereafter.

'The high general standard of health, the rareness of epidemics and the absence of evidence of the spread of contagious disease suggest that the precautions taken are effective. Verminous infestations are fortunately rare but when they occur vigorous action is taken. The cells are stripped and the door fittings and furniture are treated in an insulated container by cyanide gas, the floors and walls being sprayed with D.D.T. solution.' [1]

Finally, sanitation. On this many hard words have been written and spoken, not without some justification, against prison arrangements. There are, for cellular prisons, a chamber-pot in each cell (with cover), and one or more 'sanitary recesses' on each landing: the recess includes a slop-sink, running water (cold) and a water closet: over a period of years these have been and are being gradually reconstructed and given more modern fittings, but those remaining of the old type are not pleasant to see. There are also ranges of W.Cs. in the exercise yards, and a certain number in each workshop. The prisoner is instructed that he should normally use the W.C. during his exercise: that on the

[1] *Prisons and Borstals*, p. 53.

landing is intended only for emergency use if he requires it while he is locked in his cell, when he should ring for the duty officer. In general, prisoners have plenty of opportunity to attend to the calls of nature when they are out of their cells, and again before locking up; they should not often, therefore, need to venture a ring.[1]

Criticism of these arrangements centres first on the disadvantages of the chamber-pot, and then on the nature of the recesses and W.C. provision generally. As to this, one or two deprecatory observations may be ventured. Prisons were not designed for those from whom this sort of criticism most generally emanates; and while we should no doubt do better if we were building today, the normal habits of large numbers of the prison population still fall short of refinement. And making all due allowance for this, is either the standard of fitting or the cleanliness of a modern prison W.C. *much* below the average of similar accommodation in—say—railway stations and public places? As for the chamber-pot, the difficulties of dispensing with it have already been discussed, and it is after all not peculiar to a prison cell. The principal objection is to the unsavoury process of 'slopping out' on morning unlocking, when the prisoners line up to empty their slops at the recesses. This objection must be sustained; but the slops must also be emptied. The solution of the problem, in spite of constant thought, has not yet emerged.

(2) EXERCISE

The relevant Statutory Rule provides as follows:

'97. (1) Prisoners who are not engaged in out-door work shall be given one hour's exercise in the open air, weather permitting: provided that in special circumstances the Commissioners may authorise the reduction of the daily period to half an hour.

'(2) Wherever practicable prisoners of suitable age and physical condition shall receive physical training under qualified instructors during some part of the daily exercise period.

'(3) The Medical Officer shall decide on the fitness of every prisoner for exercise and to undergo physical training, and may on medical grounds modify the exercise of a prisoner or excuse a prisoner from exercise.'

The exercise period is divided into two half-hours, either before or after each period of work. For those who are fit for physical training, one period will be for this, the other for 'walking exercise': for the

---

[1] On this, see p. 106.

others, both periods will be walking exercise. This still takes place, in the great majority of prisons, on the paved concentric rings of the original Pentonville model, which in recent years have been widened to allow two prisoners to walk abreast. There are usually two or three exercise yards, to allow of separation of the different categories, and it is common to find them very pleasantly laid out with flowers and small shrubs. The general arrangement is for the young and active to step briskly round the outer rings, while the old and infirm potter gently round the inner. Supervising officers keep the circulation flowing evenly and without bunching. Conversation is unrestricted, but smoking is not permitted. This traditional English prison scene has sometimes aroused surprise in foreign visitors, who see it as regimented and somewhat inhuman, and ask why the prisoners should not just be left to themselves in the open air for half-an-hour—to wander round, prop up the walls or gossip in groups in a natural manner. It is a legitimate question. The answer lies partly in the view still taken, rightly or wrongly, in our prisons of the need for constant control and supervision, and partly in the terms of the Rule, which does in fact—and it may be thought, at least by an Englishman, rightly—require exercise, not just fresh air. It may be added that in women's prisons the scene and tempo are likely to be much more in the 'natural manner'.

Physical training during the exercise periods may be given by any member of the staff who has qualified as an instructor during his initial training at Wakefield, but at most prisons there is also a recognised Gymnastic Instructor, in receipt of a special allowance, who has obtained an instructor's certificate at the Army School of Physical Training at Aldershot. He has a general supervision of physical training in the prison, and he alone is authorised to take classes with apparatus in the gymnasium. These are limited to younger men passed fit by the Medical Officer and are held in the evenings on a voluntary basis. For women the position is a little different. There is no daily physical training, but a good deal is done in evening classes on lines more suitable for women—'keep fit' classes, therapeutic exercises, dancing and the like.

While outdoor games are not precluded in principle, lack of suitable space prevents them at all but a few favoured prisons, though several prisons have developed types of football or handball with local rules appropriate to the peculiarities of the pitch. There is often a large parade ground used for physical training which may also serve for cricket of a sort, though the hard surface may make football too dangerous. At some prisons with ground outside the walls cricket or football may be played at week-ends, and most of the prisons used for corrective training are so favoured, as is the central prison at Parkhurst—here the week-end game in 'the compound' is eagerly looked forward to by both players and spectators, and the privilege is so highly valued that any abuse would make the sinner's life uneasy in that prison. One man who tried to escape from the compound spent weeks of voluntary segregation in the separate cells to allow memories to fade.

In the open prisons the cricket and football clubs are often vigorous institutions with regular fixture lists against local teams, though so far the Commissioners have not thought fit to authorise 'away' fixtures. At one camp, community with village life had gone so far that the village team were borrowing players from the prison to fill gaps in their side—a practice which the Commissioners, with some regret, felt bound to frown on when it came to notice. However, the incident shows to what extent friendly relations can develop, and sport is one of the many ways by which the prisoner and the outside community can healthily and fruitfully be brought together.[1]

(3) FOOD

The morale of a prison, not less than that of an army, depends upon its stomach. All who have been prisoners of war know the disproportionate importance which food assumed in their daily life. 'When we listen to the well-known complaints to be found in prison memoirs old and new, we can be sure that the majority of them are concerned with the problem of food. From older writers, as Friedrich von der Trenck, to Macartney and Mark Benney, the quantity of the bread, the consistency of the porridge and the flavour of the cocoa become matters of utmost importance.'[2] Dr. Mannheim has traced in detail the effect of the 'principle of less eligibility' on this aspect of prison life and reference has also been made to this in earlier chapters of this book. But though it would no longer be seriously argued that a prisoner's diet should not be better than that of the poorest citizen at large, it is still necessary for it to bear a suitable relation to the general standard of life of the population. Comparisons between the dietary standards of different prison systems are therefore of little value without a wider connotation. The food in our English prisons may seem meagre and dull against the rich and various meals served in an American penitentiary, or gross in comparison with those of some European prisons; but the only proper criterion is its relation to the standard of eating among the generality of manual workers in this country.

And here there is another consideration to be borne in mind. Half a dozen cooks given the same collection of ingredients may well produce six strikingly different results. And if a visitor looking at a prison dinner is inclined to say grudgingly that it is 'better than anything he would be likely to get at home', he should reflect that a trained cook working on

[1] See Appendix K. [2] Mannheim, p. 62.

bulk materials in a well-equipped kitchen is very likely to get better results than a number of harassed and possibly indifferent housewives with such resources as they have to hand. It is not necessary to have bad cooking as part of the punishment.

The present dietary system, then, is intended to maintain not health and strength only, but also contentment. It does not seek to go beyond this, and some may think it does not even go so far. But no institutional meals will ever satisfy everybody, and one of the unpleasant aspects of prison life is that in the way of food you have to eat what you get or go without. And on the whole, in recent years, internal complaints about food have been negligible, while external criticism—which was forceful during and immediately after the war—has not lately been heard.

This situation, curiously enough, was to a large extent brought about by the national food situation during the war and post-war years. In their Annual Report for the years 1939–41 the Commissioners said:

'The introduction of civilian rationing made it imperative to review the dietary in all classes of prisons and Borstals institutions. The pre-war dietary had been based on the report of a Committee which reported in 1925. Immediately before the present war the Commissioners were arranging for a new committee to be appointed to reconsider the whole question of prison diets. This was not practicable after the outbreak of war. Nevertheless, the whole scheme of prison dietary was recast in 1940. Instead of an arrangement of set meals, a ration scale was drawn up for each prisoner in strict accordance with the civilian ration scale. Certain additions in the shape of culinary adjuncts were made. One of the criticisms of the old prison diets, and one not without force, was that they all tasted alike. The addition to the rations of such things as curry powder, herbs and dried fruit (or fresh fruit if in season) enabled the cooks to serve the food in more palatable form and with greater variation.

'The set meals were abolished, and it was left to the cook to serve the rations issued in the most suitable manner he could devise. There have been singularly few complaints from prisoners about the new dietary, and medical officers report that the general health of prisoners has been well maintained, as also have their body weights. The great majority of the cooks have risen to the occasion and have produced meals which have given general satisfaction. They are to be commended warmly for their efforts.'

There was nevertheless a considerable if contradictory criticism of the dietary, and 'In August 1944 the Prison Commissioners consulted the Ministry of Food and asked them to assist in studying the problem of prison diets. The Scientific Adviser's Department of the Ministry drew up a scheme for this investigation which was approved and the investigation commenced at the end of September, 1944.' [1] The investigator attended seven representative institutions for seven days each, and got together from each an average diet for the seven day period. Each of these diets was analysed and every calorie, protein, vitamin and other element duly weighed and estimated. Nothing could have been more scientifically thorough. It was found that the composition of the diet was generally satisfactory except for a shortage of vitamin C. Recommendations were made to remedy this, to improve the Borstal diet to meet the higher physiological requirements of adolescents, and on certain other matters. Steps were taken, as approved by the Ministry, to give effect to these recommendations, and the diets have remained on this basis, subject to the fluctuations of rationing, in the ensuing years.

At the same time the Commissioners asked the Ministry of Food to advise on the planning of menus and the preparation and serving of meals, and among the many recommendations made was that the Commissioners should appoint a full-time Catering Adviser—advice which was followed by an appointment in 1946.

The one remaining weakness of the dietary arrangements was the long gap between the evening meal, which on the one-shift staff system must in most prisons be served by 5 p.m., and breakfast next morning. To meet this it was arranged for cocoa to be served later in the evening.

The meals served, except dinners, are described on the Diet Card placed in each cell, a copy of which is shown as Appendix J. The dinners consist of a meat or fish course, with bread, potatoes and a vegetable, followed on most days of the week by a sweet pudding. Cooks have a reasonable repertoire, and they try to avoid sameness by not serving the same dish on the same day of every week: a specimen week's diet from a London prison is included in Appendix J. In their Report for 1949 the Commissioners gave the calorific value of the diets in use as follows:

Local Prisons				*Central Prisons*			
Men	.	.	3,140	Men	.	.	3,452
Women	.	.	2,790	Women	.	.	2,790
Y.P. Boys.	.	.	3,420				
Y.P. Girls.	.	.	3,114				

Borstal Institutions				*Regional Prisons*			
Boys	.	.	4,495	Men	.	.	3,452
Girls	.	.	4,329	Women	.	.	2,790

Prison kitchens are in charge of 'cook and baker officers' who are members of the established grade of prison officer. They have all gone through a special course of training and receive an additional

---

[1] *Annual Report* 1942–44, para. 209.

allowance for their specialist skill and responsibility. In the larger kitchens there may be both a cook and a baker.

A considerable effort has been made since the war to bring the kitchen buildings and equipment up to a satisfactory level: all have now been supplied with refrigerators, fish-fryers, mechanical potato cleaners, slicing machines and the like, and in some of the larger bakeries dough-mixing machines have also been installed.

Responsibility for securing that the food is 'of wholesome quality and well prepared', under the general surveillance of the Director of Medical Services and the Catering Adviser, is placed first, by Statutory Rule, on the Medical Officer who 'shall frequently inspect the food, cooked and uncooked, provided for prisoners, and shall report to the Governor on the state and quality of the food and on any deficiency in the quantity or defect in the quality of the water'. The Governor also, as part of his daily duty, inspects the meals and tastes them. A traditional feature of every prison kitchen is a small side table, laid with a white cloth, on which are set out with geometrical precision samples of every article of diet served during the day, including the special vegetarian and hospital diets. While this is aesthetically pleasing, knowledge is better gained by examining the actual meals as they are to be served. Control of the quality and quantity of the ingredients rests with the Steward, who issues the necessary amounts to the cook from his stores.

One question, in the application of the Statutory Rule, is still to be answered. Are the meals 'well served'? At present the answer must, on the whole, be no, with the usual qualifications required in so various a system. The unit of service is still, in the majority of prisons and for the majority of prisoners in those prisons, the single prisoner eating in his cell; and for breakfast this is always so. The basic system, therefore, requires the kitchen to put up some hundreds of identical meals in individual containers, which in turn are stacked in large wooden food-trays, covered with a cloth, and placed in hot-plates some time before the hour for serving the meal. These trays must contain the exact number of meals required on each landing in each hall, including vegetarian and other special diets, according to the daily state—a complicated bit of calculation and organisation. As soon as all the men are in their cells, the Principal Officer on the centre gives the signal and from all directions the 'landing orderlies' clatter down to the point where their trays await them, duly marked with the landing number and number of meals in each tray. These are checked by the landing officers and carried up to the landings, where the processions begin—an officer in front to unlock, a second officer to hand in the dinner from the tray to the waiting hands inside the door. As the time when the staff get away to their own dinners depends on the speed of the operation, time is not wasted. Another method, for dinners only, is more usual at most prisons—here the trays are brought to a central point and placed on tables; the men as they come in from work file past, each collecting his own meal which is handed to him by prisoner orderlies, with no unnecessary ceremony, under the supervision of officers.

The source of all evil in any single unit service is the nature of the container. This from time beyond memory has been the notorious prison can—perhaps, with the broad-arrow and the mail-bag, one of the hoariest stigmata of the prison. It is a cylindrical metal tin, with a carrying handle (rarely used) and an inverted loose top which serves both as cover for the main body beneath and container for potatoes on top. It is in every way unsuitable, unhygienic, and inefficient by modern standards, though it may have served its purpose when prison meals and standards were simpler. It must be both sticky and unsafe to climb the narrow spiral stair of a prison hall with a piece of pudding in one hand and in the other this tin, with a piece of bread precariously perched on top of the potatoes. The meal is not—or should not—be eaten from the tin, for plate, knife, fork and spoon are provided in each cell: it is intended simply for transport, but apart from its inefficiency for that purpose it has the effect of reducing any meal, however well prepared, to an unpalatable slush before its gets to the plate.

Since the war experiments have been carried out with alternative methods, and at the time of writing initial supplies have been delivered of a white plastic cafeteria tray, compartmented to hold the various parts of a meal. These are to be tried in representative prisons: but the problems of storage in the hot-cupboards, transport from kitchen to cell without loss of heat, and resistance to the less than fair wear-and-tear they will get in the prisons may still delay a satisfactory solution.

It is of course axiomatic that a modern prison would avoid these troubles by communal eating in dining-rooms with a cafeteria service. Meanwhile the best arrangements possible are made in prisons with nothing like a dining-room for those prisoners in stage who do eat together. Usually this has to be on the floors of the halls, though some prisons have a number of small rooms which are used for 'messes'. Small tables, usually for six, are provided, and neatly laid with two plates and a mug, knife, fork and spoon for each man. Water and condiments are placed on each table. For these associated messes the meals are sent up from the kitchen in bulk, and served on to the plates from a service table. Every effort is made to secure a clean and decent standard of table-manners.

In the open prisons, of course, all meals are served in dining-rooms, where the standards of a good works canteen may be expected.

There are certain variations of the standard pattern. At some prisons where there is a lot of outdoor work the men prefer to have their main meal in the evening, and outside parties at all prisons who do not come back during the day take out a 'haversack ration' and have their main meal when they get back: these parties usually have their dinner together in mess. There are of course variations of diet for the hospital generally and for individuals on medical grounds. And at Christmas there is more than a variation: the cooks usually show a good deal of enterprise then, and a good roast, Christmas pudding, cake, fruit, mincemeat and the like somehow appear in quantities beyond what is necessary to maintain health and strength.

(4) CLOTHING

It is difficult to strike the right note in prison dress. One of the earliest of the changes made after the First World War was to abandon deliberately defamatory dress—the drab tunic and breeches, sown with broadarrows, which are still cherished by cartoonists. In place of this came a plain suit of jacket, waistcoat and trousers, worn with a shirt, collar and tie, woollen socks and black leather shoes. But the result was disappointing: no-one could feel that it helped to stimulate self-respect. In particular the practice of boiling all outer garments before re-issue, though hygienically sound, did not make for good appearance. Women at this time wore jean dresses, with aprons and white washable caps, woollen cardigans for colder weather, and underclothing that approached the normal scarcely more in principle than in detail.

After the late war, the Commissioners reconsidered the whole position, and in view of the difficulties of providing suits cut on normal civilian lines to look well on such a large and constantly changing population, other possibilities were discussed, such as something along the lines of the 'battle-dress' suit popularised during the war. However the balance of advantage seemed to be in favour of a suit, and much care was devoted to getting a suitable cloth which would stand up to the conditions, and a style that would look well and could still be made up in prison work-shops. Two important innovations were the substitution of dry-cleaning for boiling, and the provision of protective clothing for use at work. The underclothing and shoes were also brought into line with normal wear.

A more radical change was made for the women, who may now have a choice of frocks (in four colours to their own taste) made in a 'zephyr' material to a normal (though uniform) design. Two dresses are issued, one for work, one for the evening. Maternity frocks of similar material are also available. The underclothing, stockings and shoes were also revised and would probably now be acceptable, in the circumstances, to most women: those who wish to use their own corsets and brassieres may do so, if they are fit for use. The grey wool cardigans remain, and aprons, overalls, raincoats, boots etc., are issued as required by the nature of the work.

The men's suits are of plain grey cloth for the convicted, and of brown for untried and civil prisoners who choose to wear prison dress. Men in the higher stages of a long-term sentence wear navy blue jackets. The shirts are cream coloured with a pin-stripe, have attached collars, and are worn with a plain blue or brown tie. A second shirt is issued for night wear. It is a little early yet to pronounce on the general effect, but though it is an improvement, it does not so far look like fulfilling the hopes of the designers: and time will not improve it. There is, however, no doubt that the working dress, of ordinary blue bib-and-brace overalls, is a pronounced success: the appearance of prisoners at work is normal and workmanlike.

The outer clothing is diversified by stripes and badges of varying significance, the proliferation of which has recently been brought under control. Star class prisoners in local prisons wear a red cloth star, men on the sleeve below the shoulder, women above the left breast. Young prisoners in local prisons wear a yellow triangle in the same position—in their separate centres they need no distinguishing mark. They no longer wear shorts and stockings: this attire, for robust young men of 19 or 20, was felt on the whole to be unsuitable—indeed at times it seemed to verge on the 'defamatory'. For women the different stages of the long-term stage system are marked by different coloured ties or bows on the front of the dress; for men by a stripe on the cuff.

There are local variations in different types of prison. In prisons where there are 'leaders', these wear a blue armlet. In central and regional prisons where there is much outdoor work jerseys are issued, and all outdoor parties have mackintoshes for wet weather. The standard wet-weather (or cold-weather) wear has not been changed, and is still a short grey cloth cape for men and a longer blue cape for women. There is no regular head-gear: elderly men, and others on medical recommendation, have the old prison cap, which is something like the pre-war army forage cap. Men on the 'escape list' wear a dark cloth patch on the front and back of the trousers and the breast-pocket, so that they can be easily identified:

CHAPTER FOURTEEN

MEDICAL SERVICES

(1) THE BODY

IN the medical department of the prison the principle of 'inclusion in the community' has been carried as far as in any other. Although prison Medical Officers are not themselves officers of the National Health Service, every facility offered by that service is available to every prisoner. Dentists and opticians regularly visit the prisons, which are equipped with dental surgeries, and all necessary dental treatment (including dentures) and spectacles are supplied. Venereal disease is treated by venereologists from the local clinics, whether at the prisons or at the public clinics: everything is done to secure so far as possible continuity of treatment on discharge, and at Holloway, where the problem bulks largest, the London County Council have attached a venereal disease social worker to the prison clinic to this particular end. Full use is also made of N.H.S. consultant and hospital services, and for all these purposes numbers of prisoners are taken every day to the public hospitals and clinics—a considerable additional drain on the time of the staff for escort duties.

To this extent the prisoner is as well served as if he were not in prison, and no better, for his status affords him no priority in the supply of dentures, spectacles, etc. But in so far as he is under regular medical supervision and direction from the day of his reception he is at some advantage, and it is a necessary and logical part of his treatment that this should be so: the prison may or may not succeed in removing moral defects, but it may well remove or relieve mental and physical defects which could handicap a prisoner who, on discharge, had the will to 'lead a good and useful life'. This indeed is regarded as a duty implicit in the terms of Statutory Rule 6.

The Medical Officer is, therefore, equipped with considerable autonomous powers and responsibilities, which are prescribed in detail in the Statutory Rules. He must examine every prisoner on reception, record the state of his health and other particulars and note his fitness for

238

labour and physical training. He must 'have the care of the mental and physical health of the prisoners and shall every day visit every sick prisoner, every prisoner who complains of illness, and every other prisoner to whom his attention is specially directed (S.R. 86)'; and 'attend at once on receiving information of the illness of a prisoner' (S.R. 87). Mention has already been made of his responsibilities in respect of hygiene and sanitation; food, work and exercise; and of prisoners undergoing certain forms of punishment or under mechanical restraint.

In addition, the following specific responsibilities are laid on him by the Rules:

'88. The Medical Officer shall report to the Governor any matter which appears to him to require the consideration of the Commissioners on medical grounds, and the Governor shall send such report to the Commissioners.

'89. Whenever the Medical Officer has reason to believe that a prisoner's mental or physical health is likely to be injuriously affected by continued imprisonment or by any conditions of imprisonment, or that the life of a prisoner will be endangered by imprisonment, or that a sick prisoner will not survive his sentence or is totally or permanently unfit for imprisonment, he shall without delay report the case in writing to the Governor with such recommendations as he thinks fit, and the Governor shall forward such report and recommendations to the Commissioners forthwith.

'90. The Medical Officer shall report in writing to the Governor the case of any prisoner to which he thinks it necessary on medical grounds to draw attention, and shall make such recommendations as he deems needful for the alteration of the diet or treatment of the prisoner or for his separation from other prisoners, or for the supply to him of additional clothing, bedding or other articles, and the Governor shall so far as practicable carry such recommendations into effect.

'91. The Medical Officer shall draw the attention of the Governor to any prisoner who he may have reason to think has suicidal intentions in order that special observation may be kept on such prisoner, and the Governor shall, without delay, direct that such prisoner be observed at frequent intervals.

'92. The Medical Officer shall keep under special observation every prisoner whose mental condition appears to require it, and shall take such steps as he considers proper for his segregation, and if necessary his certification under the Acts relating to lunacy or mental deficiency.

'93. The Medical Officer shall give notice to the Governor and the Chaplain when a prisoner appears to be seriously ill.'

Finally, he must examine every prisoner 'as short a time as practicable before discharge, or removal to another prison' (S.R. 25), and if a prisoner dies the Medical Officer 'shall keep a record of the death of any prisoner which shall include the following particulars: at what time the deceased was taken ill, when the illness was first notified to the Medical Officer, the nature of the illness, when the prisoner died, and an account of the appearance after death (in cases where a *post mortem* examination is made) together with any special remarks that appear to him to be required' (S.R. 27). In this event the Governor is also required to 'give immediate notice thereof to the Coroner having jurisdiction, to the Visiting Committee and to the Commissioners' (S.R. 28). The examination before discharge is intended to ensure that the prisoner is fit for the journey, and that his medical condition is on record in case of subsequent complaints: a prisoner may not be removed to another prison unless the Medical Officer certifies that he is fit for removal, and one due for discharge 'who is suffering from an acute or dangerous illness shall, unless he refuses to stay, not be sent out of prison until in the opinion of the Medical Officer it is safe to send him out, (S.R. 25).

To assist the Medical Officer in the discharge of his duties the Rules further provide that 'At every prison either a separate hospital building or a suitable part of the prison shall be equipped and furnished in a manner proper for the medical care and treatment of sick prisoners, and staffed by suitably trained officers' (S.R. 85). Most prisons have a separate hospital building within the wall. The nature and size of these vary with the size of the prison. The best of them are light, airy and well-equipped buildings, with pleasant wards and ranges of separate rooms which are larger than the ordinary cell, painted white, lighted by normal windows and equipped with hospital beds and furniture and head-phones for wireless. There will also be a dispensary, treatment rooms, offices, etc. Others are less satisfactory, and could only be put right by rebuilding. In smaller prisons a few hospital rooms and offices in one of the halls may suffice for normal purposes.

The hospital will also control a number of cells in the main building set aside for certain cases who do not require 'hospitalisation'—epileptic cells, with padded floor, walls, etc.; special cells for itch, verminous and venereal cases; and others, with large windows and washable walls, for tubercular cases. In dealing with tuberculosis, full use is made of the resources of local T.B. clinics and, where necessary, sanatoria.

The nursing in men's prisons is done by male nurses who are called Hospital Officers. They are recruited mainly from men with suitable nursing experience in the Royal Navy, the R.A.M.C. or the R.A.F., or as mental hospital attendants: some are State Registered Nurses and some hold certificates in mental nursing, but these qualifications are not essential. Selected candidates are first given the ordinary course of training of a prison officer: those who are successful are later sent to a course of training in prison nursing at a large prison hospital, and if they pass the examination they receive a certificate and are posted for duty as Hospital Officers.

For women's prisons there is a service of Nursing Sisters recruited from fully trained State Registered Nurses, with assistant nurses in the larger hospitals. There are one or more Sisters at every women's prison, and in the large hospital at Holloway there would be 30 or more if the staff were at full strength. Unfortunately since the war there has been a serious shortage of qualified Nursing Sisters in the prison service as elsewhere. The head of the women's Nursing Service is the Nursing Matron-in-Chief, who though stationed at Holloway periodically visits all the women's hospitals. The Commissioners also receive advice on nursing matters, and on the conditions of service of the female nursing staff, from a Voluntary Advisory Nursing Board, consisting of the Matrons of certain large London hospitals and other qualified ladies: the Board meets quarterly, with the Governor of Holloway and the Matron-in-Chief, from the latter of whom it receives a regular report. Members of the Board visit the Holloway hospital on a regular rota, and other hospitals from time to time.

The prisons are thus equipped to deal with most medical contingencies, including minor surgery, and some hospitals have operation theatres in which major operations can be performed. There is, however, power under the Criminal Justice Act 1948 to remove to an outside hospital any prisoner who requires surgical or medical treatment which cannot be given in the prison. This power is freely used. The majority of cases requiring major operations are however removed to Wormwood Scrubs prison, where there is a large modern operating theatre and surgical unit staffed by Nursing Sisters: the operations are performed by outside surgical consultants.

Until 1949 it was the practice for births to take place in the prison hospitals, and all Sisters were required to be qualified midwives. Following the Criminal Justice Act, however, the Secretary of State decided that any woman who wished to be delivered in an outside hospital should be removed to one if suitable arrangements could be made, and the great majority of women have since opted to do this so that their babies may not be under the stigma of having been born in prison. The hospital authorities have in general co-operated most helpfully, and the arrangements have worked well: mother and child are however, usually returned to the prison a day or two after the birth. These babies get an excellent start in life, in spite of their inauspicious nursery, for their mothers have not only had skilled pre-natal care but are given a good training in child welfare and management, and the babies are provided with a nice little outfit to go home in. A woman may have her baby with her in prison, whether it be born there or brought in at reception, 'during the normal period of lactation and longer if required in special circumstances' (S.R. 20). The creche is usually the most cheerful feature of a women's prison, except when feeding-time is overdue.

(2) THE MIND

In this section we approach a subject which is highly specialised, of increasing interest today both inside and outside the prison world, and also, because of its scientific immaturity, in many of its aspects still controversial. The impact of psychological medicine on the treatment of offenders is nevertheless no new thing. As long ago as 1932 the Departmental Committee on Persistent Offenders stated, in the course of its recommendations, that 'The mental condition of offenders is a matter calling for careful attention. There is reason to believe that certain delinquents may be amenable to psychological treatment. The application of this method to criminal cases is, in this country at any rate, in its infancy. Its scope is probably limited and is applicable chiefly to children, juveniles and adolescents. Further experience is desirable to show to what extent this method can be used effectively. A certain number of offenders might benefit by attending under probation approved mental hospitals or out-patient clinics. Use should also be made in suitable cases of child-guidance clinics. A medical psychologist should be attached to one or more penal establishments to carry out psychological treatment in selected cases. He should be assisted by voluntary women workers who should visit the offender's home and obtain information as to his history and circumstances. This system should be applied to offenders who are willing to be treated during a sentence of Borstal detention or imprisonment, and are recommended for such treatment by the Medical Officer as being hopeful cases if transferred for this purpose to a special establishment.'

All these recommendations have since been realised, either by developments in prison medical practice or by legislation, and the position before the war was set out in the well-known 'East-Hubert' Report on the Psychological Treatment of Crime.[1] This four-year investigation was undertaken, the writers tell us, largely as a result of the recommendation of the Departmental Committee.

It is not within the scope of this section, nor the competence of the writer, to attempt either to summarise or to comment on this authoritative work, nor on the post-war reports of the successors to Sir Norwood East and Dr. Hubert in this field which have appeared in the Annual

[1] By W. Norwood East, M.D., F.R.C.P., late Medical Commissioner of Prisons, and W. H. de B. Hubert, B.A., M.R.C.S., L.R.C.P., late Psychotherapist, H.M. Prison, Wormwood Scrubs. Published in 1939 for the Home Office by H.M. Stationery Office, price 2s. 6d.

Reports of the Commissioners: readers can but be referred to the originals, and more particularly to the Appendix to Chapter Seven of the 1949 Report, which contains full accounts of their work by the two consulting psycho-therapists at Wormwood Scrubs, Dr. John C. Mackwood and Dr. Jonathan H. Gould.[1]

The primary purpose of this section will be the more limited one of describing the 'set-up' within the prison system for dealing with diseases and disorders of the mind, and the duties which fall on the Medical Officers and their assistants in this connection: it will however be necessary for completeness to consider also the provision made by law for dealing with any offender, whether he be sentenced to imprisonment or not, who may suffer or be thought to suffer from such diseases and disorders, since the prison Medical Officer may have an essential part to play at any stage of these proceedings. We shall consider also the role of the Medical Officer *qua* psychiatrist, and of the psychologist, in the general treatment of prisoners, especially in relation to classification. For a synthesis of contemporary international expert views on all these, and other, aspects of the function of psychiatry in.the prison, attention is drawn to the Resolution on Question Two of Section I in Appendix F. How far English practice conforms with these views will appear as we proceed.

An essential preliminary here is the definition of terms, since these are not always used in the same sense internationally or even professionally within the same country: this is not to claim any authority for the following definitions, but simply to make clear the sense in which these terms will be used. By psychology, psychiatry and psychotherapy we shall mean the branches of science concerned respectively with the nature and functions of the mind, with mental abnormality and disease and with the specific treatment of mental abnormality and disease. Our psychologist will therefore be a professionally qualified layman, our psychiatrist a medical man skilled in diseases and disorders of the mind, our psychotherapist a medical man who undertakes the treatment of such diseases and disorders. By 'lunatic' we shall mean a person certifiable as insane under the Lunacy Acts. By 'mental defective' a person certifiable under the Mental Deficiency Acts, i.e. one who suffers from an incomplete or arrested development of mind, existing before the age of 18 years; these fall into the categories of idiots, imbeciles, feeble-minded persons and moral defectives. By 'mentally subnormal', we shall mean persons of inferior intelligence who are not certifiable as mentally defective. By 'psychoneurotics', those who suffer from minor mental disorders such as neurasthenia, hysteria, anxiety and obsessive neuroses. With the major mental diseases classed as 'psychoses' we shall be little concerned: they will commonly lead to certification. There remains the difficult group commonly described as

[1] Dr. Gould resigned in 1950 and was replaced by Dr. D. S. Macphail.

'psychopaths', of which so far as the writer is aware no comprehensive definition exists which has been generally accepted by medical psychologists. 'The term,' says Sir Norwood East, 'has been frequently abused, so that some observers consider it to be little more than a waste-paper basket nomenclature.' [1] East's own 'tentative' definition is 'a person who, although not insane, psychoneurotic or mentally defective, is persistently unable to adapt himself to social requirements on account of abnormal peculiarities of impulse, temperament and character', and he adds that 'Many cases seem to lie on the borderline between mental disease and anomalies of character rather than between mental health and mental disease.'

Offenders suffering from any of these disorders may come to prison, either before or after trial, and the most onerous and exacting of the duties falling on the Medical Officer is that of recognising them and taking the appropriate action. In respect of untried prisoners, he must prepare reports to the courts on their state of mind when the courts require such information, or when he considers it necessary, and give evidence if required: remands for 'state of mind reports' are increasingly used by the courts, and the medical officer of a busy local prison may be required to prepare many hundreds in the course of a year. Where prisoners are committed for trial for serious offences, he must also be prepared to inform the Director of Public Prosecutions of any abnormal mental condition that may be relevant, and if the defence decide to put their client's state of mind in question, the Medical Officer may be called by either the prosecution or the defence to give evidence based on his findings, which may be in conflict with those of medical experts called by the defence. In murder cases, the accused is invariably placed under mental observation, and a medical report is sent to the Director of Public Prosecutions and to the defence. This (as in other cases) may be directed either to the question whether the prisoner is fit to plead, since if he is mentally incapable of instructing his defence or following the proceedings there may be a verdict of 'insane on arraignment', or to the question of whether at the time of committing the offence he was insane within the meaning of the 'MacNaghten Rules', in which case there may be a verdict of 'guilty but insane'.[2]

There are still other circumstances in which the Medical Officer may be required to make reports or give evidence on 'states of mind'. It may be explained that English law does not recognise the conception of

---

[1] *Society and the Criminal*, p. 41.

[2] It should be understood that these Rules, which were laid down by the Judges in 1843, purport to provide a definition of criminal irresponsibility, not of insanity. It is possible for an offender to be certifiably insane and at the same time to be criminally responsible under the MacNaghten Rules, the essence of which is that if at the time of committing the offence the offender, by reason of some defect of reason from disease of the mind, did not know what he was doing or did not know that it was wrong, then he cannot be held to be criminally responsible.

'partial responsibility' arising from an abnormal state of mind falling short of insanity. It does however recognise indirectly that the culpability, though not the responsibility, of an offender may be modified by the presence of mental abnormality, since by certain provisions of the Criminal Justice Act 1948 it gives the Courts powers to have expert inquiry made in such cases with a view to measures which seek rather to remove the abnormality than to punish the offender. In particular, by section 4 of the Act, if the Court is satisfied by expert medical evidence that the mental condition of an offender is such that he may benefit by medical treatment, though he is not certifiable as a lunatic or as a mental defective, and that such treatment is available and he is willing to undergo it, they may place him on probation with a condition that he undergoes such treatment. For this purpose again the offender may be remanded to prison, the Medical Officer providing the 'expert medical evidence' and making the necessary arrangements, through the Regional Psychiatrist of the National Health Service, for the carrying out of the treatment in a mental hospital or otherwise.

It is of interest to note in this connection a report issued in 1950 by the Advisory Council on the Treatment of Offenders which makes proposals towards taking this process a stage further. The Council was concerned with those offenders of the 'non-certifiable mentally abnormal' group in respect of whom the Courts might feel that action under section 4 of the Criminal Justice Act was inappropriate, in view of the gravity of their offences or their danger to society. In such cases the Courts might see no alternative to sending them to prison, though they might be reluctant either to do this at all or to impose a sentence long enough for effective treatment within the prison system. The Council therefore proposed further legislation to give the Courts powers to commit such offenders to a special psychiatric institution to be provided by the Home Office (though not as a prison), for such period as may be necessary within the maximum period prescribed by law as a sentence for the offence in question. The Home Secretary would have power to release within the period of the sentence on evidence that the offender had obtained maximum benefit from the treatment. These proposals are a compromise with the more logical if drastic system of 'psychiatric internment' in use, e.g. in Denmark, where such an offender may be committed until he is cured, however long that may be.

Returning to the actualities of the system, it will be evident that the prison Medical Officer must not only be or become a psychiatrist, but that when he has obtained sufficient experience he will also be an expert in forensic psychiatry. For these reasons experience in psychiatric medicine, and if possible the D.P.M., are sought in all candidates. This expertise of the senior Medical Officers is so far recognised that some of the leading psychiatric hospitals attach their Registrars to certain prisons for instruction in forensic psychiatry.

To turn from the untried to the convicted, the first duty of the Medical Officer is to diagnose lunacy or mental deficiency where it exists, to arrange for certification as prescribed by the Acts, and then to get the prisoner removed as soon as possible to a mental hospital or an institution for mental defectives. It is also necessary to arrange for the disposal to appropriate institutions of persons in prison under verdicts of guilty but insane or insane on arraignment, and of mentally defective offenders committed pending the presentation of an order or to await removal to an institution. While they remain in prison, such persons are by Statutory Rule placed under the special care of the Medical Officer.

The next category calling for medical treatment is the non-certifiable but mentally abnormal. These fall into two groups, those whose symptoms indicate that they may benefit by psycho-therapy, and the remainder. For the former group there is the fullest provision, described as follows in *Prisons and Borstals*—'All Medical Officers are given guidance on the type of case likely to benefit by such treatment and the prisoners they select, or those to whom the courts have drawn attention, are, in the case of men, removed to Wormwood Scrubs or Wakefield where the Principal Medical Officers investigate their condition. Here are psychiatric clinics (in one of which there are remedial workshops and a biochemical laboratory) and visiting psychiatrists conduct assessments and carry out such treatment as they consider necessary. Most recognised physical methods of various kinds and group therapy are employed, and the psychiatrists are assisted by non-medical psychologists and psychiatric social workers. Women in similar circumstances are removed to Holloway where there is a visiting psychiatrist.[1] Treatment is practicable in prison only for prisoners who comply with the necessary criteria of suitability. It is necessary, *inter alia*, not only that the mental condition should be such as in the opinion of the psychiatrist will respond to treatment, but that the patient should be willing and able to co-operate and that the sentence should be of sufficient length to enable a course, which may be prolonged, to be carried out. It may therefore happen that an offender sent to prison with a recommendation by a court for psychological treatment will not in fact be able to receive it, though all such cases will be fully considered. It follows that where such a recommendation is made by a court it is better not to announce it. Prisoners who are not certifiable under the Lunacy Act but who require physical psychiatric treatment in a mental hospital are released as voluntary patients under Section 60 (2) (*b*) of the Criminal Justice Act 1948 for so long as may be necessary. This privilege is very rarely abused and great care is taken to ensure that other inmates of the hospital do not become aware of the fact that the patient is a convicted prisoner.' In their Annual Report

[1] And also a psychiatric social worker and a psychologist.

for 1949 the Commissioners gave full particulars of the types considered unsuitable for treatment as follows:

'(a) Those who are certifiable under either the Lunacy or Mental Deficiency Act.

'(b) Those who are suffering from permanent organic cerebral changes.

'(c) Those who show intellectual inferiority of such a degree as to render them incapable of co-operating in treatment.

'(d) Those who do not exhibit a genuine anxiety for cure.

'(e) Those who are unwilling to co-operate in measures designed to modify their abnormal practices.

'(f) Adult prisoners whose criminal activities show evidence of marked chronicity.

'(g) Adolescents whose abnormality has existed from an early age and is combined with a closely related psychopathic heredity.

'(h) Those showing excessive resentment or undue resignation at their conviction or sentence.

'(i) Those whose attitude suggests that they have ulterior motives in seeking treatment.

The nature of the work carried out at the Wormwood Scrubs clinic, and its results, are fully described and discussed by the two consultant psychotherapists in an appendix to the same Report. The Commissioners have also begun to make arrangements, through the Regional Hospital Boards, for prisoners whose sentences are too short for treatment in prison to be seen by psychiatrists from the public clinics under whom they may continue treatment after release. As much as possible is also done by way of follow-up after release for those treated in the prison clinics: but the specifically personal relationship between psychotherapist and patient imposes a difficulty here.

For the remainder, the provision is less clear-cut. From simpler days, when provision would be made in a prison for the 'weak-minded party', it has been accepted that there exists a class of prisoner who, while not requiring or likely to profit by psychotherapeutic treatment, do require special management under medical supervision. It has for many years been the practice to concentrate long-term prisoners of this class at Parkhurst. Such a group would include the mentally subnormal, inefficient and constitutionally unstable, and today one would add at any rate some of those who might be called psychopaths. To these 'chronic' cases should also be added those who become temporarily unstable or unduly depressed through failure to adapt to prison life, or whose reactions to discipline present special difficulties. Ideally, such a group in every prison should be under 'psychiatric management', designed primarily to improve their adaptation to present circumstances and prevent them from being a nuisance to others, but looking also to helping their re-adaptation to normal social life after discharge.

But the ordinary local prison is not the ideal milieu for this sort of treatment, nor has the long and serious shortage of medical staff since the war been propitious to its development. For these reasons, and in order to place the whole treatment of mentally abnormal prisoners on a satisfactòry scientific basis, the Commissioners proposed as soon as the war was over to give first priority, in any new building programme, to the provision of a special psychiatric institution within the prison system on the lines recommended in the East-Hubert Report (para. 172). This would not only concentrate psychotherapeutic treatment in a suitable building suitably equipped and staffed, and provide favourable conditions for the training and treatment of the mentally abnormal generally, but serve as a centre of research into the relationships between mental disorder and crime.

Even without such a research centre, however, the prison Medical Service, sometimes in conjunction with outside experts and institutions, has since the war made many interesting contributions to knowledge in this field. Among those listed in the Annual Reports for 1948 and 1949 were:

'(a) In conjunction with the Maudsley Hospital, an analysis of the clinical histories and electroencephalographic recordings of 64 cases of murder.[1]

'(b) Observations by the Medical Officer at Wormwood Scrubs on the results of encephalography in 38 cases.

'(c) An investigation, including encephalography, in conjunction with the Maudsley Hospital, into psychopathic personalities at Wandsworth and Wormwood Scrubs.

'(d) At Bristol, in collaboration with the Medical Superintendent of Bristol Mental Hospital, research into the endocrinological aspect of psychopathic personality.'

It having been necessary to deal at so much length with the treatment of mental disorder, it would be well before leaving the subject to give some quantitative information to put the question in its proper perspective. The widespread interest in psychology which developed between the wars, and the valuable work done in applying the teachings of psychological medicine, so far as it has progressed, to the causation and treatment of delinquency, has led to an over-emphasis which in some quarters might seem to have led to the conclusion that crime is itself a form of mental disease, and that its removal as a social evil is a matter more for medicine than for the penal law. A more balanced

[1] Reported in the *Journal of Neurology, Neurosurgery and Psychiatry*, Vol. 12, 1949.

view has been stated as follows: 'Some psychiatrists in recent times have emphasised the fact that crime is not a disease though it may be due to disease.' [1]

Apart from the questions raised in Chapter 1 (pp. 5, 6) as to the nature of crime, some impression of the actual extent to which crime may be 'due to disease' may be gained from the following facts cited by East and Hubert in their Report of 1939:

'Among 278,667 persons received into prisons in England and Wales during the five-year period 1932–6, 1,164 or 0·41 per cent were certified as mentally defective, and 2,039 or 0·73 per cent were certifiably insane' (para. 20).

'The "normal" group will include at least 80 per cent of offenders' (para. 19).

Again, as regards psychopaths, Sir Norwood East [2] cites Healy and Bronner as having found 2·8 per cent of psychopathic personalities in a series of 4,000 juvenile delinquents.

The reports by Dr. Mackwood and Dr. Gould in the Annual Report for 1949 deal with 313 cases referred to them over a period of 5 years from 1943, an annual average of 62·6.

It is also necessary to strike a cautionary note about the results of this form of treatment. In the Annual Report for 1947 the Director of Medical Services said: 'It is sometimes assumed that cure by psychological treatment is, or should be, a sure preventive of further criminal activity. Criminal acts may arise from abnormal psychological factors of which the subject is unaware or only partially aware. The function of psychotherapy is to bring these factors into consciousness in such a way that any repetition of the act can only take place if the subject has the will and intention to do it. To expect more from psychological treatment is to give it credit for greater powers than it possesses.' And Dr. Mackwood added in 1949 that: 'The heading "greatly improved" is as near to "cure" as one feels justified in stating. The results of psychotherapy in some ways resemble those of surgical cancer; years have to go by before one can talk in terms of cure' (p. 77). The same thought has been expressed by Dr. J. R. Rees in *Mental Health and the Offender*: 'There is no mystery about the aims or methods of psychological treatment. Granted the co-operation of the patient, one hopes through careful and detailed discussion of the nature and origins of his particular difficulty, or abnormal reactions, to make it possible for him to alter and reshape his point of view or his conduct. To 'pull yourself together' is rarely possible in cold blood unless you know what to get

[1] *Mental Health and the Offender*, by J. R. Rees, M.D. The Seventh Clarke Hall Lecture, p. 6.
[2] *Society and the Criminal*, p. 127.

hold of and how to pull. Analytical psychotherapy seeks to provide this understanding.'

We may now pass to the functions of psychiatry and psychology in relation to the suitability of offenders for particular forms of treatment: these fall into two groups, the first concerned with advice to the Courts on the type of sentence appropriate to particular cases, the second with advice to the administration on the classification of sentenced offenders.[1] By sections 20 and 21 of the Criminal Justice Act 1948, the Courts are required, before passing sentence of Borstal training, corrective training or preventive detention, to consider reports made to the Prison Commissioners as to the suitability of the offender for such a sentence. These reports [2] are in practice made by Governors on behalf of the Commissioners, and invariably include in addition to the general recommendation a medical report as to mental and physical fitness. The report on mental fitness is yet another psychiatric function of the Medical Officer, in so far as questions of mental abnormality may arise and their bearing have to be considered, but in making these reports Governors and Medical Officers should have the assistance of a psychologist. So far, however, this situation has been reached in principle only: in practice, psychologists are not available in anything like sufficient numbers. In their Annual Report for 1949 (p. 69) the Commissioners described their intentions as follows:

'In order to meet the requirements of the Criminal Justice Act 1948, arrangements are being made for the setting up of a psychological staff in this department. This scheme will necessitate the employment of:

1 Chief Psychologist
4 Principal Psychologists
7 Senior Psychologists
5 Basic Psychologists
14 Psychiatric Social Workers
13 Psychological Testers.

'Psychologists are in post at all the allocation centres through which persons sentenced to Corrective and Borstal training pass. The allocation, whether to open or closed establishments, and if so, to which, is determined here by Boards, of which the psychologist is a member. It is here that decisions on referring cases for psychological treatment are taken and observations on the form of training recommended are made at this point. The psychological reports made at all the remand and trial prisons by psychologists with the assistance of psychiatric social workers, and testers, as it becomes possible to fill these posts, will be reviewed here.

[1] See Appendix K.
[2] They will be discussed more fully in the context of Borstal training and the treatment of persistent offenders.

'The duties of these psychologists, who will work to the medical officers at remand and trial prisons in their respective groups, will be (1) to assist in the preparation of reports to courts under Section 21 of the Criminal Justice Act; (2) to provide medical officers with the assistance necessary to enable them to fulfil the increasing demands by courts for reports on the psychological condition of untried prisoners, under Sections 4 and 26 of the Criminal Justice Act. They will also give the same assistance in the preparation of reports on Borstal cases under Section 20 as in older age groups under Section 21; (3) they will be available for making reports where necessary on convicted prisoners or Borstal inmates. Their work will include the ascertainment of intelligence, the application of performance tests, education attainment tests, mechanical and other aptitude tests and general attainment tests, and an opinion on the personality and character of the offender. The medical officer will take these data into account when submitting his report to the Court on the mental and physical condition of the accused.

'That much depends upon the psychological assessment as a basis of opinion on the suitability of the offender for Corrective Training has been shown by the results obtained at Reading Corrective Training Allocation Centre, where a psychological staff has been in operation for several months. Here an attempt is being made to overtake the leeway due to the lack of psychologists at receiving prisons and approximately 40 prisoners a week are being dealt with. A not inconsiderable number of these would have been reported as unsuitable for corrective training if the evidence subsequently obtained at Reading had been available at the time of trial.'

The functions of the psychologist in relation to classification are also touched on in the foregoing statement, to which there is little to be added. It may be, however, that as psychologists come to be employed in the local prisons they will also play their part there in assessing the suitability of prisoners for transfer to regional training prisons and for other special forms of training. The Medical Officer already plays his part as a member of the Reception Board.

Finally, the Medical Officer *qua* psychiatrist should have a valuable role, in collaboration with other members of the staff, in the general 'man-management' of the prison, along the lines suggested in para. 1 and para. 2 (2) and (3) of The Hague Congress resolution. At present the serious medical under-staffing of the prisons hampers the fullest development of this function, but in the regional training prisons where there are full-time Medical Officers they do take an active part as regular members of the team, as also in central prisons and Borstals.

The Hague resolution, in para. 5, refers also to the assistance which can be given by the psychiatrist in the training of staff. Such assistance is fully used at the Imperial Training School at Wakefield in relation to the selection of staff, both the Medical Officer and the psychologist of the prison taking an active part in the testing of the candidates and in making personality reports to the Board. The Medical Officer also gives a series of lectures to each course on the psychological aspects of delinquency.

CHAPTER FIFTEEN

AFTER-CARE

(1) PRINCIPLES AND PROBLEMS

'IT has been said that a prisoner's real punishment begins when he is discharged; and, again, that the true test of a prison system is what happens to a man when he comes out. Modern methods of prison treatment seek the social rehabilitation of the offender, endeavouring to prepare him to take his place once more as a normal member of society, and to help him retain the feeling that he is still part of the community and that the community takes a continuing interest in his welfare. But this effort may be fruitless unless the difficult transition to life in the world outside the prison gates is helped and guided by a humane and efficient system of after-care; but for organised help and guidance on release, recovery would often be very difficult, if not impossible.' [1]

It would be morally indefensible, nor would the protection of society against crime be secured, if the offender, having purged his offence by undergoing his punishment, were then put out of the prison gate without thought or care for his future. So much has been recognised, at least in principle, from Howard onwards: but there is a wide gap between a simple humanitarian urge to relieve misery and distress and the statement in the foregoing quotation, which implies that the social rehabilitation of the offender *as a duty of society* does not cease when he leaves the prison. 'The trend from private charity to public responsibility corresponds to a change in the underlying theoretical conceptions. As long as the principle of retribution dominated the administration of criminal justice, the State contented itself with executing the penalty in accordance with the law. With the expiration of a prison term, however, the social effects of punishment were by no means extinct. It was left to society to help the ex-prisoner with shelter, work and bare necessities of life, and thereby to compensate for any additional hardship beyond the limits of legal punishment proper. With the recognition of social

[1] *Prisons and Borstals*, Chapter 9, para. 1.

253

adjustment as a primary object of penal policy, the negative intention of avoiding undesirable after-effects became a positive aim and an essential stage in the rehabilitative process.' [1]

The history of 'aid-on-discharge' and 'after-care' during the last hundred years has been that of the movement of thought and practice towards this principle and its implementation; and it may be said at the outset that this movement is by no means complete—as will appear, the post-war years in this field of work may well mark a significant point of fresh departure.

The problems facing a discharged prisoner are twofold—the emotional or psychological, and the economic; and both will vary widely according to the temperament and circumstances of the person, the length of time he has been in prison and the number of times he has been in prison. Individualisation of treatment is even more necessary, and certainly more practicable, after release than before it.

Attention must first concentrate on the economic problems, though the others may often be more pressing. These comprise, in a word, the re-settlement of the prisoner—return to his home district, and the provision of shelter, immediate financial and material needs and work —all that is included in the phrase 'aid-on-discharge' as distinct from 'after-care'. That society has an obligation to see to these things has not for a long time past been in doubt: both pity and prudence dictate their necessity. There is, as we shall see, a well-developed machinery for dealing with them, and on the whole the needs have been and are being met. The main problems still arising are two, and of these the first is now as it has always been that of providing work.

That a discharged prisoner should get into work as soon as possible is of the first importance both economically and psychologically. If he is not to be tempted to revert to crime, he must be able to support himself and his family by honest work. Even if he is out of work but supported by the State through unemployment pay or other regular channels of assistance, he is yet in a more difficult position, making him more vulnerable to temptation, than those equally unhappily placed who have not been in prison: he is *ex hypothesi* one who has already shown some weakness of control, and whatever effect of deterrence or reform his prison experience may have had on him, he is likely to imagine himself inferior, tainted, persecuted even, and from such imaginings to develop feelings of self-justification and resentment which may well drive him to dishonesty again as soon as opportunity offers. And if his normal associates are already so disposed, opportunity will not wait long.

Yet there are serious difficulties to be faced. No one would wish to claim that because a person has been punished for a criminal offence he should therefore have some special priority as against those who, in

1 Grünhut, pp. 318, 319.

the face maybe of equal temptation, have not offended. So in times of unemployment, when the right to work is denied to many, the ex-prisoner must take his chance with the rest. But whether employment be full or scarce, he may not always get that chance. 'Distrust and resentment against the man who has been in prison has always proved an obstacle to the work of welfare agencies as well as to the honest efforts of the former prisoner himself.' [1] For many this must be so, if they think to return to their former work; the public servant who has committed a breach of the trust placed in him, the dishonest clerk and many other such cannot reasonably expect reinstatement: and these are commonly the sort who have no trade to turn to. Nor is it easy to turn any reproach against an employer who prefers a-man of known good character to one with a record of crime. One can only be grateful to all those employers, and they are many, who do not pass by on the other side. From the offender's fellow workpeople one might hope for an even wider charity, but it must be said that this is not always found; nor has it always been easy to secure the full co-operation of Trade Unions in the problems of re-absorbing prisoners into industry.

And finally there is the ex-prisoner himself: all too many are difficult, too apt still to the same self-regarding motives that drove them to crime, and to weary the patience of their welfare officers and of helpful employers by declining good work or leaving it for no good reason. And where there is a reasonable willingness, many are virtually un-employable by reason of physical or mental inferiority, while others have never had a trade or are precluded from re-entry to such work as they can do. Even those who have learned a trade in prison which they are willing and able to practise must be prepared for disappointment: to come out of prison with long training in and practice of a skilled trade is no passport to entry into that trade, whether as a journeyman or a labourer. No regular apprenticeship is likely to mean no union card, and no card usually means no job.

To all aspects of this problem of work-finding the Commissioners and the welfare agencies, in consultation with all interests concerned, continue to give unremitting attention.

The second of the main problems of the time is much wider: it con-cerns that 'trend from private charity to public responsibility' of which Dr. Grünhut has spoken. As we shall see in the following section, the system of aid-on-discharge in this country was based almost from its beginnings on some sort of partnership between the State and private benevolence. More recent years have seen a marked tendency for the State to become the predominant partner, on grounds in part of finance and in part of an increasing disposition to hold that the rehabilitation of the offender after release is a duty not only of society but of the penal system itself: the whole process, inside the prison and out, is one and

[1] Grünhut, p. 322.

indivisible. A related aspect of this problem derives more recently still from the full development in this country of the conception of the Welfare State. We have already noted (Chapter Twelve) how far the prisoner's social insurance position is preserved. And when the position is reached that his fare home on discharge is paid from public funds; that the Assistance Board (which may already have been looking after his family) at once assumes responsibility for his maintenance; that the National Health Service looks after him if he is sick; and that the Ministry of Labour seeks to find him work, while so long as it fails he and his family are maintained either through Unemployment Insurance or by the Assistance Board—in such a position it seems that the assumptions on which the present system of aid-on-discharge was built up cannot remain unquestioned.

It may be, therefore, that the time is ripe for a radical reassessment both of the nature of 'aid-on-discharge' and of the relative responsibilities of the State and of private benevolence in providing and administering it. It may also be that in any such reassessment emphasis will be shifted from the economic to the psychological problems, from 'aid-on-discharge' to 'after-care'.[1]

What is the nature of these psychological problems? It will already have appeared that they sensibly interpenetrate the economic: the two can only formally be considered as if they were in separate compartments. Their nature will of course vary widely with the nature of the individual concerned, the kind of sentence he has undergone and its length, and the circumstances to which he is to return. Prolonged segregation from normal life creates difficulties of re-adaptation not only for the ex-prisoner—the conditions are not dissimilar for one coming out of a prisoner-of-war camp, or a hospital. This was recognised during the late war by the setting up of Civil Resettlement Units for ex-prisoners of war, with a régime specially designed to assist them to overcome these difficulties. But prison life, save in special types of prison, may be more abnormal, create more difficulties, even than these: it may certainly have a weakening effect on the will, and create a sense of inferiority or even dread of normal contacts, a fumbling and fearfulness in facing the future in what may be, or seem, a hard and unsympathetic world.

Again, there are often painful family difficulties: a home may have been broken up, economically or emotionally, or both, by prolonged separation. It may be essential to re-establish it if relapse is to be avoided.

And in the case of one whose associations have been criminal, there are difficulties of the opposite kind. The sheep may be all too kindly received in the old fold, and it may take more moral courage than he has to maintain in that company that he is now a good white sheep, not a bad black one, especially if being white cannot be shown to pay.

[1] See Appendix K.

The training inside the prisons seeks to provide, so far as it may, against these problems, but in many cases it will be wasted effort unless, after discharge, it is continued through a system of after-care based on close personal attention to the needs of the individual. After-care in this sense means more than attention to material needs, though it includes this: it means understanding, watchful sympathy, bracing oversight—for some a friend at hand to advise and help, for others a supervisor to admonish and warn, with the sanctions of authority behind him.

And to close this introduction, it should be explained that, in so far as they can properly be regarded as distinct processes, there is in some sense a legal distinction between aid-on-discharge and after-care. When a person sentenced to simple imprisonment has earned his remission and been discharged his sentence has terminated: he is under no further obligations in respect of it, and owes no duty but gratitude to any agency that may be assigned to help him. For these, after-care may be provided if they wish to have it, but for many of them the first thought may well be to put everything connected with the prison behind them and have no more to do with it. In general, what they receive is aid-on-discharge.

But for those categories who are released on a conditional licence the position is quite different: until the sentence expires by efflux of time they are by the terms of the licence under the supervision of a Society named in the licence, and if they do not comply with the directions of that Society they may be recalled to prison to continue their sentence. It is true that the intentions of the Society are wholly benevolent, and seek nothing but the welfare of those in their charge—they provide after-care in the fullest sense. Nevertheless, experience shows that if after-care is to be effective with the majority it requires this sort of sanction to make it so, even though the flavour of compulsion and constraint may often militate against its success.

(2) DISCHARGED PRISONERS' AID SOCIETIES

The principle that a prisoner should be assisted to regain his own parish was recognised by Parliament in 1792. Peel's Gaol Act of 1823 went further, and authorised Justices to provide, at the expense of the County Rate, for the provision of necessary clothing, and a sum not exceeding twenty shillings, to deserving prisoners whose sentences were shortened for good conduct: the Justices were further authorised to divert the various charitable bequests for providing poor prisoners with food and clothing to providing them with the means of returning home and with 'implements of labour'.

The next step was marked by the Discharged Prisoners' Aid Act of 1862, which set out that: 'Whereas divers Societies, hereinafter referred to as Discharged Prisoners' Aid Societies, have been formed in divers parts of England by persons subscribing voluntarily for the purpose of finding employment for discharged prisoners and enabling them by loans and grants of money to live by honest labour', these Societies might be recognised as the medium through which the Justices might assist prisoners, provided the Society had been certified by the Justices as an approved Society, and any sum which the Justices might have paid to the prisoner they were authorised to pay to the Society for the prisoner's benefit. Justices were also given power to pay grants to these Societies for the benefit of each discharged prisoner. These powers were by the Prison Act 1877 passed on to the Prison Commissioners.

When the Prison Commissioners took over in 1878 they found 29 Aid Societies in operation, but they promoted their formation with such diligence that by 1885 there were 'sixty-three Discharged Prisoners' Aid Societies working in connection with all prisons in England and Wales except one or two'.[1] The sum expended by the Government on aid to Discharged Prisoners in 1884 amounted to £7,280, made up in part of gratuities earned by prisoners under the Progressive Stage System, which were paid to the Discharged Prisoners' Aid Societies for their benefit, and in part of a Government Grant of £4,000 distributed to the prisons in proportion to the number of prisoners discharged, but 'with a proviso that an equal amount shall be provided by private subscriptions as a guarantee of that local and private interest in the work without which it cannot prosper'.[2]

'Here are contained two important assertions of principle on which has been based the action of the Government since this date:

'1. That it is the duty of the Government to make a charitable donation in aid of discharged prisoners in addition to the gratuities under the Stage System, which are an affair of prison discipline.

'2. That the sum should be regulated by the amount of private subscriptions, provided that a maximum calculated on the total number of discharges is not exceeded.

'In short, the State goes into partnership with bodies of charitable and benevolent persons, duly certified under the Act, in order to secure a double object: (*a*) the State object, that steps shall be taken at least to lessen the chances of a man's relapse into crime, (*b*) the private and charitable object of relieving misfortune and distress.' [3]

The Gladstone Committee in 1894 found that 'To each prison are attached one or more Societies. Some do admirable work—but it does not appear that there is either uniformity of action under definite principles, or that the various societies are so far organised as a whole

1 Du Cane, p. 197.   2 ibid.   3 Ruggles-Brise, p. 170.

that the effect of aid can be satisfactorily ascertained. There seems to be a great and unnecessary variation in the methods of working.' While emphasising the importance of maintaining the voluntary and local side of Prisoners' Aid Society work, they thought there should be some central organisation and supervision, and 'a representative conference in London for the purpose of securing common and uniform action providing for the most effectual distribution of the Government Grant, and for stimulating the considerable number of Societies which do little work or exist but in name'. They also recommended that arrangements should be made for the agents of approved societies to see prisoners and make the necessary arrangements with them before discharge, instead of waiting for them at the gate.

In consequence of these recommendations the Commissioners made a special inquiry into the methods of Aid Societies, and a notable improvement in the work resulted. Uniformity of procedure and organisation was secured, and in order to secure the Secretary of State's 'certificate of efficiency' the Societies were required to comply with certain Regulations, and the government grant was paid only to certified Societies conforming with these Regulations.

This grant was divided into two parts—a capitation grant and a variable grant. In 1913 the earning of gratuities by convicted prisoners was abolished, and in addition to the existing grant of 1s. a head in respect of each convicted prisoner discharged to its care, each Society now received, as an equivalent of the gratuity, a further sum (averaging 1s. a head) which varied, as the gratuities had done, according to the length of the prisoners' sentence. In 1931 this complicated system was abolished, and a flat capitation rate of 2s. was substituted. For the first time now the grant was also paid in respect of debtor prisoners, in consequence of the abolition of the system of paying them allowances for their work in prison, and debtors and convicted were assisted on the same basis. In addition to the capitation grants there was a supplementary grant of (at that time) £1,500 a year, which after consultation at an annual conference was distributed by the Commissioners 'in such a manner as they think best for the furtherance of the work'. This procedure was found valuable both in stimulating the less active societies, and in redressing to some extent the disparity between the richer and the poorer.

In 1933 the total sum raised by Aid Societies by voluntary effort was over £23,000, and the total Government grant, including both the capitation and supplementary grants, was £7,398.[1]

In the meantime, there had been a further organisational development. In 1918, in order to secure co-ordination of effort and ideas, there was instituted a Central Discharged Prisoners' Aid Society, with offices in London, and a Central Executive on which the various

[1] Departmental Committee on the Employment of Prisoners, Part II.

Societies were represented; this Society also dealt with special cases referred to it by the local Societies. Co-ordination with the Prison Commissioners was secured by the oversight of the Chaplain Inspector, who was especially charged with the care of education, aid-on-discharge, and other branches of welfare work,[1] and by the institution of an annual representative conference with the Commissioners for discussion both of general questions and of the distribution of the Annual Grant.

In 1932 the Secretary of State appointed a Departmental Committee, under the chairmanship of Major Sir Isidore Salmon, C.B.E., J.P., M.P., 'to review the methods of employing prisoners and of assisting them to find employment on discharge'. Their Report was published in two parts, the latter (1935) dealing with the second part of the terms of reference. This Committee, like the Gladstone Committee, began by deciding to exceed its terms of reference and to consider also 'the methods and organisation of the Prisoners' Aid Societies and other organisations . . . responsible for the after-care of prisoners'. On these matters they made a number of recommendations; there should be only one Society for each committal area, and each should have a full-time Organising Secretary and an office separate from the prison; there should be a National Council to co-ordinate and direct their work, and allocate the Government grant; all Societies should concentrate on the re-instatement of the ex-prisoner in employment as their primary object.

The Committee expressed themselves as satisfied that 'it is of great importance to preserve the voluntary principle to the fullest possible extent' . . . 'after-care work . . . is not a duty which can be adequately discharged by the staff of any Government Department alone, although the policy of official co-operation and of Government contributions should undoubtedly continue. The work is one for which the sympathy and active interest of the whole community need to be enlisted, and that, we are convinced, can best be done through an efficient voluntary organisation' (paras. 22 and 23). Their main concern, based on the view that 'the Central Society has failed to achieve the main objects of its foundation', was to secure better co-ordination of the work, and this was the purpose of the proposed National Council, which would 'embrace the aims of the existing Central Society, but its scope would be much wider': the Chairman of the Council and of its Executive Committee should be nominated by the Secretary of State (though he should not be a Government official), and a representative of the Commissioners should sit on the Council and the Executive Committee, as should the Director of the Borstal and Central Associations (as to which, see following section of this chapter).

[1] On the abolition of his office in 1921 these duties passed to one of the Assistant Commissioners, and in 1948 to the newly appointed Director of Education and Welfare. The office of Chaplain Inspector was re-created in 1950.

Although the Committee appeared to be satisfied that its views were consonant with those of the Societies generally, it shortly became all too clear that this was not so. Stimulated by the affronted Central Society, a conference of Aid Societies was held in London within two months of the appearance of the Report. The resolution which was passed made it clear that the Societies thought first that the Committee had indulged in unwarranted trespassing—'we feel that such reorganisation as is necessary should come from within our movement rather from without'; then that the Committee had been unfortunate in its choice of witnesses (and certainly only two representatives of Aid Societies were heard, in addition to the Chairman of the Central Society); and finally that the recommendations should be rejected in *toto*, principally because 'they make State control almost certain in the near future'.

Finally, the conference set up a Committee under the Chairman of the Central Society 'to inquire into the present position from inside our movement, and to report what reforms, if any, are desirable and necessary'.

This incident is of interest as showing the strong spirit of independence in the Societies, and their wish to retain in its completeness the spirit of self-reliance and voluntary effort on which they had been built. The result was in every way fortunate. The Home Office did not proceed with the National Council on the lines proposed by the Salmon Committee, and in 1936, following the report of the committee set up by the conference of Aid Societies, the Central Society was reconstituted as the National Association of Discharged Prisoners' Aid Societies (Inc.). To this Association all certified Societies are now affiliated. It is managed by Committees elected by the representatives of the Societies at their annual meetings, and on these the Prison Commissioners have from the outset been represented. Indeed from this time there was a new atmosphere of confidence and co-operation between the Commissioners and the Societies which has stood the test of time and change.

The new Association actively promoted the consolidation and more efficient organisation of its constituent Societies, and has admirably served its purpose as the channel of communication between the Commissioners and the Societies. It is on the recommendation of the Association that the Commissioners advise the Secretary of State as to the grant, continuance or withdrawal of the statutory Certificates of Efficiency of Aid Societies, one condition of which is that the model Rules prescribed by the Commissioners should form part of the constitution of each Society. Through the Association again, and on its advice, the Commissioners distribute the Government grants paid to the Societies, and to it they naturally turn for advice on all matters concerning aid-on-discharge. The Association also acts directly as an Aid Society, firstly for difficult cases referred to it by any constituent

Society, and secondly, with the development of Regional Training Prisons and other specialised prisons which take prisoners away from their own locality, for supervising the aid-on-discharge arrangements from such prisons. It is an excellent example of that sort of intricate partnership between statutory and voluntary bodies towards which in this country we empirically feel our way.

As a result of the war, that partnership has become closer, with the statutory body taking a more active part: this situation, fully if at first reluctantly accepted by the Societies, has resulted in no loss of the spirit of free co-operation. The reason for the change was financial. It became necessary first to make a subvention from public funds to help the Association, and then to meet the whole of its administrative expenses. With this, control by the Prison Commissioners (and ultimately by the Treasury) of the numbers and conditions of service of its staff became necessary; but this has not derogated from the freedom of the Association to manage its own affairs within the financial limits imposed, and the staff has on the whole benefited from its *quasi* civil service status. At the same time, it became necessary to come to the help of the Societies by a further Government grant of one-third of their administrative expenses. Shortly after the war the capitation rate was increased from 2s. to 3s., and requests have been pressed for a further increase which, in face of the changes in price levels since the 2s. rate was fixed, have every appearance of reasonableness. But in finance as in function, the positions of the State and private benevolence in relation to aid-on-discharge seem now to require radical review rather than further patching. [1]

In 1948, £22,000 was raised by voluntary subscription, while the Government grant consisted of £4,750 capitation rate, £2,000 special grant, and £3,000 grant towards administrative costs, or £9,750 in all.

No general statistics of the work of D.P.A. Societies are published, but in their Report for 1949 (p. 50) the Commissioners recorded that during 1949 over 31,000 men and women were discharged to the care of the Societies, while the N.A.D.P.A.S. dealt with over 1,000 discharges from Regional Prisons and over 3,300 from special Local Prisons, as well as with 445 cases referred to its Head Office from the constituent Societies or other quarters.

The operation of the Societies is relatively uniform. The Secretary, under the control of the Executive Committee, is responsible for getting in subscriptions and managing the affairs of the Society generally: in the largest Societies he may be a paid full-time officer, in others a paid part-time officer, and in others again an honorary officer. The Treasurer, under the Finance Committee, manages and accounts for the funds. Every Society employs a Welfare Officer who works in the prison, sees the prisoners and under the direction of the Case Committee makes all

[1] See Appendix K, note on p. 256.

necessary arrangements: he is usually a full-time paid worker, though not always so in the smallest prisons. The Statutory Rules require that 'From the beginning of the sentence of every prisoner consideration shall be given, in consultation with the Welfare Officer of the appropriate Aid Society or After-care Association, to the future of the prisoner and the assistance to be given to him on and after his discharge' (S.R. 72). Accordingly the Welfare Officer is always a member of the Reception Board, and should seek from the beginning to enlist the co-operation of the prisoner in the arrangements to be made for his future after release. Every prisoner has in his cell a card giving him information about aid-on-discharge, and this tells him that he may apply to see the Welfare Officer at any time. No prison officer is present at these interviews. Some weeks before his discharge, if he wishes or if it is otherwise desirable, he appears before the Case Committee of the Society, at which final arrangements are settled. The most important of these will be for employment, where the prisoner needs help to find it, and here, since 1949, there has been an important development. Following a local experiment at Wakefield prison, the Ministry of Labour, as a result of consultation with the N.A.D.P.A.S., agreed to co-operate in a scheme 'whereby every prisoner serving a sentence of more than six months may, if he so wishes, be interviewed before discharge by an officer of the Ministry in the hope that suitable employment may be found for him within a few days of his release. Should he have been serving his sentence at a distance from his home, his case will, after the interview, be brought without delay to the notice of the Employment Officer of the Ministry in his own locality.' [1]

For the rest, the first need is to see that the prisoner goes out suitably clad both for the time of year and the job he has to do, and if his own clothing is inadequate the Society may supplement it. The next is to get him home: the State by law pays for his fare back to his place of arrest or conviction (whichever is the nearer) or the equivalent in cost, and if he wishes to go further the Society may pay the difference: it will also give him a small sum to cover expenses till he can get a grant from the Assistance Board at his destination. Where the prisoner has no home to go to, the Welfare Officer will arrange for lodgings at the destination if the prisoner so wishes. In suitable cases the Society may also provide tools for a tradesman or a small stock for shop or stall, and in general will be prepared to consider the special needs of any deserving case. The deserts of cases in a local prison must of course vary widely. There is the stage army of ins-and-outs with longer or shorter sentences whose faces are all too familiar, though they generally think it worth while to try some fresh story on the Committee: these will usually leave with 2s. 6d. or so and their fare home—if it is beyond walking distance. There are others on whom much may be spent both

[1] *Annual Report for* 1949, p. 49. See also Appendix K.

in time, money and sympathetic consideration. For many the Societies will do their best, if it is needed and desired, to provide after-care as well as material aid; but as we have already seen, their powers are limited to setting a man on the right road—they cannot interfere to keep him on it. Nor, indeed, are they equipped to do so: such work requires the friend to be on the spot, and the Welfare Officer can only deal with people in his immediate neighbourhood, though he may, and often does, arrange by correspondence for the help of some benevolent agency near the home of a person who needs it.

In an attempt to fill this gap, at any rate for women, an interesting experiment was suggested at the end of 1950 on the initiative of the W.V.S. The proposal was that their members, who are to be found in every town and village, should act as the agents of the Holloway D.P.A.S. in providing a 'friend' for every Star prisoner discharged from Holloway who wished to have one. The procedure proposed was that the Aid Society should co-opt on to its Case Committee two representatives of the Headquarters of the W.V.S. Each Star woman when seen by the Committee would be asked if she would like help of this sort: if she said yes, the W.V.S. representative present would arrange for a suitable member to be selected in the woman's home district. She would have as her first duty to get to know the prisoner's family and prepare the ground there for her return: if possible, she would also come to Holloway and get to know the prisoner before discharge. Having done what she could to smooth the way for her return home, she would, after release, visit her at fairly frequent intervals and see what help or advice she might need, any need for material help being referred to the Aid Society. At the end of the first month she would send in a report in a prescribed form, and from these reports it was hoped that useful knowledge would be gained of the problems confronting women on discharge and how best to overcome them.

The experiment was initiated early in 1951, and should it prove successful at Holloway its extension to other women's prisons might be considered. The advantage of using the W.V.S. for a service of this sort is twofold—their members are everywhere at hand, and being entirely voluntary and unofficial their coming and going in a home raises no awkward questions among curious neighbours.

Another aspect of the same problem has also begun of late to receive attention. The Commissioners have been invited, both by the Prisons and Borstals Committee of the Magistrates Association and by the Howard League, to consider the employment in prisons of trained Social Welfare Officers, who would concern themselves with the whole of a prisoner's 'external relations' during his sentence and prepare for his resettlement after discharge. Such a service exists in the 'Assistance Sociale' of the French and Belgian prison systems, and the idea is certainly in tune with modern thought. On the other hand such work is being done already, in one way or another, by Chaplains, Assistant Governors and Welfare Officers, who properly regard it as an essential part of their function. Whether the introduction of another full-time worker in this field would on the whole be advantageous remains, at the time of writing, an open question.

All these considerations emphasise the gradual shifting of emphasis, in relation to prisoners not subject to 'statutory after-care', from the purely economic problems which face them on release to those other problems which may often have a more significant influence on their ultimate rehabilitation.

(3) THE CENTRAL AFTER-CARE ASSOCIATION

We pass now to the organisation of after-care for those categories who are released on a conditional licence, and certain others. It will be necessary to include here reference to the Borstal Association, though Borstal after-care will be dealt with in a later chapter.

Prisoners sentenced to penal servitude had always been outside the scope of local Aid Society arrangements, the convict prisons having been from the beginning the affair of the central government, but the government had for long made no central arrangements for their assistance and after-care. The fact that they were released on a conditional licence did not necessarily involve such arrangements, for this licence, like the transportation ticket-of-leave which it succeeded, was a police measure of security and sanction against subsequent offence: it had no flavour of welfare. This situation continued until 1910, when Mr. Churchill, on the advice of Sir E. Ruggles-Brise, established the Central Association for the Aid of Discharged Convicts. The Association was from the outset wholly financed from public funds. It was nominally placed under a General Council, of which the Secretary of State was President, and on which the Societies and Institutions hitherto operating in this field of charity were represented. In fact, after the first four years, the Association was managed by its Director, in consultation with the Prison Commissioners, and the Council ceased to have an effective existence. After the late war, this Association was brought into close co-operation with the N.A.D.P.A.S.: both occupied the same premises, and the General Secretary of the N.A.D.P.A.S. was Hon. Director of the Central Association.

The origin of the Borstal Association was rather earlier. In the early years of this century, when Sir Evelyn Ruggles-Brise was experimenting with that system of treating young offenders between the ages of 17–21 which was by the Prevention of Crime Act 1908 established as the Borstal system, he started among his personal acquaintances an Association of Visitors to these young men. When the Borstal system was legally established, it incorporated a new principle of vital importance to the future of after-care. Unlike the negative convict licence, the licence under which a Borstal boy or girl was released was positive: its main object was not a sort of police control, but to ensure that the boy was placed under the supervision of a Society whose first object was his rehabilitation, and that he should have regard to their directions and advice at the risk of being recalled if he failed to do so.

For this purpose Sir Evelyn Ruggles-Brise's Association of Visitors was established as the Borstal Association [1] under the direction of a voluntary committee, and so continued, as the Society named in the licence of a Borstal boy, until the Central After-care Association was set up. Here again the partnership with the Prison Commission was gradually extended, till in recent years the whole of the expense of administration as well as that of after-care came to be met from public funds.

The arrangements for convict women and Borstal girls were similarly centralised, but on rather different lines. Until 1928 responsibility for their after-care rested with the Central Association and Borstal Association respectively. The work was carried out at a branch office in London by a lady who was an Assistant Director of these Associations. The arrangement was neither convenient nor economical, and it was thought that there would be many advantages in bringing the after-care work into closer association with the work carried on at Aylesbury, which comprised both the only Borstal at that time for girls and the convict prison for women of the Star class. Accordingly a new Society was set up known as the Aylesbury Association, of which the Council was the Visiting Committee of the Institution and the first Director was the then Governor of the Institution, who is now Dame Lilian Barker. In more recent years, when more girls' Borstals were set up, and the convicts at Holloway assumed greater importance than those at Aylesbury, it was found desirable to separate the offices of Governor and Director, and a separate Director was appointed and provided with offices in London. As with the Borstal and Central Association, the Aylesbury Association was financed wholly from public funds.

This was the situation at the time of passing of the Criminal Justice Act, which had several important provisions affecting the field of after-care. On the one hand, it increased the categories of offenders to be released conditionally on a 'positive' licence—a licence which places them, for the purpose of assisting their rehabilitation, under certain obligations during the unexpired portion of their sentences These categories now include, as well as Borstal boys and girls, men and women released on licence from sentences of Corrective Training and Preventive Detention, and young persons under 21 released on licence from sentences of imprisonment. In all these cases the Act provides

[1] The first Director of the Association, one of the original Visitors, was Sir Wemyss Grant Wilson, who continued in office till his retirement in 1935.

that they should be under the supervision of an appointed Society. On the other hand, by abolishing penal servitude and with it the convict licence, it left prisoners serving sentences of 3 years and upwards, [1] in whatever type of prison, in the same position as local prisoners, i.e. their sentences were terminated on discharge and they had no further obligations. As some set-off to this, the higher courts were given power, under section 22 of the Act, to impose certain security conditions, in specified conditions, on persons discharged after serving sentences of 12 months or more for certain more serious offences.

This provision was evidently influenced by recommendations made by both the Departmental Committee on Persistent Offenders in 1932 and that on Employment of Prisoners in 1935. The latter, looking forward to legislation which might 'obliterate the distinction between prisoners and convicts', made the following observations (para. 62):

'In view of the dangers to which police supervision is alleged to expose a well-intentioned prisoner (though, as we have said, we do not by any means accept all that has been represented to us on this subject), we are of opinion that the mode of supervision should be one which, while securing to the police all that information about the movements of dangerous criminals which they ought to have in the public interest, would safeguard the interests of the prisoner who is really seeking to make good. We are disposed to think that this object might be achieved if in proper cases the prisoner were allowed to report to a suitable Society instead of to the police, on the understanding that the Society would on request supply the police with his address and communicate to them any information which indicated an intention to revert to crime.

'We have considered the objection that the undertaking of the duty of supervision might prejudice the relationship of the Societies to the discharged prisoner, but we do not anticipate that it would have this result. Supervision by a Society would be an alternative to supervision by the police, and we think prisoners would be quick to appreciate that it was a concession and a privilege rather than an attempt to convert the Societies into agents of the police.'

This in fact was the sort of arrangement which Parliament adopted in section 22, with results that we shall notice in due course.

Finally, the Act (5th Schedule, para. 3 (5)) enumerated among the duties of probation officers 'to advise, assist and befriend, in such cases and in such manner as may be prescribed, persons who have been released from custody'. This development had also been adumbrated by the Salmon Committee, which had given some attention to 'the desirability of instituting a National Parole Service, which should include the work both of Probation Officers and of the D.P.A.S.'. While the

[1] Except for life sentences, as to which see Appendix K.

Committee was 'not prepared to recommend any such far-reaching proposal', they did find themselves able to 'welcome an extension of the association of Probation Officers with the work of after-care' (paras. 86, 87).

In considering how this vitally important question of supervision and after-care for all these different classes of people, men and boys, women and girls, ought to be handled in the light of the great responsibilities now to be placed on the after-care organisations, the Secretary of State was faced with two problems. The first was to bring together the existing unrelated bodies in such a way as to ensure that what is in essence one problem should be treated on common principles, with a proper co-ordination of all the parts in a common whole. The second was to ensure that the actual work in the field, the supervision and help of persons released on licence and others requiring centrally organised after-care, should equally be co-ordinated and treated on common principles by a competent body of qualified social workers.

The first end was achieved by the setting up of the Central After-care Association, which is the appointed Society for all the purposes of the Act; the second by establishing *de lege* a situation which had long existed *de facto*, though in a partial and somewhat unsatisfactory condition—that is, that this work of after-care and social rehabilitation under statutory supervision falls naturally, indeed inevitably, to the Probation Service.

The constitution of the Central After-care Association (England and Wales), hereinafter referred to as the C.A.C.A., sets out its objects as follows:

'(1) To be a Society which may be specified by the Prison Commissioners to undertake the care and supervision of a person after his release:

'(i) from a Borstal Institution (section 20 (2) of the Criminal Justice Act 1948, and paragraph 2 of the Second Schedule to that Act):

'(ii) on a licence from Corrective Training or Preventive Detention (section 21 (3) of the Criminal Justice Act 1948, and paragraph 2 of the Third Schedule to that Act):

'(iii) on a licence from imprisonment (section 56 (2) of the Criminal Justice Act 1948, and paragraph 1 of the Sixth Schedule to that Act):

and to undertake such care and supervision.

'(2) To be a Society which may be approved by the Secretary of State and appointed by the Prison Commissioners to receive information of an offender's address on his discharge from prison and thereafter from time to time in accordance with the provisions of section 22 of the Criminal Justice Act 1948, and to receive such information.

'(3) To undertake the supervision of such other persons who have been released from custody as the Secretary of State may from time to time require.

'(4) To consult and co-operate with the National Association of Discharged Prisoners' Aid Societies with a view to the most effective and economical use of the resources of both bodies, whether jointly or in their respective spheres, in all matters affecting the after-care of persons released from custody.

'(5) To consider and report to the Secretary of State on questions arising out of the aforementioned objects, and in particular such questions as may from time to time be referred to the Association by the Secretary of State.'

The categories mentioned in paras. (1) (i) (ii) and (2) have already been mentioned. Para. (1) (iii) refers to young prisoners. Para. (3) includes prisoners released from central (formerly convict) prisons.

The form of the Association represents still the desire to preserve a partnership between the State and the spirit of voluntary social service. Although entirely financed from public funds as to both its central administration and its direct expenditure on the welfare of those in its charge, it is managed by a voluntary Council of not more than 20 members appointed by the Secretary of State for such period as he may think fit: the Chairman of the Council is also appointed by the Secretary of State,[1] and the General Secretary by the Prison Commissioners. The constitution requires that the Chairman and Vice-Chairman of the N.A.D.P.A.S. shall be *ex-officio* members of the Council: the other members represent Government Departments with a relevant interest (Ministry of Education, Ministry of Labour and National Service, War Office, National Assistance Board), the Prison Commissioners, the Probation Service, the National Association of Prison Visitors, the Visiting Committees of Aylesbury and Holloway, the W.V.S., and the former committee of the Borstal Association, together with certain non-representative members with special interest or experience in the field.

The Council has hitherto met twice a year, and its Executive Committee, which manages the business of the Association in detail, four times a year. An annual report is made to the Secretary of State, and it is proposed to publish this for the year 1950 and thereafter.

The work of the Association is organised in three Divisions, corresponding roughly with the three pre-existing organisations, each under a Director. The Men's Division deals with men prisoners, the Women's and Girls' Division with women and girl prisoners and Borstal girls,

---

[1] The first Chairman was the Chairman of the Prison Commissioners, but this precedent need not be followed again.

the Borstal Division with Borstal boys and male young prisoners. The three Directors attend all meetings of the Executive Committee and of the Council.

Broadly, the work of the Association is preparatory: their officers regularly visit the prisons and Borstals, interview their prospective charges, and, in co-operation with the Ministry of Labour and the 'associates' who will actually receive and supervise them on release, make all necessary arrangements with families and—so far as possible —employers. Direct after-care by employees of the Association is given only in the London area for men, though the Women's Division have their own supervisors in some other centres. The Association also receives reports from its associates in the field on all persons under supervision, and where necessary makes recommendations to the Commissioners as to revocation of licence. And finally it receives, dispenses and accounts for the funds provided for the work.

With few exceptions, the associates who undertake the actual work of after-care in the field are the probation officers, under the authority of the Criminal Justice Act and the statutory Probation Rules, which prescribe the classes of person released from custody whom it shall be 'the duty of a probation officer to advise, assist and befriend', and also his duties in respect of reporting to the C.A.C.A. It may be said that the probation service has welcomed this addition to its duties, and the fullest co-operation in spirit is already assured, though practical details are still in process of being worked out. Provided always that the local authorities employing probation officers make proper allowance for this addition to their case-loads in assessing the number of officers required at each court, this essential part of the process of rehabilitation should now be firmly based and effectively furthered.

Details of method in this work can never become stereotyped: broadly, they fall into three parts—pre-release case work, reception case work, and supervisory case work. In the first stage the associate should some months before release receive from the C.A.C.A. the fullest information about an offender to come under his care—his record, character and aptitudes in prison and out, physical and mental characteristics, family and social relations and so forth. He should then become acquainted with the family situation, and do his best to smooth the way there. He should also get into touch with the offender himself—if possible by visits, if not, by correspondence—so as to make himself known and encourage friendly consideration of future plans for work and living.

When the second or 'reception' stage is reached, both the offender and his associate should be ready to meet with a common knowledge of the problems to be faced and what is to be done about them. This is the critical stage of re-settlement, and whatever previous plans may have been made it will call for the associate's constant attention.

If the initial problems of re-settlement have been successfully overcome, it may be that the subsequent supervision will not be exacting on either side. But for the reasons given in the opening section of this chapter this is by no means to be expected, and the associate cannot be content with mere routine reporting. He should know what is happening, if he can, inside the person in his charge as well as round about him, and always be ready to take quick action in a crisis, to instil courage or give sharp warning, to advise the C.A.C.A. if material help is needed, or in the last resort to suggest recall to prison.

Two points in conclusion. Although men and women sentenced to terms of imprisonment of more than 3 years are not subject to any statutory obligations or supervision, their after-care is the business of the C.A.C.A., and the probation service 'befriends, assists and advises them', so far as they need and desire such help, in the same way as if they were on licence, though without the sanction of the licence. The extent to which assistance is given in these cases is nevertheless considerable, as shown on pp. 52–54 of the Annual Report of the Prison Commissioners for 1949. In that year 1,354 long-term prisoners were discharged to the care of the Men's Division: of these 175 'required no help', and 961 were given all necessary material help and placed in employment—512 being found work through the Association, and 449 finding their own work. Of 188 it was said that they 'were given advice and maintenance but would not co-operate'. The remainder were returned to the Forces, repatriated, deported, or certified as Institution cases. The Women's Division received 48 long-term women, of whom 26 returned to their homes, some to resume their duties as housewives, others to start work: of the remainder 6 were found resident work; 3 went to hostels and found daily work, 8 returned to friends or relatives, and 2 went to lodgings—'a number of these started work'. Three only were lost sight of.

On the other hand men discharged from prison against whom a 'section 22 order' has been made, unless they come under the C.A.C.A. by virtue of length of sentence, are dealt with by the local Aid Societies in the ordinary course: the C.A.C.A. merely receives their addresses, passes them on to the police, and notifies the Criminal Record Office if they lose touch with them. There is a certain inconsistency of function here, in that the C.A.C.A. carries out what is in effect a security measure without exercising any function of after-care: but the purpose of the section was to keep the police in touch with the whereabouts of known criminals who commit serious offences, and not to put such criminals in a specially favourable position as regards after-care.

This chapter may well close on a statement of the position by one who had at least the merit of being able to express it with imaginative insight and force. Oscar Wilde wrote in *De Profundis* [1]:

[1] *De Profundis. The Complete Text*, p. 84, Methuen 1949, price 10s. 6d.

'Many men on their release carry their prison about with them into the air, and hide it as a secret disgrace in their hearts, and at length, like poor poisoned things, creep into some hole and die. It is wretched that they should have to do so, and it is wrong, terribly wrong, of society that it should force them to do so. Society takes upon itself the right to inflict appalling punishment on the individual, but it also has the supreme vice of shallowness, and fails to realise what it has done. When the man's punishment is over, it leaves him to himself; that is to say, it abandons him at the very moment when its highest duty towards him begins. It is really ashamed of its own actions, and shuns those whom it has punished, as people shun a creditor whose debt they cannot pay, or one on whom they have inflicted an irreparable, an irredeemable wrong. I can claim on my side that if I realise what I have suffered, society should realise what it has inflicted on me; and that there should be no bitterness or hate on either side.'

CHAPTER SIXTEEN

RESULTS

(1) GENERAL OBSERVATIONS

WHILE it is right, indeed necessary, that the public should be informed of the results of a system for which it is morally and financially responsible, there is no recognised method by which the results of a prison system can be assessed, either absolutely or relatively, nor does it appear that such a method could be devised. Imprisonment is only one of the means at the disposal of the Courts for the prevention of crime, and the general statistics of crime can only reflect the total effect of the use which the Courts make of those means. Nor is it possible to compare one period with another, either over the whole field or in relation to prisons as one part of the field, on a purely statistical.basis: for this a wide social study would be necessary to take account of such extraneous factors as changes in social and economic. conditions relevant to the causation of crime, variations in the practice of the police and the Courts, and the effect of fresh legislation. *A fortiori*, there is no possibility of useful international comparison: the U.N. Secretariat is at present studying the practicability of some common form of general criminal statistics which may enable such comparison, but the prospects have not hitherto appeared hopeful. In the more restricted field of imprisonment and its results, there is insufficient published material to work on, even if it afforded any valid comparative basis.

The figures to be given in this chapter, therefore, while they are of considerable interest in themselves, afford no basis for conclusions as to whether our contemporary prison system is more or less effective for its purpose than earlier phases in this country or than the systems of any other countries. They are based on the figures for 1949 in the series published by the Commissioners in their Annual Reports, and at least they give some answer to certain basic questions. If, for example, one were asked to frame a criterion of complete 'success' for a prison system, one might put it that no-one who had once been sentenced to imprisonment should ever have to be sent to prison again: and from these figures we can learn with some accuracy how close our system has come to that standard of success over a period of some 15 years. Again, since the system does not in fact reach that standard, and a proportion of those sent to prison for the first time are again punished by imprisonment, the figures tell us something of these failures, and of how many of them, by repeated returns to prison, go to make up that body of 'recidivists' who form the hard core of penal problems in general and prison problems in particular.

It is necessary to resist the temptation to read more into these figures than they claim to say, or to draw inferences from them on such broad general questions as the effect of the prison system on general or individual deterrence. The difficulties of assessing the effects of general deterrence on any scientific basis have already been suggested, and as Dr. Grünhut points out, 'the reasons for avoiding conflict with the law are even more multiple and obscure than the causes of crime' (p. 454). As for the effects of imprisonment on the individual subjected to it, 'only an extensive social research could show, of any group of persons released who have not returned to prison, whether they were reformed, or deterred, or would have been unlikely to revert to crime in any case; or of any group of those who do return, whether they were in fact better or worse human beings, more or less likely to revert to crime, as a result of their imprisonment'.[1]

Such research has in fact been carried out in the United States, over a long period of years, by Sheldon and Eleanor Glueck, and their illuminating conclusions have earned world-wide attention. But while they have shown the way, their results are, in general, valid only in the conditions in which they were obtained, and it remains for us to seek similar light in the conditions of our own problems. Scientific research on these lines in this country is scarcely yet in the state of conception. Provision is made in the Criminal Justice Act empowering the Secretary of State to spend money for this purpose, and consultations have taken place between the Home Office and the Universities and Foundations concerned with these matters as to the best lines of approach. But the field is wide, both funds and qualified research workers are limited and contemporary interest in juvenile delinquency has tended to swing available resources in that direction. In the field of the effects of various forms of treatment on adult delinquents, the little that has been completed since the war is by way of individual post-graduate research theses which have not yet been published. At present, it is understood that a study group of social and research workers in Oxford University, under the direction of Dr. Grünhut, is preparing to make a study of penal and correctional treatment, based on a large number of criminal careers, with a view to establishing information about response to treatment and post-treatment behaviour.

[1] *Prisons and Borstals*, p. 21.

Material is also being collected in the London and Middlesex probation areas with a view to an assessment of the results of probation by a Cambridge University research group.[1]

(2) RESULTS OF TRAINING

The published figures available are in three separate groups: publication of each was started at a different time and for a different purpose, and they are not easily synthesised.

The first group is that which has been published for some years past as Appendix 10 of the Annual Reports, which is headed 'Prisoners who have not returned to prison after a first sentence of imprisonment for a finger-printable offence'. This table as published for 1949 shows, from 1930 onwards, by age-groups, the total number of these 'first-timers' received during each period and the percentage of that number who had not returned to prison before the end of 1948. It is important to be clear as to just what this table does and does not cover before considering its effect. It relates to:

(1) Persons received in prison for the first time, not to persons convicted for the first time: the figures shown are divided between those with previous proved offences and those with no previous proved offences.

(2) Persons convicted of 'finger-printable offences' only, i.e. indictable offences and some more serious non-indictable offences which are akin to crime rather than to social nuisance: it is therefore a review of criminal offenders in the stricter sense, not of all offenders.

(3) Persons sentenced to imprisonment as it was before the Act of 1948, and not to sentences of penal servitude: this means that the sentences concerned may be from 5 days to 2 years.

(4) Persons serving sentences in all prisons except what prior to 1949 were 'convict prisons', i.e. the table *includes* those discharged from the special training prisons for whom separate figures are given later, provided they were not serving sentences of penal servitude.

The total effect of this table may be expressed as follows:

Year of First Reception	Number received for first time	Number not again received so far as is known before 31.12.48	Percentage (3) of (2)
1930–1935	47,010	34,536	73
1936–1940	42,996	34,827	81
1943	12,671	10,118	80
1944	12,094	9,648	80
1945	13,167	10,973	83
1946	12,539	10,286	82

Note: No accurate figures are available in respect of prisoners first received during 1941 or 1942.

[1] See also p. 367 as to a Borstal research project.

It should be noted in respect of the 1946 entry that the 2 year prisoners committed during that year would all have been released (excepting losses of remission for disciplinary reasons) between 1 May 1947 and 30 April 1948, so that on 31 December 1948 none would have been out of prison for less than 8 months or more than 20 months.

The fuller details given in Appendix 10 provide additional information.

For persons with no previous proved offences the percentages in column 4 of the foregoing table, from 1936 onwards, are remarkably steady at 93, 94, 92, 93, 94; but it would be unwise to infer from this that as a method of treatment for a first offence imprisonment is 13 per cent more likely to be successful than any other method!

The analysis of the percentages by age-groups is particularly suggestive:

Period	Without previous offences				With previous offences			
	17–21	21–30	30–40	40 & over	17–21	21–30	30–40	40 & over
1930–35	67	78	84	89	37	60	67	78
1936–40	78	85	90	93	63	70	79	84
1943	83	86	91	94	48	55	68	78
1944	81	86	92	96	50	50	68	78
1945	86	89	93	96	56	57	74	79
1946	89	89	94	96	71	58	74	81

At this point there exists the possibility of a comparison of the results shown with other authenticated figures, though the relativity is by no means exact. The '500 criminal careers' followed up by Sheldon and Eleanor Glueck in the first of their studies on these lines covered '500 ex-inmates of the Massachusetts Reformatory, mostly property offenders with previous violations of the law, and they regarded as recidivists those relapsing into any sort of punishable conduct, whether reconvicted or not. The result was a shock to any criminologist inclined to complacency. By these rather severe standards in the first five-year post-treatment span, when the average age of the men was thirty, the ratio of those relapsing into crime was 80·1 per cent; in the second, with an average age of thirty-five, 69·9 per cent; and in the third, at the time of the general depression, 69·2 per cent, but only 58·2 in the fifth year of the last period.' [1] So far as the case-material is concerned, the comparable material in the foregoing table would be the age-groups 17–30 with previous offences: as regards results, the English material relates not only to reconvictions but to recommittals to prison, whereas the American material relates to 'punishable conduct whether reconvicted or not'. It is impossible to discount this variation, but the

[1] Grünhut, p. 388.

comparable figures, for what they may be worth, in respect of the 'first five-year post-treatment span' seem to be 80·1 'relapsed' on the Glueck findings and 48·6 recommitted to prison on the figures of Appendix 10.[1]

The next group of figures relates to prisoners discharged from the three Training Prisons at Wakefield, Maidstone and Askham Grange (women): unfortunately the figures published for these three prisons cover neither the same periods nor the same case-material, so that each must be considered separately.

The Commissioners have published in their Annual Reports in respect of every year since 1931 the numbers discharged from Wakefield in that year and the number of those discharges reconvicted up to a recent date. The figures cover two categories of prisoner, Star Class and Special Class,[2] though the figures for the latter cease after 1945, when this class was discontinued. The sentences would be, broadly, 1–3 years, giving a maximum of 2 years to be served. For this prison the figures published in 1949 show that of 5,883 Stars discharged from 1939–46 inclusive, 507 or 8·6 per cent had been reconvicted up to 31 December 1948, i.e. after not less than 2 years at large. The comparable figure for the Special Class was 24·7. This gives a 'success' percentage of 91·4 for Stars as against the overall Star figure in Appendix 10 of about 80, and 75·3 for Specials as against about 55 for the 21–30 age-group with previous offences which is the comparable class in Appendix 10. If for stricter comparison the four Wakefield years 1943–6 are compared with the years 1943–6 in the first of two tables given above as abstracts from Appendix 10, the Wakefield 'success' figure for Stars becomes 95·3.

The Maidstone figures cover a much shorter period, but are here given for what they may be worth as quoted in the Annual Report for 1949, p. 36.

Numbers discharged from Maidstone Prison from 1945 to 1948 and since reconvicted up to 31 December 1949

Year	Stars			Ordinaries			Total		
	Dis-charged	Reconvicted		Dis-charged	Reconvicted		Dis-charged	Reconvicted	
		Num-ber	Per cent		Num-ber	Per cent		Num-ber	Per cent
1945	59	4	7	91	22	24	150	26	17·3
1946	177	12	7	265	29	11	442	41	9·3
1947	161	7	4	186	23	12	347	30	8·6
1948	252	4	2	196	25	13	448	29	6·5

[1] 3,087 offenders of the age-groups 17–30 are shown in Appendix 10 as having been received with previous offences in 1943. On 31 December 1948, 1,587 of these had not again been received into prison, i.e. 51·4 per cent.

[2] The Special Class was for young men between the ages 21–30 who by record and character were unfit for the Star Class.

In the foregoing table the Stars are as case material comparable with the Wakefield Stars: taking the 1945–7 discharges only, so as to allow a two-year gap to the end of 1949, this gives 23 reconvictions out of 397 discharges, or a success percentage of about 94. Particular interest attaches to the figures for the Ordinary Class discharges, since these (so far as they go) indicate what measures of success may attend the experiment of treating recidivists in the special conditions of a Training Prison: again taking only the 1945–47 figures, we find that of 542 discharges 74 had been reconvicted up to the end of 1949, giving a 'success' percentage of about 86·3. If these figures are taken with the Special Class figures for Wakefield they suggest that this method of training recidivists may hope to achieve a success rate round about 80.

Encouraging as these figures may be, they must bow to those achieved by the women trained at Askham Grange in the first three years of that prison's life (1947–9), though over this short period, during the greater part of which only carefully selected Stars were received, the fact that only two reconvictions had been recorded before the end of 1949 does not merit statistical assessment.

The third group of figures supplements Appendix 10, though indirectly and incompletely, by giving information about the reconvictions of prisoners with sentences of 3 years and over discharged from central and local prisons. This comes from the reports of the Men's and Women's Divisions of the C.A.C.A. at pp. 52 and 54 of the Annual Report for 1949: the figures given for men relate to the position of 1947 discharges at the end of 1949. For Stars the 'satisfactory' percentages are, Leyhill 96·7: [1] Wakefield 87·8. For Ordinaries, Parkhurst 46·6: local prisons 56·3. For women the figures are given for discharges over a three-year period 1945–47 and again relate to the position at the end of 1949—they are Stars, 96·8,[2] Ordinaries, 67·7.

From the total effect of these three groups of figures it seems possible to deduce some answer to the question of how the actual results of the contemporary prison system compare with the criterion of complete success postulated in the opening section of the chapter. If we take the Star Class as representing those who come to prison for the first time,[3] it appears that of all those who have served up to 2 year sentences some 80 per cent will not return to prison, and if they have served their sentences in training prisons, over 90 per cent will not return: for those who have served longer sentences in central prisons the figure may be 95 for men and tends to approach 100 for women.

[1] The 1946 discharge figure for Camp Hill, which preceded Leyhill as a long-term Star prison, was 95·5 satisfactory at the end of 1948.

[2] This represents 2 reconvictions out of 63 discharges: in most years no reconvictions are reported.

[3] In fact a small proportion of Stars may have been in prison before, but to balance this a small proportion of 'first-timers' may have been reclassified as Ordinaries owing to bad conduct or influence.

Of those who do not come back to prison these figures tell us nothing, and nothing, on any statistical basis, can be known. For them, imprisonment must be supposed to have served its purpose, for some in one way, for some in another. Many personal accounts still unhappily suggest that for the writers at least Wilde could speak today as he wrote in *De Profundis*: 'Prison life with its endless privations and restrictions makes one rebellious . . . and he who is in a state of rebellion cannot receive grace. . . . The most terrible thing about it is not that it breaks one's heart . . . but that it turns one's heart to stone.' But there is much in the records of Aid Societies, and in letters to Governors and Chaplains and other officers of the prisons, to count on the other side of the assessment—as this from the parents of a young woman recently released:

'My wife and I feel we would like to express our appreciation for your sympathetic consideration towards our daughter, which meant so much to her in the very unfortunate circumstances. We are quite certain that had your attitude been more in keeping with what one usually associates with prison life, she would have come back to us very much the worse for her experiences. Instead, we find the shining light of an unbroken spirit and renewed faith in humanity. This is quite contrary to our expectations, and so you will understand the extent of our gratitude.'

(3) RECIDIVISM

A recidivist, for an English writer, is no easier to define than a psychopath. It is not, in English usage, a term with any legal definition: it appears in no statute and in no statutory rule. We are therefore thrown back on its dictionary definition, which is given in the O.E.D. as 'one who habitually relapses into crime'. This is the sense in which the word will be used here, and in which it is perhaps most generally understood, *pace* Dr. Grünhut, who refers to the 'legal term' of recidivist, and defines recidivism as 'the commission of a new offence after the expiration of a sentence for a previous breach of the law' (p. 387). It would certainly be convenient if there could be some accepted definition of the point in an offender's career at which relapse could be said to have become habitual, and in some English-speaking countries legal or at any rate administrative definition is given to the term recidivist: no doubt Dr. Grünhut had the practice of those countries in mind rather than the English practice.

However that may be, it will have appeared sufficiently from the foregoing section that since of those who come to prison for the first time not more than 20 per cent are likely to return, a substantial proportion of that 20 per cent must return very often and for a very long time for them to bulk so large in the prison population. That this is

indeed so is shown by figures published on p. 39 of the Annual Report
for 1949, from which it appears that in 1948 there were 15,589 receptions of men and 1,143 receptions of women convicted of offences who
were known to have been in prison before: the analysis of their previous
offences is given as follows:

	Men	Women
1 to 5 previous offences . .	11,916	939
6 to 10 previous offences . .	2,207	128
11 to 20 previous offences . .	1,046	39
Over 20 previous offences . .	420	37
	15,589	1,143

The Report also gives, in Table VIIA of the Appendices, analysed by
offences, the number of previous sentences of imprisonment (other
than for non-payment of fines) which had been served by the prisoners
received in 1948. This enables the inquiry to be narrowed down to crime
proper by the omission of the less serious non-indictable offences. On
this basis it appears that the number of men received on conviction of
indictable offences or 'non-indictable akin to indictable' who were
known to have served previous sentences was 14,247. The number of
known previous sentences were:

One	Two	Three	Four	Five	Six to ten	Eleven to Twenty	Above Twenty
4,077	2,996	1,789	1,297	887	1,972	904	325

For women, of a total of 902, the numbers were:

One	Two	Three	Four	Five	Six to ten	Eleven to Twenty	Above Twenty
303	214	109	64	54	106	32	20

From these figures the size and nature of the problem of recidivism
begin to take shape. Whatever definition one gives to the term it can
be fairly applied to one who is serving a fourth sentence of imprisonment for a serious offence: on this limited basis alone it appears that
we are concerned with nearly 7,200 men and 400 women, who represent
the failures of the penal system in general and the prison system in
particular. Looking back at these figures, and considering that nearly
2,000 men had served 6–10 sentences and over 1,200 had served more
—and often many more—than ten, one need not hesitate to draw 'the
inference that the present methods not only fail to check the criminal
propensities of such people, but may actually cause progressive

deterioration by habituating the offenders to prison conditions',[1] or to agree with Dr. Grünhut that 'the crime risk increases with every subsequent conviction' (p. 455).

There is one ray of comforting light in this dark picture—depressing as it may be, it is in some respects better now than it was before the war. In the Annual Report for 1938 the number of men shown in Table VIIA as having served three or more previous sentences was 57·3 of the total receptions of men known to have been in prison before for serious offences. as compared with 50·3 in 1948. And serious recidivism as shown by the number received with 6 or more previous convictions fell from an average of 43 per cent for 1935–39 to less than 38 per cent for 1945–48.

It is against this background that we must assess the significance of the Maidstone 'success' figure for recidivists quoted earlier in this chapter, and the importance of the new methods of dealing with 'persistent offenders' to be described in Chapter Eighteen.

[1] Report of the Departmental Committee on Persistent Offenders 1932, para. 5.

PART FOUR

SPECIAL CLASSES OF PRISONERS

CHAPTER SEVENTEEN

MISCELLANEOUS CLASSES

(1) UNTRIED PRISONERS

THESE representatives of the original function of the prison are today an awkward anomaly. The law presumes them to be innocent, and the Prison Act 1877 required that 'a clear difference shall be made between the treatment of persons unconvicted of crime' and the treatment of convicted prisoners, and that special rules should be made 'regulating their confinement in such manner as to make it as little as possible oppressive, due regard only being had to their safe-custody, to the necessity of preserving order and good government . . . and to the physical and moral well-being of the prisoners themselves'. These provisions were repealed by the Act of 1948, but their moral force remains, and public opinion would be properly disturbed by any suggestion of undue harshness in the conditions in which untried prisoners are detained.

But although their innocence must be presumed, and their treatment regulated accordingly, there are other presumptions which work in rather different directions. Since in all proper cases the courts will normally release an untried offender on bail, it must be assumed that in at any rate a great many cases of those received into prison, the courts have decided that detention is necessary either to ensure further appearance or to prevent interference with the course of justice: exceptions would include remands for 'state of mind reports', and cases where bail has been allowed but sureties have not been found. Further, the special Rules have continuously since 1877 laid on the administration the duty to 'prevent contamination or conspiracy to defeat the ends of justice'.

The conditions of detention must therefore secure, as absolute obligations, safe-custody, good order, and the prevention of contamination or conspiracy: and they must be applied in, and be compatible with the régime of, an establishment primarily designed for and populated by convicted prisoners, although from these the untried must be strictly separated. It must also be recognised that the majority of these prisoners, whether or no they have committed the offences currently charged, are not in fact respectable and innocent persons but old hands well known to the prison staffs.

In the light of these considerations it is possible to understand why the lot of an untried prisoner may seem in practice to be more depressing, even if 'less oppressive', than that of a convicted prisoner. He may work if he wishes, though he may not be required to do so: those who choose to work will be given some mail-bags to sew or patch, and will be paid 6d. a day. It must be difficult to decide which is more boring, to work or not to work, for the mandate to prevent contamination and conspiracy precludes any kind of free association. Nor will the untried find their evenings relieved by the educational and other activities provided for the convicted, or even by the conversation available to those who have to sleep three in a cell—a practice strictly forbidden for the untried.

In what sense, then, can it be claimed that the treatment of the untried prisoner is 'less oppressive' than that of the convicted? Apart from the freedom to be idle, he may wear his own clothes, if they are sufficient and suitable and not required for the purposes of justice, and retain his personal possessions 'so far as is consistent with discipline and good order'; he may be supplied with food and drink at his own expense or that of his friends; he may have books, newspapers, writing materials, etc. sent in to him; he may on reasonable grounds be attended by his own doctor or dentist; he may write and receive as many letters as he likes, and receive daily visits from his friends. He may also, on payment, be allowed 'to occupy a suitable room or cell specially fitted for such prisoners' and 'to be relieved from the duty of cleaning his room or cell or from other such tasks or offices', and he may 'have at his own cost the use of private furniture and utensils approved by the Governor'.

The man with a little money, or friends to look after him, who does not mind spending his whole time in his cell except for the usual exercise periods, and can pass the time in reading or writing, may therefore be reasonably comfortable. But the cell remains a cell. The 'specially fitted room' does not offer a lot of comfort, and the conditions under which food and drink may be sent in fall short of the epicurean—alcoholic liquors are limited to a pint of ale, etc. or half a bottle of wine a day, and spirits are prohibited. But the respectable novice prepared to seclude himself in this way need come to little harm.

These conditions are perhaps the best that can be provided in the local prisons as they are, and even in a prison designed today little more could be done, though it would perhaps be reasonable to provide a separate block with its own work-room in which the rooms were of a higher standard than ordinary cells and more comfortably furnished. They have never excited public comment of a general nature, and even the Gladstone Committee found little to say on the subject. It should be understood that except so far as the special Rules apply, untried prisoners are subject to the general Rules: if they commit offences against discipline they may forfeit any of their special privileges except visits and letters required for procuring bail or preparing a defence; if they do not wear their own clothes they wear prison dress, though of a different colour from the convicted; and their food, except so far as they buy their own, is the ordinary prison food.

But in what is the most important aspect of their position, the preparation of their defence, the Rules provide the fullest facilities and protection. An untried prisoner is allowed to see his legal advisers in private on any week-day at any reasonable time, and may hand to them personally any documents he has prepared as instructions for his defence without examination by a prison officer. The prison authorities are also required to provide him with all reasonable facilities, including writing materials, for preparing notes and instructions and writing to his legal advisers and friends. Where medical evidence is required, he may be examined by a doctor chosen by himself, his friends or his legal adviser.

Special facilities are granted to those who are trying to obtain sureties for bail, and to foreigners who wish to communicate with their consulate or other representative; and every prisoner is made aware by printed notices in his cell not only of the regulations relative to his class, but of the steps he should take if he wishes to seek bail, or to secure legal assistance under the Poor Prisoners' Defence Acts.

The Welfare Agencies are available to the untried as to the convicted. They are informed on their cell-cards how to seek help if they are troubled about their family or other private affairs, or about the future. And in special cases the Prison Visitors may help them too.

(2) APPELLANTS

Under the Criminal Appeal Act 1907 a prisoner convicted at Assizes or Quarter Sessions may, under prescribed conditions, appeal against either conviction or sentence to the Court of Criminal Appeal; and from the day on which he signs his notice of appeal to the day on which it is either abandoned or determined by the Court, his sentence is held to be suspended and he is treated under the special Rules for Appellants. It should be noted that these Rules do not apply to persons appealing to Quarter Sessions against convictions by Courts of Summary Jurisdiction: a person so appealing may be, and normally is, released on bail, but if he is not so released he continues to serve his sentence until his appeal is heard.

The object of suspending an appellant's sentence is primarily to discourage frivolous appeals, and where the Court thinks fit, even if the appeal is unsuccessful, it may order the time spent as an appellant to count as part of the sentence. The special Rules do not therefore provide any specially favourable treatment for the appellant, but only regulate certain technical details, and ensure for the prisoner the same freedom of access to his legal advisers, and facilities for preparing his appeal, as the trial prisoner has for the preparation of his defence. If the Court discharges him, he may be paid for his work in prison while an appellant at rates fixed by the Commissioners.

(3) CONVICTED PRISONERS AWAITING SENTENCE, OR REMANDED FOR INQUIRY

Prisoners falling into these categories are treated like other convicted prisoners save in one respect. They may, if they wish, for the purpose of preparing any representations to the Courts before which they are to appear for sentence or otherwise, have the same special facilities as the Rules allow to Appellants.

(4) PRISONERS CONVICTED OF SEDITION, ETC.

By section 52 (4) of the Criminal Justice Act 1948, rules are to be made providing for the special treatment of persons who have been sentenced to imprisonment on conviction of sedition, seditious libel, or seditious conspiracy. This provision, taken with the repeal by the first section of the Act of the arrangements of 1898 for the 'triple division' of offenders, brings to an end that curious failure of the English penal system, the First Division.

The history of this experiment goes back to the Prisons Act 1865, section 67 of which provided as follows:

'In every Prison to which this Act applies, Prisoners convicted of Misdemeanor, and not sentenced to Hard Labour, shall be divided into at least Two Divisions, One of which shall be called the First Division; and whenever any Person convicted of Misdemeanor is sentenced to Imprisonment without Hard Labour it shall be lawful for the Court or Judge before whom such Person has been tried to order, if such Court or Judge think fit, that such Person shall be treated as a Misdemeanant of the First Division, and a Misdemeanant of the First Division shall not be deemed to be a Criminal Prisoner within the Meaning of this Act.'

The next step was taken by section 40 of the Act of 1877, which provided that 'the Prison Commissioners shall see that any prisoner under sentence inflicted on conviction for sedition or seditious libel shall be treated as a misdemeanant of the first division within the meaning of section 67 of the Prisons Act 1865'.

Finally, section 6 (2) of the Prison Act 1898, as amended by section 16 (2) of the Criminal Justice Administration Act 1914, provided that 'where a person is convicted by any court of an offence, and is sentenced to imprisonment without hard labour, or committed to prison for non-payment of a fine, the court may, if it thinks fit, having regard to the nature of the offence and the antecedents of the offender, direct that he be treated as an offender of the first division or as an offender of the second division'. And sub-section (5) further provided that any reference in section 40 of the Prisons Act 1877 to a misdemeanant of the first division should be construed as reference to an offender of the first division within the meaning of this section.

So much of this story as concerns the Second Division, and the reasons for the failure of that attempt to set up a system of classification by the courts, we have already considered. The original purpose of the First Division was different: it was to separate out a category of misdemeanants who were to be given special treatment as 'non-criminal' prisoners. As to the qualifications for admission to this category, however, the Act of 1865 was silent, and as to the nature of the non-criminal régime, para. 102 of Schedule I did no more than empower the Justices to 'make such Rules as they may think expedient'.

The Act of 1877 made no fundamental alteration of this position: its effect was limited to ensuring that a certain category of prisoners, whose offences were in essence political, were included in the First Division. This clause was inserted in the Bill on the motion of Mr. Parnell, and was primarily intended to provide for the Irish Fenian prisoners, though in the course of discussion in Committee the Chartists were also mentioned. In fact the Fenians were usually convicted of 'treason-felony', and Parnell's attempt to include treason-felony in the clause was defeated on the technical ground that these persons being sentenced to penal servitude were confined in convict prisons which were outside the scope of the Bill. It seems clear that the reason for dealing with the matter by a direction to the Prison Commissioners, rather than by leaving it to the discretion of the court, was distrust of the Judges—and especially the Irish Judges: only one Hon. Member raised this point, and his intervention enlisted no support.[1]

The transfer in 1877 of the power to make Prison Rules from the Justices to the Secretary of State did not make for clarification of the nature of the special 'non-criminal' régime: Sir E. du Cane's comment on the position in 1884 is as follows—'The rules for misdemeanants of the first division guard against the possible abuse of interest or influence which might lead to an unwarrantable difference in the treatment of prisoners, by prescribing that no prisoner shall be placed in this division except as provided by statute or by order of the court of law which sentenced him. They permit the visiting committees to authorise the

[1] *Hansard*: 5 April 1877, pp. 616–638; and 14 June 1877, pp. 1789–1800.

modification of certain ordinary rules and routine to suit the special circumstances of any particular prisoner of this class.'[1]

The effect of the Act of 1898 was to remove the limitation to misdemeanants imposed in 1865 for admission to the First Division, and to leave the courts complete discretion 'having regard to the nature of the offence and the antecedents of the offender'. But the admission of those convicted of sedition or seditious libel was still mandatory. From this time on, the Rules provided in detail for the treatment of the First Division, the general effect being that of simple imprisonment in the plain meaning of the words—confinement and no more.

The effect of the Act of 1948 and the Rules of 1949 is to abolish the First Division as such, but to preserve the régime of 'simple imprisonment' solely for the political category for whom it was made mandatory in 1877. The courts no longer have any powers or discretion in the matter; the treatment automatically follows imprisonment for the offence, as for this special category it has done since 1877.

It would be of more than historical interest to attempt to establish the real intentions of the legislature in this matter, and to ascertain how in practice those intentions have been understood and applied by the courts and the administration, since the questions raised, though temporarily at rest in this country, might well in certain circumstances arise again. That they still excite interest elsewhere is evident from the discussion at a meeting of the Swedish Association of Criminalists on 11 November 1949.[2] There exists, in the law of the Scandinavian countries, a form of sentence known as *custodia honesta* or 'honourable confinement': in the course of discussion of the ever-green topic of the 'single form of penalty involving deprivation of liberty', this form of sentence came under review. It appears that in Norway it may be applied 'for political offences and other crimes, where in a particular case it may be assumed that the offence is not due to a depraved disposition'. The Danish representative thought it should be retained for offenders who 'act as they do because of their adherence to a particular political ideology'. Another speaker 'considered that subjects for *custodia honesta* were offenders by conviction, in the sense of group conviction, that is to say, behind their offence was the pressure of a group'. It would appear that with the possible exception of Denmark this form of sentence is now little used: in Norway 'the punishment has not acquired any appreciable significance, though opportunities for applying it have not been lacking. It has hardly been used at all after the war. . . . The provisions now in force for the execution of imprisonment are such that there is no need for a special form of punishment requiring lenient treatment.'

[1] Du Cane, p. 76.
[2] *Yearbook of the Northern Association of Criminalists*, 1949–50; Stockholm 1950; pp. 21–26.

Was it the intention of Parliament, in setting up this First Division, to create a *custodia honesta* in our penal system? Sir E. Ruggles-Brise appears to have thought not. 'It is difficult', he says, 'to say whether the legislature intended this division, which, on the face of it, was a bold step in the way of differentiation, to be more than a reservation in favour of a few exceptional cases, such as are actually mentioned in the Act. The presumption is, having regard to the fact that prisoners treated as First Class Misdemeanants were not to be deemed criminal prisoners, that there was no intention to anticipate an elaborate classification such as is now laid down. . . .' [1] In this statement Sir Evelyn follows his predecessor in stressing the 'few exceptional cases', and goes further in suggesting that these cases would only be the political offenders envisaged by the Act of 1877.

That this was more than a purely personal view is borne out by the circumstances in which, as Home Secretary, Mr. Winston Churchill found it necessary in 1910 to secure the approval of Parliament to the following additional Prison Rule:

'In the case of any offender whose previous character is good, and who has been convicted of, or committed to prison for an offence not involving dishonesty, cruelty, indecency or serious violence, the Commissioners may allow such amelioration of the conditions prescribed in the foregoing rules as the Secretary of State may approve in respect of the wearing of prison clothing, bathing, hair-cutting, cleaning of cells, employment, exercise, books and otherwise.

'Provided that no such amelioration shall be greater than that granted under the rules for offenders of the First Division.'

Notwithstanding the general terms of this Rule and the carefully guarded phraseology in which Mr. Churchill proposed it,[2] its purpose was in fact limited. The Government had been placed in a politically embarrassing position by the imprisonment of the militant suffragettes in Holloway and elsewhere, and particularly by their recent technique of the hunger-strike. Similar problems had also arisen in connection with other offenders from 'group conviction', such as the 'passive resisters' to the levying of the Education Rate under the Education Act of 1902; but it was primarily with a view to meeting the suffragette situation that this Rule was introduced.

The question at once arises why, since the practical effect of the new Rule was to give very little short of First Division treatment to those to whom it applied, its introduction was thought to be necessary. Was not the First Division provided precisely for persons who broke the law, but not from 'criminal' motives? This view was strongly pressed on the Government at the time by influential supporters of the

[1] Ruggles-Brise, p. 71.
[2] Reply to Question by Mr. John O'Connor, *Hansard*, 15 March 1910, p. 177.

292   SPECIAL CLASSES OF PRISONERS

suffragist movement. The answer to be deduced from the reply to a deputation by the Home Secretary, Mr. McKenna,[1] and from his reply to a subsequent Parliamentary Question,[2] is twofold: the First Division was for 'political offenders', and persons who were sent to prison for offences of violence (e.g. such assaults and breakings of windows as the suffragettes were wont to commit) could not be placed in that category on the ground that their motives were political. Further, the Home Secretary believed 'that the infrequency of the use of the First Division arises from the fact that the conditions are so easy that Judges and Magistrates are unwilling to pass a sentence that can have little or no deterrent effect. The conditions of Rule 343A are somewhat more stringent.'

Whatever view may be taken today of the validity of this reasoning, it is at least clear that it did not embrace that conception of the function of the First Division which has been defined as *custodia honesta*. Nor indeed does it appear to have coincided with the actual practice of the courts up to that time. From the Annual Report of the Prison Commissioners for 1910–11 (p. 23) it appears that since 1899 no less than 572 persons had in fact been placed by the courts in the First Division. Analysis of Appendix 16 to the Annual Reports for the years 1906–10 shows that during those 5 years, of 348 persons placed in the First Division, only 2 were convicted of offences 'against the State and Public Order'. On the other hand there were 119 offenders against the Education Acts, who may be assumed to have been 'passive resisters', and in 1906 there were 127 women committed for offences against the Metropolitan Police Acts, who are stated in para. 19 of the Report for that year to have been London Suffragettes: there were also, *eiusdem generis*, 27 offenders against the Vaccination Acts. The balance were an assortment ranging from larceny and embezzlement to drunks and indecent exposure. With the exception of the two quasi-politicals, virtually all these persons were committed by courts of summary jurisdiction. One can only infer that many magistrates were prepared to use the discretion which the Act of 1898 had reposed in them in the sense which Parliament would appear to have intended.

However that may be, the conception of *custodia honesta* was soon to be eliminated by the inevitable if unconscious movement of English thought and practice towards the 'single sentence'. Between the wars both the First Division and the special Rule fell into desuetude, and finally disappeared in 1948–49. However devious the means, this end may perhaps be justified by the reasons advanced by the Norwegian representative at Stockholm, that in modern conditions of imprisonment 'there is no need for a special form of punishment requiring lenient treatment'.

[1] Reported verbatim in *The Standard* of 24 May 1912.
[2] Question by Mr. McVeagh, *Hansard*, 3 July 1912.

What remains is of little practical significance in the prison system, since long years may elapse without the reception of any prisoner convicted of one of these offences. Should one be received, he would find that his conditions were almost precisely those of an untried prisoner, except that he 'may work at his own trade, employment or profession, so far as the conditions of the prison and the requirements of discipline and safe-custody permit'. He would however have an inducement to choose to work in the service or industries of the prison, since he would not be eligible to earn any remission of his sentence unless he regularly did so.

(5) CIVIL PRISONERS

This class of prisoner was known, until the Statutory Rules of 1949, as 'debtors', and indeed the great majority of them are still persons committed by courts of summary jurisdiction, or by county courts, for the non-payment of sums of money ordered by the courts to be paid under non-criminal process, e.g. wife-maintenance or affiliation orders, non-payment of rates or taxes, or civil debts. They do however include certain miscellaneous classes who are not debtors, and the term civil prisoners (which followed pre-existing Scottish practice) is therefore more accurate: these classes include persons committed for contempt of court or for non-payment under various orders of court, and aliens committed for deportation or otherwise.

As the following table shows, civil prisoners are a much less important element of the prison population than they were before the war: in 1931 they accounted for 24·2 per cent of the receptions of male prisoners, in 1949 for 11·8 per cent. The table also makes it clear that this change is broadly due to a very great reduction, accentuated as a

Civil Process Prisoners

Annual averages or Calendar years

| | Total | Under Wife Maintenance or Affiliation Orders | In default of payment of | | By County Courts | Others |
			Rates	Income tax		
1913 [1]	14,026	3,554	2,379	—	5,759	2,334
1926–30	12,463	6,701	2,001	141	3,172	448
1931–35	11,642	5,054	2,609	156	3,359	464
1936–40	7,305	2,605	1,101	152	2,410	1,037
1941–45	3,462	1,974	272	34	404	778
1946	3,567	2,650	144	9	220	544
1947	4,247	3,272	191	12	234	538
1948	5,289	3,899	187	22	318	863
1949	5,205	3,808	204	15	383	795

[1] Year ended 31 March.

result of the late war, in the committals by county courts for non-payment of civil debts and by courts of summary jurisdiction for non-payment of rates. Nearly three out of four of the civil prisoners of today are men who cannot or will not pay the amounts due under wife maintenance or bastardy orders.

Although the number of county court debtors has been insignificant in recent years, their position calls for some explanation, since they are committed under an 'Act for the Abolition of Imprisonment for Debt'. The legal theory is that the debtor is not imprisoned for the debt but as a punishment for contempt of court, the intention being, as stated by Halsbury in *The Laws of England*, that 'a fraudulent debtor shall be punished, but that an honest debtor shall not'. Thus the law [1] requires the court, before making an order for committal to prison, to be satisfied that since the debtor was ordered to pay the sum found by the court to be due, he has or has had the means to pay such sum but has refused or neglected to pay. In practice, however, the court often makes in the first instance an order for payment by instalments, and only commits to prison if and when the creditor applies for committal because the instalments are not being paid. There is therefore some ground for the view that whatever the legal theory the Act is used in fact as an instrument to enable creditors to enforce the payment of debts by the sanction of imprisonment, and from time to time doubt has been expressed whether under present practice committals are always confined to the 'fraudulent' debtors, and there has been 'controversy as to whether it is or is not right to retain a power of imprisonment in respect of county court orders'. [2] In 1908 a Select Committee inquired into this question, but no agreement was reached.

In 1933 the Home Secretary appointed a Departmental Committee to try to find ways to reduce the number of committals by courts of summary jurisdiction in default of payment of fines and rates and of sums due under wife maintenance and affiliation orders, and a number of practical recommendations were made. We have already noted the useful effect of these in reducing the numbers of committals for fines (p. 81), and the foregoing table shows that in the five years following 1935 the number of committals by courts of summary jurisdiction under non-criminal process was practically halved.

This use of the prison for the coercion of debtors is not satisfactory in principle or in practice. So far as 'county court debtors' are deemed, with Halsbury, to be 'fraudulent' there seems to be no reason for treating them differently from persons convicted of fraud—indeed it is not easy to draw an ethical line between the person who steals a pound of sugar from the grocer and the person who buys a pound of sugar

---

[1] Debtors Act 1869, section 5, and Summary Jurisdiction Act 1879, section 35.

[2] Report of the Departmental Committee on Imprisonment by Courts of Summary Jurisdiction in Default of Payment of Fines, etc., 1934, para. 1.

and refrains from paying for it. And the doubt remains whether in practice all such debtors are in fact fraudulent. For the rest, notwithstanding the recommendations of 1934, it is still not clear why many of them come to prison. The Annual Reports of the Commissioners since the war have shown the concern which many Governors feel about these men 'mainly on two grounds—first, that many are genuinely convinced, and often with apparently good reason, that the fault lies as much or more with their wives as with them, and they have no intention of paying; second, that insufficient consideration appears to have been given to individual circumstances before committal to prison, and that more patient attempts to investigate and advise with a view to avoiding imprisonment wherever possible would perhaps avert much unfruitful hardship to both man and wife. Of recent years many of this class have been ex-service men who, for one reason or another, have not resumed normal married life. Attention has also been drawn to the marked variations in the periods of imprisonment ordered by courts in respect of similar sums of money.' [1]

The treatment provided by the Rules reflects this confusion, being a sort of compromise between the custodial treatment of untried prisoners and the corrective treatment of the convicted. Civil prisoners must be kept separate from criminal prisoners, but may associate among themselves: it was found however that in some prisons there were so few civil prisoners that association was scarcely practicable, and the Rules of 1949 therefore provide that 'Where owing to the small numbers of civil prisoners or otherwise suitable arrangements for association of such prisoners cannot be made, such a prisoner may if he so desires, with the approval of the Governor, be allowed to associate with prisoners of the Star Class at such times and in such manner as the Commissioners determine.' They are required to work at the normal prison work, and earn money on the same basis as convicted prisoners: they may be included in 'outside parties'. They do not earn remission, since they can secure discharge by paying what they owe, and they receive only 'out of stage' privileges. They receive the normal prison diet without supplement, and are subject to the normal prison discipline. But they may wear their own clothes, if these are sufficient and suitable, and they receive more letters and visits than convicted prisoners—one letter a week each way, and a half-hour visit once a week. On discharge they are eligible for assistance by the D.P.A.S. on the same basis as convicted prisoners.

The maximum period of imprisonment is 3 months if committed by a court of summary jurisdiction; 6 weeks if by a county court; 12 months if by the High Court under section 4 of the Debtors Act 1869. A contempt of court prisoner is held at the pleasure of the court, [2] and aliens until the necessary arrangements for deportation can be made.

[1] *Annual Report for* 1946, pp. 29, 30. [2] See Appendix K.

(6) PRISONERS UNDER SENTENCE OF DEATH

Every care is taken to prevent a condemned prisoner from coming into contact with other prisoners, or from being exposed to their view at exercise or chapel. The 'condemned cell' is usually set at the end of a landing, and is of at least double the ordinary size, with a bed for the prisoner, a table, and chairs for the prisoner and the two officers who remain in the cell day and night: washing facilities and water-closet are placed in an adjoining cell, and the visiting room also adjoins, with a separate entrance for the visitors. The execution chamber is reached through an intervening lobby, the whole set of rooms being self-contained.

The condemned prisoner wears prison dress, and except as to labour —which is not required of him—is subject to the general Rules so far as they are applicable. The prisoner may, at the discretion of the Medical Officer, receive additions to the usual diet, and be allowed to smoke, while books, games, and other means of occupation are freely permitted. He may see his friends and legal advisers at any reasonable time, in the presence of prison officers, but otherwise no person except an official of the prison or a member of the Visiting Committee may see him without the authority of the Prison Commissioners. He may if he wishes see the Chaplain, or a Minister of his own denomination, at any reasonable time. Ample facilities are granted for correspondence and for the preparation, if desired, of an appeal.

Responsibility for carrying out the execution rests with the Sheriff of the county, whose Under-Sheriff fixes the date of execution, engages and pays the executioner, attends the execution and decides whether representatives of the Press should be admitted. Immediately after the execution the Coroner for the district holds an inquest on the body at the prison. The burial takes place within the prison walls: a register of the graves is kept, but they are not distinguished by names or other marks.

CHAPTER EIGHTEEN

PERSISTENT OFFENDERS

(1) THE PROBLEM

THROUGHOUT this century the penal systems of Europe and America have sought, with little enough success hitherto, the answers to many questions arising from that central problem of penal law, the habitual criminal—the man who forms the statistical unit in the depressing figures given at the end of Chapter Sixteen. In this matter England took the lead early, and has retained it with the interesting and novel provisions of section 21 of the Criminal Justice Act 1948 and the Rules made in 1949 for implementing those provisions.

The Gladstone Committee recognised the problem as early as 1894 and prescribed broad principles for its solution which the subsequent half-century has sought to translate into practice. The first part of the prescription was to cut off the supply at the source, to dam 'the headsprings of recidivism'. 'It is certain,' they said, 'that the age when the majority of habitual criminals are made lies between 16 and 21. . . . It appears to us that the most determined effort should be made to lay hold of these incipient criminals and to prevent them by strong restraint and rational treatment from recruiting the habitual class' (para. 29). From this suggestion there developed the Borstal system, which, as we shall see in a later chapter, succeeds in diverting from 'the habitual class' some seven out of ten of those whom it receives. This 'cutting off' process continues throughout the prison system: we have seen that of those who come to prison for the first time less than 20 per cent return, and that of that 20 per cent, under modern methods of training, a substantial majority may not return again.

But in the end we are left with a certain number, small though it be, of those who are committed to a life of crime and remain ostensibly unaffected by any number of sentences of whatever severity. What is to be done with them? The suggestion of the Gladstone Committee was as follows: 'To punish them for the particular offence in which they are detected is almost useless; witnesses were almost unanimous in approving of some kind of cumulative sentence; the real offence is the wilful persistence in the deliberately acquired habit of crime. We venture to offer the opinion formed during this inquiry that a new form of sentence should be placed at the disposal of the judges by which these offenders might be segregated for long periods of detention during which they would not be treated with the severity of first-class hard labour or penal servitude, but would be forced to work under less onerous conditions. As loss of liberty would to them prove eventually the chief deterrent, so by their being removed from the opportunity of doing wrong the community would gain' (para. 85).

These ideas, or something like them, have since found expression in most European thought in this matter; but the first attempt to translate them into practice was made in England, when the Prevention of Crime Act 1908 made the two-pronged attack on recidivism recommended by the Committee—the Borstal system for young offenders on the one flank, the Preventive Detention system for habitual criminals on the other.

So far as it concerned habitual criminals, the system of 1908 failed. To understand the reasons for that failure, and for the changes introduced in 1948, it is necessary to take a wider view of the elements of the problem. These may be divided into four: the definition of an habitual criminal, the juridical basis of their treatment, the conditions of their detention and the determination and method of their release.

The Definition of Habitual Criminality

However we may define a recidivist, it is clear that the habitual criminal, or, in the current English term, persistent offender, is something more than a recidivist. First, his offences must be of a serious nature—we are not concerned with the petty misdemeanant. Then, there must be something more than mere repetition of offence: it is generally accepted that the repetition must be indicative of a significant character trait, defined by Dr. Grünhut after the Austrian criminologist Wahlberg as 'criminal tendency' (p. 389). Dr. Grünhut points out that terms having this meaning appear in the Italian Penal Code of 1930—*tendenza a delinquere*, and in the Swiss Criminal Code of 1937—*penchant au crime*, while the German Supreme Court defined an habitual criminal as 'a person who on account of an inner tendency due to the constitution of his character, or acquired by habit, has repeatedly committed criminal offences and tends to a further repetition'.

It is also generally accepted that these offenders fall broadly into two classes. The first, who have been described as 'a-social', and who constitute more of a nuisance than a danger, relapse into crime because through physical, mental or social inadequacy they are incapable of the effort to keep out of it. The second, who have been described as 'anti-social', are usually persons of adequate intelligence and competence who deliberately persist in a career of crime because they prefer it and hope, according to their own scale of values, to make it pay.

English law has never sought to define the habitual criminal: the Act of 1908 provided, as does that of 1948, for a minimum number of previous convictions of crime before an offender can become eligible for consideration, but it remains with the court to decide whether he is to be treated as 'habitual'. Under the Act of 1908 the decision rested with the jury: the procedure of section 21 of 1948 is quite different:

'Where a person who is not less than 30 years of age:

'(a) is convicted on indictment of an offence punishable with imprisonment for a term of two years or more; and

'(b) has been convicted on indictment on at least three previous occasions since he attained the age of 17 of offences punishable on indictment with such a sentence, and was on at least two of those occasions sentenced to Borstal training, imprisonment or corrective training;

then, if the court is satisfied that it is expedient for the protection of the public that he should be detained in custody for a substantial time, followed by a period of supervision if released before the expiration of his sentence, the court may pass, in lieu of any other sentence, a sentence of preventive detention for such term of not less than five nor more than 14 years as the court may determine.'

This procedure is in complete accord with the recommendation of The Hague Congress in para. 2 of the relevant resolution (II, 2, Appx. F). There is first the legal condition of 'a certain number of sentences undergone or of crimes committed', then a complete discretion in the court governed only by the need to satisfy itself that for the protection of the public it is expedient to segregate the offender for a substantial time.

It is noteworthy that there is no longer any attempt to distinguish between the 'a-social' and the 'anti-social'. Under the 1908 procedure, when the offender was specifically charged with being an habitual criminal and the jury had to find on the charge, prosecutions were deliberately limited to the 'anti-social', the 'persistent dangerous criminals'. The memorandum issued to courts by the Home Office when section 21 of the Act of 1948 came into force made it clear that in the opinion of the Secretary of State the terms of the section imposed no such limitation on the discretion of the courts. This view appears to accord with common-sense: if Bill Sikes invariably resumes his career of house-breaking when he is discharged from prison, the mental attitudes which lead to this tendency do not seem to be relevant to the question of protecting the public. It would seem also to have been the view of the Departmental Committee of 1932, which said: 'For some types of offenders—particularly those between 21 and 30—the object of detention will be reformative training: for others—particularly those whose criminality appears to be mainly determined by mental inertia and other innate negative qualities—little in the way of positive training may be practicable, and the main object may be to provide for the control of the offender and for the protection of the public' (para. 40).

It remains, in considering the definition of an habitual criminal, to examine the procedure for assisting the courts to arrive at a decision. The Hague Resolution suggests 'that the declaration of habitual criminality . . . should be in the hands of a judicial authority with the advice of experts' (10 (a)) and that 'before the sentence . . . these offenders should be submitted to an observation which should pay particular attention to their social background and history, and to the psychological and psychiatric aspects of the case' (6). The procedure established under section 21 to these ends is described in *Prisons and Borstals* (pp. 39, 40) as follows:

'To assist the court here, it is required to consider any report (a copy of which must be given by the Court to the prisoner or his legal representative) on the offender's physical and mental condition and his suitability for Corrective Training [1] or Preventive Detention which may be made by or on behalf of the Prison Commissioners. The report is ordinarily made on behalf of the Prison Commissioners by the Governor of the local prison concerned. It sets out all relevant information about the offender obtained from reports by police, employers and, where he has been on probation, by the probation officer, and is supplemented, where the offender has been in custody, by an estimate of his character. It concludes by expressing an opinion as to his suitability for Corrective Training—'suitability' connoting both that the offender is in need of prolonged training and that he is likely to profit by it.[2] Where the offender is eligible for Preventive Detention only, no opinion on suitability is given, the question whether the protection of society requires a long period of detention being regarded as a matter for the court alone. These reports also give the Medical Officer's conclusions about the mental and physical fitness of the offender for the sentence.'

To this it may be added that the Commissioners have expressed their intention, as soon as conditions permit, to set up regional Observation Centres, which will have the function of observing and reporting to the courts on untried prisoners, including those eligible to be dealt with under section 21, as well as of advising on the classification of appropriate convicted prisoners. These will include staff qualified to advise on the 'psychological and psychiatric aspects of the case': in the meantime, psychologists are being posted, as they become available, to groups of local prisons to assist the Governors and Medical Officers in the preparation of reports to courts under section 21 and otherwise.

[1] See p. 302.   [2] See Appendix K.

The Juridical Basis

'Traditional punishments,' says the first paragraph of The Hague Resolution, 'are not sufficient to fight effectively against habitual criminality. It is, therefore, necessary to employ other and more appropriate measures.' That this pronouncement in 1950 does no more than echo that of the Gladstone Committee in 1895 sufficiently indicates the caution with which this question has been approached. 'Traditional punishments' must traditionally be proportioned to the gravity of the offence. But if society is to be effectively protected against the habitual criminal, regard must be had not to the nature of the offence but to the nature of the offender; and where this is such that traditional punishments cannot restrain him, the only 'appropriate measure' seems to be to place him, for a very long time, in a position from which he is no longer able to prey on society.

Here a difficulty of principle arises. At one time banishment or transportation would have seemed entirely appropriate—and advocates of some such measure, in terms of an 'island colony', may still be heard. But so long as these resources are not available, the fact must be faced that the 'measure', under whatever name, is confinement within a prison wall. Continental systems have long drawn a distinction in law between 'punishments' and 'measures of security', and have established the doctrine that the prolonged detention of a persistent offender falls within the latter category. English law does not draw this distinction, nor, in the light of the contemporary conception of imprisonment, does it appear to have any reality in practice. Given that punishment by imprisonment means punishment by confinement in a prison, with no implication of a régime directed towards causing 'pain and suffering' over and above what is implicit in the confinement, then the imprisonment of a persistent offender as a 'measure of security' does not differ in essence from that of another offender as a 'punishment'.

It was over this difficulty, in part, that the English system of 1908 broke down. 'Some countries,' says Dr. Grünhut, 'have introduced a cumulative system which enables the Court to inflict legal punishment for the expiation of the offender's guilt, together with a further sentence awarded as a measure of public security to check his unabated dangerousness' (p. 392). This was precisely the system of 1908, the effect of which was that if a person with three previous convictions of crime was again convicted of crime and sentenced to penal servitude, and was found by the jury to be an 'habitual criminal', the court might pass a further sentence of not less than five nor more than ten years of preventive detention. No doctrinal camouflage could prevent prisoners, courts and juries from regarding this as what in fact it was—a double punishment, and after the first few years it fell into general disfavour; in 10 years from 1921 only 346 men and 8 women were sentenced to preventive detention. There were other reasons for this—the reluctance of the prosecution to prefer the charge of habitual criminality, and the requirement that the preceding sentence must be one of penal servitude, which meant that an offender, whatever his record, could only be caught in this net on conviction of a particularly serious offence.

In 1931 therefore the Home Secretary appointed a Departmental Committee 'to enquire into the existing methods of dealing with Persistent offenders', and its Report of 1932 [1] is one of the landmarks of English penological thought. From its suggestions came not only the provisions of the Act of 1948 dealing with persistent offenders and the abolition of penal servitude, but the subsequent inquiries into prison employment and the re-absorption of prisoners into industry, the development of the 'open prison' system, and the establishment of psychiatric services in the prisons. On the question under immediate consideration, they recommended the abolition of the 'cumulative sentence' system, and the substitution of a procedure such as is now provided by section 21. This again is in accord with the recommendation at (3) of the Hague Resolution that 'the special measure should not be added to a sentence of a punitive character. There should be one unified measure. . . .'

Their major contribution to the problem, however, was an entirely novel one in practice, though in principle it was no more than an extension of the 'cutting off' procedure already described. They proposed to divide persistent offenders into two categories—those 'still in the early stages of a criminal career, including the large number of such offenders as are between the ages of 21 and 30', and the rest. What the Committee wished to ensure for the first group was no more than a period of imprisonment of sufficient length to enable them to profit from the régime of 'training' already well established in the English prisons, in the hope that this might succeed in diverting them from a career of crime. But to do this it was necessary, as for the confirmed habitual, to establish a fresh juridical basis. Again, in order to make the punishment fit not the offence but the offender, it was necessary to break with the traditional practice in the infliction of traditional punishments. It had been laid down by the Court of Criminal Appeal that if the offender's specific offence did not warrant a sentence above a·certain length, a longer sentence should not be awarded for the purpose of giving him a period of training appropriate to his needs.[2] The proposal of the Committee was that, for 'those persistent offenders who are likely to profit by a period of training . . . a new form of sentence should be introduced and that courts should be given power, as an alternative to their present powers of ordering imprisonment or penal

---

[1] Report of the Departmental Committee on Persistent Offenders, 1932. Cmd. 4090. 1s. 6d.

[2] Case of Stanley Oxlade (13 Cr. App. R. 65), cit. p. 25 of the Report of the Departmental Committee.

servitude, to order, in suitable cases and subject to proper safeguards, detention for any period being not less than two nor more than four years with the object, not of imposing a specific penalty for a specific offence, but of subjecting the offender to such training, discipline, treatment or control as will be calculated to check his criminal propensities' (p. 16).

These were the proposals which in section 21 of the Act of 1948 found legislative form in the new sentence called 'corrective training', as follows:

'Where a person who is not less than 21 years of age:

'(a) is convicted on indictment of an offence punishable with imprisonment for a term of two years or more; and

'(b) has been convicted on at least two previous occasions since he attained the age of 17 of offences punishable on indictment with such a sentence;

then, if the court is satisfied that it is expedient with a view to his reformation and the prevention of crime that he should receive training of a corrective character for a substantial time, followed by a period of supervision if released before the expiration of his sentence, the court may pass, in lieu of any other sentence, a sentence of corrective training for such term of not less than two nor more than four years as the court may determine.'

We have already noted (p. 300) the procedure to be followed by the courts when offenders eligible for corrective training are before them.

Conditions of Detention

The problem here is related to the difficulty of distinguishing in principle between the confinement of an offender as a 'measure of security' and as a 'punishment', and a study of international practice in this matter published by the International Penal and Penitentiary Commission [1] confirms the statement of Dr. Grünhut that 'No existing system has succeeded in differentiating between ordinary prison routine and the régime applicable to preventive detention' (p. 399). The Finnish report says, 'It must be admitted that it is difficult to arrange the conditions so as to make much difference from those of ordinary prisoners, at least of those who are promoted to the higher stages. The loss of liberty in itself, the discipline, and the maintenance of order entail the essential restrictions.' The German report stresses the same point, adding that this necessary resemblance gives prisoners in 'internment' a sense of grievance which it is difficult to eradicate.

This problem was clearly envisaged by the Home Office when the

[1] *Recueil de Documents en Matière Pénale et Pénitentiaire*, Vol. XIII, 1. Staempfli et Cie, Berne, 1947.

draft Rules under the Act of 1908 were laid before Parliament, and was set out in the accompanying memorandum in the following terms:

'The present draft Rules have been prepared by the Prison Commissioners, who have done their utmost to carry out the intention of the Statute and to make the conditions of Preventive Detention as easy as circumstances will allow. But it should be clearly understood that no modification of the conditions which prevail in Convict Prisons can alter the essential fact that Preventive Detention is a form of imprisonment. Several hundred criminals of the most skilful and determined class will have to be confined for considerable periods within prison walls and to be controlled by a staff which cannot be made very numerous without undue expense. During their detention, they must always be either within locked cells or under close supervision; discipline must be firmly maintained; and hard work enforced. If there were neglect or relaxation in the supervision and discipline, it would inevitably lead to escape, or mutiny or vice.

'While, therefore, it is possible to maintain the conditions of sufficient food, adequate clothing, warmth and shelter, which all convicts enjoy, and to allow further relaxations in the way of conversation and association, of minor luxuries, and to some extent of recreation, the essential fact remains that, after every possible mitigation has been allowed, the convict is completely deprived of his liberty and is subject to constant supervision, control and compulsion in all that he does.'

The Departmental Committee, in its consideration of this question, described the appropriate régime as 'custodial and remedial'. By 'custodial' they appear to have intended first, safe custody, and second, the absence of specifically 'penal' or 'repressive' aspects of ordinary imprisonment: by 'remedial', reformative treatment in conditions which will be 'more strenuous' than ordinary prison conditions, and designed 'so far as practicable to fit them to take up life on release under normal social conditions' (paras. 40, 46, 48, 52, 65, and 160 (8)).

When it became necessary to reconsider the problem in 1948, two fresh factors were apparent. First, that in spite of the strong words of the Home Office memorandum of 1911, the system established in the first preventive detention prison at Camp Hill [1] had degenerated, no doubt owing to the dwindling of its population, until the atmosphere so far from being strenuous was rather that of a 'home for aged convicts', in which any attempt to secure firm discipline or hard work would have come as a serious shock. Second, since 1911, and indeed since the Report of 1932, the conditions of normal imprisonment had so far developed that practically all the features introduced into

---

[1] Subsequently transferred to Portsmouth, then to Lewes and finally to a wing of Parkhurst.

preventive detention in 1911 as 'mitigations' had become quite usual in all prisons. Nor was it easy to define the 'penal' or 'repressive' features of imprisonment which could be removed from preventive detention: it was still the case, as the Home Office had pointed out in 1911, that this system would be required to handle many hundreds of the most difficult and dangerous prisoners in the country, with whom there could be no relaxation either of security or of control.

Although a serious attempt was made to make a fresh approach to the problem in the light of past experience both at home and abroad, it will be apparent when we come to describe the present system that it differs even less from the long-term imprisonment of today than did the system of 1911 from penal servitude. Whether it will prove, as it is intended to prove, more 'remedial' than that system, we shall not know for many years. The solution to the difficulty of principle may perhaps be stated as follows. In a prison system in which there is a complete system of classification, providing different methods of training and forms of custody appropriate to different categories of prisoners, the provision of a régime appropriate to habitual criminals detained for very long periods requires no more than the application to the particular case of the general principles of the system, which include due regard to the purpose for which the sentence was awarded.

Length and Determination of the Sentence

Consideration of what is an appropriate length of sentence to be applied as a measure of prevention rather than of punishment inevitably raises the question of the 'indeterminate sentence'. This is not the place for a discussion of the merits of this system, since in spite of its established favour in America and some European countries the idea has never succeeded in naturalising itself in this country, save in the restricted sense of the Borstal sentence, where release is indeterminate within a statutory minimum of 9 months and a maximum of 3 years. For this evasive action there is good precedent in the Report of the Departmental Committee, which said (para. 50) 'We have considered the general question of the indeterminate sentence, but we do not think it necessary to enter into a discussion of the general considerations for and against a sentence wholly indeterminate in length, because we feel that the scheme we have suggested will give powers as extensive as any Court in practice will wish to use.'

Nevertheless the systems of the majority of European and American States have committed themselves to a sentence of indeterminate length for habitual criminals, and the law of some American States has gone even further, the Baumes Law of New York making the indeterminate sentence subject to a *minimum* of 15 years, and the Californian law imposing a life sentence from which release on parole is not permissible before 12 years. In these circumstances it is noteworthy that the Hague Resolution goes no further than to suggest that the 'measure' should be of a 'relatively indeterminate duration'.

The provisions of the Criminal Justice Act left it open to the administration, in framing the Statutory Rules governing corrective training and preventive detention, to allow the date of release to be (as in the Borstal sentence) indeterminate within the statutory maxima of 2 to 4 years for corrective training and 14 years for preventive detention; but the decision was deliberately taken not to do this in respect of corrective training. For preventive detention, however, which stands on a different basis, the Rules do provide, as we shall see, a modest concession to the Hague principle of 'relative indeterminacy'. English prison administrators have never felt that for adult prisoners, particularly those of the types now under consideration, the theoretical advantages of this system outweigh the practical disadvantages. If a man gets a sentence of 3 years' corrective training he knows from the start that he can get out in two years if he does not play the fool: he settles down to it and gets on with his training. If the date of his release is entirely vague, and dependent on the decision of some Board or Committee which will be taken on grounds that are never likely to commend themselves to a disappointed prisoner even if he understands them, he will be in a state of constant unrest, always 'sweating on the next Board' instead of concentrating on the job in hand, and thrown into a fury of resentment whenever A is lucky and B is not, whether B be himself or one of his friends. This does not make for 'a happy prison'. Nor is it certain that either the prison staff or a Board—with or without the advice of psychiatrists—on the basis of past records and of behaviour in prison conditions, could make enough good guesses about the behaviour of prisoners after release to justify a system of selective discharge in the face of these disadvantages.

There is the further difficulty that the courts might well view with distrust a system under which an habitual criminal might be released some years before the expiration of the period they had fixed as necessary for the protection of the public. Hitherto English law and practice have been such that this question has not become prominent. Where the sentence is wholly indeterminate it may be of primary importance; indeed one of the principal points of controversy in the discussion of the Hague Resolution centred on the question whether the date of termination of a preventive sentence should be fixed by a judicial authority or otherwise, and para. 10 (b) of the Resolution has the characteristics of the 'formule agréable' required to resolve such a situation.[1]

English practice in this matter, under the Rules of 1949 relating to

[1] The proceedings have not yet been published, and are not therefore available for reference: the writer is in a position to make this statement since he acted as President of the Section concerned.

preventive detention, is consonant with the latter alternative of 10 (*b*). It accords also with para. 7, which suggests that 'the final discharge of the habitual offender should, in general, be preceded by parole combined with well-directed after-care'. All prisoners discharged from corrective training or preventive detention, after the expiration of that part of their sentences specified in the Rules, are released on a conditional licence of the 'positive' type, which places them under the care and supervision of the Central After-Care Association.

(2) CORRECTIVE TRAINING

Corrective training is a new name in our penal terminology, but it does not describe any new method of treatment or training: it is the statutory application of an existing method to a category of prisoners selected not by the administrative classification system but by the Courts. This method is the system of training, formerly known as the Wakefield System, as it is now applied in the regional training prisons. But those who, under the normal classification system, are found suitable for the system practised in those prisons are carefully selected as being likely to respond to and co-operate in a system based on the maximum of trust and self-responsibility, and it was evident from the outset that among the wide variety of offenders who were likely to receive sentences of corrective training there would be many who would not be found suitable for training in these regional prisons: indeed this was foreseen by the Departmental Committee, which said 'we do not suggest that the Wakefield methods would be generally applicable to all Detention Establishments', and envisaged another type of establishment with the same purposes but with 'a régime of strict discipline and firm control' (paras. 58, 59).

Accordingly the Statutory Rules provide as follows:

'151. A sentence of corrective training shall be served in:

'(*a*) a regional prison set aside under sub-paragraph (ii) of paragraph (2) of Rule 7, or

'(*b*) some other prison or part of a prison set aside for the purpose.

'152. (1) When a prisoner sentenced to corrective training is received in a local prison his suitability for training in a regional prison shall be considered, and for this purpose he may be removed for special observation to a prison set aside under sub-paragraph (i) of paragraph (2) of Rule 7.

'(2) If the character or previous history of a prisoner are such that he appears to be unsuitable for a regional prison, he shall serve his sentence in some other prison or part of a prison set aside for the purpose.

'153. A prisoner sentenced to corrective training shall before removal to the prison in which he is to serve his sentence be treated as a prisoner of the Ordinary Class.'

Since it was of the essence of this scheme that the prisoners sent to regional training prisons, whether open or closed, should participate fully in the training without differentiation from the other trainees, it was necessary to secure most careful classification. Accordingly, Reading Prison was set aside as an Allocation Centre for the observation and allocation to the appropriate type of prison of all men sentenced to corrective training, and to Reading [1] they are removed as soon as possible after reception in a local prison. 'Here the causes of his anti-social behaviour will be studied in relation to his social history, mental and physical constitution, personality and temperament, by a selected staff, which includes psychologists and social workers. When the investigation is complete, his case is considered by a Board consisting of the senior members of the staff which, on the basis of the case-study, will decide his allocation in one of the following ways:

'(1) To an "open" regional training prison. Such an allocation postulates that he is likely, from the outset, to co-operate in his training and to respond to a system of trust and self-discipline.

'(2) To a "closed" regional training prison, where there is greater security and where the conditions of training can be graduated according to the response shown. These prisons have camps attached to them and suitable prisoners may obtain a remove to "open" conditions as their training proceeds.

'(3) To a corrective training prison, for those from whom there is little hope of spontaneous co-operation, at any rate at an early stage of the sentence, and whose training can only proceed under conditions of maximum security and close supervision.' [2]

On 30 January 1951 there were 367 men serving sentences of corrective training in regional training prisons, of whom 15 were in the open prison at Sudbury and 63 in the 'medium security' of The Verne. Their assimilation presented no special problems: one Governor in his Annual Report for 1950 said 'Nearly all the trainees received during the past six months have been carefully selected and are likely to benefit by positive training,' and another 'Nevertheless, the majority of the corrective training prisoners played their part as well as the Star prisoners. Eight became Leaders; and one of the best examples set was that by a corrective training prisoner who was the Leader in charge of a party of men employed on the construction of the Sports Ground.' We can therefore leave these men there, in the hope that the

---

[1] See Appendix K.   [2] *Prisons and Borstals*, p. 40.

numbers diverted from their careers of crime will be not less than those of the 'trainable Ordinaries' whom they have largely displaced.

As for the women, their much smaller numbers do not call for such an elaborate system. They all go to Holloway in the first instance, and there the great majority remain, since the only regional training prison for women is the open establishment at Askham Grange. However, by January 1951 eleven women had been found suitable for transfer to Askham.

It was thought by the draftsmen of the Statutory Rules to be desirable to set out, in the 'Special Rules for Prisoners Sentenced to Corrective Training', a definition of the training to be given in the regional prisons to prisoners so sentenced, although this training is not exclusive to corrective trainees: it is as follows:

'154. The training in a regional prison of prisoners so sentenced shall be designed to carry out the purposes specified in Rule 6, and shall include:

'(i) the provision of work which will so far as practicable help to fit them to earn their living after release, with technical training in skilled trades for suitable prisoners;

'(ii) special attention to education;

'(iii) the exercise of personal influence on the character and training of individuals by members of the prison staff;

'(iv) the provision of every opportunity for the development of a sense of personal responsibility, including for suitable prisoners training in open conditions.'

The next Rule carries into effect the above quoted intention of·the Departmental Committee in these terms:

'155. The training in other prisons set aside for the purpose of corrective training shall be designed to carry out the purpose of the foregoing Rule, with such modifications of method as are necessary for ensuring closer supervision and safe custody.'

These provisions, on the coming into force of section 21 in April 1949, presented the Commissioners with formidable difficulties. All their prisons were at that time full and overfull, and there was no more cellular accommodation to be had. There was no means of knowing the extent to which Courts would wish to use their new powers against the thousands of eligible candidates who would in due course be appearing before them, or of divining how many of those selected for the new treatment would be suitable for regional training and for how many it would be necessary for 'other prisons or parts of prisons' to be set aside. And it was clear that if the intention of the Rules was to be properly implemented these other prisons would have to combine with maximum security adequate accommodation and facilities for this type of training, and, where parts of prisons had to be used, adequate separation from other types of prisoner, which virtually ruled out all prisons built on the normal radial plan. It was out of the question to empty prisons or any parts of prisons in readiness for a new influx which might be either a trickle or a torrent.

However, in the course of 1949 and 1950 these difficulties were somehow overcome. In the eight months of 1949 sentences of corrective training were passed on over 1,000 men and 52 women, and in their Annual Report for that year the Commissioners were able to say that 'while at present all men and women sentenced to corrective training are receiving it, in full accordance with the Rules, in separate and suitable accommodation and without undue delay, it may not prove possible to preserve the situation throughout 1950 if the number of committals to corrective training increases without a corresponding fall in other categories of the prison population'. This situation was achieved by setting aside Chelmsford Prison and the former Nottingham Prison, then in use as a Borstal, two wings of Liverpool, two wings of Wormwood Scrubs, and a wing of Durham. Chelmsford had formerly been a training prison for young convicts, the accommodation at Durham and Liverpool had been centres for young prisoners, who were now concentrated at Stafford and Lewes, and the two wings at Wormwood Scrubs had been the Star prison for the south-east. All, therefore, provided the best available facilities for training and for segregation in separate blocks. This was the position in May 1950. For the rest of the year the corrective training population continued its steady increase and there was no diminution in the overall population. No further prison accommodation could be spared, so it became necessary to squeeze the Borstals again, and at the end of the year Camp Hill, the former preventive detention prison, was taken over as a corrective training prison. On the 30 January 1951 there were in these corrective training prisons.1,247 men,[1] and it was calculated that the accommodation thus provided would suffice until the flow of release of 3-year men began in April: thereafter the rate of discharge should balance the rate of intake, if that did not significantly change.[2]

On this date the distribution of corrective training prisoners was as follows:

Men
In Regional Training Prisons	. .	367
In Corrective Training Prisons	. .	1,247
In the Allocation Centre	. . .	129
In local prisons awaiting removal, etc. .		386
	Total	2,129

[1] At that stage only 80 had been removed to Camp Hill.
[2] See Appendix K.

Women

At Askham Grange	.	.	.	.	11
At Holloway	.	.	.	.	.	76
In local prisons	.	.	.	.	.	4
			Total	91

It would evidently have been better if all the corrective training prisons could have been separate institutions, but in the circumstances that was impracticable, and towards the end of the second year of the system it was possible to say that it had satisfactorily established itself in the available premises, in which the régime prescribed by the Rules was still being fully applied. Let us now look at the practical working of that régime, as it is set out above in Rule 152.

A prisoner sentenced to corrective training, as soon as he comes into his local prison, is given a special cell-card which aims to make him see his sentence in a proper light. It tells him why he has got this form of sentence, and warns him squarely that if he is charged with one more serious offence he may become liable to preventive detention for up to 14 years. There has been some evidence that these provisions have come as a considerable shock to the regular members of the criminal class, who had been under the mistaken impression that the main purpose of the Act was to make life easier for them.[1] Many of them in the early stages took it far from well, and were in no frame of mind to co-operate in any sort of training. However, it was thought well to leave no doubt in their minds as to their position, even at the cost of seeming to 'rub it in': if they could not be reformed, they might still be deterred. The next purpose of the card was to remove the illusion, prevalent at least in the early days of the system, that corrective training was a sort of 'Butlin's Borstal'—an idea too often fostered by well-meant but illconceived remarks made by some Courts in passing sentence. All Governors agree that an almost universal characteristic of these men is the desire to avoid any kind of effort of their own: they regard 'training' as a sort of beneficent influence to be applied by the staff for their good, but calling for nothing from them. They must, therefore, be told at the outset that while the staff is there to help them the outcome of the business is entirely 'up to them'. Those ideas are again pressed home during their stay at Reading, and it seems that most of the men leave there in a reasonable frame of mind and willing to make the best of it.

Arrived at his corrective training prison, the offender finds himself for the first 8 weeks 'out of stage'. This is a period of orientation during which the staff get to know him and he gets to know what will be expected of him. During this time he will be seen once or twice by the Reception Board (or Planning Board as some corrective training prisons

[1] See Appendix K.

call it) to discuss how he can best make use of his time in the prison in the light of what his future after release is likely to be. The representative of the Central After-Care Association will take part in this planning. While 'out of stage' he receives all the privileges which he would have in stage in a sentence of imprisonment except association for meals and evening recreation. When he comes into stage, he has all meals and the evenings in full association. Indeed from then on the conditions are very similar to those already described at Wakefield or Maidstone, except that there is less trust and closer supervision by the staff.

The industries available are all of a good class—there is no mailbag sewing—and in every prison there are some shops which provide 'technical training in skilled trades', though it is neither possible nor necessary to provide this for all of them. Many are incapable of learning.[1] Many more start by demanding 'vocational training' as of right, under the impression that it is a 'cushy job', and then do their best to get out of it when they find it means hard work and sustained effort. These are the men who all claim to be cooks in the winter and gardeners in the summer; who on discharge will be found work, given a kit of tools, and helped in every way; who will throw up their jobs a fortnight later and appear in court the following week plausibly pleading that they 'have never been given a chance'. However, there are many more who are willing and able to stick it, become good workmen, and write after they have settled in work to say how grateful they are for the help that was given them.

The next thing required by the Rule is special attention to education, and this is given as fully in corrective training prisons as in regional prisons. There is nothing to add here to what has already been said in Chapter Twelve (3).

To 'the exercise of personal influence by members of the staff' the greatest importance is attached. Assistant Governors are appointed to all these prisons who take special responsibility for the individual training of groups of men. It is their job to get to know and understand them as individual human beings, to fortify their weakness, encourage their strength, help them in their troubles inside and outside the prison, and try to make them face reality with courage and confidence.[2] In this difficult task they have the help and co-operation of all

---

[1] One Governor of a corrective training prison, in his Annual Report for 1950, estimated at 60 per cent those 'quite unfitted for Vocational Training through lack of manipulative ability, interest or mental capacity.'

[2] The Governor of a corrective training prison, in his Annual Report for 1950, mentioned the case of a man who failed at the end of a V.T. class after a promising start. The man 'eventually admitted that he had not wanted to pass because he thought the fact would be recorded and having been taught a trade might well be held against him should he have to face a court in the future. This reason may not have been valid but such a depressing and pessimistic outlook is not uncommon among corrective trainees.'

grades of the staff. It is usual for groups of men to have 'supervising officers', who are encouraged to study them and make full reports at regular periods on their development and behaviour, as do their instructors on their performance at work. This is possible because of the stability of the staffs in these prisons, which enables them to concentrate on the job of getting to know the men in their charge and so handling them as to get the best out of them.

The last requirement, to develop a sense of personal responsibility, cannot in the nature of these prisons and of the men who come to them be taken so far as in the regional prisons. A large proportion of them, having already passed most of their lives in Approved Schools, Borstals and prisons, are 'over-institutionalised', which means *inter alia* that while they normally give no trouble they can only be trusted as far as the staff can see them. But the régime is nevertheless made as open as is compatible with safe custody and proper control. The periods of association are observed rather than strictly controlled. At all the prisons but one there is ground on which football can be played at the week-ends, and though there are no camps, as at Wakefield and Maidstone, there are opportunities for work in parties outside the prisons for selected men towards the end of their sentences. And the whole effort of the staff is devoted to making the men face precisely this question of self-responsibility in their general attitude to life.

'In order not to jeopardise the success of this system, or to sacrifice the welfare of the majority of prisoners under training to the interests of the vicious or incorrigible few, strong sanctions are necessary against those who will not co-operate. To this end parts of Manchester (for men and women) and Pentonville (for men) have been set aside for the reception of prisoners removed as unsuitable for training in the ordinary corrective training prisons: here the Rules are applied to the extent practicable, but they are not eligible for corrective training stage privileges. Their cases are reconsidered by the Commissioners from time to time' (A.R. 1949, p. 32, para. 20). At the time of writing it has been necessary to exercise this sanction against some 50 men and two or three women, and the result has been most salutary. A proportion return in due course to a corrective training prison: the others appear to give little or no trouble—indeed many of them prefer the more routine and less exacting life of a local prison, and it may be that they are neither more nor less likely to offend again as a result of the change.

For women the principles are the same, and are applied in the same way. They are located in a separate wing at Holloway, under the specific charge of an Assistant Governor. Such differences as there are are such as are inevitable in the training of women and have been mentioned elsewhere. Thus there is no 'vocational training', but the industrial training follows the pattern described at Askham Grange, and if the evening education programme is less strenuous it is as much as these women are willing or able to take.

As we have seen, a corrective training prisoner is released on a conditional licence, after he has served a period which is fixed by the Rules as two-thirds of his sentence: his release may however be postponed as a punishment for an offence against discipline, for not more than 14 days at any one time on an award by the Governor or 6 months on an award by the Board of Visitors. This licence is of the 'positive' kind, which imposes on him a duty not only to lead an honest, sober and industrious life, but to place himself under the supervision of the Central After-care Association, and to obey any directions of the Association as to where he shall work and live, and as to when and how he shall report to his supervisor.

The Rules provide that 'From the reception of a prisoner in the prison in which he is to serve his sentence consideration shall be given, in consultation with the Central After-care Association, to the provision to be made for his welfare and supervision after release.' Accordingly the representative of the Association visits the prison at frequent intervals, sees all the men soon after their reception, and consults with the prison staff and the Ministry of Labour representative about their ultimate disposal. Towards the end of the sentence, when plans can be finalised, he will make contact with the Probation Officer who will take the case on after release, in accordance with the procedure described in Chapter Fifteen (3).

Behind a conditional licence there must be the sanction of recall, and on this the Rules provide as follows:

'159. (1) A prisoner sentenced to corrective training who has been recalled after release on licence shall on his return to prison in consequence of such recall remain in a local prison and be treated as a prisoner of the Ordinary Class until such time as the Commissioners, in their discretion, order his removal to a prison or part of a prison set aside for prisoners sentenced to corrective training.

'(2) A prisoner who has been so recalled shall not be eligible for release on licence until he has served two-thirds of the unexpired portion of his sentence.'

At the time of writing little experience has been gained of the operation of the recall procedure, though its use has already been necessary in a few cases. In general, other than in cases of reconviction, it is not intended to use it arbitrarily on a mere technical infringement of the conditions of licence: the Probation Officer reports to the Association, which makes a recommendation to the Commissioners, who consider on the merits of each case whether recall is necessary. No regular practice has yet developed as to return to a corrective training prison on recall; it is unlikely that in many of these cases further training will have a positive effect, and the presence of recalled men would not be helpful to the training prisons. At present these men are located in part of a local prison which has been set aside as a 'recall centre'.

It is not yet possible to assess or even to forecast the results of corrective training. So far the only discharges have been the earlier cases with 2-year sentences. Nor will it perhaps be fair to judge the system by the results of the first two or three years. Without doubt, in the early stages, a number of offenders have been received who were beyond the aid of any penal system. Nor can this be ascribed in any large measure to failure of the courts to pay regard to the recommendations made to them by Governors on behalf of the Commissioners. It may be hoped that with the enlargement of experience, and more expertise in assessment before reports are made to courts, fewer offenders will be recommended who are unlikely to profit from this form of training. But for the proper application of such expertise it would certainly be necessary for the methods adopted at Reading after sentence to be applied in Observation Centres before sentence, and to make this possible in every case changes would be necessary in the machinery of justice. Adequate reports can never be made on offenders who are only in custody for a few days before trial, or who are never seen because they are on bail.

One feature of the corrective training system which may be open to question is the variable sentence, of from 2 to 4 years, which it is open to courts to pass: during 1949 and 1950 the great majority of the sentences were for 3 years. While in principle it may seem right that the courts should have power to vary the length of training according to the needs of the offender, Governors of corrective training prisons have expressed the view that these variations cause much resentment among the prisoners, and that for their part, having no information as to what reasons influenced the courts, they are unable to offer any satisfactory explanations in their attempts to secure the co-operation of the disgruntled prisoners—nor do comparisons of the criminal records of the prisoners always avail to clear up these doubts. It has not been the practice for the reports made by the Commissioners to the courts to include any recommendation as to the length of training required.

The Prison Commissioners in their Annual Report for 1950 gave full information showing how the courts have used their powers, and the type of offender to whom the sentence of corrective training was applied, in the first full year of the system.

(3) PREVENTIVE DETENTION

The threefold problem confronting those charged in 1948 with devising a new system of preventive detention has already been defined. The system should conform with the penological principle that this sentence is a preventive, not a punitive measure. Nevertheless, it must provide maximum security and firm disciplinary control for a large number of men who are *ex hypothesi* difficult and potentially dangerous. And notwithstanding that they have received this sentence because they have proved impervious to all other forms of training, it must still seek to be 'remedial'.

The solution of the problem was complicated by the circumstances of the time. After the Act of 1908, a special preventive detention prison was built at Camp Hill in the Isle of Wight, neighbouring Parkhurst, and the administration had ample advance notice of the numbers it would have to deal with since all had first to serve a sentence of penal servitude. In 1948 there was no prospect either of building a new prison or of emptying an existing one. To be suitable for its purpose the prison selected must be one of those suitable for long-term prisoners and that limited the choice to Parkhurst or Dartmoor, since Camp Hill was then in use as a Borstal. Parkhurst, therefore, virtually chose itself, and it already housed the handful of men serving sentences under the Act of 1908. How many persistent offenders would be sent there, and how fast the flow would be, there was no means of knowing.

Accordingly the Act made no provision that preventive detention was to be served in a prison set aside for the purpose, and the Rules provided simply that the second stage of the sentence should be served in a central prison, where the preventive detention prisoners 'shall so far as practicable be accommodated in a separate part of the prison and shall not be allowed to associate with prisoners serving sentences of imprisonment except in the course of industrial or agricultural employment'. No principles of classification are affected, for these are all the same sort of men, whether they happen at the moment to be serving 7 years' imprisonment or 7 years' preventive detention. The situation moreover was likely to solve itself, for the rate of flow from the courts into preventive detention during 1950 was such as, if continued, would fill Parkhurst in 1951: already in 1950 it had become necessary to limit transfer to central prisons of long-term Ordinaries to those with sentences of over 4 years.[1]

The two assumptions on which the new system was based were that it was neither necessary in principle nor possible in practice that it should throughout be separate from and different from that for long sentences of imprisonment; and that instead of a normal progressive stage system, which seemed inappropriate to sentences of such length, there should rather be progress through a series of establishments of different types, each serving a particular purpose, with a total effect of breaking up the monotony of a long sentence.

[1] On 30 January 1951, 517 men and 18 women were in custody under sentences of preventive detention.

Accordingly the new Rules provided that a sentence of preventive detention should be served in three stages. The first stage should be served either in a regional prison set aside as an observation centre or in a local prison: it should last for not less than one year nor more than two years, and in this stage a prisoner 'shall be treated in all respects under the Rules applicable to prisoners serving a sentence of imprisonment'.

The original intention of this arrangement cannot be given full effect until the proposed observation centres have been set up. The purpose was that treatment should be preceded by diagnosis, and also perhaps by some measure of classification if this could be put to practical use by making two prisons available, possibly allowing for a more open régime for those for whom it might be appropriate. At present the whole of the first stage is passed in a local prison. This serves to induce a certain humility, to stamp out the idea prevalent among men of this type that they are a privileged class entitled to special consideration and peculiar rights, and to suggest to them rather that they have deservedly received a long sentence because of their bad records, and though they will shortly enjoy the very different conditions of the second stage they will not do so as of right but by earning them—and if they don't continue to deserve them they may find themselves back where they are, in the first stage.

The Rules provide that 'The Governor of the regional or local prison shall report to the Commissioners on the expiration of the first twelve months of the sentence, and thereafter at such intervals not exceeding three months as the Commissioners determine, on the suitability of the prisoner for removal to the second stage.' In practice, during 1950, men were almost invariably sent on to the second stage at Parkhurst after the first 12 months.

'The second stage' says Rule 163, 'shall be served in a central prison and the arrangements in this stage shall be such that the treatment of a prisoner (other than a prisoner in the penal grade) shall be not less favourable than that of a prisoner serving a sentence of imprisonment in a central prison.' This is a necessary statement of principle, but the practical conditions derive rather from the further provisions of Rule 165, viz:

'165. Arrangements shall be made under which a prisoner who has passed into the second stage may become eligible to earn privileges over and above those allowed to a prisoner serving a sentence of imprisonment, including:

   '(a) payment for work done at a higher rate,

   '(b) facilities for spending money earned in prison either at a prison store or on such articles, including newspapers and periodicals, purchased outside the prison as may be approved, '(c) the cultivation of garden allotments and the use or sale of the produce in such manner as may be approved,

'(d) the practice in the prisoner's own time of arts or crafts of such kinds and in such a manner as may be approved,

'(e) additional letters and visits,

'(f) association in common rooms for meals and recreation.'

The effect of these two Rules, as they are being put into effect at Parkhurst, is that a preventive detention prisoner, after his year in the first stage, moves straight into a minimum way of life which it would take him 4 years to reach on a sentence of imprisonment, and then only by consistent good conduct. He has his meals in association in a large dining-room specially provided for this purpose, and a period of each evening is spent in recreation in the same conditions. He spends, or need spend, very little time in his cell, but he can make it homely with things of his own, and keep in it the materials for any craft or hobby that, with approval, he may wish to practice. These conditions are similar to those of the final stage of a long sentence of imprisonment. But he can also earn a higher standard of wages than an ordinary prisoner: this is arranged not by any variation of the earnings scheme, but by an additional payment, related on a percentage basis to his actual earnings, which ensures first that his addition is related to his industry and second that he can earn more in total than if he were drawing the appropriate 'stage allowance' on a sentence of imprisonment. The canteen also offers him rather more facilities—he can, for instance, purchase through it not only periodicals but daily newspapers.

For work the prisoners have the full range of the useful industrial and agricultural trades of this prison, and every effort is made to interest them in educational activities in the evenings: classes are taken by L.E.A. teachers, as well as by voluntary teachers and members of the staff. These, apart from such normal activities as band, choir and gymnastics, include at the end of 1950 building construction, elementary and advanced English, current affairs, art, chess, and a dramatic class which stages periodical shows. Education is of course voluntary, and the Governor noted in his Annual Report for 1950 that less than half the men had applied for classes and only 18 per cent attended regularly: out of over 200 men only 15 were taking correspondence courses. It will be a necessary part of the régime to seek to overcome this disposition to enjoy any privilege except those which call for some effort. One weapon may well prove to be the arrangements for promotion to the Third Stage: if it comes to be understood that this is not automatic progress for the man who keeps out of trouble, but careful selection based on general attitudes and real progress, something may yet be done to make this system 'remedial' as well as 'custodial'.

Before passing to the Third Stage, it may be noted that the allotments mentioned in Rule 165 (c) are in fact available, though their number is limited and entails a waiting-list, and that the letters and visits under (e) are one letter a week each way and a visit once a fortnight (or additional letter and reply in lieu).

The arrangements for the Third Stage are novel, complicated and at present largely notional, since they were devised for men sentenced under the Act of 1948 who cannot become eligible for consideration for some time yet. The remaining 1908 Act men, however, are deemed to be serving their sentences under the Act of 1948 and the Rules of 1949 must therefore be applied to them so far as practicable.

The first feature to be noted of the Third Stage is that it introduces into the system, to a limited extent, the Hague principle of 'relative indeterminacy'. This is explained to the prisoners, on the cell-card issued in the prevention detention prisons, as follows:

'Admission to the Third Stage is not automatic: it depends on the view taken by the Advisory Board both of your conduct in the Second Stage and of your prospects on release. If you get into the Third Stage, you may become eligible for release on licence when you have served two-thirds of your sentence. If you stay in the Second Stage, you will not become eligible for release on licence till you have served five-sixths of your sentence.'

The Rules provide that 'the date of admission of any prisoner to the Third Stage shall not be more than twelve months before the date on which he will have served two-thirds of his sentence' and that 'the period to be served in the Third Stage shall not in any case be less than six months and shall not normally exceed twelve months'.

The Advisory Board for which the Rules provide, as the operative instrument of this system, is appointed by the Secretary of State, and is required to consist 'of three members of the Board of Visitors approved by the Secretary of State, and such other persons not exceeding four, of whom one may be a Commissioner or Assistant Commissioner, as the Secretary of State may appoint. The chairman of the Advisory Board shall be appointed by the Secretary of State.' The members additional to the Board of Visitors members so far appointed are a Commissioner, a Principal Probation Officer, and the Chairman, who is one of the Metropolitan Magistrates. The Board is required to meet at the prison once a quarter. In form it is 'advisory' to the Board of Visitors, on whom the Act places the duty of reporting to the Commissioners on the advisability of releasing a preventive detention prisoner on licence.

The further provisions of the Rules require that the Advisory Board, when a prisoner who has become eligible for consideration for the third stage is brought before them, 'shall consider not only his conduct in the second stage, but whether they expect to be able, within the period to be served in the third stage, to recommend his release on licence'. This should mean that this is not automatic promotion for the 'well-conducted prisoner': the Board will look not so much at what he does but at what he is, and what is the likelihood of his making a real effort after release to keep out of trouble—a difficult task indeed, but one which with this sort of sentence must be attempted, so long as the attempt continues to make the system in any sense 'remedial'.

If a man is not placed in the third stage on his first appearance, his case must be reconsidered at intervals of not less than 3 months, and once he has been placed in the stage, the question of his date of release on licence must be considered at each quarterly meeting of the Board.

Under this system therefore the indeterminate factor rests primarily on the decision of the Board as to admission to the third stage, and it normally affects the date of release only within the limits of two-thirds or five sixths of the sentence. This variation however may be considerable on the longer sentences, amounting to the difference between 2 years 4 months and 4 years 8 months on the maximum sentence.

This then is the administrative framework. We come now to the more interesting questions—What is the third stage? What are its purposes? How does it work? It is described in the Rules as follows:

'168. (1) The third stage shall be designed both to fit the prisoner for release and to test his fitness therefor, and may be served in such conditions of modified security as are available for the purpose, whether in connexion with a central prison or elsewhere.

'(2) During this stage every effort shall be made, by special industrial and social training and otherwise, to fit a prisoner to take his place in normal social life on discharge.

'(3) As and when suitable arrangements can be made, prisoners in this stage, or in the latter part thereof, may be permitted to live in conditions of modified security designed to form a transition from prison life to freedom.'

Since the practical implementation of the Rules lies in the future, it may here be discussed as a theoretical problem, the solution of which may take various forms. It is a problem as old as the transportation system, long discussed in principle and experimented with in practice in the prison systems of the world—how best to regulate the transition from prison to freedom. In our own system we have noted the various gradations to freedom of the transportation system, Sir Walter Crofton's 'intermediate stage' in the Irish penal servitude system, and the 'satellite camps' of more recent practice. At Camp Hill too, in its time as a preventive detention prison, there was an experiment of this sort, notable in its day, in that selected men towards the end of their sentence were allowed to live in 'parole cabins': these were a single-storey row of small rooms detached from the main prison, though within the wall, in which the favoured prisoners slept and kept house on their own. This however was an administrative arrangement and formed no part of the statutory basis of the system as does the third stage of today.

The processes involved in a complete solution of the problem appear to be as follows.

First, the psychological preparation of the prisoner for release, which requires that he should be brought face to face with all the problems that he will have to meet in adjusting himself both to normal life and to the initial period of supervision; that he should be made to think about them realistically; and that he should be brought to appreciate the best ways of meeting them.

Second, his vocational preparation for release, which requires that his industrial training should so far as possible be adapted to fitting him to earn a living in the occupation he seems likely to take up.

Third, his 'de-institutionalisation', which requires the 'tapering off' of supervision and control, and the gradual increase of personal responsibility, from the conditions of confinement through certain stages of supervised freedom to complete freedom.

Each of these features, under the general heading of 'pre-release procedure' has already received a good deal of consideration in different penal systems, particularly in the U.S.A.,[1] and the question was touched on in the last paragraph of Resolution III, 2, of the Hague Congress. And it should be said at once that while they are here discussed only in the context of preventive detention, their importance is beyond doubt in relation to all long-sentence prisoners.

The first presents little difficulty. It seems probable that the technique of group-discussion, under the leadership of suitable experts from the outside community, would provide the most effective approach.

The second is easier in principle than in practice. The resources of any prison for real industrial training in trades in which men of this type can usefully be trained must be limited, if a realistic view is taken of the prospects of their employment in the trades they have been taught. Nevertheless, whatever is reasonable and possible should be done.

The third is both the most difficult and the most interesting. On the basis of various practices already well established in different penal systems, one may conceive of a 'tapering off' in four stages.

First, the provision within the prison wall of a special 'pre-release', or in our preventive detention prison, 'third-stage' block, in which staff control would be reduced to the minimum and responsibility for a degree of self-government placed on the inmates. This would be a variation of the old 'parole-cabins'. This practice has been followed in certain American prisons, of which that of the Federal Penitentiary at

[1] Cf. *Handbook on Pre-Release Preparation in Correctional Institutions*, 1950, prepared and published by the American Prison Association.

Lewisburg, Pa., may be singled out for mention since the writer was able to see it in operation, and a well-developed example in the National Penitentiary at Buenos Aires was described in a paper presented to theHague Congress by the Argentine delegate (Question III, 2).

Second, weekly leave for the inmates of this block, after a certain time, to go for walks in the country, or visit the neighbouring town, without supervision and with money to spend. This is already usual in English Borstals, and is practised in France at the central prison of Loos, where since 1948 a bold experiment has been in progress to provide graduated steps to freedom for the relégués who are no longer transported to Cayenne.[1]

Third, removal to conditions, preferably in a hostel away from the prison, from which the inmates will go out to normal work like free men. This stage may be seen in various forms in different systems. The Cornton Vale Borstal in Scotland is in effect a hostel for selected boys from the parent Borstal who go out to work in various employments in the neighbouring town. At Witzwil in Switzerland the men live in a hostel on the edge of the extensive prison estate, near the village, but they work on the estate. At Loos the men go out to work in the town, but return to the central prison after the day's work.

Which of these forms, or which fresh combination of them, may eventually be adopted for the third stage of preventive detention it is not yet possible to say. If it is not possible to provide suitable new buildings, consideration may be given to adapting some large house as a hostel in a suitable urban centre, or—by a variation of the Loos system—to creating hostel conditions within a local prison, if one can be found in a good centre for employment with a suitable block or hut to spare.[2] But this conception may not be so easy to realise as it is to state. These men will only require employment in this centre for short periods, in no case more than a year. If they have been trained for a trade, work in that trade may not be available. And the special co-operation of local employers will have to be secured if any work is to be found at all. If these difficulties are too great, it may still be possible to fall back on the Witzwil model, employing the men on the prison farm and in other extra mural work, with perhaps a different form of remuneration.

It is to be understood that throughout these three phases the prisoner will still be serving his sentence under prison control: they are designed not only to prepare him for greater freedom but to test his fitness for it. The Rules therefore provide that 'The advisory board may at any

[1] 'Le Problème des Relégués,' par MM. Cannat, Gayraud, Vienne, et Vallien. Published in the *Revue Pénitentiaire et de Droit Pénal*, 1950, no. 1.

[2] There is an example of this method in the West German youth prison at Herford: the youths live in a pleasant hostel hut within the walls, and though they work in the prison they may go into the town without supervision.

time order the return of a prisoner to the second stage if it appears to them to be in the interests of himself or of others to do so, and the Governor, if he considers it necessary, may so order in his discretion subject to confirmation by the board at its next meeting.'

The fourth phase is the release on a conditional licence, the procedure for which, and for after-care, does not differ materially from that described for corrective training prisoners. This licence is also subject to the sanction of recall, the procedure for which is set out in the Rules as follows:

'173. (1) A prisoner who has been recalled from release on licence shall on his return to prison in consequence of such recall be placed in the first stage, and may at the discretion of the Commissioners be removed to the second stage within a period of twelve months from his return to prison as aforesaid:

'Provided that if the unexpired period of the sentence is less than two years, the whole of it may be served in the first stage.

'(2) A prisoner who has been recalled shall not again be eligible for release on licence before he has served five-sixths of the unexpired portion of his sentence and, if that period is completed in the first stage, the question whether he shall be released on licence shall be decided by the Commissioners on a recommendation of the Governor of the local prison.'

The time has not yet come for the establishment of any practice in this matter.

Finally, the Rules make provisions for the maintenance of discipline in a preventive detention prison which differ from those in a central prison. In addition to the normal punishments of restricted diet, close confinement and stoppage or reduction of earnings, the special privileges of a preventive detention prisoner may be suspended for up to 28 days for 'the abuse of any privilege or for an offence arising from the enjoyment of a privilege'.

A sanction peculiar to preventive detention is removal to the 'penal grade', which involves forfeiture of all association and privileges and accommodation in a separate part of the prison. The Rules provide, however, for the prisoner to continue his normal work in association unless the Governor 'considers it necessary to exclude him in the interests of the prisoner himself or of others'. So long as the prisoner does his normal work he is eligible to earn on the ordinary prison rate, i.e., excluding the special addition for preventive detention prisoners. It is also provided that 'The diet of prisoners in the penal grade may be restricted, so long as it is not reduced below a nutritional standard adequate for health and strength at normal work.' Removal to the penal grade is for so long as may be necessary up to 28 days on a Governor's award, and for so long as may be necessary without limit on an award by the Board of Visitors, though no prisoner may be kept for more than three months consecutively unless he has again been brought before the Board and the Board continues the order.

In addition to these punishments the Board of Visitors have power to defer, for a period of not more than 6 months at any one time, the date on which a prisoner will become eligible for release on licence.

Finally, 'This attempt to establish a system in which some attempt will be made to apply remedial methods which require the co-operation of the prisoners makes it necessary, as in corrective training, to have available severe sanctions for the minority who by refusal or failure to co-operate jeopardise the system and with it the good of the majority. Accordingly the Rules provide not only for a penal grade within the second stage, but for removal to the first stage in a local prison when a prisoner persistently misconducts himself and is not influenced by reprimand or punishment: this can only be done by the Commissioners on the recommendation of the Board of Visitors, and the Commissioners are required to reconsider such cases at least every three months and order return to the second stage as soon as they consider it expedient.' [1]

So far it has not been necessary to use this power.[2]

[1] *Prisons and Borstals*, p. 45.
[2] For later developments in preventive detention see Appendix K.

PART FIVE

YOUNG OFFENDERS

CHAPTER NINETEEN

THE PENAL SYSTEM AND THE YOUNG OFFENDER

(1) BEFORE 1908

'IN 1816,' says Sir E. du Cane, 'when the population of London was under a million and a half, there were in London prisons above 3,000 inmates under 20 years of age—half of these were under 17, some were 9 or 10, and 1,000 of these children were convicted of felony.' [1] What these prisons were like, and what must have been their effect on these young people, we have sufficiently considered. Nor did the other arms of the penal law make any concession to youth: many of the 1,000 convicted of felony would without doubt be hanged or transported. These conditions, however, were sufficiently known and abhorred to excite active and practical interest among people of good will from the earliest years of the century—indeed from the eighteenth century such interest had been moved to action at least of a preventive kind. In 1756 the Marine Society had established a school for waifs and strays and the children of convicts, to clothe and feed them and eventually send them to sea, and in 1788 the Philanthropic Society had established in London another school for the children of convicts.

In the first half of the nineteenth century this movement, entirely under the impulse of private benevolence, began to gather force. The first Ragged Schools were founded by John Pounds in 1818, but attention began now to turn to reformation as well as to prevention, and there began that struggle to keep young people out of prison altogether of which the penultimate stage was marked by the Criminal Justice Act 1948. This was the period in which the reformatories and industrial schools which have so honourable a place in the history of our penal system first developed: the latter were in origin rather preventive than corrective—they were intended to provide training in decent conditions for the lost children of the new industrial age, in the hope of preventing them from recruiting the ranks of criminals. The reformatories were

[1] Du Cane, p. 200.

for the correction of young people who had actually been convicted of crime. They were in no sense State institutions, but they were recognised and indeed encouraged, and their use was made possible by the flexible instrument of the Prerogative, under which a young offender would be granted a Pardon on condition of placing himself under the care of a Charitable Institution—though he would still be sent to the Colonies when his 'reformation' was deemed to have been effected.

One of the first of these reformatories was established at the Stretton Colony, in Warwickshire, in 1818; and Sir E. Ruggles-Brise tells us that when in 1847 a Parliamentary Committee was established to enquire into Juvenile Crime, the authorities of this Colony said in evidence that their experience had been that 'with prisoners between the ages of 16 and 20 . . . no less than 60 in every 100 might be permanently reformed and restored to Society.' [1] England was not alone in this field, and development here was much influenced by similar work in France and Germany, in particular that of the pioneer agricultural colony established at Mettray in France in 1839. It was on the pattern of Mettray, with its cottage 'family' system, that the Philanthropic Society in 1849 modelled their new Farm School at Redhill, Surrey, which from the time of its first Warden, the Rev. Sydney Turner, exercised a notable influence in reformatory development.

A series of Parliamentary Committees resulted in 1854 in the first Reformatory Schools Act, which enabled the Courts to commit offenders under 16 to a reformatory, after not less than 14 days' imprisonment, for periods of not less than 2 nor more than 5 years. The reformatories remained under voluntary management, but were now given legal powers to detain and control their charges, and were subject to certification by the Secretary of State and inspection by an Inspector of Prisons: Treasury contributions were also authorised. By a later Act of 1857 Local Authorities were enabled to contribute towards the establishment of reformatories, and power was given to license the inmates when they had served not less than half their period of detention. In that year also Sydney Turner was appointed an Inspector of Prisons, to devote himself to the reformatories, and in 1866 his post was converted into Inspector of Reformatories. But it was not until 1899 that the last link between reformatory and prison was severed by the repeal of the provision requiring a period of imprisonment as a preparation for reformatory treatment.

Industrial Schools were first placed in a legal setting by the Act of 1857, which, as amended by later Acts of 1860, 1861 and 1866, established them as primarily training schools for children under 14 years old who would today be described as 'care or protection' cases, including those beyond the control of their parents. Children under twelve who had committed offences might also be sent there. Local Authorities

[1] Ruggles-Brise, p. 89.

were also (in 1872) empowered to establish these schools. The State interest was similar to that for reformatories: there were Treasury contributions, and control by the Secretary of State through the approval of plans and rules, and by inspection. The Inspector of Reformatories, with Assistant Inspectors, now became Inspector of Reformatories and Industrial Schools. The scope of the Schools was extended by the Elementary Education Acts 1870 and 1876, which empowered justices to send children to Industrial Schools for truancy.

While this movement for keeping children out of prison was developing, the Government had taken an important step for dealing with those in prison. The Parkhurst Act of 1838, observing in its preamble that it would be 'of great public advantage that a prison be provided in which young offenders may be detained and corrected, and receive such Discipline as shall appear most conducive to their Reformation and to the Repression of Crime', enabled the buildings of the former military hospital at Parkhurst in the Isle of Wight to be used for such a prison. Here were sent offenders under 18 sentenced to transportation, to be subject for a few years to what Sir E. du Cane described as 'a system of treatment distinguished from that applied to adults, by being composed more largely of the reformatory than the strictly penal element' [1]; there was also some classification, those under 10 years old forming a junior class. In due course the inmates might be either pardoned on condition of going to a reformatory, or transported to the Colonies. The Gladstone Committee found that it was 'almost impossible to ascertain to what extent the Parkhurst Government Reformatory was a success. It died a natural death after the passing of the Reformatory Acts'.

The system of reformatories and industrial schools thus established did succeed, in the latter part of the nineteenth century, in keeping a very large number of young people out of prison—but a very large number also came into the prisons: Sir E. du Cane states (p. 201) that 'there were on 31 March 1884 only [sic] 275 prisoners under 16 years of age, and 3,226 between 16 and 21', while on 31 March 1894 there were 100 prisoners under 16 and 2,226 between the ages of 16 and 20.[2] Those under 16, officially known as 'juveniles', were by the Prisons Act 1865 required to be kept separate and given special treatment.

The Gladstone Committee did not devote a great deal of attention to the question of juveniles. They did not find 'practicable or desirable' the suggestions made by several witnesses 'in favour of the total discontinuance of committing this class of offenders to prison'. They did however speak strongly about their treatment in prison: 'We think that the ordinary prison discipline and regulations should not be applied to juveniles, but that governors and the visiting committees should be made responsible for their treatment subject to general instructions which should be issued by the Secretary of State. The

[1] Du Cane, p. 202. [2] Report of Gladstone Committee, p. 29.

principle of these instructions should be that each child should be treated according to its own peculiarities of temperament; that the fact of imprisonment should be the main deterrent; and that treatment should be altogether of a reformatory character. We think that the age of 16, above referred to, should be raised to 17.'

It was many years before this suggestion of the Committee as to raising the age of 'criminal majority' was implemented, although as Sir E. Ruggles-Brise tells us, there had been strong pressure as early as the 'eighties' to have it raised to 18. He adds the interesting comment that 'The age of 16 was adopted at that time by universal consent for no other reason, so far as I can gather, than that it was the age of "criminal majority" in the French Penal Code, and it had become notorious owing to the success of the French Colony of Mettray, established in the "thirties" and which prescribed 16 as the age of "discernment" under French Law.' [1]

The Committee were much more concerned with the next higher age-group, that of 16–21. 'It is certain that the ages when the majority of habitual criminals are made lies between 16 and 21. And from the interesting figures supplied by Mr. Merrick, the Chaplain of Holloway Prison, the most fatal years are 17, 18 and 19. This is corroborated by other experienced witnesses. It appears to us that the most determined effort should be made to lay hold of these incipient criminals and to prevent them by strong restraint and rational treatment from recruiting the habitual class. It is remarkable that previous inquiries have almost altogether overlooked this all-important matter. The habitual criminals can only be effectually put down in one way, and that is by cutting off the supply.' They were impressed by the Redhill Reformatory system, and recommended that the age of admission to reformatories should be raised from 16 to 18: this proposal was not followed. Their next proposal however, was more fruitful, since it developed directly into the Borstal system as it is today. It deserves the respect of full quotation.

'We are of opinion that the experiment of establishing a penal reformatory under Government management should be tried. It should be begun on a moderate scale, but on a design which would allow of large expansion if the results were proved to be satisfactory. The court should have power to commit to these establishments offenders under the age of 23, for periods of not less than one year and up to three years, with a system of licences graduated according to sentence, which should be freely exercised. In the event of any inmate of a reformatory being contumacious and beyond the power of the managers to control, power should be given to a court of summary jurisdiction, on cause being shown by the managers, to transfer him or her to a penal reformatory for a period not exceeding the unexpired portion of

1 Ruggles-Brise, p. 90.

the term which was to be served in the reformatory. And power should also be vested with the Secretary of State similarly to transfer prisoners under 23 from prisons to the penal reformatory, if satisfied that the treatment there would be more suitable to the particular case.

'The penal reformatory should be a half-way house between the prison and the reformatory. It should be situated in the country with ample space for agricultural and land reclamation work. It would have penal and coercive sides which could be applied according to the merits of particular cases. But it should be amply provided with a staff capable of giving sound education, training the inmates in various kinds of industrial work, and qualified generally to exercise the best and healthiest kind of moral influence. Special arrangements ought to be made for receiving and helping the inmates on discharge. It would be necessary to adopt a careful system of classification, which should limit the number of inmates in each building, as at the Redhill Reformatory, in order to insure proper individual treatment.

'We look upon this plan, in conjunction with the raising of the age for admission to reformatories, as the best proposal that is open to us for the rescue of young offenders. Under the present system numbers of them come out of prison in a condition as bad or worse than that in which they came. They go out with the prison taint on them. The available prison staff and the rigid system of prison discipline, without any fault on the part of the officials, preclude the possibility of bringing to bear on the prison population the moral suasion and the healthy practical advice which we think could be exercised by a trained and selected staff in the penal reformatory. The inmates upon discharge would be provided for and looked after much as in the case of the lads and girls who leave reformatories, and if they relapsed into crime it would be of their own deliberate choice, in spite of every effort to save them, and they would subsequently be exposed to the far sterner penalties of prison life.' [1]

It is also fitting that Sir Evelyn Ruggles-Brise, the founder of the Borstal system, should now take up the story in his own words.[2] 'The proposal to found a State, or Penal Reformatory, confirmed and emphasised the opinion that had been rapidly gaining ground, both in England and abroad, and especially in the United States, that *up to a certain age*, every criminal may be regarded as *potentially* a good citizen: that his relapse into crime may be due either to physical degeneracy, or to bad social environment: that it is the duty of the State at least to try and effect a cure, and not to class the offender off-hand and without experiment with the adult professional criminal. . . . I

[1] *Gladstone Committee*, pp. 30, 31, para. 84 (*b*).
[2] The following quotations are from Chapter 8 of *The English Prison System*.

obtained the authority of the Home Secretary, Sir M. Ridley, who was in warm sympathy with my views, to go to the United States in 1897 to study at Elmira the working of what is known as the American "State Reformatory System". The annual reports of the authorities at Elmira had begun to attract considerable attention in Europe. The American System classified as youths all persons between the ages of 16 and 30. While we classified our boys as adults, the American adopted the converse method, and classified his adults as boys. I thought myself that the truth lay midway between these two systems, between the system that ends youth too early and that which prolongs it too late, between the voluntary system of England and the State Reformatory System of the United States. The point I was aiming at was to take the "dangerous" age—16–21—out of the Prison System altogether, and to make it subject to special "*Institutional*" treatment on reformatory lines. I was impressed by all that I saw and learnt at the principal State Reformatories of America, at that time chiefly in the States of New York and Massachusetts. The elaborate system of moral, physical, and industrial training of these prisoners, the enthusiasm which dominated the work, the elaborate machinery for supervision of parole, all these things, if stripped of their extravagances, satisfied me that a real, human effort was being made in these States for the rehabilitation of the youthful criminal. It was on my return that, with the authority of the Secretary of State, the first experiments were begun of the special treatment, with a view to the rehabilitation of the young prisoners, 16 to 21, in London Prisons.'

The next stage in this experiment was to give it 'a local habitation and a name'. Near the village of Borstal in Kent, on a hill above the Medway two miles from Rochester, stood one of the old 'public works' convict prisons built in connection with the prison at Chatham. 'There were still,' says Sir Evelyn, 'a few convicts there; but there was available space for an experiment, which it was decided to make (and which is described later) for the special location and treatment on reformatory lines of young prisoners, 16–21, selected from the ordinary Prisons, where the length of sentence afforded a reasonable time for the application of the system. The title "Juvenile-Adult" was invented to describe the class—too old for commitment to Reformatory Schools, and too young to be classified with the ordinary grown-up criminal.' The grounds on which the name of this prison was first attached to the system are of considerable interest, in the light of the regular but fruitless attempts that have since been made to find for it some other name. 'At that time, there was a confusing medley of appellations; and children, young persons, and youthful offenders, were all jumbled together in the same category. The specific proposal was to deal with the age, 16 to 21, and it was decided, in order to emphasise this fact and make a clear distinction between this age and all other ages, to make use of the word "Borstal", that is, the name of the village where the experiment was being carried out. I think that this appellation has been singularly fortunate in its results, as it has made it quite clear that we are not dealing with the youthful offender as usually conceived, that is, a boy, or even a child, who may have lapsed into some petty or occasional delinquency, and who was being sufficiently provided for by the Reformatory School Acts and by the Rules concerning juvenile offenders in prisons. Our object was to deal with a far different material, the young hooligan advanced in crime, perhaps *with many previous convictions*, and who appeared to be inevitably doomed to a life of habitual crime.'

The system which Sir Evelyn established in this 'juvenile-adult' prison at Borstal is thus described. 'The object of the System was to arrest or check the evil habit by the "*individualisation*" of the prisoner, mentally, morally and physically. To the exhortation and moral persuasion of a selected staff, we added physical drill, gymnastics, technical and literary instruction: inducements to good conduct by a system of grades and rewards, which, though small and trivial in themselves, were yet calculated to encourage a spirit of healthy emulation and inspire self respect. Elaborate rules for giving effect to the system were introduced by the Authority of Parliament, but at this stage, Parliament had not recognised the system in any other way, and *we had to work within the limits which existing Penal law afforded*: that is, the cases we dealt with were by the *transfer* of young prisoners of this age, who happened, for their particular offence, to have been awarded sentences of imprisonment for *six months and upwards*. It soon became clear that the *element of time*, that is, a longer sentence than the law permitted, was essential for the success of the scheme. Experience showed that something may be done in twelve months, little or nothing in a shorter period, that the system should be one of stern and exact discipline, tempered only by such rewards and privileges as good conduct, with industry, might earn: and resting on its physical side on the basis of hard, manual labour and skilled trades, and on its moral and intellectual side on the combined efforts of the Chaplain and the Schoolmaster. Such a sentence should not be less than three years, conditional liberation being freely granted, when the circumstances of any case gave a reasonable prospect of reclamation, and when the Borstal Association, after careful study of the case, felt able to make fair provision on discharge.'

The translation of this system into law, and the subsequent developments, up to the Second World War, in the Borstal system and the other methods which had been and were to be provided by Parliament for the treatment of young offenders, are described in the following section.

(2) 1908–1938

The years 1907 and 1908 laid the foundation stones of the contemporary penal system in England: they were three—the Probation of Offenders Act 1907, the Children Act 1908, and the Prevention of Crime Act 1908, of which the first or Borstal part only will now concern us. The probation system is not for discussion here, except to note its enduring value in enabling the courts to provide suitable treatment for young offenders [1] without imprisonment or detention in a training institution.

The Children Act, popularly known at the time as The Children's Charter, ranged over the whole field of child protection, and in the particular field of delinquency clarified and codified the law relating to reformatory and industrial schools, established juvenile courts, and took further steps towards restricting the imprisonment of young offenders and providing alternative methods of dealing with them. The Act began by establishing the definition of a 'child' as a person under the age of 14 years, and of a 'young person' as one who was 14 years of age and over but under 16. It then provided that a child should not be sentenced to imprisonment or committed in default of payment of a fine, etc.; that a young person should not be sentenced to penal servitude; and that a young person should not be sentenced to imprisonment, or committed in default 'unless the court certifies that the young person is of so unruly a character that he cannot be detained in a place of detention provided under this Part of this Act, or that he is of so depraved a character that he is not a fit person to be so detained'. All persons under the age of 16 apprehended by the police and not released on bail, and all such persons remanded or committed for trial by the courts and not released on bail, were also to be sent to 'places of detention', except on a certificate of unruliness or depravity. These 'places of detention' were to be provided by police authorities for every petty sessional division: they might be in specially provided premises or in any existing premises suitable for the purpose, the 'registered occupier' being the responsible custodian.

The Act made no change in the age of 'criminal majority', nor in the ages qualifying for admission to a reformatory, which remained at 12 and over but under 16, or to an industrial school, which remained at under 14. The treatment of young offenders under 16, on the basis of these statutory provisions and under the guidance of a new department of the Home Office called the Children's Branch, developed steadily and without further legislation for the next twenty-five years. At the outbreak of the First World War, there were 223 reformatory and industrial schools, containing 25,357 children and young persons.[2]

For those whom Sir Evelyn Ruggles-Brise had called juvenile-adults,

---

[1] And of course for adults also. [2] *Making Citizens*, p. 9.

aged 16–20, provision was made by Part I of the Prevention of Crime Act 1908. In 1906 Sir Evelyn, satisfied with the success of his Borstal experiment, had advised the Home Secretary that if its fruits were to be harvested it would be necessary to introduce legislation to give the courts power to commit suitable offenders of this age-group direct to a 'juvenile-adult reformatory', for a period long enough to allow of their training, and subject to release under supervision on a conditional licence. It was at this time that Mr. Herbert Samuel, now Lord Samuel, joined the Home Office as Parliamentary Under-Secretary of State, and became responsible for the introduction of the Bill to effect these purposes. He has told in his *Memoirs* (p. 53) how he firmly refused to sponsor anything called a 'juvenile-adult reformatory', how no other suitable name could be found, and how in the end he suggested 'Borstal Institutions'. So 'Borstals' they became, and in spite of recurrent attacks on the name, Borstals they still are—among the few public institutions to survive contemporary euphemism in names of any embarrassing connotation. It may be doubted whether those who work in Borstals regret this; for them, as for all who understand their work throughout the world, it is a name of honourable significance which should not be lightly put aside.

It is unnecessary at this stage to describe in detail either the legal basis of the sentence of Borstal Detention as it was laid down in 1908 or the Borstal system as it was developed in the following years, since the Act of 1908 was repealed by the Criminal Justice Act of 1948, which will be fully considered in the following section, and the system as it works today will be described in the following chapters. To fit it into the general picture of the treatment of young offenders up to the Second World War, it is sufficient to say that it provided a method of correctional training for persons aged 16–20 who had been convicted of indictable offences for which they might be sentenced to imprisonment, and who 'by reason of criminal habits or tendencies, or association with persons of bad character' appeared to the courts to require 'detention under penal discipline'. As subsequently amended by the Criminal Justice Administration Act 1914, section 11, the Act provided for a term of not less than two years nor more than three years, to be followed by a year under supervision. Within the maximum imposed by the court, however, the sentence was 'indeterminate', since the Prison Commissioners had power to release a boy on a conditional licence after six months, a girl after three.

It is sufficiently clear from the phraseology of the section that those who framed it still had in mind Sir Evelyn's 'young hooligans well advanced in crime', and that 'shades of the prison house' still hung about their conception of the appropriate treatment. Indeed of the three Borstals for boys first taken into use, two were old convict prisons—Borstal and Portland: the third, at Feltham in Middlesex, was one of the earliest local authority industrial schools. All three buildings were substantially altered to adapt them to their new use. For girls provision was made in the premises of the former State Inebriate Reformatory within the high wall of the women's prison at Aylesbury. This was still the position when the writer joined the Prison Commission in 1925, to find Alec Paterson leaving in his colleagues' rooms large cards inscribed with the words 'Borstalium quartum aedificandum est'. When that fourth Borstal came to be built it embodied all that enlargement of the spirit of Borstal for which Paterson was especially responsible. He substituted self-discipline for 'penal discipline', introduced the house system, and made the house-master the centre of his staff—'It is men,' he said, 'not buildings, that will change the hearts and ways of misguided lads.'

The new Borstal, at Lowdham Grange in Nottinghamshire, embodied Paterson's view that 'you cannot train men for freedom in a condition of captivity'. In the summer of 1930 took place the historic march from Feltham to Lowdham of a party of Borstal boys, who camped on the hill-side and began to build their own institution—without walls, cells, locks or bars. They are still adding to it. Lowdham was the first and last Borstal to be built for its purpose. With two exceptions all those to come were established in hutted camps or large country houses. In 1938 there were nine Borstals for boys (including a special wing of Wandsworth Prison for those who had been recalled from licence or had seriously misconducted themselves in their institutions) and Aylesbury for girls. At the end of the year there were over 2,100 boys in the male Borstals, and the provision of a new institution was in preparation.

We must now retrace our steps to 1927, when the Report of the Departmental Committee on the Treatment of Young Offenders provided a fresh point of departure of which the consequences were not exhausted until the Criminal Justice Act 1948. Their recommendations ranged over the whole field—the juvenile court, bail and remand, probation, fines, whipping, detention, reformatory and industrial schools, imprisonment, Borstal, capital punishment and after-care; and subsequent legislation in this field has been largely concerned with translating them into practice.

The Children and Young Persons Act 1933 revised the constitution and procedure of juvenile courts, raised from seven to eight years the age below which a child cannot be adjudged guilty of a criminal offence, and redefined a 'young person' as one over 14 and under 17 years of age, bringing all children and young persons within the jurisdiction of the juvenile court.

The distinction between reformatory and industrial schools was abolished, and they were renamed 'approved schools'. The normal minimum age for committal was raised to 10, the maximum to 17:

this gave an overlap of the Borstal age of 16–21 of one year, thus allowing the courts a discretion in the cases of the more mature young people of sixteen. Here we must leave these partners of the Borstal system, junior in their material but senior in their experience, observing only that a friendly co-operation is maintained between the Children's Department and the Prison Commission, and that regular visits are arranged between Headmasters of Approved Schools and Governors of Borstals and their staffs. Those who would learn more of the schools should read the full account of their work in the Home Office booklet called *Making Citizens*.[1]

The restrictions on the imprisonment of children and young persons imposed by the Children Act 1908 were re-enacted in relation to children and young persons as now re-defined, with the effect of extending this special protection from those under 16 to those under 17. The age below which sentence of death could not be pronounced was rasied to 18, and in lieu of that sentence there was substituted one of 'detention during His Majesty's pleasure'—the one truly indeterminate sentence which our law provides. For certain grave offences of violence against the person by a child or young person 'the court may sentence the offender to be detained for such period as may· be specified in the sentence; and where such a sentence has been passed the child or young person shall, during that period, notwithstanding anything in the other provisions of this Act, be liable to be detained in such place and on such conditions as the Secretary of State may direct'. In practice such an offender may be sent to an approved school, a Borstal or a prison according to the circumstances of the offence, his age, maturity, character, mental condition and all other relevant considerations.

For the 'places of detention' of 1908 the Act substituted 'remand homes', the provision of which for their areas was made a duty of county and county borough councils, and detention for not more than one month in a remand home, as a punishment in place of imprisonment, was by section 54 substituted for detention in a 'place of detention'. Since 1933 therefore all young persons committed to prison by courts of summary jurisdiction, whether on remand or under sentence, have come under a certificate of unsuitability, through 'unruliness or depravity', for detention in a remand home.

Certain other recommendations of the Young Offenders Committee, including those relating to Borstal, were gathered together in the Criminal Justice Bill introduced by Sir Samuel Hoare (now Lord Templewood) in 1938. The outbreak of war in 1939 put an end to this Bill, the provisions of which were with certain modifications included in the Criminal Justice Act of 1948.

---

[1] Stationery Office 1945. Price 1*s*.

(3) THE CRIMINAL JUSTICE ACT 1948

With the general scope of this Act we have already dealt. In the field of the treatment of young offenders it supplements the Children and Young Persons Act 1933 by taking what may prove to be the final steps, so far as concerns legislative action, in the long-drawn process of removing young people under 21 from the scope of the prison system.
These steps may be summarised as follows:

'(1) To provide some place other than a prison to which courts may send, before conviction, persons between the ages of 17 and 21 and young persons under 17 who are unsuitable for detention in remand homes.

'(2) To prohibit altogether the imprisonment of persons under 15 years of age; to limit the imprisonment of young persons under 17 to those more serious cases which are dealt with in the higher courts; and to restrict still more closely the imprisonment of persons between the ages 17–21 by courts of summary jurisdiction.

'(3) To provide alternative methods of treating young offenders for less serious offences, so as to avoid short sentences of imprisonment.

'(4) To remove, in the qualifications for Borstal training, the limitation to criminal habits and associations.

'(5) Finally, when the alternative methods of dealing with young offenders have become available, to extend from 17 to 21 the age of complete prohibition of imprisonment for young offenders found guilty by courts of summary jurisdiction.'

The eventual enforcement of complete prohibition of the imprisonment of persons under 21 by summary courts is left to the Secretary of State, who may proceed by Order in Council when he is 'satisfied that the methods, other than imprisonment, available for the treatment of offenders afford to courts of summary jurisdiction adequate means of dealing with the persons to whom the Order relates'. It is left open to the Secretary of State to proceed in this matter step by step as regards age, and to deal with one sex at a time.

If, therefore, we may assume a time when the Secretary of State has exhausted his powers under this provision, the position will be that no person under 15 can be sentenced to imprisonment at all, and no person under 21, convicted or unconvicted, can be sent to prison by a court of summary jurisdiction. The only persons under 15 in prison will then be those sentenced under the Children and Young Persons Act 1933 to detention, whether at His Majesty's Pleasure in lieu of the capital sentence [1] or for grave offences of violence against the person, in so far as the Secretary of State may direct their detention in prison: the only persons between 15 and 21 will be those convicted by the higher courts of serious offences for which the court finds, and states as a considered opinion, that no other method of dealing with them is appropriate. Whether Parliament will ever find it both desirable and practicable to go beyond that stage can now be no more than a matter of speculation. Whether and when that stage may be reached at all depends first on the extent to which the alternative methods can be made available. It may be also, though this is perhaps a question of the interpretation of the statute, that it will depend on the view formed by the Secretary of State of the success of those methods—they may well have been provided, but he may nevertheless not be satisfied that they are 'adequate'.

Let us therefore proceed to consider, one by one, what those methods will be in so far as they go beyond cautions, bindings over and fines: all those, in short, which involve some limitation of the freedom of the offender. [2]

The first group concerns young people who are not yet found guilty. For those under 17 there are the existing remand homes, which by section 49 are brought under closer Home Office control, and empowered to provide 'facilities for the observation of any person detained therein on whose physical or mental condition a medical report may be desirable for the assistance of the court in determining the most suitable method of dealing with the case'. For those of 17 and over, there is to be a new type of institution called a remand centre, which will serve the same purpose as a remand home, but will be provided by the Secretary of State, not by local authorities. To these centres also may be sent the 'unruly and depraved' from remand homes, provided they are 14 years old or over, and any of 14 or over who require special observation for which the local remand home does not provide facilities. They will perform the present function of the prisons in respect of the young offenders concerned.

For those found guilty, perhaps the mildest form of treatment at the disposal of the courts will be an entirely novel method known as Attendance Centres. The idea behind the Attendance Centre is 'deprivation of leisure' without removal from home: the offender must attend at the place specified, at such hours, not exceeding 12 in all, as will not interfere with his school or working hours, and not more than once a day nor for more than 3 hours at once. Physical exercise and useful occupation will be provided.

[1] This is now covered by section 16 of the Act of 1948.
[2] The following order of consideration is one of convenience only, and is not intended to carry any implications as to the manner in which they may be used by the courts.

The next group of treatments rests on the probation system, and is in three tiers, the first being the normal order placing the offender for a stated period under the supervision of a probation officer. The second carries the idea of deprivation of leisure one stage further, by making it a condition of the order that the offender shall reside in a probation hostel, from which he will go out to school or work. The third involves complete deprivation of liberty, by making it a condition of the order that he shall reside in a probation home, where he will both live and work: these probation homes are the 1948 equivalent of the institutions proposed by the 1938 Bill under the name of Howard Houses, which were to perform a similar function but were not linked with the probation system.

While the Bill of 1948 was under consideration, the view was expressed by many magistrates, and supported by the Advisory Council on the Treatment of Offenders, that it was necessary to have some sanction behind these milder measures that had not been provided in the Bill of 1938. It was argued that many young people come before the courts who can be taught respect for the law only by something in the nature of a 'short sharp shock': it is not yet necessary or desirable to send them away for residential training in an approved school or Borstal, but they laugh at probation, and will not stay or behave in a home or hostel. For these the only measure short of prison had been detention for a month in a remand home under section 54 of 1933, and that was not regarded as adequate. This procedure in fact had been little used, and almost the only information available about it is a survey of the Liverpool experience, issued under the auspices of the School of Social Sciences of Liverpool University, by Mr. J. H. Bagot.[1] Mr. Bagot's conclusions on the value of this form of treatment were that 'in general the results may be considered disappointing', but that punitive detention 'as a form of treatment has its uses'; these however would be more effective in a separate institution devoted to this purpose. He quotes with approval Mr. John Watson's remarks on this question: 'In theory it would seem that this provision meets the case where no long period of training is called for, and all that is necessary is a short sharp punishment to bring the offender to his senses and act as a deterrent. There is a very definite demand for some form of treatment of this kind, which would be of short duration but thoroughly unpleasant, and available as a penalty for minor offences, including minor breaches of probation. What is needed is a small local establishment in which the discipline is of the sternest, the food of the plainest, where everything is done "at the double", and where there is the maximum of hard work and the minimum of amusement; the kind of establishment a young offender would not wish to visit twice, and of which he would paint a vivid picture on his return home.'[2]

[1] *Punitive Detention*, 1944, Cape.   [2] *The Child and the Magistrate*, 1942, Cape.

It was precisely such an establishment as Mr. Watson describes that was envisaged by the Advisory Council, and in due course was provided for in the Act of 1948 under the name of 'detention centre'. These centres are to be provided by the Secretary of State, and in a case where a court would have power to impose imprisonment it may commit to one of them a person who is not less than 14 but under 21 years of age for a term of three months, or in 'special circumstances' (which the section does not define) not more than 6 months. There is a still further qualification in respect of offenders of compulsory school age, for whom the term may be reduced to not less than one month.

Committal to a detention centre is hedged about with conditions to prevent the committal of persons who have previously been sentenced to imprisonment or Borstal training, or have previously (if aged 17 or more) been sent to a detention centre, and to ensure that this method is not used 'unless the court has considered every other method (except imprisonment) by which the court might deal with him and is of opinion that none of those methods is appropriate'.

This power will become available to courts when the Secretary of State has notified them that detention centres are available for the reception of their committals. When a court has been so notified, it will no longer have power to commit young persons to a remand home under section 54 of 1933: meanwhile that section remains in force.

Finally, if the time comes when a young offender must be sent away for prolonged residential training, the court may send him to an approved school if he is under 17, or to a Borstal if he is not less than 16 and under 21. With approved schools we have already dealt, and with the Borstal system, as it stands after the Act of 1948, we shall deal in subsequent chapters.

Of these various alternatives to prison, only those institutions to which the Prisons Acts apply, and which therefore are placed under the control of the Prison Commissioners, come within the scope of this book: these are the remand centres, detention centres and Borstal institutions. Probation hostels and homes existed before 1948, and are controlled by the Probation Division of the Home Office: the provisions of 1948 may however extend their use and value. Attendance centres come under the Children's Department of the Home Office: three have already been set up by way of experiment, but no report is yet available as to their methods and success.[1]

So far no remand centres have been established, nor has any provision been made for doing so in the near future. If these centres are to do the work required of them, they will be not only places of safe custody but laboratories of research into the causes and treatment of juvenile delinquency, with large and specialised staffs of medical, psychological and social workers. Their number must therefore be

[1] Four more are expected to be ready by the end of 1951.

limited, so that except for the largest urban centres they will have to provide for both sexes and all ages in the same premises. They will therefore require a number of separate blocks, some of which at least will have to provide complete security against escape. These requirements could only be met in buildings designed and erected for the purpose, and so far it has not been possible to provide funds for this purpose.

The Commissioners originally took the view that specially provided buildings would also be required for detention centres, but when it became clear that such buildings could not be provided, they decided at least to experiment with adapted buildings, if any suitable could be found. In their Annual Report for 1950 they announced that negotiations were in progress for two sites in south-east England, which they hoped might be ready for use in 1951. It is therefore too soon to speak of the methods and management of these centres, though it is possible to give certain broad indications of intention.

The first point of interest is that the Prison Commissioners will now be responsible—as also, in due course, in remand centres—for offenders of 14 years and over who would otherwise come under the care of the Children's Department. It has therefore been decided that there shall be separate centres for the older and younger age-groups, and that in respect of the latter the Commissioners shall act in consultation with the Children's Department, whose Inspectors may visit the centres.

The next concerns method. *Ex hypothesi*, the primary purpose of the centres is deterrence, nor does the very short period of the sentence offer the possibility of constructive training: indeed it is a second hypothesis that an offender who really needs such training ought not to be committed to a centre, but to an approved school or a Borstal. And it is certainly a third hypothesis that these centres shall not be prisons for young people under a new name.

To devise a régime which will comply with these intentions, in such buildings as may be found, will not be easy. It must clearly be such that the youngster who has once been through it will leave with the feeling that he would rather not do it again. Yet so purely negative an attitude to the task is unthinkable. Some constructive and formative influences must be brought into play, though it may be granted at once that among these the insistence on a brisk and disciplined activity will itself rank high. Further, for those of compulsory school age, provision for continuing their education will be essential.

At this stage, therefore, one can predicate only certain essentials. A centre must be separated entirely not only from the premises of a prison but from the idea and ambience of a prison—there must be no names or practices in it connecting it with the prison system in any way. The régime must be deterrent in the sense that the offender will be deprived not only of liberty but of every element of what he thinks is 'a good time', with a minimum of physical amenity, and he will have to work hard and do as he is told. But it must surely not be based on any idea that its purpose is to frighten young people into well-doing. The key to the enigma can lie only in a sympathetic and well-selected staff, who within the limits of what is possible in the conditions will be prepared to make a real effort to find out what is wrong with a boy or girl and set it right. Finally, although the Act makes no provision for after-care, which can therefore be provided only with the willing co-operation of the offender, whatever can be done in this way must be done—no doubt through the provision of after-care committees at the centres and a close liaison with the probation service.

CHAPTER TWENTY

YOUNG PEOPLE IN PRISON

(1) THEIR NUMBERS AND CHARACTERISTICS

THE Annual Report of the Prison Commissioners for 1949 shows that in 1948, the last year before the Criminal Justice Act came into force, 17,485 males and 2,783 females aged 16 and over but under 21 were found guilty of indictable offences. In 1945 the numbers had been 21,133 and 2,919. These post-war years had shown an alarming increase in the volume of crime committed by young people as compared with 1939, when the equivalent figures were 13,655 and 1,780, and public opinion was deeply concerned as to the causes of this situation and the measures to be taken to deal with it. It is therefore satisfactory to note that the courts were not driven by this public concern to a more frequent recourse to imprisonment, and that in fact the percentage of imprisonments to convictions fell from 16 per cent in 1947 to 13·5 per cent in 1948.

But if there is so much ground for satisfaction, the further analysis of those whom the courts did send to prison presents no such ground. Of the 2,479 youths and 277 girls received in prison on conviction in 1948, some 30 per cent and 35 per cent respectively had not, so far as was known, been previously proved guilty of any offence. On the other hand, 1,740 or 70·2 per cent of the youths had previous proved offences, and of these 536 had previously served sentences of imprisonment.

'The numbers of their previous sentences of imprisonment were:

1 previous sentence of imprisonment . .	350
2 previous sentences of imprisonment . .	131
3 previous sentences of imprisonment . .	25
Over 3 previous sentences of imprisonment .	30

'Their previous proved offences were:

One	.	.	. 313
Two	.	.	. 300
Three	.	.	. 295
Four	.	.	'. 266
Five	.	.	. 190
Six to ten	.		. 355
Eleven to twenty		.	20
Over twenty	.		. 1
			1,740

The figures for girls present a similar picture.[1]

The necessity of the measures taken in the Act of 1948 is abundantly shown by these disturbing figures. In one year 2,756 young people under 21 were sentenced to imprisonment, no less than 836 of them for their first proved offence, and of the youths there were over 1,100 with more than two previous convictions of whom many must surely have been qualified for Borstal training. Further, 1,362 of the sentences on youths, and 192 of those on girls, were for not more than three months.

Their numbers by ages were as follows:

Age	16	17	18	19	20
Males .	25	221	483	753	997
Females .	4	23	51	93	106

Their offences were as follows:

	Males	Females
Burglary and housebreaking .	615	—
Other offences against property .	1,174	160
Assaults and wounding . .	180	—
Sexual offences . . .	94	—
Other offences	416	117

Reference to Table II on pp. 154 and 155 of the Report shows that, of the youths, less than 20 per cent were convicted of non-indictable offences, and of the girls, less than 30 per cent. One might expect to find this much lower proportion of young people than of older people in prison for non-indictable offences, firstly because courts would be reluctant to send them to prison for 'social nuisance', and secondly because they would on the whole be less prone to commit such offences. Of these minor offences by males, almost all were committed by youths

[1] *Annual Report* 1949, p. 22.

of 17 and over, and the only ones reaching significant figures were assaults (118) and 'Highway Acts' (105): drunkenness produced only 28. For girls the only classified offences which reached double figures were 11 drunks and 13 sleeping out: prostitution produced only 8.

The number of persons under 17 received under section 53 of the Act of 1933 is small: in 1949 only two such cases were received under the direction of the Secretary of State. The number of convicted boys under 17 received as so 'unruly or depraved' that they could not be detained in a remand home was 29; of girls there were none. The numbers of young persons of both sexes sent to prison for this reason *before* conviction however was very much higher, the average for 1947 and 1948 being about 300 boys and 46 girls. An average for these years of those under 17 committed to await removal to an approved school was 81 boys and 18 girls, and to await removal to Borstal 254 boys and 13 girls.

The real need for the proposed remand centres is shown by the figures quoted in the Annual Report for 1949 of young offenders who were received in prison on remand and did not return to prison on conviction. These numbered in 1948 no less than 1,633, of whom 446 were found not guilty and discharged and 1,187 were dealt with other than by imprisonment or Borstal training. It is to be supposed that the explanation lies in the desire of the courts to have full information about a young person before deciding how to dispose of his case: nevertheless, it is deplorable that so many young people, many of them innocent, should thus have the taint of prison thrust upon them—deplorable also that when the remedy is known, and Parliament has prescribed it, it should be out of our power to make it available.

(2) TREATMENT AND TRAINING OF YOUNG PRISONERS

It was unfortunate that Sir E. Ruggles-Brise, in his enthusiasm for Borstal methods, chose to describe his system for the treatment of 'juvenile-adults' in prisons as the Modified Borstal System, and to set up at each prison 'Borstal Committees' for the after-care of these young people.[1] The intention was good, but it had the result of suggesting to the courts that since some sort of Borstal training was given in prison, a sentence of imprisonment might serve the same purpose as one of Borstal training. His successors, on the other hand, were so strongly impressed with the necessity of keeping young people out of prison that while they continued this system they not only dropped the name, so as to avoid any suggestion that prison could be a substitute for Borstal training, but almost 'fell over backwards' in their reluctance to admit that imprisonment could have any constructive effect at all.

The system as it is today endeavours to steer a middle course, forti-

[1] Ruggles-Brise, p. 96.

fied by those provisions of the Criminal Justice Act which are designed to ensure that if young people do come to prison, it is because the courts, after proper consideration of all alternative courses, have decided that imprisonment is the most suitable treatment. And indeed, even when detention centres are fully available, it is difficult to see how the courts can entirely dispense with the use of prison, at any rate for young offenders over 17. There will always be those whose offences are so serious that a severe sentence is essential, and they may be either unsuited for Borstal or already qualified as 'Borstal failures'. And as we shall see in considering the Borstal system, it is a necessary part of that system that there should be power to commute to imprisonment the Borstal sentences of those who refuse to profit by the training it provides.

The prison system must, therefore, be prepared to do what it can to provide suitable treatment and effective training for young people, but its efforts must also be conditioned by certain qualifications. First, the conditions of local prisons, as they have been described in earlier chapters, do not now and never will provide a suitable framework for the treatment of young offenders. But in these prisons short sentences must be served, until we have detention centres. It may be that for some, who come to it for the first time, this experience will at least have the effect of deterrence and to that extent serve its purpose: but it will almost certainly be quite useless a second time. Nor can young people in these conditions hope to escape the prison taint, however carefully they may be kept from direct contamination by older men and women. The second qualification is that the advantages of open prisons have not been made available for young offenders: they are for the most part too unstable and irresponsible to be trusted in these conditions—the analogy of open Borstals does not hold good, for the conditions are quite different. And lastly, whatever may be done for boys outside the local prisons, nothing similar can be done for girls: their numbers are so small that it is impossible to make any suitable arrangements for their segregation in special centres.

The system therefore concentrates on getting young men out of the local prisons into separate prisons, or separate wings of specialised prisons, called Young Prisoners' Centres. There are three of these. A detached wing at Wakefield takes the majority of those with long sentences (over 3 years) including those detained during His Majesty's Pleasure. Lewes, a pleasant country prison, receives in one wing all those who have not been in prison before and others suitable to associate with them, in another wing those of recidivist type. A detached block at Stafford, which is otherwise a Star prison, takes the rest of the recidivists and any overflow of 'Star' types from Lewes.

The qualifying length of sentence for removal to a centre is 3 months or over, which allowing for remission means 2 months to serve. This is not to suggest that constructive training can be given in two months: but it does remove as many as possible from the local prisons, and it is not worth while to arrange transfers for a shorter period. There is another reason for making a distinction at three months. In order to secure for young persons sentenced to imprisonment the same positive after-care and supervision as is provided by a Borstal licence, the Criminal Justice Act gave power to release such persons on a conditional licence, and that power is exercised in respect of sentences of three months and over. It would not be worth while to issue a licence to those who would only be under supervision for two or three weeks. Thus all the young prisoners in the centres are in the same position as regards release on licence, and all come under the care of the Central After-Care Association.

It follows that if a young man receives a sentence of three months and upwards, it may be hoped that at least it will do him no harm, and the system certainly aims, as we shall see, to do him some good. And when he is released he will be well looked after. But let us first see what happens to those left in the local prisons.

Under the Rules all prisoners under 21 are placed in the Young Prisoner Class, and kept separate from all other classes. This means that in a local prison all those under 21, with or without previous convictions, including those awaiting removal to Borstal, are treated together as one group. Admittedly an illogical and unsatisfactory arrangement, and one that can be modified in the largest prisons, but in the average prison it is simply not possible to subdivide this class into 'homogeneous groups', unless some boys are to spend their time in what would amount to separate confinement. In London it is possible to do better: all young prisoners go to Wormwood Scrubs which has a separate 'Boys' Prison', including a block for the untried which forms a sort of remand centre within prison walls.

But in the normal local prison on the radial plan separation of the young prisoner class can mean no more than locating them together on one landing, giving them exercise at a separate time or in a separate yard, and keeping them separated from the men while at work.[1] As work they must do what the prison has to offer in the way of unskilled jobs—they cannot be put on to skilled work for the few weeks they are there. Usually Governors try to employ them on the gardens or other odd jobs in the open air: if they have to be in a workshop they will be put together somewhere at the front or back by way of notional separation—sometimes behind a screen if there are enough of them. And in all their comings and goings during the prison day they are in the sight and hearing of the general prison population. They will be

---

1 At Holloway the girls for once have the advantage, since with the larger numbers in this prison it is possible to place them in a separate block, with Star women only, under the special charge of an Assistant Governor.

given physical training instead of walking exercise, and allowed to play such recreational games as space permits. 'Special attention' should, in principle, be paid to their education, but it is hardly practicable to have regular classes for boys who change at least every few weeks, and many of them every few days.

This somewhat pessimistic picture could be improved if conditions permitted a full working day, for at least the boys would get 7 or 8 hours work; but as things are it can be nothing but a dreary round of unexacting routine, dull, comfortless and perhaps for the younger novice frightening till he has got used to it, but of little significance to those who have had it before. Indeed it cannot be too strongly emphasised that to send a young person to prison for a short sentence is likely to make certain one thing and one thing only—that by removal of the dread of the unknown a great part of the deterrent effect of prison for the future will have been lost. One small point may be added, which mitigates the dangers of contamination within these very mixed groups—the Rules allow the Governor to remove from the Y.P. Class any prisoner over 17 years of age whom he regards as unsuitable by character for that class, and to place him in the Star Class. It is better for an aggressive young tough to find himself among older men who are not impressed by his exhibitionism.

Turning to the Y.P. Centres, we find at Wakefield a difficult collection of young people, some of whom may be mere children detained under the Act of 1933, who have for the most part committed homicides or other grave offences. Many of them present psychological problems, and since Wakefield is one of the psychiatric centres they are well cared for in that way—in his Report for 1948 the Governor said, 'The improvement in some of these youngsters after treatment has been sometimes quite amazing.' [1] They are a small group, usually less than fifty, and lead a fully communal life of their own in their detached wing, though they mix with the other prisoners in the workshops: this does more good than harm in the conditions of a specialised prison with a selected population like Wakefield. They have a choice of several skilled and interesting trades with vocational training classes, and a full working day. Their evenings are productively active, with a wide selection of educational classes and correspondence courses, and other fruitful organised activity. Above all a carefully selected and stable staff, with an Assistant Governor who gives his whole time to the group, are responsible for the personal training of the boys: in the same Annual Report the Governor said, 'I am more than ever convinced that what success we have had, is, in the main, attributable to the fact that the Housemaster, Principal Officer and the Discipline Staff, are in close contact with the boys, study their individual characters, gain their respect and often their affection and so are able to

[1] *Annual Report for* 1948, p. 28.

influence them in a way which would be impossible under more rigid conditions.'

These lads mature at different ages, and they are transferred to the adult central prison for Stars at Wakefield as soon after they are 21 as is appropriate to their individual needs.

Not all long-sentence young men go to Wakefield—it is a rather specialised group, and it would not be possible to include in it some of the hardened and depraved young men who get 3 years or more. These go to Stafford or Lewes if their sentences do not exceed 4 years— otherwise they must, at present, go to Dartmoor with the long-term prisoners of the Ordinary Class. Such cases however are rare, and are looked at with care before they are finally allocated.

Of the other centres the more satisfactory is at Lewes, which except for a detached block holding the untried prisoners of the locality is entirely devoted to the young prisoners, who number about 250. Those of 'Star' type who come here are kept apart from the others except to some extent at work. There is a brisk and tonic discipline, a full working day, and a coherent scheme of training. The industries are good, with vocational training classes in carpentry, shoe repairing, bricklaying and painting and decorating. Evening education is well organised under the direction of a full-time teacher appointed by the Local Education Authority, and there is a good library. Finally, as always, there is personal training by the staff, with two Assistant Governors to divide this special charge between them.

Stafford takes a much smaller group, and their surroundings are less attractive. They are housed in a detached block of a prison with a good general atmosphere, since all the men are Stars, and they have their own workshops, with one or two training classes. The L.E.A. take a great interest in their education, which offers a wide variety of classes. An Assistant Governor has special charge of the block.

At all the centres there is a Young Prisoners' Committee, which includes members of the Visiting Committee, specially charged with the oversight of the training, welfare and after-care of the young prisoners. The representatives of the Central After-Care Association visit regularly, and great care is taken, with the help of the Ministry of Labour and the probation service, to secure suitable placing in work and helpful supervision after discharge.

The Special Rules for young prisoners are concerned only with the setting up of the centres and of the young prisoner committees: other- wise the General Rules, and general practice as it has been described in previous chapters, apply to them, with such modifications as have been suggested above. Their stage system however is more akin to that of the corrective training prisons than to that of the local prisons: they are out of stage for 8 weeks, and then receive all available privileges.

In effect, this operates only in the centres, since no young prisoner is likely to remain more than 8 weeks in a local prison. This period enables them to be observed and 'conditioned', and in doubtful cases to have their classification checked, before they are placed in full association. They have one stage privilege not enjoyed by adults—a letter once a week instead of once a fortnight.

CHAPTER TWENTY-ONE

THE BORSTAL SYSTEM

(1) THE LAW

THE Criminal Justice Act of 1948 follows the tradition of the Prevention of Crime Act 1908 in placing young offenders and persistent offenders next door to each other. The statutory framework of the Borstal system is entirely contained within section 20, preceding section 21 on persistent offenders, and the Second Schedule to the Act: the Act of 1908, and the amending sections of 1914, are entirely repealed.

This framework is basically that of 1908, but there are several new features which derive for the most part from recommendations of the Departmental Committee on Young Offenders. The qualifications for a Borstal sentence have been changed so as, in the words of the Committee, 'to give more young offenders the advantage of this form of training' and to give 'prominence . . . rather to the need of training than to the existence of formed criminal habits'. The section requires that the court shall be 'satisfied having regard to his character and previous conduct, and to the circumstances of his offence, that it is expedient for his reformation and the prevention of crime (hallowed words!) that he should undergo a period of training in a Borstal institution'.

The qualification by age remains the same—not less than 16 but under 21: but the provision of 1908 enabling the Secretary of State to raise the maximum age to 23 has not been repeated. In fact between the wars the age was so raised, but it was found that Borstal training was unsuitable for men of this age and after World War II the Order was repealed.

The third and last qualification is that the person should have been convicted on indictment of an offence punishable with imprisonment.[1]

The sentence itself is now one of 'Borstal training' instead of 'Borstal detention', a change which speaks for itself. Another change recommended by the Committee affects the length of the sentence: under the

[1] See Appendix K as to absconders from approved schools.

352

Act of 1908 this was for not less than 2 nor more than 3 years, plus 1 year's supervision: the Committee thought the 2-year sentence should be abolished, and a flat rate of 3 years provided. Given a normal period of about 2 years of institutional training followed by release on licence, this would give a total period of control of 4 years, of which two would be 'inside' and two under supervision outside. Under the provisions of the Act of 1948, the court does not prescribe a period at all, but simply passes a sentence of Borstal training: the effect of such a sentence, as defined in the Second Schedule, is that the person may be detained in a Borstal institution for such period, being not less than 9 months or more than 3 years from the date of sentence, as the Prison Commissioners may determine, and after release from a Borstal he shall, until the expiration of four years from the date of his sentence, be under the supervision of a specified society or person. During this period of supervision he may, in specified conditions, be recalled to a Borstal and detained until the expiration of the original 3 years, or for 6 months from the date of being taken into custody under the order of recall, whichever is the later.

This method of approach has the advantage of emphasising first, the indeterminacy of the period of detention, and second that the whole period of four years is a unity, one part being training under detention, the other part being training in controlled liberty.

In one respect the Act does not follow the Committee's recommendations. They proposed that under certain restrictions summary courts should be empowered to pass Borstal sentences, so as to avoid what was often a wait of several weeks in prison for an offender who had been convicted by a summary court and referred to a higher court for sentence. This has always been a point of controversy, but in 1948 Parliament decided to leave the power to pass a Borstal sentence with the higher courts. If therefore a person is convicted by a court of summary jurisdiction of an offence punishable with imprisonment, and the court is satisfied that he is qualified for Borstal training, they may commit him in custody to quarter sessions for sentence.

As in 1908, a court of summary jurisdiction before committing for sentence, or a higher court before passing sentence, must consider a report by the Prison Commissioners on the offender's physical and mental condition and his suitability for the sentence. The observations in Chapter Eighteen on the preparation of the similar reports required for corrective training are equally applicable here.

Such is the legal basis of the Borstal sentence. There are certain other administrative provisions in the Act. By section 48 the Secretary of State is empowered to provide Borstal institutions, and the Prison Acts 1865 to 1898 are applied to them 'subject to such adaptations and modifications as may be made by rules of the Secretary of State'. This is a legal formality: it does not have the effect of turning the Borstals into prisons either in principle or in practice. By section 52 the Secretary of State may make rules 'for the regulation and management of (*inter alia*) Borstal institutions, and for the classification, treatment, employment, discipline and control of persons required to be detained therein': the rules now in force are the Borstal (No. 2) Rules 1949. Section 53 provides for the appointment by the Secretary of State of a Board of Visitors at each Borstal (see Chapter Six).

Section 59 provides for transfers from prison to Borstal, and *vice versa*, in the following circumstances. By sub-section (1), 'If the Secretary of State is satisfied that a person serving a sentence of imprisonment is under 21 years of age and might with advantage be detained in a Borstal institution he may, after consultation where practicable with the judge or presiding chairman of the court which passes the sentence, authorise the Prison Commissioners to transfer him to a Borstal institution; and the provisions of the Second Schedule to this Act shall thereupon apply to him as if he had on the date of the transfer been sentenced to Borstal training: provided that if on that date the unexpired term of his sentence is less than three years those provisions shall apply to him as if he had been sentenced to Borstal training three years before the expiration of that term.' This provision repeats a similar provision of 1908, with the addition of prior consultation with the court. It is used on occasion with advantage, but since the court must be deemed to have decided on imprisonment rather than Borstal in full knowledge of all the facts, it is normally invoked only on the basis of considerations which were not before the court at the time.

Sub-section (2) provides as follows—'If a person detained in a Borstal institution is reported to the Secretary of State by the board of visitors to be incorrigible, or to be exercising a bad influence on the other inmates of the institution, the Secretary of State may commute the unexpired part of the term for which the said person is then liable to be detained in a Borstal institution to such term of imprisonment as the Secretary of State may determine, not exceeding the said unexpired part; and for the purpose of this Act the said person shall be treated as if he had been sentenced to imprisonment for that term.' This also repeats a provision of 1908, which the Departmental Committee considered at some length. They found that in some cases 'it has worked fairly well', but that in others 'particularly with girls, the result has been an unhappy one. A bitter sense of injustice has been created in the inmate's mind by finding that he or she has to serve a long time in prison, when the offence for which he or she was originally committed was no worse than those for which other people in the same prison have been sentenced to a few weeks. A large reduction of the term of imprisonment, on the other hand, is impracticable, because it would place a premium on misconduct at the institutions. On account of these drawbacks the power is not now used, and the institutions deal with their ill-conducted members themselves.' They therefore recommended that this section should be repealed. Whatever the conditions in 1927, it would be difficult to dispense with this power today, and it has unfortunately been necessary to use it fairly often since the war: this question is further discussed in the following chapter.

There remains only; among the statutory provisions which call for special mention, section 65. This was inserted to bite on all persons who escape from penal institutions, including Borstals, by providing that, unless the Secretary of State otherwise directs, time during which the escaper is unlawfully at large shall not count towards calculating the period for which he may be detained. In its application to Borstal, it does not apply to the person who does not respond to an order of recall, and cannot serve to extend the total period for which a person is liable to supervision.

(2) THE PRINCIPLES

In 1932 the Prison Commissioners published the second and revised edition of a little grey book called *The Principles of the Borstal System*. Written by Alexander Paterson, this expressed the spirit which he had brought into Borstal during the ten previous years. Though much has changed in practice since then, the spirit still holds, and cannot be better explained than in the words of its first expression. Where unidentified quotations follow, therefore, they will be from this source.

'At the back and at the bottom of this Borstal System of training there lies a fundamental principle. There have always been bad lads and the supply will never cease entirely. Once upon a time the method employed to deal with them consisted simply in the use of force. The lad was regarded as a lump of hard material, yielding only to the hammer, and was, with every good intention, beaten into shape. Sometimes there were internal injuries, and the spirit of the lad grew into a wrong shape, for sometimes the use of force produces a reaction more anti-social than the original condition. There ensued a second method which has flourished for fifty years in many schools and places where boys are trained, and might be termed the method of pressure. The lad is treated as though he were a lump of putty, and an effort is made to reduce him to a certain uniform shape by the gentle and continuous pressure of authority from without. In course of time, by perpetual repetition, he forms a habit of moving smartly, keeping himself clean, obeying orders and behaving with all decorum in the presence of his betters. These are in themselves very useful qualities, and it is hoped by those who use this system that, after some years of constant admonition and daily habit, all lads will retain the same pleasing shape when no longer subject to the pressure of those in authority. But the springs of action lie deeper than the laws of habit or the voice of the mentor are likely to reach, and character is determined ultimately not by the outside shape that has been fashioned, but by powers within that possibly have not been touched. It happens, therefore, sadly often that the lad who has been merely subjected to the pressure of authority from outside will, when exposed to the different influences of free life, assume quite another shape. In other words, having been treated like a lump of putty, he will behave like a lump of putty and respond successively to the influences of each environment.

'The third and most difficult way of training a lad is to regard him as a living organism, having its secret of life and motive-power within, adapting itself in external conduct to the surroundings of the moment, but undergoing no permanent organic change merely as a result of outside pressure. So does Borstal look at him, as a lad of many mixtures, with a life and character of his own. The task is not to break or knead him into shape, but to stimulate some power within to regulate conduct aright, to insinuate a preference for the good and the clean, to make him want to use his life well, so that he himself and not others will save him from waste. It becomes necessary to study the individual lad, to discover his trend and his possibility, and to infect him with some idea of life which will germinate and produce a character, controlling desire, and shaping conduct to some more glorious end than mere satisfaction or acquisition.

'This is indeed the more difficult way, for it passes from the external things that can be seen, which are dealt with so much more easily, to the inner things unseen. Further it requires that each lad shall be dealt with as an individual and shall not be regarded as being the same as any other lad, requiring the same universal prescription.'

A system which seeks to work in this way must depend first and foremost on the men who are to do the work. 'The Borstal System has no merit apart from the Borstal Staff. It is men and not buildings who will change the hearts and ways of misguised lads. Better an institution that consists of two log-huts in swamp or desert, with a staff devoted to their task, than a model block of buildings, equipped without thought of economy, whose staff is solely concerned with thoughts of pay and promotion. The foundations of the Borstal System are first the recruitment of the right men, then their proper training, and finally their full co-operation with one another in an atmosphere of freedom and mutual understanding.'

The first step in a system aiming at this individual training of the young offender must be careful classification, to ensure that, in the words of the relevant Statutory Rule, 'in the light of his history, character and capacities he may be sent to the Borstal best suited to his character and requirements'. 'It may be maintained that, as no two lads are the same, only a policy of separate confinement can provide a perfect system of classification. This *reductio ad absurdum* shall not, however, deter us from proceeding with as sensible a scheme as we can devise. The first purpose of classification is positive, and consists in putting a lad in such a milieu as is likely to draw out what is best in him. Ideally, therefore, each Borstal lad should be drafted to a group of honest and intelligent lads, to whose level he would wish to aspire. This, by the nature of things, is impossible; there are too many rogues and not enough honest lads. For this reason the courts rightly hesitate before committing a first offender to a Borstal Institution. But it is possible within rather narrow limits, in assigning a lad to an Institution or a House or group, to put him in a place where there is someone or something that will stimulate the better side of him. The second purpose of classification, and it should always be kept in the second place, is the avoidance of contamination. One evil spirit can poison the tone of a whole House, and every Borstal Officer is keen to watch the effect of one lad upon the others. A clique may form whose influence on each member is undoubtedly evil. Such a clique will be scattered among different Houses or Institutions. Transfer and reclassification are ready to our hand to prevent corruption, and should be employed without hesitation where the reasonable prospect of a risk has been established by those who have observed. The community must be protected even at the cost of disturbance to the individual.'

'The purpose of a Borstal Institution is to teach wayward lads to be self-contained men, to train them to be fit for freedom. It is impossible to train men for freedom in a condition of captivity.' The conditions of Borstal training must therefore be as little like those of a prison as is compatible with compulsory detention: they must be 'based on progressive trust demanding increasing personal decision, responsibility, and self-control. These are qualities which can only be attained by practising them', [1] and they cannot be practised in conditions where safe-custody is an over-riding consideration. Thus Borstals must provide varying conditions of security to suit different types of character, and in all there must be freedom to earn progress to a stage of complete trust and self-discipline. But this progress must be *earned*. 'Steps must repeatedly be taken to ensure the difficulty of ascent, so that the minimum of promotion may reward a maximum of effort. This can be done by emphasising the responsibilities rather than the privileges associated with each grade, and by a merciless reduction when these responsibilities are not fulfilled. Each grade carries a lad a little further towards freedom. He is practising his wings, developing his power of choice between right and wrong. This is a more difficult life than that of confinement and repression. He must show that he justifies the trust and is indeed growing more fit for freedom. If he fails, he must return to the lower order where it is easy to be good, and wait a little while

[1] *Prisons and Borstals*, p. 60.

before taking a step forward again towards liberty. Further, we must scrutinise very closely the claim of the lad for promotion. Let it not come to him. Lay rather the onus on him to show that he has stretched himself to reach it.'

The essential instrument of this individual study and personal training is the House—a group which should ideally be of not more than about fifty, leading its separate and corporate life under the House-master or Housemistress and House Staff. 'Thus corporate pride is nurtured and a great natural force is brought into play. No lad is proud, or should be proud, of being a Borstal boy. The smaller the unit, however, the stouter the allegiance of the lad. He becomes proud of his House. He can be induced sometimes so to change his habits as to conform with its traditions. The Housemaster and his staff set a standard, the boys catch the spirit, and on it rolls to successive generations. This division into smaller entities releases the two great weapons of moral training—personal influence and the corporate spirit.'

These principles are summed up in the Statutory Rules governing Borstal training as follows:

'4. (1) The objects of training shall be to bring to bear every influence which may establish in the inmates the will to lead a good and useful life on release, and to fit them to do so by the fullest possible development of their character, capacities, and sense of personal responsibility.

'(2) Methods of training may vary as between one Borstal and another, according to the needs of the different types of inmate allocated to them.

'6. In order to ensure so far as practicable the prevention of contamination and the best use of training facilities, the Commissioners shall arrange that each Borstal receives inmates who have been selected as suitable for that Borstal in age, character, and capacities.

'7. (1) To enable members of the staff to exercise their personal influence on the character and development of individual inmates, and to understand the needs of each for the purposes of training, inmates of Borstals may be grouped in houses.

'(2) A Housemaster shall be responsible to the Governor, with the assistance of a Matron and such other staff as may be appointed, for the administration of each house, and for the personal training of the inmates in his house.

'8. (1) To encourage the progressive development of responsibility, and to assist in the assessment of fitness for release, inmates may be placed in such grades as the Commissioners approve.

'(2) Promotion from grade to grade or reduction in grade otherwise than as an award for an offence against discipline shall be decided by the Governor with the advice of an institution board composed of such officers as the Commissioners determine.

'(3) Inmates who have been promoted to an appropriate grade may be given positions of special responsibility and leadership.

'9. (1) There shall be established at every Borstal such system of privileges as the Commissioners approve in the interests of good conduct and training.'

So much for the broad principles of training in the institution: but 'Borstal training falls into two parts. In the first part a lad is trained in custody at an Institution: in the second part he enjoys the comparative freedom of licence or supervision, and is under the training of the Borstal Association.[1] The functions of the two bodies dovetail closely into one another. . . . The Borstal Association represents one-half of the Borstal System. Its method of after-care starts to discover the lad and plan his future from the date of his conviction, following him through the Institution, finding him employment and guiding him for some years after his discharge.'

The unity of these two parts of Borstal training, as we have seen, is emphasised by the form of the sentence, and the principles of 1932 are implemented by the following Statutory Rule:

64. (1) From the beginning of the training of every inmate consideration shall be given, in consultation with the Central After-care Association, to the future of the inmate and the assistance to be given to him on and after release, and for this purpose the Association or their representatives shall be given all necessary information and assistance.

'(2) Facilities shall be afforded to the representatives of the Association to visit every inmate before release.'

(3) THE RECEPTION CENTRES AND CLASSIFICATION

A Borstal Reception Centre has four functions: to decide, as the Rules require, after careful examination of each inmate, which is 'the Borstal best suited to his character and requirements': to straighten out the inmate's affairs, to relieve his mind of any difficulties, to look into his mental and physical state and so far as possible relieve any conditions that might handicap his training, and generally to prepare him to receive his training in a fit and ready state of body and mind: to give him instruction in what he is to expect in Borstal, with certain elementary training: and to furnish the Governor of the Borstal to which he will go with all the information necessary to help in charting his course.

There are two of these centres, one in a separate wing of Wormwood

---

[1] Now the Borstal Division of the Central After-care Association.

Scrubs prison, the other at Latchmere House, near Kingston-on-Thames, formerly a war-time military detention establishment. It is wrong that the former should be part of a prison, but security is necessary for young men at this stage, and no other suitable accommodation has become available. For girls there is at present no separate centre, nor is one strictly necessary since the only decision to be made is whether she is or is not suitable for the one open Borstal, at East Sutton: they all go first, therefore, to the closed Borstal at Aylesbury, where they are kept under observation for some weeks before allocation.

The team working under the Governor of a reception centre will include the housemasters, a psychologist, an educational guidance officer, a vocational guidance officer, and two or three women social workers who make out the case histories and pay home visits where necessary. At Wormwood Scrubs the services of the Chaplain and medical staff of the main prison are available; at Latchmere House the Chaplain and doctor are part-time, and there is a visiting psychiatrist to see such boys as the psychologist refers to him. The period of observation and testing lasts about 6 weeks, and when members of the above team, and the Borstal officers in charge of the boys, have completed their reports the institution Board meets to consider the case.

The possibilities of allocation are wide, as there are thirteen institutions to choose from, each with slightly different characteristics, and each taking, on the whole, a slightly different type of boy. Broadly speaking, there is one group of Borstals for the more mature, another for the less mature. Within these two groups, some take those with better records and some those with worse. The Board will also take account of a boy's vocational aptitudes and wishes, and so far as possible allot him within his group to the Borstal best able to help him in that way. Often too, with particular cases, they will have in mind that a particular Governor or member of a Borstal staff is likely to bring the best out of a boy.

Among the thirteen Borstals are four which are generally described as 'closed', since they are situated in buildings with security walls, locks and bars. To these are sent the more unstable, who present the greatest escape risk, and the older and tougher types. One of these, in the former prison at Hull, takes those who are thought unlikely to co-operate in or profit from the normal training system, particularly those with second sentences of Borstal training.

(4) THE INSTITUTIONS

Only one Borstal was built for its purpose—Lowdham Grange. All the others are adapted premises of various types. Of the three originals of the Ruggles-Brise era, Borstal and Portland were early convict prisons, but the buildings have been radically reconstructed and serve their purpose pretty well. Each provides five self-contained houses with their separate dining and common rooms: at Portland all houses are cellular, at Borstal one is a dormitory house, the others cellular. Feltham, on the other hand, which was one of the first industrial schools, has four dormitory houses and one cellular house added later. All these have extensive farms or market-gardens outside the walls, the gates stand open all day, and there is little feeling of confinement. The security they provide is that of having their inmates safe once the gates are shut in the evening. All are on the large side, housing over 300 boys each.

The contemporary girls' Borstal of these three is also, unhappily, within a prison wall. The mixed establishment at Aylesbury comprises a small cellular prison, part of which is used for the initial stages of the Borstal girls, and the pleasanter premises of what was once a State Inebriate Reformatory, which now provide two houses with separate bedrooms and suitable dining and common rooms. Here too there is a small farm with a dairy outside the wall, and room for playgrounds, gardens and a swimming pool inside. The Borstal now houses about 150 girls, though at its peak during the war it had some 250. Even so, it is too big and too prison-like for training young girls: a first priority is the building of two small Borstals to take its place. This would be so even if it had not the added disadvantage of neighbouring the long-term Star women in the other part of the prison block.

The next to be added, Lowdham Grange, was Alec Paterson's 'Borstalium quartum', the origin of which has already been described. It is designed as an entirely open institution with four dormitory houses for sixty boys connected by a covered way: in appearance it might be a pleasant hospital. It stands in a large estate which is farmed by the institution, and has been built—indeed is still being built—with the institution's own labour. Two more open institutions followed before the war: Hollesley Bay Colony was taken over from the London County Council, who had developed it as a farm training colony for unemployed. Its four hutted houses, with dormitory sleeping accommodation, are widely dispersed about the broad acres of farmland and orchard, with an administrative centre of more substantial structure. This is one of the largest Borstals, primarily agricultural in its interests, breeding prize sheep and Suffolk Punch horses, which are used for work on most of the prison and Borstal farms. North Sea Camp was another pioneering experiment in the heroic spirit of those days. At least since the days of the Empire men have embanked the shores of the Wash to reclaim rich Lincolnshire land from the sea-marsh, and in 1938 a party of Borstal boys was set down in a hut under the Roman Bank to continue the work. Today a thriving little colony of about 100 boys still toil in the deep mud and bitter winds to add to the protecting banks, and farm some 200 acres of the richest land in the country which before the war were under salt water.

The last pre-war Borstal was at Usk, and is again different. Its base is the old county gaol, where the boys are received to begin with, and from which they go out to work on various jobs around the premises and neighbourhood. The main body however are in a farm-camp some miles away. There is a good deal of to-and-fro on bicycles, boys from the camp cycling out to local farms to work or back into town for classes, and boys from the town cycling out to work at the camp. There is no definite purpose in this arrangement—it just happened so.

The first post-war Borstal, at Gringley-on-the-Hill in Nottinghamshire, was an experiment on still another basis. The Ministry of Agriculture had, for war purposes, taken over a large tract of low-lying country, poorly and partially farmed, and turned it into a fine estate, largely worked by the Women's Land Army. When the W.L.A. was disbanded, Borstal came forward to take over their hostel and their work. The sixty or so men here also provide large work-parties for the local authorities responsible for keeping up the river banks and other such work. A few years ago, when a bank broke and a disastrous flood submerged the estate, they worked for days and nights on end rescuing lives and property, and an inscribed radio set in the camp marks the great gratitude of the neighbourhood. The five Borstals that followed in the post-war years present less striking features, excepting perhaps at Hewell Grange. Here, in the former seat of a noble family, reproductions of the lovely mediaeval tapestries of the 'Dame aux Licornes' strangely encompass the Borstal boys at their meals, and from its famous glass-houses First ·Prize blooms still regularly emerge at the National Chrysanthemum Society's exhibition in Vincent Square.

Gaynes Hall and Huntercombe have each the same pattern of a large country house with a war-time camp in the grounds, though in the latter the 'camp' is cellular in construction, having served as a wartime Army detention establishment: it is however 'open' in all essentials, as the Army removed all the locks and the Borstal has removed the barbed wire. Hatfield and Pollington, the two latest, are training camps borrowed from the Army, unadorned but lending themselves well to Borstal purposes. All these post-war camps will take about 150 boys in three houses.

Since the war it has also been possible to provide for the girls as well as for the boys an open Borstal: two were intended, but before the second was acquired it became clear that one small unit of 50–60 would suffice for all the girls found suitable for these conditions. East Sutton Park is placed in an Elizabethan house of considerable beauty and character, in a natural setting not less beautiful.

Such are the ordinary 'training institutions'. There are also several institutions serving special purposes. The special Borstal established in

1950 at Hull is also a training Borstal, but it provides a different sort of training for young men who do not fit into the normal scheme. It is in the buildings of the former local prison, almost completely destroyed by enemy action in the war, and its tough but constructive task is first to clear away the ruins and then to build afresh inside the wall. This is a small unit which will probably not exceed 100.

In a separate wing of Wandsworth prison, declared to be a Borstal, is a 'correction centre' for absconders who cannot at once be taken back to a training Borstal, and others who persistently misbehave to an extent beyond the normal resources of a training Borstal to correct. The removal of this centre from its unsuitable milieu has been sought long but unsuccessfully.[1]

In the former local prison at Portsmouth is the 'recall centre' for boys who are, for breach of the conditions of their supervision, recalled for further training. In the former women's wing of Exeter prison is a similar centre for girls.

The various methods of training followed in these different types of institution will be described in the following chapter. The purpose of this quick impression of the sort of places in which Borstals are to be found is to show that for the building round the teacher there need be no standard pattern—not that some patterns may not be better than others, and the prison pattern in particular could be lost without tears. But for a system based on diversity, elasticity, initiative and hard work, with a dash of the spirit of pioneers, this improvised and various framework has merits of its own.

(5) THE STAFF

The prison and Borstal services are two in one, indivisible and complementary. All entrants to the service, whether as Assistant Governors or officers, may indicate a preference for one branch or the other, and if the selection boards' views of their capacities support their preferences they will normally be posted accordingly. There is much value in this arrangement, and little harm. Broadly, the men and women working in Borstals are those who want to do that work and are best fitted for it: those who grow out of liking or fitness for the work can be moved to a prison, and those on the prison side who want to try Borstal work can equally cross over if they are thought to be suitable. The prisons have been constantly refreshed by the passing into them of younger or older Governors from Borstal: and since many Borstal boys and girls have been in prison, and many prisoners have been in Borstal, it is well that the staff on each side should know something of the other's ways and work. If there is a disadvantage, it is that prison ways and names carried into a Borstal, especially a closed Borstal, may tend to suggest to boys who already know

[1] See Appendix K, note on p. 308.

their prison language that Borstal is the same sort of thing, under another name.

Throughout the Borstal service, therefore, the grades of the staff are the same as those of the prison service—Governor, Deputy and Assistant Governors, Chief Officer, Principal Officers and Officers, and a similar complement of instructors and specialists, with of course a Chaplain and a Medical Officer—full-time or part-time according to the size of the institution. The one variation is that in boys' Borstals there is in each house a house matron. In two respects the conditions of service of Borstal officers differ from those of prison officers—they wear plain clothes, receiving an allowance in lieu of uniform, and receive a special additional allowance of 4s. 6d. a week.

Their functions however differ considerably. Apart from specialists —cooks, works and hospital staffs—the duties of the officers fall mainly into three groups; the house officers, who are about the houses from getting-up till bed-time supervising the boys and helping the house-masters; party officers, in charge of parties at outside work; and instructors, in charge of workshops. At every point these officers are in close touch with the boys or girls in their charge, slowly getting to know them, studying their individualities, encouraging what is good and controlling what is bad, and always setting an example of firmness, fairness, good humour and upright decency. 'The silent example will appeal where often the reiterated advice will only annoy.' [1]

The Principal Officers, who are usually attached to the houses, assist the housemasters, while the Chief Officer controls the whole staff, arranges their duties, and by example and precept secures the maximum of efficiency with the minimum of friction.

The house Matron does much more than see to such things within her sphere as the care of clothing and meal service—she should be the 'house mother', and many go still further and take classes in crafts, music, literature or wherever their special interests may lie. The mere presence about the house of the right sort of woman has a sufficient value of its own.

The housemaster (an Assistant Governor II) is, under the Governor, the key-man in the organisation. He is responsible not only for the general administration of his house as a self-contained unit, but for the personal training of each of the 50–60 boys in the house. Each house-master will in addition usually carry some institution duty—such as education, sports and recreation, employment or earnings—and cor-porately, with the Governor and Deputy Governor, they will form the Institution Board. At the larger Borstals which carry a Deputy Gover-nor (Assistant Governor I) he will generally be a housemaster with an assistant housemaster to help him: at such Borstals too the housemaster charged with education may have an assistant—in this way the recruit

[1] *Principles of the Borstal System*, p. 22.

may learn his work before he takes charge of a house himself. At most Borstals the Governor begins the day with a housemasters' meeting, at which the Chief Officer and other senior officials as necessary will also be present. The arrangements for girls are the same in principle and include women officers with the same grades and functions as the men. The pattern is however a little different to suit the particular circumstances of the three institutions. Aylesbury has a house system, but East Sutton is a single unit and though its staff conforms in grading it works, under the Governor, as a 'classless society' differentiated not by rank but by function. The Recall Centre at Exeter is in charge of an Assistant Governor I, with an Assistant Governor II and a few officers, under the general control of the Governor of the combined prison and Borstal.

In addition to the regular Borstal staffs there are at all the larger farms Farm Bailiffs, or Garden Managers, and farm workers of various kinds, who work with the boys and commonly play a helpful part in their training in their own way—a way that may often do something for a boy that could not come so easily from an officer of the regular staff.

(6) THE BORSTAL POPULATION

In their Annual Reports prior to the outbreak of war the Commissioners were calling attention to a steep rise in the Borstal population, which by the end of 1938 had reached over 2,100 in the male institutions. In September 1939, 'at the outbreak of war the Commissioners were required to discharge forthwith approximately two-thirds of the Borstal population. Those released were the seniors in the institutions, and with them disappeared overnight the carefully built-up tradition of 30 years'. It is to be doubted whether the Borstal system has even yet recovered from that shock, followed as it was by the loss to military service of a high proportion of its trained and experienced staff. The difficulties of the war years were great, but they were intensified when in 1945 the number of committals to Borstal, already greater than in 1938 or 1939, began to mount even faster: in that year they rose from 1,386 (males) to 2,166 and remained about that level in 1946. So long as hostilities continued there was no possibility of increasing either accommodation or staffs to meet this situation, and the resulting conditions raised most serious difficulties, so that in their Annual Report for 1945 (p. 5) the Commissioners recorded that towards the end of the year they had 'to take on the unprecedented task of producing 6 more Borstals and 5 more prisons more or less simultaneously'. In the subsequent years it was necessary, therefore, to rebuild the shattered tradition of 1939 in a vastly expanded system and with a staff of whom the great majority had only joined the service since the war. The daily average population in those years, up to and including

1950, has been rather less than 3,000 boys and about 250 girls: it is noteworthy that the effect on this total of the wider qualifications for Borstal training in section 21 of the Criminal Justice Act 1948 has not so far been significant.

The following extracts from Table XI of Appendix 8 of the Annual Report for 1949 give certain statistical information in respect of receptions during 1948:

Borstal Detention—Receptions during 1948

Analysis by age and previous convictions

Age on Conviction	Total	Males	Females	Previous Convictions	Total	Males	Females
16 years	248	237	11	None known	158	136	22
17 ,,	653	634	19	One . .	397	355	42
18 ,,	493	444	49	Two . .	398	363	35
19 ,,	350	319	31	Three . .	413	390	23
20 ,,	236	214	22	Four . .	296	290	6
21–23 ,,	135	127	8	Five . .	220	211	9
				Six to ten .	225	222	3
				Above ten .	8	8	—
Total	2,115	1,975	140	Total	2,115	1,975	140

Their offences were as follows;

	Male	Female
Indictable		
Against the person . .	45	3
Against property . .	1,770	94
Frauds and false pretences .	6	2
Forgery . . .	10	4
Other indictable offences .	17	4
Totals	1,848	107
Non-indictable . . .	127	33
Totals	1,975	140

The following extract from the Annual Report for 1950 of the Governor of one of the Reception Centres gives a further useful sample of information:

'723 lads were received (for the first time) in 1950 and of these 270 (37·3%) had been at Approved Schools. This is 5% less than in 1949. The ages of lads on reception were 16—7·3%, 17—32·9%, 18—27·3%, 19—20%, and 20—12%. Lads were therefore on the whole much younger than in 1949 when 71% were over 18 years of age.

'Of the 723 receptions 50 (6·9%) had no previous convictions and 45 (6·2%) had been convicted more than 6 times previously. Maxima were at 2 previous convictions (20·2%) and 3 previous convictions (19·5%).

'Only 4·6% of the lads had had previous prison sentences, 2 lads having been imprisoned 3 times. This compares very favourably with 1949 when 10% had served sentences of imprisonment.

'Some of the causative factors in the delinquency of lads were again very roughly assessed and home difficulties appeared to be of the highest significance. The death of a parent appeared to be a factor in 20·7% of the cases, separated parents in 11·3%, illegitimacy in 6·6% and parental mismanagement in 22·8%. 4·1% of the lads appeared to have an uncongenial step-parent and in 2·6% of the cases a parent suffered from some specific mental trouble.

'Other environmental factors were criminal or immoral background (10·4%), overcrowding (4·6%), Service difficulties (2·6%) and unemployment (only 1·7%).

'Some of the constitutional factors were subnormal intelligence (5·5%), subnormal health (5·3%), undue immaturity (15·5%) and drink (5·1%).'

It may be hoped that our knowledge of this case material will in due course be increased, since in 1950, following the power given in the Criminal Justice Act to spend public funds on research, the Home Office set on foot a project under the direction of Dr. Hermann Mannheim based on research into the pre-sentence and post-discharge records of some 1,000 boys who had passed through the Borstal Reception Centres.

CHAPTER TWENTY-TWO

BORSTAL TRAINING

(1) CHARACTER TRAINING

THIS chapter will describe various aspects of the system of training which today implements the principles set out in the preceding chapter. But the task is not easy. All the parts of the system form an integrated whole, and are not easily separated for convenient description: this section heading does not imply that the other sections are not equally concerned with character training. Methods are fluid, and what is done one way today may be done quite differently tomorrow. And above all they are elastic: within the general framework of the principles and the Rules, Governors are allowed, indeed encouraged, to use their own initiative and to act—within reason—according to their own faith and personal disposition. In a system which relies primarily on personal influence those exercising that influence cannot be required to use slide-rule methods. So even within one Borstal housemasters have a good deal of latitude to run their houses in their own ways. So too each member of the staff will exercise his control and impart his instruction in a personal relationship varying with each of the varying individuals with whom he must deal.

Of that first principle then, personal influence, no more need in general be said—it must permeate the whole action of the system through every member of the staff. But the subject cannot be left without a special reference to the work of the chaplain and the doctor. In all Borstals religion is 'awarded the first place among all forms of character training',[1] and in all the chaplain is in a position to bring to bear not the least of those influences which make for the development of right thought and feeling. This is especially so in the few larger Borstals where there is a full-time chaplain. Nor is influence of this sort left only to the chaplain, though it is for him to give systematic instruction. On Sundays all must go to church, and in the open Borstals this usually means the local parish church, where the boys or girls are always

---

[1] *Principles of the Borstal System*, p. 48.

welcome members of the congregation—indeed in more than one village the church depends largely on the Borstal for organ-blowers, stokers, bell-ringers or voices in the choir. What has been said of the place of religion in prison is true for Borstal too, but it must be said that the ground here seems even stonier: reports by Governors and Chaplains alike make it all too clear that on the teachings and meaning of Christianity the minds of most of those who come to Borstal are quite blank—the idea of religion, let alone its practice, has never touched them.

Only the few largest Borstals have full-time doctors, but these have a valuable part to play in the training, as well as in the care of health. They are of particular help with 'problem' boys or girls, not only helping them directly but helping the housemasters by talking over with them difficult cases. They do not practise psychiatry in the stricter sense, but their skilled approach to psychological problems is of great value.

The house system helps to intensify personal influence, and serves also a second purpose, that of bringing into play the corporate spirit, the public opinion of the boys themselves, which may be even more potent than that of the staff. In some houses there may be a further division into groups, each group with its own 'leader'. But groups are not essential to the leader system. In every house boys who have reached a certain stage, and who may—so far as judgment will carry— be trusted to exercise a good and helpful influence in the general interests of the house and the preservation of a right 'public opinion', are appointed as leaders. This is part of the training in responsibility. It is a position of obligation rather than of privilege, though they may wear a special badge and have perhaps the use of a 'leaders' room'. They have no disciplinary powers.

On the material plane, the house is the boy's home, where he sleeps, eats and passes his indoor leisure, and from which he goes out for work, education, sport and entertainment. The housemaster and his staff stand 'in loco parentis'.

A dominating factor of the training is the system of progressive grades. Although certain specific privileges attach to the higher grades, the system is not to be thought of as primarily a method of earning privileges. Its real purpose is to record progress in the attainment of that self-discipline and self-responsibility which must reach a certain stage before the boy is ready for discharge. So the privileges to be earned are not, for the most part, material privileges: they are rather the extension of trust and relaxation of institutional control.

There is no prescribed system of grades, but they follow a general pattern. Usually there are three—the first or beginners grade may last for 4–6 months, and is a period of preliminary training and observation. The second or training grade is indefinite in its duration, for it is not till a boy begins to display marked response to his training, and fitness to be trusted, that he will begin to be considered for promotion to the third or special grade. Little privilege is usually attached to the second grade, except perhaps permission to join certain clubs, or the Cadet Force, or occasionally to go out on escorted walks or trips. In the third grade a boy's status changes completely—he may become a leader; he may go about the place and do his work unsupervised; join in all clubs and institution activities; go for walks or to the cinema or to a local youth club or the like on his own, or in charge of a party of junior boys; go out to tea with his parents when they visit; and become eligible for home leave. The list is illustrative rather than exhaustive, and details will vary from place to place. A few institutions add a 'discharge grade' to their special grade, for boys whose dates of discharge have been fixed, reserving for them the greatest freedom, sometimes including the right to go out in their own civilian clothes.

Promotion in grade is a serious business and receives serious attention. It is made by the Governor on the advice of the Institution Board, over which he presides. This will comprise the housemasters and the chief officer, and sometimes the principal officers who are primarily on house duties. It usually meets monthly, and considers all the cases 'in the field', reading or hearing reports from every member of the staff concerned in the training of the boy, and often seeing the boy himself for a frank discussion of his position.

These then are the three tried and traditional methods of personal training—the house, leadership and progressive grades: but they should be seen rather as the main limbs of the tree, from which stem many branches varying in shape and fruit with the institutional tree from which they spring. Since these tend on the whole to relate to activities which may be brought under the heading of 'education and recreation', they will be discussed under that heading. But it may be said here that their broad effects on training are to increase the sense of trust and responsibility, to create a diversity of healthy interests related to normal life, to counteract 'institutionalisation' and to bring the boys and girls into regular touch with ordinary people leading ordinary lives who by treating them as friends will give them confidence and hope.

The last test and privilege—for it is both in one—is home leave. All boys and girls have the opportunity once during their training to go home for five days: this is done under a statutory power to release on parole,[1] which may also be used exceptionally for other purposes, e.g. to visit sick or dying relatives. After a long lapse the practice was resumed in 1947, and its purpose, value, and results are emphatically

[1] Criminal Justice Act 1948, section 52 as amended by Criminal Justice (Scotland) Act 1949, 11th Schedule. The practice was followed before 1949, but its legality having been questioned, the hospitality of the Scottish Bill was sought to validate it.

stated in the following extracts from Governors' reports published in the Annual Report for 1948.

'Generally I am convinced that Home Leave is extremely valuable and in many cases has been the making of some of our lads. Strained relations with parents have been rectified, especially so in cases where they have the lads back for a few days just to see what they are like. Numerous parents have written saying what a difference they notice in their lads. It does too, give the Probation Officer or B.A. Associate a chance to have a look at them a few months prior to release as in nearly all cases lads go along to see their prospective supervisor. Quite a few have found jobs for themselves during the leave and, last but not least, it presents them with an opportunity of getting to know the conditions of the very difficult world they will be returning to.'

'The scheme is of great value, particularly in that it allows the lad a salutary glimpse of the reality of outside conditions and dispels some of the fancies and fantasies born of life in a closed and specialist community.'

'Of all the additional forms of training that have fully come into being during the 12 months, I consider Home Leave one of the most important. 142 inmates have been recommended and sent home, and of these, all with the exception of one returned to the Institution to time, having as far as one may judge, used their leave to the best advantage. The staff are all of the opinion that this very natural but hard and exacting expression of trust is providing a most useful addition to our curriculum of training, and that it is doing much to help lads to see themselves, their homes and the outside world in a better perspective, and also that they have a much better understanding towards their training. Must we not always remember what a hard test we are putting them to in allowing this leave, and be grateful to them for their splendid response to our trust.'

'On several occasions leave has opened a lad's eyes to Home conditions and has given him food for thought on his return to the institution. Such lads have discussed their home problems with their Housemaster, the Borstal Association visitor, and have tried to adjust themselves mentally to the conditions they will live under on discharge. Apart from these most useful points, Home Leave is a "high spot" in Borstal life and a welcome addition to the common round of training.'

'Some of the most unlikely lads, of whom the Housemasters and I had certain doubts, have returned punctually, proud that they have done so. This is possibly the first act in their lives for which they have had cause for pride and the novel experience may be said to open up a new outlook on life for them. To my mind this has greater importance than the more obvious advantages.'

'The desire to be included in the list for Home Leave has also had a marked effect on the behaviour of Special Grade lads. They have realised that only by retaining their Special Grade and keeping to a good standard of progress are they likely to get their Home Leave sooner rather than later.'

The Commissioners prescribe no special time at which the leave is to be granted, but Governors tend to leave it till a boy has reached the senior grade, when it has the added value of serving both as a preparation for discharge and as a test of fitness. In special cases, where it may serve a useful purpose at a critical point of training, it may be allowed earlier. It is a condition that there should be a suitable home to go to, and the Borstal Division of the Central After-care Association report on this before hand. For those with no homes or unsuitable homes, kind friends of the Borstal often provide hospitality. The proportion failing to return is inconsiderable compared with the advantages of the scheme.

Although the foregoing has been written mainly in the masculine gender, it may be taken to apply also to the girls—at least to those at Aylesbury—with but slight variations, one being that the system of leaders is not found to be suitable, or at least not in so formal a way. At the open Borstal at East Sutton, however, with its carefully chosen population of under 60, they manage things quite differently. There are no houses and grades are used merely as an indication of progress towards discharge; but there is a much stronger·training in individual responsibility amounting almost to a system of 'self-government', with the minimum of direction and supervision by the staff. 'The aim throughout has been to establish a working democracy with which every girl and every member of the staff could identify herself, and whatever may be the future developments it can be said that this aim has been reached.' [1]

It may here be added by way of footnote that 'self-government' in our Borstals, with this exception, has scarcely attempted to establish itself. In one other Borstal only, since the war, has a sustained experiment along these lines been attempted, based on a system of house committees and an institution committee. On this the Governor is quoted in the Annual Report for 1948 as follows: 'My last observation is on the Committee system. I am sure that the introduction of the Committees has had a profound effect upon the discipline of the place. House staffs are brought face to face with their lads week by week. A good Housemaster takes his place simply as a member of the committee, leaving the chair and the secretaryship to lads. No topic is barred, full minutes are kept, and in good hands public opinion is moulded and mutual trust and respect strengthened. When the four elected members

[1] *Annual Report* 1947, p. 60.

from each house meet centrally as a committee I take my place as a committee member with a lad in the chair and a lad as secretary. This committee deals with matters above house level. Inevitably there are many matters over which the committee has no control but I endeavour to explain frankly what the position is and we begin to understand quarterly estimates, annual estimates, grants for this, that and the other and, most important of all, the need to stand well with our neighbours.' Although the subject has been discussed with sympathy and interest by the Governors in conference, other Governors have not so far been disposed to follow this lead. At all Borstals, however, the boys take a good deal of responsibility in the management of their sports and social clubs and other such matters.

(2) WORK

The basis and back-bone of the Borstal day is eight hours solid work, for if there is one thing that characterises the shiftless lads who drift into Borstal it is that hard and honest work is what they will not do. There may well be more than one way of approaching this, as the 'Principles' put it, 'very wonderful transformation that is to be accomplished'. The emphasis there was laid on work itself as the homœopathic cure, with the intention that the boy 'by the end of his training must have become so industrious that he will be able to keep any sort of job, however laborious and monotonous it may be. . . . Many were born to be hewers of wood and drawers of water. . . . For them labouring work, arduous and continuous, is the best preparation for the life that ensues. . . . It is the duty of every Borstal officer to preach the gospel of work, not because it is easy or healthy or interesting, but because it is the condition of an honest life.'

The truth of much of this cannot be denied. These boys must learn how to work hard, and above all they must learn to stick to a job— all too characteristic was the boy who, asked by his Governor how many jobs he had had before his last, replied with cheerful pride, 'Forty-eight, sir'. The disposition to throw up his job the moment he feels 'browned off' is the thing to be fought first and foremost in the training of such lads as this.

Nevertheless, the emphasis in recent years has shifted a little from the arduous doctrine of the Principles. It is important not only that boys should be made to work hard and consistently, but that they should be brought to see that it is good to do this, so that they will seriously want to go on doing it when they go out. While this frame of mind should be induced by the whole of the training, it is unlikely to be attained if his Borstal work never comes to mean more to him than an irksome daily grind—his reaction to this on release may be quite the contrary of 'becoming so industrious that he will be able to keep any sort of job'. Every effort therefore is now made to enlist 'the discipline of interest', and to see that the work is obviously purposeful and well organised. As an example, the sea-marsh reclamation at North Sea Camp, which before the war was done entirely by hand, is now done much more efficiently and quickly with certain mechanical aids: it is still hard and heavy work, but not more so than it must be, and the boys saw the difference.

The Principles, while not ignoring the desirability of trade training for those with the necessary aptitude, did not give it primary importance. 'The first purpose of the shops must necessarily be to instruct, for the Institution is a State Reformatory and not a State Factory, and its object is to make men rather than money. It is, however, a truism among those who have had experience of industrial training that the apprentice must receive his instruction, not in the academic atmosphere of the classroom or the laboratory, but in the busy workshop whose atmosphere is saturated with the spirit of production. We cannot teach a lad to lay bricks by building a surplus wall and pulling it down again, or train him to be a machinist in a shop where time and material are alike unchecked, and the tension of having to produce so much in so short a time or lose the job, is altogether absent.' Again there is sound truth behind this statement, but it is now felt not to be the whole truth. Much more effort is devoted to reducing to a minimum those who must be deemed to be 'hewers of wood and drawers of water', and to providing for the others a sound training in a skilled trade, even though that does involve building walls and pulling them down again.

A digression is necessary here to explain the present system of 'vocational training' and its shortcomings in so far as it seeks to give a boy a trade which he can hope to practise after release. In the penal systems of countries more fortunately placed in this respect, it is possible for a young person in a youth prison or reformatory to take a full apprenticeship course in a trade, to complete one started before arrest, or to complete after discharge a course started in prison. In any of these events, he takes the normal examination held for that trade by the State or Guild authority, and receives the normal certificate issued by the authority bearing no trace of the fact that the course was taken in prison. The writer has since the late war personally observed these arrangements, and noted their value with envy, in the United States, Switzerland and Germany. No doubt they obtain in other countries which have apprenticeship schemes organised on this basis.

In England, however, the apprenticeship system is quite otherwise— or at least in the trades with which we have so far been concerned in Borstals. It calls for no specific course of training and requires no examination, but it does require that the young person should serve from the age of 16 to 21 in the trade. Every effort has been made to obtain recognition of the training given in a Borstal as counting towards an apprenticeship, but so far without result, though the negotiations still 'drag their slow length along'. So a Borstal boy, who has probably learned more in a year's intensive instruction and practical work than he would in three years' work as a boy in the trade, can only go out with a certificate that he has completed a course of theoretical and practical training in such-and-such a Borstal. Whether this document will get him a job of any sort in the trade depends on local circumstances and the discretion with which it is used: towards recognition as a tradesman it will probably be useless. Indeed it is not given to the boy at all, but sent direct to the Borstal After-care Division to use in his interests at discretion.

Pending a solution of these difficulties, the Commissioners decided as a *pis aller* to base vocational training on the 6 months' courses introduced by the Ministry of Labour and National Service during the war for the training of ex-servicemen in various skilled trades. With the co-operation of the Ministry their syllabus for each selected trade was applied under the direction of a qualified officer or of a skilled craftsman recruited direct as a trade instructor.

At the end of 1950 the number of such classes in operation, and the trades taught, were as follows:

Carpentry	6
Woodworking Machinists	5
Motor Mechanics	4
Sheet Metal work	1
Farming	9
Bricklaying	10
Painting	10
Blacksmith	3
Engineering Fitters	2
Boot and Shoe making and Repairing	2
Cookery	12
Horticulture	5
	69

The number of boys under training in these classes was about 600. The normal size of a class is about twelve.

The system, which is under the control of the Senior Vocational Training Officer and his assistants at the Head Office, begins with the findings of the Vocational Guidance Officer at the Reception Centre, which serve as a guide to the authorities of the training Borstal.

The courses include both theoretical and practical training. Many boys who could do well on the practical side are handicapped by inadequate education on the theoretical side, and much is done both to link up trade training with evening education and to provide 'prevocational training' courses to fill these educational gaps. The examinations are necessarily internal but are centrally controlled to ensure a good and common standard. In 1950 a start was made in linking the courses with an external examination (the Intermediate City of London and Guilds) and a few passes were obtained. This arrangement, if it can be successfully developed, may go some way towards filling the gap left by the peculiarities of our apprenticeship system.

On completion of his course, the trainee will be passed on to practical work in the trade for the rest of his institutional training: indeed in many of the courses practical work will be interspersed with the normal run of the syllabus. One interesting development may be noted here. To secure a practical follow-up for boys trained in motor mechanics, arrangements have been made at one Borstal for their employment as ordinary workers in local garages, returning to the Borstal in the evening: this may be the thin end of a very useful wedge. It may be that in future training and production will be integrated in the Borstals as in the 'industrial training' system now used in prisons: change awaits some definite outcome of the negotiations about apprenticeship.

Another aspect of our contemporary life tends to obscure the purely vocational value of this training—the majority of the boys go direct from their Borstals to their national service in the Armed Forces.[1]

It is fortunate therefore that this system has more to commend it than its actual vocational value on release. These other values have been well expressed by various Governors in comments published in the Annual Reports for 1948 and 1949, as follows:

'There is no doubt of the great value of trade training nor of its incidental character training. Indeed, for some lads, the effect of the discipline of study and practice on their character outweighs even the vocational value of the course.'

'Though the courses are of the greatest value as instruments of training because they give lads in them an objective and a definite and interesting form of daily work, I believe that it will be found that few of those who have passed through the courses will take up the same type of work in ordinary life. This is partly due to the break which occurs in the great majority of cases between leaving and taking up civilian work because army service supervenes.'

'Reviewing the past 20 years of Borstal Training in trades and the establishment of these Vocational Trade Training Courses, one cannot but be glad of them. They fill a need and provide an aim for more lads than ever before, and create a variety of interest in the Institution that lightens the atmosphere and gives a more purposeful air to the week's work.'

'Of the lads who have passed out of the Painters and Decorators V.T. Course, about 70 per cent have been up to Improver's Standard, a

[1] In 1951 the C.A.C.A. estimated that approximately half the boys trained in a trade who do not go into the Forces follow their trades on release.

satisfactory result when one considers the apparently unpromising human material with which each course started. This Course, and the influence of the Instructor, has a marked moral effect on some of the most difficult lads. There have even been cases of lads, whom even their Housemasters have considered almost hopeless, who have volunteered to stay in the Institution beyond what would have been their discharge date in order to complete the Course.'

'I am convinced that, apart from any utilitarian advantage derived from teaching a lad a trade and giving him the knowledge and skill to earn his living, the Trade Training Classes are immensely useful in keeping lads contented, happy, and fully occupied during their Borstal training and are educational in the widest sense of the word.'

'I think I can say that all the work is purposeful. It is not all obviously designed for fitting a boy for discharge. I record my firm conviction that the introduction of trade training in its present form has done more to convince the boy of our intentions than any other piece of training. Even those who are not actively engaged on the classes recognise this fact.'

Apart from the trade training, the work is all useful and purposeful, once a boy has got through his beginner's stage of domestic chores—and these too have to be done by some one. The various wood and metal work shops turn out high quality work; large numbers are employed on skilled jobs with the Works Department, often including the building of staff quarters and other major works; and some hundreds will at most seasons be working on the institution farms and gardens or for neighbouring farmers. The kitchens and bakeries too provide excellent training, with special courses and examinations from which certificates can be gained. Except at North Sea Camp and Gringley, the special features of which have already been described, no Borstal is now purely agricultural in its interests.

The girls do not conform very closely with this picture. Work will not form the basis of their after-life in the same way as for boys: for the most part, they think of it as a means of earning enough to provide a good time and a good appearance on the way to marriage, and little more. They are not seriously interested. Nevertheless, advice has been taken as to possible trades in which they could be given vocational training, but without result. Even had such trades been forthcoming, the chances are that most of them would have gone into simple repetitive factory work for higher pay at the first opportunity. Work therefore centres round the domestic crafts—dressmaking, laundering, cooking, housework, farms and gardens, though in these the girls are given a thorough training which will equip them not only to get good work but to run good homes. At Aylesbury there is also a workshop, now devoted to dismembering telephone and other such equipment: this is quite useful and interesting work, requiring some care and skill, but it is sad to remember that during the war the shop was used for assembling complete wireless sets.

East Sutton also concentrates, in a more homely atmosphere, on the domestic crafts. The girls also take a good deal of pride in their ability to help the Engineer in almost any kind of works job about the place, whether as electricians, bricklayers or carpenters: there is little need to import masculine labour here. There are extensive market gardens run on a highly skilled basis, and a growing farm, while many of the girls work regularly for the neighbouring farmers alongside their usual workers.

(3) EDUCATION AND RECREATION

Although education plays a large and valuable part in Borstal training, so much that has already been said about education in prisons is equally applicable that a few notes on particularities will suffice. The system is based on the recommendations of the Education Advisory Committee, and is under the direction of the Local Education Authorities, who now provide a full-time teacher at most of the Borstals to take general responsibility. Every boy or girl is required to spend at least 6 hours a week in evening education; while for the backward and illiterate education forms part of the normal working day, 2 hours each morning being usual. Technical and other correspondence courses are also used, and courses are sometimes taken at local technical schools. The provision for vocational education has already been mentioned.

As in the prisons, education shades imperceptibly through art classes, handicrafts, play readings, musical appreciation and the like into recreation. Every institution is likely to have its clubs for producing live art—an Amateur Dramatic Society or a Music Society—its Wireless or Gramophone Club, or even at one boys' Borstal a Television Club. Many Governors have noted the enthusiasm for good music which can be aroused among young people who have never yet heard anything but 'boogie-woogie'. It would take much space to record the fertile variety of expedients used by Borstal staffs to awaken and encourage interest in any and every rewarding aspect of art and nature.

Two regular forms of activity of a quasi-educational nature are the Young Farmers' Clubs and the Cadet Forces, both of which have the added value of linking the boys—and in the case of the farmers the girls too—with other young people engaged in similar activities. At every Borstal with a substantial farm there is a branch of the national Young Farmers' Clubs linked with the county organisation, in which the Borstal branch often comes to play a prominent part—in one year one Borstal provided a prize-winning team for the county, another the local chairman, in this case 'Madam Chair'. The Cadet Forces exist only at those Borstals taking younger boys who will go into the forces on discharge, and they are a great help in giving the boys confidence and a good start in their service life. Generally, thanks to the devotion of the Borstal officers who, as Cadet Officers, give their time to this training, they reach a standard which brings credit on their Borstal in competition with other companies, and is of some value to the morale of the whole institution. The following report from a Governor, quoted in the Annual Report for 1948, is typical:

'The Company of Army Cadets has been a distinct success and, I believe, has added to the general morale of the whole institution. They are smart and well disciplined, and have developed a sense of loyalty and *esprit de corps* that is most encouraging. Their Borstal training and physique provides a standard second to none in the Battalion and the Commanding Officer of the Battalion is extremely pleased with the whole set up. 18 ranks attended the annual camp near Aldershot for a week: the Guard of Honour was formed by lads from this institution and were personally congratulated by Lord Montgomery: they took part in everything that was going on in the camp and behaved as ordinary decent lads and good soldiers in the making. Their conduct and trustworthiness was beyond reproach, in fact, I am told they set a most excellent standard in every way.'

Sport is another channel which brings boys and girls alike into healthy contact with other young people. Borstal football, cricket, net-ball and tennis teams often do well in the local Leagues, and some of them in local athletics as well.

'In June we joined with the local Youth Organisations in a combined Sports Day and an excellent afternoon's sport was enjoyed by all. Several of our lads won their events, going on to compete and represent the District in the County finals. One lad came first in the mile race and the following is an extract from a letter received from the County Youth Organiser:

' "I feel that I must write you concerning the participation of your boys in the sports on Saturday last. I must congratulate them on the excellent manner in which they contested the various events and I had great personal satisfaction on congratulating young . . . on his success in the mile.

' "Several of the County Committee members were very impressed with the conduct and general bearing of your boys and I can only hope that your co-operation in this direction will be continued in future years."

'The Institution joined the Youth Club Table Tennis League, and played 28 games. Fourteen of these were away matches, played at Clubs most of which were part of a larger organisation.

'There was free association with other members, some of whom were girls from the age of 16 upwards. The general standard of behaviour of the lads was excellent and they fitted in remarkably well.

'Several cross-country runs were arranged between the institution, the Army and the Grammar School. Although we did not win any of these matches, the spirit of the contests was good. Regular football matches were played each week with Youth Clubs, local works' teams and Football clubs. The standard of play and sportsmanship of the institution 1st, 2nd, and 3rd elevens has done much to give us a good name.' (Annual Reports for 1949 and 1948.)

Another regular break is camp—holiday camps of all kinds, week-end camps, weeks by the sea, weeks on a farm helping to get in the harvest, week-ends with undergraduates or Brothers of St. Francis, even one with 'pot-holers and cavers'. These serve not only as a refreshing break in institution life, and a meeting-ground with new friends and faces, but they enable the staff and the boys to get to know each other on much more revealing terms.

Then there is a variety of activities specifically directed to 'de-institutionalisation' and the making of normal social contacts. Apart from country rambles and visits to places of local interest, trips to the town for shopping, the cinema, or a football match and so forth, most institutions organise some regular social contacts with neighbouring youth. Some link up with local Youth Clubs, others are adopted by Toc H, some run an occasional dance, and one 'closed' institution has started its own Youth Club, described by the Governor as follows:

'The Compass Club was opened in July and caters for about 80 Special Grade lads. It is managed by an outside Leader provided by the Education Committee. It is run just the same as an ordinary Youth Club outside and has the same facilities. Contacts have been made with outside clubs and social functions have been held. Whist Drives, Dances and Concerts are well attended and valuable outside contacts have been formed. The conduct of the members generally has been extremely satisfactory: up to date only one expulsion has been enforced. The equipment has so far not been mishandled but treated with the utmost respect. I wouldn't say that bad language has been completely eliminated but from the many female helpers who visit the club I have had nothing but praise for the lads' behaviour and courtesy shown to them. I believe that if we can inculcate a desire for club life and a sense of loyalty and responsibility to the other members, Leaders and the club, then the crave for pin-table saloons, undesirable dance and billiard halls and street corners may disappear.'

All these multifarious activities, it must be remembered, take place in the leisure time of the boys and girls when their work and education are done, and all form a valuable part of their social training. Not less valuable is the spirit of good-neighbourliness which they foster between a Borstal and those who live around it, a spirit essential to the effective working of such an institution. Much gratitude is due to all these good neighbours and friends who do not pass by on the other side, but gladly expend time and spirit in helping 'to save the young and careless from a wasted life of crime'.

(4) DISCIPLINE

Discussion of discipline in Borstal institutions must import more than an interpretation of the Statutory Rules dealing with offences and punishments: the first thing is to understand what, in Borstal training, discipline means. The importance of such an understanding has been emphasised by certain observations in the report, published in June 1951, of the Departmental Committee to Review Punishments in Prisons and Borstal Institutions. The Committee based these observations on their conclusion that there existed in Borstals what they described as 'a policy of leniency', and, on the basis of certain evidence given before them and of their personal observation of the demeanour of certain Borstal boys, they stated 'that discipline in general requires tightening, even at the cost of an increase in punishments, and that the policy of leniency, appeasement, or soft treatment as at present interpreted is not having the success expected or desired' (para. 33).

Since the Prison Commissioners did not accept the existence either of this 'policy of leniency' or of the deterioration in discipline believed to have resulted from it, the present account must proceed on the basis of what has hitherto been the declared policy of the Commissioners, leaving its effect as *sub judice* pending any further official pronouncement. For this policy we must again go to the Principles, which opened the chapter dealing with discipline as follows:

'There can be few words so frequently used, but in so many different senses, as the word "discipline". There is a form of discipline in the army, another in the navy, a third in a school, a fourth in the factory and so on. Each section of the community has its own form of discipline, and is frequently under a dangerous illusion that this is discipline, and that any other form is an inferior imitation. The real fact is, of course, that discipline is the first condition of life in a civilised community, and without it chaos must ensue. Each community, according to its size or nature, ultimately discovers and adopts the form of discipline most appropriate to it. We therefore in our Borstal Institutions must have our own brand of discipline appropriate to our needs.

'In its simplest form, discipline is a mere obedience to orders. That is where it starts, and unless the basis is secure, and every order given by those in authority is obeyed with alacrity and without question, no superstructure can be built. But the higher manifestations of discipline advance far from this simple beginning. The most highly disciplined form of society is that where every man is free, and his every act, free and unbidden, contributes to the good of the community.' Later we find: 'Order is kept now not by the mere weight of authority, but by the use of *control*, a far more difficult power to acquire than mere authority, on the part of the Officer, and the growth of consent among the lads. This is a far higher standard of discipline to have attained than that of years ago.

'It must be said again that, if the Institution is to train lads for freedom, it cannot train them in an atmosphere of captivity and repression. They must learn to exercise aright their power to choose. If they are forever forced by weight of numbers to do right, their faculty to choose will atrophy, and on discharge they will wait for promptings from without because there is no voice from within. In the Institutions, therefore, we must have a form of discipline which exacts something from the lad, fostering the will to do well, putting it up to him to choose right, not forcing, through fear of punishment, the right choice upon him. . . .

'It may be argued, with some show of reason, that this is no doubt a good way of running a lads' club, but can hardly be applied to a Borstal Institution, composed of three or four hundred young criminals, very different from the average member of a club. The difference, indeed, exists. The Officer, mindful of it, will be led by common sense and experience to take certain precautions which he would neglect in a lads' club. But if a Borstal Officer is to make the most of his lads, he will keep his caution in the background, and treat them generally as though they were members of his club. If he is constantly thinking of them as young criminals, they will so think of themselves. There is no telepathy more sure and rapid than the perception of attitude. If, however, an Officer can, without losing his balance, control and common sense, treat his lads as he would treat working lads in a rough club outside, the great majority will rise to the suggestions and live up to the level on which they have been set. . . .

'On the other hand, the Governor or his deputy is a student of boy nature, and knows that many of the silly things they do are merely symptoms of a certain condition, and it is the business of the Institution to deal with the condition rather than the symptoms. A doctor would justifiably refuse to prescribe certain treatment for a lad merely because another lad, showing the same symptoms, received that treatment the week before. Similarly, in discipline, the punishment must fit the offender rather than the offence. Sometimes it will seem that the lad has been dealt with rather lightly when he has committed an offence and is only reprimanded, the truth being that in his case the offence is not so heinous as it would be in the case of another lad. At other times a slight irregularity may point to a collapse which requires drastic action. Punishment is regulated not by an exact tariff according to the offence, but a perception of the condition that is revealed by this particular act. On occasion this principle may be overridden by the necessity that one should suffer in the interest of the rest. . . .

'On the Borstal Officer is cast a decision just as difficult as that of the Governor at adjudication, when he has to decide whether or not he shall report a lad. He too will distinguish between his lads, giving some lads more rope, figuratively speaking, than others. Some of the feebler specimens he will father, with others he will stand no nonsense, others again he will call aside and speak to them with quiet and unhurried emphasis. There is no golden rule which can be given to him save this, that he shall learn the nature of all his lads and do the best for each. If he can only work by a fixed rule, and insist on knowing 'where he is', guarded in every emergency by an exact regulation that fits the circumstance, a Borstal Institution is no place for him. The System trusts the Officer by outlining principles rather than imposing rules, and those who visit the Institutions from far countries see nothing in them that compels their admiration so much as the wisdom with which the Officers exercise their discretion and the firmness with which they maintain their control.'

These Principles, in the absence of subsequent qualification, must be taken as representing the spirit in which Borstal Governors and their staffs have been expected, at least for the past twenty years, to exercise control over the inmates of the institutions.

It must also be assumed that the Commissioners require Governors and their staffs to act in conformity with the first of the Borstal Rules under the heading 'Discipline and Control', which reads as follows:

'25. The purpose of Borstal training requires that every inmate, while conforming to the rules necessary for well-ordered community life, shall be able to develop his individuality on right lines with a proper sense of personal responsibility. Officers shall therefore, while firmly maintaining discipline and order, seek so to do by influencing the inmates through their own example and leadership and by enlisting their willing co-operation.'

The remainder of the Rules under this heading follow the general pattern of the Prison Rules, setting out the acts which constitute an offence against discipline, the permitted punishments, and the procedure for dealing with offences, including provision for more serious offences to be dealt with by the Board of Visitors. They also include similar provisions as to the use of mechanical restraints and as to facilities for inmates to make complaints.

The main differences from prison practice lie in the nature of the punishments which may be used. In the first place, corporal punishment may not be used at all. The permitted punishments are as follows:

If awarded by the Governor under Rule 37 (1):

'(a) removal of an inmate from his house;

'(b) deprivation of privileges for a period not exceeding twenty-eight days;

'(c) deprivation of association for a period not exceeding twenty-eight days;

'(d) stoppage of earnings for a period not exceeding fourteen days;

'(e) reduction in grade, or delay in promotion to a higher grade, for a period not exceeding three months;

'(f) confinement to a room for a period not exceeding three days;

'(g) restricted diet No. 1 for a period not exceeding three days;

'(h) restricted diet No. 2 for a period not exceeding fifteen days.

If awarded by the Board of Visitors under Rule 38 (1):

'(a) any award authorised under Rule 37 (1);

'(b) stoppage of earnings for a period not exceeding twenty-eight days;

'(c) reduction in grade, or delay in promotion to a higher grade;

'(d) confinement to a room for a period not exceeding fourteen days;

'(e) restricted diet No. 1 for a period not exceeding fifteen days;

'(f) restricted diet No. 2 for a period not exceeding forty-two days.

'Removal from house' in these Rules replaces what was formerly called 'the penal class'. It means removal from the normal life of the house to a separate part of the institution, where each is confined in a separate room and association is restricted to work. Diet is also restricted to the essentials of the normal diet—no jam, puddings or extras. The further effects of this punishment may be varied to meet individual needs: the normal work of those undergoing this punishment is something dreary and disagreeable, but the Governor may allow a boy to remain at his usual work if he thinks fit. He may also attend education classes. He will not attend any entertainments, club-meetings or the like or take part in any games. The general intention is that the conditions may be varied to meet different cases from a severe punishment to a period of retirement for reflection in appropriate austerity.

The other punishments set out above speak for themselves but it is necessary to say something about dietary punishment.

In 1948 the use of dietary punishment was suspended in Borstals, by direction of the Secretary of State, for an experimental period of two years. 'The reasons given for this decision were that dietary restriction was a completely negative form of punishment; that it was not consonant with the principles and ideals of the Borstal system; and that discipline could be maintained satisfactorily without it.' [1] The Committee, having been appointed before this experimental period expired, naturally considered this, as they described it, 'highly controversial question', on which they 'were not surprised to hear widely divergent views expressed'. Their recommendations on the subject were that No. 1 punishment diet should be restored, but that No. 2 should be abolished. Pending a decision on this question by the Secretary of State, it is expedient to leave it as being also *sub judice*.[2]

With one exception, which will be noted later, the other recommendations of the Committee were concerned with minor questions of procedure under or interpretation of the Rules.

These then are the powers and procedures available within the Borstals for maintaining discipline and control, but there are still others, for use in exceptional cases, involving removal from the normal training institutions temporarily or permanently. The first is removal to the Correctional Borstal at Wandsworth:[3] this is reserved mainly for absconders who cannot be dealt with locally or have committed further offences while at large. Now that open Borstals have been provided with security blocks for 'removal from house', it is rarely necessary to use Wandsworth for other forms of serious misconduct. An Assistant Commissioner visits periodically to consider the re-allocation of the boys there, only those who have received a concurrent sentence of imprisonment for further offences being kept more than a few months.

Next in order of seriousness comes removal to the special Borstal at Hull. This is not intended as a means to enable Governors to get rid of any and every difficult boy, nor would Governors generally be disposed to use it in that defeatist manner. But there are some who are not only totally irresponsive to and unco-operative in their training, but have an evil influence that must be excised for the good of the others in the house. It may also, since it provides complete security, seem to be the best place for some of the persistent absconders. Hull, as has been said earlier, is a training Borstal and those transferred from other Borstals [4] are sent to complete their training there, not for temporary correction. The régime contains the elements of Borstal training, but trust and privileges are limited and delayed, and physical

---

[1] Departmental Committee's Report, Part II, para. 51.
[2] See Appendix I, Part II,
[3] New Reading, see Appendix K, note on p. 308.
[4] These so far are a small proportion of the Hull population.

conditions are more those of a prison than of a normal Borstal. At the time of writing Hull as a Borstal is but 6 months old, and it is too early to speak in detail of a system which is still in the making, or to speak at all of its results. The establishment of such an institution was recommended by the Departmental Committee.

The third and final power is that of commutation of the Borstal sentence to one of imprisonment. We have already noted (p. 354) the legal provision governing this power, and the views expressed thereon by the Departmental Committee on the Treatment of Young Offenders. Since the war it has been necessary to use the power more frequently, the average number per year for 1946–1950 being about ten. The Punishments Committee of 1951 thought that there would be 'obvious objections to encouraging any substantial extension of the practice, among them it would involve over-riding the verdict of the Court which imposed a sentence of Borstal training': they thought the setting up of a special Borstal might prove a better way of dealing with the types for whom commutation had been used. This may prove to be so for some of them, but probably not for all—Hull must remain a training Borstal, and certain young men of today make it clear both that they will not tolerate the kind of training Borstal seeks to give and that Borstal cannot tolerate them.

In view of the special reference made by the Young Offenders Committee to the 'unhappy' results of commutation for girls, it is worth while to note that in the few cases in recent years in which a girl's sentence has been commuted the result has almost invariably been the opposite. The prison staffs, in a different environment, have often succeeded in setting right girls who in Borstal have been completely intractable, and their reconviction figures have not been high.

Before leaving the question of punishments, mention should be made of the fact that housemasters are authorised, by delegation of the Governor's powers under the Rules, to punish for minor offences. The Punishments Committee (paras. 81, 82) said that they fully approved of this practice and were 'satisfied that housemasters use their powers reasonably and do not accept jurisdiction in cases which should properly be dealt with by the Governor'. There is less formality of procedure in these cases, and serious punishments are not awarded.

The Rules provide a method of treatment which may properly be considered under the general heading of discipline, though it is in no sense a punishment.

Rule 26 provides as follows:

'(1) If the Governor is satisfied that the behaviour of an inmate is such that, in the interests of his own training or of the good conduct of his house, he should be temporarily removed from normal community life, he may order the removal of the inmate from his house.

'(2) Inmates removed from their houses shall be accommodated in a separate part of the Borstal under such restrictions of association, diet, earnings, and privileges as the Commissioners determine:

'Provided that where diet is restricted it shall not be reduced below a nutritional standard adequate for health and strength at normal work.

'(3) An inmate shall not be removed from his house under this Rule for longer than is necessary to achieve the purpose of the removal, and during this period every effort shall be made to ascertain the causes of the inmate's behaviour and to correct it.'

Since confusion may arise between removal from house under this Rule, and removal as a punishment, it may be well to clarify this distinction and explain the purpose and operation of the Rule by quoting the Commissioners' directions thereunder in full:

'It is first necessary to emphasise the fundamental difference between removal under Rule 26 and removal under Rule 37. The former is a method of treatment, to be used entirely in the Governor's discretion; the latter is a punishment, to be awarded only as prescribed by the Rule. Rule 26 should not be used where the circumstances clearly require that the inmate should be reported and dealt with under Rule 37.

'An inmate may be removed under Rule 26 in many different sorts of situation, sometimes in the interests of the House, sometimes in his own interests. In the former category might come the case of an inmate known to be exercising a bad influence who manages to avoid being put on report, or one who has an outburst of bad temper or hysteria disturbing to the House, but not such as to call for action under Rules 37 or 43: [1] in the latter, one who is being bullied or worried, or for any other reason might benefit by a temporary withdrawal from ordinary House life.

'The essence of removal under Rule 26, therefore, is change of location, and it need have no other consequences beyond those which must result from the change of location. It is in every way preferable, for example, that an inmate so removed should carry on his work in his usual party, and attend his usual educational classes: but it remains within the Governor's discretion to make different arrangements to suit the needs of different cases.

'The Commissioners' directions on the matters set out in the Rule are accordingly as follows:

'*Association*—should not be restricted beyond the necessities of the case, and the restriction should never, except in special cases for the shortest necessary period, amount to confinement to a room.

[1] Rule 43 provides for the temporary confinement of violent or refractory inmates in a special room, but not as a punishment and only for so long as is necessary.

'*Diet*—should not be altered.

'*Earnings*—will depend on the Governor's directions as to work. If the inmate remains with his party his earnings will not be affected. If he works on his own, they need not be affected, but they may be adjusted if necessary to the effort he makes and to the nature of the work. If through his own fault he does not work, he will not earn. The Governor may direct, if he thinks fit in a particular case, that amounts earned be withheld until the inmate returns to the House.

'*Privileges*—Removal from House under Rule 26 will not automatically affect promotion in grade, though naturally, where it has become necessary through the inmate's own fault, the nature of that fault and its bearing on promotion will be taken account of by the Institution Board in the normal course of considering that inmate's case.

'Privileges will normally be affected only to the extent that the change of location requires. Such privileges as taking part in games, walks, etc., or attending clubs or entertainments, should be dealt with by the Governor according to the circumstances of each case.

'Care should be taken that all inmates who are being dealt with under Rule 26, Rule 37 (1) (*a*) or (*f*),[1] or Rule 43 [2] understand what measures are being applied to them and why.'

It is, unfortunately, impossible to close this section without reference to the problem of absconding, which in post-war years had grown so serious that the Commissioners in their Annual Report for 1948 described it as 'one of their gravest concerns' and 'a challenge to the Borstal system'. The Punishments Committee naturally considered this question at length, and quoted figures which showed that the number of abscondings had risen from 514, or 16 per cent of the total number detained, in 1945, to 1,031 or 23 per cent of the number detained in 1949. As compared with these figures, the average number of abscondings for the 5 years 1935–39 was 124 or 4 per cent of the average numbers detained.

It has been made sufficiently clear that it is of the essence of the Borstal system that safe-custody cannot be an over-riding consideration, and Borstal boys and girls being what they are, to run away from trouble is their natural course. This being so, these figures may seem less disturbing if their effect is stated as being that of every five boys or girls who could abscond if they chose only one in fact does so. Indeed it would no doubt be true to say that whatever might be the concern of the administration about this situation, public opinion would scarcely concern itself at all if absconders did not commit offences while at large. Unhappily they do, though no large proportion: indeed if the proportion were much larger the 'challenge to the Borstal system'

[1] See p. 384.   [2] See p. 387.

would be critical, since such offences are concentrated around the Borstals in the attempt to get food and civilian clothing to assist escape. It is this aspect of the problem which causes 'the gravest concern', for there is no satisfactory answer to the just indignation of the neighbours of Borstal if they are subject to constant fear of such depredations. Quick and generous compensation is paid for loss and damage—unless covered by insurance—but that can be no more than a palliative.

What are the reasons for this serious deterioration of the situation in post-war years? As stated by the Commissioners to the Punishments Committee (para. 71), they are mainly as follows:

'1. That the Borstal system was almost completely disintegrated during the war and there is even now a bare nucleus of staff who had experience of the system before the war.

'2. That the young men who are now in Borstals belong to the generation which suffered most the unsettling conditions of the war years. Evacuation, bombing, interrupted schooling, lack of proper parental control all helped to produce boys and girls who are not able, or are not disposed, to count the cost of their actions and are therefore more difficult to train.

'3. That the Commissioners have taken into use additional open Borstals to accommodate the increased population. One consequence of this development is that many lads have to be sent to open institutions who by pre-war standards would have been sent to closed Borstals.'

And what, finally, is the answer to the challenge? So far as the foregoing reasons are valid, the passage of time alone can remove them. The slow rebuilding of the pre-war tradition and morale depends both on greater stability and responsibility in the young people received and on greater experience in the staff. The third condition must remain unless more secure Borstals are to be built to house some of those who are now placed perforce in open conditions. Even so, there will always be abscondings so long as Borstal training is not confined within a prison wall. It is impossible to remove the reasons for a wholly irrational act, and most of these boys and girls have very little idea why they run away, or even in many cases that they are going to do so till it happens. For many it is almost essential to do it, just to work it out of their systems, and when it is over they settle down and do perfectly well. From the point of view of their training, it is only a serious matter when it becomes persistent. Absconders are of course severely punished, often very severely, but if Borstal boys and girls were of the sort that stop to count the cost of foolish acts before doing them they would not be in Borstal: it may legitimately be doubted whether greater severity of punishment would make a significant difference.

No quick or easy solution of this difficult problem is therefore to be expected, and its consideration can end only on a note of qualified hope.

(5) GENERAL

An analytical description of this sort cannot convey any real impression of what a Borstal looks like, or the general run of a Borstal day. The former is in any case impossible, for no two Borstals look alike: one can only say that in the prison and camp types the physical austerity of the buildings is matched by the furnishings, which are much like the prison style except in the dining and association rooms—here small tables for four and suitable chairs give a pleasant appearance. A good deal is done to brighten things up with flowers, framed posters and the like, so that most dining and common rooms look cheerful enough. Though it might equally have been mentioned under education, one might here notice that a scheme is working, financed from non-official funds, for circulating sets of framed reproductions of fine pictures, from Giotto to Picasso, which are changed periodically. There are generally plenty of class-rooms, good work-shops, an assembly-hall which serves also as a theatre, a gymnasium and in the more permanent premises a chapel. Outside will be gardens, a parade and physical training ground and sports fields, with a swimming pool at most places.

The boys at work look very much like other young men at work, wearing grey trousers, a blue wind-jammer, and a general appearance of robust health. For evening and better wear they have blue jackets of blazer type with a grey pull-over, shirt, collar and tie and grey trousers. The traditional brown jackets and shorts disappeared after the war, and grades are now distinguished by a badge, not by different coloured clothes. They wear their hair far too long, and their general demeanour is boisterous and friendly.

The girls too have been re-dressed since the war, and can make their own choice of dresses from a fair variety of not too institutional patterns and colours. At work they wear overalls for house or shop work, and suitable garments for the farm or garden or other outside jobs. Their demeanour, if a little more complex than that of the boys, also suggests cheerful health.

The medical officers, in fact, are more concerned with the care of the mind than that of the body, though their general duties and responsibility are the same in principle as those of prison doctors. It is, therefore, only at the largest Borstals that there are full-time doctors, and to these are allocated so far as possible boys who would benefit from their presence, including those few who require special physical attention.

Healthy adolescents, working hard and often out of doors in all weathers, need a lot of food, and the calorific value of the Borstal diet for both boys and girls is higher than that of the prison diet. There are four meals a day—breakfast, dinner, tea and supper.

They have a long and busy day in which to work off their energies. Get up, clean up, physical training, breakfast, four hours work, dinner, another four hours work, change and clean up, tea and then a break when the dart-boards and ping-pong tables are thronged amidst the competing noises of radio, laughter and heavy feet on hard floors. Then a 'silent hour' in their rooms for reading or writing, followed by classes or an hour in the gymnasium, supper, a little more free time, house prayers and bed. Such at least is the general pattern, though it will vary, especially after tea, from one Borstal to another, from house to house, from grade to grade and often from boy to boy. To find out what is going on in a Borstal in any detail, the only safe plan is to go and see.

CHAPTER TWENTY-THREE

RELEASE AND AFTER

(1) RELEASE

RULE 94 provides that 'an inmate shall become eligible for release in accordance with the Second Schedule to the Criminal Justice Act 1948 [1] when the Commissioners are satisfied that there is a reasonable probability that the objects of training as defined in Rule 4 have been achieved': that is to say, that there has been established in the inmate the will to lead a good and useful life on release, and that he has been fitted by his training to do so.

The Rules further provide to this end that the Institution Board shall keep under review the progress of each inmate throughout his training, and make a report to the Governor when they consider a boy or girl fit for release. If the Governor is satisfied he refers the case to the Board of Visitors who, if they agree, 'shall thereupon recommend to the Commissioners that the inmate be released under supervision'. When the Commissioners have decided that an inmate shall be released, the arrangements for release shall be made in consultation with the Central After-Care Association.

The key words in these provisions are 'reasonable probability'. In dealing with human material of this sort certainty in human judgment is not to be looked for: whether this fallibility may be modified by the use of 'prediction tables' is for the future to determine. Meanwhile, the Borstal staffs in the light of their experience and intuition record their views on the progress and prospects of each of the young people in their charge, and from the time the minimum period of 9 months is reached the institution boards periodically weigh them up.

'The principle implicit in the methods of selection for release under the Act is that each boy's readiness for release must be assessed on his own merits, and this is carefully observed. There is, therefore, no set period of training or automatic discharge' [2]. . . . Nevertheless, something like an average expectation must come to be established, though

---

[1] See p. 352.　　　　　[2] *Annual Report* 1949, p. 56.

this varies a good deal between institutions according to the type of youth received in each. Thus in those taking the more hopeful type the averages have recently been 12–15 months, and in others 15–20 months. The average over all the boys' Borstals in 1949 was 17·6 months; for girls it was 22 months at Aylesbury and 20 months at East Sutton. 57 boys were released at or before 12 months, and 203 were detained for over 2 years: no girl served less than 13 months, and the longest period was 31 months.[1]

Sooner or later, then, the Governor and the board have to make up their minds, on the basis of what they think they know about the boy or girl and of what the C.A.C.A. representative tells them about his or her prospects, whether the time has come to recommend release. In many cases they can be fairly sure that the purposes of the training have been achieved, in many there must be doubt, and in some they can be fairly sure not only that the purposes have not been achieved but that they are not likely to be. It is not possible to attempt an appraisement of the general accuracy of their findings: perhaps a boy with a good pre-sentence record who has done well in Borstal is released in 12 months—a month later he is again before a court, which may make an acid comment on the circumstances. But there are so many reasons for failure on release, and who can say that another 3 or 6 months training would have prevented this one? In the doubtful cases there may often be as great a risk in holding a boy too long as in releasing him too soon—'it is often true that the boy or girl may "go off" rather than "come on" if the training is further prolonged'.[2] Then there are the cases that seem hopeless: they would probably not become more hopeful by keeping them for the full 3 years, and except where release has been delayed by resolute misconduct it must often seem wise to read the Rule as meaning 'achieved, so far as they are likely to be achieved'. It must also be remembered that relapse into crime may well be prevented by proper supervision outside, and that the longer the training inside the shorter the period of supervision.

These perplexities are no doubt inherent in any system of indeterminate sentences, and it can only be said in conclusion that everyone concerned addresses himself seriously to the task of carrying out the intention of the Act and the Rules in the spirit as well as in the letter, and that when Borstal boys and girls relapse after release their failure is not necessarily to be attributed to errors of judgment in the timing of release.

(2) SUPERVISION AND AFTER-CARE

The essential part played by this second part of Borstal training, and the importance attached to it in the Principles and the Rules, have

---

[1] The figures quoted in this para. are from pp. 55 and 59 of the *Annual Report* for 1949.   [2] *Prisons and Borstals*, p. 64.

already been indicated (p. 359): it remains only to fill in the details.

The Central After-Care Association is in close touch from the beginning with every boy or girl who will eventually come under its care, and the Directors of the Borstal Division for boys and the Women and Girls' Division for girls, or their representatives, regularly visit the institutions to see the inmates and discuss their future with them and with their Governors and housemasters.

For plans to be made there must be full knowledge of the local conditions to which the inmate will return—the home and family, the prospects of work and the social 'milieu'. To obtain this knowledge the Borstal Division works through its local associates, who today are the members of the Probation Service assigned to this recognised part of their statutory duties. The Women's Division, with its much smaller numbers, has its own full-time Supervisors in different parts of the country, though it can equally rely on the co-operation of the Probation Service where necessary. Thus the associates who will be responsible for supervision are also 'in the picture' and preparing the way from an early stage of the sentence: and many of them find that they can do a lot of useful ground-work with the family meantime.

When the day comes for this difficult change from the regulated life of an institution to controlled liberty, the boy will be handed a copy of the statutory 'notice' which sets out the conditions of his release as follows:

'1. On your release the Central After-Care Association will tell you where to go, and you must go there and not change your address without the permission of the Association or the person under whose supervision you are placed.

'2. If told to do so you must report, either by letter or by personal visit as required, to the Association or the person under whose supervision you are placed.

'3. Being under supervision means that you must do as the Association or your supervisor tells you. You must work where you are told. You must be punctual and regular at your work and must lead a sober, steady, and industrious life to the satisfaction of the Association.

'4. You must not break the law, or associate with persons of bad character.'

The Governor will carefully explain to him all that this implies, and the boy will sign it in witness that he has read and understood. The signed copy will go to his supervisor, and he will keep one lest there be any doubt that he knows what he is in for: the wisdom of this has been questioned, on the grounds that he is likely either to flaunt it vaingloriously, to reveal it carelessly, or at best to throw it away as soon as he passes the gate. So far however the formally correct view has prevailed, particularly since the Commissioners have been informed that some boys or girls who have been recalled claim that they never knew the conditions of their release.

Then with final admonitions and good wishes the boy will set off, with a railway warrant, enough money to see him to his destination, a new suit of his own choosing and such other outfit as is necessary. A girl will probably have made all except the tailored items of her outfit herself. The official destination will be the office of the supervisor, to whom the boy must report as soon as possible after he arrives: he will then be told what is expected of him as regards reporting and so on, and any loose ends of plans not already arranged for will be tidied up.

These plans of course primarily concern the boy's work and his home. All boys who are capable of being employed have work to go to as soon as they are available, and the supervisor has a copy of any certificate of trade training the boy may have earned: the co-operation of the Ministry of Labour is willingly granted, but it has not been found necessary to introduce into boys' Borstals the system under which, in prisons, the Placement Officer personally visits the establishment. There is more difficulty about the home: often it is quite unsuitable, but even a bad home has the pull of home, and except in extreme cases more harm than good may be done by trying to keep a boy away from it—in the worst cases, he must be found work and lodgings in another district. The problem of the homeless boy is one with which the Borstal Division takes very great pains to ensure satisfactory arrangements. Many of the older 'boys', of course, are married, and here different problems of establishing reconciliation and a proper sense of responsibility may have to be faced.

It is necessary to qualify the foregoing picture in respect of the high proportion of boys [1] who are discharged direct to the Armed Forces, either to rejoin their units or to start their National Service. There is complete and satisfactory liaison between the Commissioners, the War Office, and the Ministry of Labour and National Service, and between the C.A.C.A. and the military and M.L. & N.S. authoritories with whom they deal, at all stages of this procedure. Arrangements for 'call-up' and reporting to units, including medical examination, are made well before-hand, and a boy leaves his Borstal knowing exactly what he must do and where he must go. The War Office do their best to arrange that there are no concentrations of Borstal boys in particular centres. Military service does not however entirely relieve the Borstal Division of its responsibilities, and they maintain indirect supervision by correspondence and through contact with the homes.

The separate problems arising in the re-establishment of girls were

[1] Reported in the *Annual Report for* 1947 as being over 50 per cent.

comprehensively surveyed by the Director of Women and Girls' After-care, in the Annual Report for 1949 (p. 61), as follows:

'From 1st January 1949 to 31st December 1949, 142 girls were discharged from Borstal Institutions at Aylesbury, Exeter, and East Sutton Park, and 60 from Holloway after recall for further training. Of original discharges, 102 returned home or went to live with relatives, 14 went to hostels, 2 to approved lodgings, 20 to resident domestic work and 2 directly into the Women's Services. Most girls were found employment within a week of discharge and it is here that the co-operation of the Ministry of Labour and National Service is of such value, every girl being interviewed by their representatives at the Borstal Institutions prior to her discharge.

'The majority of girls get work in factories, mills, canteens, or hospital work as ward maids, ward orderlies, or as cooks and waitresses. Some girls prefer private domestic work and some have got work on farms. Many girls ask to join the Women's Services, but experience has shown that it is advisable to let them earn a reference before they apply. Those who join subsequently have done well. The same thing applies to training for specialised work such as that of a Nursery Nurse, where the training is long and the wage small in comparison with wages in factory or domestic work, where the untrained can and do earn high wages and acquire skill while earning.

'The unmarried girl with a baby is a very different proposition. Of the original discharges, 11 girls were unmarried with babies, 6 were able to return home, while homes for mothers and babies had to be found for the other five. In addition, 14 girls discharged after recall were either pregnant or had already been confined. Of this number, only one was able to return home, 2 went into private domestic work with their babies, 9 were found accommodation in Hostels for mothers and babies and 2 went to Public Assistance Institutions.

'At the end of 1949 there were under supervision 37 unmarried girls with babies, or pregnant. The problem is further complicated when the baby is coloured.'

In these different ways all these young people are re-established in normal life—but that is the easy part: what matters most is what happens next. Now the associate must, with sympathy and firmness, combine the roles of friend and of supervisor. Persistent patience is needed to keep the feet of wayward boys and girls along the narrow path in which they have been set. The Associate must always wish to appear as the friend, anxious above all to help and to keep his charges from the danger of being sent back to Borstal: and indeed, except on reconviction, the sanction of recall is not invoked without most earnest consideration. But there comes a time with some when neither friendly advice nor stern admonition will prevail, and the associate has no option but to advise the C.A.C.A. that the young person should be recalled.

Before passing to consider the law and practice relating to recall, it may be noted that the Commissioners have power, under the Second Schedule of the Act of 1948, to 'modify or cancel any of the said requirements or order that a person who is under supervision as aforesaid shall cease to be under supervision'. This is useful on occasion to encourage a boy or girl who has been released early and has clearly settled down—a very long period of supervision in such a case may do more harm than good. Conversely, the power may be used where a long sentence has followed reconviction, and further Borstal supervision would be either impracticable or out of place.

(3) RECALL

Power to order recall to a Borstal institution is by the third para. of the Second Schedule vested in the Commissioners. A person recalled is 'liable to be detained in the Borstal institution until the expiration of three years from the date of his sentence, or the expiration of six months from the date of his being taken into custody under the order, whichever is the later, and if at large shall be deemed to be unlawfully at large'. There are certain other provisions in the Schedule to prevent any 'cat-and-mouse' prolongation of the total period of the original sentence: thus any order of recall ceases to have effect when the original four years have expired, unless the person is then in custody thereunder, and any sentence of imprisonment passed on a person under supervision counts as part of the period for which he is liable to be detained under the Borstal sentence. The total period of the original sentence cannot, therefore, under the recall procedure, be extended to more than four years and six months—and that only in the extreme case of a person taken into custody under an order on the last day of the period of his four-year sentence. A person who has been recalled may again be conditionally released if his period of supervision has not expired.

There are separate Borstals, known as Recall Centres, for the further training of those who have to be brought back, since it is on many grounds undesirable for these failures to mix with the ordinary trainees. If the failure has resulted in a reconviction, and there is a prospect that further training might be effective, another Borstal sentence may be passed: this however can rarely be recommended save in the case of a quite young boy or girl who has failed after an early release. The purpose of the Recall Centre is, therefore, first to serve as a sanction *in terrorem*, and the conditions are by no means as agreeable as those in a training Borstal: the régime is however a Borstal training régime under the Borstal Rules, and is not intended to be simply repressive. Its second purpose is to find out why failure has occurred, and to do its best to straighten out what needs straightening out. The staff is a normal Borstal staff, with the addition at the Boys' Centre of a psychologist, for much useful research can be done here into causes of failure and weaknesses in both training and after-care. The Girls' Centre is much smaller, and there are not often more than about 20 girls there, with two Assistant Governors and a small staff.

The average number at the Boys' Centre is about 150, and some 340 boys were received there in 1950: of these, 32 had been recalled for not observing the conditions of their release, the remainder in consequence of a reconviction. The arrangements where a person under supervision is charged with a fresh offence are set out in *Prisons and Borstals* as follows—'The practice is for Courts to consider whether, having regard to the facts of the case, it will be sufficient for him to be dealt with by recall. In that event, the convenient course is to make this view known to the prison authorities and to remand the offender so that the Prison Commissioners can make the necessary arrangements for recall. Whenever the Commissioners are aware that a young person under supervision is on remand, they make a report to the court indicating the position, and stating whether they have issued or propose to issue an order of recall.' If the court passes a short sentence (6 months or less) the boy will generally be recalled to Borstal and sent to the Recall Centre; where a longer sentence is passed he will serve it in prison—in a Young Prisoners' Centre if he is under 21.

The date of release is decided by an Investigation Committee, which meets monthly under the chairmanship of an Assistant Commissioner. Where there is a prison sentence on reconviction, a boy will be detained at least as long as he would be required to serve under the sentence in a local prison. Generally, the date of discharge does not depend on 'response to training' but on the assessment by the committee of his conduct while under supervision. A boy is rarely kept more than six months.

The procedure at the Girls' Centre is similar.

The C.A.C.A. resume supervision on discharge from the Recall Centres, and take equal pains to ensure proper placement, the Directors personally interviewing each boy or girl some time before discharge. In the cases where a sentence of imprisonment is served in a prison, and the young person is still nominally under Borstal supervision on discharge, a decision must be made in each case whether he is to be discharged under Borstal supervision or on a Young Prisoners' licence.

(4) RESULTS OF THE BORSTAL SYSTEM

It is easy to write the heading of this section, less easy to proceed. By what criteria may we discern and assess the results of the system we have described? The first might be to ask how far it has achieved the objects set before it in Rule 4—in how many of the young people who have passed through Borstal has their training established 'the will to lead a good and useful life on release', and fitted them to do so? In our present state of knowledge this question can have no objective answer, though it is not impossible that an extensive social research on the lines of that carried out by Sheldon and Eleanor Glueck in the United States of America would go some way towards supplying one. The statistics of re-conviction are only pointers. Many who through innate weakness or unhappy circumstances have failed in this way may well have left Borstal, with every good intention and ability, better human beings than others who have not again come into court.

For a criterion with any objective basis, however, we can rely only on these statistics of reconviction, which have been carefully recorded over a long period of years. And at least they show how far the system has succeeded in 'the prevention of crime', though they are an uncertain guide to 'the reformation of the offender'. In assessing these figures we should not forget that many young people who have 'reverted to crime' may nevertheless be better people as a result of their training, while it may also be that some, whether they offend again or no, could say with justice that it did them more harm than good. There is no means of weighing and valuing these subjective judgments: let us, therefore, look at the figures, and see whether within their limits they tell a clear story—a result which is not necessarily to be expected.

In their Annual Report for 1949 the Commissioners published tables showing for each year from 1937–1947, for boys and girls separately, the numbers (1) discharged, (2) not reconvicted, (3) reconvicted once only, (4) reconvicted two or more times. The figures covered a period of 7 years from the year of discharge, or where 7 years had not elapsed they gave the position up to 31 December 1949, i.e. all had been discharged for at least two years. It will perhaps be well, rather than to consider the tables as a whole, to select two years from the pre-war, the war, and the post-war periods. The result, for boys, is as follows:

	Numbers of Dis-charges	Not reconvicted		Reconvicted once		Reconvicted twice or more	
		Number	Per cent	Number	Per cent	Number	Per cent
1937–38	1,741	1,039	59·5	340	19·5	362	21·0
1942–43	2,795	1,320	47·3	618	22·1	857	30·6
1946–47	3,714	1,857	50·0	945	25·5	912	24·5

From this table one fact appears to be firm and unqualified, that is that the boys' Borstals at their best, before the disruption of the war, were achieving complete success with about six boys out of every ten discharged, and if we include also those who after one conviction settled down, with very nearly eight out of ten. This latter figure may reasonably be accepted, since further lapses after so long a period are hardly now to be expected.

The figures for the war period, as was to be expected, are less satisfactory. Even so, the falling off from the pre-war figure is not great, taking account of the much larger numbers which were handled in conditions of the greatest difficulty. This may however be to some extent attributable to the external conditions in war time, every fit young man going at once to active service in the armed forces or to other essential national work.

On the post-war figures judgment must be suspended. *Prima facie* they show an improvement, but this may not last: the percentage of 'no reconvictions' for the 1946 discharges was 55·4 at the end of 1948, but it had fallen to 46·2 at the end of 1949. Some hope may be derived from the records of the C.A.C.A., which show that at the end of 1950 the percentage of reconviction among those who had been discharged for at least 12 months was only 28·5.

The 1937–38 figures show what the Borstal system has done, and therefore what it can do again: they may be compared with the statement in the Principles that 'of the 9,000 lads who passed through the Borstal training in the first twenty years it can be stated with certainty that only about 35 per cent have again come into conflict with the law . . . about three out of every four Borstal lads are reclaimed and continue to live as honest citizens'. Let us hope that when the figures for 1950 and 1951 come to be assessed they will show that Borstal has fought its way back to at least its pre-war standard. And surely, given the records and characters of the young men who come to Borstals, most often after many other resources of our social, educational and penal systems have failed to affect them, that standard can be judged a high one. In most examinations a mark of 75 per cent achieves distinction'.

The picture presented by the table for girls is curiously different, and may be summarised as follows. For the two pre-war years, the percentage with no reconvictions was 45; for the two war years it was 57·5; for the two post-war years 71·5° The percentages with two or more reconvictions were 31, 16·8, and 14·5 respectively. Of the girls discharged in 1947, 83·2 per cent had reached the end of 1949 without a reconviction. To establish the significance of these figures would be an interesting but complicated task which will not be attempted here. Again one must enter the caveat that these post-war figures may change for the worse: the 1946 discharges, which showed a 61·6 percentage of no reconvictions at the end of 1948, had fallen to 59·7 at the end of 1949. But if the 1947 figure does even worse, it will remain a remarkable achievement.

It is necessary to record these facts, even though they do not contain the whole truth, for better or worse, about the Borstal system, because it is unfortunate if natural that the minority of failures attract a great deal more publicity than the majority of successes. It is also desirable to consider other results of the system. Dr. Grünhut records [1] the 'great interest' and 'admiration' for the Borstal system aroused among visitors from abroad, and its widespread influence is undisputed. As recently as 1949 a Report to the Senate of the United States from the Committee on the Judiciary, to whom had been referred a Bill to provide an improved Federal system for the treatment of young offenders, stated that 'the concept of the instant bill had its origins in a system initiated in England . . . known as the Borstal system. . . . The Borstal system has been successful in England. The American Law Institute has fathered a similar program of youth correction in the United States.' [2]

On the whole, therefore, there is reason to end this account of the Borstal system with, in Dr. Grünhut's words, 'a feeling that it is something to be proud of'. [3]

[1] Grünhut, p. 382.
[2] 81st Congress, 1st Session, Report No. 1180, p. 4.
[3] Grünhut, p. 382.

APPENDIX A

Extracts from

An Inquiry whether Crime and Misery are Produced or Prevented
by our Present System

By Thomas Fowell Buxton, Esq., M.P.: London, 1818

PREFACE

'BEING at Ghent during the early part of this winter, I took some pains in examining the excellent prison of that city, known by the name of the Maison de Force. On my return to England, I communicated to the "Society for the Improvement of Prison Discipline, and for the Reformation of Juvenile Offenders," the intelligence which was thus acquired. The members of that institution had accurately investigated the state of almost every jail in the metropolis and its vicinity. Their inquiries had led them to a decided and unanimous conviction, that the present alarming increase of crime arises more from the want of instruction, classification, regular employment, and inspection in Jails, than from any other cause; and that its prevention could only be accomplished, by an entire change in the system of prison discipline. These views were strongly confirmed by the practical illustration afforded by the Maison de Force; and this led to a request from the Committee, that the description of it might be published.

'When I sat down to this task, the work insensibly grew upon my hands. It was necessary to prove, that evils and grievances did really exist in this country, and to bring home to these causes, the increase of corruption and depravity. For this purpose, repeated visits to various prisons were requisite.

'Again, a detail of the regulations of the Maison de Force alone, did not seem to establish the point contended for, with sufficient certainty. An experiment might succeed abroad, which might fail at home. Local circumstances, and the habits of the people, might have rendered a plan very judicious in the Netherlands, which was quite impracticable in England. It appeared therefore desirable to shew, that, whether the attempt be made on the Continent, in England, or in America, the same results are invariably displayed.

'Feeling no uneasiness as to the accuracy of the facts related, I must confess I have felt some repugnance to the disclosure of scenes, which may be considered as reflecting discredit on those who ought to have prevented them; but against the pain which this pamphlet may give to the affluent and the powerful, must be weighed the secret sufferings, the unknown grievances, the decay of health, and corruption of morals, which, by its suppression, may be continued to the inmates of many dungeons in this country. I have great confidence in the power of public opinion, in preventing detected wrong; and if this confidence be not misplaced, all option upon my part ceases; the publication becomes a matter of imperative duty; to conceal would be to participate.

'I will conclude this Preface by stating that none of the grievances represented, are occasioned by the jailers; that class of men are often subjected to undistinguishing abuse; my experience would furnish me with very different language. Without any exception, I have had reason to approve, and sometimes to applaud their conduct; and I can truly say, that of all the persons, with whom I have conversed, they are the most sensible of the evils of our present system of prison discipline.'

PRELIMINARY AND GENERAL OBSERVATIONS

'It is therefore evident, I conceive, that where the law condemns a man to jail, and is silent as to his treatment there, it intends merely that he should be amerced of his freedom, *not that he should be subjected to any useless severities*. This is the whole of his sentence, and ought therefore to be the whole of his suffering.

'If any one should be disposed to hesitate in the adoption of this opinion, and should still cling to the idea, that prisons ought to be, not merely places of restraint, but of restraint coupled with deep and intense misery; let him consider the injustice, and irresistible difficulties, which would result from such a system. If misery is to be inflicted at all in prisons, it ought surely to be inflicted in some proportion to the crime of the offender; for no one could desire to visit very different degrees of guilt, with the same measure of punishment. Now this is utterly impracticable. Our prisons are so constructed, as in many instances to prevent the possibility of any separation at all, even between the tried and untried, the criminal and the debtor, the insane, the sick, and the healthy. If it be difficult to separate those amongst whom the difference is so broad and palpable, how would it be possible to relax or to aggravate imprisonment, according to the varying circumstances of each case? There must be as many distinctions as crimes, and almost as many yards as prisoners. And who is to apportion this variety of wretchedness? The Judge, who knows nothing of the interior of the jail, or the jailer, who knows nothing of the transactions of the Court? The law can easily suit its penalties to the circumstances of the case. It can adjudge to one offender imprisonment for one day; to another, for twenty years; but what ingenuity would be sufficient to devise, and what discretion could be trusted to inflict, modes of imprisonment with similar variations?' .

'But besides the rights of the individual, there are duties to the community —*Parum est improbos coercere pœna, nisi probos efficias disciplina.*—One of the most important of these duties is, that you should not send forth the man committed to your tuition, in any respect a worse man, a less industrious, a less sober, or a less competent man, than when he entered your walls. Good policy requires that, if possible, you dismiss him improved.' 'Punishments are inflicted, that crime may be prevented, and crime is prevented by the reformation of the criminal.'

'I have already noticed the benevolence displayed by the legislature, in their provisions for the regulation of prisons; but their intentions will be, as they have hitherto been, of little avail, if they do not enforce them.'

THE BOROUGH COMPTER

'This prison belongs to the city of London, and its jurisdiction extends over five parishes.—On entrance, you come to the male felons' ward and yard, in which are both the tried and the untried—those in chains, and those without them—boys and men,—persons for petty offences, and for the most atrocious felonies;—for simple assault,—for being disorderly,—for small thefts,—for issuing bad notes,—for forgery and for robbery. They were employed in some kind of gaming, and they said they had nothing else to do. A respectable looking man, a smith, who had never been in prison before, told me that "the conversation always going on, was sufficient to corrupt any body, and that he had learned things there he never dreamed of before."

'You next enter a yard, nineteen feet square; this is the only airing place for male debtors and vagrants, female debtors, prostitutes, misdemeanants, and criminals, and for their children and friends. There have been as many as thirty women; we saw thirty-eight debtors, and Mr. Law, the Governor, stated, when he was examined, that there might be about twenty children.

'On my first visit, the debtors were all collected together upstairs. This was their day-room, workshop, kitchen, and chapel. On my second visit, they spent the day and the night in the room below; at the third, both the room above, and that below, were filled. The length of each of these rooms, exclusive of a recess in which were tables and the fireplace, is twenty feet. Its breadth is three feet, six inches for a passage, and six feet for the bed. In this space, twenty feet long, and six wide, on eight straw beds, with sixteen rugs, and a piece of timber for a bolster, twenty prisoners had slept side by side the preceding night: I maintained that it was physically impossible; but the prisoners explained away the difficulty, by saying, "they slept edgeways." Amongst these twenty, was one in a very deplorable condition; he had been taken from a sick bed, and brought there; he had his mattress to himself, for none would share it; and indeed my senses convinced me, that sleeping near him, must be sufficiently offensive.

'I fear I shall hardly be credited when I assure my readers, that as yet, I have not touched upon that point in this prison which I consider the most lamentable—the proximity between the male debtors and the female prisoners. Their doors are about seven feet asunder, on the same floor, these are open in the day time, and the men are forbidden to go into the women's ward; but after the turnkey left us, they confessed that they constantly went in and out; and there is no punishment for doing so. That this is the fact, appears by the evidence of the Governor before the Police Committee. *Ques.* Is it possible for the men to get into the sleeping wards of the women? *Ans.* I cannot say that it is impossible. Is any thing done to prevent them, if the parties consent? No.

'There is no school; no soap is allowed; and a prisoner, when he arrives, is turned in amongst the rest without any examination as to the state of his health. This may account for a remark in the apothecary's book, January 5th,

1818—"Some of the prisoners have contracted the itch." The case of one man struck me much: he was found in a most pitiable state in the streets, and apprehended as a vagrant; he was at first placed with the debtors, but he was so filthy, and so covered with vermin, (to use the expression of the turnkey, "he was so lousy") that his removal was solicited. I saw him lying on a straw-bed, as I believed, at the point of death, without a shirt, inconceivably dirty, so weak as to be almost unable to articulate, and so offensive, as to render remaining a minute with him quite intolerable; close by his side five other untried prisoners had slept the preceding night, inhaling the stench from this mass of putrefaction, hearing his groans, breathing the steam from his corrupted lungs, and covered with myriads of lice from his rags of clothing; of these his wretched companions, three were subsequently pronounced by the verdict of a jury, "not guilty".'

TOTHILL FIELDS PRISON

'Many of the wards in which the prisoners sleep, are sunk below the level of the ground, and this level is considered to be below high water mark. The up-stairs rooms of the Governor's house are much affected with damp; hearing this from himself, I could not suspect the truth of the statements of the prisoners, who complained bitterly of the cold and moisture of these cells. To obviate these inconveniences, as many as possible crowd together at night into the same cell; how injurious this must be to health, can be conceived by the statement of the jailer, who told me that having occasion lately to open one of the doors in the night, the effluvia was almost intolerable.'

BOROUGH JAIL AT ST. ALBANS

'We first went to the Borough Jail, which is a *wooden building*.

'A girl was confined in the day-room; the window at which she sits, opens to the street, with which it is nearly on a level. We, standing in the street, conversed with her, and the bars are wide enough to admit any thing, of which the bulk is not very considerable; of course spirits could not be excluded. On the Sessions day, this window is closed by a shutter, as it was found that the prisoners got drunk, and were in that state during their trial. The jailer opened a door of what appeared to us a dark closet, assuring us that when we entered we should be able to see—and in fact, we could discover, by the light admitted through a small lattice-window, that it was a room of considerable dimensions.

'The bed-rooms were equally incommodious. The men and women, when in bed, are separated by an open railing, the bars of which are about *six inches* distant from each other, and the only air, or light, admitted to the men's apartment, is through this lattice. The allowance of food, is one pound and a half of bread per day, and no firing is provided; in fact, it would be needless, for there is no fire-place. It is to be observed, that there is no yard. How far the exposure at all times, by this open intercourse with the male prisoners at night, and with all persons in the street in the day, may improve the morals and delicacy of the females, and how far the seclusion from exercise may affect the health of the men, experience alone can determine.'

JAIL FOR THE LIBERTY OF ST. ALBANS

'No separation, except between men and women. One of the men's sleeping-rooms is without air or light, except what may be received through a grating, which opens into a passage, which opens into the day-room, which communicates with the yard. The building is an old fortification, and in this room there is one of the loop-holes, which are common in such buildings; but this was stopped by the prisoners to exclude the cold air. When the door was open, it was so dark, that we hesitated about entering, being unable to perceive whether there was or was not a step. We were informed there was a load of straw, which we did not see: one blanket and some straw is the bedding allowed.'

JAIL AT GUILDFORD

'In this jail the prisoners complained much of cold, and not unreasonably, as I thought, for the day-room for all of them, at this time amounting to thirty-five, and at one period of the year for a short time amounting to as many as one hundred, is nine feet ten inches by nine feet six inches; eight feet three inches high. It is therefore evidently impossible, in snow or rain, or frost, for them to obtain shelter or warmth. A prisoner, however, has the privilege, if he requires it, of being shut up all day in his sleeping cell, with unclosed windows and without fire, and these cells are opened in very severe weather.

'There is no chapel. There is no work. There is no classification. There is no privy. No prison dress is allowed.

'The irons are remarkably heavy, and all who are confined for felony, whether for re-examination, for trial, or convicted, are loaded with them; and those who are double-ironed cannot take off their small-clothes.'

JAIL AT KINGSTON

'The town jail is a public house, in the tap-room of which, the debtors were sitting, in the center of a crowd of other visitors.'

USE OF IRONS

'Nothing can be more capricious than the existing practice with regard to irons.

'In *Chelmsford, and in Newgate,* all for felony are ironed.

'At *Bury, and at Norwich,* all are without irons.

'At *Abingdon,* the untried are not ironed.

'At *Derby,* none but the untried are ironed.

'At *Cold-bath-fields,* none but the untried, and those sent for re-examination, are ironed.

'At *Winchester,* all before trial are ironed; and those sentenced to transportation after trial.

'At *Chester,* those alone of bad character are ironed, whether tried or untried.

'And there is as much variety in the weight of the fetters; some are heavy, others are light: in one prison they are placed on one leg, at another on both.'

FOOD

'The quantum of food is equally variable.

'*Tothill Fields, and Ipswich.* No allowance for debtors except from charity.

'*Bedford,* three quartern loaves per week for all prisoners.

'*Bristol,* a four-penny loaf per day.

'*Borough Compter,* fourteen ounces of bread per day, two pounds of meat per week.

'*Bury,* one pound and a half of bread per day, one pound of cheese, and three-quarters of a pound of meat, per week.

'*Norwich,* two pounds of bread per day, half a pound of cheese per week.

'*Penitentiary, Milbank,* one pound and a half of bread, one pound of potatoes, two pints of hot gruel, per day, and either six ounces of boiled meat, without bone, or a quart of strong broth mixed with vegetables.

'Fourteen ounces of bread per day with two pounds of meat per week, are not enough to support life; besides, in some prisons, the allowance is withheld for a considerable time. The hour of delivery is fixed, and if a prisoner arrives after it, he receives nothing till the next morning. Persons may steal for immediate sustenance.'

BEDDING AND CLOTHING

'There are differences with regard to bedding:—
'From—No bedding, or coverlid,
A blanket for two men,
A blanket for each,
Two blankets for each,
Two blankets and a rug each,
Three blankets and a rug for each,
'To—three blankets, a rug, a hair bed, and two pillows, each.

'The same dissimilarity exists in clothing. Some prisons provide a dress, others do not; some prisoners are comfortably clad, and some are almost naked.'

PROCEEDINGS OF THE LADIES COMMITTEE, NEWGATE

'About four years ago, Mrs. Fry was induced to visit Newgate, by the representations of its state, made by some persons of the Society of Friends.

'She found the female side in a situation, which no language can describe. Nearly three hundred women, sent there for every gradation of crime, some untried, and some under sentence of death, were crowded together in the two wards and two cells, which are now appropriated to the untried, and which are found quite inadequate to contain even this diminished number, with any tolerable convenience. Here they saw their friends and kept their multitudes of children, and they had no other place for cooking, washing, eating, and sleeping.

'They slept on the floor, at times one hundred and twenty in one ward, without so much as a mat for bedding; and many of them were very nearly naked. She saw them openly drinking spirits, and her ears were offended by the most terrible imprecations. Every thing was filthy to excess, and the smell was quite disgusting. Every one, even the Governor was reluctant to go amongst them. He persuaded her to leave her watch in the office telling her that his presence would not prevent it being torn from her. She saw enough to convince her that every thing bad was going on. In short, in giving me this account, she repeatedly said—"All I tell thee is a faint picture of the reality; the filth, the closeness of the rooms, the ferocious manners and expressions of the women towards each other, and the abandoned wickedness, which everything bespoke, are quite indescribable." One act, the account of which I received from another quarter, marks the degree of wretchedness to which they were reduced at that time. Two women were seen in the act of stripping a dead child, for the purpose of clothing a living one.

'At her second visit she requested to be admitted alone, and was locked up with the women, without any turnkey, for several hours; when she mentioned to those who had families, how grievous and deplorable she considered the situation of their offspring, and her desire to concur with them in establishing a School; the proposal was received, even by the most abandoned, with tears of joy.

'Having thus obtained the consent of the females, Mrs. Fry's next object was to secure the concurrence of the Governor. She went to his house, and there met both the Sheriffs and the Ordinary. She told them her views, which they received with the most cordial approbation; but, at the same time, unreservedly confessed their apprehensions that her labours would be fruitless. At the next interview they stated, that they had thoroughly examined the prison, and were truly sorry to say, they could not find any vacant spot suitable for her purpose, and therefore feared the design must be relinquished. Conclusive as this intelligence appeared, her heart was then too deeply engaged in the work, and her judgment too entirely convinced of its importance, to allow her to resign it, while one possibility of success remained. She again requested to be admitted alone amongst the women, that she might see for herself; and if her search then failed, she should be content to abandon her project. She soon discovered a cell which was unused, and this cell is the present school-room. Upon this she returned to the Sheriffs, who told her she might take it if she liked, and try the benevolent, but almost hopeless experiment.

'The next day she commenced the school, in company with a young lady, who then visited a prison for the first time, and who since gave me a very interesting description of her feelings upon that occasion. The railing was crowded with half naked women, struggling together for the front situations with the most boisterous violence, and begging with the utmost vociferation. She felt as if she was going into a den of wild beasts, and she well recollects quite shuddering when the door closed upon her, and she was locked in, with such a herd of novel and desperate companions. This day, however, the school surpassed their utmost expectations: their only pain arose from the numerous and pressing applications made by young women, who longed to be taught and employed.

'These ladies, with some others, continued labouring together for some time, and the school became their regular and daily occupation; but their visits brought them so acquainted with the dissipation and gross licentiousness prevalent in the prison, arising, as they conceived, partly from want of certain regulations, but principally from want of work, that they could not but feel earnest and increasing solicitude to extend their institution, and to comprehend within its range, the tried prisoners. This desire was confirmed by the solicitations of the women themselves, who entreated that they might not be excluded. Their zeal for improvement, and their assurances of good behaviour, were powerful motives, and they tempted these ladies to project a school for the employment of the tried women, for teaching them to read and to work.

'When this intention was mentioned to the friends of these ladies, it appeared at first so visionary and unpromising, that it met with very slender encouragement; they were told that the certain consequence of introducing work, would be, that it would be stolen; and though such an experiment might be reasonable enough, if made in the country, among women who had been accustomed to hard labour; yet it was quite destitute of hope, when tried upon those who had been so long habituated to vice and idleness. It was strongly represented that their materials were of the very worst descriptions; that a regular London female thief, who had passed through every stage and every scene of guilt, who had spent her youth in prostitution, and her maturer age in theft and knavery, whose every friend and connexion are accomplices and criminal associates, is of all characters the most irreclaimable.

'With these impressions, they had the boldness to declare, that if a committee could be found, who would share the labour, and a matron, who would engage never to leave the prison, day nor night, they would undertake to try the experiment; that is, they would find employment for the women, procure the necessary money, till the city could be induced to relieve them from the expense, and be answerable for the safety of the property committed into the hands of the prisoners.

'This committee immediately presented itself; it consisted of the wife of a clergyman, and eleven members of the Society of Friends. They professed their willingness to suspend every other engagement and avocation, and to devote themselves to Newgate; and, in truth, they have performed their promise. With no interval of relaxation, and with but few intermissions from the call of other and more imperious duties, they have *lived* amongst the prisoners.

'The Sheriff expressed the most kind disposition to assist her, but told her that his concurrence, or that of the City, would avail her but little—the concurrence of the women themselves was indispensable; and that it was in vain to expect that such untamed and turbulent spirits would submit to the regulations of women, armed with no legal authority, and unable to inflict any punishment. She replied—"Let the experiment be tried; let the women be assembled in your presence, and if they will not consent to the strict observance of our rules, let the project be dropped." On the following Sunday, the two Sheriffs, with Mr. Cotton and Mr. Newman, met the ladies at Newgate. Upwards of seventy women were collected together. One of the committee explained their views to them; she told them that the only practicable mode of accomplishing an object, so interesting to her, and so important to them, was by the establishment of certain rules.

'They were then asked, if they were willing to abide by the rules which it might be advisable to establish, and each gave the most positive assurances of her determination to obey them in all points. Having succeeded so far, the next business was to provide employment. It struck one of the ladies that Botany Bay might be supplied with stockings, and indeed all articles of clothing, of the prisoners' manufacture. She, therefore, called upon Messrs. Richard Dixon & Co. of Fenchurch Street, and candidly told them that she was desirous of depriving them of this branch of their trade, and stating her views, begged their advice. They said at once, that they would not in any way obstruct such laudable designs, and that no further trouble need be taken to provide work, for they would engage to do it.

'She then told them, that the ladies did not come with any absolute and authoritative pretensions; that it was not intended they should command, and the prisoners obey; but that it was to be understood all were to act in concert; that not a rule should be made, or a monitor appointed, without their full and unanimous concurrence; that for this purpose, each of the rules should be read, and put to the vote; and she invited those who might feel any disinclination to any particular, freely to state their opinion. The following were then read:

Rules

'1. That a matron be appointed for the general superintendence of the women.

'2. That the women be engaged in needlework, knitting, or any other suitable employment.

'3. That there be no begging, swearing, gaming, card-playing, quarrelling, or immoral conversation. That all novels, plays, and other improper books, be excluded; and that all bad words be avoided: and any default in these particulars be reported to the matron.

'4. That there be a yard-keeper chosen from among the women: to inform them when their friends come; to see that they leave their work with a monitor when they go to the grating, and that they do not spend any time there, except with their friends. If any woman be found disobedient in these respects, the yard-keeper is to report the case to the matron.

'5. That the women be divided into classes, of not more than twelve; and that a monitor be appointed to each class.

'6. That monitors be chosen from among the most orderly of the women that can read, to superintend the work and conduct of the others.

'7. That the monitors not only overlook the women in their own classes, but if they observe any others disobeying the rules, that they inform the monitor of the class to which such persons may belong, who is immediately to report to the matron, and the deviations to be set down on a slate.

'8. That any monitor breaking the rules shall be dismissed from her office, and the most suitable in the class selected to take her place.

'9. That the monitors be particularly careful to see that the women come with clean hands and face to their work, and that they are quiet during their employment.

'10. That at the ringing of the bell, at 9 o'clock in the morning, the women collect in the work-room to hear a portion of scripture read by one of the visitors or the matron; and that the monitors afterwards conduct the classes from thence to their respective wards in an orderly manner.

'11. That the women be again collected for the reading, at six o'clock in the evening, when the work shall be given in charge to the matron by the monitors.

'12. That the matron keep an exact account of the work done by the women, and of their conduct.

And as each was proposed, every hand was held up in testimony of their approbation.

'In the same manner, and with the same formalities, each of the monitors was proposed, and all were unanimously approved.

'When this business was concluded, one of the visitors read aloud the 15th chapter of St. Luke—the parable of the barren fig-tree seeming applicable to the state of the audience. After a period of silence, according to the custom of the Society of Friends, the monitors, with their classes, withdrew to their respective wards in the most orderly manner.

'A year is now elapsed since the operation in Newgate began, and those most competent to judge, the late Lord Mayor and the present, the late Sheriffs and the present, the late Governor and the present, various Grand Juries, the Chairman of the Police Committee, the Ordinary, and the officers of the prison, have all declared their satisfaction, mixed with astonishment, at the alteration which has taken place in the conduct of the females.'

APPENDIX B

Extracts from the First Reports of the Inspectors, 1836

NEWGATE

Male Side

'THE beer-man comes into the prison every day from twelve to one, with four three-gallon cans: when they are empty, he sends his boy for more. Sometimes an officer is at the yard gate, who may be present at the distribution of the beer; but this is not generally the case. We observed the beer-man distributing the beer, no officer being present to see that no more than the proper quantity of beer was received by the prisoners, who in fact might, unchecked, have obtained as much as they chose to purchase. And from our own observation, the statements of prisoners, and those of officers at present in the prison, we have no hesitation in expressing our belief, that almost any quantity of beer which the prisoners can afford to purchase may be brought into the wards.'

'In ward No. 12 were six prisoners. We found a man aged 38, under a sentence of 12 months' imprisonment for an assault on a lad, with an intent to commit an unnatural offence; two lads of 17 and 18 years of age, one under a 14 days' sentence; the other untried, being charged with a slight offence for which he was afterwards sentenced to a month's imprisonment; a man, aged 35, under sentence of transportation for life, for forgery; another aged 34, under sentence of seven years' transportation; and the sixth, aged 34, for the nonpayment of several small sums of money.'

'At the time of our visit to this ward, the wardsman was obviously in a state of intoxication. We took pains to ascertain the fact, by observing the man closely, and by asking him questions; and we satisfied ourselves that the man was drunk. He admitted that he had drank two pints of porter that morning.'

'With the exception of the wardsmen (who have beds and bedsteads), the prisoners all sleep on mats on the floor, with rugs to cover them; and some two, three, and even four, under the same covering. So closely, indeed, do they lie together, that in our night-inspections we have found it difficult, in stepping across the room, to avoid treading upon them.

'That gaming goes on in the wards is a matter of moral certainty. The practice is not only attested by every prisoner whom we have examined, and by the acknowledgment of its existence on the part of the officers, but by the appearance of the tables throughout the prison, scarcely one of which is without the marks of gaming-boards deeply cut on them, for the playing of low games.

412

'Rioting, uproar, and fighting, are frequently going on; the serious nature of which may be best understood from the number of severe accidents which have occurred. We would likewise refer to the statement of officers, who have been under the necessity of going among the prisoners, armed with cutlasses; and even on such occasions windows have been broken, and forms and tables burnt, before order could be restored. The act of locking-up becomes, from the consequent removal of all superintendence, a signal for the commencement of obscene talk, revelry, and violence; and that gaming, swearing, singing, narration of adventures, instruction in crime, proceed unchecked, and without ceasing, until a late hour of the night.

'When this division of Newgate was first inspected by us, we found in it seventeen prisoners under sentence of death: in the lower room were three, who expected to suffer: in the upper room were fourteen, nine of whom were not more than twenty years of age; five of them were fifteen and under; one of them was no more than thirteen years old, and, in appearance as well as in years, quite a child.

'Early in the morning, each day during the session week, all the male prisoners against whom bills of indictment have been found, are mustered in the Master's Side Yard, and, before the sitting of the court, are taken down to the Bail Dock sometimes as many as 60 or 70 together. Here they are often kept day after day expecting their trials, sometimes from eight or nine o'clock in the morning until 11 at night. Some of the prisoners have spoken of this as the time of their greatest sufferings: one in particular said, "There we are mixed up with horrid characters, and are like wild beasts in a den. The conversation is gross and horrible; some behave more as if they were going to a fair than to a trial. They annoy all those who are not of their set, and who seem alive to a sense of their situation." Here, as everywhere else in Newgate, we find the evils of prison association.'

Female Side

'Intoxication has been found to occur even among the women. A gate-woman, named Saunders, was removed from her situation not many months ago, for drunkenness.

'Prisoners sleep on the floor upon mats, with rugs and blankets. Here, also they lie two, three, and even four, under the same covering, and much crowded together on the floor. The matron informed us that the bedding was insufficient, that some of it was ragged, and that it generally wanted washing. Neither the clothing nor the shoes of the women were good. The matron said it was some time since any had been issued, and that it was much wanted. There was an exceedingly offensive smell in all the water-closets; the arrangements for cleansing them not being efficient.'

'Here again we find that the 2d, 3d, 6th and 7th Rules of the Gaol Act, which require that female prisoners shall be constantly attended by female officers, are constantly infringed. The female prisoners, when taken down for trial, are often under the care of male officers only.'

'Better provision is made for the instruction of the females, in consequence of the constant and valuable attention which has been paid to them by the Ladies' Association for the Improvement of the Female Prisoners. To assist Mrs. Fry in her exertions the Ladies' Association was formed, about twenty years ago. Whatever may be our opinion as to the propriety and advantage of such associations, and of the expediency of encouraging generally the visits of ladies to well-regulated gaols, no one can for a moment doubt that in a miserable prison like Newgate the visits of the Ladies' Committee have greatly contributed to lessen the depravity of the place, and cannot fail to be highly beneficial, so long as the present state of the prison shall continue. It is only due to these Ladies to say, that they have been the means of introducing much order and cleanliness; that they have provided work for those who had before passed their time in total idleness; that they have introduced much better regulations than had been heretofore observed for the government of the women on their passage to New South Wales, furnishing them with many necessaries and with materials for keeping them employed during the voyage.

'The women sometimes, whilst washing themselves, expose their necks; this is certainly not decent, as the female yards are overlooked by the principal male turnkeys' apartments.'

General Observations

'The Association of Prisoners of all ages, and of every shade of guilt, in one indiscriminate mass, is a frightful feature in the system which prevails here; the first in magnitude, and the most pernicious in effect. In this prison we find that the young and the old; the inexperienced and the practised offender; the criminal who is smitten with a conviction of his guilt, and the hardened villain whom scarcely any penal discipline can subdue, are congregated together, with an utter disregard to all moral distinctions, the interests of the prisoners, or the welfare of the community.

'If human ingenuity were tasked to devise a means by which the most profligate of men might be rendered abandoned to the last degree of moral infamy, nothing more effectual could be invented than the system now actually in operation within the walls of the first metropolitan prison in England!

'Another feature in the Newgate system, to which it is our duty to call your Lordship's attention, is the utter absence of all employment for the prisoners: an evil which imparts to indiscriminate association nearly all its force and malignity.

'The last evil which we have to notice is the subjection of convicted prisoners to the same degree only of restraint and privation (with the single exception of a restriction upon the number of days for receiving visits) to which they had to submit when merely awaiting their trial. That the law should inflict upon an individual whom, as yet, it regards as innocent, the same measure of privation and restraint to which it subjects the convicted culprit as a punishment, involves a confusion of moral distinctions, and a disregard for individual suffering.

'We now return to the consideration of Newgate as a Prison of Detention for the Untried. We are aware that we shall be encountered by a measure which has been suggested as a specific and sufficient remedy for the enormous and acknowledged evils of the present system: we mean the classification of the prisoners. It is maintained that, by a proper classification, we may get rid of the apprehension and mischief of gaol contamination. We deliberately deny this. The opinion is based upon a foundation which both reason and experience abundantly prove to be delusive. Classification is professedly regulated by one or other of these two standards—gradation in crime, or diversity of character. Now we submit, that an attempt to classify according to the degree of imputed guilt is entirely futile; the standard itself is purely technical, inasmuch as the law places in the category crimes which, in moral atrocity, are separated by the widest assignable interval. But, even granting that the legal denomination embraces crimes of the same degree of moral turpitude, the imputed guilt of the prisoner will not necessarily consign him to the society of his equals in moral depravity; because a most atrocious character may happen to be committed on a charge involving only trivial criminality. Is this accident, then, to associate him with trivial offenders? By the system of classification by crime, it must be so. But the advocates of this system seek to avoid the lamentable consequences of this branch of the arrangement by taking refuge in the other. They offer to determine the class in which the prisoner shall be placed, by the actual moral habits and character of the offender! They profess to determine the case by a reference to a test of which they cannot have any cognizance; by an inquiry into circumstances which are impenetrably veiled from all human scrutiny—the internal habits and disposition of the mind and heart! We will not trifle with the subject, by further needlessly exposing a doctrine, the fallacy of which is so apparent; and shall therefore proceed to state to your Lordship the nature and advantages of the Separate System, by the adoption of which we feel a strong conviction that most of the evils which attach, more or less, to all other plans, will be guarded against, and the benefits aimed at by a judicious and well-digested system of prison discipline will be secured. If we venture to express ourselves confidently upon this subject, it is because a long and patient investigation, pursued under circumstances peculiarly favourable to an intimate acquaintance with it, in all its various aspects and bearings, both in this and other countries, has forced a conviction upon us of the various merits of this most valuable system, and justifies us in strongly recommending its adoption. But before we proceed, we deem it right to guard against any misconception of our meaning, as to the sense in which we employ the expression "separate confinement". By these terms we mean the confinement of the prisoners individually in cells, so as effectually to keep them separate from each other. In this sense it will be perceived that "separate confinement" is not the same as "solitary confinement", with which it is often inadvertently confounded. It does not contemplate the utter seclusion of the prisoner from all human intercourse: on the contrary, it expressly secures to him that intercourse, so far as his circumstances admit of and require it. It provides, that he shall see the Chaplain both in public worship and in private converse: upon a due performance of this latter duty are founded the strongest hopes of the reformation of the offender, whose spiritual good this system provides for with an earnestness proportioned to its importance, and with a rational expectation of success which no other system can venture to entertain. Under this plan, also, the prisoner sees the medical officer when he needs his assistance: he sees constantly the officers of the prison, and is permitted to confer with his legal adviser; and, under proper regulations, with his relations and friends. He only sees not those whom it is his own interest, and the interest of the State, and of Public Justice, that he should not see. The system, in short, is not an instrument to oppress; it is a shield to defend. It denies the prisoner no advantage which he ought to possess. It guards him against those evils to which the present system unfeelingly exposes him. In order to mitigate the discomfort necessarily attendant upon this mode of confinement, we propose that, for those who desire it, means and materials for employment should be provided. But in any provision which the prison regulations may make for the employment of the accused, we must never lose sight of the protection due to the rights of the Untried. His guilt is but contingent: he may be innocent: therefore, no occupation which may be provided for him should be characterised by marks of compulsion, or degradation, or severity.

'In the enumeration of the advantages of this system, we must not overlook the effect which it will have even upon those who shall eventually be found guilty. Upon their minds it will impress the conviction that a prison is what the law designs it to be, and that its regulations cannot be defeated. The gloom with which their imaginations will infallibly connect the interior of a prison, will make a powerful impression; and thus from the first moment that Justice lays her hand upon the offender, he will feel that he is suffering for his misdeeds.

'Amongst the evils against which the Separate System affords a safe-guard we may enumerate the following: it prevents, in the first place, the most alarming of all evils which attend imprisonment as now conducted, viz., gaol contamination. This it does simply and effectually. And when we say that it provides against this evil, we entreat one moment's reflection upon the magnitude of the mischief it at once destroys.

'The dreadful state of terror and alarm in which prisoners are constantly kept, and the exposure of the weak to the oppression of the strong—evils against which the present system can provide no remedy—have no place in the Separate System; and consequently cannot operate against those habits of self-examination and reflection, which are totally discouraged and over-borne by the present unhappy and fearful circumstances of the prisoners.

'The last evil which we shall notice is that of Recognition, against even the apprehension of which, separate confinement fully secures the prisoner. This is a measure which justice, as well as humanity, loudly demand. Regulations which fail of completely effecting this, have not even the merit of palliating the evil.

'In support of the views which we have thus taken of the necessity of Separate Confinement for the Untried, we beg to call your Lordship's attention to what has been done, and is now doing, in the United States of America, for the advancement of the same end. Whatever differences of opinion may prevail in the United States as to the expediency of adopting a rigid system of separation for convicts, the advantage of its application, in a modified form, to prisoners before trial is becoming generally acknowledged. In Pennsylvania two county gaols have been erected on this principle; and even the Authorities of the city of New York, attached as they have hitherto been to the Silent System, have yielded to the general conviction that it is most unjust to subject the Untried Prisoner to association with other prisoners. A County Gaol, or House of Detention, is now building in the city of New York, on the Separate System.'

'In another part of that Report we have proposed the construction of large, airy, separate cells at Milbank, with every needful accommodation for the prisoner. The value of the plan suggested will be further felt, when it is considered that by carrying it into effect in a place so central and important as the Metropolis, at a time when the magistrates in several parts of the kingdom are contemplating the erection of separate cells, a model will be presented for general imitation. This circumstance is the more important, as much ignorance and misconception prevails throughout the country relative to the construction and fitting up of separate cells.'

CAMBRIDGE

House of Correction

'*Labour.* There are two tread-wheels in separate yards, which are divided from each other by a passage walled on each side, leading to the interior of the mill. The power is applied to grinding grist for the public, or, when that is not to be procured, to pumping water into a tank, which, by the use of a waste pipe, affords the means of endless labour. The tread-wheels are each 12 feet 6 inches in length, and 16 feet in circumference, and allowing them to revolve twice in a minute, and that the men are at work ten hours, they ascend 12,800 feet daily. Each revolution of the wheel is denoted by a bell, and the men rest after every 40 rounds. The female prisoners are employed in washing.'

'Prisoners of all descriptions, tried and untried, are permitted to labour in the keeper's garden, outside the prison, for which they have received, occasionally, from him small gratuities, such as onions, potatoes, and ale; and the keeper stated that the magistrates permitted this, and that it was an understood part of his remuneration.'

Spinning House

'This establishment, situate in St. Andrew's Street, was founded by Thomas Hobson, in 1628, for the purpose, as expressed by him, in the endowment, "of setting the poor people of the University, and Town of Cambridge, to work, and for a House of Correction, for correcting unruly and stubborn rogues, beggars, and other poor people which shall refuse work, and to provide wool and flax for their occupation." '

'The University make use of their allotted portion of the Spinning House, for the inclusion of prostitutes, who are apprehended by the Proctors; they are taken there generally at night. The Vice-Chancellor attends in the morning, and the prisoners are brought before him. A Proctor is present, and the information is taken without the formality of an oath, and the offenders dealt with by sentences of imprisonment for periods not exceeding two months, or discharged upon admonition.'

'*General Discipline.*—This prison appeared, upon first inspection, particularly that portion applied to vagrants, to be in a neglected and uncleanly state, but on a second visit, it was much improved in this particular. There is no sort of discipline maintained; several escapes have taken place. The prisoners are not searched, nor deprived of money, nor any other article.

'They occasionally climb over the walls of one airing yard into another; they pass their time huddled round the fires, in obscene talk, or occasionally in singing and dancing. The keeper gives it as his opinion, "that any girl not very bad, would be far worse on going out than when she came in. He has observed shades of difference, as to feeling their situations, among some of the females upon first coming in, but this has worn off by association"

'The confinement has no other effect but that of keeping them out of the streets in term time. The females now come in at a much younger age than formerly; they have generally been servant girls in lodging-houses in the town.'

HUNTINGDON

County Gaol

'Treadmill and crank machine. The treadmill is divided into compartments for the purpose of preventing communication between the prisoners while on it. The divisions are made of thin deal; the space allotted for each prisoner is 22½ inches.

'This arrangement does not appear to me to answer the purpose for which it was intended; the men on the wheel loll, and rest themselves against the partitions, and the free circulation of air is much impeded; and they contrive to make holes in, and injure the partitions whenever they can do so unperceived.

'Without the constant presence of the taskmaster, the treadwheel is a very inefficient agent of correctional discipline.'

Borough Gaol

'The following are the dimensions of the six apartments appropriated to prisoners:

'Felons' day room, 17 ft. 3 in. by 17 ft.; and 8 ft. 9 in. high.

'Felons' sleeping room, 16 ft. 6 in. by 16 ft. 6 in.; and 7 ft. 6 in. high, containing three large wooden bedsteads, for three men each.

'*Observations.*—This apartment is four feet under ground, descended by a trap door and staircase. It is quite unfit for the confinement of any human being. The floor is rotting with damp, and is broken through in many places; is imperfectly ventilated, and almost without light.

'Solitary cell, 10 ft. 6 in. by 3 ft. 10 in.; 5 ft. 10 in. high.

'*Observations.*—This den, for it can only with propriety be so termed, is built below ground, in the shape of a barrel; it is without light, and is entered through the felons' sleeping room. Misdemeanants' sleeping room, 18 ft. by 17 ft.; 7 ft. 3 in. high. Three wooden bedsteads.

'Females' day and sleeping room, ·18 ft. by 15 ft. 6 in.; 7 ft. 6 in. high.

'A female felon, under sentence of two years' imprisonment, was the only prisoner in the gaol at the period of inspection. Had there been male prisoners, she must have been confined wholly to this room, and precluded from air or exercise.'

NORWICH

County Gaol

'*Moral and Religious Instruction.*—The Chaplain reads prayers twice, and gives one sermon on Sundays; and is in the habit of paying a visit on that day to all the prisoners; particularly attending to those in the infirmaries.

On week-days prayers are read at half-past nine; and after this duty is performed, he retires to the room set apart for him by the Magistrates, and receives the Schoolmaster's report of the conduct of the prisoners during the day preceding. He examines the prisoners who have come in, and before they are classed, and he states this to be the time when, previous to their intercourse with others, he finds he has the greatest influence over them. He is frequently occupied several hours in obtaining information from them, as to their former habits, connexions, and conduct. He then proceeds with those who are about to be discharged, and gives them suitable advice; and, if they can read, accompanies it with the present of a Testament, Prayer Book, or Tracts. He then examines into the progress the different classes have made who are under the Schoolmaster. The prisoners do not attend Chapel until examined by the Surgeon and classed by the Chaplain.'

'*Schoolmaster.*—Under the direction of the Chaplain. He states that no prisoner is ever taken from his labour for the purposes of instruction; it is done in the intervals allowed for rest, in the day rooms and cells. He thinks there are many prisoners who seek to be taught for a good purpose, but there are others who resort to it merely for employment of time, and to relieve the tediousness of a prison. The prisoner in solitary confinement is always the first to ask for books. He is sure that it would tend much to reformation and improve the discipline of the prison, if the prisoners were confined apart and provided with books. Still the instruction now has a beneficial effect. He keeps a book for each class under his tuition, noting down their daily advancement, and a list of the books in their possession; likewise a journal of the disposal of his time, and how employed.

'*Observations.*—The instruction of the prisoners is not altogether voluntary on their parts. When a prisoner refuses to be taught, he is removed from his class, and placed in close confinement in his own cell; but allowing him exercise. The Chaplain states this only to last two or three days before the individual is glad to get back to his class. It is done with the sanction of the Magistrates. The prisoners are cautioned, that if they do not make that use of the day rooms for which they were intended, they will be removed from them; that they are not for the purpose of idle communication and talk, and that those who do not choose to learn themselves, must not be there to disturb the others. I examined several of the prisoners who had been under the schoolmaster, and as far as reading fluently, and learning by rote, their proficiency was satisfactory; their spelling was much less so.

'The books used in the process of instruction are wholly of a moral and religious tendency.'

Borough Gaol

'The principal front and gateway presents a massive and appropriate architectural elevation. The lodges on either side the entrance contain accommodation for turnkeys, searching room, hot and cold water baths, and reception cells. The disposition of the interior is a centre, with four detached radiating wings. The central building contains the Keeper's dwelling and the chapel; it comprises a basement, with kitchen, store-rooms and domestic offices. First floor, magistrates' room, two parlours, and office. Second floor, two chambers, and chapel, with fourteen divisions, for as many classes. Upper story, two chambers.

'The sleeping cells for the prisoners are 8 feet 10 inches long; 6 feet wide; 8 feet 10 inches high. Four square towers or attics are raised at the extremity of each radiating wing, containing four cells each, for the reception of prisoners sentenced to solitary confinement. The floors of the cells are of stone, the doors of iron, and the light and air are admitted to them by wooden shutters which have three panes of glass.

'*Observations.*—The prison is altogether well ventilated, the drainage effective, and quite free from any danger of accident by fire; its divisional arrangements are convenient, and from the balcony which runs round the Keeper's dwelling, a sufficiently commanding view of the whole prison is obtained.'

SWAFFHAM

Gaol and House of Correction

'*Scourge for Boys.*—Handle 20½ inches of whalebone, nine lashes of common whipcord, 14½ inches each in length, with three single knots in each.

'*Scourge for Men.*—Handle 21½ inches of whalebone, nine lashes of common whipcord, 20½ inches each in length, and from six to nine knots in each last. The Keeper inflicts the punishment himself. The number of lashes is never specified. The sentence runs, "to be whipped until his back be bloody." The number of lashes in his experience is only three or four, laid on very sharply, and never more than twenty. No medical man attends.

'*Observations.*—The Keeper considers it necessary that there should be the power to inflict corporal punishment, although it is but seldom requisite to resort to it. The punishment he has been in the habit of inflicting, has been so slight as not to require the presence of a medical man.'

GREAT YARMOUTH

Borough Gaol and House of Correction

'The brick partitions of the sleeping cells being only 9 inches, and those between the male and female wards being little or no more, and also remote from any inspection, conversation in both situations is carried on almost uninterruptedly. In the old gaol the four underground cells are quite dark, and deficient in proper ventilation. The prisoners describe their heat in summer as almost suffocating, but they prefer them for their warmth in winter: their situation is such as to defy inspection, and they are altogether unfit for the confinement of any human being.'

'*Observations.*—Upon first visiting the prison I found several of the prisoners in the yards walking about without shoes or stockings on, and otherwise imperfectly clad. The following particulars of their condition and treatment are derived from themselves, the gaoler, and turnkey.

'*John Bowles.*—This prisoner, sentenced to twelve months' imprisonment, was without shoes or stockings, with scarcely a rag of trousers to cover him. He had been so for four months; he was limping about the yard with a leg covered with sores, greatly inflamed and swelled. He had been without medical attendance. He told the turnkey of it about a fortnight since. Had but a single shirt, and was not allowed any soap; washed it as well as he could; he got a bit of chalk and scrubbed it.

'*William Edwards.*—Twelve months' imprisonment; had no clean linen this month; had been four months without shoes. He borrowed a pair of shoes to go to trial of another prisoner in the yard.'

'*Labour and Employment.*—Many of the prisoners are sentenced to hard labour, but none is provided; shoemakers and tailors are permitted to carry on their trades and procure work from the tradesmen in the town; the masters send their wages to them in the prison. Until the Resolutions of the Lords' Committee were communicated by the Magistrates, they were allowed to purchase whatever articles they pleased, but the money is now received and kept by the Keeper until their discharge.'

'*Sarah Martin.*—This most estimable person has, for the long period of seventeen years, almost exclusively given up her time to bettering the wretched condition of the prisoners confined in this gaol. She is generally there four or five times a week, and, since her first commencing these charitable labours, she has never omitted being present a single Sabbath-day. On the week-days she pursues, with equal zeal, a regular course of instruction with the male and female prisoners. Many of the prisoners have been taught to read and write, of which very satisfactory examples were produced; and the men are instructed and employed in binding books, and cutting, out of bones, stilettoes, salt spoons, wafer stamps, and similar articles, which are disposed of for their benefit. The females are supplied with work according to their several abilities, and their earnings are paid to them on discharge; in several instances they have earned sufficient to put themselves in decent apparel, and be fit for service. After their discharge, they are, by the same means, frequently provided with work, until enabled to procure it for themselves.

'Only a single instance is recorded of any insult being offered to her, which was by a prisoner of notoriously bad character; upon which she gave up her attendance upon the ward to which he belonged; after his discharge, the other prisoners came forward, and entreated most earnestly that she would be pleased to resume her visits.

'There are several cases where her attentions have been successful, and have apparently reclaimed, if the continued good conduct of the discharged be admitted as satisfactory proof. That of four smugglers is singular from the fact that, upon their discharge after a long imprisonment, they addressed the felons, and entreated them to listen to her advice and treat her with respect.'

County Gaol and House of Correction

'The interior structure originally consisted of a central building, with four attached wings, upon the radiating principle.

'Dimensions of the cells—Original building, 7 feet 9 inches, by 6 feet 3 inch wide, and 10 feet high.

'New buildings, 9 feet 6 inches long, 5 feet wide, 10 feet high.

'Cells, where three sleep, 9 feet 6 inches long, 9 feet 6 inches wide, 10 feet high.

'The materials used in the first construction of the prison were of the best quality; it is perfectly ventilated and free from damp. It was erected in 1790, on the plan of Mr. Howard, and was then supposed to answer every possible purpose of such an establishment; but subsequent experience has so improved the details of prison architecture, as to leave this structure far inferior to many of a later construction.'

'*Labour.*—Treadwheel. The buildings with the treadwheels are among the later erections in the prison. The six wheels are all placed contiguous to each other; and the prisoners for hard labour are taken there from all parts of the prison to perform their daily tasks upon the wheel.

'The Matron states, that in one instance a female was sentenced to six months' imprisonment, the last to be solitary; her dread of it was so great, that she refused her food for the six weeks previous, for the purpose of making herself ill, and avoiding it. She pursued this conduct till she became speechless, and was obliged to be taken to a sick room and attended by a nurse.'

Borough Gaol

'*Officers of the Prison.*—Keeper, a widow, aged 60: her husband held the situation of Keeper 35 years ago. Upon his death, in 1811, the Magistrates permitted her to succeed him. There is no established turnkey, but she employs one at her own expense, who boards and sleeps in the prison.

'*General Observations.*—Without going into the question of the propriety of a female holding such an appointment as that of Keeper, the indifferent state of this prison is quite sufficient to manifest the utter incompetence of the person entrusted with its governance. She is a very respectable person, and it is impossible not to feel regret at her being placed in this anomalous position. She stated, upon examination, that she was quite unaware that there were Acts of Parliament for the Regulation of Prisons. She had no instructions, no rules. That prisoners, in many instances, were brought to the prison without commitments from the Magistrates, and have lain four or five weeks, and been discharged without any having been sent.'

REPORT OF THE INSPECTOR FOR THE S. AND W. DISTRICT

General Observations

'In all the County Gaols which I have entered, a remarkable degree of cleanliness and neatness has reigned throughout, equalling that which is usually maintained among the middle classes in England, and largely surpassing the standard which generally prevails in the most splendid residences of Continental Europe. This observation will not be considered trivial by those who appreciate the influence which these two qualities daily exercise over the health of the body, and the discipline of the mind. Among the Borough and Town Gaols, and those placed under local jurisdiction, these characteristics are far less prominent, and sometimes, indeed, are scarcely visible; but these blemishes appear to me, in the various shades in which they exist, to be derived rather from the narrow space and unsuitableness of the building, from the limited funds, the scanty salaries, and the insufficient service, than from wilful neglect on the part of the keepers, who, indeed, are often sensible of evils which they do not possess the power of remedying.'

'From the recent introduction of silence into some prisons I have not yet been able to trace a single instance of mischievous consequences. My conversations with prisoners, officers, surgeons, chaplains and magistrates, have not led to the discovery of any case in which disease, either of body or of mind, has been affirmed by any party to have grown out of this mode of discipline. The experiment, it is true, has not yet been practised for a long period; but I am bound to add, that all the persons most conversant with the interior of prisons who have favoured me with their conclusions on this head, pronounce decidedly in its favour, and entertain an expectation of its probable efficacy in increasing the repugnance to incarceration.'

'The branch of my inquiries which has afforded me the most unmixed satisfaction is that which relates to the proportion of deaths which occurs in the principal gaols which I have visited. The rate of mortality is, in most of these abodes, so remarkably low, that I can confidently affirm, that in very few situations of life is an adult less likely to die than a well-conducted English prison.'

Gloucester County Gaol and Penitentiary

'The County Gaol and Penitentiary are both comprehended within one building, although separate in arrangements and in position. This edifice reflects honour on the memory of Sir George Paul, who appears to have had the entire direction of the plan, and who anticipated, in his own time, certain improvements, which were not much noticed then, and have been since regarded as the discovery of later individuals. His presiding genius watched over the most minute details; thus, for instance, he has made all the doors of passages very low, in order that a prisoner, if running at an officer to attack him, might be suddenly arrested in his course.'

'The ventilation is good; the windows and privies in complete order. The Prison is a secure one. Although the situation is not very dry, the Prison is usually dry internally.

'There are 13 Wards in the Gaol, with six Day Rooms, and six Airing Yards. There are 88 Light Cells for sleeping-rooms. There are only two Dark Cells and both of these are above ground. There are no other Refractory Cells specially appropriated for punishment.

'In the Penitentiary there are 79 Day Cells, and 69 Sleeping Cells. The entire number of the cells, in the whole Penitentiary, is 148.'

'The Gaol is appropriated to Untried Prisoners (excepting fines in execution, also admitted). The Penitentiary is for the Convicted.

'The Convicted Prisoners are confined in separate cells, both by day and by night, whenever there is sufficient room for the practice of such a system. They are always separated at meals and at night. Solitude appears to be that part of the discipline which is most severely felt. Amongst these classes the observance of silence is strictly enforced. When the Prison is crowded, 15 or 20 are placed in a large day-room together.'

'Cleanliness, neatness and steady discipline are visible throughout, and the Prison has been fortunate in long possession of a zealous and judicious Governor.

'Silence appears to have been introduced here on the opening of the Gaol in 1792; but it was not then so methodically pursued as at present. This appears to have been the fountain-head of information on the subjects of silence and solitude. Labour in separate day cells was only given up in 1822, when the treadwheel was introduced.'

'Each Penitentiary prisoner has daily for breakfast and supper, half a pint of milk mixed with half a pint of boiling water, and 1½ lb. loaf of bread daily.'

'*Labour*.—There are two treadwheels here, containing 40 divisions or compartments. Each side has 10 of these divisions; and the total number of prisoners which the wheels can employ at the same time is 40. The height of each step is eight inches, and the ordinary velocity of the wheels is twice in the minute. The other lighter employments consist in cooking, washing, cleansing, but no trade. Certain trades are performed by the Debtors, when the prison does not happen to be crowded, and they receive all their earnings.

'The hours allotted to hard labour are about five in the winter, and about nine in the summer.'

Winchester County Gaol

'*Construction*.—Large, substantially built, and imposing in form, this Gaol is probably less secure than it appears at first sight. It is overlooked by the windows of neighbouring houses in several points. There are Nine Yards; five for Male Felons, two for Debtors, and two only for the Women. In consequence of this want of accommodation for the females, classification among them becomes impracticable to any extent. The wall of the Women's Yard is so low, that they may easily converse across. A great evil here is, that the Felons look up from their yards, and observe the Debtors in their galleries, while the Debtors look down from their galleries, and obtain an extensive view of all that passes in the Felons' yards. Thus a mutual source of amusement is established, and a sort of amphitheatre is formed for reciprocal survey. There is no Kitchen, nor Bathing-house.'

'*Labour*.—No hard labour is practised here, nor indeed is any regular employment carried on. The washing for the whole prison is performed by the prisoners, so also is whitewashing, and trifling repairs of the premises make an occasional occupation.'

APPENDIX C

Extracts from Report of the Select Committee of the House of Lords
on Prison Discipline, 1863

(1) SEPARATE CONFINEMENT (pp. v and vi)

'IN all questions of prison discipline, it appears to the Committee that the principle of separation, or association, stands first for consideration. Next in importance is the question of solitary confinement.

Association, or a mixed system of association and separation, prevails, as has already been shown, in many gaols. Such anomalies, however, are, in the opinion of the Committee, very objectionable. They should be removed at the earliest practicable time; and their present existence can only be justified by the difficulties of reconstruction, and the natural reluctance of the local authorities to incur a heavy expenditure. The Committee entertain a very decided opinion on this head, and having reference to the course of legislation now extending over many years, and the agreement in opinion and practice of the highest authorities, they consider that the system generally known as the separate system must now be accepted as the foundation of prison discipline, and that its rigid maintenance is a vital principle to the efficiency of county and borough gaols.

The Committee concur entirely in the opinion expressed by the Commissioners of Pentonville, who in their Fifth Report, dated 5 March, 1847, give the following decisive testimony in its favour:

'We concluded our Third Report by strongly urging the advantage of the separation of one prisoner from another as the basis and great leading feature of all prison discipline.

'On reviewing this opinion, and taking advantage of further experience, we feel warranted in expressing our firm conviction that the moral results of the discipline have been most encouraging, and attended with a success which we believe is without parallel in the history of prison discipline.'

'And in conclusion they state as their deliberate opinion that

'The separation of one prisoner from another is the only sound basis on which a reformatory discipline can be established with any reasonable hope of success.

'It is clear that this kind of separation must depend upon the judgment and capacity of those who are locally responsible for the administration of the prison. The newest and most elaborate form of construction is an insufficient safeguard if there is any relaxation of the necessary precautions by the local authorities, whilst an old and defective gaol may in some degree, by care and proper arrangement, be adapted to the requirements of our present system.[1] Looking, however, to the ordinary arrangements which exist in most gaols, there are so many interruptions to the regularity of prison discipline, instruction is given at such various times, and the communications which pass between prisoners and other persons are so frequent, that separation, though it exists nominally in many, is really to be found in few gaols; but where it does exist, it exercises both a reformatory and a deterrent effect. Under these circumstances, the Committee are of opinion that the principle of separation should be made to pervade the entire system of the prison, and no adequate reason has been assigned for the relaxation of the rule in school, in chapel and at exercise. It is, however, to be understood that this conclusion is not intended to limit the *cellular* and other religious instruction which the chaplain may think fit to administer to any prisoner.

'The justice of this view is generally admitted, except as regards the association of prisoners in chapel. Upon this point the evidence is conflicting.

'The main objections to the use of separate compartments in chapel appear to resolve themselves into two; one moral, the other mechanical. The first is grounded upon the opinion that a gaol chapel ought to be as much as possible like a parish church; the second arises from the belief that the compartments, from the mode of their construction, tend to facilitate rather than impede communication between the prisoners, and to induce them to deface the panels of the stalls by indecent writings or drawings. Neither of these objections seems to the Committee to be valid. With regard to the first, they conceive that the benefits which may be derived from giving a more devotional character to the chapel cannot outweigh the advantages of preventing the communication of prisoners with each other, and of rendering difficult their recognition by their fellow-prisoners on their discharge. With regard to the second objection, the Committee think that by adopting arrangements of the same nature as those which are in force in Bristol Gaol, the separation of the prisoners may be effected without difficulty. For these reasons the Committee recommend that the separate system should be carried out in the chapel as well as in every other part of the prison.'

(2) LABOUR (pp. vii and viii)

'There can be little doubt that a large proportion of the discrepancies which exist in the discipline administered in different prisons is due to the different

---

[1] This appears actually to be done in the city gaol of Bristol. See Mr. Gardner's evidence. Sir J. Jebb has added his testimony to the complete success, so far as separation is concerned, which is obtained by the system that is there pursued. 'I know of one prison,' he says, 'which is on the old construction (I speak now of the prison at Bristol), where a most effective discipline is well kept up by the Governor, with very inadequate means as regards construction: he has small cells, which are only fit for sleeping in, and cannot be certified for separate confinement; but by dividing his treadwheel into close compartments, and letting out the prisoners from their cells at certain distances from each other, and shutting them up in the compartments of the treadwheel, and marching them back again to their cells in the same way, no two prisoners can ever see each other, and you really obtain the advantages of separate confinement without the expense which is entailed by the construction of a prison.' (1207.)

constructions placed by the local authorities upon the sentence of hard labour ordered by the Court. Committees of both Houses have repeatedly recommended, and various statutes have distinctly required, the infliction of hard labour: but it is clear from the evidence that there is the widest possible difference in the opinions held as to what constitutes hard labour. The Committee believe that, with the best intentions on the part of the local authorities, there is in many gaols a great and unfortunate misapprehension on this head, and that until some more precise definition of hard labour is assigned, the grave public inconvenience and injustice which now arise from the inequalities of penal discipline in neighbouring counties or even in parts of the same county, must continue in full force. The first step towards a better and more uniform system throughout the country, would, in the opinion of the Committee, be found in an authoritative definition, by Act of Parliament, of the term of hard labour. Nor does there seem to be in this any practical difficulty. Of the various forms which are in force in the several prisons, the treadwheel, crank and shot-drill alone appear to the Committee properly to merit this designation of hard labour. Of these, the treadwheel and the crank form the principal elements of penal discipline, and might be safely prescribed as such in any future Act of Parliament. But whenever the local authorities may think it necessary to supplement the treadwheel or crank by further hard labour, recourse may satisfactorily be had to shot-drill, and this form of hard labour may be combined with the industrial employment in the later stages of imprisonment. Industrial occupation, though it may vary in amount and character, is so much less penal, irksome and fatiguing, that it can only be classed under the head of light labour. The picking of oakum must be regarded as an intermediate form of work; but under no circumstances, and to no class of prisoners, can industrial occupation be made an equivalent for a corresponding amount of hard labour as administered by means of the wheel, the crank or the shot-drill.

'It has been alleged in the course of the evidence, that the use of the treadwheel and crank degrades, irritates and demoralises the prisoner; but the Committee, after full consideration, see no reason for entertaining this opinion, and, under certain conditions, they highly approve of the use of both these instruments of prison discipline. Productive labour, indeed, holds out to the local authorities the hope of some profit, and is somewhat less irksome to the prisoner; it is therefore frequently urged, that the crank and wheel, if used at all, should be confined to the pumping of water, or the grinding of corn, or some other remunerative work. The Committee cannot subscribe to this view. If the local authorities can make use of the crank or treadwheel for productive work, the Committee see no objection to such an arrangement, but they think it essential that every prisoner sentenced to hard labour should be employed upon the crank or treadwheel for a minimum period, and that in no case should the regular enforcement of this system be relinquished or impaired for the sake of making the labour remunerative.

'As regards the short sentences or the earlier stages of imprisonment, the Committee believe that they are adopting a safe and a moderate standard when they recommend that every prisoner sentenced to hard labour shall, unless exempted by medical authority on grounds of health, be employed at the treadwheel or crank not less than eight hours per day the first three, and not less than six hours per day during the next three months of the first year of imprisonment.'

(3) REFORMATORY INFLUENCES (pp. xii and xiv)

'The possible reformation of offenders is an object which successive Committees of both Houses have had in view. The House of Lords Committees of 1835 and 1847 both refer to it; the House of Commons Committee of 1850 recognises its importance in marked terms. The Committee fully admits that it forms a necessary part of a sound penal system, but they are satisfied that, in the interests of society and of the criminal himself, it is essential that the other means employed for the reformation of offenders should always be accompanied by due and effective punishment. Sir W. Crofton, indeed, whose experience on this subject entitles him to much consideration, does not hesitate to go so far as to say that moral reformation of character is greatly assisted by a preliminary course of stringent punishment.[1]

They also believe that the inefficiency of the present system of administering the law in ordinary prisons is shown in the large proportion of prisoners who, after undergoing a period of confinement, are again committed to prison under fresh sentences. The relapse of such prisoners is partly due to the difficulty which any one of tainted character has in finding employment.

'In this view, the question of rendering assistance to prisoners on discharge, as a preventive measure calculated to reduce the rate of re-convictions, appears to the Committee to be deserving of serious consideration.

'2. The Committee, whilst they are compelled to admit that the reformation of individual character by any known process of prison discipline is frequently doubtful, believe that the majority of prisoners are, within certain limits, open to the influences of encouragement and reward. They therefore attach importance to the establishment, in every prison, of various gradations, which shall rise from the penal and disciplinary labour of the treadwheel, crank or shot-drill, into the higher and less irksome stages of industrial occupation and prison employments. And with that view they would make the entire system strictly progressive throughout its several stages.

---

[1] Q. 'Your view would be, that, having regard to the requirements of prison discipline, and the ultimate reformation of the prisoner, the penal element, whether it be by the treadwheel or by the crank, ought to form a constituent part of that system?

A. 'I am quite satisfied about that, and more now than ever, because nine years since we established reformatory schools at a great cost of money and time: and I think that when we do so much to prevent crime, and to train those youths up, so that they shall not pursue criminal avocations, we are bound, on the other hand, to be more stringent in the punishment of those who still pursue a course of crime in spite of what we have done for them; and I am quite satisfied that the managers of reformatory schools would consider their hands to be strengthened by the prisoner knowing that pursuing a course of crime would lead to really stringent punishment, and other procedure externally, which I shall, I hope, point out presently.

Q. 'It has been given in evidence before this Committee by some of the witnesses, that, in their opinion, the effect of the treadwheel and the crank is to create a sense of degradation in the mind of the prisoner; is that your opinion?

A. 'I have no doubt it may do so; but, combined with other industrial pursuits, I think it might be counteracted. I believe that the penal element is so necessary that the feeling of degradation I must place on one side altogether in my mind.'

'7. The Committee give full credit to both the inspectors for their wish to improve the general condition of the gaols placed under their supervision; but they feel bound to express their dissent from many of the ruling principles of prison discipline, which they, and especially Mr. Perry, have laid down. They do not consider that the moral reformation of the offender holds the primary place in the prison system; that mere industrial employment without wages is a sufficient punishment for many crimes; that punishment in itself is morally prejudicial to the criminal and useless to society, or that it is desirable to abolish both the crank and treadwheel as soon as possible.'

(4) PRISON PUNISHMENTS (p. xiii)

'Punishments for offences committed in prison form so important a part of prison discipline, that, under any system, they cannot be overlooked. The Committee believe that in many cases misconduct is best punished by degradation from a higher to a lower and more penal class, combined with harder labour and a more sparing diet; in òthers, by the ordinary penalty of reduction of food, or by solitary confinement in dark cells—if separated by a sufficient distance from each other, and from the other parts of the prison—but that where the offender is hardened, and the offence deliberately repeated, corporal punishment is the most effective, and sometimes the only remedy. The most experienced witnesses are unanimous as to the wholesome influence of corporal punishment; some, indeed, have stated that they have never known it ineffective; and the Committee wish to record their opinion of its great value as one form of disciplinary correction.'

(5) STATE OF CERTAIN PRISONS (p. xv)

'Some of these minor prisons, such as that of Falmouth, have repeatedly been condemned in the inspectors' reports as altogether unfit for the custody and penal discipline of prisoners, and it would almost seem that the inspector in such cases has given up the fruitless duty of making his inspection, and republishing his annual censure. There is frequently an unrestrained association of untried with convicted, juvenile with adult prisoners, vagrants, misdemeanants, felons; dormitories wholly without light or control or regulation exist, and in one case the governor admits that, in the event of a disturbance at night amongst the prisoners, the warder on duty would not be allowed to enter the room, for fear of an assault being made upon him; occasionally two and more prisoners have been allowed to sleep in the same bed. In one instance the beds themselves have been removed, lest the prisoners should break them up and make use of the fragments, whilst in another gaol the beds form so large an element of the life of the prisoners that no less than 15 hours out of the 24 are allowed to be given to sleep. It appears that in several places the building itself is out of repair, or is overlooked by adjoining houses; that sometimes one man alone is in charge of the gaol, and responsible for its security; that, in one case, so little facility is there for carrying on the ordinary administration of the establishment, that the prisoners' food is supplied daily from the neighbouring inn, and that the innkeeper's bill constitutes the only accounts which are kept; that there are times of complete idleness, when neither penal labour nor light employment is given, and that amongst many other abuses communications of a contaminating and injurious tendency take place between the prisoners.

In reviewing this unsatisfactory and discreditable condition of many of the minor borough gaols, the Committee cannot conceal from themselves that it is in a great measure due to a disinclination on the part of the town councils or governing bodies to provide the necessary means for the proper administration of the prison. In one instance, where the visiting justices of the borough, as a measure of common prudence, appointed a warder to assist the governor, who is the only functionary in the gaol, the Town Council have declined to confirm this order, and the warder remains unpaid.

'In the same prison no chaplain has been appointed, although the 2 & 3 Vict., c. 56, s. 15, makes this obligatory upon the authorities of every gaol.'

APPENDIX D

NUMBERS AND SALARIES OF STAFF IN ENGLISH PRISON SERVICE

Numbers	Grades	Salaries
	HEAD OFFICE	
	(Senior and Specialist Posts)	£
1	Chairman of Commissioners . (Commissioner)	2,850
1	Deputy Chairman . . . (Commissioner)	2,125
1	[1]Secretary . . . . . (Commissioner)	1,500–2,000
1	Director of Prison Administration (Commissioner)	1,500–1,800
1	Director of Borstal Administration (Commissioner)	1,500–1,800
1	Director (Woman)	1,340–1,625
1	[1]Establishment Officer	1,500–2,000
1	Director of Medical Services	1,850–2,125
1	Assistant Director of Medical Services . . .	1,725–2,000
1	Director of Industries	1,800
1	Director of Works	1,500–1,750
1	Deputy Director of Works	1,050–1,270
6	[2]Assistant Commissioners	1,250–1,500
1	Chaplain Inspector	1,050
1	Senior Vocational Training Officer . . .	830– 930
2	Vocational Training Officers	775– 875
1	Catering Adviser	700– 950
1	Physical Training Organiser.	650– 850

NOTES:

[1] Assistant Secretaries of the Administrative Class: there are also 3 Principals of the Administrative Class.

[2] One Assistant Commissioner is in charge of Education and Welfare.

The Finance Officer and the Controller of Stores and Manufactures rank as Chief Executive Officers. There are two other Chief Executive Officers, one in the Secretariat and one in Establishments Branch.

Numbers	Grades		Salaries
	PRISONS AND BORSTALS		
	Superior Officers		
10	Governors, Class I	Men	1,400
		Women	1,300
18	Governors, Class II	Men	1,100–1,275
		Women	925–1,100
36	Governors, Class III	Men	850–1,050
		Women	700– 900
33	Assistant Governors, Class I . .	Men	650– 750
		Women	530– 650

431

NUMBERS AND SALARIES OF STAFF IN ENGLISH PRISON SERVICE—*continued*

Numbers	Grades		Salaries
	PRISONS AND BORSTALS—*continued*		
	Superior Officers—*continued*		£
95	Assistant Governors, Class II . .	Men	395– 650
		Women	365– 525
26	[1]Chaplains (full-time)		520
9	Senior Medical Officers		1,725–2,000
38	[2]Medical Officers (full-time)		1,250–1,725
	Psychological, Educational and Welfare		
2	Principal Psychologists		1,050–1,270
2	Senior Psychologists	Man	750–1,000
		Woman	650– 850
5	Psychologists		350– 750
1	Educational Psychologist . . .	Woman	495– 600
2	Psychiatric Social Workers . . .	Women	407– 562
10	Psychological Testers	Men	350– 400
		Women	280– 320
1	Vocational Guidance Officer . . .		775– 875
5	Social Workers	Women	350– 480
	Nursing and Medical		
1	Nursing Matron-in-Chief		380– 530
6	Principal Sisters		504– 582
50	Nursing Sisters		364– 485
10	Pharmacists		509– 606
20	*Works*		a week
22	Foremen of Works		190s.–202s.
63	Engineers, Class I		180s.–190s.
	Engineers, Class II		165s.–180s.
23	*Industries*		
3	Industrial Managers		570– 675
	Farm and Garden Managers . .	Two	500– 600
		One	400– 525
25	*Prison Officers*		a week
	Chief Officers, Class I . . .	Men	200s.–218s.
63		Women	175s.–193s.
	Chief Officers, Class II . . .	Men	180s.–192s.
386		Women	160s.–174s.
	Principal Officers	Men	160s.–174s.
3,250		Women	139s.–150s.
	Officers (established)	Men	118s.–158s. 6d.
		Women	103s.–136s. 9d.

NOTES:

[1] There is also one full-time Roman Catholic Priest, and a number of part-time Chaplains and Priests at various rates.

[2] There is also a number of part-time Medical Officers at various rates.

The foregoing represent the main grades only, excluding Civil Service Executive and Clerical grades, and numerous miscellaneous and temporary grades.

APPENDIX E

PARTICULARS OF ESTABLISHMENTS IN USE

Note. The establishments listed do not accommodate women prisoners except where this is specifically stated.

Prison	Special Features	Address
	LOCAL PRISONS	
	(a) General	
Bedford	—	St. Loyes Street, Bedford
Birmingham	Also a women's prison	Winson Green Road, Birmingham
Bristol.	—	Cambridge Road, Bristol
Brixton	(1) Untried adults from the London area	Jebb Avenue, Brixton Hill, S.W.2
	(2) 'Stars' from the London area serving a sentence of six months' imprisonment or less	
	(3) Civil prisoners from the London area	
Canterbury	—	Longport Street, Canterbury
Cardiff	Also a women's prison	Knox Road, Cardiff
Dorchester	—	North Square, Dorchester
Durham	(1) Also a women's prison	Whinney Hill, Old Elvet, Durham
	(2) See also under corrective training prisons	
Exeter	(1) Also a women's prison	New North Road, Exeter
	(2) See also under Borstals	
Gloucester	—	Castle Lane, Gloucester
Holloway	(1) All classes of women and girls	Parkhurst Road, Holloway, N.7
	(2) See also under central prisons	
	(3) See also under corrective training prisons	
Leeds	—	Gloucester Terrace, Armley Road, Leeds
Leicester	—	Tower Street, Leicester
Lewes	(1) Untried prisoners only	Brighton Road, Lewes
	(2) See also under regional prisons	
Lincoln	—	Greetwell Road, Lincoln
Liverpool	See also under corrective training prisons	Hornby Road, Walton, Liverpool
Manchester	(1) Also a women's prison	Southall Street, Manchester
	(2) See also under corrective training prisons	

Prison	Special Features	Address
	LOCAL PRISONS—*continued* (a) *General—continued*	
Norwich . .	—	Knox Road, Norwich
Oxford . .	—	New Road, Oxford
Pentonville . .	(1) Prisoners of the Ordinary class from the London area (2) See also under corrective training prisons	Caledonian Road, Holloway, N.7
Shrewsbury . .	—	The Dana, Shrewsbury
Swansea . .	—	Oystermouth Road, Swansea
Wandsworth. .	(1) Prisoners of the Ordinary class from the London area (2) See also under regional prisons.	Heathfield Avenue, Trinity Road, Wandsworth, S.W.18
Winchester . .	—	Romsey Road, Winchester
Wormwood Scrubs	(1) 'Stars' from the London area serving a sentence of more than six months' imprisonment, while awaiting transfer (2) Untried youths from the London area (3) Convicted youths from the London area serving a sentence of less than three months' imprisonment or awaiting transfer to Lewes (4) Surgical Centre (5) Psychological Centre (6) See also under Borstals (7) See also under corrective training prisons	Ducane Road, Shepherds Bush, W.12
	(b) *Special*	
Eastchurch . .	An open prison for, Civil prisoners, 'Stars' with sentences of 6 months' imprisonment or less, and prisoners of the Ordinary class with not more than 4 months of their sentences still to serve, all specially selected and transferred from other prisons	Eastchurch, Isle of Sheppey, Kent
Northallerton .	'Stars' with sentences of less than 12 months' imprisonment and youths from Leeds prison	East Road, Northallerton
Preston . .	Civil prisoners and 'Stars' with sentences of under 12 months' imprisonment, from northern prisons	Ribbleton Lane, Preston
Stafford (and Fauld Camp) . .	(1) 'Stars' serving sentences of from one to three years' imprisonment, collected from northern prisons for transfer to appropriate regional prisons if and when vacancies occur (2) See also under regional prisons	Gaol Road, Stafford

Prison	Special Features	Address
	CENTRAL PRISONS	
Aylesbury . .	Women of the 'Star' class	Bierton, Aylesbury, Bucks.
Dartmoor . .	Prisoners of the Ordinary class	Princetown, Yelverton, Devon
Holloway . .	(1) Women prisoners of the Ordinary class (2) Women sentenced to preventive detention (3) See also under local prisons and corrective\training prisons	Parkhurst Road, Holloway, N.7
Leyhill. . .	An 'open' prison for 'Stars'	Leyhill, nr. Falfield, Glos.
Parkhurst . .	(1) Prisoners of the Ordinary and Star classes transferred for medical or other special reasons (2) Prisoners sentenced to preventive detention	Lonsdale Avenue, Cowes Road, Newport, Isle of Wight
Wakefield . .	(1) Prisoners of the 'Star' class (2) See also under regional prisons (3) Selected youths serving sentences of more than three years' imprisonment	Love Lane, Wakefield
Training Prisons	REGIONAL PRISONS	
Askham Grange .	An open prison for women	Askham Grange, Askham Richard, nr. York, Yorks.
Sudbury Park .	An open prison	Sudbury Park, Derbyshire
The Verne . .	A prison of medium security	The Verne, Portland, Dorset
Maidstone (and Aldington Camp)	A closed prison with attached camp	County Road, Maidstone, Kent
Wakefield (and New Hall Camp) .	(1) A closed prison with attached camp (2) See also under central prisons	Love Lane, Wakefield
Young Prisoners' Centres		
Lewes . . .	See also under local prisons	Brighton Road, Lewes
Stafford . .	See also under local prisons	Gaol Road, Stafford
Allocation Centre		
Wandsworth .	For corrective training prisoners	Heathfield Avenue, Trinity Road Wandsworth, S.W.18
Camp Hill . .	CORRECTIVE TRAINING PRISONS	Camp Hill, nr. Newport, Isle of Wight
Chelmsford . .		Springfield Hill, Chelmsford, Essex
Durham (1 wing) .		Whinney Hill, Old Elvet, Durham
Liverpool (2 wings)		Hornby Road, Walton, Liverpool
Nottingham . .		Perry Road, Nottingham
Wormwood Scrubs (2 wings) . .		Ducane Road, Shepherds Bush, W.12

Prison	Special Features	Address
Allocation Centre	CORRECTIVE TRAINING PRISONS	
Manchester (small part) . .	⎱ For prisoners who prove unco-operative ⎰	Southall Street, Manchester
Pentonville (small part) . .		Caledonian Road, Holloway, N.7
Holloway . .	For women	Parkhurst Road, Holloway, N.7

Selected corrective training prisoners are also sent for training to regional training prisons

	BORSTALS	
	(a) For Girls	
Aylesbury . .	A closed Borstal	Bierton Road, Aylesbury, Bucks.
East Sutton Park .	An open Borstal	East Sutton Park, Maidstone, Kent
Exeter . . .	Recall Centre	New North Road, Exeter, Devon
	(b) For Boys	
	OPEN TRAINING INSTITUTIONS	
Gaynes Hall. .	—	Gaynes Hall, Great Staughton, nr. St. Neots, Hunts.
Hatfield (and Gringley) . .	—	Nr. Doncaster, Yorks.
Hewell Grange .	—	Hewell Grange, nr. Redditch, Worcs.
Hollesley Bay Colony . .	—	Church Road, Hollesley, Woodbridge, Suffolk
Huntercombe .	—	Huntercombe, Nuffield, Henley - on - Thames, Oxon
Lowdham Grange.	—	Lambley Lane, Lowdham, Notts.
North Sea Camp .	—	Freiston, nr. Boston, Lincs.
Pollington . .	—	Pollington, nr. Snaith, Yorkshire
Usk . . .	—	Mayport Street, Usk, Mon.
	CLOSED TRAINING INSTITUTIONS	
Borstal . .	—	Borstal, nr. Rochester, Kent
Feltham . .	—	Bedfont Road, Feltham, Middlesex
Hull . . .	—	Hedon Road, Kingston-upon-Hull
Portland . .	—	The Grove, Portland, Dorset
	SPECIAL INSTITUTIONS	
Latchmere House ⎰ Wormwood Scrubs . ⎱	Reception Centres	⎰ Nr. Richmond, Surrey. Ducane Road, Shepherds Bush, W.12 ⎱
Portsmouth . .	Recall Centre	Milton Road, Portsmouth
Reading . .	Corrective establishment for those who persistently misbehave	North Forbury Road, Reading

Note. This list represents the position as in June 1951.

APPENDIX F

Resolutions of the XIIth International Penal and Penitentiary
Congress relevant to matters discussed in the text

SECTION I   *Second Question*

How can psychiatric science be applied in prisons with regard both to the
medical treatment of certain prisoners and to the classification of prisoners
and individualisation of the régime?

Resolution

1. The purpose of prison psychiatry is to contribute by the co-operation of
the prison psychiatrist with other members of the staff towards a more
efficacious treatment of the individual prisoner and to the improvement of
the morale of the institution thereby attempting to decrease the probability
of recidivism, whilst at the same time affording society a better protection.

2. The psychiatric treatment should be extended to include: (1) the recognised mentally abnormal prisoners; (2) a number of borderline cases (including those with disciplinary difficulties) who may, possible for comparatively short periods only, require special treatment; (3) prisoners with more
or less severe disturbances resulting from prison life; lack of treatment would
lessen their chances of rehabilitation.

3. It is desirable, and would be highly advantageous, to have prisoners
classified and separated into groups for special treatment, e.g. groups of
feeble-minded persons and groups of inmates with abnormal personalities.
An establishment for the treatment of inmates with abnormal personalities
should have facilities for dealing only with a suitably homogeneous group,
not exceeding about two hundred persons. It is of decisive importance that
the treatment be not limited to a previously fixed period, and that the end
of detention should not mean cessation of treatment—this should continue
after discharge until adequate rehabilitation is obtained. It is desirable that
social psychiatric after-care facilities be provided.

4. The general methods of psychiatric treatment—e.g. shock treatment,
psychotherapy (including group therapy)—may advantageously be applied to
criminals with due regard to occupation and prison routine. For prisoners
with abnormal personalities it is necessary to work out indirect forms of
treatment, not attempting to force upon them definite patterns of response.
Direct and active co-operation on the part of the prisoner is of decisive
importance, and his readiness to be treated is, therefore, a necessary condition. This state of readiness is stimulated under a system of indeterminate

sentence which is morally justified on the grounds of public safety. The indefinite term element must, in all cases, be utilized with due regard to the risk of society which the prisoner would constitute if at large.

5. The assistance of the psychiatrist is essential in the classification of prisoners and in the training of the staff. Only when psychiatric centres are established within the prisons, permanently employing skilled forensic psychiatrists, is it possible to direct the special treatment of personality problems ascertained at the general classification, besides those spontaneous nervous reactions that may manifest themselves in prisoners previously classified as fully normal.

The forms of psychiatric treatment would, of course, depend on the degree and nature of the development of the general correctional system in the country or locality in question as well as on the number of psychiatrists available.

6. By his own example and in collaboration with the other members of the staff, the psychiatrist can contribute towards making individualised treatment a reality. In his guidance and teaching, the psychiatrist should build on careful analyses of individual cases actually encountered, and he should avoid all temptations to dogmatise.

SECTION I   *Third Question*

What principles should underlie the classification of prisoners in penal institutions?

Resolution

1. The term classification in European writings implies the primary grouping of various classes of offenders in specialised institutions on the basis of age, sex, recidivism, mental status, etc., and the subsequent subgrouping of different classes of offenders within each such institution. In other countries however, notably in many jurisdictions of the U.S.A., the term 'classification' as used in penological theory and practice lacks philological exactitude. The term should be replaced by the words 'diagnosis (or, if desired, classification), guidance and treatment', which more adequately portray the meanings now inaccurately included in the *one* term 'classification'.

2. In view of the foregoing, it is concluded that for the purpose of distributing offenders to the various types of institutions and for sub-classification within such institutions the following principles be recommended:

(a) While a major objective of classification is the segregation of inmates into more or less homogeneous groups, classification should be flexible;

(b) Apart from the imposition of the sentence further classification is essentially a function of institutional management.

3. For the purpose of individualising the treatment programme within the institution, the following principles are recommended:

(a) Study and recommendations by a diversified staff of the individual's needs and his treatment;

(b) The holding of case conferences by the staff;

(c) Agreement upon the type of institution to which the particular offender should be sent and the treatment plan therein;

(d) Periodic revision of the programme in the light of experience with the individual.

SECTION II   *First Question*

To what extent can open institutions take the place of the traditional prison?

Resolution

1. (*a*) For the purposes of this discussion we have considered the term 'open institution' to mean a prison in which security against escape is not provided by any physical means, such as walls, locks, bars, or additional guards.

(*b*) We consider that cellular prisons without a security wall, or prisons providing open accommodation within a security wall or fence, or prisons that substitute special guards for a wall, would be better described as prisons of medium security.

2. It follows that the primary characteristic of an open institution must be that the prisoners are trusted to comply with the discipline of the prison without close and constant supervision, and that training in self-responsibility should be the foundation of the régime.

3. An open institution ought so far as possible to possess the following features:

(*a*) It should be situated in the country, but not in any isolated or unfavourable location. It should be sufficiently close to an urban centre to provide necessary amenities for the staff and contacts with educational and social organisations desirable for the training of the prisoners.

(*b*) While the provision of agricultural work is an advantage, it is desirable also to provide for industrial and vocational training in workshops.

(*c*) Since the training of the prisoners on a basis of trust must depend on the personal influence of members of the staff, these should be of the highest quality.

(*d*) For the same reason the number of prisoners should not be high, since personal knowledge by the staff of the special character and needs of each individual is essential.

(*e*) It is important that the surrounding community should understand the purposes and methods of the institution. This may require a certain amount of propaganda and the enlistment of the interest of the press.

(*f*) The prisoners sent to an open institution should be carefully selected, and it should be possible to remove to another type of institution any who are found to be unable or unwilling to co-operate in a régime based on trust and self-responsibility, or whose conduct in any way affects adversely the proper control of the prison or the behaviour of other prisoners.

4. The principal advantages of a system of this type appear to be the following:

(*a*) The physical and mental health of the prisoners are equally improved.

(*b*) The conditions of imprisonment can approximate more closely to the pattern of normal life than those of a closed institution.

(*c*) The tensions of normal prison life are relaxed, discipline is more easy to maintain, and punishment is rarely required.

(*d*) The absence of the physical apparatus of repression and confinement, and the relations of greater confidence between prisoner and staff, are likely to affect the anti-social outlook of the prisoners, and to furnish conditions propitious to a genuine desire for reform.

(*e*) Open institutions are economical both with regard to construction and staff.

5. (*a*) We consider that unsentenced prisoners should not be sent to open institutions, but otherwise we consider that the criterion should not be whether the prisoner belongs to any legal or administrative category, but whether treatment in an open institution is more likely to effect his rehabilitation than treatment in other forms of custody, which must of course include the consideration whether he is personally suitable for treatment under open conditions.

(*b*) It follows that assignment to an open institution should be preceded by observation, preferably in a specialised observation institution.

6. It appears that open institutions may be either

(*a*) separate institutions to which prisoners are directly assigned after due observation, or after serving some part of their sentence in a closed prison, or

(*b*) connected with a closed prison so that prisoners may pass to them as part of a progressive system.

7. We conclude that the system of open institutions has been established in a number of countries long enough, and with sufficient success, to demonstrate its advantages, and that while it cannot completely replace the prisons of maximum and medium security, its extension for the largest number of prisoners on the lines we suggest may make a valuable contribution to the prevention of crime.

The rules and regulations obtaining in open institutions should be framed in accordance with the spirit of point 4 above.

SECTION II   *Second Question*

The treatment and release of habitual offenders.

Resolution

1. Traditional punishments are not sufficient to fight effectively against habitual criminality. It is, therefore, necessary to employ other and more appropriate measures.

2. The introduction of certain legal conditions so that a person can be designated an habitual criminal (a certain number of sentences undergone or of crimes committed) is recommended. These conditions do not prevent the giving of a certain discretionary power to authorities competent to make decisions on the subject of habitual offenders.

3. The 'double-track' system with different régimes and in different institutions is undesirable. The special measure should not be added to a sentence of a punitive character. There should be one unified measure of a relatively indeterminate duration.

4. It is desirable, as regards the treatment of habitual offenders who are

to be subject to internment, to separate the young from the old, and the more dangerous and refractory offenders from those less so.

5. In the treatment of habitual offenders one should never lose sight of the possibility of their improvement. It follows that the aims of the treatment should include their re-education and social rehabilitation.

6. Before the sentence, and thereafter as may be necessary, these offenders should be submitted to an observation which should pay particular attention to their social background and history, and to the psychological and psychiatric aspects of the case.

7. The final discharge of the habitual offender should, in general, be preceded by parole combined with well-directed after-care.

8. The habitual offender, especially if he has been subjected to internment, should have his case re-examined periodically.

9. The restoration of the civil rights of the habitual offenders—with the necessary precautions—should be considered, particularly if the law attributes to the designation of a person as an habitual criminal special effects beyond that of the application of an appropriate measure.

10. It is desirable

(a) that the declaration of habitual criminality, the choice, and any change in the nature of the measure to be applied, should be in the hands of a judicial authority with the advice of experts;

(b) that the termination of the measure should be in the hands of a judicial authority with the advice of experts, or of a legally constituted commission composed of experts and a judge.

SECTION II   *Third Question*

How is prison labour to be organised so as to yield both moral benefit and a useful social and economic return?

Resolution

1. (a) Prison labour should be considered not as an additional punishment but as a method of treatment of offenders;

(b) All prisoners should have the right, and prisoners under sentence have the obligation to work;

(c) Within the limits compatible with proper vocational selection and with the requirements of prison administration and discipline, the prisoners should be able to choose the type of work they wish to perform;

(d) The State should ensure that adequate and suitable employment for prisoners is available.

2. Prison labour should be as purposeful and efficiently organised as work in a free society. It should be performed under conditions and in an environment which will stimulate industrious habits and interest in work.

3. The management and organisation of prison labour should be as much as possible like that of free labour, so far as that is at present developed, in accordance with the principles of human dignity. Only thus can prison labour give useful social and economic results; these factors will at the same time increase the moral benefits of prison labour.

4. Employer and labour organisations should be persuaded not to fear competition from prison labour, but unfair competition must be avoided.
5. Prisoners should be eligible for compensation for industrial accidents and disease in accordance with the laws of their country. Consideration should be given to allowing prisoners to participate to the greatest practicable extent in any social insurance schemes in force in their countries.
6. Prisoners should receive a wage. The Congress is aware of the practical difficulties inherent in a system of paying wages calculated according to the same norms that obtain outside the prison. Nevertheless, the Congress recommends that such a system be applied to the greatest possible extent. From this wage there might be deducted a reasonable sum for the maintenance of the prisoner, the cost of maintaining his family, and, if possible, an indemnity payable to the victims of his offence.
7. For young offenders in particular, prison labour should aim primarily to teach them a trade. The trades should be sufficiently varied to enable them to be adapted to the educational standards, aptitudes, and inclinations of the prisoners.
8. Outside working hours, the prisoner should be able to devote himself not only to cultural activities and physical exercises but also to hobbies.

SECTION III   *Second Question*

How should the conditional release of prisoners be regulated? Is it necessary to provide a special régime for prisoners whose sentence is nearing its end so as to avoid the difficulties arising out of their sudden return to community life?

Resolution

1. The protection of society against recidivism requires the integration of conditional release in the execution of penal imprisonment.
2. Conditional release (including parole) should be possible, in an individualised form, whenever the factors pointing to its probable success are conjoined:

(a) The co-operation of the prisoner (good conduct and attitudes);
(b) The vesting of the power to release and to select conditions in an impartial and competent authority, completely familiar with all the aspects of the individual cases presented to it;
(c) The vigilant assistance of a supervising organ, well trained and properly equipped;
(d) An understanding and helpful public, giving the released prisoner 'a chance' to rebuild his life.

3. The functions of prisons should be conceived in such a way as to prepare, right from the beginning, the complete social re-adjustment of their inmates.
Conditional release should preferably be granted as soon as the favourable factors, mentioned under 2, are found to be present.
In every case, it is desirable that, before the end of a prisoner's term, measures be taken to insure a progressive return to normal social life. This can be accomplished either by a pre-release programme set up within the institution or by parole under effective supervision.

SECTION IV   *Third Question*

Should not some of the methods developed in the treatment of young offenders be extended to the treatment of adults?

Resolution

The Congress agrees that both fields, that of the control of adult crime and that of the control of juvenile delinquency, are involved in the gradual change from crime and delinquency control through punishment to control through correction. For varying reasons much more progress in that direction has been made in the juvenile field and it is therefore advantageous to look to that field for suggestions and leads for further developments in adult crime control.

The Congress considers that many adults are capable of response to the kind of training and conditions which in several countries are applied only to juveniles. Because a young man or woman is legally an adult, it should not mean that he or she must be condemned to a form of imprisonment which is shorn of all chances for education, training and reformation.

More specifically, the Congress suggests that the experiences acquired in the field of juvenile delinquency with regard to preparation of case histories, probation and parole and judicial pardon should be utilised also in the adult field.

APPENDIX G

Extracts from Reports, etc., illustrating contemporary international opinion on the principles of penal punishment and their application

AUSTRALIA

Annual Report of the Comptroller-General of Prisons, Queensland, for 1949.

'It is generally realised that the deprivation of personal liberty is the greatest penalty which any man can suffer and that it is the function of the prison service of the country to take positive measures towards rehabilitation rather than the wholly repressive measures of the past, which achieved nothing to remedy crime, but which bred a race of bitter, warped, and anti-social men.

'While there is little doubt that it will always be necessary to maintain closed prisons, many countries have in addition established prison farms or camps for suitable prisoners where security measures are sharply modified.

'The inmates of the prisons themselves retard progress to a great degree, as it is the small, troublesome, and unreliable minority who make the rigid security measures of the closed prisons necessary.'

BELGIUM

Extracts from *Vers une nouvelle architecture pénitentiaire* by Jean Dupréel, Director-General of the Administration of penitentiary establishments, Ministry of Justice, Brussels.

'Car on ne repétera jamais assez que la privation de liberté est en elle meme un chatiment très dur et que, sauf de rares exceptions, il est inutile, et par conséquent nuisible, de le renforcer par un régime systematiquement pénible.'

'En d'autres termes, il faut associer le condamné au traitement dont le but final est d'assurer son reclassement dans la société. La détention ne doit pas être une sinistre parenthèse, qui, s'ouvre lors de l'incarcération et se ferme a la libération. Elle doit être la continuation de la vie sociale, sous une forme différente, plus austère, mais néanmoins constructive.'

SCOTLAND

Report on The Scottish Prison System by the Scottish Advisory Council on the Treatment and Rehabilitation of Offenders, 1949.

'Punitive methods aimed solely at deterrence, we have suggested, not only fail to achieve their purpose but may aggravate the state they are trying to remedy. "Warehousing" is, in our view, a negative policy, which encourages recidivism, and results in an appalling waste of human lives and money. Is it possible to formulate a reformative policy which in practice will be effective?

'The main difficulty appears to be to combine an effective reformative policy with a punitive régime. The social stigma of a prison sentence; the loss of liberty; the enforced discipline; the deprivation of the comforts and amenities of ordinary life are all punitive. It must not be forgotten, however, that a convicted prisoner is sent to prison as a result of committing an offence and that the intention of the Court is not only to punish the offender but also to protect the community and to deter potential offenders from committing similar offences. The protection of the community can best be achieved if the training within the prison is such as to ensure, so far as it is possible, that the prisoner on discharge will lead a law-abiding life. In our view the shame attached to a prison sentence, the loss of freedom, the separation from family and friends, the difficulty of being accepted as a normal member of the community after release, constitute a heavy punishment and will always be a deterrent to potential offenders. In a word, the sentence and all it implies is the punishment; the object of prison treatment should not be to increase the punishment but to reform the prisoner.

'We have recommended that the administrators of the prison system should place reformative treatment of prisoners as their first consideration. In other words the primary object should be to train each prisoner to return to the community as a law-abiding citizen. To achieve this it will be necessary, in our view, to train prisoners while living apart from the community to stand on their own feet on release; and to be capable of doing right.

'The main factor in the training should be to instil a sense of responsibility and, as a secondary factor, which should lead naturally from the first, a sense of self respect. The best method of instilling a sense of responsibility is to give responsibility. This should be a gradual process. Without wishing to lay down any hard and fast régime we suggest that this category of convicted prisoners should be housed in "open" prisons, that is, prisons without bars and surrounding walls.

'The chief value of the "open" institution is, to our mind, the choice it gives to each individual prisoner to abide by the rules or to abscond. Here is an acid test which, if successfully borne, goes a long way towards instilling a sense of responsibility. But in addition, the "open" institution allows opportunity for giving each prisoner further responsibility in a number of ways. Supervision is not so close and is certainly less obvious, thus presenting the choice of idling or working; the choice of breaking or keeping the rules of the institution; the opportunity of living with members of that particular community in harmony or in disharmony. All these and other opportunities of choosing the social or the anti-social mode of behaviour form the basis of training for the acceptance of responsibility in the outside world, where choice is in a number of matters completely free. So far these experiments have shown sufficient success to call for further efforts in the same direction. They have indicated that prisoners can be trusted to a far greater degree than was previously thought possible.'

SWEDEN

Report of the Swedish Penal Code Commission 1942, on which is based the Swedish Prison Act 1945, quoted by Professor Thorsten Sellin in *Recent Penal Legislation in Sweden*, Stockholm, 1947.

'The loss of liberty can never be outweighed by any benefits . . . and need not be accentuated by repressive means to be deterrent. Neither can it be assumed that the generally deterrent effect of imprisonment becomes great or small with greater or less severity in the execution of this punishment.

'Nothing should be done to the prisoner that would counteract the aim of penal treatment, i.e. the reformation of the offender. He should not be set apart in a way likely to lower him in his own opinion or that of others.

'Many of the principles of traditional prison treatment are the products of hoary theories. Our present prison system has never taken adequate note of the imperative need of preparing a prisoner for a life of freedom, making him useful and conscious of his responsibilities: Prison life so easily becomes artificial and even stupefying. . . . Instead, one should strive to make the conditions resemble life in free society as far as possible.

'Walls, bars, and locked doors are the traditional features of a prison, but it is likely that they are required to a much less degree than at present.

'Every effort must be made to counteract the deteriorating effect of imprisonment . . . by placing on certain agencies the responsibility of maintaining contacts between life in the institution and the free world outside.'

SOUTH AFRICA

Report of the Penal and Prison Reform Commission appointed by the Government of the Union in 1945.

'Punishment by the courts is the infliction of some kind of pain or loss upon a person who transgresses the law. The fundamental purpose of this punishment in the view of the modern penologists and the opinion of this Commission is the protection of the community from the depredations of the lawbreaker. Obviously the best way to protect the community is so to educate and train people that they obey the laws, either because they accept them as their own, or at least because they realise that it is the better part of wisdom so to do. No community, however, achieves full obedience to its laws without penal sanctions, and there must therefore be punishment or penalty as a sanction for disobedience. Compliance with the law may be obtained by inflicting a sanction involving physical pain or by material loss in the form of fines, or it may be achieved by greater or less deprivation of liberty of action together with a smaller or greater degree of rigid control of conduct. The most fundamental principle of modern penal methods is loss of liberty of action in some degree by those persons who break the laws and by their behaviour show that they are not fully responsible members of the community. The loss of liberty of action may be partial, such as submission to the guidance of a probation officer or the necessity to refrain from certain conduct for a certain period, or complete as when imprisonment is imposed. Complete loss of liberty through imprisonment with its strict discipline and enforced obedience is now-a-days being used less, but in certain cases it is essential. In all these cases of deprivation of liberty of action there is the punitive element, i.e. the penalty for the offence, but positive treatment during this period, e.g. guidance and help by the probation officer and practical training or retraining and character development during imprisonment, is emphasised in all modern penal systems.

'The general objects of punishment accepted by the Commission then are conversion of an offender into a law abiding citizen, if possible, or at least his deterrence (and if possible of others likeminded) from entering or continuing upon a course of criminal or anti-social behaviour, so that the community may be protected. In pursuing these purposes, a court of justice must have regard, firstly, to the individual characteristics of the offender before it and, secondly, to the kind of penalty or treatment which is best suited to bring him to a proper state of mind. If detention is necessary, a suitable institution must be chosen.

'Mr. Herbert Morrison, then Home Secretary in England, in a speech made on 28th March 1944, dealing with the questions of Penal Reform, put the present trend of penal methods thus:

' "The first principle . . . is to keep as many offenders as possible out of prison. In the eighteen-sixties it was laid down in plain terms that sole object of imprisonment was punitive deterrence with the emphasis on the punitive. Just that: and so for a generation we had the most strictly deterrent penal system ever devised.
' "The experiment had to be made at some time. The belief in the efficiency of severe punishments is always cropping up and without the devastating failure of this experiment we might never have known better. The failure was so complete that a departure to fresh principles became essential."

'Punishment, whether harsh or mild, sometimes fails of its purpose and therefore reform must go with it. There is only one way to combine punishment and reform in prison and that is to regard the loss of liberty with its obloquy and separation from family and friends as the punishment, while the treatment of the offender during the period he is deprived of liberty is aimed at his reformation. Though prison must not be made a place of desirable residence, the treatment there, while discipline must be emphasised, must not assume a punitive character. This view of the position has already been adopted to some extent in our penal institutions, but needs greater development.

'While methods aimed at rehabilitation must still be the main remedial measure employed with this hardened group, the treatment and discipline required will obviously be very different. But the persistent effort for reform must ever be maintained notwithstanding frequent lack of success. There will always be a percentage of human kind who are and will remain anti-social —persons who, having the ability generally to resist pressures leading to criminality, lack the desire to do so. The steady increase over the years in the number of recidivists shows clearly that imprisonment under existing conditions in these cases is not achieving its object fully. Imprisonment is not deterring enough criminals from repeated anti-social conduct. The effect of repeated imprisonment has been rather to weaken the will towards law-abiding conduct and to make some offenders resentful, callous and desperate. To strengthen the individual will to resist, when this is possible, is wise: to diminish the forces, in so far as these are personal, which overcame such will, and are likely to overcome it again, is wiser.

'It is for this reason that most civilised communities today realise that the punishment of the offender is of itself not enough, but that combined with it reformative methods must be used in an attempt to adjust treatment in penal institutions to the individual after a study of the causes which led to his downfall as shown by his history, environment and character. It is obvious that the best method of securing the safety of society is to transform the anti-social individual into a co-operative one if this is possible. The present system of returning an offender to freedom, often with the knowledge that he is still a dangerous man, is a poor way of protecting society. The prison authorities have presently no discretion—the prisoner must be discharged when his sentence has expired.'

U.S.A.

Report for 1948 of the Director of Federal Prisons.

'To some, prisons are nothing but "country clubs" catering to the whims and fancies of the inmates. To others the prison atmosphere seems charged only with bitterness, rancor and an all-pervading sense of defeat. And so the whole paradoxical scheme continues, because our ideas and views regarding the function of correctional institutions in our society are confused, fuzzy, and nebulous.

'Of the various civic institutions, the prison has been most relegated to the background of the social conscience. Ordinarily the prison comes to the attention of the public only when it reaches the headlines because of an escape or riot. Yet the prison cannot be a fully effective agency of society unless its work is known and understood by the citizens it serves and unless it can utilise the resources of the community.

'It was encouraging to note this year an increased public interest and partici-pation in our work. Such participation has been described in connection with the sponsorship programme at the National Training School for Boys and with pre-release preparation at the various institutions. At the Federal Correctional Institution, Seagoville, Texas, for example, some thirty public-spirited citizens of nearby Dallas contributed their services in the development of the pre-release programme. In increasing numbers, educators, lecturers, musicians, actors, members of religious and civic organisations, and others who have contributions to make in education, counselling, and recreation are assisting us in making our institutions a constructive force in the lives of our charges. At best the artificial restrictions and barriers to normal social behaviour of prison life make difficult the development and maintenance of healthy attitudes and interests. The infiltration of normal community interests through visits of public-spirited citizens is a hopeful trend, both in the develop-ment of a healthy outlook among the inmates and in the interpretation of our problems, activities, and objectives in the community at large.

'Now, three years after its reopening as an institution for men, Seagoville serves as a demonstration that the prison of bars and cells, walls and gun towers, is not necessary or even desirable for many of the men sentenced to confinement. Of the 472 men confined on June 30, 1948, 187 were serving sentences of 5 years and over, with 117 sentenced to 10 years and over, including 4 with life sentences. They represented practically every offence in the Federal statutes. Yet there is no institution in the Federal system where the morale of inmates is higher nor where they work harder. Despite the almost complete absence of security facilities, the escape rate has been low, with only four escapes (all promptly recaptured) from the 1,514 prisoners received during the three years of the institution's operation. One cannot spend a few days at the institution without the realisation that the atmosphere, the "climate" of the institution, is healthy; that attitudes of the men are changing from suspicious, disgruntled, and anti-social, to those of self-respect and regard for the rights of others.

'It is not implied that what has been accomplished is due to the physical setting alone. The entire staff at Seagoville recognised the problems with which they were faced but approached their solution through positive leadership in the development of constructive activities, rather than through a programme based on fear, restrictions, and bars.' ·

From Chapter VI, *The Prevention of Repeated Crime*, by John Barker Waite, Professor of Law, University of Michigan: The University of Michigan Press, 1943.

'But though punishment is still clearly the purpose of the law, the purpose of the punishment is not so clear. The once academically popular notion that punishment should be imposed only for the purpose of retribution, to the end of exacting an owed expiation, has passed into obsolescence. In the main it has yielded place to concepts of punishment as a preventive of new wrongdoing. But it is by no means obsolete. It still affects both the content of the law and its administration. Today's newer legislation can be accounted for in part only by recognition of the extent to which the motivation of revenge for injury accomplished has coloured it. The instinctive desire for revenge, for the compelled repayment by an offender of a quid pro quo in suffering, is a social force which has never been wholly argued down, which has definitely influenced the whole process of dealing with convicted criminals and which must necessarily be taken cognizance of in any proposal of legislation to be enacted. It seems safe to say, therefore, that the purpose of treatment of discovered criminals is a composite, in fluctuating proportions, of retrospective, retributive satisfaction and of prospective hope. But no matter how strong the latter element of purpose, regardless of how emphatically the preventive purpose is stressed, the commonly accepted method of treatment, almost wholly relied upon, is still the infliction of unpleasant consequences for the sake of their effect upon the will of the sufferer—it is punishment, in the usual connotation of that term.

'A second unavoidable conclusion is the relative ineffectiveness of this punitive process, particularly as a preventive of *repeated* crime by wrongdoers who have been subjected to it. The light of history precludes an assumption that its failure lies in the mildness of its punishments; the most drastic of penalties have proved equally inefficient. Nor is there substantial evidence that its failures are caused by the infrequencies of its application. On the contrary its most obvious failures and its most notable ones are precisely with the very individuals to whom it has in fact been applied once, twice, or repeatedly. Whether or not a greater assurance of punishment, a greater modicum of inevitability, would more effectively decrease the amount of first criminality one cannot say. Nor need one speculate—the problem of creating that greater assurance has already been struggled with too long to raise a probability of its attainment. The effective possibilities of punishment as a preventive method must be measured by the actualities of the past and of the present. And by that measurement the punitive method, particularly in its operation upon those to whom it has in fact been applied, has demonstrated its unsatisfactoriness beyond dispute.

'The reasons for this failure constitute a fairly obvious further deduction. In the main the method fails because, though it may return its victims to social freedom with a strengthened desire to refrain from crime, it returns them also without the slightest increase in ability to do so. Too often it returns them to freedom with only a wish to evade renewed punishment, no desire at all to abstain from crime. But whether it succeeds in creating a will to abstain, or merely a will to sin more safely, it operates only upon the will, not upon the capacity to abstain. Only when the treatment applied ceases, in part at least, to be a punitive method can it actively seek to better its subjects' ability in self-support.

'The failure of punishment cannot be prevented while the process of punishment is retained as the primary method of treatment. Yet that the faults, and therefore the method, must be eliminated if society is to be successfully protected against repeated crime is an inescapable conclusion. Some fundamentally different method of treatment must be substituted. The only question is as to the essentials of that substitution.

'Presumably the substitute could not wisely, even were attainment practicable, depart entirely from the notion of unpleasant consequences as a result of conviction of wrong-doing. Prevention of repeated crime is but one objective, though the main one, of criminal law enforcement. The prevention of first crime cannot be ignored. Nor might it be altogether safe to disregard that vigorous insistence of the man on the street that wrongdoers be punished because they deserve to be punished. It may well be doubted that disorder would increase and private persons might take into their own hands the exaction of retribution if instincts of revenge were left unsatisfied by official action. More likely, a public which believes that its freedom from crime is being adequately protected will acquiesce peaceably in whatever reasonable means are adopted for that end. Still, satisfaction of that undeniably prevalent wish for retributory suffering as a consequence of injury done must be given some heed in consideration of any substitute for the common, punitive method of dealing with convicted criminals.

'In so far as the prevention of crime by others than the person dealt with is concerned, psychologists agree and history demonstrates that neither fear of monetary amercement nor the physical distress of imprisonment are of material effect. What deterrence there may be springs from more subtle influences; from the fear of public condemnation demonstrated through punishment, from the conduct habits and inhibitions created by open and notorious application in specific cases of what might otherwise be mere abstract formulations of right and wrong, from the instinct of individuals to conform with the expressed beliefs and demanded conduct of the herd.

If this be so, punishment, in the sense of treatment administered for the primary purpose of causing suffering, is not necessary tó attainment of the end sought. All the deterrent effect, the explicit expression of group reprobation, the demonstration of its standards of right and wrong, its insistence upon conformity with its group ideas, can be expressed by conviction and individualised corrective treatment as effectively as by conviction and stereotyped punishment.'

INDIA

Report of the Jail Reforms Committee appointed by the United Provinces Government in 1946. (Reference by Minister for Jails, United Provinces, in Presidential Address to Indian Conference of Social Work, 1949).

'The committee envisaged a large number of changes to modernise our penal system and to accord that treatment to the criminal which may be conducive to the realisation of a sense of responsibility and respectability in him, which he definitely loses during the long process of his detection, detention and incarceration. In recent years a number of amenities and facilities have been accorded to him with a view to assert his right as a prospective citizen in a free country. It is unfortunate that such facilities and concessions have been misunderstood and there is an impression in some misguided quarters that such steps will lead to a pampering of the prisoner. It is easy for a personality to be distorted but it is a tough job to reconstruct it, so as to enable the individual to take his proper place in society. This is the basic principle in our treatment of prisoners and it is with this object in view that attempts are being made to soften the life of an individual while undergoing his period of sentence.'

APPENDIX H

STAGE SYSTEM AND PRIVILEGES

The following is a copy of the information given to prisoners on the appropriate cell card:

PRIVILEGES

All prisoners are allowed certain privileges, whether they are in Stage (see next paragraph) or not. But these privileges may be forfeited under the above Rules if you abuse them or as a punishment for misbehaviour. They are as follows:

Additional letters and visits.
Library books.
Educational note-books.
Books and periodicals.
Attendance at educational classes or taking of correspondence courses.
Attendance at concerts or lectures in so far as accommodation permits.
Purchase from earnings of tobacco or other articles from the prison canteen.
Possession or smoking of tobacco.

STAGE SYSTEMS

The Stage systems for prisoners sentenced to imprisonment vary according to classification (Star or Ordinary) and length of sentence (Short-term or Long-term). They are as follows:

ORDINARY CLASS

Short-term prisoners, i.e., those with sentences of imprisonment up to and including 3 years. Short-term prisoners will be either 'Out of Stage' or 'In Stage'. A prisoner will be 'Out of Stage' for four calendar months from the date of admission on conviction, and will then be 'In Stage'. The privileges will be as follows:

Out of Stage. Out of Stage privileges are as in paragraph 'Privileges' above.
In Stage. In addition to the foregoing:

Attendance at concerts and lectures.
Dining in association by selection at the discretion of the Governor and to the extent that accommodation is available.
A general note-book and, if the prisoner so desires, a drawing-book.
Games and other permitted occupations in cells.

After 12 months in stage: Extension of visit to 30 minutes.

Tea and evening association for three evenings each week, by selection at the discretion of the Governor and to the extent that accommodation is available.

Long-term prisoners, i.e. those with sentences of over 3 years. The Stage System will be progressive, as follows:

On admission on conviction—1st Stage.
After 18 months in the 1st Stage eligible for 2nd Stage.
After 12 months in the 2nd Stage eligible for 3rd Stage.
After 18 months in the 3rd Stage eligible for 4th Stage.

The privileges attached to the Stages are as follows:

1st Stage—Privileges as in paragraph 'Privileges' above plus general note-book and drawing book if desired.

2nd Stage—Attendance at concerts and lectures.
Games and other permitted occupations in cells.
Evening association (twice weekly).
Extension of visit to 30 minutes.

3rd Stage—Dining in association.
Evening association (three times weekly).
Personal possessions in the cell.

4th Stage—On each day of the week, dinner and tea in association and evening association.
Certain additional facilities for obtaining newspapers and periodicals.

N.B. All association is by selection at the discretion of the Governor and subject to the accommodation available.

Stage Allowances.—In addition to payments received under the earnings scheme long-term prisoners will be paid a weekly stage allowance on reaching the Second Stage subsequently at the following rates:

Second Stage—2*d*.
Third Stage —3*d*.
Fourth Stage—4*d*. to be increased by 2*d*. per week per annum up to a maximum of 1*s*. 2*d*. per week.

Distinctive Dress. Second Stage—Grey dress, blue stripe.
Third Stage —Blue dress.
Fourth Stage—Blue dress with grey stripe.

STAR CLASS

Star prisoners whether long-term or short-term will be 'Out of Stage' for the first month after admission on conviction and 'In Stage' thereafter. An 'Out of Stage' Star prisoner will be treated in the same way as an 'Out of Stage' prisoner of Ordinary class: when 'In Stage' the Star prisoner will receive all the privileges available, according to the prison in which he is located.

Long-term Star prisoners will become eligible for stage allowances on a time basis similar to that for Ordinary prisoners:

After 18 months—2*d*. a week.
After 2½ years —3*d*. a week.
After 4 years —4*d*. a week to be increased by 2*d*. per week per annum up to a maximum of 1*s*. 2*d*. per week.

YOUNG PRISONERS

Young prisoners retained in local prisons will be 'Out of Stage' for the first 8 weeks of their sentences, and will then receive the stage privileges of the short-term Ordinary class.

CORRECTIVE TRAINING

If you have been sentenced to corrective training:

(a) On reception in a regional training prison you will receive the privileges granted to men in that prison.

(b) On reception in a corrective training prison you will be 'Out of Stage' for the first 8 weeks; during this period you will receive the privileges (though not the stage allowances) of the long-term 2nd Stage. Thereafter you will be 'In Stage'. The Stage privileges, as far as facilities permit, will correspond to those of the 4th Stage long-term prisoner. Corrective training prisoners with sentences of over three years will become eligible for stage allowances on a time-basis similar to that for Ordinary prisoners—After 18 months—2*d*. per week. After 2½ years—3*d*. per week.

(c) The Governor of a corrective training prison may in his discretion temporarily remove a prisoner from association if he is satisfied that it is in the interests of the prisoner's own training, or of the good conduct of the prison, to do so.

APPENDIX I

Summary of the principal recommendations of the Departmental
Committee to Review Punishments in Prisons, etc.

PART I—PRISONS

1. The Committee advised that the No. 2 punishment diet should be replaced by an alternative (para. 54).

2. There should be a special prison for recalcitrant and dangerous prisoners (para. 90).

3. A prisoner reported for an offence should be given in good time written notice of the offence charged and an opportunity to make his defence or explanation in writing (para. 100).

4. For adjudication on prison offences, Visiting Committees and Boards of Visitors should sit not less than two nor more than five at a time, the adjudicating members being called on in rotation from a 'judicial panel' (para. 115).

5. Visiting Committees and Boards of Visitors should follow the procedure of courts of summary jurisdiction when dealing with prison offences (para. 116).

6. An explanatory card about the procedure which will be followed under the preceding recommendation should be handed to every prisoner who is to appear before the Visiting Committee or Board of Visitors (para. 117).

7. Prisoners charged with offences against prison discipline should not be entitled to representation by a 'friend' or legal adviser (para. 128).

The Secretary of State accepted these recommendations in principle, subject to consultation with the Magistrates Association on 4, 5, and 6. No. 1 will require an amendment of the Prison Rules before it can be implemented. No. 2 must wait till a suitable prison is available. No. 3 is already in force.

PART II—BORSTALS

1. The power to award restricted diet No. 1 should be restored to Governors and Boards of Visitors (para. 58).

2. Restricted diet No. 2 should be abolished (para. 59).

3. A special closed institution should be established for lads who by persistent misconduct or subversive activities interfere with the training of others (paras. 61–66).

4. Absconders should be dealt with by the Board of Visitors (para. 76).

5. A notice of the offence for which he has been reported should be served on an inmate in good time before adjudication (para. 78).

6. The Governor should be obliged to remit to the Board of Visitors every case where an inmate is reported for assaulting an officer, gross personal violence to an officer or another inmate, or mutiny or incitement to mutiny (para. 79).

7. As for 4 and 5 under PRISONS.

The Secretary of State accepted these recommendations in principle, subject as to 1 to the qualification 'that this punishment should be used only as a last resort when other forms of punishment have failed or in exceptional cases of serious misconduct where no other form of punishment is deemed appropriate'; as to 2, 4 and 6, to the amendment of the Borstal Rules, though punishment diet No. 2 is not now being used; as to 7, to consultation with the Magistrates Association. Recommendations 1, 3 and 5 are already in force.

It may be noted here that in connection with the amendments to the Prison and Borstal Rules required to give effect to the foregoing recommendations, a series of further amendments will be proposed of which it is unfortunately impossible to take account here as they have not yet been presented to Parliament. These may affect some matters dealt with in the text.

APPENDIX J

PRISON DIETS

Dietary Card Issued to Prisoners

ORDINARY DIET

1. Statutory Rules, 98, 100 and 101 provide as follows:

'98. The food provided for prisoners shall be of a nutritional value adequate for health and strength and of wholesome quality, well prepared and served, and reasonably varied.

'100. Except as determined by the Commissioners, or on medical grounds, no prisoner shall be allowed to have any food other than the normal prison diet.

'101. Except as provided under Rules 43 and 44 for an offence against discipline, or on the written recommendation of the Medical Officer in the case of a prisoner who persistently wastes his food or on medical grounds by direction of the Medical Officer, no prisoner shall have less food than is provided in the normal prison diet.'

2. (a) The meals are not prepared on a fixed dietary scale. Excepting breakfast they may vary from day to day. They cannot be measured by weight and it is no use complaining about the quantity unless there is clearly something wrong.

(b) You may not like some dishes but the kitchen staff cannot meet individual tastes. If you waste your food it may be cut down; if you are in real trouble about it you should apply to see the Medical Officer.

3. The meals served are as follows:

Breakfast consists of oatmeal porridge, bread, margarine, and tea.

Dinner varies from day to day.

Supper consists of bread, margarine, tea and (normally) an extra dish according to what the cook can make available from the rations, e.g jam, cheese, salad, or a cooked dish.

Evening cocoa.

4. (a) If you are a Jew, a Mahommedan or a Hindu the food which will be issued to you will include a substitute for those items which you are precluded from eating on religious grounds.

(b) You may receive a vegetarian diet if you are a registered vegetarian and report this fact on admission, but you cannot change about. The vegetarian diet is the ordinary prison diet without meat with additional cheese and bread. Vegetarians may, should they so desire, take fish when it forms part of the meal issued to the prison as a whole.

Specimen Week's Diet in a London Prison, 1951

Day	Breakfast	Dinner	Supper	Evening
Mon.	Bread, marg., tea, porridge	Fried fish, peas, mashed potatoes, semolina pudding	Meat, onion and potato savoury, bread, marg., tea	Cocoa
Tues.	,,	Irish stew, potatoes, cabbage, savoury dumplings	Cheese. bread, marg., tea	,,
Wed.	,,	Soup, meat pie, potatoes, cabbage, fruit pudding	Bread, marg., jam, tea	,,
Thurs.	,,	Steamed fish, parsley sauce, cabbage, mashed potatoes, semolina pudding	Cheese savoury, sweet buns, bread, marg. and tea	,,
Fri.	,,	Savoury bacon pie, haricot beans, potatoes, cabbage, treacle pudding	Bread, jam, marg. and tea	,,
Sat.	,,	Vegetable soup, potatoes, savoury dumplings	Cheese, bread, marg. and tea	,,
Sun.	,,	Roast meat, roast potatoes, cabbage, date pudding	Cake, bread, marg., tea	,,

APPENDIX K

ADDITIONAL NOTES

(*to December* 1951)

p. 25. The origin and development of the Amsterdam Rasp House are very fully described, from the original sources, by Professor Thorsten Sellin in his *Pioneering in Penology* (University of Pennsylvania Press and Oxford University Press, 1944). From this it is clear that in its origin the Rasp House was intended as a place of correctional imprisonment for all sorts of offenders, even for sentences of many years. The memorandum of Jan Spiegel, an Amsterdam magistrate, on the principles to be followed in its administration is a remarkable document in the literature of penal reform, anticipating by 200 years the teaching of Howard and his followers (Sellin, pp. 27 and 28). Professor Sellin deals also with the Spin House, founded a few years later for women. The gate of the Rasp House still stands at the entrance to the Public Baths in the Heiligenweg: its present form, which may derive from the late seventeenth or early eighteenth century (Sellin, p. 33) appears to symbolise the deterioration of the original conception, the dominant motifs being chains, chastisement, and terror.

p. 25. *Bridewell*—It is not without interest to note that in the City of New York progress has led in precisely the opposite direction. From p. 1 of the Annual Report of the Dept. of Correction for 1950 we learn that in September 1950 'the Penitentiary and Workhouse situated on Rikers Island, Brooklyn, N.Y., was reorganised to permit the establishment of two divisions operating as separate and distinct institutions.'

p. 31. A parallel development on the continent, which led to the damming up in hulks of convicts who could no longer be disposed of as galley-slaves (an alternative to transportation) is described by M. Jean Dupréel as follows:

'Mais dès la fin du XVII⁰ siècle les progrès de la navigation à voile brisèrent l'avantageuse communauté d'intérêts qui s'était ainsi établie entre la défense sociale et la propulsion des vaisseaux de ligne. Les marines de guerre eurent donc de moins en moins l'emploi de galériens, et comme on continuait à leur en envoyer, elles durent les entasser dans des installations de fortune, tantôt à terre, dans les locaux disponibles des ports militaires, tantôt dur l'eau, dans des navires désaffectés et immobilisés à l'ancre.

'Ce fut l'origine des bagnes qui, en France, existèrent à Toulon, Brest, Rochefort et Lorient et dont le nom provient, dit-on, du fait qu'un des premiers parmi ces lieux de détention fut installé à Constantinople dans un ancien établissement de bain.'[1]

p. 38. It is of some interest to note the history of the plan established at Pentonville, since so many prisons in Europe built since that date have been influenced by it. Theoretically, it appears to derive from a combination of the circular panopticon of Bentham's imagining and the well-known plan of the 'maison de force' at Ghent which was followed at Millbank: instead of radiating from an open court, as at Ghent, the separate blocks radiate from a closed central space, from which the complete and simultaneous supervision sought by Bentham is obtained. But this plan had been adopted as early as 1817 in the Philadelphia Penitentiary which was reported on in 1834 by the English Inspectors who had visited the U.S.A. to study the Separate System, and the writer has been assured by Professor Thorsten Sellin of Philadelphia University that the architect derived his plan from that of the London Hospital. This form of prison was adopted in Belgium through the influence of the Belgian Inspector-General Edouard Ducpétiaux, who had made a visit to England in 1835, and M. Dupréel, in the article above quoted to which I am indebted for this information, mentions that in Belgium some thirty prisons of this type were built between 1844 and 1919, fifteen by Ducpétiaux himself before his death in 1868. This influence also spread to Germany, and on visiting the Lehrterstrasse prison in Berlin the writer was informed that it was built in 1846 from the plans of Pentonville brought from London by the King of Prussia.

p. 45. It is interesting to note the following from an address given to the Institute of Comparative Law in Paris as recently as May 1949 by the Director-General of Prisons, Chili—'Le réglement pénitentiaire chilien, en usage, établit le système irlandais, connu aussi sous les noms de système de Crofton ou système progressis . . .'

pp. 51, 78, 83. The I.P.P.C. met for the last time at Berne in July, 1951. After long negotiation, it had been agreed that its functions should be taken over by the United Nations. Under the terms of the agreement 'consultative groups' of experts will meet in different regions of the world at least once in two years, and the first such group to be set up will be composed of the former members of the I.P.P.C. The U.N. also undertakes to organise quinquennial Congresses after the manner established by the I.P.P.C., and to publish regular Bulletins. The work will be organised by the Social Defence Section of the U.N. Secretariat.

p. 80. Following the retirement of the first Director, it was decided in consultation with the Ministry of Education that the duties of this post might in future be carried out by a suitably qualified Assistant Commissioner.

pp. 100, 144. During 1950 it became necessary to reserve part of Parkhurst for men passing into the second stage of a sentence of preventive detention (see Chapter XVIII). As their numbers grew, the Ordinary class prisoners were gradually squeezed out, and by mid-1951 there were no more transfers of this class to Parkhurst except for medical or special reasons.

[1] 'Vers une nouvelle architecture pénitentiaire' ; Revue de Droit Pénal et de Criminologie ; Mars 1951.

Dartmoor, therefore, became the only central prison for the general run of long-term Ordinaries, and it was necessary to prescribe 'over four years' as the qualifying term for transfer from a local prison.

p. 144. *Star Class Prisons*—Continued increase of population and inability to obtain an additional open prison has prevented the full development of these plans. The present situation is that in the Northern group all Stars with sentences of 12 months to 3 years inclusive are collected at Stafford, from where they are allocated to the two regional training prisons for that group. Stars with sentences of less than 12 months, and civil prisoners, go to Preston or Northallerton, which take only those categories. These are all cellular prisons. In the Southern group there is an open prison (Eastchurch, Kent) for civil prisoners and Stars with sentences of less than 12 months who are not found to be unsuitable for open conditions: others of this category are concentrated in Brixton and Wormwood Scrubs prisons in the London area, and elsewhere remain in their local prisons. Stars with sentences of 12 months and over are allocated to the three regional training prisons for the group from their local prisons or from Wormwood Scrubs.

p. 146. During 1950, in consequence of the development of the system of corrective training (see Chapter XVIII) the 40 per cent of places allotted to 'trainable ordinaries' at Wakefield and Maidstone were gradually filled by corrective trainees selected as suitable for the regime of these prisons—on the whole a similar type of man. The 'trainable ordinary' may still however find room in the open regional prisons.

p. 157. Mention should have been made in the text that arrangements for classification and for training programmes are made in each local prison by a Reception Board of the Governor (or deputy) and senior officials, including the Welfare Officer. The Board sees every prisoner as soon as possible after reception, and those with longer sentences about whom decisions have to be made are seen again when the necessary material has been collected and observation made. At training and central prisons similar boards meet to arrange the training programmes of the prisoners transferred to them.

p. 187. It is satisfactory to be able to report a marked improvement in the position during 1951. Whether as a result of the new arrangements of 1950, or of the re-armament programme, or of both, there was no shortage of work except to a limited extent for the unskilled short-sentence prisoners.

p. 195. In July, 1951, the Secretary of State approved an interesting extension of this scheme. Hitherto it had been limited to out-door work on public utilities, except for a party working in a privately owned quarry. On this occasion a party of women prisoners were allowed to go out daily to work in a civilian spinning factory under normal conditions, but under the supervision of a woman prison officer, who wears plain clothes and voluntarily works alongside them. The arrangements as to wages, etc., were made through the Ministry of Labour and National Service and the Trade Union concerned in the usual way. This arrangement has so far worked well, and no untoward incident has resulted. The women work in a separate group, but they are indistinguishable in appearance from the other workers.

p. 197. In view of the recommendation on this subject in the relevant Resolution of the Hague Congress (II(3) of Appendix F), and of the reasoned proposal on similar lines made by the Scottish Advisory Council in their report on the Scottish Prison System, it seems desirable to examine this idea further. The proposal as stated is that the prisoner should be paid an 'economic wage' for his work in prison, and that out of this wage he should pay for his keep in prison, maintain his family, keep up his insurance contributions, and 'if possible' pay compensation to the victims of his crimes. The purposes of his training would then be furthered by the greater 'normalisation' of his position, the increase in his self-respect, the strengthening of his sense of responsibility to his family and society, and the greater stimulus to his industry and skill. If indeed these results could be assured, they might well be worth a high price in administrative cost and labour. But can they be assured?

It appears to the present writer that for such a scheme to succeed it must appeal to the prisoner as bearing a realistic and comprehensible relation to ordinary life: if the effect so far as he is concerned is merely that the prison authorities, after a complicated piece of book-keeping in which he exercises no personal choice or self-determination, inform him that the weekly balance due to him is so much, then it may be doubted if in the minds of the great majority of prisoners any of the desired effects will in fact be aroused.

And how is 'a wage calculated according to the same norms that obtain outside the prison' to be fixed in the labour conditions described in the text? It is sufficient, for the present purpose, to state the question. No answer has yet, to the writer's knowledge, been put forward. The Scottish Report, if it may be said with respect, merely shirks this issue by proposing a general rate of £3 a week: such an arrangement could bear no relation to economic conditions either inside or outside the prison, and could in the writer's submission only degenerate into the artificial book-keeping system above-mentioned.

If the rate is to bear any relation to the calls to be made on it, it may be noted that it costs £4 3s. 7d. a week (including all overhead costs) to keep a prisoner in an English prison, that a Class I National Insurance contribution is 5s. 1d. a week (the State would also have to pay the employer's contribution of 4s. 4d.) and that the National Assistance Board rate for a wife and—say—two children would be at least £2 10s. 0d. a week.

Among the various difficulties that spring to the mind, are such questions as, who would decide the amount due by way of compensation to the victims of the great variety of offences of dishonesty and violence to be found among prisoners, and relate the payments to the prisoners' wages? Would the man in prison for refusing to maintain his family be subject to compulsory stoppage of his prison wage? Is the bachelor or widower with no dependants to enjoy the balance of his wage, or is a system of family allowances to be super-added to the structure?

Further reflection only serves to confirm the view that any such system must, in the end, lead to some such result as was attributed to it by the Salmon Committee, and that the cost to the State and the administrative work involved would be wholly disproportionate to the effects achieved.

p. 215. An interesting account of the history, use, and organisation of prison libraries is given by Mr. Richard F. Watson, Lending Librarian of the Harris Public Library, Preston, in Library Association Pamphlet No. 7.

'Prison Libraries,' 1951. (The Library Association, Chaucer House, Malet Place, London.) Mr. Watson is a prison visitor and for two years acted as Prison Librarian at H.M. Prison, Preston.

pp. 219, 222. In 1951 the Howard League published a pamphlet, 'The Legal Disabilities of Ex-prisoners', price 1*s.*, which deals in greater detail with many aspects of these questions. I am indebted to this publication for drawing my attention to two statutory disqualifications which I had over-looked, as follows:

'A clergyman sentenced to imprisonment, or to any greater punishment, following a conviction of treason, felony or misdemeanour (if tried on indictment) forfeits his preferment and continues during his lifetime incapable of holding preferment. (The Clergy Discipline Act, 1892, Section 1).'

'The Licensing Laws contain various provisions for the disqualification of convicted persons. (The Beerhouse Acts of 1830 and 1840. The Licensing Acts, 1910 and 1949). The most important of these which disqualified a person convicted of felony from being a licensee during his lifetime was repealed by the Criminal Justice Act, 1948.'

p. 220. On 15 February 1951 the Secretary of State told the House of Commons that 'the question of altering the law will be considered when an opportunity for amending legislation occurs.' (*Hansard*, 15.2.51, col. 94).

p. 220. In 1951 the Secretary of State decided that in future a prisoner might be released under escort, to be married at the nearest place to the prison licensed for the purpose, if a child would otherwise be born before the expiration of his or her sentence. This practice is now in force.

p. 226. The Prison Rules 1951, which are now in force, add to the prison Rules a new Rule in the following terms:

'*Parole*

'84A. (1) A prisoner may be allowed by the Commissioners, on conditions and for reasons approved by them, to be temporarily absent from the prison on parole, for a stated length of time.

'(2) If the Commissioners are satisfied that a prisoner absent on parole has broken any of the said conditions, he shall, notwithstanding that the said length of time has not elapsed, be liable to be recalled to the prison.'

This new power has so far been used for two purposes. First, to allow to long-term Star prisoners who apply for it a short period (five days) of home leave, towards the end of the sentence, provided their applications are approved by a special Board at the prison after consultation with the C.A.C.A. Second, to allow a prisoner to visit a dying relative if the Governor is satis-fied that during his temporary absence he is likely to abstain from crime and that he may reasonably be counted upon to return to prison at the proper time. This latter concession does not apply to untried, unsentenced, appellant or civil prisoners, nor to any who are certifiable as insane or mentally deficient or under sentence of death. If a prisoner is unsuitable for parole, he may nevertheless be allowed to make such a visit under escort.

p. 231. With a view to the further development and better organisation of physical training and recreational games a Physical Training Organiser has now been appointed as a full-time member of the Head Office staff.

p. 250. It is becoming increasingly clear that the whole question of the scientific examination of offenders, with a view to assisting the courts to select the appropriate treatment and the administration to classify and individualise treatment, is ripe for reconsideration and much fuller development. In December 1951 the U.N. organised a Seminar in Brussels, attended by experts from eighteen countries, entirely devoted to this question, and its findings when published will be of first-rate importance.

Experience already suggests that a *complete* examination will include:

(a) Analysis of the criminal record.

(b) Social examination by a qualified social case-worker.

(c) Medical examination by a general practitioner.

(d) Psychological examination, including the educational and vocational fields.

(e) Psychiatric examination, where any question of mental abnormality arises.

Not all parts of this examination will be required for all offenders, and for many no examination will be required at all, but there should be properly co-ordinated arrangements for making such examinations both before and after sentence. At present the position in England is only partially satisfactory. Complete examinations can be and are carried out *after* sentence in Borstal Reception Centres and the Corrective Training Allocation Centre, but it is abundantly clear that this work ought to be done *before* sentence, so that the results of a complete examination may be available when reports are made to courts on the suitability of offenders for different forms of treatment. Unfortunately the machinery of administration of justice makes no provision for these needs, and it is often necessary to report on persons who have only been under observation for a few days, or even on bail and not under observation at all. What is required is a series of regional observation centres, on the pattern of the existing allocation centres, where both pre-sentence and post-sentence examinations can be made. Courts will then be advised, and classification carried out, on a reasonably full and scientific basis.

pp. 256, 262. In April 1951 the Secretary of State appointed a Joint Committee of the Prison Commissioners and the N.A.D.P.A.S., under the Chairmanship of Sir Alexander Maxwell, G.C.B. (formerly Permanent Under Secretary of State of the Home Department) to enquire into the functions and finance of the D.P.A.S's.

p. 263. The following are extracts from the instructions issued by the Ministry of Labour and National Service to its local offices:

'It is not the intention that the arrangements should in any way curtail the activities of the Discharged Prisoners' Aid Societies and Central After-Care Association in finding employment for persons released from prison or Borstal Institutions by such personal contacts as they may have with employers of labour. The purpose of the scheme is solely one of securing closer co-operation between the Ministry of Labour and National Service and the two organisations. In carrying it out the fundamental aim is to secure that the maximum number of men, women and girls are placed in employment and given a fair start on their release from prison or a Borstal Institution.'

'When the prisoner is interviewed before discharge by the Welfare Officer of the Discharged Prisoners' Aid Society or a representative of the Central After-Care Association as the case may be, his attention is drawn to the assistance which the Ministry of Labour and National Service can give him in finding suitable employment. If the prisoner wishes to take advantage of this help, the Employment Exchange in whose area the prison is situated is advised about two months before the prisoner's discharge. The Employment Exchange then arranges for a Placing Officer to interview the prisoner in prison. This Officer finds out as much about the prisoner's experience and qualifications as possible, taking account of any training he may have been given whilst in prison. Full particulars are then sent to the Employment Exchange in whose area the prisoner intends to live on release, so that efforts can be made to find him employment in advance. When the prisoner is discharged he is given an introduction to this Employment Exchange in order to make it more easy for him to register for employment.'

'In the case of prisoners conditionally discharged, the Central After-Care Association is notified of the name of the Employment Exchange to which particulars of the prisoner have been sent; the Association then advises this Exchange of the date the prisoner is due to be discharged and the name and address of the local Associate with whom the Exchange should co-operate in placing the prisoner in employment.'

'It is realised that persons who have served terms of detention need particularly sympathetic treatment. Employment Exchanges, therefore, are most careful to deal with such persons with great tact and to limit reference to their offences and subsequent detention to a minimum. Interviews are conducted in conditions of privacy, and everything is done to win their confidence and to impress upon them that the whole aim of the Employment Exchange is to place them in employment which will give them an opportunity of leading a useful and happy life.'

'Employment Exchanges endeavour to strike a proper balance between their responsibility to assist a discharged prisoner to obtain suitable employment and their responsibility to assist an employer to find a suitable worker for the vacancy he has notified. The fact that an applicant has served a prison sentence is not, however, disclosed to an employer without the applicant's consent. Such consent would, for example, be sought where it would obviously be in the applicant's interest to be considered for a particular vacancy but the circumstances of the job are such that it would not be right to ask an employer to consider an applicant in ignorance of his past record.'

p. 267. Section 57 of the Criminal Justice Act 1948 provides as follows:

'The Secretary of State may at any time if he thinks fit release on licence a person serving a term of imprisonment for life subject to such conditions as may be specified in the licence; and the Secretary of State may at any time modify or cancel any such condition.

'The Secretary of State may at any time by order recall to prison a person released on licence under this section, but without prejudice to the power of the Secretary of State to release him on licence again; and where any person is so recalled his licence shall cease to have effect and he shall, if at large, be deemed to be unlawfully at large.'

Each case is reviewed by the Home Office, on a report from the Prison Commissioners, at 4-yearly intervals, and the period to be served is decided on the merits of each case. Under recent practice it has been rare for release to be postponed beyond 9 or 10 years.

p. 295. The cases referred to in the text may be said to be subject to the coercive function of the prison, since they may secure release by obedience to the order of the court. There are however, other cases which are in principle correctional, since the offender is committed for a specified term in respect of a specific act deemed to be in contempt of the court, e.g. violent or abusive behaviour in court. Both categories are treated as civil prisoners.

p. 300. In the case of Rex v. Murray, 16 October 1950, the Court of Criminal Appeal said:

'Because the Prison Commissioners report that a man is suitable for corrective training or preventive detention, this is not in itself a reason why the court should pass such a sentence, but if they report that he is not suitable for corrective training, it is a very strong thing to disregard their opinion.'

pp. 308, 363. In December 1951 a change-over took place between the C.T. Allocation Centre and the Correctional Borstal at Wandsworth (see p. 363). The change was made with regret so far as concerns the C.T. allocation work, but the necessity to move the Borstal into a separate establishment had become over-riding, and it is now established at Reading. There seems to be no reason why the C.T. work should not prosper in the separate wing of Wandsworth, though ideally it should be in a separate prison if one could be made available.

p. 310. These calculations were borne out by the event. Committals to corrective training in 1951 did not reach the level of 1950, and the accommodation provided amply sufficed throughout the year.

p. 311. In confirmation of this view formed in the prisons, the following extract from the Report of the Commissioner of Police of the Metropolis for 1949 is of interest:

'It is interesting to speculate on the causes of this striking fall in 1949. Many could be adduced and all would be debatable except one on which experienced officers of the C.I.D. are unanimous, namely the Criminal Justice Act of 1948. Section 21 of this Act, which created new sentences of corrective training and preventive detention, came into force on 18 April 1949, and there is no doubt that its implications have been fully appreciated by the criminal community. When habitual criminals are found on arrest to be in possession of copies of an Act of Parliament it is a safe assumption that their study of the new criminal law is dictated by something more than an academic interest, and indeed it is reported that in some cases house-breakers have disposed of the tools of their trade and have decided that the possibility of a long period of detention raises the risks of their calling beyond the point where it is remunerative. Experience will show whether the effect of the new Act is permanent or not and whether, contrary to what has so often been said, it is in fact possible to make men honest by Act of Parliament. The omens are at any rate encouraging.'

p. 324. By the end of 1951 the number of men serving sentences of preventive detention had risen to 693, of whom 467 were in the second stage at Parkhurst. If the numbers increase at the same rate in 1952, the provision of additional accommodation elsewhere will present difficult problems.

Arrangements for the third stage have now been made on the lines suggested on pp. 321 and 322. A separate third-stage block with a pleasantly furnished common-room is provided: the cells stand open, and the men go to and from work without supervision. The idea of a 'weekly leave' has however been deferred pending further experience. A full programme of talks and discussions has been arranged, with an informal atmosphere. It has also been decided in principle to set up an 'intra-mural hostel' within a suitable local prison, and arrangements are proceeding.

On the whole question of habitual criminals and preventive detention, reference should be made to *The Habitual Criminal* by Dr. Norval Morris (Longmans, Green and Co., 1951), price 27s. 6d. This valuable work, unfortunately received too late for notice in the text, deals comprehensively with all the problems treated in the text, both of principle and practice, and contains a valuable section on comparative law and practice in this field.

p. 352. Under section 82 of the Children and Young Persons Act 1933 and section 72 of the Criminal Justice Act 1948, a person who has attained the age of 16 years may be sentenced to Borstal training by a court of summary jurisdiction if he is brought before them as an absconder from an approved school or as guilty of serious misconduct therein.

The initiative is taken by the managers of the school with the authority of the Secretary of State.

This provision of 1933 had been much criticised, mainly on the grounds that it was possible for a young person who had never committed a criminal offence to be sent to Borstal, and even possibly to prison, since his Borstal sentence might in law be commuted to imprisonment. Section 72 of 1948 therefore provides that the Secretary of State may by Order in Council bring this power to an end when he 'is satisfied that adequate methods, other than Borstal training, are available for dealing with the persons to whom the Order relates.' It is understood that the provision of one or more 'closed' schools, or of closed blocks within normal schools, is under consideration.

INDEX

A

Absconding from Borstals, 388–9
Accommodation
  in Borstals, 360–2, 390
  in prisons, 101–4
Adult education (see under Education)
Advisory Council on the Treatment of Offenders
  advises on use of notebooks by prisoners, 216
  membership and functions, 78
  on treatment of mentally abnormal offenders, 245
After-care
  in Borstal system, 393–7
  of prisoners, 253–72
American National Prison Congress, 52
American Prison Association, 142
Annual Reports of Prison Commissioners, 84
Appellants, treatment of, 287–8
Approved Schools, 336–7
Art, in education, 209, 390
Askham Grange, open prison for women, 148, 154, 157, 278
Asquith, H. H. (Earl of Oxford and Asquith), 53, 57
Asquith, Lord Justice, 9, 14
Association of prisoners
  for meals, 69, 235
  for recreation and education, 209 *seqq.*
  forfeiture of association, 168–71
  under stage-system, 150, Appendix H
Attendance Centres, 339
Auburn prison, N.Y., and system, 33
Australia (Queensland), Report for 1949 . . . 444
Aylesbury Association (former), 266
Aylesbury prison, 148, 157

B

Babies, in prisons, 241
Bathing, of prisoners, 227
Beccaria, C. B., 26, 31
Beds and bedding, 107
Benefit of Clergy, 23
Bennett, James V., 64
Benney, Mark, 223, 231
Benson, George, M.P., 169
Bentham, Jeremy, 31, 130, 133
Bibles, provision of, in prisons, 204
Birkett, Lord Justice, 5, 6, 7, 8, 9, 11, 78
Births in prisons, 241
Blackstone, W., 26, 27
Boards of Visitors (see Visiting Committees)
Books for prisoners
  devotional, 204
  library, 50, 62, 149, 214
Borstal Association (former), 265
Borstal institutions
  absconding from, 388
  accommodation in, 360–3, 390
  Correctional Institution, 385
  population of, 365–7
  Recall Centres, 363, 397–8
  Reception Centres, 359, 360
  staff of, 363–5, 368
Borstal system
  after-care and supervision, 393 *seqq.*
  amended by Act of 1948 . . . 352
  arrangements for release, 392–3
  commutation to imprisonment, 354, 386
  established by Act of 1908 . . . 335
  influence of system, 401
  originated by Sir E. Ruggles-Brise, 331
  principles of system, 355 *seqq.*
  recall to a Borstal, 397
  results of system, 398 *seqq.*